Competing Capitalisms: Institutions and Economies
Volume II

Critical Studies in Economic Institutions

Series Editor: Geoffrey M. Hodgson
Research Professor, University of Hertfordshire Business School, UK

Wherever possible, the articles in these volumes have been reproduced as originally published using facsimile reproduction, inclusive of footnotes and pagination to facilitate ease of reference.

For a list of all Edward Elgar published titles visit our site on the World Wide Web at
http://www.e-elgar.co.uk

Competing Capitalisms: Institutions and Economies Volume II

Edited by

Richard Whitley

Professor of Organisational Sociology
University of Manchester, UK

CRITICAL STUDIES IN ECONOMIC INSTITUTIONS

An Elgar Reference Collection
Cheltenham, UK • Northampton, MA, USA

Published by
Edward Elgar Publishing Limited
Glensanda House
Montpellier Parade
Cheltenham
Glos GL50 1UA
UK

Edward Elgar Publishing, Inc.
136 West Street
Suite 202
Northampton
Massachusetts 01060
USA

A catalogue record for this book is available from the British Library.

Library of Congress Cataloguing in Publication Data

Competing capitalisms : institutions and economies / edited by Richard Whitley.
  p. cm – (Critical studies in economic institutions ; 1)
  Includes bibliographical references and index.
  1. Capitalism. 2. Comparative economics. I. Whitley, Richard. II. Series.

 HB501 .C715 2002
 330.12'2—dc21   2002021989

ISBN 1 84064 749 3 (2 volume set)

Printed and bound in Great Britain by MPG Books Ltd, Bodmin, Cornwall

Contents

Acknowledgements

The editor and publishers wish to thank the authors and the following publishers who have kindly given permission for the use of copyright material.

John Benjamins Publishing Company for excerpt: Sigrid Quack and Glenn Morgan (2000), 'Institutions, Sector Specialisation and Economic Performance Outcomes', in Sigrid Quack, Glenn Morgan and Richard Whitley (eds), *National Capitalisms, Global Competition, and Economic Performance*, Chapter 2, 27–52.

Cornell University Press for excerpt: Robert Boyer (1996), 'The Convergence Hypothesis Revisited: Globalization but Still the Century of Nations?', in Suzanne Berger and Ronald Dore (eds), *National Diversity and Global Capitalism*, Chapter One, 29–59.

Walter de Gruyter GmbH and Co. KG for articles: Richard D. Whitley (1991), 'The Social Construction of Business Systems in East Asia', *Organization Studies*, **12** (1), 1–28; Arndt Sorge (1991), 'Strategic Fit and the Societal Effect: Interpreting Cross-National Comparisons of Technology, Organization and Human Resources', *Organization Studies*, **12** (2), 161–90; Steven Casper (2000), 'Institutional Adaptiveness, Technology Policy, and the Diffusion of New Business Models: The Case of German Biotechnology', *Organization Studies*, **21** (5), Special Issue, 887–914.

Journal of Asian Business for articles: D. Eleanor Westney (1996), 'The Japanese Business System: Key Features and Prospects for Changes', *Journal of Asian Business*, **12** (1), 21–50; Linda Y.C. Lim (1996), 'The Evolution of Southeast Asian Business Systems', *Journal of Asian Business*, **12** (1), 51–74.

Oxford University Press, Inc. for excerpt: J. Rogers Hollingsworth and Wolfgang Streeck (1994), 'Countries and Sectors: Concluding Remarks on Performance, Convergence, and Competitiveness', in J. Rogers Hollingsworth, Philippe C. Schmitter and Wolfgang Streeck (eds), *Governing Capitalist Economies: Performance and Control of Economic Sectors*, Chapter 11, 270–300.

Princeton University Press for excerpt: Paul N. Doremus, William W. Keller, Louis W. Pauly and Simon Reich (1998), 'The Strategic Behavior of MNCs', in *The Myth of the Global Corporation*, Chapter 5, 84–137, references.

Stanford University Press (www.sup.org) and the Board of Trustees of the Leland Stanford Jr. University for excerpt: David L. Wank (1999), 'Producing Property Rights: Strategies, Networks, and Efficiency in Urban China's Nonstate Firms', in Jean C. Oi and Andrew G. Walder (eds), *Property Rights and Economic Reform in China*, Chapter 11, 248–72, notes.

Taylor and Francis Ltd (http://www.tandf.co.uk/journals) for articles: Lane Kenworthy (1997), 'Globalization and Economic Convergence', *Competition and Change*, **2**, 1–64; Richard Whitley (1998), 'Internationalization and Varieties of Capitalism: The Limited Effects of Cross-national Coordination of Economic Activities on the Nature of Business Systems', *Review of International Political Economy*, **5** (3), Autumn, 445–81.

University of Chicago Press for article: Gary G. Hamilton and Nicole Woolsey Biggart (1988), 'Market, Culture, and Authority: A Comparative Analysis of Management and Organization in the Far East', *American Journal of Sociology*, **94**, Supplement, S52–S94.

Every effort has been made to trace all the copyright holders but if any have been inadvertently overlooked the publishers will be pleased to make the necessary arrangement at the first opportunity.

In addition the publishers wish to thank the Marshall Library of Economics, Cambridge University and the Library of Indiana University at Bloomington, USA for their assistance in obtaining these articles.

Part I
National and Regional Capitalisms –
East Asian

[1]

Market, Culture, and Authority:
A Comparative Analysis of Management
and Organization in the Far East[1]

Gary G. Hamilton and Nicole Woolsey Biggart
University of California, Davis

Three frameworks purport to explain industrial arrangements and practices: a market approach that emphasizes economic characteristics, a cultural approach that sees organization as the expression of patterned values, and an authority approach that explains organization as a historically developed structure of domination. The efficacy of each approach is tested in explaining the organizational structures of three rapidly growing East Asian economies: Japan, South Korea, and Taiwan. The paper argues through comparative analysis that organizational *growth* is best explained by market and cultural factors but that authority patterns and legitimation strategies best explain organizational *structure*.

Several social science disciplines have been interested in the structure and functioning of economic organizations. This widespread interest is largely grouped around three perspectives. Especially in economics (Chandler 1977, 1981; Teece 1980; Williamson 1981, 1985) but also in anthropology (Orlove 1986) and sociology (White 1981), scholars have studied economic decision making in regard to the conditions under which business firms

[1] Versions of this paper have been presented in the following locations: Pan Pacific Conference in Seoul; Tunghai University Seminar Series in Taiwan; Stanford University Organizational Studies Seminar Series; Regional Seminar on Chinese Studies, University of California, Berkeley; and the All-University of California Conference in Economic History at Asilomar, California. We greatly appreciate the helpful comments from many who attended these sessions and thank the following people who carefully read one or more drafts of this paper: Howard Aldrich, Manuel Castells, Tun-jen Cheng, Donald Gibbs, Thomas Gold, Chalmers Johnson, Cheng-shu Kao, Earl Kinmonth, John W. Meyer, Ramon Myers, Marco Orrù, Charles Perrow, William Roy, W. Richard Scott, and Gary Walton. We also wish to acknowledge and thank the following individuals for their help in some part of the research: Wei-an Chang, Ben-ray Jai, Hsien-heng Lu, Hwai-jen Peng, Cindy Stearns, Moon Jee Yoo, and Shuenn-der Yu. Hamilton also wishes to acknowledge the support of the Fulbright Foundation and the National Science Foundation (SES-8606582), which made this research possible. Request for reprints should be sent to Gary G. Hamilton, Department of Sociology, University of California, Davis, California 95616.

arise and operate in relation to market-mediated transactions. We call this general perspective the "market approach." The second perspective on economic organization is the "cultural approach," which suggests that cultural patterns shape economic behavior. This perspective was formerly a preserve of anthropologists (e.g., Benedict 1946; Douglas 1979; see also Orlove 1986) but is now widespread among a large number of scholars from diverse backgrounds. Studies of corporate culture (Deal and Kennedy 1982; Peters and Waterman 1982; Kanter 1983) and comparative culture studies of Japanese (Ouchi 1981, 1984; Pascale and Athos 1981; Vogel 1979), Swedish (Blumberg 1973; Foy and Gadon 1976), Yugoslavian (Adizes 1971), and other nations' industrial practices have increased manifold in the past 10 years. The third perspective is a political economy perspective, which we call the "authority approach." Scholars in all social science fields have worked on economic organization from this wide-ranging perspective, from the seminal work of Marx (1930) and Weber (1958, 1978) to such recent studies as Granovetter (1985), Perrow (1981, 1986), Portes and Walton (1981), Haggard and Cheng (1986), Reynolds (1983), and Mintz and Schwartz (1985).

This paper assesses the relative efficacy of each of these three approaches in explaining the industrial arrangements and strategies of three rapidly developing countries of the Pacific region—South Korea, Taiwan, and Japan. We argue that, while market and culture explanations make important contributions to understanding, neither is alone sufficient. A market explanation correctly draws our attention to state industrial policies and entrepreneurial responses. But a market explanation cannot account for the distinctive and substantially different organizational arrangements that have appeared in the three countries. A cultural explanation, however, enables us to see, correctly, organizational practices in Japan, South Korea, and Taiwan as generalized expressions of beliefs in the relative importance of such social factors as belongingness, loyalty, and submission to hierarchical authority. But looking at culture alone obscures the fact that business organizations, no matter how well they accord with cultural beliefs, are fundamentally responses to market opportunities and conditions. Enterprise may be culturally informed, but it remains enterprise. Moreover, cultural variables are insufficiently distinguishable in the region to have clear explanatory force.

In this paper, we argue that the political economy approach with a Weberian emphasis produces the best explanation of the three. This approach incorporates elements of the market and culture explanations but does so from the point of view of the historically developed authority relations that exist among individuals and institutions in each society. We argue that market opportunities do indeed lead to innovations in organi-

American Journal of Sociology

zational design but that these innovations are not simply a rational cal-
culus of the most efficient way to organize. Organizational practices,
instead, represent strategies of control that serve to legitimate structures
of command and often employ cultural understandings in so doing. Such
practices are not randomly developed but rather are fashioned out of
preexisting interactional patterns, which in many cases date to preindustrial times. Hence, industrial enterprise is a complex modern adaptation of
preexisting patterns of domination to economic situations in which profit,
efficiency, and control usually form the very conditions of existence.

We pursue this argument in the following sections. First, we introduce
the recent economic history of the three countries of interest and describe
their current patterns of industrial organization. South Korea, Taiwan,
and Japan offer an unusual opportunity for comparative analysis. The
economy of each was virtually destroyed by war, World War II in the
cases of Japan and Taiwan and the Korean War in the instance of South
Korea. In recent years, all three nations have rebuilt their economies and
achieved extraordinary rates of economic growth, yet each has a different
dominant form of organizational structure. Second, we employ in turn
market, culture, and authority relations explanations, suggesting the distinctive contribution and limitation of each to analyzing the three cases
and explaining their differential outcomes. Finally, we suggest how our
analysis of these three East Asian economies, and the relative superiority
of the authority relations approach, has implications for industrial analysis, including the American case as it is currently understood.

RECENT ECONOMIC DEVELOPMENT IN JAPAN, TAIWAN, AND
SOUTH KOREA

Forty years ago, at the end of World War II, Japan lay in ruins, its
industrial core shattered and its colonial empire of Korea and Taiwan
severed. Taiwan, a largely agricultural society, was also leveled by the
war, and "three-quarters of [its] industrial capacity was destroyed" (Little
1979, p. 454). Moreover, Taiwan absorbed fleeing migrants from the
Chinese mainland, who arrived with Chiang Kai-shek's armies and government. Taiwan's population jumped from fewer than 6 million people
in 1944 to 8 million in 1950, a more than one-third increase in about five
years (Kuznets 1979, p. 32). Similarly, 32 years ago Korea emerged from
a civil war that destroyed its economy and killed 1.3 million of its people.
The southern agricultural portion of the country was separated from the
industrial north. South Korea lost its supply of manufactured goods,
hydroelectric power, and the bituminous coal that powered its railroads
(Bunge 1982, p. 24).

Far East

TABLE 1

VALUE OF EXPORTS IN JAPAN, SOUTH KOREA, AND TAIWAN IN
MILLIONS OF U.S. DOLLARS

	Japan*	South Korea†	Taiwan‡
1965	8,452	175	450
1970	19,318	835	1,481
1975	55,753	5,081	5,309
1980	129,807	17,505	19,810
1984	170,132§	29,253§	30,456

* From *Abstract of Statistics on Agriculture, Forestry and Fisheries*, Japan, 1982.
† From *Korea Statistical Handbook*, National Bureau of Statistics, 1985.
‡ From *Statistical Yearbook of the Republic of China*, Directorate General of Budget, Accounting, and Statistics, 1984.
§ From United Nations, *Monthly Bulletin of Statistics*, 1985.

Yet, in the 1980s, these three countries are the centerpiece of a rapidly industrializing Asia (Hofheinz and Calder 1982; Linder 1986). They have not only rebuilt their economies but have also become the wonder of the developing and developed worlds. Japan's success is the envy of American and European nations: in 1984, Japan's gross national product was the second highest in the capitalist world (Economist Intelligence Unit 1985a), with growth and investment rates double the United States' (Vogel 1979). Taiwan's GNP increased an average of 10.6% a year in the decade 1963–72, and in the decade 1973–82, a period that includes a world recession, it increased 7.5% a year (Myers 1984). In 1949, Taiwan's per-capita income was less than $50 U.S. In 1970, it was around $350, and, in 1984, $2,500 (Minard 1984, p. 36). South Korea's economic development did not accelerate until the 1960s, but in the decade 1963–72 manufacturing exports grew 52% a year (Little 1979), and between 1962 and 1984 industrial production increased at an average rate of 17% (Economist Intelligence Unit 1985b). In 1962, South Korea's per-capita GNP was $87 U.S., in 1980, $1,503 (Bunge 1982, p. 109), and in 1983, $1,709 (*Monthly Bulletin of Statistics* 1985). All three countries' economic success has largely been fueled by exports. Table 1 shows the extraordinary growth in the countries' export sectors. In 1984, Japan's trade surplus to the United State was about $40 billion (*Direction of Trade Statistics* 1985, p. 242); Taiwan's was nearly $10 billion (more than twice Japan's on a per-capita basis) (*Taiwan Statistical Data Book* 1985, p. 205); and South Korea's was $3.2 billion (*Direction of Trade Statistics* 1985, p. 248). By any economic measure, the growth of these northeast Asian economies is

American Journal of Sociology

unprecedented and has led many to refer to this economic success story as the "Asian Miracle."

The similarities of Japan, Taiwan, and South Korea go beyond economic recovery in the wake of wartime destruction; in fact, other similarities might seem to account for their common economic development (Cumings 1984; Hofheinz and Calder 1982). All three countries have few natural, especially mineral, resources. Their success cannot be explained by the discovery of oil reserves, as in some comparably successful developing nations in the Middle East. Nor is land the source of their wealth. Taiwan, South Korea, and Japan are among the most populated countries in the world in relation to cultivable land, "higher even than Egypt and Bangladesh and four times as high as India" (Little 1979, p. 450). Clearly, these are nations dependent on industry for wealth. They received economic aid and direction from the United States to repair and restart their economies, but the aid alone, which was given to other countries as well, cannot explain the rapid development there (Amsden 1979; Haggard and Cheng 1986; Little 1979; Hofheinz and Calder 1982; Barrett and Whyte 1982). Historically and culturally, the three are intertwined. Japan colonized Taiwan in 1895 and Korea in 1910, pursuing similar colonial policies in each (Cumings 1984; Myers and Peattie 1984). While each nation has its own language and ethnicity, China has, historically, had influences throughout the region. Korea and Japan, like Taiwan, have been deeply influenced by Confucian and Buddhist traditions. All three have relied on exports as a means for economic expansion.

In sum, the similarities are substantial. In fact, they are so great and the fate of the three countries so interlinked historically that Bruce Cumings (1984, p. 38) insightfully argues that "the industrial development in Japan, Korea, and Taiwan cannot be considered as an individual country phenomenon; instead it is a regional phenomenon. . . ." He further argues: "When one [country] is compared to another the differences will also be salient, but when all three are compared to the rest of the world the similarities are remarkable."

Despite these similarities, Japan, South Korea, and Taiwan have substantially different forms of enterprise or firm organization, particularly in the export sectors of their economies. Moreover, in each country the firm is embedded in a network of institutional relationships that gives each economy a distinctive character.[2] The important point here is that, if one looks only at individual firms, one misses the crucial set of social and

[2] Although true for all three societies, Japan is best known for these extrafirm networks. So prevalent and important are these networks in Japan that Clark (1979, pp. 95–96) suggests that they constitute a "society of industry": "No discussion of the Japanese company can disregard this context. The society of industry circumscribes, for example, the organization and administration of the company."

political institutions that serves to integrate the economy. Taking advantage of Granovetter's very useful discussion (1985), we argue that the firm is "embedded" in networks of institutionalized relationships and that these networks, which are different in each society, have a direct effect on the types of firms that develop, on the management of firms, and on organizational strategies more generally. The particular forms of economic embeddedness in each society, particularly in relation to political institutions, allow for the activation of different organizational designs to achieve industrialization.

THREE PATTERNS OF INDUSTRIAL ORGANIZATION

In Japan, two interrelated networks of firms are crucial for understanding the operation of the Japanese economy, and particularly the export sector. These networks represent two types of what Caves and Uekusa (1976) call "enterprise groups." One type of enterprise group consists of linkages among large firms. These linkages are usually loosely coupled, basically horizontal connections among a range of large firms. Although such firms differ in terms of size and prestige (Clark 1979, p. 95), the linkages between them are what Dore (1983, p. 467) calls "relational contracting between equals." These groupings of firms are intermarket groups and are spread through different industrial sectors (Vogel 1979, p. 107). The second type of enterprise group connects small- and medium-sized firms to a large firm, creating what economists (e.g., Nakamura 1981; Ozawa 1979; Patrick and Rosovsky 1976) call a "dual structure," a situation of "relational contracting between unequals" (Dore 1983, p. 465). Both types of enterprise groups make centrally located large firms and associations of large firms the principal actors in the Japanese economy. As a result of these enterprise groups, assets are distributed throughout a range of different types of firms, as shown in table 2.

The best-known networks of large firms, or *grūpu,* are the *kigyo shudan,* or intermarket groups, which are the modern-day descendants of the pre–World War II *zaibatsu.* These networks are normally groups of firms in unrelated businesses that are joined together by central banks or by trading companies (Clark 1979; Caves and Uekusa 1976). In prewar Japan, these groups were linked by powerful holding companies that were each under the control of a family. The *zaibatsu* families exerted firm control over the individual firms in their group through a variety of fiscal and managerial methods. During the U.S. occupation, the largest of these holding companies were dissolved, with the member firms of each group becoming independent (Bisson 1954). After the occupation, however, firms (e.g., Mitsui, Mitsubishi, and Sumitomo) regrouped themselves, but this time allowing for only limited concentration of fiscal resources in

American Journal of Sociology

TABLE 2

DISTRIBUTION OF ASSETS OF LARGE JAPANESE CORPORATIONS, BY GROUP AFFILIATION

	PERCENTAGE OF TOTAL ASSETS		
AFFILIATE GROUP	1955	1962	1965
Public corporations whose capital is wholly or partly government owned	62.2	50.1	38.3
Affiliates of long-term credit banks whose capital is partly government owned	2.1	3.3	4.3
Affiliates of *zaibatsu* and large private banks	23.3	28.4	29.2
Mitsui	6.1	3.8	5.0
Mitsubishi	5.0	6.4	7.2
Sumitomo	3.2	5.9	5.4
Fuji Bank (Yasuda)	2.9	3.6	3.8
Dai-ichi Bank	3.1	3.5	3.2
Sanwa Bank	1.4	2.2	2.6
Giant industrial corporations with vertical and conglomerate structures of subsidiaries and affiliates	5.6	9.5	8.8
Foreign-owned enterprises	1.0	1.4	1.4
Companies outside the affiliate system	5.8	7.3	18.0
Total	100.0	100.0	100.0

SOURCE.—Caves and Uekusa (1976, p. 64).

banks and none whatsoever in family-run holding companies (Johnson 1982, p. 174; Caves and Uekusa 1976). In addition to the former *zaibatsu*, another variant of the intermarket groups emerged in the postwar period. This is what Clark (1979, p. 72) calls the "bank group," which consists of "companies dependent for funds on a major bank" (e.g., Fuji, Dai-ichi, and Sanwa).[3]

The second type of enterprise group consists of vertical linkages between major manufacturers (*kaisha*) and their related subsidiaries (Abegglen and Stalk 1985; Clark 1979, p. 73), linkages that produce a dual structure in the Japanese economy (Yasuba 1976; Nakamura 1981). Ma-

[3] Usually, overlapping networks founded on banks are the networks of firms linked by general trading companies (*sōgō shōsha*) (Young 1979; Kunio 1982). These trading companies market and distribute the products of the firms that are affiliated with them. Some companies handle as many as 20,000 individual items and have offices in over 100 locations outside Japan (Krause and Sueo 1976, p. 389). Each bank-based network has its own trading company that supports its affiliate firms. Otherwise unaffiliated companies, usually small- and medium-sized businesses, also form their own trading-company cartels to market their products overseas as well as in Japan (Ozawa 1979, pp. 30–32).

jor firms in Japan are directly connected to a series of smaller independent firms that perform important roles in the overall system of production.[4] According to Nakamura's analysis (1981, pp. 171–93), with the exception of some assembly industries (e.g., automobiles), "The prevailing pattern is that large firms are in charge of the raw materials sector while small firms handle the transformation of these materials into manufactured goods." This system of subcontracting allows large firms to increase their use of small firms during times of expansion and to decrease their use during times of business decline. So common are these relations between large and small firms that the "subcontractorization" of small firms by the large has been seen as the "greatest problem" confronting the Japanese economy because of the inequality and dual-wage system that it spawns (Nakamura 1981, p. 175).

In sum, the Japanese economy is dominated by large, powerful, and relatively stable enterprise groups. These groups constitute a "society of industry" (Clark 1979, pp. 95–96), "where *zaibatsu* and other affiliations link industrial, commercial, and financial firms in a thick and complex skein of relations matched in no other country" (Caves and Uekusa 1976, p. 59).

Unlike in Japan, with its diversity in business networks, in South Korea, the dominant industrial networks are large, hierarchically arranged sets of firms known as *chaebol*. *Chaebol* are similar to the prewar *zaibatsu* in size and organizational structure. In 1980–81, the government recognized 26 *chaebol*, which together controlled 456 firms (Westphal et al. 1984, p. 510). In 1985, there were 50 *chaebol* that controlled 552 firms (*Hankook Ilbo* 1985). Their rate of growth has been extraordinary. In 1973, the top five *chaebol* controlled 8.8% of the GNP (Koo 1984, p. 1032), but by 1985 the top four *chaebol* controlled 45% of the GNP (*Business Week* 1985, p. 48). In 1984, the top 50 *chaebol* controlled about 80% of the GNP (*Hankook Ilbo* 1985).

While the *chaebol* resemble enterprise groups in Japan, the member firms of the *chaebol* are closely controlled by central holding companies, which are owned by an individual or a family. In turn, the central holding companies of the *chaebol* do not have the independence of action that the enterprise groups possess in Japan. Instead, they are directly managed by the South Korean state through planning agencies and fiscal controls. Whereas the intermarket groups in Japan are based on a central bank and trading company, in South Korea *chaebol* rely on financing

---

[4] Many of these major firms are independent of the established *keiretsu*. According to Abegglen and Stalk (1985, pp. 189–90), these firms represent the fastest growing sector of the Japanese economy. As these firms grow larger, however, they come to resemble the *keiretsu*: "Some have become so large and successful that through subsidiaries and affiliates they now control groups of their own."

American Journal of Sociology

TABLE 3

CONTRIBUTION TO GROSS DOMESTIC PRODUCTION IN THE
MANUFACTURING SECTOR BY *Chaebol* GROUPS IN SOUTH KOREA (in
percentages)

Number of *Chaebols*	1973	1975	1978	1984–85
4 largest*	...	...	...	45.0
5 largest†	8.8	12.6	18.4	...
10 largest†	13.9	18.9	23.4	...
20 largest†	21.8	28.9	33.2	...
50 largest‡	...	...	...	80.0

* From *Business Week* (1985).
† From Koo (1984, p. 1032).
‡ From *Hankook Ilbo* (1985).

from state banks and government-controlled trading companies. With this type of support, the *chaebol* have developed at a phenomenal rate, as shown in table 3. In addition, in contrast to Japan, outside the *chaebol* networks there are few large, successful independent firms and less subcontracting between large and small firms.[5]

In Taiwan, the family firm (*jiazuqiye*) and the business group (*jituanqiye*) are the dominant organizational forms throughout the economy, especially in the export sector. Unlike in either Japan or South Korea, in Taiwan there are relatively low levels of vertical and horizontal integration and a relative absence of oligarchic concentrations. Family firms predominate, and they are usually small to medium in size (i.e., fewer than 300 employees or total assets of less than $20 million U.S.). According to Zhao (1982), of the 68,898 firms registered in 1976, 97.33% were small to medium in size. These firms employed about 60% of Taiwan's workers and accounted for 46% of the GNP and 65% of Taiwan's exports. (For GNP contributions of the largest firms, see table 4.) Some of these firms form production, assembly, or distribution networks among themselves, often linking together through informal contracts. Other firms, however, perform subcontracting work for larger firms.

Jituanqiye, or large business groups, cross-cut family firms. Most groups are networks of firms controlled by a single family (Zhonghua

[5] Public sector enterprises are important in South Korea, even in export manufacturing. This sector continues to grow in importance in tandem with the *chaebol,* at the same time that the public sectors in Japan and Taiwan are declining both in size and in their involvement in export manufacturing. As in Japan, in South Korea there also are large associations of firms: the Korean Federation of Small Business, the Korean Traders' Association, the Federation of Korean Industries. But these associations do not have the influence of their Japanese counterparts, and "they have been accused of meekly obeying government directives" (Bunge 1982, p. 122).

Far East

TABLE 4

CONTRIBUTION TO GROSS NATIONAL PRODUCT BY FIRM SIZE IN
TAIWAN (in percentages)

Number of Firms	1980	1981	1982	1983
5 largest	5.52	4.90	5.02	5.45
10 largest	8.70	7.91	7.69	8.23
20 largest	12.66	11.73	10.96	11.85

SOURCE.—*Tianxia zazhi* (World Journal), September 1, 1983, pp. 63–84.

TABLE 5

CONTRIBUTION TO GROSS NATIONAL PRODUCT BY THE LARGEST 100 BUSINESS GROUPS
IN TAIWAN

	1973	1974	1977	1979	1981	1983
Percentage of GNP	34.0	29.5	29.1	32.8	30.0	31.7
Percentage of employees	5.1	5.1	5.0	4.9	4.6	4.7

SOURCE.—Zhonghua Zhengxinso (1985, pp. 46–47).

Zhengxinso 1985). These networks, however, do not rival the size of
business groups in Japan and South Korea. Instead, most consist of conglomerate holdings of small, medium, and a few modestly large firms. As
shown in table 5, a survey of the 100 largest business groups in Taiwan
between the years 1973 and 1983 revealed remarkable stability in the
overall economy, especially when compared with the rising corporate
holdings in Japan and the phenomenal growth of the *chaebol* in South
Korea (Zhonghua Zhengxinso 1985).

We develop the details of these patterns of business networks as we
discuss the market, culture, and authority explanations for these differences.

THE MARKET EXPLANATION

The market explanation for organizational structure is associated most
importantly with Alfred D. Chandler's analysis of the American business
firm. *The Visible Hand* (1977) attempts to account for the development
and rapid diffusion of the modern corporation. The invention of the
corporation, what Chandler calls "multiunit" business enterprise, accelerated the rate of industrialization in the United States and, as American management ideas spread abroad, in the industrializing world generally. Although Chandler (1984) recognizes local differences in the

American Journal of Sociology

spread of the multiunit firm to Western Europe and Japan, he attributes such differences largely to market characteristics. The United States was the "seed bed" of managerial capitalism, not Europe, because of "the size and nature of its domestic market" (1977, p. 498).

The logic of Chandler's analysis is a straightforward developmental thesis of institutional change based on changing market conditions.[6] Chandler shows that the preindustrial American economy was dominated by small, traditional organizations: partnerships or family-owned businesses with limited outputs. The traditional business typically received its raw materials and tools from a general merchant who in turn purchased at wholesale the business's finished goods and distributed them in nearby markets at retail prices. The general merchant was the kingpin of the colonial economy (1977, p. 18). After the colonial period and until the advent of the railways, traditional businesses became more specialized, with the general merchant giving way to the commission merchant. But even with these changes, the essential organization of the traditional firm stayed the same. They "remained small and personally managed because the volume of business handled by even the largest was not yet great enough to require the services of a large permanent managerial hierarchy" (1977, p. 48).

The development of a nation-spanning railroad network in the United States in the mid-1800s had two important consequences for industrial organization (1977, pp. 79–187). First, the railroads, the first geographically dispersed business, were compelled to develop innovative strategies of management; they developed the first multiunit firm organizations. Second, and more important, the railroad made it possible for small, traditional businesses to buy and sell in much larger markets, and larger markets made it possible for them to increase the volume of production manifold. Newly enlarged businesses now found it more efficient to perform under one corporate roof the multiple services performed by various commission merchants. Each business arranged the purchase of its own raw materials, the financing of its debts, the production of goods, and the location of and distribution to markets. Managerial or administrative coordination of these multiple activities "permitted greater productivity, lower costs, and higher profits than coordination by market mechanisms" (1977, p. 6). Chandler argues for the technical superiority of administrative over market coordination under conditions of mass markets created by the development of transportation networks.

[6] In a personal comment, William G. Roy reminded us that Chandler's explanation is economic only in a narrow sense. Chandler considers mainly the flow of goods within and between firms. He does not include in his explanation the dynamics of money and finance. Inflation and deflation, busts and booms, credit and capital—none of these factors are a part of his explanation for the rise of modern corporations.

Chandler's argument rests largely on technological causes. A related but much more economy-oriented argument has been developed by Oliver E. Williamson (1975, 1981, 1983, 1985). Building on the work of earlier economists (Commons 1934; Coase 1937), Williamson argues that the basic unit of economic analysis is the economic transaction—the exchange of goods or services across technological boundaries (e.g., the transformation of raw materials into finished goods or the purchase of goods for money). Every transaction contains costs, and especially those costs associated with ensuring that each party to a transaction lives up to the terms of the agreement. The more the uncertainty within the marketplace, Williamson argues (1985, pp. 30–32, 47–50, 64–67), the greater the likelihood that some parties will cheat, "will act opportunistically with guile." The more such opportunistic behavior occurs, the less reliable, the less efficient, and the less profitable the marketplace becomes. At this point, businesses reorganize to correct the deficiencies of the marketplace; they expand their organization through vertical or horizontal integration, thereby creating a "governance structure" that internalizes transactions, reducing transaction costs and increasing efficiency (1985, pp. 68–162).

Using transaction-cost theory, Williamson develops a theory of modern business organization. Multiunit firms arise when internally conducted transactions cost less than market-mediated transactions. The more complex and uncertain the economic environment, the more likely it is that businesses will expand their organization. Expansion reduces uncertainty and transaction costs and maximizes efficiency. For Williamson, the forms of organization that survive in specific economic arenas are the ones that deliver products more efficiently.[7]

To Chandler, multiunit firms offer superior coordination; to Williamson, lower transaction costs. Chandler acknowledges the influence of historical factors in explaining organization; Williamson explains the variety of organizations according to transactions: "There are so many kinds of organizations because transactions differ so greatly and efficiency is realized only if governance structures are tailored to the specific needs of each type of transaction" (1981, p. 568). Both, however, are efficiency theorists and see organization structure as the calculated expression of economically rational persons pursuing profit (Perrow 1981; Perrow 1986, pp. 219–57).

Chandler's market explanation of multiunit businesses can be applied to Japan, Korea, and Taiwan in a straightforward fashion but with am-

---

[7] This idea is a central thesis in the work of other economists as well: "Absent fiat, the form of organization that survives in an activity is the one that delivers the product demanded by customers at the lowest price while covering costs" (Fama and Jensen 1983, p. 327).

American Journal of Sociology

biguous results. Williamson's central concepts are more difficult to operationalize, particularly "transaction costs" and "contracts" (Perrow 1986, pp. 241–47). Although both Chandler and Williamson qualify their theories at various points, they restrict their explanations to decisive economic variables.[8] Therefore, differences in organizational structure necessarily would have to be explained in terms of crucial differences among the three countries. We find, however, that all three countries are very similar in regard to the crucial variables Chandler pinpoints. Moreover, even loosely applied, Williamson's theory does not seem to explain adequately the differences among the three.

First, in all three countries internal transportation and communication systems are well developed, modern, and certainly far beyond what they were in late 19th-century America (see, e.g., Ranis 1979, p. 225). External transportation and communication systems are also well developed. Second, the three countries possess substantial and growing internal mass markets, which have already risen above the level of early 20th-century America. But more important, all the countries have vast external markets. Third, Japan, South Korea, and Taiwan use, have available, or have developed, the most advanced technologies in the various industrial sectors. This level of technology, of course, is far advanced over that discussed by Chandler. Fourth, business enterprises in all three countries operate on principles of profit in the marketplace. By any definition, they are capitalist enterprises; they practice cost accounting, depend on free labor, develop through invested capital, and, if unsuccessful, may go bankrupt.[9]

Yet, despite these extensive similarities, as well as the others discussed earlier, among the three countries on all macroeconomic variables, the organizational structures of business enterprises are quite different. Moreover, even when each country is considered individually without regard to the other two, the enterprise structure is only partially explained by the market approach.

On the surface, Japanese business enterprise would seem to satisfy the conditions of Chandler's interpretation the best. The intermarket groups now include firms ranked among the largest in the world. They are vast, complexly organized, multiunit enterprises. They are successful in the world economy, where each of them has a sizable share of the total

---

[8] Writing with Ouchi, Williamson acknowledges that different societies may have preferences for either a "hard" or a "soft" form of making contracts (Williamson and Ouchi 1981). Chandler (1977, pp. 498–500) implicitly qualifies his theory by noting that in some other societies there were social factors blocking what would otherwise be the natural development of managerial capitalism.

[9] Although state/business cooperation is greater in Japan and South Korea than in the United States, these countries do not protect enterprise from business failure.

Far East

market in their respective sectors. Moreover, as is well known, these enterprises attempt to control the marketplace through administrative means (e.g., cartelization) insofar as it is possible (Johnson 1982; Vogel 1979). When Americans speak of emulating Japanese management practices, it is the management techniques of the intermarket groups, such as Mitsubishi and Sumitomo, or the giant *kaisha,* such as Toyota, to which they refer. In fact, Chandler (1977, p. 499) acknowledges that Japanese corporations satisfy his definition of the modern managerial business enterprise.

The South Korean case fits the market explanation less well than the Japanese case seemingly does. But if one includes the state as an aspect of business organization, then the Korean case might be squeezed into a market explanation. East Asian political organization has, of course, been a "multiunit" organization for centuries, but if one ignores this fact, then one could argue that, because of market conditions and the circumstances of a late-developing economy, the rapid industrialization in South Korea favored the formation of a type of state capitalism. [10] Vertical integration in South Korea occurred both at the level of the *chaebol* and at the level of the state, and both forms of integration were structurally and causally linked. Therefore, unlike the firm in the United States and somewhat unlike the firm in Japan, the South Korean multiunit business firm is not independent from state organization. As we will discuss later, important functional operations of the firm are controlled by bureaucratic departments of government. The firm is not an independent creation of market forces, even though state organization and the managerial corps of the *chaebol* attempt administratively to control the marketplace.

If the South Korean case can be made to fit Chandler's thesis, the Taiwan case obviously cannot. [11] Here we find, relative to the other cases, a conspicuous lack of vertical integration and the absence of the oligarchic concentration that occurred in the United States, Japan, and especially South Korea. The unwillingness or inability of Taiwanese entrepreneurs to develop large organizations or concentrated industries appears to have defied even the encouragement of government. Ramon Myers (1984) cites an example: When the government persuaded a successful businessman, Y. C. Wang, to establish a plastics factory, the Chinese impulse was immediately to copy Wang's success. "Three other businessmen without any experience in plastics quickly built similar fac-

[10] There is now a considerable literature on the Gerschenkron (1962) thesis that, among developing societies, strong states are able to promote industrialization better than those having different state formations (see Evans, Rueschemeyer, and Skocpol [1985] for a survey of this literature).

[11] For another, related treatment of Taiwan as a deviant case, see Barrett and Whyte's (1982) insightful use of Taiwan data to criticize dependency theory.

American Journal of Sociology

tories, and many more entered the industry later. Between 1957 and 1971 plastic production grew 45% annually. In 1957 only 100 small firms fabricated products from plastic supplied by Wang's company, but in 1970 more than 1,300 small firms bought from plastic suppliers" (1984, p. 516).

The plastics industry is one of the most concentrated in Taiwan's private sector. The tendency in this industry is the rule elsewhere: the "unusual feature of manufacturing and service firms in Taiwan is their limited size: each operation is usually owned by a single proprietor or family" (Myers 1984, p. 515). Moreover, the organization of such firms is usually of single units, functionally defined in relation to a finished product. These small firms join together in what is called the *weixing gongchang*, which is a system of satellite factories that join together to produce a finished product. Such interorganizational networks are based on noncontractual agreements sometimes made between family members who own related firms but more often between unrelated businessmen. On personalistic terms, these businessmen informally negotiate such matters as the quality and quantity of their products. For instance, in Taiwan, the world's leading exporter of bicycles, the bicycle industry is organized in a vast array of separate parts manufacturers and bicycle-assembly firms.[12] Similarly, Myers reports that Taiwan's television industry is composed of 21 major firms and hundreds of satellite firms: "Since this industry [requires] thousands of small parts such as picture tubes, tuners, transformers, loudspeakers, coils, and antennae, countless Chinese firms sprang up to supply these in ever greater quantities" (Myers 1984, p. 517).

Although there are exceptions, the small-to-medium size, single-unit firm is so much the rule in Taiwan that when a family business becomes successful the pattern of investment is not to attempt vertical integration in order to control the marketplace, but rather is to diversify by starting a series of unrelated firms that share neither account books nor management. From a detailed survey of the 96 largest business groups (*jituanqiye*) in Taiwan, we find that 59% of them are owned and controlled by family groups (Zhonghua Zhengxinso 1985). Partnerships among unrelated individuals, which, as Wong Sui-lun (1985) points out, will likely turn into family-based business organizations in the next generation, account for 38%. An example of such a family-controlled business group is the Cai family enterprise, until recently the second largest private holding in Taiwan.[13] The family business included over 100 separate firms, the

[12] Information based on interview material.

[13] The family enterprise was rocked by scandals in the early months of 1985. The scandal forced the family to open their books and to account for their economic success. For one of the better descriptions of the Cai family enterprise, see Chen (1985).

Far East

management of which was divided into eight groupings of unrelated businesses run by different family members, each of whom kept a separate account book (Chen 1985, pp. 13–17).

Taiwan does not fit Chandler's evolutionary, technology-based model of modern business organization. But neither does it seem to fit Williamson's model of business organization. Although the variables for transaction-cost theory are more difficult to operationalize than the variables for Chandler's theory, it seems apparent that the growth of large business groups in Taiwan cannot be explained by either transaction-cost reduction or market uncertainty, two key factors contributing to the boundary expansion of firms.

In the first place, a normal pattern by which business groups acquire firms is to start or buy businesses in expanding areas of the economy. Often, these firms remain small to medium in size, are not necessarily integrated into the group's other holdings (even for purposes of accounting), and cooperate extensively with firms outside the holdings of the business group. As such, firm acquisitions represent speculation in new markets rather than attempts to reduce transaction costs between previously contracting firms.

Second, uncertainty is a constant feature in Taiwan's economic environment.[14] Family firms, many no larger than the extended household, usually do not have either the ability or the means to seek out or forecast information on demand in foreign export markets. They produce goods or, more likely, parts for contractors with whom they have continuing relationships and on whom they depend for subsequent orders. The information they receive on product demand is second- and thirdhand and restricted to the present. They have limited abilities to plan organizational futures and to determine whether their products will find a market and elicit continuing orders. In fact, misinformation and poor market forecasting are common, as is evident in the high rate of bankruptcy in Taiwan.

Conditions like these are the very ones that Williamson predicts should produce vertical integration. These conditions should prevail especially during business depressions in the world economy, such as those that occurred in 1974–78 and again in 1980–81. Tables 4 and 5, however, show no discernible trend in this direction. If anything, one might argue that in Taiwan uncertainty leads in the opposite direction, away from

---

[14] Very little research has been done on the business environment in which small- and medium-sized firms in Taiwan operate. Some hints are found in Myers (1984), Peng (1984), Hu (1984), and DeGlopper (1972). In the popular press, however, the topic is discussed frequently, particularly in the very good business magazines, which are among the most widely read magazines in Taiwan. The following discussion draws particularly on Chen (1983).

American Journal of Sociology

strategies of vertical integration and toward a strategy of spreading investment risks.

Chandler's and Williamson's theories do not explain the organizational structure of Taiwan business. But if one looks more closely at the Japanese and South Korean cases, then it becomes equally obvious that they, too, do not fit the market explanations well.[15] Intermarket business groups date from the beginning of Japanese industrialization, in some cases even before. Therefore, growing technology, expanding communication, and the increased volume of manufacturing transactions are not the *causes* of Japanese industrial structure because the structure precedes the economic growth.

In the Tokugawa era, from 1603 to 1867, a rising merchant class developed a place for itself in the feudal shogunate. Merchant houses did not challenge the traditional authority structure but subordinated themselves to whatever powers existed. Indeed, a few houses survived the Meiji Restoration smoothly, and one in particular (Mitsui) became a prototype for the *zaibatsu* (Bisson 1954, p. 7). Other *zaibatsu* arose early in the Meiji era from enterprises that had been previously run for the benefit of the feudal overlords, the *daimyo*. In the Meiji era, the control of such *han* enterprises moved to the private sphere where, in the case of Mitsubishi, former samurai became the owners and managers (Hirschmeier and Yui 1981, pp. 138–42). In all cases of the *zaibatsu* that began early in the Meiji era, the overall structure was an intermarket group. The member firms were legal corporations, were large multiunit enterprises, and could accumulate capital through corporate means. As Nakamura (1983, pp. 63–68) put it, "Japan introduced the [organizational] framework of industrial society first and the content afterward."

Zaibatsu clearly emerged from a traditional form of enterprise. Although they adapted spectacularly well to an international, capitalist economy, they did not develop in response to it. Therefore, Chandler's assertion that the United States is the "seedbed of managerial capitalism" (1977, p. 498), that this form of organization "spread" to Japan (p. 500), is dubious and at the very least must be substantially qualified.

The organizational structure preceded economic development in South Korea as well. The organizational structure of *chaebol,* as well as state capitalism in general, although encouraged and invigorated by world economic conditions, can be traced more persuasively to premodern political practices, to pre–World War II Japanese industrial policy (Myers and Peattie 1984, pp. 347–452), and to the borrowing of organizational de-

[15] See Dore (1983) for an excellent critique of Williamson's theory as it would be applied to Japan.

signs for industrialization from Japan than to those factors specified by either Chandler or Williamson. At the very best, causality is unclear.

The market explanation neither explains the organizational differences among the three countries nor offers an unqualified explanation for any one country. Still, at one level the market explanation is certainly correct. Transportation systems, mass markets, advanced technology, and considerations of profit all influence the organization of modern business, and it is inconceivable that modern business firms would have developed, as they have in fact developed, in the absence of these factors. Nonetheless, to equate these factors with organizational structure, to make them the sole causes of organizational design, is not only theoretically and substantively to misinterpret business organization but also to make a serious methodological blunder. Chandler and Williamson, each in his own way, concentrate their entire causal argument on proximate factors. Their cases are analogous to arguing that the assassination of Archduke Ferdinand caused World War I or that the possession of handguns causes crime. Clearly, important causal links are present in all these relationships, but secondary factors play crucial roles in shaping the patterns of unfolding events. To banish all secondary factors, such as political structures and cultural patterns, is to fall into what David Hackett Fischer (1970, p. 172) calls the "reductive fallacy," reducing "complexity to simplicity, or diversity to uniformity. . . . This sort of error appears in causal explanations which are constructed like a single chain and stretched taut across a vast chasm of complexity." This is what Chandler and Williamson do in their attempts to derive organizational structure solely from economic principles.

THE CULTURE EXPLANATION

Cultural explanations for the diversity of organizational structures and practice are many. Smircich (1983) identifies no fewer than five ways researchers have used the culture framework. Some analysts, for example, see culture as an independent variable, exerting pressure on organizational arrangements (e.g., Harbison and Meyer 1959; Crozier 1964), or as a dependent variable in comparative management studies (Peters and Waterman 1982). Most important recent approaches see culture as socially created "expressive forms, manifestations of human consciousness. Organizations are understood and analyzed not mainly in economic or material terms . . ." (Smircich 1983, p. 347). While market analysis sees organizations striving toward maximum efficiency, cultural theorists probe the nonrational, subjective aspects of organizational life.

Culture studies tend to link organizational patterns with the cultural

American Journal of Sociology

practices of the larger society. For example, Nakane's classic study, *Japanese Society* (1970), combines cultural and structural analyses to show how the group relations of the Japanese family serve larger social institutions, including Japanese enterprise: ". . . the characteristics of Japanese enterprise as a social group are, first, that the group is itself family-like and, second, that it pervades even the private lives of its employees, for each family joins extensively in the enterprise" (1970, p. 19). Swedish shop-floor democracy can be traced to strong socialist sentiments in the country (Blumberg 1973). Worker self-management in Yugoslavia is linked to an ideology of social ownership (Tannenbaum et al. 1974). Americans' strong central values of individualism and free enterprise lead to segmentalist organizations (Kanter 1983) and fear of central planning by government (Miles 1980).

Most culture studies do not concern themselves with the economic implications of corporate culture, but a few more popular works do, often to critique economic approaches to management. Peters and Waterman's *In Search of Excellence* (1982, pp. 29–54) repudiates the "rational model" of organizations, citing, as more successful, organizations that promote shared values and productivity through people-centered policies.

William Ouchi's recent works (1980, 1984) are important links between culture studies and the economic tradition.[16] Whereas Williamson describes organizational structures ("governance structures") as emerging from market transactions, Ouchi claims that cultural values such as "trust" influence whether individuals will resort to contracts and other devices of control of mediate transactions (see Maitland, Bryson, and Van de Ven 1985).

If the market explanation errs by emphasizing proximate causes, then the culture explanation of organization errs in the opposite direction. By concentrating on secondary causes, primordial constants that undergird everything, the cultural explanation works poorly when one attempts to examine a changing organizational environment or to analyze differences among organizations in the same cultural area. Therefore, to use this explanation to account for differences among organizational structures of enterprise in Japan, South Korea, and Taiwan, one must demonstrate cultural differences that would account for different organizational patterns. Such cultural differences, we argue, are difficult to isolate.

The first step in locating cultural differences is to ask what factors would be included in a cultural explanation and what factors would not (see, e.g., Gamst and Norbeck 1976). Many scholars define culture as the

---

[16] It is important to note the collaborative work of Williamson and Ouchi (1981), which is an attempt to introduce a cultural variable concerning trust into Williamson's transaction and Chandler's visible-hand theories.

S70

socially learned way of life of a people and the means by which order-liness and patterned relations are maintained in a society. While the concept of order suggests its link to a sociological authority-relations understanding of society, in practice culture theorists tend to be con-cerned with the symbolic, rather than the material, impulse behind social life—with norms, values, shared meanings, and cognitive structures (see Harris [1979] for an exception). Basic culture ideals, and myths and rituals in relation to those ideals, are explored for their ability to integrate persons and to reinforce and celebrate common understandings.[17] Recent works about corporate culture, for example, refer to "weak" versus "strong" corporate cultures: how engaging and encompassing corporate life is for employees. While culture may be understood as universal to the society and changing only slowly, culture theory tends not to look beyond a culture of immediate interest, and especially not at long-term historical trends. In organizational analysis, culture study is social science writ small: either rich, detailed ethnographies of a single people during a relatively short historical period or, at most, the comparison of a limited number of bounded cases. Without a wider scope, such an approach is of only limited use in explaining differences in business organization among societies. Fortunately, in regard to the cases at hand, there have been numerous attempts to develop more broadly based cultural explanations.

The culture explanation has been used often to understand Japanese corporate practices (see Abegglen 1958; Benedict 1946). Although a num-ber of points of departure have been taken, many share the belief that it is the central Japanese value of *wa*, or harmony, that explains Japanese organizational arrangements. *Wa* denotes a state of integration, a har-monious unity of diverse parts of the social order. The organizational consequences of *wa* are numerous, but most important is the subordina-tion of the individual to the group and the practices to which that leads: the necessity to check with colleagues during contract negotiations; the routine and calculated movement of personnel among functional areas to promote wider understanding at the expense of specialization; the promo-tion of cohorts, not individuals, up the organization ladder; and the de-velopment of lifetime employment, internal labor markets, and seniority systems (*nenkō*) to maintain the integrity of the group. The wearing of uniforms, the performance of group exercises, the singing of corporate anthems, and even intercorporate cooperation have been explained as expressions of *wa*. At the societal level, cooperation is orchestrated by the

---

[17] From a cultural perspective, organizations can be seen in two ways: first, as culture-producing entities and, second, as expressions of the larger culture of the society. Recent studies of corporate culture reflect the first approach, but the second holds more promise for understanding the development of organizational arrangements in a given society.

American Journal of Sociology

state: "The Japanese government does not stand apart from or over the community; it is rather the place where *wa* deals are negotiated" (Sayle 1985, p. 35).

As persuasive as the culture approach seems in explaining the Japanese case, it has suffered substantial attack. An analysis of one practice, *nenkō* (seniority system), suffices to suggest the nature of the critique. *Wa* and its expression in practices such as *nenkō* have been described by culture theorists as part of a cultural continuity extending to preindustrial times. But there are many examples of different practices and of discontinuity. For instance, labor turnover rates were high before 1920 and very high in the late 1930s and early 1940s (Evans 1971; Taira 1970). Why, then, were apparently expensive lifetime employment and seniority preferences offered by enterprise group firms? Economics provides the alternative explanation that it is economically rational to maintain a stable work force and protect training investments. "It appears that some of the industrial features thought to be traditionally Japanese . . . are in fact fairly recent innovations, supported by traditional values to be sure, but consciously designed for good profit-maximizing reasons" (Dore 1962, p. 120). Jacoby further argues that, although economic interests are important in understanding the institution of lifetime employment and its adoption before World War II, they cannot explain why it exists only in some firms and not others, applies only to some worker groups in the same organization, and appeared at a given historic juncture. He suggests an explanation in line with an authority relations approach: "More careful historical research on the circumstances surrounding the introduction of internal labor markets in Japan indicates the importance of the increase in firm size and complexity, the change in skilled labor organization, and the desire to forestall unionization. These factors are causally connected to the emergence of an emphasis on stability and control in input markets, as well as the creation of new pressures to maintain employee effort and loyalty" (1979, p. 196). That *wa* provides a socially accepted justification for *nenkō* and that *nenkō* accords easily with Japanese culture cannot be denied. Culture constants, however, are insufficient to explain changing organizational practices.[18]

Similar culture arguments have been made for Chinese management practices (Chen 1984; Chen and Qiu 1984; Hou 1984; Huang 1984; Silin 1976; Zeng 1984). For the most part, they focus on the Confucian belief system and its expression in enterprise. Confucianism promotes individual self-control and dutiful conduct to one's superiors and particularly to

---

[18] For a very persuasive argument, in line with the one we present here, assessing the contribution of culture to Japanese corporate practices, see Dore (1973, pp. 375–403); also, see Johnson (1982, p. 307).

one's family. At some level, modern Chinese organizations reflect these patterns. Comparative management studies show that Chinese entrepreneurs maintain more distance from workers than do the Japanese and are likely to promote competitive relations, not cooperation, among subordinates (who may be family members) (Fukuda 1983). But, unlike in Japan, where loyalty to the firm is important, Chinese loyalty is not firm specific and may extend to a network of family enterprises. Because a Chinese businessman can with some assurance trust that people in his family network will respect the Confucian obligation to act with honor toward relatives whenever possible, business is conducted with members of one's kinship network (Chan 1982; Huang 1984; Chen and Qiu 1984; Omohundro 1981; Redding 1980). Moreover, Confucianism has been described as a system that promotes strong bonds at the local level when face-to-face relations are paramount but that, in mediating broader relations, is a weak form of social control.

Despite an appearance of cohering, the Confucian culture argument, if pressed, falls apart. It is used to explain the conduct in large factories (Silin 1976) as well as in small, premodern commercial activities (Yang 1970). The question here is why today's enterprise organization in Taiwan is composed of relatively small to medium-sized, family-run firms. The Confucian culture argument alone will not work well because the culture is a broadly based underlying cognitive factor (Redding 1980) that affects the society in general and for that reason explains nothing in particular.

This criticism of the cultural explanation gains force especially when one considers that both South Korea and Japan have been deeply influenced by Confucianism, as well as by Buddhism and various folk religions, which China also shares. In fact, in regard to underlying cultural values, Japan, South Korea, and Taiwan are not three separate cultures, but rather parts of the same great tradition. All societies in East Asia have many cultural traits in common, which can be traced to the long-term interaction between the societies in the region. Some of the intermixing of cultures can be explained politically. Imperial China always considered Korea a tributary state and exacted submission during many long periods. More recently, Japan conquered and colonized both Korea and Taiwan and set out systematically to impose Japanese language and behavioral patterns on Taiwanese and Korean societies.

Intermixing due to politics is only part of the picture, however. A much more significant interaction occurred at the levels of language, elite culture, and religion. The direction of the cultural borrowing was usually from China to Japan and Korea. Both Korea and Japan borrowed and used Chinese script. Chinese was the written language of the Korean court until *hangul* was introduced in the 16th century. In Japan, the court

American Journal of Sociology

language was a mixture of Chinese and Japanese, which itself had been adapted to written expression through the use of Chinese script. Scholars in both locations learned classical Chinese and used it in government and in arts. Beyond the Chinese script, poetry, painting styles, motifs on all artifacts, literature of all types, elite styles of dress and expression, architecture, and elements of cuisine—all these and more intermixed, so that no aspect of elite life in Japan or South Korea can be said to be untouched by cultural diffusion from China.

Besides politics and elite cultural intermixing, there was religious diffusion that permeated all levels in all three societies. Two religions are particularly important. Confucianism, which contains an elaborate ideology of familism and an equally elaborate ideology of statecraft, was supported by the elites in all three societies. In imperial China, this was more or less the case from the time of the *Han* period (established in 221 B.C.) to the fall of the empire in A.D. 1911. Confucianism had less continuous influence and came later in the other two societies but was extremely important in Korea and Japan during the most recent dynastic periods. Buddhism entered China from India in the 2d and 3d centuries A.D. and later became very important before it was finally proscribed at the state level. Thereafter, Buddhism was primarily a local religion in China, merging with other folk practices. In Korea and Japan, after diffusing from China, Buddhism became an important religion at both the state and local levels. In all three societies, Buddhism and Confucianism continue to be important, with the symbolism and values of each being key components of modern life.

We are not arguing that these three societies have the same culture. In the same way that England and France do not have the same culture, these three societies do not either. But just as France and England belong to the same cultural complex (Western civilization) so do Japan, Korea, and China (Eastern civilization). The decisive point here is that we are not dealing with three distinct cases, but rather three societies that share many of the same cultural patterns. Therefore, using the cultural explanation, we can argue, as have others (Berger 1984; Tu 1984), that this common culture helps to explain common patterns in all three societies, such as the importance of the family, obedience to authority, high rates of literacy, the desire to achieve, and the willingness to work hard. What the culture explanation, however, is not able to do is to distinguish the many differences that exist among these societies, including the organizational structure of business enterprises. The culture explanation cannot explain changes and differences well because the causal argument is concentrated on secondary factors, especially in primordial constants, and thus the explanation only with difficulty deals with factors that underlie historical changes.

Far East

AUTHORITY STRUCTURE AND ORGANIZATIONAL PRACTICE

The third approach to understanding organizations that we employ is a political economy approach primarily derived from the work of Max Weber (1978). One of the best examples of this approach is Reinhard Bendix's *Work and Authority in Industry* (1974), a historical study of the development of managerial ideology and practice in England, Russia, and the United States. Bendix covers some of the same territory as Chandler in *The Visible Hand* (1977) but provides an alternative explanatory framework.[19]

Briefly, in the Weberian view, many factors contribute to organizational structure. The structures of armies, tax collection, business enterprises, and officialdoms are influenced, most importantly, by the task at hand. But even when we consider task requirements, there is much room for variation, and historical and situational factors such as available technology, conditions of membership (Weber 1978, pp. 52–53), and the class and status composition of the group (1978, pp. 926–39) will have an influence.

But all organizations, no matter what their purpose or historical setting (although related to both), have an internal pattern of command and compliance. Organizations only exist insofar as "there is a probability that certain persons will act in such a way as to carry out the order governing the organization" (1978, p. 49). This probability rests in part on normative justifications that underlie given arrangements—who should obey and the distinctive mode of obedience owed to the powers that be. Weber called the underlying justifications "principles of domination."[20] In this context, principles of domination are not abstractions but rather serve as the substantive rationale for action. They provide guides, justifications, and interpretive frameworks for social actors in the daily conduct of organizational activity (Hamilton and Biggart 1984, 1985; Biggart and Hamilton 1984).

The Weberian approach incorporates economic and cultural factors and allows for historical diversity. Principles of domination are clearly related to culture but are not reducible to it. Bendix has shown how economically self-interested strategies of worker control were expressed

---

[19] First published in 1956, Bendix's work has long been noted as one of the most important attempts to analyze management structure in modern industry. For this reason, it is more than surprising that Chandler seems totally to have ignored the one key work in which a clear alternative hypothesis to his own work could be found. For a recent expression of his thesis, see Bendix (1984, pp. 70–90).

[20] For Weber's chief statements on a sociology of domination, see Weber (1978, pp. 941–1211; 1958, pp. 77–128). For general works commenting on Weber's sociology of domination, see Bendix and Roth (1971) and Schluchter (1981); on Weber's sociology of domination in regard to Asia, see Hamilton (1984).

American Journal of Sociology

as management ideologies in industrializing nations. These ideologies were based on an economic rationale, but "ideologies of management can be explained only in part as rationalizations of self-interest; they also result from the legacy of institutions and ideas which is adopted by each generation . . ." (1974, p. 444).

Recent extensions of Weberian views are found in the works of Karl Weick, John Meyer and W. Richard Scott, and Charles Perrow.[21] Weick (1979) discusses how people in organizations enact role-based strategies of organizational control; the enactments contain ritual, and tradition (organizational culture) builds around ritualized enactments. While enactments are certainly related to patterned behavior and the maintenance of predictable orders, they have no necessary connection with efficiency. Indeed, Meyer and Scott (1983) show that whole organizations adopt management practices for reasons of legitimacy; the organization enacts patterns understood and accepted by important constituents, not for reasons of economic rationality.[22] Perrow (1981, 1986) argues that firms are profitable not merely because they are efficient but because they are successful instruments of domination.

The market explanation concentrates on immediate factors and the culture explanation on distant ones. Both explanations are obviously important, but neither deals directly with organizations themselves; although both claim to account for organizations, they make organizations appear rather mysteriously out of a mix of economic variables or a brew of cultural beliefs. The authority explanation deals with organizations themselves and conceptualizes them broadly as patterned interactions among people, that is, as structures of authority. It aims at understanding how these structures came into being, how they are maintained, and to what consequence. As such, it attempts historically adequate explanations and therefore differs from both general cultural theories and specified, predictive economic models.

In applying this approach to account for business organization in East Asia, one must demonstrate decisive differences among the three societies

[21] After this article had been revised for publication, two articles appeared that independently call for the kind of institutional analysis of culture that we attempt to develop with the authority approach. Swidler (1986) calls for a "culture in action." "Cultural end values," she argues (1986, p. 284) do not "shape action in the long run. Indeed a culture has enduring effects on those who hold it, not by shaping the ends they pursue, but by providing the characteristic repertoire from which they build lines of action." Arguing for an institutional approach, Wuthnow (1985) applies a very similar line of reasoning in his critique of the "ideological" model of state structure.

[22] It is, of course, true that, for purposes of legitimizing authority in modern industry, concepts of profit and efficiency are extremely important, as important in political as in economic ways. On this point, see Bendix (1974) and particularly Zucker (1983) and Perrow (1986).

in terms of the structures of authority and further demonstrate that these differences affect organizational practices. Two factors seem particularly important and in need of explanation. First, What are the relationships established between the state and the business sector in the three societies? And second, given that relationship between state and enterprise, What are the structures of authority in each type of business network?

In each of the three societies, the state has pursued similar policies promoting industrialization. Economists describe these policies in terms of a product-cycle industrialization pattern (Cumings 1984) in which import substitution was gradually replaced by aggressive, export-led growth policies (Ranis 1979). What is apparent but left unanalyzed is that such state policies are administered in very different political contexts.

In South Korea, government/business relations follow in the form of what can be called the "strong state" model. In South Korea, the state actively participates in the public and private spheres of the economy and is in fact the leading actor (SaKong 1980). The state achieves its central position through centralized economic planning and through aggressive implementation procedures. The entire government is "geared toward economic policy-making and growth. . . . Economic decision making [is] extremely centralized, and the executive branch dominate[s]" (Bunge 1982, p. 115; Mason et al. 1980, p. 257). Implementation procedures aim at controlling the entire economy. For public enterprises, control is direct and bureaucratic. This sector of the economy, which is relatively small but rapidly expanding, is run as departmental agencies of the state with civil servants as managers. Although not in as direct a fashion as occurs in the public sector, the state controls the private sector "primarily from its control of the banking system and credit rationing" (Westphal et al. 1984, p. 510) and through other financial controls. The state, however, does not hesitate to use noneconomic means to achieve compliance with policy directives. "A firm that does not respond as expected to particular incentives may find that its tax returns are subject to careful examination, or that its application for bank credit is studiously ignored, or that its outstanding bank loans are not renewed. If incentive procedures do not work, government agencies show no hesitation in resorting to command backed by compulsion. In general, it does not take a Korean firm long to learn that it will 'get along' best by 'going along' " (Mason et al. 1980, p. 265).

These procedures apply to all sizes of firms but especially to medium and large firms, which are in fact favored by such planning and implementation procedures (Koo 1984, p. 1032). This is particularly the case for business groups, the *chaebol.* State policies support business concentration, and statistics indeed reveal a rapid change in this direction (Jones and SaKong 1980, p. 268; Koo 1984; *Hankook Ilbo* 1985). In addition,

American Journal of Sociology

many medium and all large firms are tethered by government-controlled credit, by government regulation of the purchase of raw materials and energy, and by government price-setting policies for selected commodities (Weiner 1985, p. 20).

In Japan, the government has developed quite a different relationship with business. The state policy toward business is one of creating and promoting strong intermediate powers, each having considerable autonomy, with the state acting as coordinator of activity and mediator of conflicting interests (Johnson 1982).[23] In business, the most important of these strong intermediate powers are the intermarket groups of large firms. The *zaibatsu* rose to great power in the pre–World War II era, and, because of their link to Japan's imperial past and because of their monopoly characteristics, American occupation authorities legally dissolved them and attempted to set up a new economic system based on the U.S. model. They promoted a union movement and encouraged small- and medium-sized competitive enterprises (Bisson 1954). After the American occupation ended, however, the Japanese government, through both action and strategic inaction, has allowed a maze of large and powerful intermarket groups to reappear.

These business networks and member firms are independent of direct state control, although they may acquiesce to the state's "administrative guidance." This administrative guidance has no statutory or legal basis. Rather, it "reflects above all a recognized common interest between MITI (Ministry of International Trade and Industry) and the leading firms in certain oligopolistic industries, the latter recognizing that guidance may occasionally impair their profits but in the long run will promote joint net revenues in the industry" (Caves and Uekusa 1976, p. 54). As Johnson (1982, p. 196) points out, this political system has led "to genuine public-private cooperation."

The strong state model in South Korea and the strong intermediate power model in Japan contrast sharply with what might be called the strong society model of state/business relations in Taiwan. The state in Taiwan is by no means weak. It is omnipresent, and, ceremonially at least, it repeatedly exacts obeisance. But, in regard to the export business

---

[23] The best analysis of state/business relations is found in Johnson (1982, pp. 196–97, 310–11). He notes that, of the various types of state/business relationships occurring in the past 50 years, "that of public-private cooperation is by far the most important. . . . The chief mechanisms of the cooperative relationship are selective access to governmental or government-guaranteed financing, targeted tax breaks, government-supervised investment coordination in order to keep all participants profitable, the equitable allocation by the state of burdens during times of adversity (something the private cartel finds very hard to do), governmental assistance in the commercialization and sale of products, and governmental assistance when an industry as a whole begins to decline."

sector, the Taiwan government promotes what Little (1979, p. 475) identifies as "virtually free trade conditions" and what Myers (1984, p. 522) calls "planning within the context of a free economy." Such policies have allowed familial patterns to shape the course of Taiwan's industrialization; this has in turn led to decentralized patterns of industrialization, a low level of firm concentration, and a predominance of small- and medium-sized firms.

Before we explain the strong society model further, three aspects of active state/business relations should be stressed. First, the state owns and manages a range of public enterprises that provide import-substituting commodities (e.g., petroleum, steel, and power) and services (e.g., railways and road and harbor construction) and that have been very important to Taiwan's economic development (Gold 1986; Amsden 1985). Unlike this sector in South Korea, public enterprises in Taiwan have steadily decreased in importance, and the government shows no signs of reversal (Gold 1986; Myers 1984). Second, the state imposes import controls on selected products and promotes industrial development in export products through special tax incentive programs and the establishment of export processing zones (Gold 1986; Amsden 1985). These incentives for export production, while they have certainly encouraged industrialization, have not favored industrial concentration, as has occurred in South Korea. Third, as in Japan and South Korea, the state in Taiwan exerts strong controls over the financial system, which includes the banking, insurance, and saving systems. Having one of the highest rates of savings in the world, Taiwan has also developed what Wade (1985) calls a "rigid" fiscal policy of high interest rates to control inflation, a preference for short-term loans, and an attitude of nonsupport for markets in equity capital (e.g., the stock market). Unlike Japan's and South Korea's, however, this financial system favored the development of a curb market, "an unregulated, semi-legal credit market in which loan suppliers and demanders can transact freely at uncontrolled interest rates" (Wade 1985, p. 113). Because most small- and medium-sized firms require only moderate to little investment capital and because such firms have difficulty obtaining bank loans, the curb market has played an extremely important role in financing Taiwan's industrial development (Yang 1981).

The difference in the role of the state between Taiwan and the other two societies is revealed in state planning. Like the South Korean state, Taiwan's government develops economic plans, but unlike South Korea there are no implementation procedures. State planning is done in a "loose, noncommand style," is "unsupported by controls," has no credibility in its economic projections, and has "no importance" in determining economic behavior (Little 1979, p. 487). This unimportance of planning, Little (1979, pp. 487–89) further believes, is even true in public sector

American Journal of Sociology

enterprises. Moreover, of great importance in Taiwan's pattern of industrialization has been the absence, until recently, of spatial planning, including industrial zoning, at the municipal, provincial, and state levels. Considered together, these factors have led Little (1979, p. 488) to argue "that Taiwan planning has not even been intended to be indicative (authoritative). The mechanism usually associated with indicative planning is lacking. There are no standing consultative committees with private industry; any consultations are ad hoc. There are virtually no teeth either."

The lack of strong government intervention in the domestic economy, unlike that in South Korea, and the absence of active support for large firms, unlike that in Japan, has left the economy in Taiwan, especially the export sector, free to work out its own patterns. Using either Chandler's or Williamson's model, one would expect rapid concentration and the development of managerial capitalism. What has in fact emerged is something quite different, almost the opposite of what either theorist would predict: a low level of business concentration and a decentralized pattern of industrial development. And with this approach, Taiwan's sustained rate of economic growth during the past 30 years is one of the highest in the world.

Why did the state officials in each case choose one form of business relationship over other possible alternatives? For each society, it is clear that their choices were neither random nor inevitable. In each case, there was latitude. For instance, after the American occupation, the Japanese government could have supported and built on the system the Americans established, which was based on competition among small- and medium-sized firms. But instead they opted for creating strong intermediate powers, in terms of both economic and social controls (Johnson 1982, pp. 198–241). South Korea could have chosen the Japanese route, by building on the *zaibatsu* model they had inherited from the Japanese. Or they could have adopted the model found in Taiwan, by supporting the small-to-medium-sized private-sector firms that had developed in Korea before World War II (Juhn 1971) and still operate there to some extent. Instead, they opted for a strong state. Finally, Taiwan could have followed the other courses as well. In the early fifties, in fact, Taiwan clearly was moving toward the strong state model: the state had incorporated the former *zaibatsu* into the state apparatus, had aggressively forced the landowning class to accept sweeping land reform policies, and with a strong military presence was making ready to return to the mainland. On the other hand, the state could have supported a strong business class, as the Chiang Kai-shek regime had done with the Shanghai industrialists in the early thirties on the mainland. But, after some hesitation, the Nationalist government developed and since then has pursued a nonfavoritist policy of "letting the people prosper." In each case, the decisions about the state/business relations were not inevitable, and certainly for the case of Taiwan it takes no imagination to envision a different course, because another outcome occurred across the Taiwan straits, in mainland China.

Therefore, what determined the choice? Many factors were important, but it seems likely that the most important were not economic factors at all. Rather, the key decisions about state/business relations should be seen in a much larger context, as flowing from the attempt on the part of political leaders to legitimize a system of rule. Each regime was at a crucial point in its survival after wars and occupations and needed to establish a rationale for its existence. In fashioning such a rationale, each regime in the end resorted to time-tested, institutionally acceptable ways of fashioning a system of political power. In each case, the first independent regime of the postwar era attempted to legitimize state power by adopting a reformulated model of imperial power of the kind that had existed before industrialization began. Such a model built on the preexisting normative expectations of political subjects and contained an ideology of rulership. Moreover, some of the institutions to support these models were still in place.

In Japan, the decisive factor was the presence of the emperor, who continues to stand as a symbol of political unity (Bendix 1977, p. 489). But the emperor was above politics and so was a weak center. The American-installed legislature also was a weak center, a place of haggling as opposed to unity. Gradually, successive decisions allowed for the creation of a modern version of the decentralized structure of the Tokugawa and Meiji periods: the center (in Tokugawa, the *shogun,* and, in Meiji, the emperor) coordinates strong and, in normative terms, fiercely loyal independent powers. In turn, the independent powers have normative responsibility for the people and groups who are subordinate to them. The symbolism of the past shaped the reality of the present.

The economic consequences of this type of legitimation strategy were to create large, autonomous enterprises. These enterprises needed to legitimize their own conduct and, accordingly, to develop distinctive "personalities." Such efforts to build corporate cultures traded heavily on established systems of loyalty—the family, community, and paternalism—but also added mythologies of their own. In addition, given their size and status, these business enterprises needed to secure oligarchic positions in the marketplace and did so through a variety of economic tactics with which we are now familiar (Vogel 1979; Abegglen and Stalk 1985). But the theoretically important point is that Japanese intermarket groups are not creations of market forces. In the middle fifties when they reappeared, they began large, they began prestigious, and their economic

American Journal of Sociology

integration followed from those facts, rather than being simply the cause of them. They enacted and, in due course, institutionalized a managerial structure that, from the outside, looks like a corporation but, on the inside, acts like a fiefdom.

In South Korea, the present form of government arose in a time of crisis, during a brutal war in which over 1 million Koreans died and 5.5 million more were dislocated (Cole and Lyman 1971, p. 22). Social disruption on an extraordinary scale, destruction of rural society, and the historical absence of strong intermediary institutions placed great power in the hands of a state structure propped up by U.S. aid and occupying forces. The authoritarian postwar government of Syngman Rhee shaped the basic institutions that the Park government later gained control of and turned in the direction of economic development. The legitimizing strategy for both governments, although articulated quite differently, centered on the imagery of the strong Confucian state: a central ruler, bureaucratic administration, weak intermediate powers, and a direct relationship between ruler and subjects based on the subject's unconditional loyalty to the state. As Henderson writes (1968, p. 5), "The physics of Korean political dynamics appears to resemble a strong vortex tending to sweep all active elements of the society upward toward central power. . . . Vertical pressures cannot be countered because local or independent aggregations do not exist to impede their formation or to check the resulting vortex once formed."

South Korean firms draw their managerial culture from the same source, the state, and from state-promoted management policies; they do not have the local character of the corporate culture of Japanese firms. Instead, they have developed an ideology of administration, an updated counterpart to the traditional Confucian ideology of the scholar-official (Jones and SaKong 1980, p. 291). For this reason, American business ideology has had an important effect in South Korea, far more than in either Japan or Taiwan. In the late 1950s, the South Korean government, with a grant from the U.S. State Department, instituted American management programs in South Korean universities (Zo Ki-zun 1970, pp. 13–14). South Korea now has a generation of managers trained in American business practice, including persons at the top levels of the state. In 1981, South Korea's prime minister and deputy prime minister (who was chief of the Economic Planning Board) were U.S.-trained economists (Bunge 1982, p. 115).

In Taiwan the state/business relationship also results from a basic legitimation strategy undertaken by the state. The Chiang Kai-shek government, after an initial attempt to create a military state in preparation for a return to the mainland, tried to secure the regime's legitimacy on a long-term basis. Composed largely of northern Chinese, Chiang Kai-shek's forces virtually conquered and totally subordinated the linguistically distinct Taiwanese. This created much resentment and some continuing attempts to create a Taiwanese independence movement. When a return to the mainland became unlikely, Chiang began creating a stable, long-term government. He actively promoted an updated Confucian state based on the model of the late imperial system. Unlike the more legalistic model of the Confucian state developed in Korea, Chiang attempted to make the state an exemplary institution and its leader a benevolent ruler: a state that upholds moral principles (*dedao*), that explicitly allows no corruption and unfair wealth, and that "leaves the people at rest." In this role, the state supervises internal moral order and takes care of foreign affairs. This policy militates against the emergence of favorite groups, which had been a weakness of the Nationalist regime in the 1930s and 1940s. This policy also limits participation of the state in what was seen in late imperial times as the private sector (*sishi*), an area that includes not only people's economic livelihood but also all aspects of family and religious life. Taiwan's state policy toward business operates within the limits established by Chiang's legitimation strategy (Peng 1984).

The consequences of this state policy have been to allow society, unfettered by the state, to respond to the economic opportunities that existed in the world economy and for which the state offered incentives. The Chinese of Taiwan, using traditional commercial practices and customary norms, quickly adapted to modern economic conditions. This outcome should not be surprising, because Chinese business practices have for some time operated competitively in the world economy. In 19th-century China, there was a thriving commercial system that functioned well in the absence of a legal framework, even in the deteriorating political conditions of the time (Hao 1970, 1986; Hamilton 1985; Feuerwerker 1984; Myers 1980; Chen and Myers 1976, 1978). The Chinese used the same patterns of business relations to gain industrial and commercial control of the economies in Southeast Asia (Wickberg 1965; Omohundro 1981; Hamilton 1977) and, more recently, to develop highly industrial societies in Hong Kong and Singapore (Nyaw and Chan 1982; Redding 1980; Ward 1972). Therefore, when we consider the similar free-market conditions that exist in these other locations, the Chinese economic success in Taiwan is perhaps not surprising but needs to be examined nonetheless.

The industrial patterns in Taiwan reflect the same invigoration of Chinese commercial practices found in late imperial China and in Southeast Asia. As analysts have noted (e.g., Wong 1985; Chan 1982; Omohundro 1981), in all these locations Chinese businesses develop on the basis of small family-run firms and personalistic networks linking firms backward to sources of supply and forward to consumers. Two sets of factors account for the prevalence of these small family firms. The first set concerns

American Journal of Sociology

the nature of the Chinese family system.[24] The Japanese family system is based on a household unit and on primogeniture; younger sons must start households of their own. In contrast, the Chinese system is based on patrilineage and equal inheritance among all sons. The eldest son has seniority but no particular privileges in regard to property or authority over property. Because all males remain in the line of descent, the patrilineage quickly expands within just a few generations. Adoption of a son into any household is considered improper, and the only approved way is to adopt the son of a kinsman (cf. Watson 1975*a*). Equally privileged sons connected to networks of relatives create a situation of bifurcated loyalties, with wealth itself becoming a measure of one's standing in the community of relatives. Accordingly, conflict between sons is ubiquitous, intralineage rivalries are common, and lineage segmentation is the rule (Baker 1979, pp. 26–70). Hence, the argument goes, besides the lineage and the state, there is no central integrating unit in Chinese society, and the lineage itself breeds as much conflict as unity. Therefore, it is difficult in Chinese society to build a large cohesive group.

This leads to a closely related set of explanations of how Chinese businesses are run.[25] The Chinese firm duplicates family structure; the head of the household is the head of the firm, family members are the core employees, and sons are the ones who will inherit the firm.[26] If the firm prospers, the family will reinvest its profits in branch establishments or more likely in unrelated but commercially promising business ventures (see, e.g., Chen 1985). Different family members run the different enterprises, and at the death of the head of household the family assets are divided (*fenjia*) by allocating separate enterprises to the surviving sons, each of whom attempts to expand his own firm as did the father. In this way, the assets of a Chinese family are always considered divisible, control of the assets is always considered family business, and decisions (in normative terms) should be made in light of long-term family interests.

[24] The material on Chinese kinship is extensive. The best general treatments are Baker (1979), Freedman (1966), Hsu (1971), Watson (1982), and Cohen (1970).

[25] For treatments of the Chinese kinship system in relation to Taiwan's business development, see Lin (1984), Chen and Qiu (1984), Chen (1984), Hu (1984), and Huang (1984). For the role of an extended lineage in modern commercial ventures, see Cohen (1970), Watson (1975*b*), and Wong (1985).

[26] The literature on large business enterprises in Japan often cites the family as having an important influence on how the firms are run. In comparison with the Chinese case, however, the Japanese family provides much more a metaphor for organization than an actual model. In Taiwan, the family structure and enterprise organization cannot be readily distinguished in many cases, so much so that the effect of the family on business in Taiwan is not metaphorical but actual and of great significance. Moreover, although the data are limited, the role of the family in modern business in Taiwan seems very similar to the role of the family in traditional agriculture (Baker 1979).

Far East

This pattern leads to what might be described as a "nesting box" system of Chinese management (see, e.g., Omohundro 1981; Huang 1984; Redding 1980). In the small, innermost box are those core family members who own or will inherit the business; in the next box are more distant relatives and friends who owe their positions to their connection with the owners and who are in a position to influence and be influenced by them; in the next outer boxes are ranks of unrelated people who work in the firm for money. Depending on the size of the firm, the outer boxes may contain ranks of professional managers, technicians, supervisors, and other craftspeople. The outermost box would include unskilled wage laborers. This pattern of business organization is most stable when the business is fairly small. Loyalty among unrelated employees is often low, which makes personalistic connections an essential part of management strategy (Huang 1984). The preference is always to begin one's own small business if one has sufficient capital to do so; as the Chinese saying goes, "It is better to be a rooster's beak than a cow's tail!"

Because everyone works in small- to medium-sized firms, Chinese have historically developed techniques to aid forward and backward linkages. These techniques include putting-out systems, satellite factory systems, and a variety of distribution networks often based on personalistic ties (see, e.g., Willmott 1972; Hamilton 1985). In fact, so complex and all-encompassing are these various techniques, and seemingly so efficient (Ho 1980), that they contribute to keeping businesses fairly small and investment patterns directed toward conglomerate accumulations rather than vertical integration (cf. Chan 1982).

In summary, as illustrated in table 6, in each of the three societies, a different combination of present and past circumstances led to the selection of a strategy of political legitimation. This strategy, in turn, had direct consequences for the relations between state and business sectors and for the formation of economic institutions.

Finally, we should note that the three types of business networks that developed in these three countries are usually not in direct competition with one another, except in a few product areas (e.g., electronics). Each possesses different economic capabilities, and each seems to fill a different niche in the world economy. Much more research needs to be done on this topic, but it appears that the following division is occurring: Taiwan's system of small family firms, which can flexibly shift from producing one commodity to another, has become a dominant producer of an extensive range of medium- to high-quality consumer goods (e.g., clothes, small household items) of the kind that fill the modern home and office but that require very little research and development. Large Japanese corporations specialize in a product area and, through research, development, and marketing strategies, attempt to create new commodities and con-

TABLE 6

FIRM STRUCTURE AND FIRM/STATE RELATIONSHIPS

	State/Business Relations	Principal Corporate Actors	Intrafirm Managerial Strategies	Extrafirm Market Strategies
Japan	Cooperative partnership	Intermarket groups	Company ideologies; consensus building; peer group controls	High R & D; manufacture and marketing of new products
South Korea	Political capitalism	*Chaebol*	State Confucianism; impersonal management; strong, centralized control	High capital ventures in established markets
Taiwan	Separation of spheres	Family firms	"Family-style" management; control through personal ties	Low capital; low R & D; manufacture of consumer expendables

Far East

sumers for those commodities (Abegglen and Stalk 1985). Exploiting their competitive advantage in technology and mass production, Japanese businesses operate on the frontiers of product development. With the entire economy orchestrated by the state, South Korean businesses are attempting to become important producers of commodities that require extensive capital investment but for which markets already exist (e.g., steel, major construction materials, automobiles). Such ventures require large amounts of capital and coordination but relatively little research and development. Each of these three strategies of industrialization may well be, in the economist's terminology, "least-cost" strategies in their respective niches of the world economy. But that fact does not make these strategies any less the outcomes of noneconomic factors. Moreover, a strategy of efficiency can only be calculated in terms of an existing array of economic and social institutions.

CONCLUSION

The theoretical question underlying this paper is, What level of analysis best explains organizational structure? We argue that, on the one hand, profit and efficiency arguments are too specific and too narrow to account for different organizational forms. Economic models predict organizational structure only at the most superficial level (e.g., successful businesses seek profit). On the other hand, cultural arguments seize on such general, omnipresent value patterns as to make it difficult to account for historical and societal variations occurring within the same cultural area. Culture pervades everything and therefore explains nothing. The authority explanation provides the most successful explanation because it aims at a middle level, at explanations having historical and structural adequacy. We argue that enterprise structure represents situational adaptations of preexisting organizational forms to specific political and economic conditions. Organizational structure is not inevitable; it results from neither cultural predispositions nor specific economic tasks and technology. Instead, organizational structure is situationally determined, and, therefore, the most appropriate form of analysis is one that taps the historical dimension.

Given this conclusion, then, this analysis suggests that the key factors in explaining economic organization may not be economic, at least in economists' usual meaning of that term. Economic and cultural factors are clearly critical in understanding the *growth* of markets and economic enterprise, but the *form* or structure of enterprise is better understood by patterns of authority relations in the society. This suggests further that the economic theory of the firm may in fact be a theory based on, and only well suited to, the American firm as it has developed historically in Amer-

S87

American Journal of Sociology

ican society. Chandler's analysis of firm formation in the United States concentrates on how firm development permitted the lowering of costs under changing market conditions. It is important to note, however, that firm development also allowed the concentration of economic interests and market control by private parties. The American state (in both the 19th and 20th centuries) exists to allow the market to function in the service of private interests; it intervenes only to prevent market break-downs or overconcentration. This state role was not an inevitability dictated by the market, however, and emerged from a historically developed vision about the "correct" state/industry relation. The American vision has always been that of a weak state and powerful private institutions (Hamilton and Sutton 1982). Industrialists of the 19th century, unfettered by transportation and communications impediments, realized that vision with the aid of a laissez-faire government. But the American firm, like the firms in Japan, South Korea, and Taiwan, had no inevitable developmental sequence to traverse.

REFERENCES

Abegglen, James C. 1958. *The Japanese Factory*. Glencoe, Ill.: Free Press.
Abegglen, James C., and George Stalk, Jr. 1985. *Kaisha: The Japanese Corporation*. New York: Basic.
Adizes, Ichak. 1971. *Industrial Democracy: Yugoslav Style*. New York: Free Press.
Amsden, Alice H. 1979. "Taiwan's Economic History: A Case of *Étatisme* and a Challenge to Dependency." *Modern China* 5:341–80.
————. 1985. "The State and Taiwan's Economic Development." Pp. 78–106 *Bringing the State Back In*, edited by Peter B. Evans, Dietrich Rueschemeyer, and Theda Skocpol. Cambridge: Cambridge University Press.
Baker, Hugh. 1979. *Chinese Family and Kinship*. New York: Columbia University Press.
Barrett, Richard E., and Martin King Whyte. 1982. "Dependency Theory and Taiwan: Analysis of a Deviant Case." *American Journal of Sociology* 87:1064–89.
Bendix, Reinhard. 1974. *Work and Authority in Industry*. Berkeley: University of California Press.
————. 1977. *Kings or People*. Berkeley: University of California Press.
————. 1984. *Force, Fate, and Freedom*. Berkeley and Los Angeles: University of California Press.
Bendix, Reinhard, and Guenther Roth. 1971. *Scholarship and Partisanship: Essays on Max Weber*. Berkeley: University of California Press.
Benedict, Ruth. 1946. *The Chrysanthemum and the Sword: Patterns of Japanese Culture*. Boston: Houghton-Mifflin.
Berger, Peter. 1984. "An East Asian Development Model." *The Economic News*, no. 3079, September 17–23, pp. 1, 6–8.
Biggart, Nicole Woolsey, and Gary G. Hamilton. 1984. "The Power of Obedience." *Administrative Science Quarterly* 29:540–49.
Bisson, T. A. 1954. *Zaibatsu Dissolution in Japan*. Berkeley: University of California Press.
Blumberg, Paul. 1973. *Industrial Democracy: The Sociology of Participation*. New York: Schocken.

Far East

Bunge, Frederica M. 1982. *South Korea: A Country Study.* Washington, D.C.: Government Printing Office.

Business Week. 1985. "The Koreans Are Coming." *Business Week,* no. 2926, December, pp. 46–52.

Caves, Richard E., and Masu Uekusa. 1976. *Industrial Organization in Japan.* Washington, D.C.: Brookings Institution.

Chan, Wellington K. K. 1982. "The Organizational Structure of the Traditional Chinese Firm and Its Modern Reform." *Business History Review* 56:218–35.

Chandler, Alfred D., Jr. 1977. *The Visible Hand: The Managerial Revolution in American Business.* Cambridge, Mass: Harvard University Press.

———. 1981. "Historical Determinants of Managerial Hierarchies: A Response to Perrow." Pp. 391–402 in *Perspectives on Organizational Design and Behavior,* edited by A. Van de Ven and William Joyce. New York: Wiley.

———. 1984. "The Emergence of Managerial Capitalism." *Business History Review* 58:473–502.

Chen, Chengzhong. 1985. "Caijia ti dajia shangle yike" (The Ts'ai Family Gives Everyone a Lesson). *Lianhe Yuekan* 44 (March): 13–17.

Chen, Fu-mei Chang, and Ramon Myers. 1976. "Customary Law and Economic Growth of China during the Qing Period," pt. 1. *Ch'ing-shih Wen-ti* 3, no. 5 (November): 1–32.

———. 1978. "Customary Law and Economic Growth of China during the Qing Period," pt. 2. *Ch'ing-shih Wen-ti* 3, no. 10 (November): 4–27.

Chen, Mingzhang. 1983. "Woguo xian jieduan zhongxiao qiye de fudao wenti" (The Difficulty in Assisting Taiwan's Present Day Small and Medium Businesses). *Tianxia zazhi* 29:137–41.

———. 1984. "Jiazu wenhua yu qiye guanli" (Family Culture and Enterprise Organization). Pp. 487–510 in *Zhongguo shi guanli* (Chinese-style Management). Taipei: Gongshang Shibao.

Chen, Qinan, and Shuru Qiu. 1984. "Qiye zuzhi de jiben xingtai yu chuantong jiazu zhidu" (Basic Concepts of Enterprise Organization and the Traditional Family System). Pp. 487–510 in *Zhongguo shi guanli* (Chinese-style Management). Taipei: Gongshang Shibao.

Clark, Rodney. 1979. *The Japanese Company.* New Haven, Conn.: Yale University Press.

Coase, R. H. 1937. "The Nature of the Firm." *Economica* 4 (November): 386–405.

Cohen, Myron L. 1970. "Developmental Process in the Chinese Domestic Group." Pp. 21–36 in *Family and Kinship in Chinese Society,* edited by Maurice Freedman. Stanford, Calif: Stanford University Press.

Cole, David C., and Princeton N. Lyman. 1971. *Korean Development: The Interplay of Politics and Economics.* Cambridge, Mass.: Harvard University Press.

Commons, John R. 1934. *Institutional Economics.* Madison: University of Wisconsin Press.

Crozier, Michel. 1964. *The Bureaucratic Phenomenon.* Chicago: University of Chicago Press.

Cumings, Bruce. 1984. "The Origins and Development of the Northeast Asian Political Economy: Industrial Sectors, Product Cycles, and Political Consequences." *International Organizations* 38:1–40.

Deal, Terrence E., and Allan A. Kennedy. 1982. *Corporate Cultures.* Reading, Mass.: Addison-Wesley.

DeGlopper, Donald R. 1972. "Doing Business in Lukang." Pp. 97–326 in *Economic Organization in Chinese Society,* edited by W. E. Willmott. Stanford, Calif: Stanford University Press.

Direction of Trade Statistics. 1985. Yearbook. Washington, D.C.: International Monetary Fund.

American Journal of Sociology

Dore, Ronald. 1962. "Sociology in Japan." *British Journal of Sociology* 13:116–23.
———. 1973. *British Factory–Japanese Factory: The Origins of National Diversity in Industrial Relations.* Berkeley: University of California Press.
———. 1983. "Goodwill and the Spirit of Market Capitalism." *British Journal of Sociology* 34:459–82.
Douglas, Mary, with Baron Isherwood. 1979. *The World of Goods.* New York: Basic.
Economist Intelligence Unit. 1985*a. Quarterly Economic Review of Japan.* Annual supplement.
———. 1985*b. Quarterly Economic Review of South Korea.* Annual supplement.
Evans, Peter B., Dietrich Rueschemeyer, and Theda Skocpol, eds. 1985. *Bringing the State Back In.* Cambridge: Cambridge University Press.
Evans, Robert, Jr. 1971. *The Labor Economics of Japan and the United States.* New York: Praeger.
Fama, Eugene F., and Michael Jensen. 1983. "Agency Problems and Residual Claims." *Journal of Law and Economics* 36:327–49.
Feuerwerker, Albert. 1984. "The State and the Economy in Late Imperial China." *Theory and Society* 13:297–326.
Fischer, David Hackett. 1970. *Historians' Fallacies.* New York: Harper.
Foy, Nancy, and Herman Gadon. 1976. "Worker Participation: Contrasts in Three Countries." *Harvard Business Review,* 54 (May–June): 71–83.
Freedman, Maurice. 1966. *Chinese Lineage and Society: Fujian and Guangdong.* London: Athlone.
Fukuda, K. John. 1983. "Transfer of Management: Japanese Practices for the Orientals?" *Management Decision* 21:17–26.
Gamst, Frederick C., and Edward Norbeck, eds. 1976. *Ideas of Culture.* New York: Holt, Rinehart & Winston.
Gerschenkron, Alexander. 1962. *Economic Backwardness in Historical Perspective.* Cambridge, Mass.: Harvard University Press.
Gold, Thomas B. 1986. *State and Society in the Taiwan Miracle.* New York: Sharpe.
Granovetter, Mark. 1985. "Economic Action and Social Structure: The Problem of Embeddedness." *American Journal of Sociology* 91:481–510.
Haggard, Stephen, and Tun-jen Cheng. 1986. "State and Foreign Capital in the 'Gang of Four.' " Pp. 84–135 in *The New East Asian Industrialization,* edited by Frederick Deyo. Ithaca, N.Y.: Cornell University Press.
Hamilton, Gary G. 1977. "Ethnicity and Regionalism: Some Factors Influencing Chinese Identities in Southeast Asia." *Ethnicity* 4:335–51.
———. 1984. "Patriarchalism in Imperial China and Western Europe: A Revision of Weber's Sociology of Domination." *Theory and Society* 13:393–426.
———. 1985. "Why No Capitalism in China? Negative Questions in Historical, Comparative Research." *Journal of Asian Perspectives* 2:2.
Hamilton, Gary, and Nicole Woolsey Biggart. 1984. *Governor Reagan, Governor Brown: A Sociology of Executive Power.* New York: Columbia University Press.
———. 1985. "Why People Obey: Theoretical Observations on Power and Obedience in Complex Organizations." *Sociological Perspectives* 28:3–28.
Hamilton, Gary G., and John Sutton. 1982. "The Common Law and Social Reform: The Rise of Administrative Justice in the U.S., 1880–1920." Presented at the annual meeting of the Law and Society Association, Toronto, June.
Hankook Ilbo. 1985. *Pal ship O nyndo hankook ui 50 dae jae bul* (The 50 Top *Chaebol* in Korea). Seoul, Korea.
Hao, Yen-p'ing. 1970. *The Comprador in Nineteenth-Century China.* Cambridge, Mass.: Harvard University Press.
———. 1986. *The Commercial Revolution in Nineteenth-Century China.* Berkeley and Los Angeles: University of California Press.

Harbison, Frederick H., and Charles A. Meyer. 1959. *Management in the Industrial World: An International Analysis*. New York: McGraw-Hill.

Harris, Marvin. 1979. *Cultural Materialism: The Struggle for a Science of Culture*. New York: Random House.

Henderson, Gregory. 1968. *Korea: The Politics of the Vortex*. Cambridge, Mass.: Harvard University Press.

Hirschmeier, Johannes, and Tsunehiko Yui. 1981. *The Development of Japanese Business 1600–1980*. London: Allen & Unwin.

Ho, Yhi-min. 1980. "The Production Structure of the Manufacturing Sector and Its Distribution Implications: The Case of Taiwan." *Economic Development and Cultural Change* 28:321–43.

Hofheinz, Roy, Jr., and Kent E. Calder. 1982. *The Eastasia Edge*. New York: Basic.

Hou, Jiaju. 1984. "Xianqin rufa liangjia guanli guannian zhi bijiao yanjiu" (Comparative Research on Management Concepts in Confucian and Legalist Philosophy in Early Ch'in). Pp. 59–74 in *Zhongguo shi guanli* (Chinese-style Management). Taipei: Gongshang Shibao.

Hsu, Francis L. K. 1971. *Under the Ancestors' Shadow: Kinship, Personality and Social Mobility in China*. Stanford, Calif.: Stanford University Press.

Hu, Tai-li. 1984. *My Mother-in-law's Village: Rural Industrialization and Change in Taiwan*. Taipei: Institute of Ethnology, Academia Sinica.

Huang, Guangkuo. 1984. "Rujia lunli yu qiye zuzhi xingtai" (Confucian Theory and Types of Enterprise Organization). Pp. 21–58 in *Zhongguo shi guanli* (Chinese-style Management). Taipei: Gongshang Shibao.

Jacoby, Sanford. 1979. "The Origins of Internal Labor Markets in Japan." *Industrial Relations* 18:184–96.

Johnson, Chalmers. 1982. *Miti and the Japanese Miracle*. Stanford, Calif: Stanford University Press.

Jones, Leroy P., and Il SaKong. 1980. *Government, Business, and Entrepreneurship in Economic Development: The Korean Case*. Cambridge, Mass.: Council on East Asian Studies, Harvard University.

Juhn, Daniel Sungil. 1971. "Korean Industrial Entrepreneurship, 1924–40." Pp. 219–54 in *Korea's Response to the West*, edited by Yung-Hwan Jo. Kalamazoo, Mich.: Korean Research and Publications.

Kanter, Rosabeth Moss. 1983. *The Change Masters: Innovation and Productivity in the American Corporation*. New York: Simon & Schuster.

Koo, Hagen. 1984. "The Political Economy of Income Distribution in South Korea: The Impact of the State's Industrialization Policies." *World Development* 12: 1029–37.

Krause, Lawrence, and Sekiguchi Sueo. 1976. "Japan and the World Economy." Pp. 383–458 in *Asia's New Giant*, edited by Hugh Patrick and Henry Rosovsky. Washington, D.C.: Brookings Institution.

Kunio, Yoshihara. 1982. *Sogo Shosha*. Oxford: Oxford University Press.

Kuznets, Simon. 1979. "Growth and Structural Shifts." Pp. 15–131 in *Economic Growth and Structural Change in Taiwan*, edited by Walter Galenson. Ithaca, N.Y.: Cornell University Press.

Lin, Xiezong. 1984. "Riben de qiye jingying—shehui zuzhi cengmian de kaocha" (Japanese Industrial Managment: An Examination of Levels of Social Organization). *Guolijengjrtaxue xuebao*, no. 49, April, pp. 167–99.

Linder, Staffan B. 1986. *The Pacific Century*. Stanford Calif.: Stanford University Press.

Little, Ian M. D. 1979. "An Economic Reconnaissance." Pp. 448–507 in *Economic Growth and Structural Change in Taiwan*, edited by Walter Galenson. Ithaca, N.Y.: Cornell University Press.

American Journal of Sociology

Maitland, Ian, John Bryson, and Andrew Van de Ven. 1985. "Sociologists, Economists and Opportunism." *Academy of Management Review* 10:59–65.

Marx, Karl. 1930. *Capital*. London: Dent.

Mason, Edward S., Mahn Ke Kim, Dwight H. Perkins, Kwang Suk Kim, and David C. Cole. 1980. *The Economic and Social Modernization of the Republic of Korea*. Cambridge, Mass.: Council of East Asian Studies, Harvard University.

Meyer, John W., and W. Richard Scott. 1983. *Organizational Environment: Ritual and Rationality*. Beverly Hills, Calif.: Sage.

Miles, Robert H. 1980. *Macro Organization Behavior*. Glenview, Ill.: Scott-Foresman.

Minard, Lawrence. 1984. "The China Reagan Can't Visit." *Forbes*, May 7, pp. 36–42.

Mintz, Beth, and Michael Schwartz. 1985. *The Power Structure of American Business*. Chicago: University of Chicago Press.

Monthly Bulletin of Statistics. 1985. March. New York: United Nations.

Myers, Ramon H. 1980. *The Chinese Economy, Past and Present*. Belmont, Calif.: Wadsworth.

———. 1984. "The Economic Transformation of the Republic of China on Taiwan." *China Quarterly* 99:500–528.

Myers, Ramon, and Mark R. Peattie, eds. 1984. *The Japanese Colonial Empire, 1895–1945*. Princeton, N.J.: Princeton University Press.

Nakamura, Takafusa. 1981. *The Postwar Japanese Economy*. Tokyo: University of Tokyo Press.

———. 1983. *Economic Growth in Prewar Japan*. New Haven, Conn.: Yale University Press.

Nakane, Chie. 1970. *Japanese Society*. Berkeley: University of California Press.

Nyaw, Mee-kou, and Chan-leong Chan. 1982. "Structure and Development Strategies of the Manufacturing Industries in Singapore and Hong Kong: A Comparative Study." *Asian Survey* 22:449–69.

Omohundro, John T. 1981. *Chinese Merchant Families in Iloilo*. Athens: Ohio University Press.

Orlove, Benjamin S. 1986. "Barter and Cash Sale on Lake Titicaca: A Test of Competing Approaches." *Current Anthropology* 27:85–106.

Ouchi, William. 1980. "Markets, Bureaucracies, and Clans." *Administrative Science Quarterly* 25:129–42.

———. 1981. *Theory Z*. Reading, Mass.: Addison-Wesley.

———. 1984. *The M-form Society*. Reading, Mass.: Addison-Wesley.

Ozawa, Terutomo. 1979. *Multinationalism, Japanese Style*. Princeton, N.J.: Princeton University Press.

Pascale, Richard Tanner, and Anthony G. Athos. 1981. *The Art of Japanese Management*. New York: Warner.

Patrick, Hugh, and Henry Rosovsky. 1976. "Japan's Economic Performance: An Overview." Pp. 1–62 in *Asia's New Giant*, edited by Hugh Patrick and Henry Rosovsky. Washington, D.C.: Brookings Institution.

Peng, Huaijen. 1984. *Taiwan jingyan de nanti* (The Difficult Problems of Taiwan's Experience). Taipei.

Perrow, Charles. 1981. "Markets, Hierarchies and Hegemony." Pp. 371–86 in *Perspectives on Organization Design and Behavior*, edited by A. Van de Ven and William Joyce. New York: Wiley.

———. 1986. *Complex Organizations*, 3d ed. New York: Random House.

Peters, Thomas J., and Robert H. Waterman, Jr. 1982. *In Search of Excellence*. New York: Warner.

Portes, Alejandro, and John Walton. 1981. *Labor, Class, and the International System*. New York: Academic.

Ranis, Gustav. 1979. "Industrial Development." Pp. 206–62 in *Economic Growth and*

Structural Change in Taiwan, edited by Walter Galenson. Ithaca, N.Y.: Cornell University Press.

Redding, S. C. 1980. "Cognition as an Aspect of Culture and Its Relation to Management Processes: An Exploratory View of the Chinese Case." *Journal of Management Studies* 17:127–48.

Reynolds, Lloyd G. 1983. "The Spread of Economic Growth to the Third World: 1850–1980." *Journal of Economic Literature* 21:941–80.

SaKong, Il. 1980. "Macroeconomic Aspects of the Public Enterprise Sector." Pp. 99–128 in *Macroeconomic and Industrial Development in Korea,* edited by Chong Kee Park. Seoul: Korea Development Institute.

Sayle, Murray. 1985. "Japan Victorious." *New York Review of Books* 33 (5): 33–40.

Schluchter, Wolfgang. 1981. *The Rise of Western Rationalism: Max Weber's Developmental History.* Berkeley and Los Angeles: University of California Press.

Silin, Robert H. 1976. *Leadership and Values: The Organization of Large-scale Taiwanese Enterprises.* Cambridge, Mass.: East Asian Research Center, Harvard University.

Smircich, Linda. 1983. "Concepts of Culture and Organizational Analysis." *Administrative Science Quarterly* 28:339–58.

Swidler, Ann. 1986. "Culture in Action: Symbols and Strategies." *American Sociological Review* 51:273–86.

Taira, Koji. 1970. *Economic Development and the Labor Market in Japan.* New York: Columbia University Press.

Taiwan Statistical Data Book. 1985. Council for Economic Planning and Development, Republic of China.

Tannenbaum, Arnold S., Bogdan Kavcic, Menachem Rosner, Mino Vianello, and Georg Weiser. 1974. *Hierarchy in Organizations.* San Francisco: Jossey-Bass.

Teece, David. 1980. "Economics of Scope and the Scope of the Enterprise." *Journal of Economic Behavior and Organization* 1:223–48.

Tu, Wei-ming. 1984. "Gongye dongya yu rujia jingshen" (Industrial East Asia and the Spirit of Confucianism). *Tianxia zazhi* 41 (October 1): 124–37.

Vogel, Ezra. 1979. *Japan as Number One: Lessons for America.* Cambridge, Mass.: Harvard University Press.

Wade, Robert. 1985. "East Asian Financial Systems as a Challenge to Economics: Lessons from Taiwan." *California Management Review* 27:106–27.

Ward, Barbara E. 1972. "A Small Factory in Hong Kong: Some Aspects of Its Internal Organization." Pp. 353–86 in *Economic Organization in Chinese Society,* edited by W. E. Willmott. Stanford, Calif.: Stanford University Press.

Watson, James L. 1975a. "Agnates and Outsiders: Adoption in a Chinese Lineage." *Man* 10:293–306.

———. 1975b. *Emigration and the Chinese Lineage.* Berkeley: University of California Press.

———. 1982. "Chinese Kinship Reconsidered: Anthropological Perspectives on Historical Research." *China Quarterly* 92 (December): 589–627.

Weber, Max. 1958. *From Max Weber.* New York: Oxford University Press.

———. 1978. *Economy and Society,* edited by Guenther Roth and Claus Wittich. Berkeley: University of California Press.

Weick, Karl. 1979. *The Social Psychology of Organizing.* Reading, Mass.: Addison-Wesley.

Weiner, Steve. 1985. "K-Mart Apparel Buyers Hopscotch the Orient to Find Quality Goods." *Wall Street Journal,* March 19, pp. 1, 20.

Westphal, Larry E., Yung W. Rhee, Lin Su Kim, and Alice H. Amsden. 1984. "Republic of Korea." *World Development* 12:505–33.

White, Harrison. 1981. "Where Do Markets Come From?" *American Journal of Sociology* 87:517–47.

American Journal of Sociology

Wickberg, Edgar. 1965. *The Chinese in Philippine Life, 1850–1898*. New Haven, Conn.: Yale University Press.

Williamson, Oliver E. 1975. *Markets and Hierarchies*. New York: Free Press.

———. 1981. "The Economics of Organization." *American Journal of Sociology* 87:548–77.

———. 1983. "Organization Form, Residual Claimants and Corporate Control." *Journal of Law and Economics* 36:351–66.

———. 1985. *The Economic Institution of Capitalism*. New York: Free Press.

Williamson, Oliver E., and William G. Ouchi. 1981. "The Markets and Hierarchies and Visible Hand Perspective." Pp. 347–370, 387–390 in *Perspectives on Organization Design and Behavior*, edited by Andrew Van de Ven and William Joyce. New York: Wiley.

Willmott, W. E., ed. 1972. *Economic Organization in Chinese Society*. Stanford, Calif.: Stanford University Press.

Wong, Siu-lun. 1985. "The Chinese Family Firm: A Model." *British Journal of Sociology* 36, no. 1 (March): 58–72.

Wuthnow, Robert. 1985. "State Structures and Ideological Outcomes." *American Sociological Review* 50:799–821.

Yang, Jinlung. 1981. "Zhongxiao qiye yinhang zhedu zhi tantao." *Jiceng jinrong* 30:58–63.

Yang, Lien-sheng. 1970. "Government Control of Urban Merchants in Traditional China." *Tsing Hua Journal of Chinese Studies* 8:186–206.

Yasuba, Yasukichi. 1976. "The Evolution of Dualistic Wage Structure." Pp. 249–98 in *Japanese Industrialization and Its Social Consequences*, edited by Hugh Patrick. Berkeley: University of California Press.

Young, Alexander K. 1979. *The Sogo Shosha: Japan's Multinational Trading Corporations*. Boulder, Colo.: Westview.

Zeng, Shiqiang. 1984. "Yi rujia wei zhuliu de chongguo shi guanli linian zhi shentao" (An In-depth Discussion of Using Confucian Philosophy as the Unifying Principle for Chinese-style Management Concepts). Pp. 101–20 in *Zhongguo shi guanli* (Chinese-style Management). Taipei: Gungshang shibao.

Zhao, Jichang. 1982. "Zhengfu ying ruhe fudao zhongxiao quye zhi fazhan" (How Should the Government Develop an Assistance Policy for Small and Medium Businesses?). *Qiyin jikan* 5:32–38.

Zhonghua Zhengxinso, comp. 1985. *Taiwan diqu jitua qiye yanjiu* (Business Groups in Taiwan). Taipei: China Credit Information Service.

Zo, Ki-zun. 1970. "Development and Behavioral Patterns of Korean Entrepreneurs." *Korea Journal* 10:9–14.

Zucker, Lynn G. 1983. "Organizations as Institutions." *Research in the Sociology of Organizations* 2:1–48.

[2]

The Social Construction of Business Systems in East Asia

Richard D. Whitley

*Richard D.
Whitley*
Manchester
Business School,
University of
Manchester,
Manchester, U.K.

Abstract

Distinctive forms of business organization have become dominant and successful in Japan, South Korea, Taiwan and Hong Kong over the past 40 years. These different business systems reflect historical patterns of authority, trust and loyalty in Japan, Korea and China. They also vary in their specialization, strategic prefer- ences and patterns of inter-firm co-ordination because of significant differences in their institutional environments, especially the political and financial systems. Similar processes exist in western societies but distinctive business systems are not so sharply bounded between nation states and cultures in Europe and North America.

Introduction: Three Business Systems

The identification of distinctive forms of dominant business organization in Japan, South Korea, Taiwan and Hong Kong over the past few decades (Hamilton et al. 1990; Orru et al. 1988; Whitley 1990) demonstrates the plurality of viable ways of organizing and directing economic activities, as well as the importance of what Maurice (1979) terms the 'societal effect' in generating this pluralism. Dominant economic actors have become established in these societies that are remarkably similar within them yet differ in key respects between them (Hamilton and Biggart 1988). These actors are: the Japanese specialized clan or *kaisha* (Abegglen and Stalk 1985; Clark 1979), the Korean patrimonial bureaucracy or *chaebol* (Amsden 1989; Jones and Sakong 1980; Yoo and Lee 1987) and the Chinese Family Business (Limlingan 1986; Redding 1990). Their major differences were described in an earlier paper in *Organization Studies* (Whitley 1990) and can be explained in terms of the quite different institutional environments in which each business system developed. In this paper, I describe the major social institutions in each economy which together help to account for the distinctive characteristics of these busi- ness systems. Essentially, I am arguing that dominant forms of business organization in Japan, South Korea, Taiwan and Hong Kong since the 1950s reflect the nature and interconnections of key social institutions in both pre-industrial Japan, Korea and China and in these contemporary societies.

Organization
Studies
1991, 12/1:
001–028
© 1991 EGOS
0170–8406/91
0012–0001 $1.00

Before continuing to describe these institutions and their connections with successful business systems, it is worth summarizing the key differences between the three forms of business organization. These can be subsumed under three broad headings: (a) the system of authoritative coordination and control, (b) enterprise domain and development, and (c) the nature of enterprise co-ordination and market organization. They reflect three key issues which all systems of hierarchy–market relationships have to deal with: how are economic activities coordinated and controlled through authority hierarchies, what sorts of activities and resources are authoritatively coordinated in firms, and how are market connections between firms organized (cf. Imai and Itami 1984)?

These three broad headings can be subdivided into 8 distinct dimensions which summarize the major differences between East Asian forms of business organization. Considering first the authority system, there are major variations in the importance of personal authority and ownership and, relatedly, the significance of formal co-ordination and control procedures. Managerial styles and authority relations also differ markedly, as does the nature and extent of employee commitment to the company. In terms of enterprise domain and development the key variations concern the degree to which businesses specialize in particular economic activities and capabilities and whether their development is primarily evolutionary within a given sector or more discontinuous in the activities and resources controlled. Finally, inter-enterprise co-ordination varies within and between sectors in its scope and longevity. The extent to which firms depend on long term and diffuse connections with suppliers and customers differs considerably, as does their co-ordination of strategies and new ventures across sectors, either directly or through banks and state agencies.

These eight dimensions cover important aspects of business organizations in East Asia which differ markedly between Japan, South Korea, Taiwan and Hong Kong as summarized in Table 1. Because I am here focusing on how these differences can be understood in terms of their societal variations and wish to clarify the major ways in which East Asian business systems vary between themselves, these dimensions differ slightly from those listed in Table 1 of the earlier *Organization Studies* paper (Whitley 1990). In particular, they highlight the significant variations in preferred managerial styles and reliance on formal co-ordination procedures as well as distinguishing more sharply between inter-enterprise connections within the same sector from those across sectors. These eight do not, of course, constitute the only ways of contrasting East Asian forms of business organizations, but they do incorporate the major differences which generate quite distinct business systems. In comparing these with western hierarchy–market configurations, additional dimensions would become relevant.

A key feature of any business organization is the basis of managerial authority. In Korean *chaebol* and the Chinese family business (CFB) this is much more closely associated with personal ownership than in Japanese

Table 1
East Asian
Business Systems

	Japanese *Kaisha*	Korean *Chaebol*	Chinese Family Business
Authoritative Co-ordination and Control			
Personal authority and owner domination	low	high	high
Significance of formal co-ordination and control procedures	high	medium	low
Managerial style	facilitative	directive	didactic
Employee commitment	emotional	conditional	conditional
Business Domain and Development			
Business specialization	high	low	high within firms medium within families
Evolutionary strategies	high	medium	medium
Inter-Firm Co-ordination			
Relational contracting	high	low	medium
Long-term intersector co-ordination	strong through business groups and state agencies	indirect through state	limited and personal

kaisha where ownership has been separate from managerial control for some time (Abegglen and Stalk 1985: 177; Aoki 1987; Dore 1986: 67–72; Orru et al. 1988; Silin 1976; Yoo and Lee 1987). Linked to this is the formalization of co-ordination and control procedures which tends to be much more significant in Japanese firms — albeit not as great as in large diversified U.S. corporations (Lincoln et al. 1986; Pugh and Redding 1985; Rohlen 1974).

Dominant conceptions of the managerial role and competences also differ in that Japanese managers are not expected to be as remote and aloof from subordinates as are Chinese and Korean ones (Rohlen 1979; Silin 1976; Smith and Misumi 1989). A key part of their role is to maintain high group morale and performance and they are less directive or didactic than managers in Korean and Chinese firms (Liebenberg 1982; Redding and Richardson 1986; Redding and Wong 1986). These differences in managerial authority are echoed by variations in employment policies and practices which together generate conditional loyalties in Chinese and Korean businesses as opposed to what Silin (1976: 127–131) terms 'emotional' loyalties in Japanese *kaisha* (Amsden 1985a; Michell 1988).

In terms of the activities co-ordinated through authority hierarchies, Japanese and Chinese firms tend to restrict them to a relatively narrow range in which their specialized skills and knowledge provide distinctive capabilities. Complementary, but dissimilar activities requiring different skills (Richardson 1972; cf. Mariti and Smiley 1983), are co-ordinated through quasi-market connections (Clark 1979: 62–64; Cusumano 1985: 186–193; Redding and Tam 1985). Korean *chaebol*, in contrast, are much more vertically integrated and control more diverse activities through a common authority hierarchy (Amsden 1989; Orru et al. 1988; Levy 1988; Zeile 1989).

Specialization in Japan is linked to the long-term employment of managers and a preference for evolutionary growth strategies within a particular sector. Diversification thus tends to be limited to related industries (Kagono et al. 1985: 55–87; Kono 1984: 78–80). Korean and Chinese businesses are more susceptible to opportunistic diversification outside their main area of specialization, partly because of the much more personal nature of ownership and control, especially when encouraged to do so by the state as in Korea (Amsden 1989; Kim 1989). Diversified business groups have developed in Taiwan but these are more like family partnerships than authoritatively integrated enterprises (Hamilton et al. 1990; Numazaki 1986).

Business specialization increases the interdependence of enterprises and so the need to co-ordinate activities and strategies to reduce uncertainty. Large Japanese companies are highly dependent on elaborate networks of sub-contractors with whom they have relatively long-term relationships that allow for the extensive sharing of information and technology, together with some commitment to be helpful during crises. Dore (1986: 77–83) describes this as 'relational contracting'. Chinese firms in Taiwan and Hong Kong also depend heavily on sub-contractors but their commitments to them tend to be less extensive and long lasting (Redding and Tam 1985). Because the Korean *chaebol* are more vertically integrated they are less dependent on intra-industry links with other businesses.

In addition to this sort of inter-firm co-ordination there are also considerable variations in the extent to which dominant firms join together in cross-sectoral business groups (Hamilton et al. 1989). Many large Japanese firms are joined together through mutual shareholdings, regular 'presidents' clubs' meetings and the exchange of senior managerial staff across business sectors and with banks, insurance and trust companies to form large, co-operative groups (Futatsugi 1986; Goto 1982; Miyazaki 1980). Similar business groups exist in Taiwan and, to a lesser extent, in Hong Kong but they are much more personal and family based than in Japan (Hamilton and Kao 1987; Numazaki 1986). Korean *chaebol* are more discrete entities which are interconnected through state agencies and political alliances (Kim 1979) rather than by separately institutionalized business networks.

East Asian Business Systems and Pre-industrial China, Korea and Japan

In seeking to explain these differences between business systems in different countries, both current characteristics of dominant social institutions and historical patterns of social development are relevant. Indeed, many of the former cannot be adequately understood without taking account of the latter, as in the case of the relationship between financial institutions and industrial firms in Britain (Ingham 1984). In the analysis of East Asian societies, pre-industrial political and social structures are especially important because of the speed and recentness of their industrialization. In particular, traditional patterns of loyalty, solidarity and trust have substantial consequences for authority patterns within businesses as well as relationships between them and for the organization and policies of state elites. Additionally, because of the weakness of what Pye (1985: 324) terms 'secondary forms of political socialization' after military defeat and occupation in many countries, traditional modes of primary socialization through the family have become more significant in generating and reproducing distinctive attitudes towards authority and power. Thus important aspects of the societal contexts of East Asian business systems include established patterns of obedience, loyalty and trust as well as the structure and legitimacy of the state. Differences in these between Japan, Korea, Taiwan and Hong Kong reflect historical variations in authority relations, political structures and belief systems in addition to patterns of village organization and social co-operation.

The major contrasts between pre-industrial China, Korea and Japan which have affected the contexts in which different business systems developed can be summarized under four headings. First, the historical extent of political pluralism and decentralization of political authority to intermediate levels of organization between the ruler and households. Second, and relatedly, the degree to which privately controlled concentrations of economic power were permitted and became significant loci of political autonomy and influence. Third, the basis on which authority is claimed and obedience justified. Fourth, the degree to which the family was the fundamental unit of social identity, loyalty and production as opposed to broader groupings which crossed kinship boundaries and which were linked to higher levels of authority.

Political Pluralism

One of the most notable differences between Japan, Korea and China is the degree of political pluralism which has developed over the past 1,000 or so years. Both China and Korea were governed by central 'bureaucratic' dynasties which controlled provincial landowners through state officials and made their status dependent on access to state offices (Jacobs 1958, 1985). The Han dynasty in China institutionalized the practice of demoting noble families by one rank each generation and was also able to reduce them to the rank of commoner at any time (Jacobs 1958: 104), a system also practised in Korea to reduce the independence of landowners and make them compete for state appointments (Jacobs 1985: 31). While the effectiveness of these policies has varied, they did prevent the emergence of an independent warrior class which competed for control over the state, as in Japan.

The failure of the Taika reforms (646–858) to replicate the Confucian patrimonial model, and the subsequent separation of the Emperor's personal powers from military control over Japan, led to the distinctive Japanese form of feudalism in which the *de facto* central power was determined by competitive military struggles between clans (Jacobs 1958; Pye 1985). Formal obeisance to the central authority of the Emperor remained important, but effective political and economic power was decentralized to the major clans and, at times, to religious orders such as Buddhist monasteries (Jacobs 1958: 81–83), who controlled land and retainers. The ability of the central political authority to control economic development and capital accumulation was therefore much more restricted in Japan than in China and Korea. Even when the Tokugawa government banned foreign commerce in 1636, feudal lords were able to engage in widespread smuggling and trade, and so increase their wealth substantially (Jacobs 1958: 37–38). In contrast, Chinese rulers could, and did, redistribute land rights to prevent concentrations of landownership and maintained tight control of urban markets and merchant activities (Jacobs 1958: 23–32).

This difference in political pluralism is linked to the existence and significance of a hereditary aristocracy and varied inheritance practices. In Japan and Korea aristocratic status was an important distinction and could not be acquired by passing examinations, whereas in Confucian China elite status was either granted by the ruler as a personal favour or awarded through the education system. Thus a hereditary aristocracy which could develop as an intermediate group between the ruler and his advisors and the mass of the population was prevented from becoming established in China.

Furthermore, whereas inheritance of property in Japan was based on the principle of primogeniture and hence concentrations of resources could be maintained over generations, this was not the case in China and Korea. The general pattern in these countries was to divide an inheritance equally between the sons, or at least equally enough to prevent large amounts of property being conserved and passed on across generations (Jacobs 1958: 149–155). This preference for equal inheritance remains an important feature of Chinese society, which helps to explain the lack of large, stable and successful businesses which have survived over many generations in a comparable manner to Japanese ones.

The combination of equal inheritance, or what Jacobs (1985: 204) terms homoyogeniture, and intergenerational demoting of the nobility in Korea meant that each generation of an aristocratic lineage had to compete for central state offices if they were to restore the family fortunes. Thus, during the Confucian Yi dynasty (1392–1910) local centres of political and economic power based on aristocratic families did not develop to nearly the same extent as in Japan because they depended on the centrally administered examinations and state offices to maintain status and income. As Jacobs (1985: 30) suggests: 'the dominance of the capital over the periphery was assured by preserving the capital as the locus of primary political patrimonial initiative. Hence individuals had to be either physically present or represented at the capital to secure and expand their prestige, power and prebends.' Although, then, the Korean local political elite remained an aristocracy of birth and retained their local power bases, they were too dependent on the centre to mount effective challenges to it and did not mobilize peasants or their retainers to oppose central authority.

Economic Pluralism

The differences in pre-industrial political pluralism between Japan, Korea and China were echoed by variations in economic pluralism. Just as the Confucian elite in China consistently fought any attempt to create local power bases or intermediate political organizations between the central state and the peasantry, so too did they ensure that potential concentrations of private economic power were controlled and limited by strong official control of markets and towns (Jacobs 1958: 30–32). During the Han dynasty, the ruler established his ethical right to prevent the accumulation of monetary power, except under his own control and sponsorship. As a result, any accumulation of property, unless it was for religious purposes or public relief measures, was automatically subject to state confiscation (Jacobs 1958: 57–60). Similar efforts to maintain central state control over mercantile activities and prevent the concentration of private capital occurred in Korea.

In Japan, on the other hand, independent mercantile wealth expanded considerably during the Tokugawa period despite official disdain for merchants and periodic refusals to pay back loans and attacks on merchants' power. By the late 18th century, both the central authority and the feudal lords were so dependent on rich merchants for loans that they could not suppress them and, in some cases, the aristocracy also undertook commercial activities (Hirschmeier and Yui 1981: 14–36). Additionally, many merchants invested their profits in land reclamation, so becoming landowners themselves, and began to blur the formal boundaries between the aristocracy and merchants. By the time of the Meiji restoration (1867–1868) many concentrations of private, family controlled economic power had become established and these dominated the economic system despite their formal subservience to the aristocracy.

The Mitsui family business, for instance, which developed into one of the largest financial holding companies (*zaibatsu*) in pre-war Japan and survives as a giant business group today, was founded in the 17th century and developed into a large chainstore enterprise during the 18th and 19th centuries, which made the family very wealthy (Hirschmeier and Yui 1981: 60–66). While more integrated into, and dependent upon, the prevailing feudal system than their European counterparts, these rich Japanese mercantile families were more powerful, stable and independent than Chinese or Korean ones and were able to establish an effective banking system (Jacobs 1958: 70–74). A further point about the large merchant houses in Tokugawa Japan is that they were organized into powerful guilds that were more stable and autonomous than their Chinese counterparts. These government regulated guilds developed intricate systems of inter-urban, inter-family connections which reinforced their independent economic power, whereas Chinese guilds were primarily local associations of craftsmen with little capital controlled by officials (Jacobs 1958: 38–40; Hirschmeier and Yui 1981: 36–38).

Bases of Claims to Authority and Obedience

In addition to the degree of political and economic pluralism varying considerably between these three pre-industrial societies, there were also major differences in how power was legitimately claimed and obedience justified. Chinese and, later, Korean rulers adopted Confucian ideologies which asserted their superior moral worth and relied on the Confucian elite to legitimate their virtue and hence their right to rule. Japanese leaders, in contrast, acquired central control through military competition between feudal clans and relied on more pragmatic justifications, primarily the ability to sustain political and social order (Jacobs 1958: 77–96). This competitive struggle for power meant that authority was relatively unstable and depended on the effective mobilization of resources and retainers and so on the development and maintenance of loyalty.

Domination in China and Korea was, then, supposed to be derived from the moral virtue of the ruler and his Confucian, virtuous, advisors, so forming a 'virtuocracy' (Pye 1985: 22–24). This meant that the political order was a moral order, so that challenges to it were regarded as attacks on virtue itself. Since state office and authority were reserved for virtuous administrators who had demonstrated their moral worth by mastering the Confucian classics, incumbents had no need to justify their rank and power by being effective administrators or by performing useful services for the uneducated and hence unworthy. By controlling the interpretation of the classics and the examination system, the Confucian 'bureaucratic' elite effectively controlled the definition of virtue, and hence authority, and were able to prevent the emergence of independent power bases by mobilizing resources against evil, unworthy and disruptive accumulations of land or goods.

In contrast, because power in pre-industrial Japan was linked more to military and co-ordinative competence than moral worth, it relied more on actively demonstrating ability and performing some services, rather than a passive exemplification of superior virtue (Pye 1985: 57–58). Feudal lords were able to attract peasants away from Imperial estates during the Taika reform period, for instance, by protecting them against forced labour service for the Imperial authority (Jacobs 1958: 29) and so domination in Japan rested upon some notion of reciprocal service, albeit to a lesser extent than in European feudalism (Moore 1966: 233–234).

A further point about subordination in China is that obedience to the Emperor and his mandarins was more a matter of following norms of filial piety, in an analogous way to fulfilling role obligations to fathers as heads of families, than a personal commitment to an individual superior (Hamilton 1984). Commitment and loyalty to superiors are thus less 'emotional' and more calculating in Chinese society than in Japan, where common identification with collective goals has been facilitated by the institutionalization of feudal loyalties which overrode purely personal and kinship based ones (Moore 1966: 254–266; Silin 1976: 127–138). Because loyalty to collective authority in Chinese society was demanded as a matter of respect for the virtuous as an extension of filial piety in the family, it did not involve active personal commitment. Thus if the leader ceases to manifest his moral superiority by, for example, behaving inappropriately in his private life or failing to be successful in maintaining order, commitment can legitimately be transferred elsewhere (Jacobs 1958: 77).

The plurality of competing clans and alliances in Japan which provided foci of loyalty and identity beyond kinship groups institutionalized collective commitments to relatively large units of social organization in a way that did not happen in Chinese society. The systematic integration of ruling groups with the peasantry, providing military protection in exchange for transferring land tenure rights, ensured that vertical loyalties were less restricted to the household or extended kinship systems than in China where the mandarins rotated and could not claim personal loyalties (Jacobs 1958: 24–27). Because the feudal lords in Japan had to mobilize retainers and peasantry in order to compete effectively, they were more involved with local production systems and social structures than the Korean aristocracy or the Chinese mandarinate who concentrated on the rewards of central favour and preferment. They thus developed integrated hierarchies of control of the peasantry through their retainers and village headmen (Smith 1959: 54–64).

Inter-Family Solidarity and Collaboration

This difference in vertical integration between China and Japan is related to the general significance of the family as the basic unit of social identity and control in East Asian societies and the ease of establishing trust and mutual obligations across family boundaries. As well as vertical loyalties being limited and conditional in Chinese society, so too commitment to horizontal groupings and collective entities which transcend kinship boundaries was restricted by the Confucian concentration on the family as the fundamental unit of harmonious society and model for all authority relations. As Silin suggests (1976: 37): 'Aside from kinship, no coherent model or set of organizing principles exists to govern inter-personal relations within the Confucian conceptual system.' Whereas the Japanese recognized the legitimacy of tensions between family members and allowed ambitious younger sons to leave the family in order to establish a new lineage (Pye 1985: 68–69), thus weakening family boundaries, the Chinese and, to a lesser extent Korean, emphasis on the family as the core institution of society implied strong boundaries between family members and outsiders and the need to maintain solidarity and harmony within families. As Pye (1985: 70) puts it: 'The Chinese were taught to recognise a vivid distinction between family members, who could be relied upon, and non-family people, who are not to be trusted except in qualified ways.'

The pervasiveness of this 'familism' in Chinese culture is demonstrated by the infrequency and limited nature of co-operation across kinship groups in Chinese villages. As Moore (1966: 208) summarizes the situation: 'The Chinese village . . . evidently lacked cohesiveness . . . There were far fewer (than in Japan or Europe) occasions on which numerous members of the village co-operated in a common task in a way that creates the habits and sentiments of solidarity . . . the primary unit of economic production (and consumption as well) was the household.' In contrast, the Japanese village was highly cohesive, with families co-operating in major agricultural tasks, in particular the spring planting of rice (Smith 1959: 50–52). Partly because individual households depended so much on the assistance of others, ostracism and banishment from the village were very powerful sanctions against deviance which, together with the collective responsibility for taxation and criminal law, limited the open expression of conflicts between families and maintained the importance of group solidarity rather than individual wishes (*ibid.*: 60–62).

This contrast between China and Japan is exemplified by the differing results of introducing into the two countries the *pao-chia* system of mutual surveillance, under which ten households were made responsible for each others' conduct. According to Moore (1966: 206, 260), the system was quite ineffective in China, but when the Tokugawa rulers adapted it in 17th century Japan — albeit reduced to five households — it proved highly successful in maintaining order and raising taxes. Such inter-family solidarity and village cohesion was lower in Korea and, in general, the Korean and Chinese families seem to have many features in common. However, although the Korean family is important as the main source of support, the consanguineous lineage is more significant than in China and forms, according to Jacobs (1985: 211), the main intermediary organization between the individual and central, formal authority.

The weakness of inter-family co-operation and solidarity in the traditional Chinese village is echoed by the lack of an effective legal system in China and of institutional processes for regulating exchanges between strangers (Jacobs 1958: 97–99). Together with the Confucian distrust of mercantile wealth which resulted in periodic confiscation and official constraints on economic activities, this meant that personal bonds and familiarity were very important in developing trust and encouraged con-

Table 2
Significant
Differences
Between Pre-
industrial China,
Korea and Japan

	China	Korea	Japan
Political pluralism	low	low	medium
Economic pluralism	low	low	high
Basis of claim to authority	moral worth	moral worth	competitive military success
Inter-family solidarity and integration into larger political units	low	low	high

siderable secrecy and defensiveness. In contrast, pre-industrial Japan began to develop more formal mechanisms for settling disputes as early as the 18th century with the acceptance of the legitimacy of private litigation in 1721.

This growth of impersonality in Japan was assisted by the separation of the warrior class of *samurai* from the land and their employment in towns as the administrative agents of the feudal lords. According to Smith (1988: 136–142), during the Tokugawa period of the 17th, 18th and much of the 19th centuries, traditional feudal ties of personal loyalty between *samurai* and their lords (*daimyo*) became more attenuated, distant and impersonal as the former lost their direct ties to the land and came to depend on the stipends received from the latter for administering their estates. They increasingly saw themselves as loyal administrators of the collective entity, and began to regard merit and competence as the key attributes of superior status and rank rather than inherited positions. While loyalty to superiors remained a necessary attribute of the ideal official, it became less personally focused on the individual leader and had increasingly to be complemented by demonstrated ability (Pye 1985: 161). These differences between pre-industrial China, Korea and Japan are summarized in terms of the four features mentioned earlier in Table 2.

The Institutional Environments of East Asian Business Systems

The differences between China, Korea and Japan described above have had substantial consequences for the institutional environments in which business systems developed. These environments can be summarized in terms of the following interrelated features. First, the system of authority relations, including the degree of vertical integration of loyalties, the importance of personal ties and conceptions of appropriate behaviour. Second, the system for establishing trust and obligation relations between exchange partners and its impact on enterprise loyalties and commitment. Third, the organization and policies of political and bureaucratic state elites, including the extent to which the state dominates the economic system and controls banks as well as co-ordinating firms' strategies. Differences in these features help to explain the development and reproduction of different business systems in East Asia.

The System of Authority Relations

One of the major differences in authority relations between Japanese, Korean and Chinese societies concerns the extent to which loyalties are systematically integrated as a series of mutual commitments between superiors and subordinates in an elaborate vertical hierarchy. Whereas the centralized feudalism of Tokugawa Japan developed a series of intermediate organizations between the state and individual households which integrated vertical loyalties, Confucian China and Korea systematically prevented the establishment of local centres of loyalty and political organization. Thus, obedience and subordination relations in Japan are tied to particular collective entities which, in turn, are subordinate to larger ones. Furthermore, the development of reciprocity norms in Japanese society between superior and subordinate — however asymmetric they may be — has helped to integrate vertical loyalties more than in Chinese or Korean societies, where the rule of collectively self-certified virtuous officials has limited the perceived need to legitimate domination through reciprocal services. While modern Japanese politicians and other leaders are expected to look after their supporters and perform useful services for them in return for deference and support (Eisenstadt and Roniger 1984: 159–162), Chinese and Korean ones restrict their obligation to kinship groupings and do not rely on extensive chains of mutual support. Coupled with the role performance model of filial piety as the exemplar of obedience in Chinese society, this lack of reciprocity and sequential integration of commitments through a succession of superiors and collectivities reduces the intensity of vertical loyalties and their mobilization for collective goals beyond the family unit.

A further difference in the system of authority relations in Japanese, Korean and Chinese societies concerns the relative importance of direct personal subordination to leaders as distinct from obedience to collective and positional authority. This in turn reflects the extent to which authority has become collective and depersonalized in a society. The patrimonial authority system of pre-industrial China and Korea which emphasized the personal moral superiority of the ruler and his advisors inhibited the development of more impersonal forms of authority. As a result, allegiance remains a primarily personal relationship to particular individuals in these societies (Jacobs 1985; Pye 1985).

In contrast, reciprocity and recognition of mutual dependence between superiors and subordinates in modern Japan are combined with strong beliefs in the common commitment to collective goals and the right of superiors to issue commands on the basis of their competence, as assessed by the education system, and subservience to joint interests (Pye 1985: 163–181). Personal commitments to immediate superiors and more senior patrons (Rohlen 1974: 122–134), are greater and more significant than in most western societies, but rest much more on shared loyalties to collective objectives and mutual trust than elsewhere in East Asia.

These variations in loyalty to non-family collectivities are also a result of different conceptions of authority within families which affect expectations about managerial authority and appropriate managerial behaviour (Pye 1985: 73–79). In the Chinese family, the father is supposed to be omnipotent and omniscient so that obedience is owed to him as a superior being who is solely responsible for the family fortunes. The mother is obliged to reinforce his authority and so cannot serve as a focus of different values and modes of conduct (cf. Ho 1986). Authority is thus monolithic and undifferentiated. Similarly, the owner of the CFB is expected to exhibit superior qualities and a didactic leadership style by allowing subordinates to learn the thoughts and beliefs which enable him to be successful (Silin 1976: 127–128). As the head of the family enterprise, he maintains a considerable distance from employees and cannot delegate or share authority because leadership is a moral quality of individuals. Thus managing by consensus in the CFB would be regarded as a sign of incompetence and weakness (Silin 1976: 71). The Korean father is supposed to be similarly omnicompetent and aloof, but authority in the Korean family is more differentiated than in the Chinese one and so children are able to play off paternal and maternal authorities against each other (Pye 1985: 75).

In contrast, the Japanese father can share his responsibilities with others and admit uncertainty. Furthermore, the mother in Japanese families can function as an alternative focus of authority so that children become accustomed to differentiated authority, in particular to what Pye (1985: 74) terms a maternalist image of authority. Together with the need to elicit subordinates' commitment and energies in competitive struggles, this legitimacy of supportive and 'nurturing' forms of authority encourages managerial styles which take account of emotional dependence needs and seek consensus among subordinates and encourage the development of their skills for group goals. Their authority is not threatened by subordinate success in the way that a Chinese or Korean manager's would be. Authority relations in Japanese society then are less focused on direct personal relationships between subordinates and the leader than in Chinese and Korean societies and obedience is owed on the basis of competence and collective loyalties rather than deference to the personal qualities of political leaders.

Trust, Reciprocity and Enterprise Loyalty

The institutionalization of norms of reciprocity and mutual obligation between superiors and subordinates is, of course, a part of the overall development of trust and confidence relationships between increasingly separate individuals and groups in an industrializing society. In considering how such norms and relations differ between Chinese, Korean and Japanese societies it is helpful to use Zucker's (1986) distinction between three major bases for generating trust between exchange partners: reputations for reliability and probity, common ascriptive characteristics such as ethnicity and, third, through some more general social institution such as the professional certification of competences and code of ethics or legal system. The more socially and geographically distant the exchange partners, the more important the formal institutional means of building confidence become, as reputation and ascription cease to be effective where cultural heterogeneity and distances are considerable. Thus the development of large national corporations in the late 19th century U.S.A., after waves of immigration had increased the size and heterogeneity of the population, depended, according to Zucker, on the establishment of formal controls and signalling institutions.

Cultural homogeneity in Japanese, Korean and Chinese societies is greater than in many western countries and so reputational and ascriptive means of developing trust and confidence remain effective over considerable distances through elaborate and extensive reputational networks, as demonstrated by the overseas Chinese (Limlingan 1986; Redding 1990; Yoshihara 1988). However, the growth of more impersonal norms of obligation and objective indicators of performance for officials in the 19th century, together with a strong emphasis among merchants on demonstrating honesty and probity to the public in order to conform with the norms of model citizenship, encouraged more generalized, formal and collective means of establishing trust relations in Japan (Hirschmeier and Yui 1981: 40–48). To be trustworthy across a wide range of transactions became a general and public indication of collective business success and social honour. Confidence in the larger merchant houses grew to the extent that their deposit notes and bills of exchange were often trusted more than cash (Hirschmeier and Yui 1981: 29–30). While not, then, developing the extensive formal mechanisms of trust generation and reproduction found in many western societies, the institutionalization of trust relations between strangers has gone much further in Japan than in Korean or Chinese society.

This more general and collective basis for generating trust in Japan is reflected in the greater ease of establishing mutual obligation relations between members of different groups there (Pye 1985: 71). While Chinese and Korean ties of reciprocal obligations are often based on ascriptive foundations such as common birthplace, school or university class, Japanese ones are more idiosyncratic and situation specific. Thus *guanxi* networks of mutual support in Chinese society are usually tied to common background characteristics (Wong 1988) whereas Japanese obligation networks are formed across such categories as well as within them, and demonstrate an ability to form strong bonds between people with different backgrounds. Reciprocity of favours and obligations is a stronger norm in Japan than in China and Korea and is a more generalized relationship in the sense that it can be developed between Japanese with different ascriptive characteristics. Thus strong loyalties and cohesive bonds can be established between different groups of people to a much greater extent than seems to be feasible in Chinese society where ascriptive ties — especially family — predominate.

These differences are, of course, related to the general pattern of co-operation and solidarity across kinship groups in Japan, Korea and China. As already suggested, the historical nature of the Chinese village and the lack of integration of households in production, consumption or common defence activities have reproduced a sharp distinction between family members and outsiders which makes the development of social cohesion and common identities between families difficult in Chinese societies. Rather, distrust tends to be pervasive, since each person is held to be responsible for his own household and to put its interests ahead of broader objectives.

This primacy of family relationships and identities in Chinese society means that commitment to one's family overrides all other loyalties, and individual prestige is based on family standing rather than being organizational or occupational. Family prestige, in turn, is linked to property ownership as well as to educational and professional success since full membership of the Chinese village was not feasible without owning land and it was also a pre-condition of establishing a family and so gaining respect. In Moore's words (1966: 212): 'no property: no family, no religion'. Especially in societies where political advancement has been inaccessible for many, such as Hong Kong and Taiwan, business success and wealth have become the major sources of family prestige and, for that reason, many managers and technicians leave to start their own businesses when good opportunities arise (Redding and Tam 1985; Tam 1990). Thus, commitment to employers among the expatriate Chinese and Taiwanese is always limited and conditional, unless strong personal obligations exist through family connections.

This limited commitment to employers and companies means that business owners feel unable to trust employees with important decisions unless they are members of the same family or have strong personal obligations and commitments to them. Additionally, since trust is such a personal phenomenon in Chinese society, and people beyond the kinship group are expected to pursue their own family interests even if they fulfil role expectations of obedience to superiors, Chinese entrepreneurs are very concerned to develop personal ties of mutual obligation with key staff and with business partners. Thus personal reputations for honesty and competence and membership of large mutual obligation networks are crucial components of business success in Chinese communities (Limlingan 1986; Ward 1972). The need for strong personal involvement in running the CFB in order to ensure trust and commitment, coupled with the dependence of family prestige on business success and wealth, encourage owner control, highly personal authority relations and centralization of decision-making in the CFB.

In contrast, the greater importance of relatively independent legal procedures for resolving disputes in Japan, and the more widespread and idiosyncratic the processes for establishing mutual obligation ties between non-family members, have facilitated the development of less personal forms of control and managerial authority which are not tied to direct ownership. Additionally, the existence of substantial concentrations of economic power in feudal Japan and the ability to transform wealth into political resources meant that owners were not so threatened by political elites as in China and so did not retain such close personal control over financial resources and decisions. Loyalty to independent collective entities was institutionalized in Japan well before the Meiji restoration and the use of unrelated retainers as managers of family businesses was not uncommon, so that the development of college educated managerial cadres towards the end of the 19th century did not present a sharp discontinuity with the Tokugawa period (Hirschmeier and Yui 1981: 165–168).

The weaker sense of family boundaries and historical commitment to broader collectivities also facilitated the growth of loyalty to firms and a greater willingness to trust employees (Silin 1976: 131–138). Since family prestige and worth were derived from the success and prestige of the collective enterprise, as well as from individual ownership, and personal identities were as much tied to such enterprises as to specific family membership, the pressure to establish an independent source of family status by setting up one's own business is much less than in Chinese cultures and loyalty to broad, non-family collectives correspondingly stronger.

State Policies and Financial Systems

Finally, the degree of political and economic pluralism in pre-industrial China, Korea and Japan has affected the ways in which state agencies and political elites have dealt with the economic system and promoted industrialization. In Japan, Korea and Taiwan both bureaucratic and political elites have been extensively involved in promoting economic change and growth and have seen the state as a central agent of modernization and development. In all three countries, the state is 'developmental' and plan rational in Johnson's terms (1982: 17–23) rather than regulatory and market oriented as in the U.S.A. Thus they are all concerned with setting substantive social and economic goals which involve particular industrial policies.

The Hong Kong government, on the other hand, has been overtly distant from economic affairs and has not sought to manage the process of economic development. The emergence of a highly efficient and rather fragmented manufacturing sector since the 1950s has taken place almost despite the state rather than with its assistance (Haggard and Chen 1987). However, Deyo (1987) suggests that the leaders of the large banks and trading companies are strongly integrated into the colonial elite to constitute a British dominated establishment that is supportive of development and fulfils some of the functions of the developmentalist state. Similarly, Nishida (1990) claims that the British banks and trading houses provided support for the Shanghaiese cotton spinners in Hong Kong in the 1950s.

Perhaps the major difference in the role of the state between Japan, Korea and Taiwan to be considered here concerns the extent to which it actively intervenes in managing the environment of corporate decision-making and influences individual firms' strategic choices. Whereas the South Korean state since 1961 has pursued a highly interventionist policy aimed at achieving high economic growth and industrial development through state co-ordination of private business, the Japanese bureaucracy has been less inclined to direct corporate decision-making through hierarchical commands and has not been so successful at obtaining compliance since the Second World War. Finally, although the Taiwanese state still controls 18 percent of industrial production and is responsible for half of the gross domestic investment (Amsden 1985), it has not attempted to manage firms' choices in the export sector or allocate resources on a discretionary basis to individual firms (Myers 1986). Thus the extent of state co-ordination of strategies and the direction of economic activities in the export sector over the past 30 years has been highest in South Korea, significant but less directive in Japan, and most indirect — although still important — in Taiwan. Let us first discuss these differences and then consider their consequences for business systems.

The South Korean military regime has assumed direct responsibility for managing economic development, arguably as the means of legitimating its domination (Kim 1988). By controlling access to foreign exchange, bank credit at low interest rates, tax concessions, imposing price controls and threatening tax investigations, the Korean state has manipulated and directed the strategic choices of major firms, especially the *chaebol* (Jones and Sakong 1980: 100–140). Jacobs (1985) has characterized this central direction of the economic system as essentially patrimonial and a continuation of the Confucian system of bureaucratic elitism in which wealth and power depended on the grace of the ruler and his virtuous advisors. However, Kim (1988) suggests that the power of the Korean 'hard state' has declined since the 1960s and the *chaebol* are becoming more autonomous; a view partly borne out by the dispute over the terms for rescuing the Daewoo shipyards (Clifford 1989).

The important role of the state bureaucracy, especially the Ministry of International Trade and Industry (MITI), in guiding Japanese economic development is well known. However, despite the Bank of Japan's strong influence on the credit policies of private banks through the 'overloaning' system (Johnson 1982: 201–204), the ability of the Japanese state to manage economic actors' strategies directly is much more limited than in Korea. This is partly because the bulk of the banking system has been privately owned and controlled, and partly because Japan has had major concentrations of economic power outside the state apparatus for a considerable time. Hence the guidance and co-ordination of private decisions have rarely amounted to direct commands and there have been a number of well publicized rejections of MITI's advice (Abegglen and Stalk 1985; Eads and Yamamura 1987). Generally, the bureaucracy has influenced strategies indirectly through field manipulation of costs and opportunities and has concerned itself more with the collective behaviour of firms and industries, rather than directing the actions of individual firms (Haggard 1988; Johnson 1982, 1987; Wade 1988). It has helped businesses to co-ordinate and plan their strategies but has not, on the whole, intervened in particular decisions of individual firms.

The Taiwanese case is superficially paradoxical because it manifests a high rate of state ownership and control of major banks and industries, with public enterprises contributing 31 percent of gross fixed capital formation on average between 1965–1980 compared to 23 percent in Korea and 11 percent in Japan (Wade 1988), at the same time as exercising a much more distant relationship between the state and firms in the export sector. In contrast to South Korea, the Taiwanese state has not sought to co-ordinate firms' strategies, to build up large national champions in particular industries or to direct firms' resources in particular ways, except to encourage investment in plastics and electronics (Myers 1986). Additionally, it has pursued a high interest rate policy in order to control inflation and has not encouraged large-scale lending at privileged interest rates for capital intensive industries (Amsden 1985; Gold 1985; Haggard 1988). Essentially, loss-making state enterprises have subsidized the export sector which has also benefited from general state support for new export such as preferential tariff rates and indicative planning which reduced investment risks (Gold 1985: 87). As Gold (1985: 126) puts it: 'in Taiwan, planners retained an aloof posture. They met to formulate policy and then relayed their decisions and attendant mechanisms to implement it to the business community, and watched what happened.' Partly as a result, Taiwanese firms have remained relatively small and in industries where flexibility and small size are advantageous (Levy 1988). Lacking strong state support for large, capital-intensive firms, the private sector has been dominated by the CFB and has avoided competing directly with dominant western firms where entry costs are very high (Hamilton and Biggart 1988).

The financial systems in all three countries are based on bank credit for industrial development rather than on capital markets and this has provided the state with substantial leverage over firms' decisions, especially where low real interest rates have stimulated a surplus demand for loans and hence encouraged their administrative rationing (Zysman 1983: 71–72). However, the close association between banks, trust companies and insurance companies with industrial firms in Japanese business groups, seems more equal and interdependent than similar relations in Korea and Taiwan. Furthermore, because the banks are much more state controlled in the latter two countries, many firms have preferred to rely for investment funds on the unofficial 'curb' money markets, even with their attendant exorbitant interest rates, or on personal contacts and family resources (Wade 1988).

In particular, the numerous small and medium sized firms in Taiwan have not developed close links with the state controlled banks and have not formed inter-market business groups through them. Such inter-sector co-ordination as does exist between Taiwanese firms occurs through family connections and strong personal ties between owners (Numazaki 1986). Thus the degree of integration of financial institutions with major firms differs between Japan, Korea and Taiwan although, in all three, it is greater than in capital-market based financial systems such as the U.S.A. While the large Hong Kong banks are not so formally tied to the state or publicly involved in long-term economic development as those elsewhere in East Asia, Haggard and Cheng (1987) suggest that they have played a major role in the long-term funding of manufacturing industries and, more recently, have been critical to the explosion of the financial services industry.

The major significance of state co-ordination and bank involvement in business strategies for the sorts of business recipes that become established concerns risk reduction and sharing, what Pye (1988) terms the 'nationalization of risk'. Particularly with regard to large-scale capital investments in new industries and markets, long-term commitment to enterprise goals by powerful agencies facilitates growth objectives and encourages risky decisions which might not otherwise be taken. Strong state control over labour movements, as in Korea and Taiwan, also encourages major investments because expected profits will be higher than if there is an independent union movement which can challenge owners' rights (Cumings 1987; Haggard 1988).

In the case of Japan, the role of the banks and the General Trading Companies, or *Sogo Shosha*, in business groups facilitated business specialization because many aspects of purchasing, selling and finance functions can be organized on a relational contracting basis with other members of each group (Yoshino and Lifson 1986: 21–53). As a result, firms could concentrate on developing relatively homogenous and specialized skills to achieve high growth rates in particular markets. State support for orderly markets and reducing excessive competition reduced the risks of business specialization and enabled specialized firms to benefit from relatively homogeneous skills and commitments to particular industries, as well as reduced co-ordination costs because of this homogeneity of activities. Thus relatively close and interdependent connection between state agencies, banks, *sogo shosha* and other major actors enabled considerable specialization of capabilities and activities to develop successfully in Japan.

The strong support of the South Korean state for favoured *chaebol*, and the associated preferential allocation of bank loans for politically desired projects (Jones and Sakong 1980: 106–109), clearly encouraged the growth of these large, integrated enterprises and their willingness to move into new, capital-intensive industries in the 1970s (Amsden 1989: 80–85). In effect, the state assumed a substantial proportion of the risks involved and also had the mechanisms for ensuring compliance with its wishes. This close involvement of state agencies also means, though, that *chaebol* are highly dependent on the goodwill of bureaucrats and their masters, which has resulted in their support for government programmes and their strong personal ties to key officials. Shin and Chin (1989) suggest that this need for continued state support and favours helps to explain the high levels of centralized decision-making in the *chaebol* and their reliance on ascriptive criteria for filling senior managerial posts (cf. Yoo and Lee 1987). The paramount need for trust and loyalty in a highly faction ridden society, where personal relationships and connections are critical, encourages the use of kinship and regional criteria for such posts (cf. Jacobs 1985). Centralization within the *chaebol* thus matches the highly centralized nature of authority in Korean society, and the formation of a personally loyal and cohesive group of top managers and advisors facilitates central control of these large enterprises.

The more removed and distant relationships between state agencies and large enterprises in Taiwan, together with a general policy of not directly building up large, integrated businesses to compete with Japanese and western ones in advanced industrial sectors (Myers 1986), have limited the growth of large-scale integrated enterprises in the export sector. Thus, Taiwanese businesses have concentrated on industries and products where economics of scale are less important than flexibility and innovation (Levy 1988). Specialization and extensive sub-contracting are also, of course, a characteristic of the CFB in Hong Kong. The centrifugal tendencies of the CFB appears to have resulted in increasing fragmentation of the industrial structure in the absence of strong central co-ordination of industrial development in Hong Kong (Tam 1990).

To summarize, I am suggesting that the major differences between East Asian business systems, identified in Table 1, result from particular features of their institutional environments. These concern authority relationships, mechanisms for generating and maintaining trust, and obligation relations between non-kin and the structure and policies of state agencies and financial institutions. Variations in these features which help to explain East Asian business systems are listed in Table 3.

Conclusions: Towards the Comparative Analysis of Business Systems

This analysis of the different forms of business organization which have become established and successful in different institutional environments in East Asia highlights both the variability of competitive business systems and their interdependence with their societal contexts. In particular, it emphasizes the continuing influence of pre-industrial political and social structures together with the critical role of state agencies and financial institutions in sharing risks and co-ordinating strategies. Differences between the modern Japanese *kaisha*, Korean *chaebol* and the Chinese family business reflect historical patterns of authority and iden-

Table 3
Major Differences
in the Institutional
Contexts of East
Asian Business
Systems

	Japan	Korea	Taiwan	Hong Kong
Authority Relations				
Vertical integration of loyalties	high	low	low	low
Significance of collective non-personal authority	high	low	low	low
Differentiation of family authority	high	high	low	low
Omnicompetence of father	low	high	high	high
Trust, Reciprocity and Loyalty				
Bases of trust of obligation	institutional	ascriptive	ascriptive and reputational	
Primacy of family commitment	medium	high	high	high
Political and Financial Systems				
Developmental state	high	high	high	low
State coordination of strategies	medium	high	medium	low
Integration of banks with firms	high	high	medium	medium

tity reproduced through current family structures and other institutions as well as variations in state structures and policies during the industrialization process. The extent to which these influences are significant factors in explaining variations between established business systems in other societies differs, however, and it is worthwhile briefly exploring these differences and their implications for a more general comparative analysis of business systems.

The continued importance of pre-industrial political and social structures in East Asian societies, as well as traditional patterns of familial authority, reflects the recentness of their industrialization and the crucial role of the family as the basic social unit. All these 'post Confucian' cultures share the common theme that 'individuals achieved their identity solely through family membership which carried with it not only the obligation of deferring to the collectivity in critical decision-making but of acknowledging that the mortal life of the individual was less important than the immortality of the ancestral family line' (Pye 1985: 62). Despite, then, differences between Japanese, Korean and Chinese family structures and boundaries, consciousness of family identities and of the importance of family relationships is much greater than in most 'western' societies. Furthermore, the relative homogeneity of each culture, which reflects considerable isolation from external influences and migration over several centuries, both encourages and is reproduced by high degrees of similarity of family authority patterns and expectations so that these have a strong influence on attitudes and beliefs within societies.

These points suggest that where industrialization took place over a longer time span and developed before the 20th century, and where the individual has become more detached from the family, pre-industrial structures and attitudes are less directly influential in affecting the sorts of enterprise structure that have developed, and the role of family authority relations is less marked. While the institutional framework in which industrialization took place remains important in understanding present differences between, say, the role of the British and German financial institutions in funding industrial investment, variations in feudal structures do not directly explain differences in the organization of manufacturing firms or in the degree of vertical integration between these countries (cf. Maurice et al. 1980; Sorge and Warner 1986). Similarly, differences in family authority patterns between western countries are less directly significant in explaining variations in co-ordination and control practices than in East Asia because of the greater importance of horizontal groupings and identities based on occupations, as well as the general emphasis on individualism and legal rational modes of authority. Additionally, most western cultures are more heterogeneous than East Asian ones so that family structures are more varied and changeable.

In comparing dominant economic actors in western societies, then, the role of intermediate collective institutions, such as the education and training system (Maurice et al. 1986), and horizontal foci of loyalty and identity are more directly significant. Where skills are formally assessed and certified in a standardized way, and are important bases of identity and labour market boundaries, loyalty to individual employers will be limited and mobility between them correspondingly greater. Because skills are 'owned' by individuals and are separately defined, their integration and co-ordination for particular tasks and problems require more systematic management and organization than if they are derived more directly from particular organizational structures and practices. Thus tasks and responsibilities in 'credential' societies (Collins 1979) tend to be more formally specified, and their performance by individuals more directly monitored and linked to reward systems, than where skills and loyalties are more organization based (Lincoln et al. 1986). Similarly, standardized skills facilitate market determination of wage rates and so the institutionalization of public training and certification of practical skills is associated with market based wage rates rather than with organizationally specific ones (Dore 1973: 71–73, 110–113).

A further feature of the societal context of business systems which becomes highly significant when comparing East Asia with western industrialized countries is the nature of the financial system and the associated extent to which the state performs a market-oriented, regulatory role rather than a plan-oriented developmentalist one. Zysman (1983) has emphasized the differences between capital market and credit-based financial systems for corporate behaviour and for the ability of state agencies to influence firms' policies. Whereas the credit-based system makes firms more directly dependent on the banks and those who can control the availability of loans, capital-market based financial systems inhibit close relations between the state, banks and firms because of, *inter alia*, specialization and competition among financial inter-mediaries. While all East Asian economies have credit-based financial systems and developmentalist states, the U.S.A. and U.K. have strong capital market oriented states which affect the sorts of business systems that have developed.

Firms in these countries are both less constrained by ties to state agencies and banks and less able to claim their support or help in reducing uncertainty than in credit-based systems. Here, the state merely provides the framework for economic activities and does not share risks or co-ordinate plans. Similarly, financial institutions provide funds and own shares on a portfolio basis and so emphasize liquidity and diversification of financial risk rather than interdependence and mutual support. Invest-ment finance is here raised from relatively impersonal and decentralized competitive capital markets, which evaluate the risks and opportunities of a range of investments, rather than from large 'universal' financial institu-tions which are tied to particular businesses and share their particular risks and returns.

These arms' length and impersonal connections between large corpora-tions, state agencies and financial institutions mean that major risks and long-term investments cannot easily be shared with other organizations and market processes are the dominant means by which firms' and banks' activities are co-ordinated. As a result, firms tend to be more risk averse and less likely to undertake major long-term investments than their Japanese or German counterparts. They are also more likely to be con-cerned with increasing their share price and achieving high returns on investment funds supplied by the capital market than with growth and market share objectives because of the much more important market for corporate control in capital market based financial systems (Abegglen and Stalk 1985: 175–178; Lawriwsky 1984: 165–177). Similarly, because they have to manage risk on their own, and are more likely to be taken over and sacked if financial results are regarded by the markets as inferior to others, the dominant coalitions of large U.S. corporations are more positive about diversification into unrelated sectors than are those of large firms in credit-based systems.

The combination of standardized, formally certified skills, legal rational authority principles, a market-oriented state and capital market financial system, then, leads to a quite different form of business organization in Anglo-Saxon societies to those found in East Asia and, in many ways, to those established in some continental European countries. In addition to relying predominantly on formal and impersonal forms of authority and co-ordination, manifesting relatively low levels of employer–employee commitment and loyalty and high levels of task and role differentiation with performance measures tied to individual efforts, these dominant economic actors incorporate a wide range of skills and activities in diverse markets with few stable, long-term relationships to other firms or banks and tend to make discontinuous, radical changes in growth strategies rather than evolutionary ones (Kagono et al. 1985).

In broadening the comparative analysis of business systems beyond East Asia, this discussion suggests that further important features of institutional environments are: the strength of occupational identities and prevalence of formally assessed and certified skills, the nature of the financial system and the strength and orientation of the state. These help to explain differences in the use of formal co-ordination and control rules and procedures, the extent to which roles and responsibilities are formally specified and allocated to separate individuals as well as the heterogeneity of skills and activities integrated and directed by authority structures, and preferred growth strategies.

As a result of these differences between institutional environments, different kinds of enterprise structures become feasible and successful in particular social contexts, especially where cultures are homogeneous and share strong boundaries with nation states. While not assuming that national contexts determine all aspects of business systems, nor denying the significance of variations between industries in heterogeneous cultures, the comparative analysis of enterprise structures does claim that dominant social institutions generate distinctive business systems which are relatively similar within nation states and strong cultural systems, but vary considerably between them. In this paper, I have suggested how particular features of dominant economic actors in Japan, South Korea, Taiwan and Hong Kong can be understood in terms of their institutional environment as an initial contribution to such a comparative analysis.

References

Abegglen, James C., and George Stalk
1985 *Kaisha, the Japanese corporation.* New York: Basic Books.

Amsden, Alice H.
1985 'The state and Taiwan's economic development' in *Bringing the state back in.* P. B. Evans et al. (eds.), 78–106. Cambridge: Cambridge University Press.

Amsden, Alice H.
1985a 'The division of labour is limited by the rate of growth of the market: the Taiwan machine tool industry in the 1970s'. *Cambridge Journal of Economics* 9: 271–284.

Amsden, Alice H.
1989 *Asia's next giant.* Oxford: Oxford University Press.

Aoki, Masahiko
1987 'The Japanese firm in transition' in *The political economy of Japan, I: the domestic transformation.* K. Yamamura and Y. Yasuba (eds.), 263–288. Stanford: Stanford University Press.

Berger, Peter, and H.-H. M. Hsiao, *editors*
1988 *In search of an East Asian development model.* New Brunswick, New Jersey: Transaction Books.

Clark, R.
1979 *The Japanese company.* New Haven: Yale University Press.

Clifford, M.
1989 'Shipyard blues'. *Far East Economic Review* (23rd February): 62–64.

Collins, Randall
1979 *The credential society*. New York: Academic Press.

Cumings, Bruce
1987 'The origins and development of the northeast Asian political economy' in *The political economy of the new Asian industrialism*. F. C. Deyo (ed.). Ithaca: Cornell University Press.

Cusumano, Michael A.
1985 *The Japanese automobile industry: technology and management at Nissan and Toyota*. Cambridge, Mass.: Harvard University Press.

Deyo, F. C.
1987 'Coalitions, institutions and linkage sequencing — towards a strategic capacity model of East Asian developments' in *The political economy of the New Asian industrialism*. F. C. Deyo (ed.), 227–247. Ithaca: Cornell University Press.

Dore, Ronald
1973 *British factory — Japanese factory*. London: Allen and Unwin.

Dore, Ronald
1986 *Flexible rigidities*. Stanford: Stanford University Press.

Eads, George C., and Kozo Yamamura
1987 'The future of industrial policy' in *The political economy of Japan, I: the domestic transformation*. K. Yamamura and Y. Yasuba (eds.), 423–468. Stanford: Stanford University Press.

Eisenstadt, S. N., and L. Roniger
1984 *Patrons, clients and friends*. Cambridge: Cambridge University Press.

Futatsugi, Yusaku
1986 *Japanese enterprise groups*. Kobe University, School of Business Administration.

Gold, T. B.
1985 *State and society in the Taiwan miracle*. Armonk, New York: M. E. Sharpe.

Goto, A.
1982 'Business groups in a market economy'. *European Economic Review* 19: 53–70.

Haggard, Stephen
1988 'The politics of industrialisation in the Republic of Korea and Taiwan' in *Achieving industrialisation in East Asia*. H. Hughes (ed.), 260–282. Cambridge: Cambridge University Press.

Haggard, Stephen, and T.-J. Cheng
1987 'State and foreign capital in the East Asian NICs' in *The political economy of the New Asian industrialism*. F. C. Deyo (ed.), 84–135. Ithaca, New York: Cornell University Press.

Hamilton, Gary
1984 'Patriarchalism in imperial China and western Europe'. *Theory and Society* 13: 393–426.

Hamilton, Gary, and C. S. Kao
1987 'The institutional foundation of Chinese business: the family firm in Taiwan'. Program in East Asian Culture and Development, Working Paper Series, No. 8. Institute of Governmental Affairs, University of California at Davis.

Hamilton, Gary, and N. W. Biggart
1988 'Market, culture and authority: a comparative analysis of management and organisation in the Far East'. *American Journal of Sociology* 94. Supplement: 552–594.

Hamilton, Gary, William Zeile, and W. J. Kim
1990 'The network structures of East Asian economies' in *Capitalism in contrasting cultures*. S. R. Clegg and G. Redding (eds.), 105–130. Berlin: Walter de Gruyter.

Hirschmeier, J., and T. Yui
1981 *The development of Japanese business 1600–1980*, 2nd ed. London: Allen and Unwin.

Ho, David Y. F.
1986 'Chinese patterns of socialisation: a critical review' in *The psychology of the Chinese people*. Michael Bond (ed.), 1–37. Hong Kong: Oxford University Press.

Imai, K., and H. Itami
1984 'Interpretation of organisation and market. Japan's firm and market in comparison with the U.S.'. *International Journal of Industrial Organisation* 2: 285–310.

Ingham, G.
1984 *Capitalism divided? The city and industry in British social development*. London: Macmillan.

Jacobs, Norman
1958 *The origin of modern capitalism and eastern Asia*. Hong Kong: Hong Kong University Press.

Jacobs, Norman
1985 *The Korean road to modernisation and development*. Urbana: University of Illinois Press.

Johnson, Chalmers
1982 *MITI and the Japanese miracle*. Stanford: Stanford University Press.

Johnson, Chalmers
1987 'Political institutions and economic performance: the government–business relationship in Japan, South Korea and Taiwan' in *The political economy of the new Asian industrialism*. F. C. Deyo (ed.), 136–164. Ithaca: Cornell University Press.

Jones, Leroy, and Il Sakong
1980 *Government, business and entrepreneurship in economic development: the Korean case*. Harvard: Harvard University Press.

Kagono, Tadao, Ikujiro Alonaka, Kiyonori Sakakibara, and Akihiro Okumara
1985 *Strategic vs. evolutionary management*. Amsterdam: North Holland.

Kim, Kyong-Dong
1979 *Man and society in Korea's economic growth*. Seoul: Seoul National University Press.

Kim, E. M.
1988 'From dominance to symbiosis: state and *chaebol* in Korea'. *Pacific Focus* 3: 105–121.

Kim, E. M.
1989 'Development, state policy and industrial organisation: the case of Korea's *chaebol*'. Paper presented to the International Conference on Business Groups and Economic Development in East Asia, Hong Kong, June 20–22.

Kono, Toyohiro
1984 *Strategy and structure of Japanese enterprises*. London: Macmillan.

Lawriwsky, Michael L.
1984 *Corporate structure and performance*. London: Croom Helm.

Levy, Brian
1988 'Korean and Taiwanese firms as international competitors: the challenges ahead'. *Columbia Journal of World Business* (Spring): 43–51.

Liebenberg, R. D.
1982 'Japan incorporated' and 'The Korean troops': a comparative analysis of Korean business organisations. Unpublished MA Thesis, Dept. of Asian Studies, University of Hawaii.

Limlingan, Victor S.
1986 *The overseas Chinese in Asean: business strategies and management practices*. Pasig, Metro Manila: Vita Development Corporation.

Lincoln, J. R., M. Hanada, and K. McBride
1986 'Organizational structures in Japanese and U.S. manufacturing'. *Administrative Science Quarterly* 31: 338–364.

Mariti, P., and R. H. Smiley
1983 'Co-operative agreements and the organisation of industry'. *Journal of Industrial Economics* 31: 437–451.

Maurice, Marc
1979 'For a study of "the societal effect": universality and specificity in organisation research' in *Organisations alike and unalike*. C. J. Lammers and D. J. Hickson (eds.), 42–60. London: Routledge and Kegan Paul.

Maurice, Marc, Arndt Sorge, and Malcolm Warner
1980 'Societal differences in organising manufacturing units'. *Organization Studies* 1/1: 59–86.

Maurice, Marc, Francois Sellier, and Jean-Jacques Silvestre
1986 *The social bases of industrial power*. Cambridge, Mass.: MIT Press.

Michell, Tony
1988 *From a developing to a newly industrialised country: the Republic of Korea, 1961–82*. Geneva: ILO.

Miyazaki, Yoshikazu
1980 'Excessive competition and the formation of *keiretsu*' in *Industry and business in Japan*. K. Sato (ed.), 53–73. New York: M. E. Sharpe.

Moore, B.
1966 *The social origins of dictatorship and democracy*. Boston: Beacon Press.

Myers, R. H.
1986 'The economic development of the Republic of China on Taiwan' in *Modes of development*. L. J. Lau (ed.). San Francisco: ICS Press.

Nishida, Judith
1990 *The Japanese influence on the Shanghaiese textile industry and implications for Hong Kong*. M.Phil. Thesis, University of Hong Kong.

Numazaki, I.
1986 'Networks of Taiwanese big business'. *Modern China* 12: 487–534.

Orru, M., Nicole W. Biggart, and Gary Hamilton
1988 'Organisational isomorphism in East Asia: broadening the new institutionalism'. Program in East Asian Culture and Development Research, Working Paper Series, No. 10. Institute of Governmental Affairs, University of California, Davis.

Pugh, Derek S., and Gordon R. Redding
1985 'The formal and the informal: Japanese and Chinese organisation structures' in *The enterprise and management in East Asia*. S. R. Clegg et al. (eds.). University of Hong Kong: Centre for Asian Studies.

Pye, Lucian W.
1985 *Asian power and politics: the cultural dimensions of authority*. Cambridge, Mass.: Harvard University Press.

Pye, Lucian W.
1988 'The new Asian capitalism: a political portrait', in *In search of an East Asian development model*. P. L. Berger and H.-H. M. Hsiao (eds.), 81–98. New Brunswick, N.J.: Transaction Books.

Redding, Gordon
1990 *The spirit of Chinese capitalism*. Berlin: Walter de Gruyter.

Redding, Gordon and S. Richardson
1986 'Participative management and its varying relevance in Hong Kong and Singapore'. *Asia Pacific Journal of Management* 3: 76–98.

Redding, Gordon, and Simon Tam
1985 'Networks and molecular organisations: an exploratory view of Chinese firms in Hong Kong' in *Perspectives in international business*. K. C. Mun and T. S. Chan (eds.). Hong Kong: Chinese University Press.

Redding, Gordon, and Gilbert Y. Y. Wong
1986 'The psychology of Chinese organisational behaviour' in *The psychology of the Chinese people*. M. Bond (ed.), 267–295. Oxford: Oxford University Press.

Richardson, George
1972 'The organisation of industry'. *Economic Journal* 82: 883–896.

Rohlen, Thomas P.
1974 *For harmony and strength: Japanese white-collar organisation in anthropological perspective*. Berkeley: University of California Press.

Rohlen, Thomas P.
1979 'The company work group' in *Modern Japanese organisation and decision-making*. E. F. Vogel (ed.), 185–209. Tokyo: Tuttle.

Shin, E. H., and S. W. Chin
1989 'Social affinity among top managerial executives of large corporation in Korea'. *Sociological Forum* 4: 3–26.

Silin, R. H.
1976 *Leadership and values. The organisation of large scale Taiwanese enterprises*. Cambridge, Mass.: Harvard University Press.

Smith, T. C.
1959 *The agrarian origins of modern Japan*. Stanford: Stanford University Press.

Smith, T. C.
1988   *Native sources of Japanese industri-
        alisation, 1750–1920.* Berkeley:
        University of California Press.

Smith, Peter B., and J. Misumi
1989   'Japanese management. A sun ris-
        ing in the west?' in *International
        review of industrial and organisa-
        tional psychology.* C. L. Cooper and
        I. Robertson (eds.). New York:
        Wiley.

Sorge, A., and Malcolm Warner
1986   *Comparative factory organisation.*
        Aldershot: Gower.

Tam, Simon
1990   'Centrifugal   versus   Centripetal
        growth processes: contrasting ideal
        types for conceptualising the devel-
        opmental patterns of Chinese and
        Japanese firms' in *Capitalism in con-
        trasting cultures.* S. R. Clegg and G.
        Redding (eds.), 153–183. Berlin:
        Walter de Gruyter.

Wade, Robert
1988   'The role of government in over-
        coming market failure: Taiwan,
        Republic of Korea and Japan' in
        *Achieving industrialisation in East
        Asia.* H. Hughes (ed.), 129–163.
        Cambridge: Cambridge University
        Press.

Ward, Barbara E.
1972   'A small factory in Hong Kong:
        some   aspects   of   its   internal
        organisation' in *Economic organisa-
        tion in Chinese society.* W. E.
        Wilmott (ed.), 353–385. Stanford:
        Stanford University Press.

Whitley, Richard
1990   'East Asian enterprise structures
        and the comparative analysis of
        forms of business organisation'.
        Organization Studies 11/1: 47–74.

Williamson, O. E.
1985   *The economic institutions of capital-
        ism.* New York: Free Press.

Wong, Siu-Lun
1988   'The applicability of Asian family
        values to other sociocultural set-
        tings' in *In search of an East Asian
        development model.* P. L. Berger
        and H.-H. M. Hsiao (eds.), 134–
        152. New Brunswick, N.J.: Transac-
        tion Books.

Yoo, S., and S. M. Lee
1987   'Management style and practice in
        Korean   Chaebols'.   *California
        Management Review* 29: 95–110.

Yoshihara, Kunio
1988   *The rise of Ersatz capitalism in
        South East Asia.* Oxford: Oxford
        University Press.

Yoshino, M. Y., and T. B. Lifson
1986   *The invisible link: Japan's Sogo
        Shosha and the organisation of
        trade.* Cambridge, Mass.: MIT
        Press.

Zeile, William
1989   'Industrial policy and organisational
        efficiency: the Korean *chaebol*
        examined'. Program in East Asian
        Culture   and   Development
        Research, Working Paper Series,
        No. 30. Institute of Governmental
        Affairs, University of California,
        Davis.

Zucker, Lynne G.
1986   'Production of trust: institutional
        sources of economic structure,
        1840–1920'. *Research in Organisa-
        tional Behaviour* 8: 53–111.

Zysman, John
1983   *Governments, markets and growth:
        financial systems and the politics of
        industrial change.* Ithaca: Cornell
        University Press.

Journal of Asian Business   Volume 12 • Number 1 • 1996

The Japanese Business System: Key Features and Prospects for Change

D. ELEANOR WESTNEY*

This paper argues that the Japanese business system cannot be adequately understood without extending the focus of analysis beyond the individual firm to the vertical *keiretsu* or business group. The vertical keiretsu structure was first identified and studied in the auto and electronics industries, where it is most strongly marked, but it characterizes virtually all sectors, service industries as well as manufacturing. Large industrial vertical keiretsu are composed of subsidiaries engaged in three distinct types of activities (manufacturing, marketing, and quasi-related business). The coordination and control systems are built on the flows of products, financial resources, information and technology, and people across formal company boundaries, with the parent firm controlling the key flows. This paper examines the prevailing explanations first for the emergence and then for the persistence of the vertical group structure, and looks at the current pressures for change and adaptation in the system.

Introduction

In the late 1980s, the efforts of the business media and academic researchers to analyze the Japanese business system were spurred primarily by the desire to explain the success of Japan's economy and its firms. In the mid-1990s, however, with the Japanese economy mired in a prolonged recession, the business press virtually unanimously has portrayed a system in crisis, whose past successes contain the seeds of current and future difficulties, as its faces a changed international and domestic environment and unprecedented strains on its internal structures and processes (e.g., *Economist*, 3 June 1995: 67-8).

The image of the Japanese business system in the popular press has changed much more dramatically than the system itself. But the image of the business system among academic researchers has also changed over the years. The intensified scrutiny to which Japan was subjected in the 1980s provided a model of the Japanese business system that built on previous work, particularly on the human resource management and decision-making systems of the large

* M.I.T. Sloan School of Management

D. ELEANOR WESTNEY

Japanese firm. But additional elements were added: assessment of strategic behavior in the mid-1980s, and an analysis of the corporate form known as the vertical *keiretsu* (business group) in the last decade. The evolving model of the business system suggests that both paradigms and the business system itself are changing. This paper provides an analysis of the key features of the Japanese business system, with a particular focus on the vertical group structure; looks at some of the pressures for change; and indicates directions for future research in assessing the prospects for change in the business system in Japan.

The Analysis of Japanese Industrial Firms

In 1958, James Abegglen's pioneering study first demonstrated to a Western audience the existence of an interrelated set of distinctive organizational characteristics in Japanese manufacturing companies. Since then, both Japanese and Western social scientists have expended considerable effort on exploring, re-defining, and explaining those characteristics. By the late 1980s, there was general agreement among both Western and Japanese social scientists that large Japanese firms exhibited strongly institutionalized and interrelated patterns in four areas: human resource management, governance and control systems, strategy, and structure.[1]

The distinctive features of the human resource management systems were the first aspects of Japanese companies to draw attention (Abegglen 1958), and for over three decades they have been seen as the key distinctive features of the Japanese business system. Those features are by now so familiar as to need little elaboration: reliance on recruiting new graduates with a generalist education; a strong but unwritten commitment of long-term employment and the assumption by the company of the responsibility for providing training and for shaping the individual's career; and a key role for seniority in promotion. This system facilitates a career structure that emphasizes rotation across positions, the development of personal networks (*jimmyaku*) as a basis for horizontal information exchange, and intense competition among employees over the long term for the rewards that come with being identified as a highly committed and highly capable employee. The centrality of the human resource management system in the coordination systems of the firm and the company's strong commitment to take responsibility for the careers of employees has led several Japanese social scientists to identify the key distinction between the U.S. and Japanese business systems as the critical role of human resources instead of financial resources in the company (e.g., Aoki 1988; Itami 1987, 1994b; Odagiri 1992).

The critical role of employees as stakeholders is reflected in the governance systems of Japanese firms, which give little scope for the role of shareholders so central to the economic theories of the firm of the 1970s and 1980s in the United States. Boards of directors are made up of current and former top managers of the company, and the position of director is one of the most coveted rewards in the internal career ladder. External representation on the Board is rare: the lead bank sometimes has a Board representative, but other shareholders, however sizeable their ownership stakes, do not (as the American corporate raider T. Boone Pickens discovered to his chagrin when he attempted to bring American-style takeovers to Japan in the late 1980s). Shareholding in Japan is dominated by institutional shareholders of two types: "portfolio" shareholders, including trust banks and insurance companies, who have traditionally looked to long-term growth in the value of the firm as a consequence of growth strategies rather than to dividends or short-term gains from trading shares) and relational investors (companies related to the firm who hold shares as a symbol of that relationship, including the firm's lead bank, key suppliers, and affiliated firms). Neither type of shareholder has traditionally taken an active interest in monitoring the management of the firm, and a 1988 survey by MITI found that fewer than 1 percent of the top managers who responded rated "increasing value for shareholders" as either the most or the second most important goal of the firm. The separation of ownership and control so marked in the large Japanese firm is accompanied by an internal coordination and control structure that emphasizes decision-making at the operating level, accompanied by dense information exchange and interaction in the decision-making process. As early as the 1960s, Western social scientists became aware of the "consensus-oriented", information-intensive coordination system embodied in the *ringisei*, a system whereby a single document detailing a decision is circulated to every department affected, collecting the seals of managers to indicate assent (Yoshino 1968). The ringisei itself was much less important than the interaction-intensive processes it symbolized, which Ikujiro Nonaka (1988) has dubbed "middle-up-down management."

Researchers were slow to extend their focus beyond workplace dynamics within firms on the one hand and below the system level of governmental industrial policy on the other to a realization that the large industrial enterprise itself differed significantly in strategy and structure from its Western counterparts. By the mid-1980s the growing competitive success of Japanese firms led to a focus on how Japanese firms competed domestically and internationally. This focus on strategy led to several studies that portrayed Japanese firms as

D. ELEANOR WESTNEY

having a widely-shared set of strategic behaviors: employing incremental strategies of continuous improvement and related diversification that built on their existing businesses and technologies, exiting from unprofitable businesses much more slowly than their U.S. counterparts, being much less integrated vertically and diversified horizontally and strongly oriented to growth strategies (Goto 1982; Kono 1984; Abegglen and Stalk 1985; Kagono et al. 1985; Itami 1987; Aoki 1988). Until the latter part of the 1980s this pursuit of growth focused on expanding market share; in the last decade it has increasingly emphasized the development of high value-added products and businesses based on technological innovation. In their pursuit of growth-oriented strategies, Japanese companies are seen to have a high propensity to engage in cooperative networks (the kind of inter-firm cooperation dubbed "strategic alliances" in the management literature of the 1980s) with suppliers, customers, and even competitors in order to develop technologies and markets (Prahalad and Hamel 1990).

However, the data on individual firms that indicated much lower levels of vertical integration and horizontal diversification did not capture the fact that each major firm extended its reach both horizontally and vertically well beyond its formal boundaries, through extensive networks of subsidiaries and affiliated firms. Each of Japan's leading industrial firms (and indeed its commercial firms as well) sits at the top of a "group" that bears its name: the Toyota group, the Hitachi group, the Toray group, etc. These vertical groups are dominated—indeed created—by a single lead (or "parent") firm, which focuses its own activities on technology development and high value-added manufacturing (or, in other terms, R&D and final assembly).

This paper argues that neither the human resource management systems nor governance and control systems nor strategies in the Japanese business system can be adequately understood without extending the focus of analysis beyond the individual firm to the vertical group. The following section provides a more detailed profile of this latest element to be included in the portrayal of the Japanese business system.

The Vertical Group

The vertical group or *keiretsu* structure was first identified and studied in the auto and electronics industries, where it is most strongly marked, but it characterizes virtually all sectors, service industries as well as manufacturing. Interest in these vertical keiretsu grew in part because of a surge of interest among social scientists in "intermediate forms" of organization between market and hierarchy (Imai and Itami 1984; Powell 1987, 1990; Hamilton and Biggart 1988; Eccles and Nohria 1992). But more pragmatically, the interest in the keiretsu extended well beyond academic circles into public policy debates and the pages of the business press, largely because of the difficulties experienced by Western businessmen in penetrating Japanese markets for industrial goods and in benchmarking their companies against their Japanese competitors. After tariff barriers had been dismantled, Western firms found that entry into industrial markets in Japan was complicated by vertical sourcing relationships in which large Japanese firms had "inside" and "outside" suppliers for most inputs. In these relationships the "insiders" seemed to have privileged positions: Western firms complained that large firms channeled information and innovations from the outside to the inside suppliers, which were legally separate companies, but had some proportion of the ownership held by the parent firm. Entrance into Japanese consumer markets also encountered the keiretsu system, as foreign companies found that many Japanese manufacturers (especially in autos and electronics) had subsidiaries engaged in sales and distribution, even to the retail level.

Simultaneously, when U.S. firms tried to benchmark their organizations against their increasingly formidable Japanese competitors, they were often frustrated by the apparently small size of the incorporated enterprise: in 1989, for example, only eleven Japanese firms had more than 40,000 employees, in terms of the unconsolidated data on which the Japanese government and business press provided the most detailed financial and product information. The data in basic Japanese sources such as the *Japan Company Handbook* were and continue to be data on the individual company, according to Japan's domestic accounting practices. Although in the mid-1980s Japanese accounting standards were changed to mandate the reporting of consolidated data (in line with international practice, which demands that firms consolidate the financial performance of subsidiaries in which they own half or more of the shares), even today the individual incorporated enterprise, without the financial data even from its wholly-owned subsidiaries, remains the major unit on which performance is measured within Japan—in the annual rankings of company size and performance published in the business press, for example. Such rankings ignore the financial data of its subsidiaries, even of those that are wholly owned by the company.

In 1987, for example, when General Motors had over 765,000 employees, Toyota was listed in the *Japan Company Handbook* as having only 65,000, Canon as having just over 15,000 (compared to Xerox with 113,000), Fuji Photo as having just over 11,000 (compared to

25

D. ELEANOR WESTNEY

Kodak's 145,300). Clearly a more appropriate target for benchmarking was the group rather the lead firm in the group. But a General Motors trying to benchmark itself against the Toyota group instead of the parent company alone ran into difficulties of how to establish comparable boundaries, and both managers and academics began to realize that fundamental differences in corporate form were signaled by the problems of defining boundaries. Comparative analysis, in other words, had to face the question of whether the key economic actor in the Japanese business system was "the firm" as understood in Western business literature, or a different kind of corporate form, the vertical group or keiretsu. But taking the vertical group as the key economic actor in the Japanese business system ran into the very pragmatic problem that whereas the formal boundaries of the corporation are defined by law, the boundaries of the group are not. They are defined by the group itself and by outside analysts as those in which the lead firm has some ownership stake, but many of the ownership stakes are too small to be identified without massive efforts in data collecting.

This creates some very real problems of cross-border comparison, and even problems of comparison across Japanese companies themselves. For example, measured by sales of the individual firm, Matsushita Electric is Japan's largest electronics firm, with 4.55 trillion yen in sales in 1992. However, Hitachi, with sales of 3.81 trillion yen in 1992, claims to be the largest electronics firm in Japan, because when its consolidated sales rather than its company sales are taken as the unit of analysis (which means including the sales of the 818 subsidiaries in which it has an ownership stake of 50 percent or more), its sales total 7.53 trillion yen (Murayama 1994: 12), whereas Matsushita's consolidated sales, with its mere 440 consolidated subsidiaries, only reach 7.1 trillion. On the other hand, one could argue that the overall sales of the Matsushita group as a whole might well exceed Hitachi's total, since the group includes 706 companies, over a third of which are not consolidated. Among those unconsolidated subsidiaries are six that are listed on the Tokyo stock exchange, including one of Japan's largest prefab housing firms (National Jutaku), one of its top elevator manufacturers (Nippon Otis) and a leading bicycle producer (Miyata Kogyo).

This complex group structure is not confined to the electronics industry. Toray Industries, a synthetic fibers and chemicals company, is listed as a single industry company in most diversification studies (e.g., Fruin 1992). However, it sits atop the Toray group of 186 companies, only 88 of whose sales are consolidated. The group includes 42 companies in the textile industry, 18 in housing and engineering, 12 in trade and distribution, and 60 in various new

The Japanese Business System

businesses (including, for example, Toray Medical, established in 1980, a pioneer in the synthesis of Interferon).

Examining the vertical groups in Japanese industry immediately raises questions about the relative importance of location effects: particularly country effects, industry effects, and individual firm effects on business systems in Japan. Comparative business system analysis explicitly states that country level effects—those that have nation-wide influence on social systems—are the most important, overriding industry and company effects (Whitley 1992; Hamilton and Biggart 1992). The principal factors assumed to produce country effects include late development (the effects on a country's social systems attributable to the timing of its industrialization, which affects the kind of technology and organizational models available, the distribution of resources for development within the society, and the world system context of the nation's economy and polity—see Dore 1973); the configuration of national institutions such as the legal system, political system, the financial system, the education and training system; and the labor system (Whitley 1992).

In contrast, some of the researchers who take an institutional approach emphasize location effects below the national level, focusing on sub-national regions or geographic clusters (Kogut 1993). Such work is likely to take into consideration the interaction effects between industry and location, since subnational clusters tend to be industry-specific. However, industry effects themselves, independent of locational factors, are assumed to be similar (though of course not identical) across countries. They are produced by the inherent features of the industry: its technology, the nature of its markets, and the structure of competition. Institutionalists would undoubtedly add an additional category of industry effects: cross-border learning within an industry, such that the organizational systems of the leading firms serve as models for emulation by other firms in the industry, whatever their home country. So-called "global industries," dominated by a small number of firms who compete across countries, are particularly likely to be characterized by cross-border learning and adaptation (Westney 1992). Subnational studies usually analyze the interaction of location effects and industry effects.

Both country and industry effects are evident in Japanese vertical groups, although the country effect dominates. The vertical group structure clearly has a strong country component: it is the dominant mode of business enterprise in large Japanese firms across industries. A recent publication mapping the major industrial groups (one of a stream of popular publications on the subject in Japanese) provides overviews of the vertical groups of forty of Japan's major firms, covering all major industries: construction, food and beverages, chemicals, energy, steel, electronics, autos, trading companies,

D. ELEANOR WESTNEY

department stores, transportation, and real estate. Each has the same fundamental structure: a lead firm with a network of subsidiaries. For manufacturing firms, the subsidiaries tend to be of three major types: supplier firms, involved in steps in the manufacturing processes which the lead firm dominates with final assembly; distribution and sales firms that handle products made by the lead firm (and its subsidiaries); and firms in diversified businesses.

Table 1 provides 1993 data on the average number of group companies per parent firm by industry for manufacturing firms. This data was taken from the annual publication, *Nihon no Kigyo Guru-pu* (Japan's Industrial Groups), which compiles information on the related firms of companies listed in the first section of the Tokyo Stock Exchange.

The average number of companies per group in all industries, including the 826 non-manufacturing firms as well as the 1,003 manufacturing companies, was 22.6. Of the 33 industry categories tabulated by the publication (of which table 1 shows a representative subset, somewhat biased toward the industries where the groups are larger), only three have an average of fewer than 10 affiliated companies per parent: machine tools (19 firms with an average group size of 9.8 subsidiaries), ceramics (34 firms, with 9.8), and bicycles (9 firms, with 9.4). And although for many Western companies, most of their subsidiaries are their foreign operations, incorporated separately out of necessary deference to local commercial law, the Japanese groups are primarily domestic, as the table makes clear. Only in consumer electronics do foreign subsidiaries outnumber domestic, and then by only a very small margin. The group is clearly a widespread mode of organizing within Japan.

On the other hand, some industries are clearly oriented to larger groups—or are populated by companies with larger groups—than others. The industries which have both a fairly large population of listed firms and relatively large groups are those which have been most internationally competitive and most widely studied: electronics, heavy electrical equipment, and autos. As one of the articles in the current *Nihon no Kigyo Guru-pu* points out, these industries lend themselves to specialization by subsidiary both in the manufacturing process (components and subsystems) and in distribution. And in these industries the major companies adopted what the Japanese call a "full set" strategy: to have a full range of products in their major businesses, with all supporting activities and technologies contained within the group—although not necessarily exclusively within the group (virtually all companies try to keep at least one outside supplier of key subsystems or components, as well as their "group" company).

The Japanese Business System

Table 1

Average Number of Companies in a Vertical Group, 1993
by Industry

Industry	Affiliates per parent	No. of parent cos	No. of subsidiaries	Domestic subs.	% of subs in Japan
All manufacturing	24.2	1,003	24,320	18,038	74.17
Cement	90.3	3	271	262	96.7
Shipbuilding	73.9	10	739	599	81.1
Petroleum	60.4	10	604	493	81.6
Consumer Electronics	55.4	36	1,996	994	49.8
Heavy Electrical	54	29	1,566	1132	72.3
Autos, parts	40.2	53	1,905	1311	68.8
Chemicals	31.6	116	3,670	2,841	77
Steel	30.9	25	772	628	81.3
Textiles	28	60	1,684	1,439	85
Precision instruments	25.9	34	869	520	59.8
Food products	22.1	80	1,604	1,398	87.1
Rubber	16.9	17	738	554	75.1
Commercial equipment	13.8	86	1186	820	69.1
Metal products	12.2	45	545	490	89.9
Machine tools	9.8	19	187	106	56.7

D. ELEANOR WESTNEY

But firm effects as well as industry effects are important. A closer look at the leading firms in the electronics (including both heavy electrical firms and consumer electronics firms) and auto industries reveals considerable variation across firms in the more fine-grained aspects of the structure of the vertical groups. Table 2 shows the number of companies in the vertical groups of nine leading electronics and nine auto firms.

The first observation that springs from these data is the variation across the size of the groups. For the three integrated electrical firms (Hitachi, Toshiba, and Mitsubishi Electric, which cover large systems as well as consumer electronics), the number of companies in each group roughly follows the scale of the firm: Hitachi, the largest, has the largest group. But Matsushita has a smaller group than Sony, its smaller rival; NEC than the less-diversified Fujitsu, and—perhaps most surprising to those unfamiliar with Japanese groups—Toyota's group is smaller by half than that of the number two firm in Japanese automobiles, Nissan. The size of the group is clearly determined not by the size of the parent's sales, but by the parent's history.

Some of that history is revealed by the data on how the group companies are distributed across two categories of "related companies" (*kankei-gaisha* in Japanese), both classified by their historical relationship to the lead firm. One type is the *kogaisha*, literally "child company". These are companies created by the lead firm, usually by spinning out a division or department from its own organization. To take just one example, Matsushita Denshi Buhin (Matsushita Electrical Components) is Japan's—and perhaps the world's—largest electrical components manufacturer, and is a kogaisha of Matsushita Electric. The parent company began making electrical components in 1931, when it set up a Parts Department in its Radio Division. In the early 1960s, the department was elevated to the status of a division in its own right; in the early 1970s, it became a Components Group within the parent. Finally, in 1976 it was spun off into a separate company, of which Matsushita Denki owns 98.6 percent of the shares, making it a consolidated subsidiary (Shimura 1986).

In both the electronics and auto industries groups, kogaisha outnumber the second category of group company: the *kanren-gaisha*, usually translated as "affiliate"—with the exception of two companies, both in the auto industry, Mazda and Fuji Heavy Industries. Affiliates are formerly independent companies with which the lead company has developed a long-standing relationship (usually as a supplier company), culminating in the lead company bringing the company into the group through the purchase of an equity stake. Often this is at the invitation of the affiliate. The size of the equity stake taken by the

The Japanese Business System

Table 2
Composition of Vertical Groups, Electronics and Autos 1993

Company	Total number of group firms	Kogaisha (Child Co's)	Affilates	% of group Kogaisha	Consolidated Subsidiaries	% consolidated
Hitachi	1004	818	186	81.47	818	81.47
Toshiba	689	532	157	77.21	134	19.45
Mitsubishi El.	237	145	92	61.18	98	41.35
NEC	293	164	129	55.97	105	35.84
Fujitsu	531	438	93	82.49	365	68.74
Matsushita*	706	706	n. a.	n. a.	313	44.33
Sharp	68	43	25	63.24	20	29.41
Sony	885	836	49	94.46	749	84.63
Sanyo	242	146	96	60.33	44	18.18
Toyota	319	182	137	57.05	45	14.11
Nissan	696	550	146	79.02	100	14.37
Honda	374	281	93	75.13	214	57.22
Mitsubishi Motors	260	199	61	76.54	63	24.23
Mazda	217	69	148	31.80	11	5.07
Isuzu	223	157	66	70.40	61	27.35
Daihatsu	83	56	27	67.47	33	39.76
Suzuki	144	130	14	90.28	124	86.11
Fuji Heavy Ind.	116	46	70	39.66	20	17.24

*Matsushita does not provide data that distinguish between categories of subsidiaries.

D. ELEANOR WESTNEY

lead firm varies considerably, depending on the circumstances. One famous example in the electronics industry is Aiwa, an electronics company established in 1951, which was brought into the Sony group in 1969 when Sony bought a substantial proportion of its shares, and which has continued to produce consumer electronics under its own brand name. It is, however, now a consolidated subsidiary of its lead firm.

As the previous example shows, either kogaisha or kanren-gaisha can also belong to another category of group company: the consolidated subsidiary, in which the lead firm has 50 percent or more of the equity. As was pointed out above, the consolidated subsidiary is a classification created by the introduction of more internationally accepted standards of accounting. There is enormous variation across companies in the extent to which the lead firm owns what Western management texts customarily call "a controlling share" in the firms in their vertical group. Some companies, like Hitachi, Sony, and Suzuki, own majority stakes in over four-fifths of the companies in their groups. Others, like Toshiba, Sanyo, Toyota, Nissan, Mazda, and Fuji Heavy Industries, own majority stakes in fewer than one-fifth of their group companies. But in most groups, the consolidated subsidiaries are a distinct minority of the group companies: in only 3 of the nine electronics firms and one of the nine auto firms are consolidated subsidiaries in the majority.

There is another categorization of group companies which has long been institutionalized in data on the groups: differentiation by function. Historically, each firm in the group tended to fit into one of three categories: manufacturing, sales and distribution, and quasi-related diversification.

Manufacturing subsidiaries: These produce subassemblies and components, and in turn have a set of subcontracting affiliates that produce simpler components, in a production value chain that stretches across multiple formal company boundaries. Most of these firms also supply other firms outside the group; few are totally tied to the lead firm in their group. And the lead firm rarely relies completely on the group firm for components, although group firms are preferred suppliers. Participation in the open market disciplines pricing on both sides and allows both the lead firm and the subsidiary to maintain a certain level of flexibility in their operations.

Turning once again for an example to Matsushita Denshi Buhin, the kogaisha that is Japan's largest producer of electronic components in the Matsushita group, we find that in the mid-1980s sales of its components to its parent and to other Matsushita group companies accounted for 45 percent of its total sales; the rest were to companies outside the Matsushita group (13 percent to customers overseas). Matsushita Denshi Buhin estimated that it supplied 50 percent of the internal Matsushita market for the kinds of components it produced; its president declared then that he aspired to raise that to 70-80 percent (Shimura 1986: 163). This was a goal that would be difficult to reach, given that other companies inside the Matsushita group produced some of the same kinds of components (the parent company itself produced film condensers and small motors like those produced by its subsidiary). But the very fact that it was publicly articulated gives some insight into the complex dynamics of competition within the vertical groups. Like other major manufacturing group companies, Matsushita Denshi Buhin has a small vertical group of its own: it has 7 *kogaisha* in Japan, and manufacturing plants offshore in 13 countries (Shimura 1986).

Many of the larger manufacturing subsidiaries have their own strong technology development capabilities; particularly in the automobile and electronics industries they work closely with their lead firms in new product development (Westney 1994). A small number of subsidiaries develop such strong capabilities in producing certain technology-intensive components or subsystems that they become an industry leader in that sector (and in an even smaller minority of cases the sole supplier of the component not only for the lead firm but also for virtually all the firms in the industry). For example, Nippon Denso of the Toyota group has achieved this position in some areas of automobile componentry.

Sales and Distribution Subsidiaries: The lead firms in most industries have tended to put the sales and distribution function into separate subsidiaries, often on a regional basis. These firms concentrate on the activities involved in physically getting final products to the customer, especially supplying and supervising the retail outlets that are dedicated to selling the product lines of the parent company. The leading firms in consumer electronics as well as in autos have built up their own chains of retail stores. Matsushita's market dominance in Japan is widely attributed to the 25,000 National (Matsushita's major brand in Japan) shops distributed throughout Japan; Toshiba and Hitachi each have about 15,000, and Mitsubishi Electric about 5,500 (Murayama 1994). Most of these stores are owned by individuals, but their activities are closely supervised by the regional sales subsidiaries. Marketing strategy and the direct interactions with lead users that feed into new product development are still the province of the lead firm.

Table 3 shows the distribution across functions of the consolidated subsidiaries within the groups for the eighteen firms in the electronics and auto firms covered by table 2 (detailed information

33

D. ELEANOR WESTNEY

Table 3
Consolidated Subsidiaries of Leading Electronics and Auto Firms, 1993
by Company by Function

Company	Consolidated Subs.	Domestic: Manuf.	Domestic: Sales	Domestic: Other	Overseas: manuf.	Overseas: Sales	Overseas: Other	% Consol. Subs Domestic	% Consol. Subs Sales
Hitachi	818	25*	10*	8*	14*	4*	1*	69.35	22.58
Toshiba	134	19*	7*	8*	16*	10*	4*	48.44	26.56
Mitsubishi El.	98	23	26	22	11	10	4	72.45	36.73
NEC	105	37	19	27	10	8	4	79.05	25.71
Fujitsu	365		119		246			32.60	32.60
Matsushita	313	40	22	14	70	23	144	24.28	14.38
Sharp	20	2	4	3	6	4	1	45.00	40.00
Sony	749	68	3		53	34		44.94	23.42
Sanyo	44	7	18	3	10	6		63.64	54.55
Toyota	45	3	4	1	7	8	22	17.78	26.67
Nissan	100	7	58	10	4	12	9	75.00	70.00
Honda	214	8	156	6	21	13	10	79.44	78.97
Mitsubishi Motors	63	4	40	3	2	5	9	74.60	71.43
Mazda	11	2	3	2		4		63.64	63.64
Isuzu	61	2	53	3	3			95.08	86.89
Daihatsu	33	3	25	3	2			93.94	75.76
Suzuki	124	10	96	5	4	9		89.52	84.68
Fuji Heavy Ind.	20	3			1	3	13	15.00	15.00

* Data on categories of subsidiaries provided only for a subset of the subsidiaries.
Source: *Nihon Kigyo no Guruppu '94*, p. 17.

on functional distribution is only readily available for the consolidated companies, and not even for all of those for the Hitachi and Toshiba groups: those two companies provide this data only for their major consolidated subsidiaries).

Clearly the electronics and auto industries differ somewhat in the relative salience of sales subsidiaries, at least among the consolidated subsidiaries: in all but one of the auto firms, domestic sales subsidiaries substantially outnumber manufacturing subsidiaries, whereas their weight in the electronics industry is much less substantial. The pattern of setting up separate <u>kogaisha</u> in manufacturing and sales is carried overseas, making, as we shall see below, for some interesting challenges in international management.

Subsidiaries in Quasi-related Businesses: Most of Japan's leading industrial groups are involved in a wider array of businesses than those of the lead firm. The lead firm assiduously develops new business areas that are closely related to its core capabilities; businesses that involve substantially different technological or market capabilities are usually put into separate subsidiaries. For example, both Toyota and Matsushita have a subsidiary in their group engaged in producing and selling prefabricated housing. Most of the large industrial firms set up financial services and real estate subsidiaries during the "bubble" years of the 1980s, when the profit opportunities in those sectors vastly overshadowed those in manufacturing. Such subsidiaries are rarely brought into the group by acquisition; they are "kogaisha" set up by the parent firm, sometimes in joint ventures with other firms, both domestic and foreign, and often staffed largely by the parent's employees, who are transferred or "dispatched" to the new venture. In addition, particularly in the electronics industries, some of the subsidiaries are engaged in final assembly of relatively mature products whose profit margins have been eroded by competition, products which at earlier stages of the product life cycle were assembled by the parent but whose production has been hived off into separate subsidiaries.

Coordination and Control in the Vertical Group

How the lead firm in the vertical group manages this extended network is still a matter of speculation rather than analysis. As we saw in table 2, ownership strategy, viewed as a basic control mechanism in North America, constitutes an important but complex element of the vertical group. The boundaries of the group are defined by the fact that the lead firm has a direct ownership stake in many of

D. ELEANOR WESTNEY

its member companies and an indirect stake in others, in the form of equity held in third or fourth tier companies by its direct subsidiaries. But the size of the ownership stake varies considerably across firms. As we saw, although Honda and Toyota have built groups of roughly comparable size, Honda has a "controlling" stake in a much larger proportion of its group companies than does Toyota (57 percent compared to 14 percent), and yet Toyota is widely seen as having stronger control over its group than Honda.

Clearly ownership is only one aspect of the coordination and control system of the vertical group. Other elements, however, are much more difficult to measure: unlike shareholding, they are not a matter of public record. They include: the interconnections of the value chains (that is, the flow of "things" across the formal boundaries of the companies); the flows of financial resources in forms other than equity; flows of information and technology, and, most importantly, flows of people.

Flows of "things:" The flow of components and sub-assemblies up an extended chain of manufacturing subcontractors is probably the model of the vertical group most frequently encountered in the Western business literature. Often this literature does not make a clear distinction between the suppliers that are regarded as members of the group (both internally and in the eyes of the outside world) and those that are not. Even recent analyses that acknowledge that two types of suppliers co-exist (the group and the independent suppliers) avoid the issue of whether the two groups are treated differently (e.g., Dyer and Ouchi 1993).

The potential power of the mutual interest of supplier and customer in a value chain is one of the key elements in the concept of the "network" models of the corporation in the West (for example, Kanter 1989; Dertouzos et al. 1989). However, the supplier flows of "things" is only one element of the flows in the group: the other major element is the flow of products to the sales and distribution companies from the parent and from those subsidiaries engaged in making complete products (more common in the electronics than the auto industry). Clearly the sales and distribution companies within the group are the most dependent on the parent: they sell and distribute only the products of the parent company, and produce none themselves. And the group companies in quasi-related businesses are least dependent on the parent and other group companies for flows of components, products, and materials. The complexities of the Japanese case, where suppliers fall into two categories, where one is used to discipline the other into efficiency, and where supplier management is part of a larger pattern of network management, have yet to be adequately explored.

Some recent data suggests that we may find significant industry effects on these network relationships. The latest volume of one of the standard reference works on the vertical groups (*Nihon Kigyo no Guru-pu '94*) contains an analysis of the profitability of the groups in autos and electronics over the last five years—admittedly based on the very small subset of the companies in each group for which detailed performance data are available. The analysis shows that the profits of the group companies in the auto industry were much more closely related to those of the parent firm than in the electronics industry, and that the group companies were consistently less profitable than the parent. In electronics, there was much greater variation in pattern across groups, and often (NEC for three years 1989-91, Fujitsu 1989 and 1990, Mitsubishi Electric in 1989, 1991, 1992, and 1993) the group companies were collectively more profitable than the parent. The analyst attributes this industry difference to the greater parent company control of transfer prices in the auto industry, due to its greater power in an industry of relatively few end users, and the greater proportion of the business of the electronics group companies that involved producing their own end products, as opposed to components and subsystems. This indicates that where the group companies are engaged in a "food chain" where assembly of the final product tends to be monopolized by the parent firm, parent control of the relationship is much stronger.

Flows of financial resources: Equity is only one means by which the lead firm supports its subsidiaries financially. The others are direct loans or shared financing of necessary investments in equipment (including information systems), and the facilitation of bank loans, which are often easier for a subsidiary to obtain if they are guaranteed by the lead firm. The company for which the financial control system is best known is Matsushita, famous in Japan both as a firm that relies heavily on financial controls and as the pioneer of organization by business divisions. (Matsushita claims to be an independent originator of the multi-divisional enterprise, introducing it in the early 1930s). The Matsushita system, put in place by its founder, Matsushita Konosuke, prevents any Matsushita business division or group company from raising financing on its own initiative: it must come to the headquarters to borrow the needed resources. Headquarters generates this funding by taking 60 percent of the profits of each division or related company. In this system, no distinction is apparently made between the internal business divisions, the kogaisha (called *bunsha* in the Matsushita lexicon, meaning companies spun out from the parent), and the *kanren-gaisha*. Matsushita also states

37

D. ELEANOR WESTNEY

that if a division or a group company loses money for three quarters, top management will be replaced (Murayama 1994: 130). Matsushita clearly has ways of drawing financial resources from its group companies in addition to the obvious routes of returns on its shares (a mechanism probably more often used for wholly-owned subsidiaries) or transfer pricing (maintaining prices advantageous to the lead firm in terms of lower prices for subassemblies and components bought in from subsidiaries and higher transfer prices on products sold through the sales and distribution subsidiaries).

Information and Technology: While the transfer of personnel is an extremely important vehicle for transferring information and technology across the vertical group, it is by no means the only method. The density of information flow between lead firms and their suppliers in general has been traced in particular detail in the automobile industry. The flow of information of all kinds, particularly between the lead firms and their manufacturing and sales subsidiaries, is extremely dense, and carried out both in highly standardized formats and through constant interpersonal interactions. It should be noted that until very recently, these systems have been managed without the benefit of the high-performance information systems made possible by the development of personal computers, local area networks, etc.

Personnel: The lead firm transfers its own employees to its subsidiaries in two ways: on temporary assignments, both as a mode of career development for the individual and as a way of improving the operations or the control of the subsidiary, and on permanent transfer. Often at the time of transfer it is not clear to the employee whether the assignment is temporary or permanent, and in many cases the lead firm's personnel department itself may be reserving judgment, depending on the employee's performance over the term of his posting. The flow of personnel is overwhelmingly from the parent to the subsidiary; reverse transfers tend to be shorter in duration and clearly designated as project-linked and temporary.

This outflow of personnel from lead firm to subsidiaries has several functions, and is critically important in the human resource management systems of the lead firm in the group. It clearly maintains strong communications links across the boundaries of the firms; it facilitates the transfer of technology and knowhow between lead firms and subsidiaries; and it enables the lead firm to stay "lean" and to select only the high-commitment and high-performance employees from its labor pool; and to provide senior management positions for its managers who have "plateaued" in the lead firm. The ability of lead firms to relegate lower-performing employees to

38

subsidiaries helps to explain the Japanese employees' continuing commitment to work and performance that so bemused Western analysts of Japanese firms in the 1970s and early 1980s. Commitment is sustained in a regime of "permanent employment" and the seniority wage system in part because of the ever-present prospect of transfer into the lower prestige and lower reward subsidiaries. And yet the move to subsidiaries was not in itself de-motivating in the new context: it provided the prospect of rising to the high-prestige position of company president or director for hundreds of managers who did not have such an opportunity in the lead firm. There is only one president of Hitachi; there are over 800 presidents in the Hitachi group.

Exactly how extensive this movement really is can be difficult to establish. Aoki (1988: 66) cites data from Japan's Central Labor Commission showing that, in 1985, 8.2 percent of the total employees in manufacturing firms with over one thousand employees were on assignment in group companies. Whether this figure would be larger or smaller if only the lead firms in the major vertical groups were included is a matter of speculation. These data cover all employees, rather than just managers. The *Nihon Kigyo no Guru-pu '94* provides some interesting data on the transfer of the top management levels (table 4).

As of 1993, for (again) a very limited subset of the consolidated subsidiaries, the proportion of company officers (including the chairman, president, vice-presidents, directors, and auditor) coming from the parent company was substantial: well over a third in six of seven electronics firms, and from nearly a quarter to a third in the three auto firms for which data were compiled. The industry effect here is demonstrable: the electronics firms show a remarkable similarity across companies, and the proportion is much higher than in the auto industry. This suggests that the various modes of coordination and control are inversely related: in the auto industry, where the flow of "things" makes the group companies more dependent on the parent, the flow of officers is a less important mechanism. That the one exception in the electronics industry is Matsushita provides some support for this hypothesis: Matsushita's justifiably famous tight control of financial flows may serve to lower the importance of the flow of company officers as a control mechanism.

Individual firms vary considerably in the way they balance these various means of coordinating and controlling their subsidiaries, and relatively little empirical research exists on the topic. Hitachi, for example, has a propensity for higher levels of ownership, and consequently has a larger "vertical group" than many other firms. Aside from the ownership linkages, however, the flows of resources within the vertical network are extremely difficult to trace. One of the

D. ELEANOR WESTNEY

most interesting questions for the management researcher—the
extent to which these coordinating mechanisms vary between
subsidiaries in the vertical network and companies outside the group
with which the lead company has a long-term relationship—is one
which in these sensitive times Japanese managers are unlikely to
want to have measured.

Table 4
Dispatch of Company Officers to Subsidiaries, Selected Companies

Company	Number of Subs. included	Total Number of Company officers	Number Dispatched from Parent	Number Dispatched from other subs
Hitachi	22	382	148 (38.7%)	5
(<20% owned)	18	18	6 (33.3%)	
Toshiba	11	184	69 (37.5%)	
Mitsubishi El.	7	129	47 (36.4%)	
NEC	10	176	66 (37.5%)	
Fujitsu	10	167	79 (47.3%)	
(<20% owned)	1	9	4 (44.4%)	
Matsushita	12	214	38 (17.8%)	21
Sony	4	60	34 (56.7%)	3
Toyota	17	400	96 (24.0%)	6
(<20% owned)	9	204	32 (15.7%)	
Nissan	26	397	129 (32.5%)	6
(<20% owned)	5	114	5 (4.4%)	
Isuzu	6	103	25 (24.3%)	
(<20% owned)	2	34	3 (8.8%)	

Explanations for the Emergence and Persistence of the Vertical Network

The dominance of the vertical group as a corporate form across industries in Japan suggests that there is a country-level explanation for its development, and indeed not surprisingly, country-level explanations have dominated discussions of the phenomenon. Just as the financial controls and management systems of the U.S. multi-divisional form of the corporation are seen to owe much to the historical circumstances and business environment of the United States (Chandler 1962; 1977), so the vertical network of the Japanese industrial firm is regarded as a product of the Japanese postwar business environment.

One factor that looms large in explanations of the development of the vertical keiretsu is fundamentally political: the postwar labor settlement. As part of the extensive management-labor compromise that ended the fierce conflicts of the immediate postwar years, management agreed that members of the enterprise union (which included all employees, including college graduates up to their first promotion into management) would receive wages calculated on homogenized criteria, in which education and seniority were the factors most heavily weighted. In consequence, it was extremely difficult for management to differentiate across jobs or departments depending on the value-added of their activities. Wages and salaries were pulled to the highest common denominator. This constituted a powerful incentive for management to put lower value-adding activities into separate subsidiaries, in which wages were internally homogeneous but differentiated from those in the parent firm.

Another set of explanations looks at strategic adaptations to the postwar business environment. In this approach, the use of subsidiaries for horizontal diversification by the lead firm in the group invokes risk-shifting: that is, in new business areas, where the firm is stretching its capabilities, a separate enterprise avoids putting the name and the resources of the parent firm at risk. This is seen as particularly important in the Japanese business context, where the lifetime employment system imposes serious barriers to exit from unsuccessful business and where reputation is seen as a more important business asset than in the United States (Aoki 1988).

Still another set of factors has been invoked to explain the resort to smaller, more focused companies through the vertical network: the limitations on the face-to-face, relational kinds of coordination and control systems favored in Japanese companies. Itami Hiroyuki has established that Japanese firms seem to run up against limits to scale more quickly than their U.S. counterparts, and has suggested that this

41

D. ELEANOR WESTNEY

may be due to the fact that, given the enormous complexities of the Japanese written language, Japan never really experienced the first office revolution introduced by the typewriter (Itami 1984). Whatever the technological basis, it is clear that the coordination and control systems of Japanese firms today do rely heavily on face-to-face interactions, and that these clearly function less effectively in very large, vertically integrated firms than do more impersonal, less information-intensive systems.

All these explanations portray the emergence of the vertical de-integration of the firm as a response to problems and constraints, both those imposed on the firm from the business environment (labor cost explanation, risk shifting) and those rooted in the limitations of the firm's own coordination and control systems. It is difficult to assess the validity of these historical explanations, however plausible they may seem, in the absence of detailed case studies of the evolution of some of the vertical groups over time.

But once the system developed, it was clear that it conferred a set of advantages on those firms who were able to use it effectively. Those advantages have sometimes been invoked to explain why the vertical group exists. These functionalist explanations are better viewed as reasons why the group has persisted and the prospects for its serving as a model for other business systems, rather than as explanations for its original development.

The vertical network form of the corporation that emerged as the dominant form in postwar Japan turned out to have a number of unanticipated consequences, many of which constituted an improvement on more vertically integrated firms:

• The disaggregation of activities along the value chain made costs more transparent and therefore controllable.
• The lead firm focused on core activities, which were primarily the high value adding activities of technology development and high value added manufacturing. This focus on technology-intensive activities made technology a more salient element of corporate strategy, and contributed to the technological dynamism of the firm;
• Even large firms stayed relatively small: in 1990, only eleven Japanese manufacturing firms employed more than 40,000 people. This smaller size also contributed to the flexibility and dynamism of the firm, helping it to move quickly into new related technologies and product markets;
• The lead firm was able to achieve a greater efficiency in wages, keeping only high value-adding activities on its employment roster and rewarding its high commitment, high value-adding employees appropriately;

The Japanese Business System

•   The ability of the lead firm to send employees into subsidiaries, often in positions higher, at least in terms of titles, than those to which they could have aspired to in the parent firm constituted an important incentive system in a status-oriented incentive system. It has only been recently that analysts of Japanese business have realized the extent to which the large firm's implicit contract with employees to ensure their employment up to retirement age meant employment within the vertical group, not necessarily employment within the lead firm.   But for managerial employees the prospect of employment outside the parent, in other group firms, came with the implicit promise of a rise in status. On the other hand, the highest-status positions remained those within the parent. The lead firm was able to keep—or to recall—the best employees. The lead firm has thereby been able to monopolize not only high value-adding activities in its value chains, but also high value-adding, high-commitment employees.

Imai Kenichi (1984) has also pointed to an advantage of the vertical network for the business system as a whole: the rapid diffusion of technology and knowhow through the industrial system. The fact that relatively few of the firms in the value chain produce exclusively for the lead firm means that innovations in product and process tend to diffuse fairly rapidly through the system. While this may be a short-term disadvantage for any single innovative lead firm, even that firm benefits in the long run from the greater dynamism and efficiency of the system as a whole.

On the other hand, the vertical network form is not without its disadvantages. The ties between the lead firm and its subsidiaries make it difficult for new firms to break into the networks of the lead firms, which are Japan's "lead users" and key players in the development of innovations. This may have constituted a brake on the expansion of new firms in Japan's major industries. A second disadvantage is that the group ties make it even more difficult for firms from abroad to break into the marketplace—which may constitute a short-run advantage for Japanese firms, but which has made the system vulnerable to outside pressures, and has contributed to the strengthening of the yen, which has in turn threatened to negate the cost advantages conferred by the vertical network. Another consequence of the vertical network, which has neither clear advantages or disadvantages, is that because one of the key management skills is managing the linkages across firms in the network, managerial capabilities are less transferable across firms/groups than in industrial forms that depend more heavily on analytical skills and impersonal coordination and control systems. The lower inter-firm mobility in Japan may therefore be as much a

D. ELEANOR WESTNEY

function of the pervasiveness of the vertical network as it is of any cultural preferences for loyalty and stability of employment.

Finally, internationalization of the vertical network is a more complex process than for more integrated forms of organization. The lead firm's focus on final assembly means that it faces serious managerial challenges when it locates production abroad. If it continues to draw its subassemblies and components from its subsidiaries in Japan, it will negate many of the cost advantages of locating production offshore and will contribute to the direct rather than the inverse link between foreign direct investment and trade that has been the hallmark of Japanese FDI. If it tries to recreate its vertical network in the new location by drawing its subsidiaries in its wake, it will be criticized for trying to "Japan-ize" the local business system. Recreating the vertical network using local firms is a politically preferable option, but it takes time and puts at risk the efficiency of the final assembly process—and local firms with the required capabilities may simply not be available. Internationalization of production therefore becomes a relatively slow and incremental process, one that for Japanese firms has been overtaken by the speed of the strengthening of the Japanese currency.

Prognosis for the Future:
The Evolution of the Japanese Business System

The last decade has seen a growing body of analysis describing the essential "system-ness"—the close interrelationship and mutual reinforcement among various elements—of the Japanese business system (e.g., Itami 1987; Aoki 1988; Whitley 1992; Imai and Komiya 1994). The flow of employees from the lead firm into the subsidiaries of the vertical group is a critical element sustaining the long-term employment commitment and the human resource management system of the lead firm, as we noted above, and reinforces and mirrors its diffuse coordination and control system. Long-term employment and the company's control of its employees' careers make the intra-firm and intra-group coordination and control system possible. The human resource management system, the coordination and control system, and the vertical group all contribute to the preference for incremental and growth-oriented strategies.

In addition to the intra-system reinforcement, key institutions in the external environment have also evolved in a mutually supporting system. The lead firm's strong control over the careers of its employees is made possible by the nature of Japan's labor markets, in which the large industrial firms have an implicit agreement not to

The Japanese Business System

"poach" each other's mid-career employees, but to recruit instead primarily new graduates, giving mid-career employees little alternative of lucrative employment outside their current employer. Mid-career employees, particularly mid-career managers, have been unlikely to find comparable jobs if they leave their company because they are reluctant to accept a posting to a subsidiary, for example. The conservatism of Japanese banks and the relatively less developed equity markets of postwar Japan have also served in the past to reinforce the importance of the financial advantages that a lead firm could bestow on its subsidiaries. And the cultivation of the hierarchical nature of supplier-customer relations cultivated by Japanese firms as a source of competitive advantage for the most deferential and cooperative supplier meant that the "food chain" of suppliers could more easily be dominated by the lead firm—the ultimate customer.

Many Japanese economists over the last decade directed considerable effort to demonstrating that the features of the Japanese business system, particularly the human resource management system, were rational adaptations to an environment of high growth rates, technology followership, and scarce human resources (see the various articles in the Imai and Komiya collection 1994). The question facing Japanese managers and researchers focused on the Japanese business system is therefore whether the business system must change significantly to adjust to the changes in the environment of the post-Bubble era within Japan. Table 5 presents the data on what many believe to be the two greatest challenges facing the business system: the domestic recession, which has persisted for the last three years and shows few signs of alleviating, and the strong yen.

The strong yen reinforces the need for Japanese companies to internationalize production more rapidly, intensifying the challenges for the vertical network structure outlined in the previous section. But more vulnerable to the economic changes is the human resource management system. Many Japanese firms responded to the onset of the recession by cutting back drastically on their hiring of new graduates. As the recession persisted, many continued to hold back on hiring, creating problems for the new graduates each year, whose employment prospects became increasingly uncertain. Japan's demography has complicated the problem: the "second baby boom"— the children of the first postwar baby boom of 1947-49—is now entering the job market. The number of college graduates in 1995 was the highest in Japan's history, but it will be surpassed by the size of the graduating class of 1996 (*JEI Report No. 43B*: 5). The difficulties for many companies are compounded by the fact that they hired unprecedentedly large numbers of college graduates during the "Bubble" years of the late 1980s and early 1990s. A seniority-based

D. ELEANOR WESTNEY

system finds it extremely difficult to cope with major imbalances in the size of cohorts, imbalances sustained over three to five years.

Table 5
Economic Indicators 1985-1994

YEAR	% change in Gross Domestic Product from previous year	Yen/U.S.$ Exchange rate
1985	6.2%	238.5
1986	4.3%	168.5
1987	4.6%	144.6
1988	6.4%	128.2
1989	6.7%	138.0
1990	7.5%	144.8
1991	5.3%	134.7
1992	0.4%	126.7
1993	-0.4%	111.2
1994	0.5%	102.2

What are the prospects for changes in the Japanese business system?   Most academic researchers and indeed most leading Japanese executives do not share the apocalyptic visions of impending transformation signaled by such headlines in the popular press as "Japan Inc's Demise" (*Time International* July 10, 1995).   But, to oversimplify considerably, one can identify three differing perspectives on change in the business system.   One is the *strategic* or *rational* perspective, most strongly represented among economists, that emphasizes the role of environmental selection regimes.   For this group, the low growth environment constitutes a selection regime that will reward companies that experiment successfully with alternative modes of organization.   Some of these may be new companies, such as arose in Japan in the wake of World War II; some may be old companies experimenting with new forms.   A key indicator in this approach is whether we see a change in the demography of key industries, involving the rise or the growth of companies experimenting with new organizational forms.   One of the current problems is the high level of uncertainty over what those new forms might be.   A featured set of articles in the July 1994 issue of *President*, the Japanese equivalent of *Fortune*, asserted that the Japanese personnel system was likely to change.   However, most of the writers

The Japanese Business System

and the numerous personnel managers and executives they interviewed admitted that they had no clear ideas of how it would change.

A second perspective is the *political,* which sees change as driven by shifts in the power of internal and external stakeholders in a business system. In this perspective, the demographic factors inside and outside the corporation may be the most significant, creating cohorts of managers who have little to gain from the perpetuation of the current system in view of the demographic imbalances in the firm. In this perspective as well, the human resource management system is the most vulnerable element of the Japanese business system, and given its centrality in its "system-ness" as presented in current analyses, this would affect the entire system. The changes that would have the greatest import for the system as a whole do not concern the specifics of the reward and employment system, but are changes that would weaken the company's control over the individual career, and hence weaken the company's ability to move people freely across departments and across company boundaries as part of the coordination and control system of the vertical group.

Finally, those who emphasize the centrality of *institutional* elements in the business system are skeptical that significant changes will occur. In the language of institutional theorists, the Japanese business system may be in a period of "de-institutionalization", in which both its normative and cognitive institutional aspects—the belief in its value and the extent to which it is taken for granted—are both under siege. However, given the embeddedness of the Japanese business system, the current process of de-institutionalization will not necessarily lead to a new process of institutionalization of alternative forms. At most, in a highly institutionalized system, one can expect to observe adaptations of existing elements of the business system. There may, however, be a prospect that just as the Japanese firm has followed incremental innovations and incremental strategies to a point of genuine change and innovation, so the business system will evolve incrementally to significantly different patterns.

Endnote

1. See, for example, the English translation of a 1988 volume on the Japanese business system, *Business Enterprise in Japan* edited by Kenichi Imai and Ryutaro Komiya (translation edited by Ronald Dore and Hugh Whittaker, MIT Press, 1994), which has five sections: the first two ("The Firm" and "Intercorporate Relations) cover the features summarized here under "governance and coordination" and

D. ELEANOR WESTNEY

"structure"; the third, "Enterprise Behavior", covers strategy, and the fourth "Human Resources". The fifth covers public and cooperative enterprises.

References

Abegglen, James 1958. *The Japanese Factory: Aspects of its Social Organization*. Glencoe, Ill: Free Press.
_____ and George Stalk 1985. *Kaisha: The Japanese Corporation*. New York: Basic Books.
Aoki Masahiko 1988. *Information, Incentives, and Bargaining in the Japanese Economy*. Cambridge: Cambridge University Press.
Chandler, Alfred P. 1962. *Strategy and Structure*. Cambridge, MA: MIT Press.
_____ 1977. *The Visible Hand: The Managerial Revolution in American Business*. Cambridge, MA: Harvard University Press.
Dertouzos, Michael, Richard K. Lester, and Robert M. Solow, 1989. *Made in America*. Cambridge, Ma: MIT Press.
Dore, Ronald P. 1973. *British Factory Japanese Factory*. Berkeley, CA: University of California Press.
_____. 1983. "Goodwill and the spirit of market capitalism."
_____ and Hugh Whittaker 1994. "Introduction" In Kenichi Imai and Ryutaro Komiya, eds. *Business Enterprise in Japan*, 1-15. (translation edited by Ronald Dore and Hugh Whittaker). Cambridge, Mass: MIT Press.
Dyer, Jeffrey H. and William G. Ouchi 1993. "Japanese-style Partnerships: Giving Companies a Competitive Edge". *Sloan Management Review* 35 (1): 51-64.
Economist 3 June 1995. "Japan Inc. Frays at the edges"
Eccles, Robert G. and Nitin Nohria, eds., 1992. *Networks and Organizations*. Boston, MA: Harvard Business School Press.
Fruin, W. Mark, 1992. *The Japanese Enterprise System: Competitive Strategies and Cooperative Structures*. New York: Oxford University Press.
Gordon, Andrew 1985. *The Evolution of Labor Relations in Japan: Heavy Industry 1853-1955*. Cambridge, Mass: Council on East Asian Studies, Harvard University Press.
Goto Akira 1982. "Statistical evidence on the diversification of Japanese large firms." *Journal of Industrial Economics* 29 (3): 271-8.
Gouldner, Alvin (1954). Patterns of Industrial Bureaucracy. Glencoe, Ill: Free Press.

The Japanese Business System

Hamilton, Gary, and Nicole Biggart, 1988. "Market, Culture, and Authority: A Comparative Analysis of Management and Organization in the Far East." *American Journal of Sociology* (Supplement): 552-94.

_____, 1992. "On the Limits of a Firm-Based Theory to Explain Business Networks: The Western Bias of Neoclassical Economics." In Nitin Nohria and Robert G. Eccles, eds., *Networks and Organizations.* 491-520. Boston: Harvard Business School Press.

Imai Kenichi 1988. "The Corporate Network in Japan." *Japanese Economic Studies* 16 (Winter): pp. 3-37.

_____ and Hiroyuki Itami 1984. "Interpenetration of organization and market: Japan's firm and market in comparison with the U.S." *International Journal of Industrial Organization* II: 285-310.

_____ and Ryutaro Komiya 1994. "Characteristics of Japanese Firms". In Kenichi Imai and Ryutaro Komiya, eds., *Business Enterprise in Japan,*19-37. (translation edited by Ronald Dore and Hugh Whittaker). Cambridge, Mass: MIT Press.

Itami Hirouyuki 1987. *Jinponshugi Kigyo.* Tokyo: Chikuma Shobo.

_____ 1994 (a). "The 'Human-Capital-ism' of the Japanese Firm as an Integrated System". In Kenichi Imai and Ryutaro Komiya, eds., *Business Enterprise in Japan* , 73-88. (translation edited by Ronald Dore and Hugh Whittaker). Cambridge, Mass: MIT Press.

_____ 1994 (b). "Maegaki." In Kigyo Kodo Kenkyu Guru-pu, eds., *Nihon Kigyo no Tekiyoryoku,* 1-3. Tokyo: Nihon Keizai Shimbunsha.

JEI Report No. 10A March 11, 1994. "Prospects for Change in Japan's Industrial Structure."

JEI Report No. 43B November 17, 1995. "Japanese Workers Still Waiting for Recovery".

Kanter, Rosabeth Moss 1989. *When Giants Learn to Dance.* New York: Simon and Schuster.

Kogut, Bruce, ed. 1993. *Country Capabilities and the Organizing of Work.* New York: Oxford University Press.

Kono Toyohiro, 1984. *Strategy & Structure of Japanese Enterprises.* London: Macmillan.

Murayama Kazuo 1994. *Denki Gyokai Haya-Wakari Mappu.* Tokyo: Toyo Keizai Shimpo Sha.

Nihon no Kigyo Guru-pu 1994. Tokyo: Toyo Keizai Shimposha

Nonaka, Ikujiro, 1988. "Toward Middle-Up-Down Management: Accelerating Information Creation." *Sloan Management Review* 29 (3): 9-18.

D. ELEANOR WESTNEY

Nonaka, Ikujiro and Hirotaka Takeuchi, 1995. *The Knowledge-Creating Company: How Japanese Companies Create the Dynamics of Innovation*. New York: Oxford University Press.

Odagiri Hiroyuki 1992. *Growth Through Competition, Competition Through Growth: Strategic Management and the Economy of Japan*. New York: Oxford University Press.

Powell, Walter W. 1987. "Hybrid Organizational Attangements." *California Management Review* 30: 67-87.

_____ 1990. "Neither Market nor Hierarchy: Network Forms of Organization." In Barry Staw, ed., *Research in Organizational Behavior* XII, 295-336. Greenwich, CT: JAI Press.

Prahalad, C.K. and Gary Hamel 1990. "The Core Competence of the Corporation". *Harvard Business Review* 68 (3): 79-91.

Shimura Yukio 1986. *Denshi Buhin*. Tokyo: Nihon Keizai Shimbunsha.

Westney, D. Eleanor 1992. "Institutionalization Theory and the Multinational Corporation". In Sumantra Ghoshal and D. Eleanor Westney, eds., *Organization Theory and the Multinational Corporation*. 53-76. London: Macmillan.

_____ 1994. "The Evolution of Japan's Industrial Research and Development". In Masahiko Aoki and Ronald Dore, eds., *The Japanese Firm: The Sources of Competitive Strength*. 154-177. New York: Oxford University Press.

Whitley, Richard 1992. *Business Systems in East Asia: Firms, Markets, and Societies*. London: Sage Publications.

Yoshino, Michael Y., 1968. *Japan's Managerial System: Tradition and Innovation*. Cambridge, MA: MIT Press.

[4]

Producing Property Rights: Strategies, Networks, and Efficiency in Urban China's Nonstate Firms

DAVID L. WANK

China's emerging market economy presents a puzzle: why such dynamic economic growth without the clarification of legal rights to private property? Since 1979, China's economy has grown about 10 percent annually, while the southeastern coastal region has been growing almost twice as fast. A main engine of growth has been the entrepreneurial nonstate economy, consisting of private and collective sector firms. Yet empirical research persistently portrays these firms as operating through ties to local government that do not conform to our own legal distinctions between public and private property.

Here I examine this puzzle from an analytic perspective different from that found in many recent studies. Drawing on the assumption of an ideal typical market, the market transition account views the ties to local government as evidence of poorly enforced legal property rights and an obstacle to the formation of a more complete market economy. The ties are said to reflect the inefficiency of firms, because they embody suboptimal incentives and higher transaction costs, resulting in lower rates of reinvestment in business.[1] But this neglects the crucial issue of how the institutions of an "incomplete" market economy can nonetheless create such economic dynamism.

A second perspective might be called the "traditional culture" account. It views economic relationships as norms of cooperation and authority rooted in traditional kinship and community institutions. These norms function as de facto property rights by stabilizing expectations in economic transactions.[2] In this account, legal property rights are of no apparent relevance, and the state's role and its policies in the emerging market economy are neglected. This potentially reductionist character is also seen in the market transition account: neither perspective sufficiently appreciates the institutionally jumbled commercial environment in which entrepreneurs must operate.

This chapter examines entrepreneurial strategies within this environment for clues about possible sources of market dynamism. This environment includes the haphazard observation of legal rights to property, changing state policies, ambiguous standards of legitimacy, and the commercial interests of local government agencies and agents. In this context, company operators cannot take for granted a single external institution to secure their property: instead they must help *produce* property rights through their own actions. They do so by creatively combining available institutional resources that stabilize expectations in their dealings with others.[3] Commercial operators can thus be considered Schumpterian entrepreneurs: their innovative strategies stimulate economic activity that would otherwise not occur.

I focus on the reasonably coherent strategies of entrepreneurs designed to produce stable expectations.[4] A strategy is a sequence of means toward an end: for entrepreneurs, the ultimate end is maximizing profit and security for their firms. Coherence occurs when diverse institutional elements such as state policies, social norms, and local government ties are successfully woven together such that entrepreneurial dealings with others further the profitability and security of their firms.[5] I use the term "reasonable" here to refer to the optimizing decisions and choices that reflect the readily available resources at hand. Such reasonably coherent strategies, as will be shown in this chapter, are expressed in networks.[6] While these networks may be suboptimal institutions from the perspective of economic theory, they are in fact the best available strategy for entrepreneurs who must cope with an emerging market economy that lacks strong legal institutions for enforcing property rights.

I describe, first, the institutions of an emerging market economy and show how networks are rational responses. Second, I describe how entrepreneurs' commercial strategies proceed through them. Third, I address the question of the economic efficiency of networks raised by the market transition account. This discussion suggests how entrepreneurial strategies serve to create market dynamism. Finally, I extend the discussion of how networks stimulate market dynamism in China by drawing brief contrasts with market economies in Eastern Europe.

My arguments are based on nineteen months of fieldwork from 1988 to 1995 in Xiamen, an old port city and now a special economic zone in Fujian

Province, along China's southeast coast.[7] Xiamen's nonstate sectors, including both the domestic and transnational sectors, have come to constitute the lion's share of local market activity, with commerce and services growing more rapidly than manufacturing.[8] This is owing to Xiamen's status as a special economic zone, making it a site of intensive commodity circulation between the domestic and international economies. Official statistics indicate about 15,000 domestic nonstate trading firms in Xiamen in 1989 when my main fieldwork was undertaken.[9] At the top end were private and collective trading companies (*maoyi gongsi*) that operated through clientelist ties with public units and government agents to trade interregionally and transnationally. At the bottom end were private shops (*getihu*) selling to one another and to retail customers in local markets. This chapter draws on a sample of 147 trading companies in the nonstate sector.[10]

As a special economic zone, Xiamen is not typical of China's market economy. What light can it shed on the nonstate sector of China's economy as a whole? As a special economic zone designed to take the lead in developing as a market economy, Xiamen has favorable economic policies, a good communications infrastructure, and ethnic advantages in attracting investment flows from speakers of the local Minnan dialect living outside the People's Republic, primarily in Taiwan, but also in Southeast Asia and Hong Kong. In such key respects as capitalization of firms, business volume, and the relative decline of the state sector, Xiamen embodies an extreme of market emergence. However, this does not correspond to the greater clarification of legal rights to property, as many of the same processes of blurring observed elsewhere in China are also seen in Xiamen. Thus, the local situation casts into sharp relief the aforementioned puzzle of China's emerging market economy.

The Institutional Environment

Business operators forge networks in response to institutional characteristics of their environment. The features of networks are responses to these characteristics. One characteristic is the enduring power of local government. In China in the 1980s, this included control over many public assets, such as land and administratively priced commodities, that constituted the best profit opportunities. Although this aspect of local government power has eroded by the 1990s, local governments have acquired greater administrative control over the market economy in their jurisdictions through new regulatory, taxation, and licensing powers. Thus, commercial firms are still dependent on local government in many aspects of their operation, although the emphasis has shifted over time from obtaining profit opportunities to reducing uncertainty.

Clientelism enables entrepreneurs to manage their dependence on local government by creating alliances to enhance business opportunities. They refer to higher-ranking patrons with greater discretionary power as "hard" (*ying*) and seek to forge ties with such officials to stimulate business. They also value the connectivity (*lianluo*) of officials. This refers to the extent that an official is linked to others in the government, providing access to information across the functional boundaries of bureaucratic jurisdictions and levels. Greater connectivity enhances access to information and communication. Access hinges on strategies of reciprocity. Reciprocity can involve quid pro quo exchange of commercial wealth for official discretion; these are idiomatically called money connections (*jinqian guanxi*). Reciprocity can also be less blatantly instrumental discharges of obligations rooted in affective bonds of kinship and familiarity, called emotive connections (*ganqing guanxi*). The mix of money and emotion in any single relation and the content of the exchange is contingent on the specific relationship between the exchange parties and the type of business involved.

A second institutional characteristic is the haphazard enforcement of legal rights to private property. This stems in part from the self-serving manner in which local governments enforce laws and regulations. Officials often put pressure on entrepreneurs for payoffs and shares in their firms, while successful private companies can be forced to sell out to local governments. Uncertainty in regard to legal rights is exacerbated by the lack of impartial courts to enforce legal rights to private property. Even after almost two decades of reform, the courts are viewed as easily influenced in any but the most petty cases. Furthermore, given the perception that "officials shield one another" (*guan guan xianghu*), private company operators are unwilling to press charges in court when malfeasance involves officials and public units.

Particularism helps compensate for the weakness of legal definitions in determining the relational statuses of exchange parties. Social distinctions between insider (*neiren*) and outsider (*wairen*) play a prominent role. One distinction is family/nonfamily, with the strongest obligations being those considered family. Another obligation is linked to the idiom of "sameness" (*tong*). Those who perceive similar characteristics among themselves, such as schoolmates (*tongxue*), colleagues (*tongshi*), and compatriots (*tongxiang*), feel enhanced obligations. Other distinctions are between familiar (*shou*) persons and strangers (*sheng*). The perception of relative statuses gives rise to use of money and emotive ties to achieve a more favorable relative position by manipulating insider-outsider distinctions. Manipulation is expressed in such typical idioms of the "art of *guanxi*" (*guanxixue*) as doing "favors" (*renqingwei*), "concern" (*guanxin*), and giving "special treatment" (*teshu youdai*) and "consideration" (*zhaogu*) to others.[11]

A third characteristic is ambiguity over what constitutes legitimate activity. In the early 1980s, the very notion of private business was controversial, and state policy discriminated against private firms by, for example, restricting their access to state bank loans and denying them the right to use mechanized transport. In the latter half of the 1980s, there was much debate over specific practices: were business commissions a legitimate incentive or an illegitimate kickback; were the operators of cooperative firms heroes for using private capital to solve public problems (e.g., unemployment) or scoundrels exploiting public status for private gain? In the 1990s, the accounting of assets in the corporatization of state firms has given rise to new debates. Given these ambiguities, the propensity is for commercial strategies to push at the boundaries of what is formally permitted. This is reflected in the entrepreneurial argot of business by such terms as "exploiting loopholes" (*zuan kongzi*) and "walking on the edge of the policy" (*zou zai zhengce de bianshang*). Business involves not so much doing what is explicitly legal but rather doing what is not expressly forbidden. The risks are greater but profits can be much higher. The perception that "if you operate within the bounds of the policy, you will never become rich" is widespread.

Networks allow entrepreneurs to cope with these environmental ambiguities by creating a corresponding ambiguity in their firms' legal structures. In the early and mid 1980s, networks enabled entrepreneurs to cope with the discrimination against the private sector. Through such practices as "red-hatting" (*dai hong maozi*), privately operated firms came to enjoy legal public status, helping them attract customers and bypassing discriminatory legislation against legally private firms. In the 1990s, the utility of this ambiguity has increasingly centered on matters of taxation, "pocket-swapping" (*huan koudai*—the shifting of public assets to legal private ownership), and socializing risk to enhance private gain in a process referred to as "private consumption of gain and public absorption of losses" (*siren chi li, guojia chikui*). Networks obscure the legal status of a firm, keeping regulatory agencies off guard and unsure of how to treat it. This reduces entrepreneurs' accountability, giving them greater freedom of action.[12]

In sum, networks enhance entrepreneurs' expectations in dealing with state agents and others by enabling them to better channel state power toward business enhancement, achieve a reasonable degree of enforcement through popular norms, and enhance freedom of action from government agencies.

Entrepreneurial Strategies

In the uncertain environment of the emerging market economy, business is largely about the forging and enhancing of supportive ties with others. The specific kind of ties forged and the legal type of firm in which strategies proceed are contingent on the social status of specific entrepreneurs. Broadly speaking, two strategies are pursued. One is forged from below, in that the entrepreneurs who pursue it hold no formal office in government and strive to develop connections with officialdom. The other is forged from above, in that its operators are current officials who use the power of their positions to enhance their connections. While the means of each strategy differ somewhat, they both establish networks for private gain with the local government that transgress the formal borders of public and private, and of state and society. In this section I describe the two strategies as they appeared in the 1980s and the trends of change observed through the mid 1990s.

STRATEGIES FROM BELOW

Nonofficials seek ties with public agencies and officials to enhance access to public resources controlled by local governments. Their strategies are pursued through cooperative (*minban jiti*) and private (*siying*) firms. The state policies that launched these firms opened up opportunities for private (i.e., nonofficial) holders of capital by prohibiting current officeholders from running them.

In the mid 1980s, links to local governments were forged through "people-run collectives" (*minban jiti*). These are enterprises established with private capital and privately managed that are usually attached to government agencies at the district level and below, or to collective enterprises. They proliferated in the mid 1980s as a state initiative to stimulate private enterprise without expanding the legal scope of the private sector, an ideologically contentious issue at the time. New regulations enabled four or more persons who were legally unemployed to pool their own capital to found cooperative firms. These firms are legally owned by a sponsoring public unit, but partners can transfer their shares freely to the other partners. The operators make business decisions independently of their public sponsors. For example, while regulations may stipulate that after-tax profits be divided among an accumulation fund, a welfare fund, wages, and dividends, it is the operators who decide on the proportions, subject only to the provision that dividends not exceed 15 percent of the value of a firm's shares.[13]

Running a cooperative firm in the 1980s had many advantages relative to private shops (*getihu*), which were restricted by the aforementioned policy. Although many limitations on private shops were removed by the mid 1980s, key ones remained, such as a limit of seven employees and a ceiling of Y 100 in the amount of receipts. This hindered the growth of private firms. Public legal status for cooperative firms let operators bypass such restrictions and enjoy tax holidays. Also, in the ideological atmosphere of the time, private business was suspect, and red-hatting let entrepreneurs represent themselves as public firms, ensuring better treatment from government agencies and inspiring confidence in consumers.

Cooperative firm operators also found that they could profit from their firms' public status by selling affiliations to private operators, leading to the proliferation of subcontracting arrangements, colloquially termed "hanging on" (*guakao*). The transportation industry is a case in point. Regulations in the 1980s required private taxis to be sponsored by a public transportation firm. Cooperative transportation firms could serve as sponsors. The average monthly sponsorship fee paid by private taxis was Y 1,000, and larger firms sponsored dozens of taxis.

Many operators of cooperative companies also lease out subsidiaries, which in turn are subleased by the lessee, generating profits all along the subcontracting chain. I found subcontracting by Xiamen's larger firms to be so multilayered that their operators had little idea of the exact number of other firms, shops, and outlets attached to their companies.

The promulgation of the Private Enterprise Interim Regulation in 1988 opened up additional strategies. This regulation permitted single-owner, joint-stock, and incorporated private companies with fewer formal restrictions. For example, there were no limits on the number of employees or the amount of receipts, leading to the emergence of 185 privately owned trading companies in Xiamen's urban districts within a year of the policy being announced. Some of these were formed by private shopkeepers (*getihu*) who had been in business since the early days of market reform and had accumulated enough capital to establish a private company. Others were formed by low- or middle-ranking cadres who resigned their posts in the late 1980s to set up private companies under the Interim Regulations. Many of these later entrants to entrepreneurship were descended from families that had belonged to the prerevolutionary bourgeoisie and received start-up capital from relatives overseas.

Despite the wholly private legal status of these companies, their operators immediately began forging links to local government. They sought the participation of officials in their firms by giving them positions as advisors, shareholders, and board members. Called "backstage bosses" (*houtai laoban*) or "backers" (*kaoshan*), these officials assist the companies by providing timely information on the supply and demand of scarce resources, ensuring lower tax bills, preventing harassment by government agencies, and helping in other ways.[14]

Licenses to run both cooperative and private firms were also obtained via networks, a process idiomatically called "getting hold of authority" (*gaodao quanli*). This is because licenses can be scarce, particularly in the first stages of policy implementation, when the state is testing out the new policy. Yet it is precisely at this early stage that holding a license confers the greatest business advantage, because there are fewer regulations and local governments eagerly support the policy to ensure its success.

Entrepreneurs obtained these licenses through networks in several ways. Some small private shopkeepers from low social backgrounds who had limited ties to officialdom did so by becoming members of the "preparatory committee" (*choubei hui*) set up to familiarize selected entrepreneurs with a new policy to ensure its smooth implementation. Such committees were established as preludes to the formal launching of both the cooperative policy in the mid 1980s and the private enterprise policy in the late 1980s. Members of such committees were among the first to be authorized to run the new types of enterprise. To ensure membership, these entrepreneurs actively participated in the Self-Employed Laborers' Association (Geti laodongzhe xiehui), the mandatory state-run association for private proprietors, which brought them into close contact with the Industry and Commerce Bureau officials who supervised it. Since the Industry and Commerce Bureau also helps establish the preparatory committees and then issues the new business licenses, the entrepreneurs were then able to prevail on supervisory officials for inclusion on preparatory committees.[15]

Other entrepreneurs used kinship ties to officials to get licenses. Many cooperatives founded in the mid 1980s had a son or daughter of a city government official among the original partners. The ties of these offspring not only secured enterprise licenses for the partnership but supported the subsequent business as well.

STRATEGIES FROM ABOVE

Officials may obtain privileged access to scarce public resources and shift public resources to private ownership by various means. Characteristic vehicles for this strategy are branch (*neilian*) and leased (*zulin*) firms. The operation of the former is restricted to current officeholders by state policy, while opportunities to operate the latter in practice heavily favor their former public managers.

Branch firms appeared in the early 1980s as part of a state effort to compensate for the perceived shortcomings of overcentralization in the planned economy by developing new lateral flows of information and resources. Public agencies and enterprises were encouraged to bypass the hierarchical channels of the planned economy by establishing branches elsewhere to obtain their own resources and outlets. Inland public units established branches in marketized coastal locales such as Xiamen to generate income. The operators of these companies enjoy user rights to orchestrate firms' assets and limited income rights to set their salaries and those of employees, but have no transfer rights.[16]

Unlike running a private or cooperative firm, running a branch or leased firm is an opportunity almost exclusively for current or recently resigned cadres. Branch firm operators are officials from geographically distant public concerns sent to Xiamen to give those entities a presence in Xiamen's special economic zone. Some of the most entrepreneurial officials that I encountered in Xiamen were branch company operators who had previously managed rural manufacturing enterprises owned by township and county governments. They had lost their positions during the retrenchment of rural public industry in the early 1980s and were given the opportunity to run a branch firm as consolation. Many had taken "internal retirement" (*neitui*) and received no wages, although they were still formally government cadres.

Their long years of public service had left them with rich and profitable networks in government. Some used their networks for the practice of official profiteering (*guandao*). In the 1980s, with the two-tier price system, goods procured at administrative prices could be resold at market prices for a profit. Indeed, a number of branch companies were little more than conduits for transferring administratively priced commodities controlled by parent units to the special economic zone, where demand is high. This practice is especially prevalent in the construction industry, which is characterized by booming demand and administrative control of key resources such as lumber and cable, resulting in scarcity of and high prices for these commodities. Another way is what is called pocket-swapping. This practice is facilitated by the geographic distance of branch firms from their parent units, making monitoring lax and giving entrepreneurs much freedom of action. Firm operators invest heavily in real estate and other fixed assets, such as cars and machinery, which they then resell at low prices to affiliated private firms operated by family members.[17] Others give sweetheart contracts to affiliated private firms to reduce their tax bills by padding their expenditures. Yet another way of using prior networks for business is called "pulling over connections" (*ba guanxi laguolai*). This involves the total shift of a branch firm's supplier and customer base to an affiliated private firm, an increasingly common practice by the late 1980s as the status of private business rose. A case in point is a firm in the seafood trade owned by a village government along the coast. It was founded in 1983 by the former manager of a rural fishing boat factory, who used his prior ties with fishing boat captains to obtain fresh fish for sale to luxury hotels throughout China. The firm's public status was an asset during the first few years in purchasing from rural fishing collectives and selling to joint-venture luxury hotels. However, by the late 1980s, the operator was confident enough to begin shifting the business to a private company established by his son in 1988. This eventually bankrupted the firm, but by then the operator had secured its commercial potential in the private firms of his offspring.

The practice of leasing (*zulin*) collective trading companies began in the mid 1980s as a state effort to turn the money-losing subsidiary collectives established in great numbers in the late 1970s and early 1980s—the so-called May 7 enterprises—into profitable firms.[18] Many state units had established May 7 enterprises to create jobs for unneeded employees and the unemployed offspring of employees.[19] To turn the firms around, lease-holders were given legal income and user rights to the firms for the leases' duration, usually three to five years. The policy intention was to create greater entrepreneurial incentives for operators without privatizing transfer rights, which was ideologically problematic at the time.[20]

The operation of leased firms is through networks, beginning with the leasing process itself, which appears to consist largely of bid-rigging. According to regulations, firms are to be leased to nonofficials through open and fair bidding. But a number of the lessees I talked to said that bidding was rigged, for reasons discussed later in this chapter. In some instances, the lessees were told the amounts of the other bids, enabling them to submit the highest, while in other cases, the auction was never publicized, and the lessee's bid was the only one.

Other practices that confound the formal legal boundaries of public and private property also occur in leased firms. Owing to its legal structure, in which transfer rights belong to the leasing public units, while income and control rights are in the hands of the lessee for a specified period, this type of firm is an especially prime site for the practice of "private consumption of benefits and state absorption of losses." It is easy for operators to allocate business risk and overhead depreciation to the firms while assigning profits to themselves. For example, a loan can be obtained from the state bank in the name of the public firm for a business venture. If the venture is successful, the operator reaps the profit, and if it fails, he or she can declare bankruptcy and default on the loan, leaving the bank and the public owner to fight over responsibility for the debt and the firm's remaining assets.

The practice of private consumption of gain and public absorption of losses can even be written into leasing contracts. The case of a firm that traded in such restricted construction goods as lumber and cable is illustrative. The firm was founded in 1983 by a senior cadre from the forestry bureau of a rural administrative region, who used the substantial ties acquired during the course of a career as long as the history of the People's Republic to obtain highly restricted lumber for sale. In 1985, his firm was investigated for irregularities, and he resigned and retired to his rural village. However, the new manager lacked the old cadre's ties and could not obtain lumber. The forestry bureau officials pleaded with the cadre to come back and run the firm. The cadre agreed, but not before negotiating a lease contract with extremely favorable conditions. He eliminated his business risk by having three clauses inserted in the contract voiding it if he became sick and unable to work, if public construction bureaus stopped selling materials to him at the lower administrative price, and if state policies changed to oppose the policy of leasing. These clauses were so broad as to let him legally abandon the firm whenever he wanted, leaving its public owner to shoulder outstanding liabilities.

Another practice is the undervaluation of public assets when determining the leasing price. This low valuation is called "favor value" (*renqing jia*), because it is forthcoming only in the context of a personal tie between the lessee and officials in the sponsoring public unit. The low charge for private user rights boosts the profits accruing to the firm operator via private income rights. For example, in leased firms, the leasing fee rarely reflects the firm's income producing potential. In the late 1980s, monthly leasing fees for district-level collective trading firms were about Y 3,000 for firms with assets worth at least several hundred thousand yuan and capable of earning profits many times the lease fees. Furthermore, many lessees subcontract out the less profitable assets of leased firms, an income potential not reflected in the leasing fee. One lessee, for example, subleased three retail counters in a leased firm for Y 1,000 a month each, generating a Y 3,000 profit, which covered the monthly lease, while the operator concentrated on more profitable wholesale trade.

The Evolution of Strategies

The strategies and networks that transgress legal property boundaries have evolved over time. One trend occurs as a firm's capital accumulates. By the late 1980s, wealthy trading firms had shifted to the more expansive network strategy of enterprise groups (*qiye jituan*). These consist of from three to several dozen firms linked by overlapping ownership and management ties embedded in kinship and friendship. These firms are diversified not only in terms of business lines but also in the legal status of constituent firms. Many of them include legally private, leased, cooperative, and even branch companies.

This diversification among legal property rights lets entrepreneurs more readily shift assets to avoid detection and obscure their origins through such practices as pocket-swapping. Various practices such as transfer pricing, in which a component firm is overcharged for services or goods purchased by another firm in the group, facilitate tax evasion by representing taxable income as expenditures. Private firms in one's group are also convenient for holding real estate or other assets purchased by a public firm in the group. Similarly, a public firm can procure certain restricted commodities, such as construction materials, for private units in the group. This diversification also gives entrepreneurs greater freedom of action in responding to sudden policy changes. For example, when I first began fieldwork in summer 1988, policies were vigorously promoting private business. In the excitement of the propaganda buildup to the new policy, even cooperative operators were enthusiastic about being seen as private. Some that I met that summer told me that their firms were really private because they had provided their own start-up capital. In the fall, an economic rectification campaign was launched that targeted deviant commercial practices, and optimism about private business evaporated. When I subsequently met these operators, they insisted that their firms were really public because they were legally owned by public units. In other words, the operators played off different criteria to represent the status of their firms as private or public, depending on which was more advantageous in a given policy climate.

The second evolutionary trend is the adaptation of strategies to new opportunities created by policy changes. This can be seen in the response to a new state policy, the 1994 Company Law (Gongsi fa), which established a legal framework for the corporatization of state enterprises. Ownership was vested in corporations defined as "legal individuals" (*faren*), while their operators were the "legal individual's representative" (*faren daibiao*). In these new corporations I heard of practices reminiscent of my earlier observations, except that the scale was far greater. Many corporations were vehicles for diverting public property from state enterprises through the practices I had observed earlier, giving rise to the state's identification of yet another economic crime—pilfering (*toudao*).[21]

Corporatization in the 1990s appears to be proceeding along the two routes apparent in the 1980s. Strategies from below have occurred when the wealthiest cooperative companies take advantage of the law to corporatize. This course is illustrated by the career of an entrepreneur who was an unemployed youth when he first began business in 1980 with a small sundries stall. By ingratiating himself with officials of the Self-Employed

Laborers' Association, he became one of the first entrepreneurs in Xiamen authorized to run a cooperative, and by the mid 1980s he was running one of the wealthiest nonstate firms in Xiamen. In 1994, his company was reputedly the first private company to make a public stock offering under the Company Law, raising Y 25 million, and it now deals mostly in real estate and public works projects all over China.

Strategies from above involve high-ranking officials who resign their posts to establish private firms and then use their *guanxi* to establish partnerships (*hezi*) with public units. For example, a high-ranking officer in the People's Liberation Army resigned in 1993 when he heard from an acquaintance that a coal mine in Shanxi Province was seeking cash to upgrade its equipment. He obtained a Y 6 million bank loan by tapping personal ties with former comrades-in-arms who had returned to their native villages, where, as former soldiers, they occupied leading positions in village and township governments: they let him use land under their jurisdictions as collateral for the loan. He thereupon founded a private company and entered into a public-private partnership with the state mining enterprise to export coal; receipts totaled Y 400 million in 1994. In 1995, the partnership became a corporation, and many assets were intentionally undervalued and then transferred to the new corporation.

It is striking how the various entrepreneurial strategies adopted in the nonstate economy of the late 1980s mostly by smaller local firms are moving up the state hierarchy to encompass larger state-sector enterprises and higher-level officials at the city and provincial levels in the 1990s. Rather than heralding a further step toward greater clarification of legal rights to property, it seems, corporatization has stimulated the spread of network strategies to higher levels of the state structure.[22]

In sum, the various strategies and their evolution show how property rights are produced, not by any single institution, but by entrepreneurial strategies that integrate various elements in their institutional environment into courses of action. These mixes include factors as varied as state policies, local government administration, entrepreneurs' social statuses, and popular ethics and norms. They are productive because they enhance entrepreneurs' expectations in interactions with others, stimulating economic activity that would otherwise be unlikely to occur.

Efficiency Considerations

Are the strategies I have described a stimulant or an obstacle to the emerging market economy? Do they create commercial dynamism or suboptimal outcomes? Answers to these questions are critical in evaluating the economic performance of networks in China's emerging market economy. My claim is that the strategies are efficient because they stimulate commercial activity that would otherwise not occur. This contrasts sharply with the market transition account, which views the networks as inefficient because the performance of firms is less than would be the case if legal rights to property were more completely observed.[23] In this section I shall seek to show that the answer to these questions largely reflects the definition of efficiency held by the analyst, and that the market transition definition, implicitly or otherwise, overlooks institutional sources of dynamism in networks.

The different definitions of efficiency just noted accord with Harold Demsetz's distinction between comparative efficiency and so-called nirvana efficiency.[24] In nirvana efficiency, existing economic activity is gauged as a deviation from an ideal typical market of completely enforced legal property rights with zero transaction costs. This definition is implicit in the market transition perspective, and by its standards existing situations are always inefficient. This is doubtless useful for making policy suggestions to improve on existing conditions, but it does not really explain how China's market economy is able to flourish in the context of such suboptimal arrangements.

Comparative efficiency, the definition that informs this chapter, refers to making choices among realistically possible alternatives. It reveals the utility of different arrangements, suggesting why one becomes the basis of strategies and organization and others not.

THE EFFICIENCY OF NETWORK STRATEGIES IN LEASED FIRMS

With respect to the practices of leased firms, the nirvana and comparative efficiency definitions generate very different conclusions about the efficiency of networks. As already noted, collective trading firms are leased to private individuals through an auction that allocates firms (or rather their legal income and user rights) among a pool of bidders. There are basically two possible auction arrangements. An open auction is characterized by competitive, sealed bids, and the lease is awarded to the highest bidder based on price alone. A rigged auction is one in which the lessee is secretly determined by the public authority and allocation proceeds through favoritism. What appears to have mostly occurred in my sample of 23 leased firms is leasing through rigged auctions. Eighteen of their operators were their former public managers, while the other five were former officials or their offspring from the parent public units. Several operators told me that they had been told the amounts of the other sealed bids ahead of time, ensuring that their bid would be the highest.

The two definitions of efficiency shed very different light on the consequences of rigged auctions for efficiency. By the logic of nirvana efficiency, rigging auctions hinders the performance of leased firms in several ways. First, it prevents more potentially talented operators from assuming control of firms.[25] Second, operators who receive control of firms through favoritism lack sufficient incentives to develop them, inasmuch as they do not bear full business risks. Taken together, these factors constitute a drag on the firms' profit potential and reduce rates of reinvestment. Also by the nirvana logic, rigged auctions are inequitable, inasmuch as they favor those with political power.

Examining the motives and perceptions held by the actors in the leasing process suggests that a rigged auction is more efficient and equitable than an open auction in certain key respects. First, while leasing often prevents operators with higher levels of human capital such as education from assuming the helm, in an emerging market economy, where information channels for supply and demand are few, the social capital of operators from the pre-market-reform era is at least as important. This can be seen in the case of the aforementioned lumber trading firm. When the original manager, the senior cadre in his late fifties, was replaced by a younger manager in his thirties, the firm's fortunes plummeted. Although the younger manager had a college degree in enterprise management, he lacked personal ties such as those the senior cadre had forged during his long career. The senior cadre had worked his way up from a lumberyard worker to a leading position in the western Fujian Forestry Bureau. He knew public lumber mill supervisors throughout Fujian and had ties to the bureau's provincial and national levels. The younger manager had never worked in a lumberyard and lacked comparable ties. Not surprisingly, he was unable to get lumber for sale. Given the restricted nature of this commodity, trading in it was branded as profiteering, and so it could only be procured through personal ties. As the firm's fortunes plummeted, the bureau beseeched the senior cadre to return. The value of his social capital is evident in the favorable leasing contract he then negotiated.

Personal ties also stimulate firms' performance. Turning unprofitable firms into profitable ones, which is the goal of leasing, is facilitated by favorable administrative decisions, which are more likely to be forthcoming in personal ties between firm operators and parent public unit officials. These ties reduce uncertainties stemming from the ambiguous character of the decisions. For example, several informants told me that in the leasing policy's early stage, the Xiamen city government decreed that a firm's existing public employees should be kept on after the firm was leased. While this stipulation was intended to protect the employees' livelihood, it worked at cross-purposes with the goal of enhancing the firms' performance. As mentioned above, many of the firms were originally set up as May 7 firms to provide jobs for the parent public units' redundant and problem workers and their unemployed offspring. Such employees were in general not suited to doing the harder work demanded by the operators once the firm was leased out. Lessees who were known to parent unit officials worked with them to get around the stipulation. For example, many public units transferred the employees back to the parent unit just before the auction.

Personal ties also enhance flows of capital to the leased firm, stimulating its performance. As can be seen in the above example of the lumber firm, goods for sale were only forthcoming in the context of personal ties. Access to bank loans is another important consideration. Legally, a lessee is a private person and should apply for a bank loan as such, in which case it is difficult to get one because of discrimination against private borrowers. However, if the lessee is known to parent unit officials, they will guarantee the loan or even let the lessee take out a loan in the name of the parent public unit. In short, rigged auctions ensure that the firm is allocated to an operator with the personal ties that can overcome many of the institutional difficulties of the emerging market economy.

While nirvana logic would see a rigged auction as inequitable because it entails the use of office for private gain, the leasing of firms in rigged auctions arguably creates more public benefits than would occur in open auction.[26] The lessee selected by rigged auction has close personal ties to the parent public unit, which can stimulate the transfer of firm profits to the public unit. For example, operators make side payments above the low lease value, held down to reduce the tax bill, to the parent unit. While some of this money undoubtedly goes into the pockets of parent unit officials as personal income, some also enters the unit's extra-budgetary funds, which can be used to provide such public benefits as higher salaries, holiday bonuses (*guojie fei*), and new housing. For example, the senior ex-cadre operating the lumber trading company has contributed to the pension fund of the forestry bureau and underwritten the cost of a research institute to find new uses for lumber by-products, several of which led to new commercial ventures by the bureau, which employed its personnel. Presumably these income flows from the leased firm back to the public unit would be reduced if the operator had no personal ties with the parent unit.

The preceding discussion has highlighted aspects of efficiency, as well as equity, that reflect realistically possible decisions. In an environment that differs significantly from the ideal typical market, rigged auctions stimulate performance and profit sharing in a leased firm that would not occur in their absence. Rather than hindering the emergence of a more complete market economy, they stimulate the emergence of a market economy by helping to institute new kinds of commercial calculations in the evolution away from a centrally planned economy.

ENFORCEMENT IN NETWORKS

The viewpoint of nirvana efficiency maintains that networks lack effective enforcement mechanisms relative to legal property rights.[27] With legal property rights, enforcement is externalized in the court system, whereas networks increase transaction costs, since entrepreneurs must bear more of the costs in terms of payoffs and much time spent in face-to-face interaction. Certainly, in a theoretical sense, a recourse to law and the court system is less costly. But in an environment where courts are considered corrupt and the self-serving enforcement of laws by local state agents is pervasive, networks that emphasize particularistic identities and personal obligations might actually be considered more effective. Therefore it is necessary to examine what kinds of enforcement possibilities can proceed in networks. In first- and second-party enforcement, the personal ethics and social norms of face-to-face interaction play a large role, while third-party enforcement also invokes the institutions of community and the state.

First-party enforcement consists of sanctions imposed by a person on him- or herself in dealings with others. These sanctions stem from the personal honor system of "upright conduct" (*zuoren*). It is frequently heard in the business world that "one must understand how to conduct oneself in society" (*yao dongde zenme zuoren chu shi*). For example, in discussing the issue of bureaucratic corruption, one entrepreneur said, "Some businesspeople blame all their problems on bureaucratic corruption. But this is wrong. It is not a question of whether officials are honest or dishonest. . . . If you know how to conduct [*zuoren*] yourself, you can work things out." In first-party enforcement, the effective sanctions are ethical imperatives. One imperative is propriety (*li*). This stresses the observation of the rituals and etiquette that conform to the relative statuses in social interaction. A closely related imperative is reciprocity (*bao*), which emphasizes the need to repay a gift or favor. Adherence to these ethics, which are diffused among the population, as well as canonized in the Confucian classics, is inculcated by prior socialization.[28] Sanctioning is through the feelings of shame produced by nonobservation. Such feelings of shame are indicated by the popular idiom of "loss of face" (*diu lian*). Thus, the aforementioned operator of the lumber firm might have been generous in his contributions to his former public unit partly because of the memories of the kindness and warm feelings shown to him by his former colleagues.

Second-party enforcement involves an understanding between two persons. Failure by either to uphold his or her end of the understanding can lead to sanctions by the aggrieved party. Enforcement is expressed in the idiom of *guanxi*. It consists of manipulating the ethics described above to create feelings of obligation in others, inducing them to provide support toward achieving self-interested goals. Sanctioning occurs in the dyadic interaction. One sanction is when the offended individual also stops honoring his or her end of the contract and withdraws support. In high-affect relationships, the sanction is to diminish emotional closeness. In more instrumental money connections, the sanction is reducing or halting material rewards. A second sanction, closely linked to the first, is reduced support in future interactions. Such processes may also help explain why the operator of the lumber firm was generous to his former public unit: perhaps its officials manipulated their ties with him to increase the payments.

There are several processes of third-party enforcement in networks. One is rooted in the community that surrounds dyads. A community in this definition consists of persons who know others by reputation (*mingyu*) and have the possibility of face-to-face encounters. Sanctioning is more diffuse but highly effective. One sanction is that malfeasance in a dyad will become known to the wider community, negatively affecting the reputation of the malefactor. This reduces the likelihood of future cooperation, not only in the dyad, but also for potential future interactions in the community. This is reflected in a young tax official's explanation to me of his willingness to give special attention (*teshu youdai*) to businesspeople introduced by mutual friends. "Xiamen is a small place and everybody knows one another," he said. "You must realize that you will live here for your entire life. You must pay attention to your reputation. If you do not show sufficient spirit of helping others then you will find it difficult to live here. No one will support you when you need it." In extreme cases, sanctioning can be through social ostracism.

Another process of third-party enforcement is linked to state agencies. Some are appendages of the Communist Party's United Front Bureau, representing such societal and occupational groups as the Xiamen Chamber of Commerce (Xiamenshi shanghui) and the Young Factory Director and Manager Association (Qingnian changzhang jingli xiehui). Some private and cooperative firm operators have pushed the chamber to lobby on their behalf in conflicts with administrative bureaus, and others use it to enforce contracts. For example, several firm operators had experienced disputes over ownership rights and responsibilities in business partnerships with public units and sought the intervention of the chamber on their behalf.[29] Other organs are the various distributive, manufacturing, and administrative units in the government that are the business partners or direct sponsors of nonstate firms. Operators prevail on these units to intercede on their behalf in disputes and when harassed by other agencies. For example, after two different departments of the Tax Bureau separately tried to tax a leased firm, one treating it as a collective firm and one as a private firm, the operator asked his sponsoring unit to negotiate with the Tax Bureau on his firm's behalf.

Another type of third-party enforcement proceeds with reference to the state's legal and regulatory apparatus. However, the sanctioning mechanism is not formal recourse to the apparatus but rather fear that it might be invoked. It proceeds by the entrepreneur giving gifts and favors to an official so that he or she will actively intervene to prevent investigation of the firm's activities. The sanctioning mechanism here is not simply the dynamics of *guanxi* but also the official's fear that investigation of the firm could implicate (*lianlei*) him or her in its dubious activities. An illustrative example is the aforementioned branch firm operator, who bought four luxury condominiums, which he registered as the legal property of family members. Whenever officials from his sponsoring township government visit Xiamen, the entrepreneur lavishly entertains them. This increases the likelihood that the officials will shield the firm from investigation during regulatory campaigns. Officials are motivated to do so not only by norms of reciprocity but also from fear that, as recipients of the operator's largesse, they might be seen as condoning any wrongdoing that is uncovered, and punished accordingly.

In yet another manifestation of third-party enforcement, the popular categories of insider and outsider inform perceptions of the utility of the state's legal apparatus for enforcement. As already mentioned, the court system is perceived as corrupt, with decisions going to those best able to influence the judges. Also, going to court exposes one's affairs to scrutiny by government agencies, which is risky given the ambiguity of many commercial practices. Hardly any entrepreneurs in Xiamen had ever used the court system to enforce contracts, and several told me that they would consider doing so only if the person involved were an outsider and the court were geographically distant from Xiamen. Outsider status is important because, with minimal expectations of future cooperation, there is no potential sacrifice of it in taking the party to court. Geographic distance is also important. Taking a party to court is a sign that interpersonal relations have failed, and so an entrepreneur who initiates court proceedings is revealing his or her failure to solve the problem through personal ties. Such a person is likely to be tagged as someone who cannot conduct themselves properly in society (*budongde zenme zuoren chushi*) because they do not understand the dynamics of personal relations, a damning reputation when so much business is conducted through just such ties. Recourse to a geographically distant court will thus better preserve an entrepreneur's reputation (*mingyu*) in his or her home base, inasmuch as news of the legal action is less likely to reach Xiamen.[30]

PATTERNS OF REINVESTMENT

Finally, let me consider the issue of reinvestment. The nirvana efficiency concept views the lack of clear legal enforcement as weakening property rights and increasing transaction costs. One result is the drain of business capital through unproductive payoffs to officials, reducing reinvestment in firms. Also, entrepreneurs are said to respond to official predation by using profits for personal consumption. The evidence for such suboptimal investment is said to be the small size of firms, which is assumed to indicate undercapitalization.[31]

My findings from Xiamen, dovetailing with research on Chinese enterprises in Taiwan and overseas, shows how reinvestment does not proceed in unitary corporate strategies but rather through interfirm networks.[32] In other words, profits are not reinvested with an eye to developing a single bounded firm into a multilayered, hierarchical corporation but rather to promote a more organizationally diffuse enterprise group of small firms connected by particularistic ties of kinship. The advantages of such network strategies in the context of China's emerging market economy have already been discussed. The point I would like to make is that the notion of nirvana efficiency rests on such concepts as "too small," "undercapitalized," and "suboptimal reinvestment," which are ambiguous, because it is not clear what the alternatives are. The strategy of enterprise groups suggests that much more reinvestment probably occurs than is recognized by the concept of nirvana efficiency. While any particular unit in a network may seem small, this is often part of the entrepreneurial strategy of "wearing a small hat" (*dai xiao maozi*): this minimizes the profile of each component of the group, masking the much larger wealth accumulation contained in the network. This strategy further enhances the entrepreneur's sense of security and willingness to reinvest.

A more relevant indicator of efficiency, in my view, is patterns of reinvestment. In the context of uncertain legal property rights, speculative forms of trade might be preferable to manufacturing or service ventures because the turnover is quicker and wealth more readily concealed, making the firm less subject to predation by officials. Therefore, if entrepreneurs perceive great uncertainties and high transaction costs, they are unlikely to diversify out of speculative trade. However, there is much diversification in the firms in my sample. For example, of 100 private and

cooperative firms, 46 have diversified out of commerce, 20 into manufacturing, 19 into services, and 7 into both. Many initially accumulated capital in speculative activities and then shifted to manufacturing and service
ventures. This suggests that stable expectations, arising from the previously described enforcement processes, do exist in the emerging market
economy despite the lack of clearly defined legal rights to property.

Transnational capital flows are an even more relevant indicator. When
uncertain property rights create high transaction costs, one might expect
an increase of capital flight and the stagnation of the domestic economy.
This does not appear to be the case in Xiamen. A number of entrepreneurs
I met no longer thought of emigrating, because business opportunities in
China seem better than elsewhere. While many held foreign passports,
this was as a means of escape should the authorities investigate their
businesses, rather than a vote of no confidence in the domestic economy.
To the extent that entrepreneurs emigrate, they stay abroad long enough
to establish foreign residence or nationality and then return, bringing their
financial capital with them. Their new legal statuses as foreign nationals or
overseas Chinese (*huaqiao*) or Macao and Taiwan compatriots (*tongbao*)
lets them establish enterprises that fall under policies that are in some
respects more favorable than those for domestic enterprises in regard to
taxes and access to state bank loans. The process of funneling money out
of the country and then back in again under these advantageous statuses,
called "round tripping," accounts for some of the huge amount of foreign
investment flowing into China.[33] In short, capital flight, which is usually
seen as indicating uncertainty, reappears as foreign investment. This is
simply part of a broader process of creating confidence and stable expectations. It is part of a strategy of shifting among legal property rights and
policies to find the legal status that provides the best returns and most
stable expectations.

In sum, definitions of efficiency that ignore the context in which means
and ends are devised shed less light on how existing arrangements promote economic activity than the alternative concept of comparative efficiency. The latter emphasizes the utility of strategies that, while far from
theoretically optimal arrangements, are nevertheless the best possible arrangement for meeting the practical opportunities and challenges of the
emerging market economy.

Conclusions: China and Eastern Europe Compared

By way of conclusion, let me address a question raised by the analysis I
have presented here: Why do clientelist networks appear conducive to a

vibrant commercial economy in the Chinese context but much less so in postcommunist economies in Eastern Europe? The networks that I have described are similar to what analysts of Eastern Europe's market transitions variously refer to by such names as *nomenklatura* privatization, hidden privatization, and political capitalism.[34] In Eastern European market economies, Kazimierz Z. Poznanski observes,

> control over capital is put in private hands, with the majority of assets made available to the Communist authorities, the party, and/or state. In the transfer, private owners are forced into a patron-client relationship with the political leadership. As a consequence, both access to and exit from production are made conditional on loyalty to the political establishment. At the same time, this support for the "super-structure" becomes essential to private owners for securing access to capital means.[35]

These ties are widely seen as a cause for the relatively poor performance of Eastern European economies.

The key issue is why network strategies appear to stimulate commercial dynamism in one situation (China) but not in another (Eastern Europe). One possible reason for the difference lies in the different state-society contexts in which networks function, a difference attributable to different state policies of reform.[36] This context is more conducive in China to connecting government officials and entrepreneurs at the local level, enhancing communication and negotiation and thereby stabilizing expectations.

A number of scholars have commented on China's more gradual reform process.[37] Whereas the Russian and other Eastern European programs conceived of reform as the dismantling of communist-era bureaucratic controls on the economy in order to release market forces, the Chinese project sought to decentralize control rather than dismantle it per se. Therefore the Chinese bureaucracy maintains a high degree of institutional continuity and structural integrity. Increased decentralization notwithstanding, Wei Li observes, "the Chinese system is not realistically in imminent danger of the disintegration that has befallen the Communist countries in Eastern Europe and the Soviet Union."[38] When looking at the more local levels of the national bureaucracy, the degree of cohesion is even more remarkable: as Andrew Walder puts it, "what strikes the researcher is not its fragmentation but its degree of integration."[39] Of particular relevance to my argument is Susan Shirk's insight that the relatively greater hierarchical integrity of the Chinese state has kept patron-client ties intact, facilitating communication, negotiation, and loyalty. The key point is that the particularistic process of Chinese policy implementation gives lower-level officials modest amounts of power, which they can then dole out to their supporters, creating lower-level support for central policies. In other words, patron-client ties have advanced rather than obstructed the market reform process and development of a commercial economy. Extending this insight to clientelist networks in the nonstate economy suggests an explanation for China's superior economic performance.

Variations in bureaucratic integrity could have several consequences for comparative efficiency. In regard to allocation, there might be several consequences. First, the Chinese reform process has to a greater extent left intact the prior social networks linking officials and citizens. Thus, while all postcommunist economies have a relative lack of effective legal instruments, in China's market economy, popular instruments are better able to compensate in creating stable expectations. Patron-client ties remain relatively intact, heightening the function of social networks as sanctioning mechanisms in exchanges. Thus, relative to Eastern European economies, clientelist networks are better able to reduce transaction costs. The evidence from Xiamen suggests that significant rates of reinvestment are occurring along the networks linking firm operators with state agents and others in the social environment.

More specifically, variations in states' bureaucratic integrity could also produce differences in the efficiency of enforcement via third-party sanctioning. In Eastern Europe, the dismantling of state control structures has led to the rise of mafia-style criminal gangs, which flourish where central states are weak, selling protection to businesspeople.[40] Reportedly, even small retail stores post guards with automatic weapons to prevent extortion by criminals.[41] Gangs have reemerged in China too, but they seem to operate more within limits defined by local governments and do not approach the scale of gangs in Eastern Europe. For example, Ole Bruun notes the rise of secret societies and criminal gangs in Chengdu City that seek to extort protection money from private shopkeepers. But many proprietors refuse to pay. Also, these criminal elements appear to operate at the sufferance of local authorities.[42] Thus, the Chinese bureaucracy plays a relatively larger role in enforcement of property rights via the third-party enforcement described in the preceding section.

Although both Eastern European gangs and the local Chinese bureaucracy enforce property rights in ways that deviate from a standard legal system, there are important differences between the enforcement possibilities they offer. First, mafias are criminal gangs, usually operating with less legitimacy than government. Consequently, they have shorter time horizons and demand larger sums from firms with little concern for their ongoing viability.[43] By contrast, local governments have a long-term interest in promoting private business in their jurisdictions as ongoing revenue sources. Thus, in China, third-party enforcement is enacted by an organization with a longer time horizon, reducing transaction costs. This difference is also suggested by the comments of other observers. The economist Anders Aslund writes that the Russian mafia "behave like robbers . . . [without] an interest in the survival of local enterprises. As a result, Russian entrepreneurs often find it impossible to collaborate with gangster syndicates."[44] In regard to China, Susan Young avers that ad hoc levies by local governments, while burdensome, have "probably been a major factor in the growth of private business. They certainly have not been so heavy as to prevent it, and they have given local officials a direct incentive to support it."[45]

Second, there might be variations in the capacity of firm operators to obtain enforcement. As illegitimate organizations, criminal gangs function in secrecy, and membership is often opaque to the local communities they operate in. In Russia and Eastern Europe, opaqueness is further enhanced by the ethnic character of gangs, such as the Chechen gangs that sell protection in urban marketplaces for agricultural produce. Ethnicity creates solidarity within the group by organizational closure to the outside. In contrast, government agents in China often reside in the communities they administer, while street-level officials in southern Fujian are often native, a reflection of the need for local dialect speakers to interact with citizens in fulfilling administrative tasks. Their social networks in the community overlap with those of the businesspeople over whom they wield authority. Therefore, Chinese entrepreneurs have lower costs in getting effective third-party sanctions to protect property rights, such as disciplining officials who transgress community-based perceptions of the amount of legitimate payoffs.

Thirdly, the greater bureaucratic integrity of the Chinese state also means that local officials are more likely to be disciplined from above by their superiors when they exceed accepted payoff levels. Such attempts can be seen in the ongoing anti-corruption drives launched by the state, which have disciplined increasingly higher levels of officials during the course of the past two decades. These campaigns have sought to define illegitimate behavior for officials and identify and punish transgressors. Presumably such disciplining would be less likely to occur in the Eastern European state structures, which have seen greater shifts in personnel, and where presumably lines of communication between locales and the center have been disrupted, with Russia again being an extreme example of this.

In sum, a process of transformation in which political reform proceeded more slowly than market reform gave Chinese entrepreneurs advantages in forging networks across local state-society borders to enhance business and stimulate the economy. Chinese entrepreneurs often faced local agents they knew, and in some cases had known for decades, whereas their Eastern European counterparts were less likely to have such an advantage. Chinese entrepreneurs were also presumably more able than their Eastern European counterparts to hold on to stable expectations in the institutional jumble of the postcommunist economy, because, given the greater integrity of the state structure, popular norms and hierarchical authority were better able to operate as enforcement mechanisms in interactions between state agents and commercial operators. The juxtaposition of the Chinese and Eastern European reform experiences also underscores the crucial point that strategies that produce property rights are highly constrained by the institutional context. Entrepreneurs do not choose as they please but rather are limited by factors beyond their control, such as the structural integrity of the state, the content of state policies, and the available local enforcement agencies.

Notes

I am grateful to Jean Oi and Andrew Walder for insightful comments on successive drafts of this chapter, and to Nan Lin, Susan Young, and other participants at the conference from which this volume stems, for numerous helpful suggestions.

1. Ding Lu, *Entrepreneurship in Suppressed Markets: Private-Sector Experience in China* (New York: Garland Publishing, 1994); Victor Nee, "Organizational Dynamics of Market Transition: Hybrid Forms, Property Rights, and Mixed Economy in China," *Administrative Science Quarterly* 37 (Mar. 1992): 1–27.

2. Nan Lin, "Local Market Socialism: Local Corporatism in Action in Rural China," *Theory and Society* 24, 3 (June 1995): 301–54; Martin L. Weitzman and Chenggang Xu, "Chinese Township-Village Enterprises as Vaguely Defined Cooperatives," *Journal of Comparative Economics* 18, 2 (Apr. 1994): 121–45.

3. I follow Harold Demsetz's definition of property rights as "an instrument of society . . . that . . . help[s] a man form those expectations that he can reasonably hold in his dealings with others. These expectations find expression in the laws, customs, and mores of a society." See Harold Demsetz, "Toward a Theory of Property Rights," in *Ownership, Control, and the Firm* (Oxford: Blackwell, [1967] 1988), pp. 104–16.

4. This chapter extends David Stark's analysis of these institutionally plural environments and of commercial action as "bricolage." See David Stark, "Recombinant Property in East European Capitalism," *American Journal of Sociology* 101, 4 (Jan. 1996): 993–1027.

5. I see institutions as the cognitive categories and social norms that construct relationships, while strategies are the actions of people who are constrained by institutions but can maneuver within those constraints to develop relationships that further their interests. Such manipulation is not the action of a fully rational actor but rather the partially unreflective routines and improvisations of a competent person. Such action is akin to what Pierre Bourdieu calls the "habitus."

6. These networks have also become an institutional element of the emerging market economy.

7. For a description of Xiamen City and discussion of the fieldwork and sample, see David L. Wank, *Commodifying Communism: Business, Trust, and Politics in a Chinese City* (Cambridge: Cambridge University Press, 1999).

8. Although not apparent in published local statistics in the late 1980s, officials at the time told me that the total value of goods and services produced by the domestic and foreign nonstate sector had surpassed that of the state sector. Such a figure was not realized in the national economy till the 1990s.

9. At the time it was impossible for a foreign or overseas Chinese firm to obtain a license for commerce. Thus the licensed trading concerns were, by legal definition, entirely domestic. However, by the late 1980s, the distinction between domestic and international was also becoming blurred. This trend is only tangentially mentioned in this chapter.

10. The sample is composed of 24 branch, 30 cooperative, 23 leased, and 70 private firms.

11. For more general discussion of these idioms during market reform, see Mayfair Mei-hui Yang, *Gifts, Favors, and Banquets: The Art of Social Relationships in China* (Ithaca, N.Y.: Cornell University Press, 1994).

12. Stark, "Recombinant Property," terms this process "organizational hedging."

13. While it is difficult to know which collective-sector trading firms are cooperatives and which are fully socialized, city government statistics suggest that there were 441 cooperative firms in the late 1980s.

14. Another private business link with government occurred in the realm of perceptions. Companies with Y 500,000 in registered capital are licensed by the city-level Industry and Commerce Bureau and authorized to use the words "Xiamen City" and "company" (*gongsi*) in their name, creating an impression of affiliation with the city government. Companies with Y 50,000 in registered capital are licensed by district-level bureau branches and lack such authorization, but some nevertheless created the impression of public affiliation by designating themselves using terms applicable to public enterprises, such as "business department" (*jingyingbu*).

15. Licenses for cooperative firms were usually issued by labor service companies (*laodong fuwu gongsi*) and for private firms by the Industry and Commerce Bureau.

16. Branch firms can also be state-sector enterprises, although this chapter is not concerned with them. By the late 1980s, there were about 500 such firms in Xiamen, mostly corporations conducting foreign trade.

17. Many branch operators buy real estate and register it in the name of family members. As purchase of a house or condominium in Xiamen confers on the owner a permanent residence permit, these operators have been able to bring their families to Xiamen.

18. In theory, leasing differs from contracting (*chengbao*) in the greater income and user rights that entrepreneurs acquire in the former, but in practice there is little difference. In Xiamen, the term "leasing" is applied to trading firms, and "contracting" to manufacturing and service firms.

19. They were called May 7 enterprises after a speech by Mao Zedong that exhorted citizens to combine productive labor with other activities. These enter-

prises constituted a quarter of the urban collective industrial labor force in the early market reform era.

20. At the time of my fieldwork, there were 205 collective trading firms sponsored by district and other levels of local government that had been leased in the mid 1980s. This figure is my own estimate, based on interviews at government agencies and published local statistics.

21. During the first half of the 1990s, it is officially estimated, Y 100 million (U.S.$12 million) was pilfered daily. According to another official estimate, in 1993, China had U.S.$416 billion in state assets, while another U.S.$57 billion had been illegally privatized. See "China's Vanishing Assets: State Prepares Crackdown on 'Pilferers,' " *International Herald Tribune*, Apr. 26, 1996, p. 11.

22. Some analysts, such as Jean Oi and Andrew Walder, see property rights reform as the devolution of legal property rights to public actors in the lower bureaucracy. This chapter suggests that this devolved control over resources also stimulates a parallel upward penetration of the state by the networks of nonstate entrepreneurs. See Jean C. Oi, "The Fate of the Collective After the Commune," in Deborah Davis and Ezra F. Vogel, eds., *Chinese Society on the Eve of Tiananmen: The Impact of Reform* (Cambridge, Mass.: Council on East Asian Studies and Harvard University, 1990), pp. 15–36; Andrew G. Walder, "Corporate Organization and Local Government Property Rights in China," in Vedat Milor, ed., *Changing Political Economies: Privatization in Post-Communist and Reforming Communist States* (Boulder, Colo.: Lynne Rienner, 1994), pp. 53–66.

23. The inefficiencies of networks transgressing state-society boundaries are more explicitly stated in the literature on East European economies cited in n. 34.

24. Harold Demsetz, "Information and Efficiency: Another Viewpoint," *Journal of Law and Economics* 12, 1 (Apr. 1969): 1–22.

25. For example, a trio of foreign advisors to the Russian government maintain that giving government officeholders shares in publicly owned firms "reduces the likelihood that control over assets will shift to managers with skills needed to restructure firms. . . . To the extent that management turnover is essential for efficient resource allocation, giving equity to politicians can entrench the old human capital and thereby reduce efficiency" (Maxim Boycko, Andrei Shleifer, and Robert Vishny, *Privatizing Russia* [Cambridge, Mass.: MIT Press, 1995], p. 59).

26. "Giving politicians equity is obviously extremely unfair. . . . Like corruption, *nomenklatura* privatization rewards arbitrary grabbing of control rights and openly acknowledges that politicians are not acting in the public interest" (ibid., p. 59).

27. According to the aforementioned Russian government advisors, sidepayments by entrepreneurs to officeholders attempt to create investment incentives by precluding officeholders from interfering in their firms. But sidepayments are ultimately inefficient inasmuch as they lack enforcement mechanisms. "The arbitrary element of a politician's control rights, which enables him to collect bribes, does not constitute a legal right that a court would protect or that he can surrender through a contract enforceable in court. In practice this

means that the politician can come back and demand another bribe from the manager, or another politician can also demand a bribe" (ibid., p. 51).

28. For example, in the Confucian classic *Li Ji* [The Book of Rites], propriety is linked with reciprocity. "And what the rules of propriety value is reciprocity. If I give a gift and nothing comes in return, that is contrary to propriety; if the thing comes to me, and I give nothing in return, that also is contrary to propriety" (quoted in Yunxiang Yan, *The Flow of Gifts: Reciprocity and Social Networks in a Chinese Village* [Stanford, Calif.: Stanford University Press, 1995], p. 124). According to Yan, popular diffusion of this ethic is reflected in the common proverb "Propriety upholds reciprocal interactions" (*Li shang wanglai*).

29. For a more detailed description of entrepreneurial strategies in regard to the Chamber of Commerce, see David L. Wank, "Private Business, Bureaucracy, and Political Alliance in a Chinese City," *Australian Journal of Chinese Affairs* 33 (Jan. 1995): 55–71, at 60.

30. For a similar discussion, see Lucie Cheng and Arthur Rosett, "Contract with a Chinese Face: Socially Embedded Factors in the Transformation from Hierarchy to Market, 1978–1989," in Tahirih V. Lee, ed., *Contract, Guanxi, and Dispute Resolution in China* (New York: Garland Publishing, 1997), pp. 192–96.

31. For example, Victor Nee writes that private business operators "are reluctant to make long-term investment in the growth of their enterprise because, in the absence of legal protection of private property rights and possible hostility directed against them in future political campaigns, they worry about possible appropriation of their assets" (Nee, "Organizational Dynamics," p. 14).

32. See, e.g., Gary G. Hamilton, ed., *Business Networks and Economic Development in East and Southeast Asia* (Hong Kong: University of Hong Kong, Centre of Asian Studies, 1991).

33. In 1995, foreign investment in China was valued at U.S.$38 billion, second only to the U.S.$60 billion in the United States, and far more than the U.S.$5.8 billion in Malaysia, the second largest recipient in Asia ("Not Quite So Sparkling China," *Economist*, Mar. 1–7, 1997, p. 30).

34. See, e.g., Jeffrey Sachs, "Spontaneous Privatization: A Comment," *Soviet Economy* 7, 4 (Oct.–Dec. 1991): 317–21; and Jadwiga Staniszkis, " 'Political Capitalism' in Poland," *East European Politics and Societies* 5, 1 (Winter 1991): 127–41.

35. Kazimierz Z. Poznanski, "A Property Rights Perspective on the Evolution of Communist-Type Economies," in id., ed., *Constructing Capitalism: The Reemergence of Civil Society and Liberal Economy in the Post-Communist World*, pp. 71–96 (Boulder, Colo.: Westview Press, 1992), at pp. 76–77.

36. In chapter 7 of *Commodifying Communism*, I further argue that differences in state policies are an important but insufficient explanation for variations in the performance of economic networks in China and Eastern Europe. Differences in institutional culture are also crucial.

37. See, e.g., Susan L. Shirk, *The Political Logic of Economic Reform in China* (Berkeley and Los Angeles: University of California Press, 1993).

38. Wei Li, *The Chinese Staff System: A Mechanism for Bureaucratic Control and Integration*, China Research Monograph 44 (Berkeley: Institute of East Asian Studies, University of California, 1994), p. 1.

39. Andrew G. Walder, "Local Bargaining Relationships and Urban Industrial Finance," in Kenneth G. Lieberthal and David M. Lampton, eds., *Bureaucracy, Politics, and Decision Making in Post-Mao China* (Berkeley and Los Angeles: University of California Press, 1992), p. 310.

40. Anton Blok, *Violent Peasant Entrepreneurs: The Mafia of a Sicilian Village* (Oxford: Blackwell, 1974); Diego Gambetta, *The Sicilian Mafia: The Business of Private Protection* (Cambridge, Mass.: Harvard University Press, 1993).

41. "Management Brief," *Economist*, Sept. 6–12, 1997, p. 67.

42. "Some suggested that the police cooperated with the gangs, obtaining assistance from them in tracing hard criminals *in exchange for granting them a certain freedom to extort* from the private sector" [emphasis added], observes Ole Bruun, *Business and Bureaucracy in a Chinese City: An Ethnography of Private Business Households in Contemporary China*, China Research Monograph 43 (Berkeley: Institute of East Asian Studies / Center for Chinese Studies, University of California, 1993), p. 181.

43. Gambetta, *Sicilian Mafia*, p. 33.

44. Anders Aslund, *How Russia Became a Market Economy* (Washington, D.C.: Brookings Institution, 1995), p. 169.

45. Susan Young, *Private Business and Economic Reform in China* (Armonk, N.Y.: M.E. Sharpe, 1995), p. 53.

Journal of Asian Business   Volume 12 • Number 1 • 1996

The Evolution of
Southeast Asian Business Systems

LINDA Y.C. LIM[*]

This paper considers how the changing regional economic, political, and cultural environments and the actions of national governments, Western and Japanese multinationals, and ethnic Chinese and indigenous capitalists, have contributed to shaping the business systems of developing market economies in Southeast Asia. It argues that as the region's enterprises, economies, political and legal systems mature, the entrepreneurial family businesses and ethnic networks heavily dependent on personal relationships and government linkages that currently dominate business systems here will change and become less dominant, but only gradually and incompletely.

Introduction

The task of articulating what constitutes "Southeast Asian business systems" is made difficult by several factors. Firstly, unlike Japan, Korea, China, or Taiwan, Southeast Asia consists of many countries, not one.   Secondly, these countries are extremely heterogeneous both among and within themselves in terms of level of economic development, political system, ethnicity, and culture. Thirdly, unlike Western countries and, arguably, Japan, business systems in Southeast Asia are very dynamic, i.e., constantly evolving due both to "immaturity" or incomplete development and to extremely rapid economic growth.   Fourthly, a long history of colonization by Western powers, early integration into the world economy, and continuous openness to foreign trade and investment have resulted in a high degree of penetration by and absorption of external forces and players.   The result is a highly complex, diverse, and ever-changing hybrid "system" which does not lend itself easily to analysis.

Nonetheless, an attempt to do so is worthwhile, in my judgment, for a number of reasons.   Firstly, despite their heterogeneity, the different national business systems in Southeast Asia are systematically similar in many ways that make an attempt to analyze them in common, both feasible and useful.   Secondly, Southeast Asia's above-mentioned characteristics arguably make it a potentially more representative "model" of business system development for other

[*] School of Business, University of Michigan

LINDA Y.C. LIM

developing regions of the world than either "Western" or "East Asian" models. Thirdly, the area's extremely rapid growth sustained over many decades suggests that conformity to either set of established models is not necessary for economic and business success. Fourthly, Southeast Asia's already significant and rapidly increasing integration into both "Western" and "East Asian" business systems makes the continued development of its own business systems of growing global as well as regional importance.

In this paper I will attempt to describe and explain existing business systems in the developing capitalist market economies of Southeast Asia,[1] and to suggest the directions that their future evolution is likely to take. I will do so by discussing, first, the regional economic, political, and cultural environments, then the evolving roles of different regional business actors, before providing an integrative overall analysis. My aim is to consider whether and why Southeast Asian business systems may or may not distinctively differ from Western and East Asian systems, and if any distinctiveness is likely to persist over time as economies, enterprises, and political systems mature, global business linkages proliferate, and the influence of "internationalization" on local cultures intensifies.

The Economic Environment

The economic environment facing business in Singapore, Malaysia, Thailand and Indonesia over the past thirty years has been one of rapid export-led growth with relatively low inflation, and high savings and investment rates (Hill 1993). Dependence on foreign investment has also been high, and there is continued though diminishing relative reliance on the export of primary commodities. Growth has led to sectoral diversification and movements up the value chain and technology ladder, impelled by both market-led adjustments and government policy. This developmental progression has led from subsistence through export-oriented primary production, to labor-intensive export manufacturing, capital-intensive and high-tech manufacturing, and labor- and skill-intensive services, for world and domestic markets. Such sectors coexist within given countries, with newer sectors displacing older ones only when resource constraints are reached.

The regional division of labor in Southeast Asia is based on differences in national comparative advantages, and on the special role of Singapore. Singapore is a commercial and financial intermediary and provider of capital, skilled labor and infrastructure services for its neighbors. It is also the location of many "high-end" manufacturing functions linked to "lower-level" activities in neighboring economies, including linkages through the internal division of labor within multinational corporations, based on comparative advantage and facilitated by the existence of free trade zones (Lim and Pang 1991; Lim 1994b). As national comparative advantages change, trade and investment also shift activities among different Southeast Asian countries e.g. by relocating labor-intensive manufacturing from Singapore to Indonesia and land- and labor-intensive agriculture from Malaysia to Vietnam (Lee Tsao 1994; Lim 1995a). Trade and investment flows also link Southeast Asia with Northeast Asia. Japan is cumulatively the region's largest trade partner, foreign investor and aid donor, with Taiwan, Hong Kong and Korea ranking close behind as sources of foreign investment (Doner 1993; Wells 1993).

Except for Singapore, the countries of Southeast Asia are still "developing", though Malaysia, and sometimes Thailand, are occasionally classified as "newly-industrializing". They are thus characterized by market imperfections and underdeveloped market institutions. As we shall see, this condition gives rise to particular organizational responses on the part of business actors to access resources and information, assess and reduce risks, and minimize transactions costs. At the same time, resource abundance, the rapid growth of markets, and new market opportunities encourage and reward opportunistic, entrepreneurial and risk-taking business behaviors, rather than the productivity-enhancing, static profit-maximizing behaviors characteristic of more mature, resource-scarce and slower-growing industrial economies like those of the West and, arguably, Japan.

Underdevelopment and rapid export-led growth in Southeast Asia mirror conditions in Northeast Asia at an equivalent stage of development, and thus might be expected to elicit somewhat similar organizational and behavioral responses from the business community. Two other aspects—resource abundance[2] and the active, often dominant, participation of foreign business actors—distinguish the Southeast Asian cases from their Northeast Asian neighbors. They introduce different forms and stronger external influences into local business systems. Thus, for example, resource-extracting multinationals like oil-and-gas companies, and plantation-based agribusiness are two prominent forms of business enterprise in Southeast Asia that are generally not found in Northeast Asia. Both import-substituting industrialization and labor-intensive export manufacturing have been led by foreign business actors. Both regions began industrializing under protective trade and investment regimes, then liberalized over time, but Southeast Asia has received much

LINDA Y.C. LIM

larger sums of foreign direct investment. And among "domestic" business actors, the dominant commercial role of the ethnic Chinese immigrant minority in Southeast Asia has no parallel in Northeast Asia.

The Political Environment

National political systems in the capitalist market economies of Southeast Asia have been for the most part authoritarian, though there is considerable diversity among countries and over time. To varying degrees, emerging nation states in the region, with the exception of Thailand, embraced nationalist ideologies in the aftermath of Western colonialism. Military-backed regimes have dominated most of the post-colonial era in Indonesia, the Philippines, and Thailand, while dominant-party governments characterize the electoral systems in Malaysia and Singapore.

Authoritarianism and militarism have been legitimated on grounds of national security concerns, given internal political tensions caused by ethnic diversity, the widespread existence of communist insurgencies and ethnic separatist movements in the immediate post-colonial period, and the triumph of socialist regimes in nearby Indochina and Myanmar. National security concerns, particularly the Vietnam War, also provided the motivation for the pursuit of national economic development, and for regional cooperation within the ASEAN grouping, as politically stabilizing forces. They also encouraged the maintenance of external economic, political and military links with Western powers, long after the end of colonialism.

Nationalism and authoritarianism both imply interventionist government in the economic sphere, which will be discussed below. In Southeast Asia there is the additional element of indigenism, which differentiates between immigrant-origin ethnic Chinese and peoples of heterogeneous indigenous origins—called *bumiputra* in Malaysia and *pribumi* in Indonesia, for example. The Chinese—now locally-born and - domiciled, and partially culturally assimilated, but still in most places a small minority[3]—dominate local private business, particularly in the modern urban-industrial sector. This is a source of internal political tension which has been managed in part by discriminatory policies designed to restrict Chinese business activities and/or to advantage their indigenous counterparts through affirmative action,(Golay et al 1969).

In response, segments of the Southeast Asian Chinese business community developed personal "clientelistic" relationships with politically powerful individuals, or the military, to protect, maintain, and advance their business interests, most notably with the Suharto regime in Indonesia. Chinese business interests thus benefitted from both the political stability engendered by, and the connections they had with, authoritarian indigenous regimes. In more "democratic" countries, they organized collectively to achieve the same end, most notably in ethnic-based business associations (e.g., the Chinese Chamber of Commerce) and political parties (e.g., the Malaysian Chinese Association) in Malaysia. In either case, political involvement has been necessary to Chinese business success, if not survival, in Southeast Asia.

Recently, democratic regimes have begun to emerge in Southeast Asia after decades of authoritarian rule. Improved information flows and popular demands for more transparency and fairness in government and business actions (relating, for example, to issues of corruption and the environment) may induce some changes in local business practices. But the position of the Chinese in Southeast Asia makes the implications of political democratization for business more complex. On the one hand, their slight representation in Southeast Asian electorates suggests that Chinese political influence is likely to decline with the rise of democratically elected governments. On the other hand, their economic power and established clientelistic relationships might enhance their political influence through the funding of sympathetic political parties or candidates (Lim and Gosling, forthcoming).

The Cultural Environment

Southeast Asia's extreme cultural diversity contrasts vividly with Northeast Asia's ethnic and cultural homogeneity, which has occasionally been advanced as one of the reasons for the latter's economic success, based on the presumption that inter-group conflicts are minimized and a "sense of common purpose" is easier to marshall among people with a common heritage. High savings and investment rates, high levels of education, and tolerance for and high standards of bureaucratic intervention, have been associated with Northeast Asia's Confucian culture, which is also found among ethnic Chinese commercial minorities in Southeast Asia.

Yet the Southeast Asian countries have virtually matched the economic achievements of Northeast Asia without the aid of cultural homogeneity or Confucian values. Indonesia, for example, has more than 300 ethno-linguistic groups and is the world's largest Islamic country, with Chinese accounting for only 4 percent of its population, yet it has had savings and investment rates of around 35 percent of

LINDA Y.C. LIM

GDP, and annual GDP growth rates of over 6 percent, for more than two decades. Thailand, where Theravada Buddhism is the major religion and cultural influence, has enjoyed even more rapid growth for a longer period of time. Malaysia's three ethnic groups—Muslim Malays, Confucian Chinese, and predominantly Hindu Indians—have achieved social harmony as well as rapid economic growth over many decades. Only in the predominantly Catholic Philippines has economic performance been lagging until recently.

One may argue from this that capitalist economic development is compatible with many different cultures, or that all Asian cultures contain elements that are conducive to capitalism. Malaysia's Deputy Prime Minister Datuk Seri Anwar Ibrahim has even argued that "collaboration between Muslim-Malay and Confucian-Chinese communities has made Southeast Asia into a prosperous region" (*Straits Times* 14 March 1995). Our interest here is in whether culture shapes aspects of the business system. Certainly the political ramifications of cultural diversity play a role, as noted in the case of ethnic Chinese business dominance. Certain elements common to all Asian cultures, such as the importance of family, gift-giving, relationships, and respect for age and education, are also reflected in regional business behaviors. Whether specific cultural attributes result in distinctive business systems and practices in different ethnic and cultural groups will be discussed below.

Regional Business Actors

National Governments

National governments have arguably been the dominant players in the evolution of modern Southeast Asian business systems to date (MacIntyre 1994). There have been many differences among countries and over time in government economic policy, but also some similarities. The early adoption and maintenance of sound macroeconomic management and realistic exchange rates by Malaysia, Singapore, and Thailand was eventually emulated in Indonesia and the Philippines, especially from the 1970s on. In the microeconomic area, policies have been more varied and variable.

Like most other developing countries, Southeast Asian governments pursued policies of import-substituting industrialization in the post-independence period, motivated economically by latecomer disadvantages and politically by nationalist aspirations. This required the erection of trade barriers, and occasionally overvalued exchange rates, but the distortions here were relatively mild by developing country standards. In most periods and places (the Philippines being the most notable exception), the competitiveness of primary commodity exports was never seriously threatened. Later, the push to export manufactures in the 1970s resulted in partial trade liberalization. Economic reforms in the wake of external debt problems and recession in the mid-1980s included more unilateral trade liberalization that continues to this day, bolstered by similar initiatives at the regional, sub-regional, and multilateral levels. (Regional policy initiatives include the ASEAN Free Trade Area (AFTA) to be completed by 2003, and the Asia Pacific Economic Cooperation (APEC) free trade area to be completed by 2020; the sub-regional policy development is the "growth triangle" linking contiguous territories of neighboring countries in limited local freedom of goods, capital, services and labor flows; and the multilateral influence is the GATT Uruguay Round agreement and the establishment of the World Trade Organization).

Most countries imposed at least some restrictions on foreign investment (Singapore being the exception here), mostly by requiring majority local ownership in resource exploitation and domestic market-oriented sectors, and/or phase-ins to increased local ownership over time (most notably in Indonesia). By the 1970s, 100 percent foreign ownership was permitted in export-oriented manufacturing, and the economic reforms of the 1980s resulted in further investment liberalization. This continued into the 1990s, with the most dramatic example being Indonesia's lifting of local ownership phase-in requirements in May 1994, which led to a record US$24 billion of new foreign investment commitments in that year, and an additional $10 billion in the first two months of 1995 alone. There have even been suggestions that Southeast Asia may be receiving "too much" foreign capital (*Wall Street Journal* 23 January 1995: 1).

Some governments in the region have been open to foreign direct investment not only for the usual reasons of access to capital, technology and foreign markets, but also because of their desire to secure a counterweight to the private sector dominance of local ethnic Chinese business. This was most clearly the case in Malaysia, where employment created in multinational subsidiaries for bumiputras and equity ownership for them in foreign-owned companies helped achieve the ethnic redistribution objectives of the Malay-dominated government's New Economic Policy (Jesudason 1989). In Indonesia, joint ventures with foreigners provided a channel of entry into business for aspiring pribumi businessmen, particularly the politically well-connected.

The dominant business presence of minority ethnic Chinese in Southeast Asia helps explain the relatively weak support provided by the indigenous-dominated state for local private business. This lack of

LINDA Y.C. LIM

support for, and in some cases even antagonism toward, local Chinese private business arguably existed even in Singapore, where an English-educated bureaucracy held the reins of political power. State-owned enterprise sectors were developed, largely in infrastructure and resource-based industry, for political (nationalism, indigenism) as well as economic (public goods, externalities, contribution to government budget) reasons. They provided an alternate economic space for the development of indigenous bureaucrat-managers, and in the case of Malaysia, of economic assets explicitly held "in trust" for the bumiputra community at large. Privatization, when it came in the 1980s and 1990s, often involved privileged distributions of such state-owned assets to politically well-connected members of this community, partly as a means of ethnic redistribution (Jomo 1995). A somewhat similar situation prevails in Indonesia, where privatization is much less advanced than in Malaysia, while in Thailand more limited state enterprises remain in the hands of the Thai bureaucracy.

Beyond policies to attract foreign investment and promote exports generally, the governments of Singapore, Malaysia, and Indonesia have also undertaken strategic industrial policy to channel resources into specific key industrial sectors or industries, most notably electronics and other high-tech industries in Singapore, automobiles, steel, and other heavy industry in Malaysia, and aircraft in Indonesia (Lim 1994a: 205-238; Jomo 1993; Bowie 1991; Lim 1995c). Foreign multinationals have played a key role in these strategic ventures, primarily as suppliers of technology, but also as joint-venture partners with state-owned enterprises. Similar policies have not been enacted in Thailand or the Philippines.

Western Multinationals

Western multinationals are the oldest-established "modern" enterprises in Southeast Asia, beginning with colonial-era multinational trading companies and export plantations. Some of these "traditional" enterprises survive today (e.g., Dole pineapple plantations in the Philippines), but most have been taken over by nationals in both ownership and management (e.g., former British rubber and palm-oil plantations in Malaysia). Some are being transformed (e.g., from trading companies into manufacturers, and from plantations into property development companies). Other Western multinationals include oil and gas companies, import-substituting "brand name" industrial enterprises established in the 1960s and 1970s, export-manufacturing enterprises established since the 1970s, financial services companies, and most recently, manufacturing ventures oriented simultaneously to both domestic and foreign markets.

Thus, even before the investment liberalizations of the late 1980s and 1990s, Western multinationals occupied a major, if not dominant, role in the modern sectors of Southeast Asian economies. They included both 100 percent foreign-owned and joint-venture companies, and in Malaysia and Singapore many were publicly listed on the local stock exchanges. Since the 1970s, the presence of Western multinationals has steadily increased as these economies have grown and developed new sectors, and barriers to foreign trade and investment have been progressively reduced (Lim 1995b).

Until the 1990s, Western investment in Southeast Asia was most attracted by the region's abundant physical resources and cheap labor, and the possibilities they provided for competitive exports to world markets. In resource-based activities such as oil and gas extraction, partnership with state-owned enterprises was required, and production-sharing agreements took the place of foreign ownership. In export-oriented manufacturing, 100 percent foreign ownership was allowed, in part because foreign technology and global sourcing and marketing networks were essential. Western enterprise was least represented in manufacturing for protected local markets, where joint ventures with local partners, often with only a minority foreign stake, were usually required. In consumer products, however, licensing to local manufacturers was common.

The 1990s surge of Western multinational investments in Southeast Asia includes both continued resource extraction and export manufacturing projects, now of a more capital-intensive, and often regionally-integrated, nature. Companies increasingly practice a regional division of labor, locating different stages of production, or producing different products, in different countries according to their respective comparative advantages. But there is also new interest in production for the rapidly growing local and regional markets. These are now either of a sufficient size to attract the interest of global companies in their own right, or are perceived as "strategic" in companies' struggle for global market share, including the need to block or counter competitors' first-mover advantages or to penetrate their profit sanctuaries. Most such projects still involve the participation of local joint-venture partners, whose contributions of capital, manpower, local market knowledge and government and business connections balance the technological, managerial and global market access contributions of the foreign investors.

Japanese Multinationals

If Western companies were the earliest foreign investors in Southeast Asia, they were soon overtaken by Japanese multinationals supplying protected local markets through minority joint-venture

LINDA Y.C. LIM

partnerships, and exporting labor-intensive manufactures to world markets from often 100 percent-owned subsidiaries (see Phongpaichit 1990; Yamashita 1991; Tokunaga 1992; Dobson 1993; Doner 1993). The relocation of Japanese export industry to Southeast Asia accelerated in the 1980s and 1990s with the appreciation of the yen. Much more so than in the case of Western firms, manufacturing investments by major Japanese multinationals were accompanied or followed by investments by other, smaller, firms in their home-country supplier networks. This helped to multiply and integrate Japanese investments, which are arguably in the process of integrating Southeast Asia into Japanese multinationals' global production networks. The Japanese influence on Southeast Asian business systems is spread through their local joint-venture partnerships with ethnic Chinese businesses and indigenous state-owned enterprises, and their growing relationships with local suppliers.

Ethnic Chinese Capitalists

Ethnic Chinese account for only a small proportion of Southeast Asia's population as a whole, but they dominate its private business sector (Wu and Wu 1980; Lim and Gosling 1983; Limlingan 1986; McVey 1992; Chan and Chiang 1994; Lim and Gosling *forthcoming*). Estimates typically have the Chinese accounting for roughly 4 percent of Indonesia's population but 75 percent of its modern private sector, with equivalent figures for the Philippines of 2 percent (40 percent), for Thailand of 10 percent (85 percent), and for Malaysia of 30 percent (65 percent).

This phenomenon has its roots in the pre-colonial and European colonial era, when trade-oriented immigrants from southeastern coastal China came to Southeast Asia. Here they were favored by both local rulers and European colonialists as tax-collectors and commercial intermediaries ("compradors") with indigenous peasant populations because, being a small immigrant minority, they did not constitute a political threat to their patrons. Their status as "outsiders", and their political vulnerability, also led the Chinese to cultivate relationships with those in power as a means of assuring political protection, accessing business opportunities in a controlled environment, and reducing risk.

Besides the sponsorship of local authorities, the Chinese had several other advantages over indigenous populations in entering into trading ventures. They were not subject to existing local cultural sanctions against trade, or indeed to any discouragement posed by the low status of the merchant in the Confucian social hierarchy in China itself. As migrants, they were not only arguably self-selected for risk-taking, ambition and entrepreneurialism, but also maintained

Southeast Asian Business Systems

international links with their home country and with fellow countrymen who had migrated to other countries in the region. These links facilitated trade. In their host countries, the Chinese immigrants were not tied to conservative established social orders, but were rather excluded from traditional modes of livelihood such as agriculture. Trade was thus often their only means of subsistence and upward mobility, and one which fit in with the migrant's short-term horizon and preference for liquid investments and quick returns. In addition, many of the early Chinese migrants to Southeast Asia had been traders at home and were motivated by trade to emigrate.

Chinese migrants set up clan, village, occupational, school, temple and other associational networks for mutual assistance in Southeast Asian host countries. These ethnic networks, which often had cross-national extensions, provided them with privileged access to scarce capital and information, and cheap loyal labor from within the Chinese community itself. This helped them to find business opportunities, assess and reduce risks, minimize transactions costs and ensure collective security to advance their business interests in economies with underdeveloped markets and institutions and imperfect information and price signals. Migrants also tended to save much of their income for repatriation to the mother country as well as for reinvestment in the host country.

After independence, Chinese communities in some Southeast Asian countries were subject to nationalist government policies which discriminated against them on the basis of race, in some cases reducing the scope of their business activities (Golay et al 1969). This reinforced the need to develop clientelistic relationships with politically powerful local patrons, who often included the military. The erection of trade and investment barriers by new nation-states in Southeast Asia, and the isolation of China after the communist revolution in 1949, further restricted the previously "borderless" reach of Chinese businesses in the region. Chinese communities lost their migrant or "sojourner" characteristics but not their minority status in their adopted lands. Even before this, permanent settlement had increased and with it, varying degrees of assimilation to indigenous Southeast Asian cultures.

With the assistance or at least tolerance of indigenous patrons and their communities, Chinese businesses took advantage of import-substituting policies (which otherwise hurt their import trade) to enter the industrial sector. This was sometimes done at the behest of national governments which wished to develop particular key industries and relied on their Chinese clients to take the risk and the initiative (e.g. steel and cement in Indonesia). In import-substituting industries, the external relationships that Chinese traders had with

61

LINDA Y.C. LIM

foreign suppliers helped provide the foreign joint venture capital, technology and expertise required in modern manufacturing for the domestic market. Chinese businesses themselves contributed some capital, local political connections, and market knowledge, and distribution networks.

Chinese businesses in Southeast Asia had long been involved in the export of primary commodities. But export manufacturing for industrial country markets in the West (since regional markets were themselves protected) required different skills and connections. These had been developed by Chinese in Hong Kong and Taiwan, who established themselves as subcontractors to, and original equipment manufacturers for, foreign buyers. They were the first to bring such labor-intensive export manufacturing to Southeast Asia in the 1970s, as foreign investors escaping third-country import quotas (as in textiles and garments), or chasing cheaper local labor and tax incentives. Some of them entered into partnerships with Southeast Asian Chinese, more because they were often the only local partners available, rather than because they were Chinese (for example, dialect-group differences existed between Chinese from Taiwan and Hong Kong, on the one hand, and those in Southeast Asia on the other, some of whom by now spoke little or no Chinese of any kind). Western and Japanese multinationals also invested in export manufacturing, but since 100 percent foreign ownership was allowed in this sector, they rarely took on local partners. However, they played a major role in developing local suppliers, who were overwhelmingly drawn from the ranks of Chinese entrepreneurs (Lim 1983; Lim and Pang 1982; Lee Tsao and Low 1990; Doner and Ramsay 1993).

Two developments since the late 1980s have increased the public profile of ethnic Chinese capitalists in Southeast Asia. The first is the increased presence of foreign Chinese investors from Taiwan, Hong Kong, and Singapore as shifting comparative advantage has caused them to relocate labor-intensive export manufacturing to the cheaper ASEAN countries. The second is the economic rise of China, which has attracted large investments from Chinese business domiciled in Southeast Asia. For example, the Sino-Thai Charoen Pokphand group of Thailand is considered to be the largest single foreign investor in China, and other cumulatively large investments in China have been made by the Salim, Lippo and other Chinese-Indonesian business groups, and by Chinese-Malaysian and Chinese-Filipino tycoons, as well as Singaporeans. These two developments have arguably led to a "re-Sinification" of otherwise partially-locally-assimilated Chinese business groups in Southeast Asia.

The "typical" Chinese business enterprise in Southeast Asia is a diversified family-owned conglomerate headed by the founder-patriarch or his immediate descendants. It is tempting to see ethnic cultural characteristics embedded in this enterprise form—particularly the Confucian family system and the inclination toward individual entrepreneurship resulting in the proliferation of autonomous business units. But it is at least equally likely that this form is dictated by environmental conditions—specifically the underdevelopment of markets and the consequential importance of relationships. These relationships then become the core competitive asset of the firm which is leveraged to provide new business that is likely to be in different sectors, given relatively small markets and rapid growth. The minority status of the Chinese, rather than their ethnic cultural characteristics (which are arguably "diluted" in the Southeast Asian context), may make relationships both within and outside the group more important to them. Similarly, the family nature of the enterprise and the use of family members to manage its different branches may simply reflect the youthful stage of enterprise development, the inadequacy of capital markets, the scarcity of skilled labor in fast-growing economies, and underdeveloped human resource management systems.

Indigenous Capitalists

My discussion here will refer only to indigenous capitalists in Malaysia and Indonesia. Thailand is excluded not only because of the overwhelming dominance of ethnic Chinese and Sino-Thai business at the medium- and large-scale enterprise levels, but also because Sino-Thai ethnic admixture makes separate identification of an indigenous capitalist class difficult.[4] In the case of the Philippines, most non-Chinese local capital is of Spanish-Chinese-mestizo, rather than indigenous Malay, origin (Yoshihara 1985).

In Malaysia and Indonesia, on the other hand, the development of bumiputra and pribumi business communities has been promoted by indigenous-dominated governments which, , for example, have given them privileged access to government contracts and credit allocations. Malaysia's New Economic Policy from 1970-1990 also included ethnic quotas favoring Malays in higher education, employment and equity ownership in larger companies, and provided scholarships to train Malays in business skills. State-owned enterprises were set up that were run by Malay managers, and subsequently privatized into the hands of privileged members of the Malay business elite. Some of these enterprises, particularly agribusiness plantations and mining companies, were taken over from foreign shareholders in "market nationalization" moves by the Malaysian government in the 1970s. The Malay ruling party UMNO has also been very active in business, generating further opportunities

LINDA Y.C. LIM

for its members. The result of these developments has been the rapid emergence of a class of Malay capitalists (Gomez 1994). Malay-Chinese joint business ventures are also evolving.

Access to higher education, especially in the pre-NEP era when it was dominated by non-Malays, has been a crucial element of the success of Malay, but not Chinese, business leaders in Malaysia. Political connections have been important to both groups, but for the Chinese these have often been connections with Chinese political leaders, who exist because of Malaysia's electoral democracy, its racially-based parties, and the large proportion (about one-third) of the electorate who are ethnic Chinese. Despite their common educational background, senior Malay business leaders are themselves a heterogeneous group. They include "products of the conservative boardroom" in publicly-listed diversified conglomerates like Sime Darby and Golden Hope, which retain a "Western organisational face" (*Far Eastern Economic Review* 3 March 1994: 48-52; *Asiaweek* 14 December 1994: 51); entrepreneurial managers of state-owned corporations like Petronas (*Asiaweek* 5 October 1994: 46-49); UMNO party members or supporters involved in party-based "money politics" ; politically well-connected private entrepreneurs (*Far Eastern Economic Review* 25 August 1994: 77-78); as well as other independent entrepreneurs who have made little if any use of political connections (*Far Eastern Economic Review* 1 December 1994: 72-76 and 6 October 1994: 77). Note that for this last group, even without explicit use of political connections, ethnicity as well as education has been an important asset in an environment where bumiputra partners or contractors are considered desirable if not officially required. Malays are also not the only non-Chinese local businessmen—there are also prominent Indian business leaders who, like the Chinese and Malays, may also make use of political connections. Probably the most prominent example here is spot oil trader and property developer, Ananda Krishnan.

Political connections are even more important to pribumi business in Indonesia, which has a less-developed, more heavily-regulated and less-transparent market economy than Malaysia, and is not an electoral democracy. Here the strategic alliance between Chinese conglomerates and members of President Suharto's immediate family as well as other individuals close to him has been oft noted as a source of monopolization of lucrative sectors of the Indonesian economy (*Far Eastern Economic Review* 30 April 1992: 54-58 and 25 August 1994: 47-49). Suharto himself has defended his children's involvement in business as both their individual right and a means of increasing pribumi participation in the otherwise Chinese-dominated private sector. More recently, some observers argue that

Suharto is beginning to distance himself from the Chinese, whose unpopularity is a political liability in a potentially liberalizing political environment (*Far Eastern Economic Review* 22 December 1994: 21). At the same time, non-Suharto-linked, non-Chinese-linked pribumi groups are on the ascendancy, and will provide more competition for the Chinese, particularly as economic liberalization proceeds. The most prominent of these is the Bakrie group (*Asiaweek*. 5 October 1994: 48-49; *Wall Street Journal*. 18 April 1994: A5A). Note that firms account for only five of the twenty-five largest conglomerates in the country, the rest being Chinese.

In terms of their structure and operations, indigenous Southeast Asian businesses greatly resemble the ethnic Chinese enterprises which operate in the same countries. They are family-based enterprises which rely heavily on personal relationships, including political connections, to access business opportunities. Using these relationships as their core competitive asset to attract foreign and local Chinese partners, they can thus access external sources of capital, technology, managerial and marketing expertise. As in the case of Chinese business, a diversified conglomerate enterprise form is the natural result.

The major differences are that indigenous Southeast Asian businesses are more likely to be directly involved in politics or state-owned enterprises, and to rely on education and previous occupational experience as secondary or even primary assets in launching and expanding their business ventures. Ethnic and village-based networks, while they exist, are probably less significant for the indigenous Southeast Asian capitalist than for the Chinese, and international connections are weaker. But the "minority" effect may be similar. Ethnic minorities have traditionally had an advantage in indigenous Southeast Asian trade (Foster 1974), and many pribumi businesses in Indonesia are drawn not from the majority Javanese community but from outer island minority groups, such as the Malay, the Bugis and the Minahasa. Further, since Chinese dominate the business community, indigenous enterprises operate as a minority within the private sector. This arguably encourages them to seek a competitive edge through privileged access to state resources, to form strategic alliances with the "majority" community and with foreigners to bolster their own position, and to network among themselves.

A Southeast Asian Business System?

The discussion in this paper has outlined several distinctive features of Southeast Asian business systems. They are located in

LINDA Y.C. LIM

underdeveloped economies, which encourages the development of private institutional mechanisms such as networks and relationships to access information and reduce costs and risks. Rapid economic growth additionally rewards opportunistic, risk-taking behavior, thereby encouraging an entrepreneurial mode of operation. This, together with the development of relationships as core competitive assets, leads to a conglomerate form of enterprise. The recentness of market economic development and the youthfulness of most firms in these economies also makes family enterprise the most common enterprise form. In addition, for historical reasons the state plays an important role in economic development as the major initiator and regulator of economic activity, and as a participant in such activity in its own right.

Thus far, there would seem to be little to distinguish business systems in Southeast Asia from those in Northeast Asia. Distinctiveness comes from the presence of an important natural resource and agricultural exporting sector, from long-established openness to international trade and foreign business participants, and from the dominant presence of an ethnic Chinese minority business community.

Control of the natural resources sector has arguably strengthened the economically interventionist role of the state. The Southeast Asian countries' long-established involvement in international trade and with foreign traders also began with the export of natural resources and agricultural products. Locally-domiciled ethnic Chinese played an important role in this trade as middlemen or agents of European colonial import-export houses. In the post-colonial period, many foreign-owned companies in the agricultural and mining sectors were taken over by the state, creating a base of Western-derived organizations run by indigenous bureaucrat-managers who themselves eventually formed the nucleus of an indigenous business class. New state-owned enterprises were also set up to develop newly discovered natural resources like oil and natural gas, and these have remained in state hands.

Western business organizations are prevalent in the modern manufacturing and services sectors too. Western organizational forms and business practices are disseminated through their hiring of mostly local employees, including managers, and their active development of local suppliers—both of which groups incubate local, particularly ethnic Chinese, business entrepreneurs. Japanese enterprises, on the other hand, have been frequently criticized for inadequate localization of both managers and suppliers. This, together with the lower turnover of local managers in Japanese subsidiaries, might be expected to limit the dissemination of Japanese business practices. But this effect is countered by the strong Japanese influence through numerous joint ventures with local partners, their position as the most important suppliers to industrial firms of all nationalities, and their increasingly proactive development of local suppliers (Doner, forthcoming).

Local ethnic Chinese enterprises are differentiated from those in Chinese-majority territories like Hong Kong, Taiwan, and Singapore by the specific nature of their relationships with the indigenous state, and with both Western and Japanese business organizations which supply them with technology and world market contacts. The Southeast Asian Chinese enterprises are arguably more likely to include both conglomerates and very large firms, and to be concentrated in trade, services, and property development, than in manufacturing on their own account without foreign joint venture partnerships. This is because they are less likely to develop internal firm competitive advantages based on technology or marketing assets, and more likely to rely on privileged external relationships. Since the numbers of ethnic Chinese are few, and many prefer to be entrepreneurs rather than employees,[5] Southeast Asian Chinese companies must employ many non-Chinese, who also form the bulk of their customers. Thus they need to develop ethnically-neutral business practices.

I have argued above that the differences between local Chinese and indigenous business enterprises in Southeast Asia are relatively minor and historically-specific. Rather, their considerable similarities are based on adaptations to similar environmental conditions, particularly the abundant opportunities for entrepreneurship, the utility of networks and relationships, and the natural evolution of family-based enterprise, in fast-growing underdeveloped but newly industrializing economies. Both groups also share a common need for state support or patronage as a response to government regulation and minority status. These politically-based relationships then become part of their competitive asset base and may be leveraged to access technology (e.g. from foreign partners) in many different sectors. This gives rise to the diversified conglomerate, which is also a means of economizing on scarce entrepreneurial and managerial skills.

Beyond shared economics and politics, it is also arguable that cultural differences between local Chinese and indigenous business enterprises are minimal, and much less than the differences that exist between Southeast Asian and Western cultural systems, (Deyo 1983; Ismail 1988; Abdullah 1992). Certainly the diversity of business cultures found in Southeast Asia, and their close interaction with each other over long periods of time, makes it difficult to argue that a single

LINDA Y.C. LIM

ethnic business culture dominates overall, though this may be the case in particular sectors of individual countries (e.g. indigenous state enterprise in petroleum in Malaysia and Indonesia). Rather, there is mutual adaptation by the various business actors, both to each other and, more fundamentally, to shared underlying economic and political conditions. This readiness to adapt to and include foreign and minority participants in the local business system has been characteristic of Southeast Asia throughout its long and very active trading history. It has certainly underlain the region's openness to foreign trade and investment, which has contributed substantially to its rapid economic growth, and may deliver a particular advantage in competing in the increasingly liberalized, diverse and "globalized" business world of the future.

Conclusion and Continuing Evolution

As described in this paper, Southeast Asian business systems are characterized by a diversity of business actors operating in rapidly-growing, underdeveloped, and politically-controlled market economies. Among local private—as distinct from foreign and state—enterprises, there is a preponderance of family firms which operate in an entrepreneurial and opportunistic mode, with many ending up as large diversified conglomerates. Closely linked to government and politics, these enterprises are heavily networked and dependent on personal relationships, which are maximized by extension to all ethnic groups and foreigners. Southeast Asian Chinese enterprises rely more heavily on ethnic and familial networks, while indigenous enterprises rely more heavily on education and the state. For both groups of firms, government and private sector connections comprise a key competitive asset that enables them to access information, capital, and specific business opportunities, and to reduce risks and transactions costs.

This business system is continuing to evolve in response to major changes that are under way in the Southeast Asian environment. In the economic arena, market liberalization policies since the 1980s are both increasing competition from new foreign and domestic entrants, and reducing the importance of government connections given deregulation and privatization. With economic development, market imperfections diminish and new legal and financial institutions become established, again reducing the need to resort to non-market institutions such as relationships and networks to access capital or guarantee contracts.

Southeast Asian Business Systems

  Some countries are also experiencing shifts in comparative advantage which, together with the emergence of newly hospitable investment locations in other developing countries, has reduced their international competitiveness in labor-intensive industry and agriculture. Labor scarcity makes retaining workers and increasing their productivity a matter of high priority. At the same time, new business opportunities elsewhere—e.g. in China, India, Vietnam and Myanmar—are enticing overseas investment by Southeast Asian companies. These developments make it necessary to compete on the basis of new firm competitive advantages—based, say, on technology, management, or marketing—that are transferable to different locations, which increases the value of alliances with foreign companies relative to local governments and ethnic networks.

  In the political arena, slow but steady movements toward more participatory democracy and institutions such as a free press and free labor organization also increase popular demands for greater transparency in business operations and reduce tolerance of close business-government relationships which are perceived as having anti-competitive, rent-seeking effects. As previously discussed, democratization is also likely to reduce the influence of the ethnic Chinese minority business community on government and politics.

  At the same time, the growing size and complexity of Southeast Asian enterprises increases their need for public sources of capital— e.g. through emerging local equity and bond markets, and participation in global financial markets—and professional management, both of which will lead to a loss of family ownership and control. Outside capital providers especially will demand more transparency in business practices and better management, just as family-based businesses face the challenge of succession from their founder-entrepreneurs to a new generation. Whether the new company leaders come from the ranks of family members or from unrelated professional managers, their ways of doing business are likely to differ from those of the founder-patriarchs. For both groups, and even for new-generation entrepreneurs, these ways are perhaps more likely to resemble those of the West due to the spread of Western managerial training and experience (*Far Eastern Economic Review* 17 November 1994: 78-86; *Asiaweek* 14 December 1994: 42-51; *Economist*. 23 Dec. 1995: 85-86). Education is likely to become a more important competitive asset to the firm.

  In short, the maturing of enterprises, economies, and political and legal systems is already initiating significant changes in Southeast Asian business systems. These changes may progress more rapidly here than in Northeast Asia, given that the established systems are less entrenched than they are in Japan and Korea.

LINDA Y.C. LIM

Change is likely to encounter both less resistance and fewer problems of transition, especially given continued rapid growth. The already high degree of market and foreign penetration of the Southeast Asian systems, their cultural diversity, the presence of many different cooperating and competing business actors, and the political weakness of the ethnic Chinese commercial minority, also weaken resistance to change.

At the same time, change is unlikely to occur overnight, or to be complete. First, except for Singapore, the Southeast Asian economies have a long way to go before they become "developed", thus the "old ways" of doing business will retain their utility for a long time to come. Second, the "old ways" will be maintained because of their continued usefulness in neighboring underdeveloped economies like China and Vietnam, in which Southeast Asian companies are increasingly involved. Third, indigenist policies are unlikely to be completely eliminated given concerns about business domination by the ethnic Chinese minority and/or foreigners, so market liberalization is unlikely to be complete.

Fourth, there is considerable utility in the "old ways" even in an advanced modern economy. For example, high-tech industry is characterized by rapid growth, the proliferation of multiple new opportunities, imperfect information, high risk and uncertainty, short product-cycles, and first-mover advantages rewarding speed to market. Trust based on long-term relationships can help in accessing information and patient capital, encouraging risk-taking, and permitting flexibility and speed in operations. The entrepreneurial mode of operation, conglomerate form of enterprise, and international strategic alliance so familiar in Southeast Asian business systems, all retain their utility under these circumstances. But high-tech industry of this type, already increasingly common in East Asia, particularly Taiwan, has yet to make its appearance in Southeast Asia outside of Singapore, where local ethnic engineer-entrepreneurs invented the computer sound-card and dominate the world market for it.

Endnotes

1. Southeast Asia consists of the six market economies of ASEAN-- Brunei, Indonesia, Malaysia, Philippines, Singapore and Thailand-- with a total population of 330 million, now joined by Vietnam's 70 million, and the three other reforming socialist economies of Myanmar (Burma), Cambodia and Laos, with a total population of another 50 million.

2. Southeast Asia has a greater relative abundance of labor than Northeast Asia and, unlike Northeast Asia, also has an abundance of land and natural resources. Capital has been readily available through domestic savings and foreign investment.

3. Apart from Singapore, which is 75 percent Chinese, their relative numbers are 2 percent in the Philippines, 4 percent in Indonesia, 10 percent in Thailand, and 30 percent in Malaysia.

4. The most prominent Thai company not founded and primarily owned by Sino-Thai capital is the Siam Cement group, which was established by the Thai government and whose main shareholder is the Thai royal family through its Crown Properties Bureau. For more on the relationship between Sino-Thai capital and the Thai state, see Hewison 1989.

5. This is a rational choice in fast-growing economies where new market opportunities are plentiful and competition often limited, and where upward mobility as an employee is limited either because monopoly of top management by family owners, or government-mandated ethnic quotas, impose a "glass ceiling" on the career advancement of ethnic Chinese employees..

References

Abdullah, Asma. 1992. "Influence of Ethnic Values at the Malaysian Workforce." *Understanding the Malaysian Workforce*. Kuala Lumpur: Malaysian Institute of Management. 2-17.

Bowie, Alsadair. 1991. *Crossing the Industrial Divide*. New York: Columbia University Press. Chan, Kwok-Bun and C. Chiang. 1994. *Stepping Out: The Making of Chinese Entrepreneurs*. Singapore: Simon and Schuster.

Deyo, Frederic C. 1983. "Chinese Management Practices and Work Commitment in Comparative Perspective" in L.A. Peter Gosling and Linda Y.C. Lim, eds., *The Chinese in Southeast Asia*. Vol. II. Singapore: Maruzen Asia. 215-230.

Dobson, Wendy. 1993. *Japan and East Asia: Trading and Investment Strategies*. Singapore: Institute for Southeast Asian Studies.

Doner, Richard F. 1993. "Japanese Foreign Investment and the Creation of a Pacific Asian Region" in Jeffrey A. Frankel and Miles Kahler, eds., *Regionalism and Rivalry: Japan and the United States in Pacific Asia*. Chicago: University of Chicago Press for the National Bureau of Economic Research. 159-216.

71

LINDA Y.C. LIM

Doner, Richard F. (forthcoming) "Japan in East Asia: Institutions and Regional Leadership" in Peter Katzenstein and Takahashi Shirashi, eds., *Japan in Asia*. Cornell University Press: Ithaca.

_____. and A. Ramsay. 1993. "Postimperialism and Development in Thailand." *World Development* 21 (5):691-704.

Foster, Brian L. 1974. "Ethnicity and Commerce." *American Ethnologist*. Vol. I, 3: 437-448.

Golay, Frank and R. Anspach, R. Pfanner and E. Ayal. 1969. *Underdevelopment and Economic Nationalism in Southeast Asia*. Ithaca: Cornell University Press.

Gomez, Edmund Terence. 1994. *Political Business: Corporate Involvement of Malaysian Political Parties*. Townsville, Australia: Centre for South-East Asian Studies, James Cook University of North Queensland.

Hewison, Kevin. 1989. *Bankers and Bureaucrats, Capital and the Role of the State in Thailand*. New Haven: Yale University Southeast Asia Studies Monograph Series 34.

Ismail, Nik A. Rashid. 1988. "Value Systems of Malay and Chinese Managers." *Economic Performance in Malaysia*. New York: Professors World Peace Academy. 95-109.

Jesudason, James V. 1989. *Ethnicity and the Economy: The State, Chinese Business, and Multinationals in Malaysia*. Singapore: Oxford University Press.

Jomo, K.S. ed. 1993. *Industrialising Malaysia*. London/New York: Routledge.

_____. ed. 1995. *Privatizing Malaysia: Rents, Rhetoric, Realities*. Boulder, Colorado: Westview Press.

Lee Tsao, Yuan. 1994. "Overseas Investment: Experience of Singapore Manufacturing Companies." Singapore: McGraw-Hill for the Institute for Policy Studies.

_____. and L. Low. 1990. *Local Entrepreneurship in Singapore, Private and State*. Singapore: Times Academic Press for the Institute of Policy Studies.

Lim, Linda Y.C. 1983. "Chinese Business, Multinationals and the State: Manufacturing for Export in Malaysia and Singapore" in Lim and Gosling. 245-274.

_____. 1994a. "Foreign Investment, the State and Industrial Policy in Singapore" in Howard Stein, ed., *Asian Industrialization and Africa*. New York: St. Martin's Press. 205-238.

_____. 1994b. "The Role of the Private Sector in ASEAN Regional Economic Cooperation" in Lynn Mytelka, ed., *South-South Cooperation in a Global Perspective*. Paris: OECD Development Centre. 125-168.

Southeast Asian Business Systems

Lim, Linda Y.C. (forthcoming, 1995a). "Models and Partners: Malaysia and Singapore in Vietnam's Economic Reforms" in Scott Christensen and Manuel Montes, ed., *Marketization in Southeast Asia*. Palo Alto: Stanford University Press for the East-West Center.

_____. (forthcoming, 1995b). "Southeast Asia: Success Through International Openness" in Barbara Stalling, ed., *The New International Context of Development*. Cambridge: Cambridge University Press.

_____. (forthcoming 1995c). "Technology Policy and Export Development: The Electronics Industry in Singapore and Malaysia" in Charles Cooper, ed., *Mobilizing Technological Capabilities in Developing Countries*. (MORE INFO)

_____. and Pang Eng Fong. 1982. "Vertical Linkages and Multinational Enterprises in Developing Countries." *World Development* .Vol. XX, 7. 582-595.

_____. and Pang Eng Fong. 1991. *Foreign Direct Investment and Industrialisation in Malaysia, Singapore, Taiwan and Thailand*. Paris: OECD Development Centre.

_____. and L.A. Peter Gosling, eds. 1983. *The Chinese in Southeast Asia*, Vol. 1, *Ethnicity and Economic Activity*. Singapore: Maruzen International.

_____. and L.A. Peter Gosling. (forthcoming) "Economic Growth, Liberalization and the Chinese in Southeast Asia" in Daniel Chirot and Anthony Reid, eds., *Entrepreneurial Minorities in East- Central Europe and Southeast Asia*. (MORE INFO?)

Limlingan, Victor Simpao. 1986. *The Overseas Chinese in ASEAN: Business Strategies and Management Practices*. Manila, Philippines: Vita Development Corp.

MacIntyre, Andrew. ed. 1994. *Business and Government in Industrialising Asia*. Australia: Allen and Unwin.

McVey, Ruth. ed. 1992. *Southeast Asian Capitalists*. Ithaca: Southeast Asia Program, Cornell University.

Phongpaichit, Pasuk. 1990. *The New Wave of Japanese Investment in ASEAN*. Singapore: Institute of Southeast Asian Studies.

Tokunaga, Shojiro. ed. 1992. *Japanese Foreign Investment and Asian Economic Interdependence*. Tokyo, Japan: University of Tokyo Press.

Wells, Louis T. 1993. "Mobile Exporters: New Foreign Investors in East Asia" in Kenneth A. Froot, ed., *Foreign Direct Investment*. Chicago: University of Chicago Press. 173-196.

Wu, Yuan-Li and C.H. Wu. 1980. *Economic Development in Southeast Asia, the Chinese Dimension*. Stanford, California: Hoover Institution Press.

LINDA Y.C. LIM

Yamashita, Shoichi. ed. 1991. *Transfer of Japanese Technology and Management to the ASEAN Countries.* Tokyo, Japan: University of Tokyo Press.

Yoshihara, Kunio. 1985. *Philippine Industrialization, Foreign and Domestic Capital.* Manila: Ateneo de Manila University Press.

Part II
Globalization, Change and Performance

[6]

The Convergence Hypothesis Revisited: Globalization but Still the Century of Nations?

ROBERT BOYER

NATION-STATES IN AN ERA OF GLOBALIZATION

The current wave of globalization has revived debates about the consequences of growing economic interdependence on the ability of national societies to preserve distinctive social, political, cultural, and economic organizations. Evidence seems to suggest that firms adopt similar technologies, that life-styles are homogenizing all over the industrialized world, and that the globalization and sophistication of financial markets are aligning national economies. Many predict that the national state will soon be obsolete and that government's room for maneuver will be limited. If lean production is destined to replace old Fordist mass production of standardized goods, then most social and economic organizations have to be redesigned to conform to the most efficient firms in each sector.

Thus convergence theory is back again, with a vengeance—the more so since the collapse of the Soviet economy. At the same time the Swedish economy, once seen as a "third way" between capitalism and socialism, is drastically reforming its social democratic institutions. So, too, the painful experience of the French socialist government suggests that the statist economies are losing direction and attractive power, as they are forced to conventional economic policies and to implement financial and political organizations more congruent with an integrated Europe.

This chapter starts from these trends but argues that they need not converge toward full and complete integration. Evidence from the

29

ROBERT BOYER

past and from the failure of past predictions of the end of national specificities should induce more caution. But even more important is the observation that few of the mechanisms that promote economic convergence are powerful enough to homogenize economic performances. Nor can we imagine the adoption of a single one best practice identical all over the world and applicable to any region or nation. Recent trends in the car industry underscore these general conclusions, as does investigation of the impact of Japanese transplants abroad. The threat of a Japanization of industrialized societies appears largely exaggerated. Indeed many of the mechanisms that translate external competition into the redesign of economic institutions have quite a different effect. Even when they try to copy strictly a supposed superior model, managers, workers, and governments finally produce a hybrid local management style and coordinating mechanisms. After a long period of trial and error, the end product usually differs widely from original intentions.

The argument proceeds along the following lines: First, ambiguities in the definition of convergence are spelled out by disentangling three distinct meanings: economic convergence, similarity in the style of development, and finally the characteristics of institutional settings that organize interactions between economy and polity. Second, when precise tests of the main macroeconomic variables are built, we see that no clear trend to convergence or divergence emerges. Third, even though the socialist bloc has collapsed, this has not reduced diversity. Rather it has revealed the coexistence and competition of various kinds of capitalism. The "regulation school" provides a taxonomy for the national trajectories since 1973 and even earlier, since World War II. No clear tendency to converge reappears.

CONVERGENCE: THREE DEFINITIONS

Productivity Levels and Standards of Living: Economic Convergence

According to the first definition of convergence, the globalization of finance, labor, technologies, and products proceeds so that each nation comes to resemble a small- or medium-size firm in an ocean of pure and perfect competition. Consequently, any Keynesian-style intervention is bound to fail, given that the competition is now international and foreign producers will capture the domestic market if local producers do not adjust to the costs and prices achieved by competitors. If the law of a single price for each commodity holds, then production costs would equalize all over the world. If knowledge about technology is a perfect public good, then Ricardian trade theory sug-

The Convergence Hypothesis Revisited

gests that productivity levels should converge under a free trade regime. Note that labor mobility via migration or capital mobility by
foreign investment is not necessary to arrive at such a result. Of
course, in contemporary capitalism, financial liberalization and a significant flow of migrant wórkers would augment the convergence
mechanisms associated with free trade in goods and services.

But no real economy exhibits the features required to deliver a general equilibrium under pure and perfect competition.[1] In a monetary
economy with imperfect competition, asymmetry in power and information, and increasing return to scale and public goods, the possible
and multiple equilibria are now closely related to the inner features of
the constitutional order, the system of incentives, and finally the configuration of organizations.[2] The argument is all the more relevant
for various national states and firms with unequal size and power,
which may struggle for and finally find niches, far away from the
abstraction of perfect competition on homogenized and standardized
goods.[3] Thus productivity levels across firms, sectors, regions, nations,
and continental zones might differ, even over the long run, without
any clear trend to convergence.

Democracy and Markets: Convergence in Development

For many social scientists, convergence has another meaning: not
pure economic performance, but the basic constitutional order, organizing interactions between polity and economy. In this tradition,
modern societies are characterized by the wide diffusion of markets,
which are supposed both to foster economic efficiency and to support
democratic order.

Convergence in this sense is to be demonstrated by the collapse of
authoritarian regimes and their replacement by more democratic con-
stitutions. Again, the basic issue concerns the generality of such a
trend and its significance. Although Chile, Brazil, Argentina, and
South Africa became more democratic, other moderately democratic
states became less democratic, as, for example, in the Islamic or African world. Moreover, democracy is a question of degree and not only
of nature. For example, there are useful distinctions between radical
developmental, legal, competitive elitist, and participatory democra-

[1] Robert Boyer, "Markets: History, Theory, and Policy," in R. Hollingsworth and
Robert Boyer, eds., *Contemporary Capitalism: The Embeddedness of Institutions* (Cambridge
University Press, forthcoming).
[2] D. North, *Institutions, Institutional Change, and Economic Performance* (New York: Cambridge University Press, 1990).
[3] J. Stopford, S. Strange, and J. S. Henlay, *Rival States, Rival Firms. Competition for
World Market Shares* (Cambridge: Cambridge University Press, 1991).

ROBERT BOYER

cies.[4] A more adequate definition of convergence would consider the precise configuration and interactions between political power and economic organization. There is no single connection between the implementation of democracy and the spread of markets and economic performances. The success of some NICs such as South Korea has been obtained by authoritarian regimes, not to speak of Chile under the Pinochet regime, Brazil during the miracle, or Mexico ruled by the PRI.

Moreover, the East European case, for example, produces not one but many configurations for democracy: the Polish system is not a variant of the Russian one, nor the Czech a copy of the Hungarian system. These differences in institutional setting seem to play some role in the pattern of economic reforms, that is, the transition toward a market economy.[5] Equally important markets are economic institutions based on explicit or implicit values, norms, and legislation. Depending on the rules of the game, the market for the same product or commodity functions quite differently.[6] Indeed from a theoretical point of view, the market mechanisms can be restricted to some products or extended to all of them. Even fictitious commodities such as futures and polluting rights can be traded in a formal market.

Thus, such a sweepingly broad conception of convergence groups under the same heading many configurations with very different implications for politics and efficiency.

Institutional Forms and "Regulation" Modes: A Third View of Convergence

The interactions of political and economic interests can have multiple configurations, depending on the balance between market and democracy and the mix between public regulations, associations, private and public hierarchies, and markets.[7] The "regulation" approach suggests that five major institutional forms combine to generate a series of dynamic patterns of adjustment.[8] For example, the mix between

[4] D. Held, *Models of Democracy* (Stanford: Stanford University Press, 1987).
[5] A. Clesse and R. Tokes, *The Economic and Social Imperatives of the Future Europe* (Baden-Baden: Nomos, 1992).
[6] C. Clague and G. C. Rausser, *The Emergence of Market Economies in Eastern Europe* (Cambridge: Blackwell, 1992).
[7] A. Przeworski, *Democracy and Market* (Cambridge: Cambridge University Press, 1991); R. Hollingsworth and Robert Boyer, *Contemporary Capitalism*; P. Di Maggio and W. Powell, eds., *The New Institutionalism in Organizational Analysis* (Chicago: University of Chicago Press, 1991).
[8] Robert Boyer, *The Regulation School: A Critical Introduction* (New York: Columbia University Press, 1990).

The Convergence Hypothesis Revisited

market mechanisms, collective agreements, and state regulation may vary widely in different product, labor, and credit markets. Various national economies would then converge if and only if their basic institutional forms were similar and responded in the same way to foreign competition, unexpected disturbances, as well as internal political conflicts and economy imbalances. Strong convergence would prevail when the mutual interaction of institutional design with market competition leads to similar performances and eventually to a convergence in productivity levels and living standards.

But the same economic performances, or at least long-run viability, can emerge from quite different institutional settings. Such a model of *mixed convergence* might prevail in countries involved in a free trade agreement (NAFTA, for example), with more or less tight financial and monetary integration, but without commitments to harmonization (as in the EC). There are other cases in which institutional inertia and pressures for coping with external competitiveness produce a relative or absolute decline in economic performances, as in Britain, a case of *partial divergence.*[9]

Yet another possibility exists. Core institutional forms and performances may not conform to the dominant development model. Strong divergence can in fact be observed at both ends of the spectrum of economic performances. Many poor African countries have distinct institutional configurations and are experiencing severe economic problems. The divergence of almost an entire continent is rarely mentioned by social scientists, although econometric studies find African countries quite distinct with significant dummy variables.[10] But such factors are a poor substitute for a deeper explanation of such long-lasting differences in institutional setting. At the other extreme, Asian NICs clearly exhibit genuine business systems and more state interventions, and they experience faster growth than old industrialized countries.[11] The conventional explanation is simple: these countries are catching up. This reason may account for dynamism, but it fails to analyze institutional patterns. The genuine strains and disequilibria affecting the Asian NICs and even Japan are another *indirect* evidence for durably distinct institutional and economic configurations. Quite intuitively—and of course this hypothesis is investi-

[9] B. Elbaum and W. Lazonick, eds., *The Decline of the British Economy* (Oxford: Clarendon, 1987).
[10] R. J. Barro, "Economic Growth in a Cross-Section of Countries," *Quarterly Journal of Economics*, May 1991: 407–43; J. Bradford deLong and L. Summers, "Equipment Investment and Economic Growth," *Quarterly Journal of Economics*, May 1991: 445–502.
[11] R. D. Whitley, *Business Systems in East Asia: Firms, Markets, and Societies* (London: Sage, 1992).

ROBERT BOYER

gated in this chapter—the world is far from exhibiting a strong convergence, when one considers the detailed and complex interactions between political and economic institutions.

ECONOMIC CONVERGENCE IN HISTORICAL PERSPECTIVE: AN AGNOSTIC VIEW

In the conventional view of convergence competition and emulation among alternative configurations lead simultaneously to homogeneity in institutional setting and common standards of living, or at least an absence of cumulative inequalities among countries. When, for example, former socialist countries implemented more or less ambitious plans for the transition to modern society, democracy, and markets, politicians and public opinion believed this would progressively deliver ways of life and productivity standards analogous to those prevailing within the Western economies. But is it true that capitalist democratic systems tend to converge toward the same macroeconomic variables? This expectation is neither unreasonable theoretically nor without empirical support, but the process of getting there is hardly automatic.

Contemporary Growth Theories: A Challenge to Convergence Hypotheses

The convergence and stability of the capitalist growth process is an old debate in political economy. Malthus and Marx conceived of industrialization as an uneven process: the cumulative growth of the most successful industries, regions, or nations was paid for by the collapse of more archaic skills, sectors, or communities. Ricardo in contrast imagined a smooth process of growth, finally leading to a stationary state with zero growth and no institutional or technological change. Any economy was bound to converge toward such an equilibrium because of the decreasing marginal returns associated with agriculture.

Modern growth theory exhibits an equivalent controversy, this time cast in a more rigorous and elegantly formalized framework. In the 1940s neo-Keynesian authors such as Harrod and Domar regarded the dynamic equilibrium of consumption and investment decisions as delivering a quite unstable macroeconomic path. Either the economy experienced explosive growth or it was trapped in a cumulative and self-defeating depression. But after the unprecedented growth of the postwar period neoclassical economists saw a more peaceful account

34

of the development process: if all the markets are competitive and if the same technology is available in each country, every economy would grow at the same rate—a growth imposed by technical change and corrected by demographic trends. Under these idealized conditions neoclassical theory provides a simple rationale for economic convergence in growth rates.

This framework has, however, been challenged by theorists dissatisfied with the assumption of automaticity in technical change, assumed to be independent of investment or policies to improve technological efficiency. If, for example, a country does not save and consequently underinvests, can it benefit from the same technological opportunities as a more innovative and virtuous country? Probably not, because learning by doing will be less efficient and the lack of domestic technological expertise may make it hard to capture advances in basic knowledge and technology.[12] Basically, for the new growth theorists, technological change is endogenous, that is, the equilibrium growth path depends on past efforts in research and development, education, and product differentiation.[13] Thus rates of productivity growth are likely to vary from one country to another, without unilinear global convergence.

Of course, if countries adopt similar educational and technological policies, they may end up on similar growth paths. Less wealthy countries, however, might be caught into an underdevelopment trap that prevents them from capturing the increasing returns to scale available, had they invested more in infrastructure, health, education, and research. This generalization of previous growth models exhibits the possible coexistence between fast-growth and low-growth countries, even in the long run. Thus some economies might follow the same pattern and catch up, whereas others are falling behind. Both convergence and divergence tendencies could be observed through time and space.

Convergence of Productivity among Major Industrial Countries after World War II

Empirical research on the convergence or divergence of performance indicators has been carried out by economists and economic historians[14] who constructed per capita GNP measures for the last cen-

---

[12] OECD, *Technology and Productivity: Challenge for Economic Policy* (Paris: OECD, 1991).
[13] For a comparison with previous theory, see P. Diamond, ed., *Growth, Productivity, Unemployment* (Cambridge: MIT Press, 1990).
[14] A. Maddison, *Dynamic Forces in Capitalist Development* (Oxford: Oxford University Press, 1991); M. Abramovitz, *Thinking about Growth* (Cambridge: Cambridge University

ROBERT BOYER

Figure 1-1. Widening disparities in productivity levels during the nineteenth century.

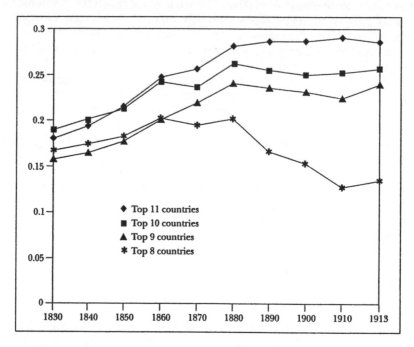

SOURCE: Data from P. Bairoch, "Europe's Gross National Product: 1800–1975," *Journal of European Economic History* 5 (1976): 286

tury. The findings are mixed: according to the period and the economy studied, sometimes they find convergence, sometimes divergence.

During the nineteenth century, productivity levels for a group of eleven advanced countries tended to diverge, especially from 1830 to 1880, which suggests the coexistence of different industrialization patterns (Figure 1-1). But when only the top eight countries are taken into account, productivity converges, particularly from 1880 to 1913. This point shows how dependent results are on the choice of countries and of periods.

After World War II economic performance indicators converged strongly, with the possible exception of the British economy (Figure

Press, 1989); W. J. Baumol, S. A. B. Blackman, and E. Wolff, *Productivity and American Leadership: The Long View* (Cambridge: MIT Press, 1989); P. Bairoch, "Europe's Gross National Product, 1800–1975," *Journal of European Economic History* 5 (1976): pp. 273–340.

The Convergence Hypothesis Revisited

Figure 1-2. A strong tendency to converge among developed countries from 1950 to 1980.

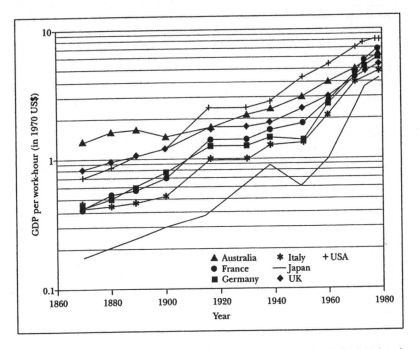

SOURCE: A. Maddison, *Phases of Capitalist Development* (Oxford: Oxford University Press, 1982), 212

1-2). In accordance with the predictions of the catch-up hypothesis,[15] more backward economies such as Japan and Italy grew faster than others between 1950 and 1980. These countries imported technologies and institutions from more advanced economies and in this way came to look more like their points of reference. The methodology of these studies has a significant bias: only currently successful industrialized countries are considered, thus convergence is partially tautological. More sophisticated analysis takes into account possible nonlinearities,[16] and the impact of innovation and educa-

---

[15] "The [catch-up] hypothesis asserts that being backward in level of productivity carries a *potential* for rapid advance. Stated more definitively the proposition is that in comparisons across countries the growth rates of productivity in any long period tend to be inversely related to the initial levels of productivity." M. Abramovitz, "Catching Up, Forging Ahead, and Falling Behind," *Journal of Economic History* 46 (1986): 386.

[16] Bart Verspagen, *Uneven Growth between Interdependent Economies* (Brookfield, Vt.: Avebury, 1993).

ROBERT BOYER

Figure 1-3. Other countries fall behind and thus diverge from developed and newly industrialized countries.

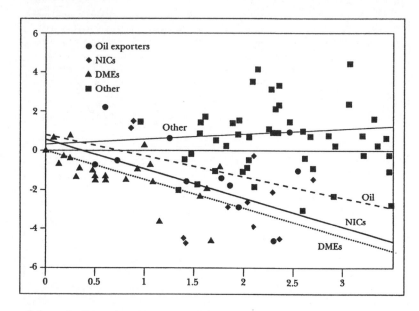

SOURCE: B. Verspagen, *Uneven Growth between Interdependent Economies* (Brookfield, Vt.: Avebury, 1993), 96–97. Reprinted with the permission of the publisher.
NOTE:
(G) is defined as the relative per capita income gap between any given country (i) and the United States. Mathematically, it is $\ln(Q_{USA}/Q_i)$ where Q_{USA} is the American per capita income and Q_i is the per capita income of country (i). Hence, negative movement in G indicates "catching up."
DMEs = Developed market economies
NICs = Newly industrialized countries
Oil exporters = Less developed oil-exporting countries
Other = Other (less developed) countries

tion[17] and examines a sample including both successful and under-developed or developing countries.[18]

The results of such efforts present quite a different picture. Over-all, the initial gap in productivity level is associated with slower rates of growth, which imply that the more advanced countries have experienced better performances than the poorer countries (Figure 1-3).

[17] B. Amable, "Catch-Up and Convergence: A Model of Cumulative Growth," *International Review of Applied Economics* 7, no. 1 (1993): 1–25.
[18] Barro, "Economic Growth"; R. J. Barro and X. Sala-I-Martin, "Convergence across States and Regions," *Brookings Papers in Economic Activity* 1 (1991): 107–82; DeLong and Summers, "Equipment Investment"; D. Cohen, *Tests of the "Convergence Hypothesis": A Critical Note* (Paris: CEPREMAP, 1992); D. Cohen, *Economic Growth and the Solow Model* (Paris: CEPREMAP, 1992).

The Convergence Hypothesis Revisited

Thus, between the early-1960s and the mid-1980s there was a widening gap between the top and bottom countries of the world, that is, diverging paths. Clearly backwardness creates a potential for faster growth, but only if adequate economic strategies and probably institutions allow such a potential to be activated by an effective development process.[19] This disparity might disappear if measures of the investment effort were taken into account, both in productive capital and in education. Unless they have invested in human capital in the previous period, less advanced countries do not appear able to catch up and move further and further away from the technological frontier of the most advanced.[20]

Convergence and Divergence

A long-term review of convergence indicators (Figure 1-4) shows that the spread among countries was rather constant from 1900 to 1930 but widened drastically during the 1930s. The significant reduction of productivity differences between countries is, therefore, a recent phenomenon, dating to the period 1950–80. The mid-1970s show a possible U-turn, with dispersion indicators once again slightly increasing. Verspagen[21] has examined and categorized the economic statistics of 114 countries during two periods: 1960–73 and 1973–88. From his work, three trends among the countries that are in a position to "catch up" (are relatively backward) emerge: very poor countries that have invested so little in manufacturing and/or in education that catch-up was impossible; countries that made moderate investments in manufacturing and education, resulting in some catching up; and countries that, because of significant investments, made significant strides in catching up. In the first period, examples of the very poor countries that were "falling behind" included Egypt and Mexico. In the "catching up" category were countries such as Jamaica and Finland; and in the "strongly catching up" category were Israel and Korea. In the second period, those who were falling behind included Rwanda and Argentina. A group of "newly catching up" countries emerged, which included Costa Rica and Iran. The third set were the "established catching up" countries, such as Greece and Poland, which continued their successes of the previous period.

Finally, a rapid review of the major statistical studies of perfor-

[19] Abramovitz, *Thinking about Growth.*

[20] Barro, "Economic Growth"; D. Cohen, "Tests"; D. Cohen, "Economic Growth"; G. Mankiw, D. Romer, and D. Weil, "A Contribution to the Empires of Economic Growth," *Quarterly Journal of Economics*, May 1992: 407–38.

[21] B. Verspagen, *Uneven Growth between Interdependent Economies* (Brookfield, Vt.: Avebury, 1993).

ROBERT BOYER

Figure 1-4. The eighties: A possible return to divergence?

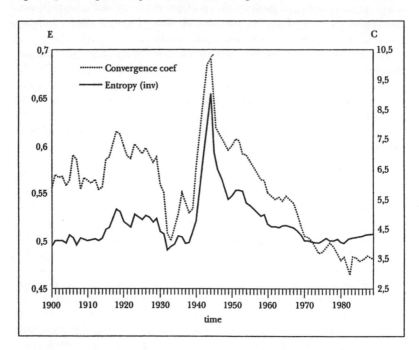

SOURCE: B. Verspagen, *Uneven Growth between Interdependent Economies* (Brookfield, Vt.: Avebury, 1993), 98–99. Reprinted with the permission of the publisher.

NOTE: The convergence coefficient (C) is the mean value across countries of the percentage deviation from the frontier (which is defined as the sample maximum of per capita GDP, which is equal to the USA value for most of the period). C is directly proportional to the degree of convergence.

The inverse of the Theil Entropy coefficient for GDP (E) indicates divergence. E is inversely proportional to the degree of divergence.

These statistics are for 16 industrialized nations.

mance across nations, summarized in Table 1-1, suggests the following conclusions, which refute both neoclassical optimism and the Marxist vision of uneven development and may reflect the character of international regimes or the features of dominant production systems.

Having the prerequisites, or *potential*, for catching up is not sufficient condition for actually growing as fast or faster than the leading country. Within the same international regime, depending on past legacies in infrastructure, health, education, and so forth, the actual strategies implemented by firms and government, a society may or may not benefit from relative backwardness.

We need to define social capability, for convergence is not mechanical and automatic, but results from deliberate attempts to copy and adapt technologies, organizations, and processes invented elsewhere. Consequently, some national institutions determine whether countries are among in the set of "catch-up" successes.

The convergence hypothesis can be confirmed for "the similar countries" in Baumol et al's sense.[22] When societies have the same development style and belong to the same economic area, then there is some strong probability that they will converge. The underlying speed of convergence has been estimated at around 2 percent, which means that it takes more than a quarter of century to reduce by half the initial productivity gap.[23]

But this does not mean that macroeconomic indicators are moving to complete convergence. The European Community shows the relevance of divergence, even as economies become more and more interdependent and exhibit similar productivity performances. When the Maastricht Treaty defined criteria for fiscal and monetary performance, the result was large speculative movements (Figure 1-7). Paradoxically, the objective of convergence triggered an opposite move toward divergence. The September 1992 and August 1993 financial crises ended with a quasi-collapse of the European Monetary System—one step backward in monetary integration. The convergence of industrial structures, productivity levels, and economic policy styles is a process far slower than ambitious monetary reforms. Complex interactions between economic convergence and institutional diversity and, conversely, an inadequate institutional harmonization may all induce economic divergence.

CONVERGENCE OF INSTITUTIONAL FORMS AFTER WORLD WAR II? THE PERSISTENCE OF NATIONAL SPECIFICITIES

It is possible to interpret the evidence on convergence in quite another way. For the "regulation" approaches, each epoch has a distinct institutional setting and a specific macrodynamics: long-run constancy of prices or cumulative inflation, moderate and unstable growth or stable and steadier growth.[24] Within this framework one can explain institutional convergence after 1950 as the product of the progressive

[22] Baumol, Blackman, and Wolff, *Productivity and American Leadership.*

[23] Mankiw et al., "A Contribution to the Empires of Economic Growth"; Barro, "Economic Growth."

[24] M. Aglietta, *Regulation and Crisis of Capitalism* (New York: Monthly Review Press, 1982); Robert Boyer, *The Search for Labour Market Flexibility* (Oxford, Clarendon, 1988); J. Mazier, M. Basle, and J. Vidal, *Quand les crises durent,* 2d ed. (Paris: Economica, 1993); A. Lipietz, *The Magic World from Value to Inflation* (London: Verso, 1985).

Table 1-1. Does productivity converge? A brief survey

Authors	Selection of countries	Periods	Convergence	Divergence	Comments
M. Abramovitz, "Catching Up, Forging Ahead, and Falling Behind," *Journal of Economic History* 46 (1986): 385–406.	16 industrialized countries	1870–1979	Coefficient of variation of productivity level has decreased	—	The potential for catching up requires social capacity to absorb more advanced technologies
W. Baumol, "Productivity Growth, Convergence and Welfare: What the Long-Run Data Show," *American Economic Review* 76 (1986): 1072–85.	16 industrialized countries	1870–1979	The growth rate is inversely related to initial levels	—	Presumption of convergence
J. Bradford Delong, "Productivity Growth, Convergence, and Welfare: Comment," *American Economic Review* 78 (1988): 1138–54.	22 "once-rich" countries based upon their status in 1870	1870–1979	No clear tendency	No clear tendency	Convergence might be limited to a small group of countries
W. Baumol, S. Blackman and E. Wolff, *Productivity and American Leadership: The Long View* (Cambridge: MIT Press, 1989).	1. Seven industrialized countries	1870–1979	Total factor productive coefficient of variation has declined	—	Convergence among a club of select countries
	2. Top 11 industrialized countries in 1870	1830–1913		GNP per capita coefficient of variation has increased	Divergence was associated with early industrialization
	3. 124 countries—no special selection noted	1965–80	Convergence among clubs of similar countries	Divergence for LDCs	Poor countries lack education and adequate social arrangements
N. Mankiw, D. Romer, and D. Weil, "A Contribution to the Empires of Economic Growth," *Quarterly Journal of Economics,* May 1992: 407–38.	98 non-oil-exporting countries	1960–85	Within OECD countries, catching up exists	Positive correlation between productivity levels and rates	Convergence is not general even for contemporary period

D. Cohen, *Tests of the Convergence Hypothesis: A Critical Note* (Paris: CEPREMAP, 1992).	100 countries	1960–85	Slow convergence but moving target		Convergence is a partial explanatory variable
J. Bradford Delong and L. Summers, "Equipment Investment and Economic Growth," *Quarterly Journal of Economics* 106 (1991): 445–502.	61 countries—no special selection noted	1960–85	Up to investment strategy	If too low investment	Investment is a privileged means for spurring growth
B. Verspagen, "A New Empirical Approach to Catching Up or Falling Behind," *Structural Change and Economic Dynamics* 2 (1991): 359–80.	114 countries—no special selection noted	1960–85	If the technological gap is small enough	If the initial gap is too large	Convergence is not general
B. Verspagen, *Uneven Growth between Interdependent Economies* (Brookfield, Vt.: Avebury, 1993).	114 countries—no special selection noted	1960–88	Only for developed and newly industrialized countries	For most African countries	Existence of a dividing line between catching up and falling behind
B. Amable, "Catch-Up and Convergence: A Model of Cumulative Growth," *International Review of Applied Economics* 7 (1993): 1–25.	59 countries—no special selection noted	1960–85	Only if sufficient investment in education	Divergence is possible and observed	Convergence is an oversimplification of limited relevance (some strategies, some countries)

ROBERT BOYER

diffusion of Fordism from America to Europe and Japan.[25] When a regulation regime enters into crisis, it would, then, trigger a period of institutional flux and experimentation that might for some time at least produce the impression of divergent development.

The Fordist Era of Economic Convergence

The impressive growth after 1950 among developed countries (see Figure 1-2) reflected not only acceleration and catch-up after interwar stagnation and wartime destruction but also the workings of a genuine development pattern, the core of which lies in capital and labor institutions. Large industrial firms advanced the division of labor with wide use of specialized equipment along with a standardization of mass-produced goods. A "social pact" linked workers and managers. The former accepted managerial authority and an unprecedented division of labor; the latter agreed to increase wages based on prices and productivity. This compromise was elaborated in a dense web of interdependent institutions: welfare, collective bargaining, accommodating monetary policy, investment or intervention by the state in education, health, and transport.

The Bretton Woods system and the Marshall Plan created a facilitating international regime and an incentive for European countries and Japan to follow the American track of mass production and consumption. Contrary to the initial expectations that the reconstruction would end with stagnation and unstability, all these transformations in the relationships between states and markets sustained a genuine growth regime and development mode. Overall, most OECD countries moved along the same path. At first, the American way of producing and living served as a model. Managers, civil servants, unionists, and politicians visited the United States to observe Fordism at work. The common model, as well as the common challenge of how to launch mass production after war destruction and limited financial resources, may have induced homogenization in the political and social structures inherited from the past.

This may explain the unprecedented convergence across nations and among regions within the same national economy.[26] Considered in isolation, neither technological change and organizational innovation, nor the conceptual revolution of Keynesianism would have been sufficient to propel such a drastic shift in "regulation" mechanisms. The rather miraculous mix of pax Americana, credit, Fordist capital

---

[25] J. Mistral, "Régime international et trajectoires nationales," in Robert Boyer, ed., *Capitalismes fin de siècle* (Paris: PUF, 1986).
[26] Barro and Sala-I-Martin, "Convergence across States and Regions."

44

The Convergence Hypothesis Revisited

and labor compromise, oligopolistic competition, and structural and cyclical state interventions together created the Fordist growth regime.

Different countries embedded the Fordist system in different institutional constellations. The monetary regime is not the same in Germany and in France because of the role of the central state. Antitrust laws like those in the United States have no equivalent in Germany or in Japan, which has a more explicit system of oligopolistic competition. As a result, the macrodynamics of credit and interest rates, price formation, and profit and investment differ across major OECD countries. The same external shocks (oil prices, interest rates, or the uncertainties at the end of the Gulf War) do not produce the same sectoral adjustments or the same macroeconomic pattern.

Persisting national specificities in basic institutional forms are rather easy to see in the capital–labor relation. France and the United States follow a rather typical Fordist path, with strong separation between conception and production tasks, quite adversarial industrial relations, and indexation of nominal wages to past inflation and expected productivity increases. Austria and Sweden accommodate Fordist methods within a highly developed social democratic state that orchestrates labor mobility, active employment policies, and large training and retraining efforts. Industrial relations are very centralized, and consequently wage bargaining shows great sensitivity to external competitiveness and unemployment. West Germany and Japan mix the Fordist principles with a long tradition of highly skilled labor and competition via quality and differentiation, and they accompany mass production with larger product differentiation. Japan shows how an imported model of technology and industrial organization are gradually incorporated and transformed. After several decades of a continuous adjustment to local conditions, the industrial relations, and the productive system, an original "regulation" mode emerged. The imperfect Fordism of the 1950s transformed itself into a flex-Fordism in the 1970s and finally into "Toyotaism," with its distinctive capital–labor relations, job tenure, continuous learning by doing, bonus payment, and a strong segmentation of labor markets.[27] Germany, too, has distinctive patterns. Its rich institutional setting enhanced quality and skills different both from those found in U.S. Fordism and Toyotaism. The United Kingdom has followed still another trajectory. Given an early industrialization and stratification of industrial relations along skills, local bargaining, and a highly conflictual bargaining

---

[27] Robert Boyer, "Rapport salarial et régime d'accumulation au Japon: Émergence, originalités et prospective: Premiers jalons," *Mondes en développement* 20, no. 79/80 (1992): 1–28; and B. Coriat, *Penser à l'envers* (Paris: Bourgeois, 1991).

ROBERT BOYER

process, the introduction of mass production of standardized products has always been difficult.

To summarize, the mesh between political and social interests on one side and economic strategies on the other makes the capital–labor relations, and by extension most other institutional forms, very dependent on localized interactions. Such institutions change mainly by marginal adaptations of the repertoire of existing coordinating mechanisms. For instance, both France and the United States exhibit a strong Fordist inertia precisely because both societies have developed an extensive set of institutions (credit markets, education system, labor laws, and so forth) designed for mass production of standardized goods.

CONVERGENCE THEORY REVISITED

Mechanisms to Best Practice Convergence

What are the mechanisms through which convergence to "best practice" might emerge? We identify several. First, even isolated social and economic systems might converge toward the same organization if they find, by chance or necessity, the same solution to common internal problems. For example, mass production systems need particular kinds of transportation, technical training, the nature of innovation, and even state intervention. In other words, facing the same problems and opportunities, national economies could finally find the same steady state and institutional arrangements after trial-and-error experimentation, even in the absence of external competition.

Other mechanisms depend on the diffusion of science, technology, and institutional "best practices." If technological determinism prevailed, every firm would tend to adopt the same industrial organization and benefit from identical productivity levels. Managers as well as governments might try to imitate best practices in institutional and organizational innovations. International consulting firms or international bodies may diffuse the same business principles and economic policies across national borders. Scientific management, for example, spread in that way, as did the U.S. mass production after World War II, quite independently of any direct pressure from product or factor competition.

Finally, other mechanisms are initiated by transnational corporations or multinational authorities who define and enforce rules of the game within a given international regime. Such mechanisms of convergence do not rely on anonymous forms of market competition but are power relations, whether they are based on economic resources (transnational corporations) or mainly political (multinational authorities)—for instance the GATT or bilateral agreements such as the Structural Impediment Initiative (SII) between Japan and the United States. These two mechanisms are not equivalent: transnational corporations usually export their best practices and thus promote a convergence toward higher efficiency. International agreements may, on the contrary, impose an economic order favorable to the leading partner and in some cases restrict efficiency.

Evaluation of Best Practice Convergence Mechanisms

In a sense none of these mechanisms are self-implementing, and they have uncertain and varied effects according to the historical context and the precise configuration of market competition, technology innovation, the degree and nature of internationalization, or the nature of national problems and the ability to diffuse new ideas, property rights, and innovations. A brief comparison of the evolution of old industrialized countries after World War II reveals the relative frequency and intensity of the seven convergence mechanisms (see Table 1-2).

Evidence suggests that until the 1970s convergence proceeded slowly, with many reverses and with many examples of divergence. But some argue that the new constraints and opportunities provided by globalization trends are accelerating convergence. Globalization of the international economy is the first premise, the argument going that financial deregulation and innovation have destroyed the national borders for credit and that firms, at least the larger ones, have equal access to finance. Similarly, modern technologies are so complex and so capital intensive, that only transnational partnerships are able to monitor innovations. The product markets themselves, which used to be segmented according to national borders, are assumed to become more and more global. The limiting case would be of a totally transnational economy without any residual disparities across countries.

The second hypothesis builds on the first one and assumes that costs and prices will tend toward the same equilibrium level once transportation costs and exchange are taken into account. Firms would be literally squeezed by the pure and perfect competition operating on both product and factor markets.

The third hypothesis is that everywhere firms facing the same optimizing problems find the same solution in terms of technology, markets, and products, for there is one best way of organizing production—a single optimum among a possible multiplicity of local optima.

47

Table 1-2. The relative frequency and intensity of convergence mechanisms after World War II

Mechanisms	Type of mechanisms	Mode of transmission	Frequency	Intensity	Impact upon the initial gap
1. Internal common trends	Facing the same constraints and problems, each unit follows the same path	Cognitivist and immaterial	Rather high	Variable across countries	Does not imply convergence but a succession of common stages[a]
2. International competition on Products	Creative destruction	External trade	Increasing	Uneven across sectors	May imply destruction of obsolete institutional forms not necessarily their convergence
Labor	Impact on wage and technical change	Immigration	Low or moderate	Quite indirect effect	Not clear: both convergence and divergence
Finance	Impact on investment	International markets	Rising with deregulation	Possibly strong	May help to converge but from a limited range of countries
3. Globalization of technology	Organizations would follow technical change	Either public knowledge or private appropriation by firms	Significant and increasing	Varies across sectors	Convergence if public knowledge. Divergence if private appropriability

4. Imitation of best practices	Learning by copying	Personal contacts, technical literature	Rather frequent, but sometimes difficult	Growing through time	Should narrow the gap; if social capabilities exist to absorb more advanced technologies[b]
5. Power of ideas Thinkers of the past	Convincing decision makers	Cognitivist and immaterial	Significant discontinuities	Could be more important than is usually considered	Possibly important for economic policy,[c] more problematic for productive system
Experts	Paying for institutional redesign				
6. Transnational corporation	Exploitation of national disparities	Direct foreign investment, trade, and technology	Few but powerful	From enclaves to embryo for institutional redesign	Help to converge if favorable initial conditions, widen gap in others
7. Harmonization by multinational authorities	Negotiation and then coercion	Political and legal apparatus	Rather low, because of intrinsic difficulties	Potentially strong if limited scope and/or duration	Theoretically helps to institutionalize convergence at the possible cost of economic convergence

[a] W. Rostow, *The Stages of Economic Growth: A Non-Communist Manifesto* (Cambridge: Cambridge University Press, 1960).
[b] M. Abramovitz, "Catching Up, Forging Ahead, and Falling Behind," *Journal of Economic History* 46 (1986): 385–406.
[c] P. Hall, *Political Power of Economic Ideas: Keynesianism across Nations* (Princeton: Princeton University Press, 1989).

ROBERT BOYER

If this is observed for each product and sector, the best organizational forms would finally prevail whatever the localization and by aggregation, the macroeconomic evolutions would tend toward the convergence of productivity and of standard of living levels.

This syllogism that equates globalization with convergence is logically flawed, and its premises may not correspond to the current state of the world economy. Given the same stylized facts, a totally different conclusion can be reached. Internationalization and globalization are hardly complete. Even if interest rates are synchronized internationally, relative levels depend on the national styles in monetary policy and the adjustment of savings and investment. National saving rates and investment rates are still strongly correlated, which implies the importance of national boundaries. Similarly, labor mobility has not equalized wages by skills. Wage levels and hierarchies are still shaped by national institutional forms, skill formation, and social values. Thus, the choice in organization and technologies will continue to depend on national legacies.

The second hypothesis about the competition in product markets is not usually fulfilled: the same product may be sold for different prices in every national market, according to the local conditions for competition. For instance, in the car industry the same product exhibits impressive price disparities with the structural competitiveness of local producers: low and competitive prices in small countries without any national car maker, higher and oligopolistic prices if the domestic producers are lagging with respect to leading producers. Competition remains largely imperfect and firms still search out niches, thus introducing possible differentiation even if production and trade are more and more international. The second pillar of convergence theory is therefore shaky: each niche may call for specific organizational forms and deliver unequal productivity levels.

The third hypothesis can be challenged, too. Technology is not a private commodity or a pure public good, so its efficient use assumes tacit knowledge or learning effects. Thus, the one best way is not necessarily available to all producers because only the leading ones, who possess sufficient past experience, can benefit from the best practices. When imperfect competition on product markets is combined with tacit knowledge for technologies, then several productive configurations may coexist even over the long run. Some simple models in industrial analysis confirm such a possibility.[28] It may be that the actual state of the international system is closer to a series of national oligopolistic markets than to a unified world market.

[28] H. C. White, "Where Do Markets Come From?," *American Journal of Sociology* 87, no. 3 (1981): 517–47.

The Convergence Hypothesis Revisited

The same argument can be made more general by using evolutionary theory. Conventionally, competition is supposed to drive out of business the more archaic and inefficient firms, whereas the most successful innovations are imitated by a cohort of followers who finally converge toward the one best way. Empirical studies of the dynamics of industrial organization do not confirm this hypothesis, as contrasted firm organizations, technologies, and capital–labor relations usually coexist within the same precisely defined sector, even in the long run. Recent advances in the modeling of evolutionary process have delivered configurations with punctuated equilibria, such as the long-run coexistence of various species for biology: various norms and organizations for social sciences. More than one solution can be given to the same problem, a feature quite common in the history of technologies and frequently observed for economic organizations. For example, consider the alternatives to Fordism. The emerging principles, such as mass production of differentiated and high-quality goods, call for a richer skill spectrum than standardized production. But given the embeddedness of education and training in each national culture, international comparisons suggest the existence of at least three distinct national models of skill formation. (See Chapter 5 in this volume.) The German occupational model emphasizes broad skills for each employee, with overlapping technical competences. In the Japanese large firms the skills are generated by internal mobility among various tasks within the firms and are largely specific to each large company. In the United States an emerging model is building skills around teamwork, but the rotation of workers is less significant than in the Japanese model and the incentives are quite different.

In both cases the firms and sectors are clearly integrated within the international economy and, nevertheless, display very different institutional forms to cope with the same challenge of structural competitiveness. Even if the economic performances are quite similar, there is no one best way. Furthermore, evolutionary approaches remind us that the success is not warranted and that failure, such as relative decline or bankruptcy, are other possibilities for coping with competitiveness. Therefore, the convergence within the club of the surviving happy few is paid by the cost of destruction of inadequate institutional forms—in other words, a kind of diverging pattern.

International Specialization and the Persistence of National Styles in Institution Building

International trade theory usually concludes that factor incomes will converge as soon as products are freely exchanged internationally. But this does not imply that the same institutional arrange-

ROBERT BOYER

Figure 1-5. National institutional diversity

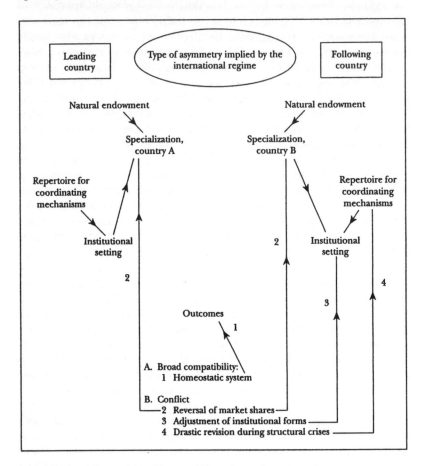

ments will be observed across countries, quite to the contrary. Imagine, for example, that a leading country is facing a follower that initially exhibits a different specialization (Figure 1-5). Basically, each country is selecting its specialization by the interaction of natural endowment, the repertoire of coordinating mechanisms, and the compatibility with the competition implied by the international regime. The architecture may display four configurations.

The first one is homeostatic equilibrium, an approximate long-run stability in specialization, industrial structures, and the nature of coordinating mechanisms. This homeostatic system does not depend on factors central to convergence. Each OECD country may, for exam-

The Convergence Hypothesis Revisited

ple, specialize in sectors that are the more efficiently run by the pre-vailing institutional setting. The Japanese economy might specialize in consumer goods (electronics and cars); the United States in software, information, and basic science; the British in chemicals and pharmaceuticals; the German in high-quality equipment goods. In each case the countries are using at their best the coordination gains typical of their national repertoire: the large firm and its subcontractors in Japan, the excellence of university research for the United States and the United Kingdom, the richness and quality of skills for Germany. In this punctuated equilibrium convergence would be the exception, not the rule.

The second configuration, the reversal of market shares, that is, shrinking for the less efficient countries and growth for the leading ones, is another mechanism in which a series of natural endowments and constructed competitive advantages are linked to the opportunities and constraints of the prevailing institutional setting. For instance, the contemporary evolution of market shares for the car industries and consumer electronics between the United States, Japan, and Asian NICs seems to fit with this mechanism. The diversity of institutions is preserved, but the relative efficiency of national economies is continuously adjusted.

But firms, business associations, or governments may react if the current economic trends hurt the welfare of the community by reducing production, employment, and/or living standards. They may try to build new institutions, to mix the various ingredients extracted from the national repertoire of coordinating mechanisms. For instance, given the weaknesses of private entrepreneurship in France, state agencies may promote special R&D programs to promote technological innovation. The Direction Générale des Télécommunications that initiated Minitel, a home-based computer network, would thus be the functional equivalent of the American Silicon Valley start-ups. Similarly, in the 1980s the British government widely opened the car and electronics industries to Japanese transplants in order to try to build a new industrial configuration, strengthening some key features of British evolutions (the search for regional autonomy), weakening others (closed shop unionization).

A third exception to convergence theory, adjustment of institutional forms, relates to the impact of European integration. The countries that traditionally had strong regional economies and political organizations have converted this inherited advantage into a new bargaining power at Brussels via clever lobbying about the use of European structural funds. The new emerging productive model gives a new opportunity to regional economies. Old norms and social values

53

ROBERT BOYER

are manufactured again into new institutional forms and sources for external competitiveness.

The fourth configuration, drastic revisions during structural crises, is quite exceptional, indeed, because it emerges when all the previous adjustment processes by market shares and the redesign of institutional forms fail. Adverse economic trends and acute social or political crises usually trigger the search for more drastic reforms in order to expand the scope and variety of coordinating mechanisms that would cope with external competitiveness and maintain a minimal social cohesiveness within the given community. "Régulation" approaches label these episodes structural crises, when the issue at stake is the redesign of institutional forms and the "regulation" modes. An example is the great depression at the end of the last century and during the interwar. The trial-and-error process, by nature quite uncertain, is very different from the smooth convergence toward a well-known growth regime. During the 1990s, the major political crisis in Italy gives a good example of a tentative complete redesign in institutional forms in order to cope with the challenge of European integration. To conclude, it is clear that the convergence hypothesis is quite challenged by these approaches.

Two Visions in Institution Building: Implications of Convergence

The issue is far more general than focused on just economic or institutional convergence and relates to alternative visions for the logic, origins, functioning, and evolution of institutions. For neoclassical theorists rational economic agents try to design optimal coordinating mechanisms (i.e., efficiency preserving or welfare enhancing). These mechanisms may result from bargaining, minimizing transaction costs, or designing by a principal of an incomplete contract to monitor a subordinate agent. Decentralized innovations prove their viability by competing efficiently on product and factor markets. If the coordinating mechanism is Pareto efficient, all other agents will have interest in adopting it; on the contrary, the agents sticking to the old mechanisms will grow slower and eventually be driven out of business. Thus, the emergence, diffusion, and maturation of institutions are the intended or unintended outcome of competition between alternative institutions.

As a consequence, the convergence toward the "best" institution is generally warranted, provided that sufficient freedom is given to economic agents and that competition prevails. Hence, according to a quite optimistic vision of how economic arrangements are reformed

The Convergence Hypothesis Revisited

and transformed, a smooth process in the evolution of institutions takes place. But however intuitive and appealing, this approach is not devoid of major flaws.

First, a unique equilibrium is not warranted: the multiplicity of equilibria in an institutionally rich economy is the rule, not the exception. Every economy can be stuck into a specific local equilibrium, without any clear mechanism for convergence, unless strong institutional mimetism prevails. Second, the transition toward a superior institution can be blocked by all the sunk costs associated with the old institutions. Even in the simplest coordination game, this pathology is quite common and the problems are still worse when agents have conflicting interests. Third, neoclassical theory assumes a quasi-divisibility of microinstitutions, which can be added in order to design a complete architecture. This divisibility principle is severely challenged by recent advances in comparative analyses: a monetary regime has to be coherent with an international system, a form of competition, and eventually a capital–labor compromise. Partners in the current discussions about a European central bank modeled on the Bundesbank recognize this social coherence: without many other closely related institutions present in the German system independence is not an insurance against inflation. Moreover, efficiency is not the key objective of many social institutions: defining the respective power and role of factors, stabilizing actors' expectations, and organizing social interactions come first. Market and system competition takes place afterward—and after assessing the relative efficiency of a complete architecture of generally interdependent institutions.

All these criticisms may be the starting point of an alternative vision. First, the economic rationale of institutions cannot be isolated from political and social contexts: the rationality of *homo oeconomicus* describes only a limited, even if increasing, fraction of human behavior. Thus the analysis has to delineate the domain in which actors interact, to provide a full description of their objectives and constraints, without an a priori restriction to either pure economic factors or political ones. Note that this extension of conventional rational choice theory strengthens the specificity of each problem and makes rationality context dependent. Thus institutional convergence is less likely, because many idiosyncratic complementarities permeate the whole system.

A second difference relates to the origins of institutions. Institutions are not designed uniquely to solve an efficiency problem or fulfill social objectives, but in most cases they are the unintended consequences of the pursuit of strategic advantage by unequal agents.

ROBERT BOYER

Figure 1-6. Convergence or divergence of institutional forms?

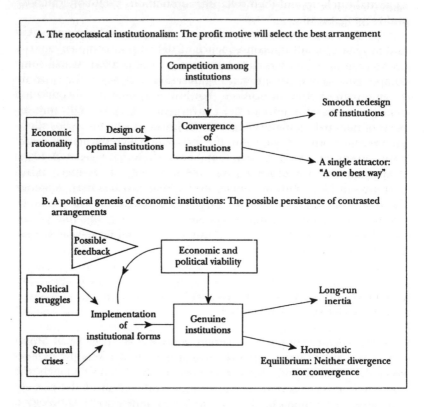

Consequently the asymmetry of power has definite consequences on the design of institutions, which only rarely enhance efficiency.[29] Thus political struggles and/or structural crises usually play a role in the invention, implementation, and the legitimation of institutional forms: this is not an accident but the very outcome of the power relations implied by any institution, in any sphere, political as well as economical (Figure 1-6).

The medium or long-run inertia of institutions is not an oddity or exception to rationality and efficiency, but it expresses the very nature of social relationships and rules of the game. Moreover, and more generally, the concept of homeostatic equilibrium describes this compatibility of an institutional architecture and the economic dynamics it generates. In such an evolutionary model, convergence or divergence

[29] J. Knight, *Institutions and Social Conflict* (Cambridge: Cambridge University Press, 1992).

The Convergence Hypothesis Revisited

are only specific cases among a large variety of other evolutions, such as partial catch-up and then collapse, autonomous evolution, catch-up and forging ahead.

Therefore convergence is not the natural "outcome" of a quite general mechanism, but the consequence of the ex post complementarity of mechanisms with unintended properties. The convergence of some components of an institutional organization may strengthen the diverging path of other institutions. For instance, financial liberalization does not necessarily lead to the convergence of more and more aspects of national regulatory regimes. In Japan during the 1980s allowing the large firms to enter into the international credit market might have produced extra profits that could then have been used to strengthen both the efficiency and the specificity of Japanese industrial organization. But, of course, in the long run this may challenge the inner stability of the large Japanese corporation. For example, because of the interlocking of corporate assets and the role of the main bank, a complete financial liberalization could destabilize the job tenure that used to prevail.[30]

PARADOXES OF CONVERGENCE THEORY: STILL THE CENTURY OF NATIONS?

Much evidence supports convergence theory: the collapse of Soviet economic regimes and the switch of their elites to markets and democracy; the erosion and structural crisis of the Swedish model; the aborted French experience of a socialist strategy out of the current crisis; the surge of Asian dragons and their impressive technological achievements; the ambition of the Maastricht Treaty to promote a fast track to real convergence via monetary integration.

But statistical evidence does not confirm any general and secular trend toward economic convergence in productivity levels and standards of living. Such convergence is restricted to the small club of nations that have been able to invest sufficiently in productive investment, infrastructure, and education. The poorest countries (for example, in Africa) have been left out of the process of economic development. Even within developed or rich countries, the long-run evolutions of Great Britain and Argentina remind us that relative or absolute decline is always a possibility and that convergence is never automatic but is associated with the choice and implementation of an

[30] M. Aoki, "Decentralization-Centralization in Japanese Organization: A Duality Principle," in S. Kumon and H. Rosovsky, eds., *The Political Economy of Japan*, vol. 3 (Stanford: Stanford University Press, 1992).

ROBERT BOYER

adequate strategy, given a changing international regime and radical changes in technological innovation.

Such conflicting views and this opposition between naive and academic representations deserve explanation. First, the idea of a single, one best way is very intuitive indeed and seems to fit with textbook neoclassical theory: if all technologies could be mastered without any cost, if institutions were totally divisible and their choice independent one from another, then economic convergence would be the rule. Note, nevertheless, that very different institutional arrangement can be imagined to solve the same economic challenge. This is precisely the strong advantage of an alternative vision. For evolutionary theory globalization is far from complete, and consequently each national economy is facing a specific system of industrial relations, money and credit, education training, and state intervention. Still more firms do not adapt passively to a given price system, but they try to discover niches more or less insulated by oligopolistic competition.

Within such a vision there may exist a multiplicity of punctuated equilibria as opposed to a single one. The simple dynamics of convergence is only one out of many other evolutions: cumulative divergence, catch-up and collapse, catch-up and then forging ahead, partial convergence and then stabilization of the productivity gap. So, the simplicity, however largely erroneous, of convergence theory is usually preferred to the complexity of evolutionary models, which nevertheless are richer and fit better with empirical evidence about long-run capitalist growth and the coexistence of contrasted national trajectories.

How to explain common belief in convergence theory? In fact, the model that is thought to be the reference point of convergence changes, either periodically or during critical episodes. In the 1990s interest in convergence theory has re-emerged precisely because the Japanese productive system and "regulation" mode are viewed as an alternative to the previous model, the American mass-production system. During such a period, because no natural law is driving convergence, the very model held up as an object of emulation and imitation is usually chosen through a political process, not only by following the evolution of the market. Which model is chosen has an important impact on the probability of convergence. If nowadays so many firms and governments want to imitate and adopt the so-called Japanese methods, this is less a proof for an invisible convergence and a Japanization of the world than an evidence of a drastic change in the model to be emulated. This triggers a process of trials and errors that may end up in a consolidation of past national trajectories.

Growth patterns after World War II may seem more favorable to

58

The Convergence Hypothesis Revisited

the convergence thesis but do not contradict this broad interpretation. Even if internationalization is now more extended, there is no strong reason to believe that the national flavor for institution building will vanish and be replaced by the diffusion of Japanese methods. Even managers translate some of Toyota's productive methods, but who would dare to transpose all the idiosyncrasies of the Japanese society?

The 1990s and the next century, too, are likely to be still the epoch of nations. The complex set of contradictory forces that are pushing simultaneously toward convergence and divergence are far from moving toward a single best institutional design. This hypothesis has proven to be erroneous and obsolete in industrial organization. Would it not be ironic if social scientists adopted such a simplistic hypothesis at the very moment when the process of trial and error is more uncertain than ever in Europe, North America, and Japan? The shakiness of convergence theory is well evidenced by the answer to a falsely simple question: who knows toward which system Russia, Poland, or even Germany might converge over the next century?

Competition & Change, 1997 Vol. 2, pp. 1–64
Reprints available directly from the publisher
Photocopying permitted by license only

Globalization and Economic Convergence

Lane Kenworthy

*Department of Sociology, East Carolina University,
Greenville, NC 27858*

Convergence among national economies is viewed by a growing number of observers as an inevitable result of increasing global integration of product and financial markets. Yet there is reason to doubt that globalization has yet brought about, or will in the future bring about, the degree of convergence assumed by some. First, markets require effectiveness, not optimality. This allows considerable space for continued differences in national economic policy choices, institutional structures, and performance patterns. Second, domestic institutions mediate the impact of international market forces. Institutions differ markedly across countries, generating substantial cross-national variation in the preferences and capacities of economic actors (firms, unions, policy makers, and so on). To assess the convergence thesis empirically, I examine developments in the 17 richest industrialized nations from 1960 to 1994. There is some indication of convergence in a few areas, but it is limited. This appears to owe partly to the fact that globalization itself remains limited and in part to the fact that globalization's convergence-generating effects are limited.

It has long been clear that national economies differ in important ways. One of the principal contributions of research in political economy over the past generation has been to enhance our understanding of such differences and why they exist. Variation across the industrialized nations in economic institutional arrangements, policy choices, and, ultimately, performance patterns has been traced to differences in labor strength, business coalitions, state structures, government partisanship, interest group size and structure, the prominence of cooperation, country size, stage of development, culture, and the influence of ideas, among other factors (Esping-Andersen 1990; Gourevitch 1986; Weir and Skocpol 1985; Hibbs 1977; Olson 1982; Kenworthy 1995; Katzenstein 1985; Cameron 1978; Gerschenkron 1952; Lodge and Vogel 1987; Hall 1986).

Ironically, just at the moment when this research has seemingly reached the height of its intellectual influence, it is deemed by a growing number of observers to be largely obsolete. According to this line of thought, global integration of product and financial markets – "globalization" – is causing national economies to converge in their structural features, policy choices, and performance results (Notermans 1993; Andrews 1994; Goodman and Pauly 1993; Bergsten 1993; Baumol, Nelson, and Wolff 1994a; Barro and Sala-i-Martin 1992).

This article offers a theoretical and empirical assessment of the convergence thesis. The first section of the article outlines the convergence thesis and suggests some reasons to question it. I argue that globalization should indeed lead to some homogenization among industrialized economies, but to less than some expect. The second section provides an overview of trends in product and financial market internationalization. The next three sections assess the degree of convergence in national economic policy choices, institutional structures, and performance outcomes, respectively. I examine the 17 richest industrialized economies – Australia, Austria, Belgium, Canada, Denmark, Finland, France, Germany, Italy, Japan, the Netherlands, New Zealand, Norway, Sweden, Switzerland, the United Kingdom, and the United States – utilizing quantitative data where available and relying on qualitative information elsewhere. The convergence trend is generally thought to have begun in the 1970s and to have accelerated since then. I compare four time periods: 1960–73, 1974–79, 1980–89, and 1990–94. (For some indicators data are available only through 1993. The years 1973, 1979, and 1989 are used as cutoffs so that the periods correspond to business cycles.) A brief conclusion discusses the principal findings and their implications.

Globalization and Convergence: Some Expectations

According to the convergence thesis, global integration of product and financial markets leads to homogenization – i.e., a reduction in dispersion or variation – among national economies. Product market integration is thought to generate convergence via two mechanisms. One is competitive selection. As economies and firms confront one another in direct competition, only the types of firm structures, interfirm relationships, and government policy choices most conducive to successful performance will survive (Alchian 1950). In the words of C. Fred Bergsten (1993, p. 57): "As the world as a whole increasingly becomes the relevant decision-making unit for corporations, they will be forced to adopt the most productive practices of their competitors." Inferior arrangements will be weeded out until only the fittest remain. As a result, economies will come to look increasingly alike in their features and in their performance results. We should not expect complete homogenization, since competition is not static. Attempts by companies to get an edge on their rivals will regularly generate new strategies and structures. According to the convergence thesis, however, the degree of variation across firms and countries should diminish.

A second mechanism is imitation. Incomplete information and limited computational capacities frequently prevent economic actors from knowing the optimal strategy in a given circumstance (Simon 1976; March 1982; Williamson 1981). One of the most common means through which they compensate for this uncertainty is imitation.[1] With product competition largely confined to domestic markets, as was the case until recently, such imitation tended to reinforce national differences. But heightened product market integration ought to produce the opposite effect. As employers, workers, and policy makers increase their direct contact with counterparts in other nations, their knowledge of alternative

---

[1] Imitation is a focus of organizational theory literature on "institutional isomorphism." See the essays in Powell and DiMaggio (1991).

structures, strategies, and policy choices is increased. They also learn more quickly about new innovations, thereby accelerating the rate at which "best practice" is diffused and adopted.

Globalization of finance has its effects primarily on policy choices and performance outcomes. Again there are two principal mechanisms. The first is capital movements. As money comes to flow more freely across national borders, governments are thought to be more tightly constrained in their policy options. In particular, financial integration is believed to impart a deflationary bias to national economic policy making (Stewart 1983). As capital mobility increases, national exchange rates come to be determined largely by speculation. Speculators generally perceive the lucrativeness of a currency as being an inverse function of the country's inflation rate, which in turn is viewed as a product of domestic interest rates and/or money supply growth. Governments and central banks thus face pressure to make low inflation a top policy priority, in order to maintain a reasonably stable and strong currency. Hence countries should converge toward tight money policy and low inflation rates.

The ability of investors to quickly shift capital and production abroad is thought to also constrain governments' capacity to tax. This, in turn, limits state capacity to increase government spending, and thereby to manipulate aggregate demand in response to an economic downturn. The convergence thesis therefore expects a homogenization of tax rates and government spending levels across nations.

Furthermore, when policy makers do attempt stimulatory fiscal policy, capital flows can prevent it from having its intended effect. As one observer puts it: "When capital is highly mobile across national borders, arbitrage between domestic and world capital markets keeps domestic interest rates from diverging widely from international interest rates, and this in turn makes fiscal policy less effective. Fiscal expansion puts upward pressure on domestic interest rates. Capital floods in as international investors take advantage of higher domestic interest rates, causing the domestic currency to appreciate. The international competitive position of domestic producers erodes, exports decline, and imports increase. Not only does the country suffer from a trade deficit, but the harm done to domestic producers can offset the stimulating effect that

fiscal expansion was intended to have on output and employment"
(Webb 1991, p. 318). Performance outcomes, in other words,
become less responsive to the individual policy styles and choices
of national governments, and therefore more alike.

There is a second convergence mechanism stemming from
financial globalization. Pressure for monetary and fiscal policy
convergence results not just from the impersonal deflationary
forces associated with financial integration, but also from
governments of countries that end up with trade or payments
imbalances. In particular, governments may attempt to respond
to internationalization by coordinating policies. As Michael
Webb (1991, pp. 309–10) has argued: "If national economies
are insulated from one another by weak market linkages and
government controls, as they were in the late 1950s and the
1960s, the international payments imbalances generated by
unilateral fiscal and monetary policymaking are small enough
to be managed without sacrificing macroeconomic policymaking
autonomy itself. But if capital is internationally mobile, as it was
by the late 1970s, the payments imbalances that emerge when
different countries pursue different macroeconomic policies are too
large to be ignored or managed; governments can reduce payments
imbalances and stabilize their external economic positions only by
coordinating their monetary and fiscal policies." The most notable
effort along these lines is the European Monetary System (EMS)
created in 1979.

The pressures for convergence generated by globalization are
real. Yet there is reason to be skeptical that they have yet brought
about, or will in the future bring about, the degree of homogenization
assumed by some observers.[2] There are two principal factors that
may be expected to limit the degree of convergence arising from
economic globalization:

1) Markets select on the basis of effectiveness, not optimality. Competition
   requires merely that economic actors do well – not that they be the best, and
   certainly not that they be the same.

---

[2] See also Hollingsworth and Streeck (1994, pp. 284–88); North (1990); Garrett
and Lange (1995).

2) Domestic institutions mediate the impact of international market forces. Institutions – interest group size and strength, government structures, policy arrangements, patterns of ideas, and so on – differ considerably across countries. Consequently, despite pressures from international capital and product markets and heightened exposure to worldwide "best practice," the preferences and capacities of economic actors vary cross-nationally.

Consider product market globalization and the selection pressures it generates. Nations have used, and in all likelihood will continue to use, protectionist measures of various types to limit the impact of international competition on certain industries. But even without such barriers, product market competition would probably induce less convergence than is commonly expected. Competition's selection effect has proved limited in domestic markets, and is likely to do so in international markets as well. Orthodox economic theory posits that firms in direct competition with one another will come to look more and more alike and experience similar performance results. But a survey of virtually any domestic industry in any nation reveals substantial variation in firm structure, practice, and performance. This owes in part to market imperfection; in some instances firms do not compete with one another for precisely the same customers, and information is frequently limited. But it is also partly due to the fact that the market mandates only that firms survive, not necessarily that they be the best. There is no reason to presume that only one structural arrangement or strategy can survive in any given product market. While some firms succeed based on efficiency, others may rely on extensive product variety, superior customer service, or effective marketing. Furthermore, there may exist a number of equally, or nearly equally, efficient means of producing the same good or service. Competition may narrow the range of feasible alternatives somewhat, but it seldom if ever reduces the choice to just one.

The same is true of government policies. For instance, given the fairly high degree of economic integration among states within the United States, one might expect little variation in economic policies across states. Yet state governments have persisted in pursuing widely different strategies on matters such as taxation, welfare benefits, and regulatory enforcement (Kenworthy 1996).

A second obstacle to market-driven selection pressures is institutions. Institutional configurations tend to be sticky; they generate preferences and capacities resistant to change. The size and strength of interest group organizations, their relationships with one another, the way government is structured (electoral systems, separation of powers, independence of bureaucracies, etc.), patterns of ideas – these and other institutions limit the effects of international pressures, thereby generating path dependence. The institutional structures and government policies of a national economy may also be interlinked in ways that form a *gestalt*, rendering the economic system more than simply the sum of its parts. Firms and other actors may therefore encounter obstacles that discourage implementation of certain organizational forms or practices. What works well in one national economy may not be effective in another (Streeck 1995; Levine and Tyson 1990).

Imitation may be similarly limited in its convergence-generating effects. In addition to the barriers just noted, there may be considerable uncertainty as to what exactly is "best practice" in any given instance. Also, as economic actors come to have greater knowledge of alternative ways of doing things, their menu of choices increases. If some companies choose to imitate the Japanese method while others select the American or German, variation across countries may continue or even increase.

Nor is it certain that financial integration will produce the degree of convergence in policy and performance that some expect. Again, international pressures may impose constraints but nevertheless allow latitude for variation in policy strategies, and policy makers typically care about more than exchange rates and capital flight. Of course, in cases of massive abandonment of a currency or flight of capital, governments may indeed be forced to bow to transnational forces. The French experience of 1981–82 is a classic and oft-cited example (Stewart 1983, pp. 78–80). But such instances, while instructive, are also exceptional. Expectations regarding the normal course of events that are based on what occurs in such unusual circumstances are often misleading. Thus, for example, Britain and Italy each recently abandoned the fixed exchange rates required by membership in the European Monetary System in order be able to lower domestic interest rates. Governments in both countries placed domestic reflation above stability of the national currency as a policy priority (*The Economist* 1993b).

These considerations suggest that expectations of convergence should be tempered somewhat. Heightened integration of national economies should indeed reduce the differences between them. But the degree of homogenization is likely to be less complete than some observers seem to expect. Globalization is like most other institutional developments; it offers incentives and constraints which push actors in a certain direction (toward convergence), but it does not mandate that they take that path. Considerable space still exists, and will in all probability continue to exist, for differences in labor strength, business coalitions, state structures, and other factors to produce a substantial degree of variation across national economies.

Globalization

Before turning to assessment of the convergence thesis, it is worth briefly examining the trend toward economic integration. Globalization has occurred in three principal areas: trade, production, and finance. I shall review each in turn.

Trade

The best indicator of product market integration is the rise in trade as a share of gross domestic product (GDP) in most industrialized economies. Table 1 shows the average of exports and imports as a share of GDP over the past three and a half decades for each of the 17 richest OECD nations. For the group of countries as a whole, this figure increased from an average of 24% during 1960–73 to 29% over 1974–79, to 31% during 1980–89. It then dropped back to 30% in 1990–94. Most of the growth in trade occurred prior to 1973; there has been little or no expansion over the past two decades.[3] The corresponding figures for the years 1960, 1974, 1980,

---

[3] This is true whether the data are unweighted, as are those in Table 1 and in the text, or weighted by population.

Table 1   Trade.

	Average of exports and imports as a share of GDP (%)			
	1960–73	*1974–79*	*1980–89*	*1990–94*
Australia	15.0	15.6	17.0	18.9
Austria	26.7	33.5	37.9	38.5
Belgium	45.5	56.7	71.5	69.2
Canada	19.9	24.6	26.2	28.2
Denmark	29.5	30.9	34.0	32.5
Finland	22.8	28.3	28.8	27.2
France	14.0	20.1	22.3	22.2
Germany	15.5	20.1	23.4	23.4
Italy	15.0	22.4	21.7	21.1
Japan	9.8	12.4	12.0	9.1
Netherlands	42.2	46.4	52.7	50.1
New Zealand	22.9	28.5	29.6	28.9
Norway	41.6	44.7	41.2	40.1
Sweden	22.5	29.1	32.2	29.9
Switzerland	30.5	33.4	36.9	34.6
United Kingdom	21.3	28.7	26.3	25.4
United States	5.3	8.8	9.6	11.0
Average	23.5	28.5	30.8	30.0
Standard deviation	11.4	12.4	15.0	14.3
Coefficient of variation	0.49	0.44	0.49	0.48

Sources: OECD 1995a, tables 6.12 and 6.13; OECD 1996

and 1990 were 23%, 30%, 31%, and 31%. Hence, convergence effects generated by heightened international product market competition should have had plenty of time to show up by the 1980s and early 1990s.

National experiences with heightened trade have differed markedly. Countries such as Austria, France, Germany, and the United States experienced substantial increases over the past several decades, but trade growth has been minimal in Denmark and Switzerland and nonexistent in Norway. In Belgium, trade accounted for an average of 46% of GDP in the 1960–73 period, the highest among the 17 countries, and it expanded to an average of 72% during the 1980s, again by far the highest. In Japan, by contrast, trade accounts for less than 10% of GDP, the lowest share among these countries, and that share was lower in the early 1990s than it had been during 1960–73. In addition to the average for the group of countries, Table 1 shows the standard deviation and the coefficient of variation for each time period. The latter, which is calculated by dividing the standard deviation by the average, is the most useful quantitative indicator of convergence.[4] It suggests that there has been no convergence in exposure to trade over the past several decades. This is one preliminary indication that national economies continue to differ substantially in their structure and functioning.

Production

The past several decades have witnessed a significant expansion of transnational production, and this increase in quantity has spurred a change in its nature. The traditional multinational firm of several decades ago "treated foreign operations as distant appendages for producing products designed and engineered back home. The chain of command and nationality of the company were clear" (*Business Week* 1990, p. 98). Today, many of the world's top manufacturing firms are much more global in their operations, conducting a substantial share of planning and production outside their base country and engaging in joint research and production ventures with companies of myriad nationalities. Robert Reich (1991, pp. 77, 81) has gone so far as to argue that "'American' corporations and 'American' industries are ceasing to exist in any form that can meaningfully be distinguished from the rest of the global economy.... The core corporation is ... increasingly a facade, behind which teems an array of decentralized groups and subgroups continuously contracting with similarly diffuse working units all over the world."

---

[4] Other indicators may be more useful for examining aspects of convergence other than homogenization. See the discussion in Baumol, Nelson, and Wolff (1994b, pp. 7–11) and in Baumol, Blackman, and Wolff (1989, chap. 5).

While Reich's portrait is somewhat exaggerated, direct investment by corporations – investment in which a firm has a controlling ownership share – in foreign countries did grow from $112 billion in 1967 to $518 billion in 1980, then to $1 trillion in 1987 (Rutter 1990, Table 1). Between 1983 and 1990 corporate investment across borders grew four times faster than world output and three times faster than world trade (Emmott 1993, p. 5). By 1994 corporations were investing some $200 billion each year across national borders (*The Economist* 1995c, p. 70). The number of multinational firms has also grown dramatically, increasing fivefold over the past two decades. A recent estimate by the United Nations suggests that by 1992 there were at least 35,000 multinational companies controlling some 170,000 foreign affiliates (Emmott 1993, pp. 9, 5). The list of companies with more than a third of their assets located outside their home country includes names such as Coca-Cola, Johnson & Johnson, Dow Chemical, Honda, Colgate, Gillette, Unilever, Electrolux, Nestle, Hewlett-Packard, and Digital Equipment (*Business Week* 1990, p. 103). According to a *Business Week* report (1990, p. 101), some world companies now "make almost daily decisions on where to shift production."

Yet, despite its rapid growth, direct foreign investment accounts for a relatively small share of overall investment by firms in the largest industrialized nations. For the period 1985–91, the ratio of direct foreign investment to total investment by domestic firms was only 5% in the United States, 7% in Japan, 7% in Germany, 7% in France, 4% in Italy, 17% in Britain, and 6% in Canada (Koechlin 1995). Although the figures are higher for some of the smaller, more open European economies – 20% in the Netherlands, for instance – this suggests that the overall degree of globalization of production remains somewhat limited.

Finance

Two developments have spurred a massive increase in capital mobility: the creation of electronic communications technology which permits a rapid flow of money around the world, and the relaxation or elimination of capital controls and other financial regulatory hurdles in many industrialized countries during the 1970s and 1980s.[5] Developments have been so rapid and far-reaching that in the view of some observers the financial markets of the major industrialized nations are now "virtually completely integrated" (Frankel 1991, p. 228).

Internationalization of finance has three components: currency trading, banking and loans, and investment in equities and bonds.

The most important of the three is currency trading. As of 1973 the daily volume of trading in national currencies totaled around $15 billion. By 1982 it had grown to $60 billion. By 1990 it had increased to $650 billion. Today, estimates put the figure at nearly $1.3 trillion (Woodall 1995, p. 10; *Business Week* 1993a, p. 94; Frieden 1991, p. 428; *Wall Street Journal* 1992a). Over the course of a year, that amounts to more than 10 times the entire annual output of the industrialized Western nations (Glasgall 1993, p. 14). Just as importantly, a change has occurred in the nature of trading, from investment-dominated to speculation-dominated. The fixed nature of currency values under the Bretton Woods regime, which existed from shortly after World War II to 1971, offered little incentive to speculate. Floating exchange rates dramatically altered this picture. According to John Eatwell (1993, p. 120): "In 1971 ... about 90 percent of all foreign exchange transactions were for the finance of trade and long-term investment, and only about 10 percent were speculative. Today [1993] those percentages are reversed, with well over 90 percent of all transactions being speculative. Daily speculative flows now regularly exceed the combined foreign exchange reserves of all the G-7 governments."[6] In some countries limits still exist on investment in foreign currencies (*The Economist* 1993a, p. 65). Nevertheless, this is by far the most mobile component of global finance.

---

[5] Capital controls were removed or greatly eased in the mid 1970s in the United States, Germany, Canada, Switzerland, and the Netherlands; in 1979 in Japan and the United Kingdom; and in the mid-to-late 1980s in France and Italy.

[6] The Group of 7 nations include the United States, Japan, Germany, France, Italy, the United Kingdom, and Canada.

Global integration of banking has also proceeded rapidly, sparked by expansion of the Eurocurrency (or Eurodollar) market – which consists of lending and borrowing of currencies outside their home country – beginning in the 1960s. The stock of international bank lending reached $4.2 trillion in 1994, up from $265 billion in 1975 (Woodall 1995, p. 10). Between 1970 and 1985 the number of foreign banking offices in the United States rose from 50 to nearly 800, and in Germany from 80 to 290 (Goldstein, Mathieson, and Lane 1991, p. 7).

The third component of financial integration is investment in bonds and equities. According to a recent report in *The Economist* (Woodall 1995, p. 10), between 1983 and 1993 cross-border sales and purchases of U.S. Treasury bonds increased from $30 billion to $500 billion. Foreign holdings of French government bonds jumped from 1% in 1980 to 43% in 1982. "Gross sales and purchases of bonds and equities between domestic and foreign residents rose from 3% of America's GDP in 1970 to 9% in 1980 and 135% in 1993. Britain's cross-border securities transactions soared from virtually nothing in 1970 to more than 1,000% of GDP in 1993." By 1993 one in seven equity transactions worldwide occurred between investors in different countries (*The Economist* 1993a, p. 65). Securities-related investing now swamps bank lending as a source of cross-border capital. Of the total funds raised on international capital markets in 1978–79, two-thirds was associated with bank lending; by 1986, 85% was accounted for by equities and bonds (Cosh, Hughes, and Singh 1992, pp. 21, 24). Despite this growth, however, equity market integration is in some respects still in its infancy. As of 1989, for instance, 93% of the aggregate value of the world's stock markets was held in domestic securities; the figure for American investors in 1995 was 94% (Reich 1991, p. 138; Pennar 1995, p. 80). As Martin Feldstein (1995, p. 72) has put it: "Although most of the legal barriers to international capital mobility are now gone, the world capital market remains essentially segmented along national lines. Capital may be free to move internationally, but its owners and managers prefer to keep almost all of each nation's savings at home."

Government Policy

Has there, then, been convergence? This section assesses convergence trends in four types of state policy: monetary, fiscal, social-welfare, and industrial. The next two sections examine economic institutional structures and performance outcomes, respectively.

Monetary Policy

Convergence in macroeconomic policy is expected even by observers who are highly attentive to national and partisan differences in policy priorities. Geoffrey Garrett and Peter Lange (1991, pp. 542–43) state the argument clearly:

Even if today there still are strong domestic incentives for governments to pursue distinctive partisan strategies ..., such incentives are now overwhelmed by international constraints. Attempts to 'fine-tune' domestic demand in open economies are of limited utility or are even harmful, leading to surges in imports, balance-of-payments deficits, and to exchange rate pressures. Perhaps more important, the integration of financial systems, the floating of exchange rates, and the removal of controls on capital flows together vitiate the possibilities for autonomous national monetary policies. Under these conditions, international bond and currency markets adjust virtually instantaneously to government attempts to affect domestic economic processes by changing interest rates, money supply growth, credit conditions, and the like. The implications of interdependence for fiscal and monetary policies are clear; governments no longer possess the autonomy to pursue independent macroeconomic strategies effectively, even if they were to seek to do so.

Monetary policy has two potential targets: interest rates and the money supply. The convergence claim is based on the notion that in a world of mobile capital, policy makers have little or no control over domestic interest rates. As Jeffry Frieden (1991, p. 431) has written: "If capital is fully mobile across borders, interest rates are constrained to be the same in all countries and national monetary policy can have no effect on national interest rates." Suppose, for instance, that a government or central bank wishes to stimulate the economy by decreasing interest rates.[7] Lower interest rates

---

[7] It may do so by, for example, lowering the reserve requirement for banks or by injecting money into the economy.

will cause an immediate outflow of funds, as investors seek a higher rate of return in other nations. This in itself, by reducing the supply of money available for loans, will push interest rates back up. In addition, the expected stimulative effect on the economy will spark fears of inflation, making the national currency less attractive to traders. The result will be a decline in the value of the nation's currency, reducing consumers' ability to purchase imported goods. This in turn results in political pressure to raise interest rates. If, by contrast, monetary authorities wish to heighten interest rates, the result is an immediate inflow of cash, which by increasing the supply of available money has the effect of pushing interest rates back down. Where capital can move freely across borders, in other words, interest rates should in theory be the same everywhere.

What about the money supply itself? Policy makers have greater capacity for control over the supply of their domestic currency, but capital mobility is believed to force all nations toward a policy of tight money. This owes chiefly to the fact that those who buy and sell national currencies base their decisions largely on expectations of inflation. Currencies of low-inflation countries are expected to hold their value and are therefore deemed attractive, whereas those of nations with high inflation are projected to lose their value and are consequently viewed as risky. Since the value of a nation's currency (i.e., the exchange rate) is important to its firms, financiers, and consumers, policy makers typically face pressure to ensure that it stays at a moderately high level. In a world of integrated capital markets, the best way to do that is by holding inflation in check, which requires tight money.

Tight money incentives also existed prior to the early 1970s, with exchange rates fixed under the Bretton Woods system. The currencies of most industrialized nations were tied to the dollar, which in turn was pegged to the value of gold. This created strong pressures for limited money supply growth, as Paul Whitely (1987, p. 186) explains: "The system put limits on the abilities of central banks to create money, since excessive monetary creation tended to produce balance-of-payments problems. These resulted from currency speculation that either anticipated inflation from such a policy, or a devaluation of the currency. Thus the system of fixed exchange rates acted as a constraint on monetary expansion." In addition, most governments in the pre-1973 era viewed fiscal policy as the tool of choice for economic management. Keynesian doctrine specified as much, and inflation was viewed in most nations as a marginal concern, as indeed it was given the strong growth rates obtaining throughout the industrialized world. The collapse of Bretton Woods in the early 1970s released nations from this constraint on monetary policy strategies at the same time that inflationary pressures were mounting. If the convergence thesis is correct, therefore, we should observe heightened cross-national variation in monetary policy in the 1974–79 period but then increasing homogenization as capital mobility begins to have its effects (Goodman 1992, p. 217).[8]

Another factor promoting convergence since the late 1970s is the various attempts that have been made to harmonize monetary policies and exchange rates across countries. Some of these have been informal, such as the attempt by the Group of 7 nations to bring down the value of the dollar in 1986. The most prominent formal effort has been the European Monetary System (EMS) established in 1979. The EMS pegged the currencies of member countries – which during the 1980s included Belgium, Denmark, France, Germany, Ireland, Italy, and The Netherlands – to the German deutschmark. The system originally permitted a fluctuation in value of no more than 4.5% (Bretton Woods allowed fluctuations of 1%) and provided mutual lines of credit among central banks to facilitate intervention to protect the established values.[9] In 1993 the band for fluctuations was widened further.

Table 2 shows trends for nominal and real long-term interest rates and money supply growth. The data suggest some convergence in long-term interest rates. For real interest rates, the standard deviation from the average for the 17 countries increased in 1974–79 compared to 1960–73, but then fell in the 1980s and early 1990s. It remains

---

[8] This is indeed what anecdotal evidence is frequently taken to suggest. Fritz Scharpf (1987, p. 66) notes, for instance, that an attempt by Austria to loosen monetary policy in 1979 was defeated "for the first time" by international constraints. There is also France's oft-cited quick withdrawal from a loose money strategy in 1981–82.

[9] A good discussion can be found in Goodman (1992, pp. 187–202). Michael Webb (1991) has argued that these efforts were a direct response to the constraints imposed by heightened capital mobility. On the effects on monetary policy choices in two EMS countries, Belgium and the Netherlands, see Kurzer (1991).

Table 2   Convergence in monetary policy?

	Nominal long-term interest rates (%)				Real long-term interest rates (%)			
	1960–73	1974–79	1980–89	1990–93	1960–73	1974–79	1980–89	1990–93
Australia	na	9.7	13.5	10.1	na	–1.9	5.1	8.2
Austria[a]	7.7	8.8	8.2	8.1	2.3	2.6	3.9	4.2
Belgium	6.5	9.0	10.7	8.8	2.6	0.9	6.0	5.3
Canada	6.2	9.2	11.7	9.3	2.6	0.0	5.7	7.1
Denmark	na	na	13.9	9.0	na	na	7.1	6.6
Finland[a]	8.1	9.8	10.1	11.4	–0.2	–2.4	2.5	8.3
France	6.9	10.7	12.3	9.0	1.8	–0.2	4.8	6.1
Germany	7.1	7.9	7.7	7.9	2.6	3.1	4.5	4.1
Italy	5.9	12.1	14.7	12.5	0.6	–4.2	2.6	6.1
Japan[a]	7.1	7.9	6.6	5.7	0.4	–0.1	4.6	4.0
Netherlands	6.1	8.7	8.2	8.1	0.1	1.3	5.6	5.7
New Zealand	5.3	8.6	14.0	9.4	1.0	–3.9	2.3	7.7
Norway[a]	5.9	7.7	12.4	9.3	–1.0	–0.4	5.0	7.5
Sweden	6.2	9.4	12.0	10.6	1.4	–1.1	3.8	5.4
Switzerland	4.3	4.9	4.6	5.9	–1.0	1.1	0.7	1.9
United Kingdom[a]	7.4	13.6	11.2	9.5	2.4	–2.0	3.5	4.1
United States	5.0	7.4	10.4	7.7	1.5	–0.6	5.1	4.4
Average	6.4	9.1	10.7	9.0	1.1	–0.5	4.3	5.7
Standard deviation	1.0	2.0	2.8	1.7	1.3	2.1	1.6	1.8
Coefficient of variation	0.16	0.22	0.26	0.19	—	—	0.37	0.32

(Continued)

Table 2 (Continued)

	Nominal money supply growth (%)				Real money supply growth (%)			
	1960–73	1974–79	1980–89	1990–93	1960–73	1974–79	1980–89	1990–93
Australia	6.0	10.6	12.0	12.4	2.5	-1.5	3.6	9.1
Austria	8.8	5.8	6.3	6.4	4.6	-0.5	2.5	2.8
Belgium	6.5	7.9	3.9	3.2	2.9	-0.5	-0.9	0.2
Canada	7.7	7.1	11.1	7.0	4.4	-2.1	4.6	3.6
Denmark	9.9	10.6	15.7	na	3.7	-0.2	8.8	na
Finland	10.2	16.7	12.2	3.8	4.5	3.9	4.9	-0.1
France	10.3	12.0	8.1	0.5	5.7	1.3	0.8	-2.3
Germany	8.3	9.8	5.9	14.2	4.9	5.1	3.0	10.6
Italy	16.6	18.6	11.6	6.9	12.7	1.9	0.4	1.4
Japan	21.0	10.9	5.1	4.6	14.8	1.0	2.6	2.3
Netherlands	9.5	9.4	6.4	7.6	4.6	2.2	3.6	4.8
New Zealand	6.2	8.5	17.8	9.4	1.4	-5.3	6.0	6.7
Norway	8.7	13.9	17.6	8.0	3.6	5.2	9.3	5.0
Sweden	2.9	12.2	7.1	na	-1.8	2.4	-0.8	na
Switzerland	8.8	6.2	2.2	0.7	4.6	2.2	-1.1	-3.9
United Kingdom	5.3	13.2	14.6	9.3	0.2	-2.4	7.2	4.2
United States	4.5	6.5	7.6	9.1	1.3	-2.0	2.1	5.2

(Continued)

Table 2 *(Continued)*

	Nominal money supply growth (%)				Real money supply growth (%)			
	1960–73	1974–79	1980–89	1990–93	1960–73	1974–79	1980–89	1990–93
Average	8.9	10.6	9.7	6.9	4.4	0.6	3.3	3.3
Standard deviation	4.4	3.6	4.8	3.9	4.0	2.8	3.2	3.9
Coefficient of variation	0.49	0.34	0.49	0.57	–	–	–	–

[a] Figures in 1960–73 columns are for 1968–73 only.
na = not available
Sources: Interest rate data are from OECD 1995a, tables 10.9 and 10.10, supplemented by earlier editions of OECD, *Historical Statistics*. Money supply data are from IMF 1990, p. 90; IMF 1992, pp. 78–79; OECD 1994b, p. 28; OECD 1995a, Table 8.11.

higher than during the Bretton Woods years, however. (The coefficient of variation can be misleading when used for a set of numbers that includes both positive and negative values, as is the case for real interest rates and real money supply growth. In such cases it is necessary to rely on the less precise method of simply comparing standard deviations and averages.) The degree of variation in nominal interest rates also was greater in the 1974–79 period than during 1960–73, but it was even larger during the 1980s. Therè appears to have been some convergence in the early 1990s, but this four-year time period is so short that it is difficult to tell if this development is meaningful. Even in this most recent period, there is a rather severe disparity between nations in both nominal and real interest rates, with nominal rates ranging from 5.7% in Japan to 12.5% in Italy and real rates from 1.9% in Switzerland to 8.3% in Finland. However, several recent studies have found a substantial degree of convergence in short-term interest rates, which suggests that the continued variation in long-term rates may be due in large measure to exchange risk rather than differences in policy (Frankel 1991; Goldstein, Mathieson, and Lane 1991).

Table 2 also shows some indication of a shift toward tighter money. The average rate of nominal money supply growth declined from 1974–79 to 1980–89 to 1990–93. But the rate of real money growth moved in just the opposite direction, contrary to what the convergence thesis would lead us to expect. This development is explainable at least in part by the vast difference in inflation between the late 1970s versus the 1980s and early 1990s. Higher-than-expected inflation reduced real interest rates in the former period, while lower-than-expected inflation increased them in the latter. On the other hand, there is no indication of convergence in rates of money supply growth. Instead, the data suggest a trend toward greater variation across countries during the past decade or so. For both nominal and real measures of change in money supply there was less variation in the 1974–79 period than previously but then heightened variability in the 1980s and early 1990s – exactly the opposite of what the convergence thesis predicts.

On the whole, then, the data suggest a mixed picture for monetary policy. There is some evidence of a general shift toward tighter money and toward convergence in interest rates. Yet there remains substantial variation in rates of money supply growth across countries, and this diversity appears to have increased.

Fiscal Policy

The expectation of convergence in fiscal policy stems in part from the growing ability of investors to shift capital and production abroad in response to policies they dislike. The type of measure most likely to provoke capital flight is an increase in taxes, typically instituted to help finance heightened government spending.

Even when not accompanied by higher tax rates, increases in state expenditures may be counteracted by currency shifts. By increasing domestic demand, fiscal stimulus will cause a rise in imports, thus reducing the country's trade balance and balance of payments. There are two potential scenarios, depending upon whether the nation's exchange rate is fixed or floating. If the exchange rate is fixed (as is the case for countries participating in the EMS), the declining trade balance will reduce the nation's external reserves and thus its supply of money. Interest rates will rise as a result. Higher interest rates themselves may cancel out the intended stimulatory effect of the fiscal expansion. Even if they do not, traders may abandon the nation's currency in fear of rising inflation. The government and its allies may try to intervene to stabilize the currency by buying large quantities of it, but this tactic tends to work only temporarily, as it signals to speculators that the currency is in trouble. Eventually the government will face overwhelming pressure to abandon the stimulatory fiscal measures by cutting back government spending.

If the nation's exchange rate floats, the declining trade balance causes a drop in the value of the currency. Inflation increases due to the resulting higher import prices and expansion of domestic production in response to accelerated exports; this in turn causes further abandonment of the currency. Again, the government will face strong pressure to give up the fiscal expansion.

Fiscal stimulation can also be attempted via deficit spending, but again internationalized capital and product markets may counteract any effect. By increasing the demand for loans, a higher budget deficit pushes up interest rates. This in turn attracts foreign capital, which increases the value of the country's currency, reducing the competitiveness of its exports, thereby partially if not entirely offsetting the intended stimulative effect.

In sum, where capital is mobile, fiscal expansion is expected to have at best no impact and at worst a deleterious one. Yet capital mobility is thought not only to discourage increases in government spending and tax rates, but to spur their reduction. As Sven Steinmo (1994, p. 10) has argued: "Globalization has dramatically increased the ease and availability of the 'exit' option for those with large incomes and capital resources. Fearing the flight of capital from their countries (and conversely wishing to attract mobile capital to their countries), governments are being forced to redesign their tax systems." Thus, as product market integration and capital mobility have increased over the past two decades, we should observe convergence toward a common, lower level of taxation and state expenditure (as shares of national wealth) and government budgets should be largely balanced.

As Table 3 makes clear, however, no such development has occurred across the 15 countries for which data are available. Contrary to the convergence thesis, the share of national wealth accounted for by taxes (shown as "government revenues" in the Table) has increased, on average, over the four time periods, and variability has been essentially constant throughout. The rate of increase in tax revenues did slow in the past decade, and four of the countries reduced the share of taxes in their GDP in the early 1990s compared to the 1980s. Yet the fact that the tax share increased at all during the late 1980s and early 1990s, especially in those nations with already-high levels, contradicts the notion that financial integration and the threat of capital flight have put a halt to fiscal activism.

The progressiveness of tax systems has changed somewhat. A number of industrialized nations reduced the marginal tax rates on wealthy individuals and corporations during the 1980s, making up for the lost revenue via higher consumption taxes or social insurance charges. This represents a genuine shift in the nature of tax policy. Yet some of the most profound shifts have been

Table 3 Convergence in fiscal policy?

	Government revenues as a share of GDP (%)				Government expenditures as a share of GDP (%)			
	1960–73	1974–79	1980–89	1990–93	1960–73	1974–79	1980–89	1990–93
Australia	25.3	29.3	33.3	34.0	24.4	33.6	36.6	38.9
Austria	38.7	43.9	47.2	47.7	38.7	46.7	51.0	51.0
Belgium	33.6	47.0	51.6	49.7	36.0	53.2	61.2	56.3
Canada	30.1	36.1	39.0	43.0	31.6	39.2	45.0	50.7
Denmark	35.4	48.3	55.6	57.0	33.8	49.1	59.0	60.8
Finland	32.6	42.3	45.4	52.3	30.3	38.7	43.5	56.3
France	37.7	40.8	46.4	46.6	38.0	43.3	50.2	51.9
Germany	37.6	44.0	45.1	44.5	37.5	47.5	47.8	47.8
Italy	30.2	33.5	37.8	44.0	33.7	42.9	49.0	54.5
Japan	20.0	24.6	30.7	33.9	19.5	28.4	32.8	33.0
Netherlands	39.5	49.8	54.3	53.7	40.8	52.8	60.4	58.3
New Zealand	na	na	na	na	na	na	na	na
Norway	40.2	49.8	53.7	55.8	36.7	48.5	49.5	55.7
Sweden	41.7	54.4	59.4	60.3	38.9	54.4	62.9	66.6
Switzerland	na	na	na	na	na	na	na	na
United Kingdom	34.8	39.0	41.2	38.4	36.7	44.4	44.9	44.0
United States	27.5	29.7	31.2	31.9	29.4	32.5	35.8	37.5
Average	33.7	40.1	44.8	46.2	33.7	43.7	48.6	50.9
Standard deviation	6.1	8.7	9.1	8.9	5.9	7.9	9.4	9.2
Coefficient of variation	0.18	0.22	0.20	0.19	0.18	0.18	0.19	0.18

(Continued)

Table 3   *(Continued)*

	Budget balance as a share of GDP (%)			
	1960–73	1974–79	1980–89	1990–93
Australia	0.9	–4.3	–3.3	–4.9
Austria	0.0	–2.8	–3.8	–3.3
Belgium	–2.4	–6.2	–9.6	–6.6
Canada	–1.5	–3.1	–6.0	–7.7
Denmark	1.6	–0.8	–3.4	–3.8
Finland	2.3	3.6	1.9	–4.0
France	–0.3	–2.5	–3.8	–5.3
Germany	0.1	–3.5	–2.7	–3.3
Italy	–3.5	–9.4	–11.2	–10.5
Japan	0.5	–3.8	–2.1	0.9
Netherlands	–1.3	–3.0	–6.1	–4.6
New Zealand	na	na	na	na
Norway	3.5	1.3	4.2	0.1
Sweden	2.8	0.0	–3.5	–6.3
Switzerland	na	na	na	na
United Kingdom	–1.9	–5.4	–3.7	–5.6
United States	–1.9	–2.8	–4.6	–5.6
Average	–0.1	–2.9	–3.9	–4.7
Standard deviation	2.0	3.1	3.8	2.8
Coefficient of variation	–	–	–	–

na = not available
Sources: OECD 1995a, Tables 6.6 and 6.5

introduced by nations whose tax systems were already among the least progressive, such as the United States.[10] Hence these changes have not produced convergence.

The same pattern holds for government spending levels. Again we observe a continuous increase and no reduction in variability. For budget balances we do see less variation in the early 1990s than in the 1980s, as suggested by the smaller standard deviation. Yet surprisingly, the average national budget was *further* in deficit during the 1980s and early 1990s than in either of the two earlier periods. Indeed, by the mid 1990s government debt totaled more than 100% of GDP in nations such as Belgium and Italy, and more than 50% of GDP in most industrialized countries. These levels are considerably higher than those of a decade or two ago (*The Economist* 1995a, 1995b). A recent study by Geoffrey Garrett (1995) finds that as of 1990 the partisan complexion of government and labor strength were more likely to cause differences in government spending and budget deficits the *more* exposed the economy was to internationalization of trade and capital. In other words, globalization has not dampened the impact of cross-national diversity in party preferences and interest group strength. This too suggests that the constraints imposed by global economic integration continue to be circumvented by national policy authorities.

Perhaps convergence has not occurred in fiscal policy because there was relatively little variation across countries to begin with. Indeed, the coefficients of variation for government revenues and expenditures during all four time periods are among the lowest for the various quantitative indicators of policy choices and performance outcomes that I examine here. Nevertheless, cross-country differences in fiscal policy are certainly not negligible. In 1993, state expenditures accounted for only 37% of U.S. GDP compared to 74% of Sweden's. This severe differential suggests little in the way of movement toward a common level of fiscal intervention.

---

[10] The United States lowered its top individual income tax rate from 70% to 33% and its top corporate income tax rate from 46% to 34% (Steinmo 1994, p. 15).

Overall, fiscal policy indicators suggest a lack of any significant shift toward austerity or convergence. The recent resurgence of market liberalism notwithstanding, there remain substantial cross-national differences in opinions and preferences regarding the conduct of both fiscal and monetary policy. To this point, heightened globalization of product and financial markets appears to have left considerable space for these differences to be translated into policy choices.

Social-Welfare Policy

If only partially evident in monetary policy and not at all in fiscal policy, perhaps convergence has occurred in other policy areas. A commonplace view holds, for instance, that globalization creates pressures for cutbacks in social-welfare programs. As product markets become more integrated, countries should be less able to remain competitive in the international marketplace while maintaining large welfare states (Pfaller, Gough, and Therborn 1991; Lindbeck 1994). In addition, investors should be reluctant to keep their money in countries with tax rates high enough to sustain expansive social-welfare programs. We should therefore observe convergence toward lower transfer expenditure levels.

On the other hand, cross-national investigations have consistently found that countries which are more heavily exposed to international trade tend to have *higher* levels of welfare spending (Cameron 1978; Hicks and Swank 1992; Garrett and Mitchell 1995). Indeed, there are several factors associated with globalization that push in favor of expanded transfer programs. Greater competition has contributed to heightened unemployment as workers in less competitive firms and sectors have been displaced. This increases the need for unemployment payments and early retirement support, much of which tends to be borne by the state. In addition, higher unemployment puts pressure on the welfare state to become a source of new jobs (Esping-Andersen 1990, chap. 6). This has been particularly true during the past several decades as the supply of labor market participants has expanded dramatically due to rising female labor force participation.

Even if globalization were to lead to cutbacks in social-welfare programs, it is possible that pressures for welfare state retrenchment could generate *increased* diversity across nations. Nations with extensive transfer systems may develop stronger coalitions in support of the welfare state and thus be resistant to retrenchment pressures, whereas moderate or intermediate welfare states may be more vulnerable to cutbacks (Stephens 1994; Stephens, Huber, and Ray 1994).

Comparative figures for government expenditures on social security and social assistance programs as a share of GDP are shown in Table 4. Almost all countries increased social-welfare spending steadily through the mid 1980s. Most then began to cut

Table 4 Convergence in social-welfare policy?

	Social-welfare transfers as a share of GDP (%)			
	1960–73	*1974–79*	*1980–89*	*1990–93*
Australia	5.6	8.3	9.1	11.1
Austria	14.9	17.8	20.1	20.4
Belgium	13.5	21.6	24.9	23.8
Canada	7.3	9.9	11.6	14.9
Denmark	9.5	14.0	17.1	19.4
Finland	6.6	11.2	13.9	21.1
France	15.5	17.5	21.2	22.3
Germany	12.8	16.7	16.5	15.1
Italy	11.9	15.4	16.7	18.8
Japan	4.5	8.4	11.0	11.5
Netherlands	16.4[a]	23.5	26.5	26.3
New Zealand	na	na	na	na
Norway	10.3	14.2	15.9	21.0[a]
Sweden	10.0	15.9	18.3	22.3
Switzerland	7.3	12.6	13.4	15.4
United Kingdom	7.8	10.2	12.7	13.3
United States	6.3	10.2	11.0	12.4
Average	10.0	14.2	16.2	18.1
Standard deviation	3.8	4.5	5.0	4.7
Coefficient of variation	0.38	0.32	0.31	0.26

[a]Estimate
na = not available
Source: OECD 1995a, Table 6.3

back. By 1989, 12 of the 16 nations for which data are available had reduced transfer expenditures compared to 1986. Around 1990, however, another upward trend commenced. The average for the 1990–93 period is nearly two percentage points higher than that for the 1980s. This is due in part to the recession of the early 1990s, which led to expanded transfer payments in response to increased joblessness. Yet the increases in transfer spending instituted by a number of countries were quite substantial, far exceeding the rises in previous recessions. It is noteworthy that as of 1993, 13 of the 16 nations were spending a higher share of their GDP on social-welfare transfers than in 1983, at a comparable point in the business cycle. The coefficient of variation for 1990-93 suggests that perhaps industrialized countries *have* been converging in their social-welfare policies. But again, assessment based on this 4-year period may be misleading. If there has in fact been convergence, it is because the traditionally low-spending nations have been catching up to their more generous counterparts, not because the latter have been engineering significant cutbacks.

Paradoxically, it was the decades immediately following World War II that witnessed the most substantial convergence in social policy among industrialized economies. Prior to the Second World War countries had moved sporadically and unevenly toward development of a modern welfare state. The war and its aftermath gave rise to widespread sentiment that strong welfare states provide a bulwark against popular discontent and communism. This view became a central component of cold war political ideology and of the U.S.-led strategy for rebuilding Europe. It was not long before almost all industrialized capitalist nations featured publicly-funded systems of old age assistance (pensions), unemployment insurance, welfare for the poor, health insurance, and child support. This process of homogenization continued through the 1960s, as the coefficients of variation for the 1960–73 and 1974–79 periods in Table 4 suggest.

The past two decades have witnessed a general expansion of the share of national wealth devoted to social-welfare programs, but little convergence in their size or characteristics. There has been some convergence in pension policy, as Einar Overbye (1994) has pointed out. Most wealthy industrialized nations have moved toward "a dual public pension structure, in which the working population receives wholly or partly contribution-based earnings-related pensions, while the non-working population receives tax-financed supplementary benefits" (Overbye 1994, p. 155). Yet profound differences continue to exist across countries in many areas of social-welfare policy. For example, the duration of unemployment benefit eligibility ranges from less than 10 weeks in Austria, Switzerland, and Italy to more than 30 weeks in The Netherlands, Denmark, and the United Kingdom (Jackman 1990, Table 5). Government support for parents with young children also varies widely across OECD nations, in terms of eligibility criteria and type and level of support provided (Kamerman and Kahn 1995). Even public pension systems differ starkly in institutional design and benefit levels (Overbye 1994). And health care systems continue to differ along two axes: who pays and whether patients may choose their physician. Britain features a single-payer system with limited patient choice, while in the German system regional associations are the principal purchasers and patients have substantial leeway in selecting doctors. The United States and Canada allow patients to choose their physician; but the former continues to rely on a mix of private insurance companies, individuals, and the government as payers, while the latter has a single-payer system.

More generally, there remains substantial variation among *types* of welfare states. Gosta Esping-Andersen (1990) has argued persuasively that welfare states in industrialized market economies cluster into three distinct "regime-types": liberal, conservative-corporatist, and social democratic. In the first type – best exemplified by the United States, Canada, and Australia – benefits are modest and targeted to the poor. The second type – which includes nations such as Austria, Germany, France, and Italy – offers more extensive benefits to a wider range of the citizenry, but an emphasis on upholding status differentials limits its redistributive impact. The third type, which exists in the Scandinavian nations, is both universalistic and highly egalitarian. Although several of the Scandinavian countries have showed signs of moving away from the extreme universalism that has traditionally characterized their social-welfare policies, the basic differences among these three types of welfare state appear to have abated only minimally, if at all, in recent decades (see Stephens 1994).

Industrial Policy

Much has been written in recent years about the purported demise of Japanese industrial policy (Eads and Yamamura 1987; Kikkawa 1983; Patrick 1986, pp. 14–17; Saxonhouse 1983; Yamamura 1986). Japan's economic bureaucracy – led by the Ministry of International Trade and Industry (MITI) and the Ministry of Finance – is said to be substantially less willing and able to impose its wishes upon Japanese firms now than it was during the 1960s and 1970s. Globalization is thought to have helped bring about this change in three ways. First, financial integration has lessened the bureaucracy's leverage over Japanese firms' access to capital. Second, globalization is believed to render government policies to assist national firms with technology development ineffective. As Richard Nelson and Gavin Wright (1992, p. 1961) argue, "policies launched by governments with the objective of giving their national firms a particular edge in an area of technology ... do not work very well any more. It is increasingly difficult to create new technology that will stay contained within national borders for very long in a world where technological sophistication is widespread and firms of many nationalities are ready to make the investments needed to exploit new generic technology." And third, as Japanese exports have flooded markets in the United States and Europe, governments have pressed Japan to curtail its preferential treatment of Japanese firms, chiefly by opening the Japanese market. Perhaps the best-known example is the 1986 Semiconductor Industry Agreement, in which Japan agreed to facilitate a substantial increase in the foreign share of semiconductors in its domestic market.

This interpretation of recent developments has some merit, but it is typically overstated. There has indeed been a reduction in the heavily interventionist role played by MITI and other industrial policy agencies in Japan. But factors other than internationalization have been of equal or greater importance in contributing to this development (Eads and Yamamura 1987, pp. 448–68). The popular consensus around state-led growth has weakened, as quality-of-life issues such as pollution control and consumer protection have become more important among the Japanese populace over the past two decades. The political hegemony of the Liberal Democratic Party (LDP) has waned, and the bureaucracy faces a more determined political challenge from Japan's parliament as politicians have become more eager to obtain a share of the federal budget for their particular constituency. Also, some influential Japanese firms no longer feel they need state financial support, and oppose state efforts to favor other industries or firms.

Moreover, even if the influence of Japanese industrial policy has subsided somewhat in the past decade, the degree of its diminution should not be exaggerated. Most careful accounts acknowledge that the economic bureaucracy continues to play an active and key role in promoting certain sectors, most often high technology or knowledge-intensive industries (Fransman 1995; Borrus, Millstein, and Zysman 1983; Anchordoguy 1988; Harris 1989; Donahue 1989; Yoshikawa 1987; Samuels and Whipple 1989). MITI has had a significant hand in promoting the development of industries such as semiconductors, computers, telecommunications, high-definition television, biotechnology, and aerospace.

The other best-known practitioner of proactive industrial policy among industrialized nations has been France, and it too has scaled back its interventionist efforts compared to the early postwar decades (Hall 1986, chaps. 7–8). At the same time, the United States under the Clinton administration has moved to take a more proactive role in relieving or preventing various types of market failure. Despite their free-market rhetoric, even the Reagan and Bush administrations engaged more actively than their predecessors in protecting U.S. industries threatened by foreign competition (Graham 1992; *Business Week* 1994b; *Fortune* 1991).

These developments taken as a whole do indicate some convergence in industrial policy approaches. But the degree of homogenization remains very limited. There continues to be a profound difference between those nations, such as Japan and France, which are willing and able to take an active, anticipatory hand in guiding domestic industries and firms, versus those, like the United States and Britain, which rely for the most part on limited, reactive measures.

Greater industrial policy convergence has occurred at the local level. Local governments in virtually all industrialized countries have responded to slower growth and higher unemployment by engaging in more active promotion and support of local industries, firms, and workers. This is especially notable in nations such as the United States, Britain, and Italy, where the national government typically has engaged in limited and uncoordinated interventionist efforts (Osborne 1987; Eisinger 1988; Totterdill 1989; Best 1990, chap. 7).

Quantitative indicators cannot adequately capture differences in industrial policy, which encompasses a wide array of objectives and a multiplicity of policy instruments. The only measure that even comes close is subsidies to firms. Despite the fact that it, too, is lacking, it is worth examining to see if there is any convergence. As with fiscal policy, the convergence thesis would expect governments to be increasingly constrained in their use of subsidies because of the pressure from international capital and product flows to cut spending. On the other hand, heightened product market competition tends to increase the domestic political pressure on national governments to provide monetary assistance to companies employing substantial numbers of citizens. Moreover, nations with high levels of corporate subsidies may develop strong societal or government coalitions favoring their continuation, rendering cutbacks difficult; those countries not inclined to subsidize industry may have greater freedom to reduce their level even further.

As the data in Table 5 indicate, the average level of subsidy provision increased in the mid-to-late 1970s as stagflation set in, and had declined only slightly by the early 1990s.[11] Countries that have decreased subsidies in recent years are primarily those that had low levels to begin with, whereas several of the nations that have increased subsidies recently, such as Denmark and Sweden, were ones that already had relatively high levels. Hence, there has been no convergence. If anything, the coefficients of variation

---

[11] These figures do not include military expenditures, which have been an important component of industrial policy in the United States (Markusen *et al.* 1991).

Table 5   Convergence in government subsidies?

	Government subsidies to industry as a share of GDP (%)			
	1960–73	*1974–79*	*1980–89*	*1990–93*
Australia	0.8	1.3	1.6	1.5
Austria	2.0	2.8	3.0	2.9
Belgium	2.6	3.9	3.8	2.9
Canada	0.9	1.9	2.3	1.7
Denmark	2.4	3.2	3.2	3.6
Finland	2.9	3.5	3.1	3.3
France	2.2	2.5	2.8	2.3
Germany	1.5	2.1	2.1	2.1
Italy	1.7	2.9	3.4	2.7
Japan	0.9	1.4	1.2	0.8
Netherlands	1.4	2.3	3.1	2.9
New Zealand	1.0	2.3	1.2	0.3
Norway	4.7	6.8	6.0	5.9
Sweden	1.7	3.7	4.8	5.2
Switzerland	0.9	1.3	1.4	1.6
United Kingdom	1.8	2.9	1.9	1.1
United States	0.5	0.4	0.6	0.5
Average	1.7	2.7	2.7	2.4
Standard deviation	1.0	1.4	1.4	1.5
Coefficient of variation	0.59	0.52	0.52	0.63

Sources: OECD 1991; OECD 1996

suggest that there is now greater diversity across the industrialized countries than a decade ago.

Institutional Structures

In this section I examine developments in three key economic institutions: labor relations, financial systems, and interfirm relations.

Labor Relations

Many observers expect nations to converge in their labor relations practices, but for two contrasting reasons. The most prevalent view is that heightened international competition in conjunction with the increasing volatility of product markets results in a need for extreme flexibility in the labor market and inside the firm. National labor relations practices should thus be converging toward the "U.S. model," which features minimal unionization, frequent job turnover, and high levels of managerial discretion in labor deployment. On the other hand, a number of studies suggest superior performance results from what might be called the "Japanese model," which features long-term employment and significant employee participation in shopfloor decision making. Ronald Dore (1989, p. 443) has suggested that such superiority should engender convergence toward this type of system: "The nature of work, and the nature of market competition in the modern world, are such that the adoption of organisation-oriented employment systems – at least for their core workforce – does confer a competitive advantage on firms, whether they be in manufacturing or service industries. And this provides a very good reason, which the empirical evidence does not controvert, for expecting such systems to become more general." (See also Lincoln and Kalleberg 1990, chap. 9.)

Four aspects of the labor relationship are worth investigating: job tenure, unions and collective bargaining, cooperative-participatory versus adversarial-hierarchical labor-management relations, and skill formation.

One of the most striking labor market differences between countries has been in patterns of job tenure. Since World War II, employees in most large Japanese companies have had a de facto lifetime employment guarantee. Labor turnover in these firms is minimal. The same holds for some large firms in Europe. In the United States, by contrast, average job tenure is quite short, with employees switching jobs frequently.

There is good reason to expect the differences between Japanese and American practices to have narrowed since the 1970s. On the one hand, heightened competition resulting from growing product market integration, the shift toward flexible specialization, and the general sluggishness that has plagued industrialized economies since 1973 have stimulated employers to rid themselves of the perceived rigidities associated with employment guarantees. Firms increasingly seek greater flexibility in labor deployment, which is impeded (in some ways) by lifetime employment. On the other hand, much has been written in recent years about the benefits associated with employment guarantees. Having long offered de facto guaranteed employment for white collar employees, large American firms may have sought to experiment with such practices for production workers as well. Perhaps firms and nations at both ends of the spectrum have moved closer to the middle.

Surprisingly, a recent study by the OECD finds that average job tenure – the average number of years workers have been with their current employer – held constant in the United States during the 1980s and *increased* in Japan (OECD 1993, Table 4.2). The difference in job tenure between the two countries remains stark. In 1991, 29% of American workers had been with their current employer for less than one year and 62% for less than five years; in Japan the figures were 10% and 37%, respectively. Average job tenure was 6.7 years in the United States versus 10.9 years in Japan. The study found Britain, Canada, and Australia to be closer to the U.S. pattern, while Germany and France more closely resemble Japan (OECD 1993, Table 4.1).

With slower growth, the shift from mass production to flexible specialization, and the ascendence of free market policy views during the 1980s, unions have come under increasing pressure in virtually all industrialized nations. Has there been convergence in union size and strength? With regard to size, exactly the opposite has occurred. As David Blanchflower and Richard Freeman (1990) were among the first to note, rather than coming together, national labor movements have been "going different ways." Table 6 shows union density figures for 1970, 1980, and 1990. The pattern of divergence over the past two decades is clear, as indicated by the coefficients of variation. High-density countries such as Sweden, Norway, Denmark, Finland, and Belgium experienced a substantial increase during the 1970s and then little or no change in the 1980s. Of the middle-density nations, some – Canada, Germany, Italy, Switzerland, and the United Kingdom – were essentially unchanged between 1970 and 1990. Others, including Australia, Austria, and the Netherlands, suffered declines. The three countries with the lowest rates of unionization – the United States, France, and Japan – experienced substantial drops.

Several factors appear to lie behind this divergence. The large, encompassing union movements in Scandinavia have greater economic and political resources with which to maintain or

Table 6   Convergence in unionization rates?

	Union density (%)[a]		
	1970	1980	1990
Australia	50.2	48.0	40.4
Austria	62.2	56.2	46.2
Belgium	45.5	55.9	51.2
Canada[b]	31.0	36.1	35.8
Denmark	60.0	76.0	71.4
Finland	51.4	69.8	72.0
France	22.3	17.5	9.8
Germany	33.0	35.6	32.9
Italy	36.3	49.3	38.8
Japan	35.1	31.1	25.4
Netherlands	38.0	35.3	25.5
New Zealand	na	56.0	44.8
Norway	51.4	56.9	56.0
Sweden	67.7	79.7	82.5
Switzerland	30.1	30.7	26.6
United Kingdom	44.8	50.4	39.1
United States	23.2	22.3	15.6
Average	42.6	47.5	42.0
Standard deviation	13.7	18.0	20.0
Coefficient of variation	0.32	0.38	0.48

[a]Employed union membership as a share of the total employed labor force. Actual years differ slightly for some countries.
[b]Data are for recorded (rather than employed) union membership.
Source: OECD 1994a, Table 5.7

increase their position. Also, as Joel Rogers (1990) has argued, employer strategies vary depending upon the existing extent of unionization. If competitor firms are also unionized, labor costs tend not to be a source of competitive disadvantage for employers, who may then resign themselves to the existence of unions. On the other hand, if the current level of unionization is low, and particularly if there is intra-industry variation in unionization, employers may feel the optimal strategy is to attempt to roll back unions entirely.

What about union structure? Much has been written about the dissolution of coordinated wage bargaining in the corporatist nations of northern Europe (Lash and Urry 1987; Offe 1985; Streeck 1984; Windolf 1989). But several recent studies suggest that popular perceptions of corporatist demise are exaggerated, or at least premature. A report by the OECD notes that "in a majority of the OECD countries the sectoral level has remained the principal arena for wage determination. In addition, during the 1980s and early 1990s, economy-wide bargaining continued or was re-established in a number of, mainly European, countries" (OECD 1994a, p. 186). Furthermore, labor movement structure has two principal dimensions: centralization and concentration. The former refers to the power and authority of national union confederations, while the latter denotes the number of competing confederations and unions. In a careful study, Peter Lange, Michael Wallerstein, and Miriam Golden (1995) have found that the degree of labor movement centralization indeed declined somewhat in Sweden and Denmark during the 1980s. Coordinated wage bargaining, however, is as much or more a function of union concentration as it is of centralization; the two are functional substitutes (Kenworthy 1995, chap. 5; Golden 1993). And there has been relatively little change in labor movement concentration during the past several decades. Change has occurred in some countries, but developments have offset one another so that the overall degree of concentration has not shifted (Lange, Wallerstein, and Golden 1995).[12]

One of the most noteworthy developments in labor relations since the 1970s has been the growing adoption of cooperative, participatory modes of labor-management interaction. A variety of studies heightened awareness of the extensive role Japanese employees play in shopfloor decision making (Nakamura and Nitta 1995, pp. 334–40). The 1970s was also the decade in which factories across the industrialized world, from Sweden to the United States, began experimenting with various, though usually limited, forms of workplace democratization. This trend has continued in the 1980s and 1990s. Quality circles and production teams have given workers a greater role in shopfloor decisions, while works councils and codetermination offer employees a voice in broader

---

[12] In Sweden and the other Nordic nations, for instance, the share of union members accounted for by the largest confederation declined in the 1980s. But at the same time the number of unions affiliated to the major confederations decreased.

company decision making (Blinder 1990; Rogers and Streeck 1995).

Yet while employee participation has increased in one form or another in all industrialized nations, the movement toward greater decision making rights has been rather uneven. In particular, the United States and Britain have been laggards compared to Japan and the rest of Europe. Thus, for instance, in a review of recent trends in the rights and practices of works councils, Joel Rogers and Wolfgang Streeck (1994, p. 148) conclude: "There is striking convergence among developed nations, *with the sole exceptions of the United States and Great Britain*, that works councils or similar institutions, intermediate between managerial discretion and collective bargaining, are part of a well-functioning labor relations system. In most of Europe, the past decade witnessed both an expansion of the collective participation rights of workers and more extensive production-related communication and cooperation between managements and work forces." The same is true of other participatory forms, such as work teams (Applebaum and Batt 1994; Blinder 1990).

Even outside the United States and Britain, considerable variation exists with respect to the form and extent of employee participation in decision making. In Japan, workers continue to have strong (informal) decision-making rights and responsibilities on the shopfloor, but at best only a consultative voice on broader issues. Beyond the shopfloor the Japanese labor relations system is perhaps best characterized as one of benevolent paternalism. By contrast, in a number of northern European nations, such as Germany and Sweden, employees enjoy codetermination rights, whereby they elect members to their firm's board of directors (*European Industrial Relations Review* 1981; Ferner and Hyman 1992).

A final aspect of labor relations to consider is skill formation. Recent studies have identified a marked contrast in the form and extent of employee training across industrialized economies, which does not appear to have abated in recent years (Commission on the Skills of the American Workforce 1990; Lynch 1993; OECD 1993; Office of Technology Assessment 1990b). In the United States, employees receive relatively little formal training in the workplace.

The public goods nature of employee skills discourages unilateral training expenditures by firms. Other nations have institutions that enable companies to overcome this barrier. In Japan lifetime employment and seniority-based pay alleviate the threat that workers will take their skills and move to another firm. In Germany, firms collectively force themselves to invest in in-house training. Industry associations and trade unions require companies to participate in an apprenticeship system offering extensive job training to future and present employees. Finally, countries such as France and Sweden levy a training tax, whereby firms can either spend a percentage of their payroll on certain specified types of training for their workforce or contribute the equivalent amount to a public training fund.

Industrial relations have been characterized by substantial change in recent decades. Increases in employers' search for flexibility, employment instability, employee participation in decision making, and attention to workforce skills have been common to most industrialized economies. These trends are due in no small measure to heightened internationalization and the competition it has unleashed. Yet these developments have not produced marked convergence in labor relations practices. In their conclusion to a recent volume assessing developments in a variety of countries, Richard Locke and Thomas Kochan (1995, p. 359) aptly sum up the situation: "Although a new approach to employment relations has emerged in all the advanced industrial nations included in our research, the particular forms it has taken and the extent to which it has diffused vary considerably ... across countries with different institutional arrangements."

Financial Systems

Already by the mid 1980s Ralph Bryant felt confident in stating, in his review of financial integration, that "Relative to earlier decades, there is much less scope for an individual nation to maintain financial conditions within its borders different from those prevailing abroad" (1987, p. 1). The banking industry and bond and equity markets have become notably more internationalized since then, as noted earlier. The question is: Has the nature of financial systems converged? Have they in fact become more alike in their structure and functioning?

Analysts of financial systems have identified two important differences across industrialized economies, illustrated most strikingly by the contrast between the Japanese and German systems on the one hand and the U.S. system on the other (Porter 1992; Zysman 1983; Ellsworth 1985; Office of Technology Assessment 1990a, chap. 3; Jacobs 1991; Wellons 1985; Berglof 1990; Hodder 1988). First, companies based in Germany and Japan have tended to rely less heavily on equity than U.S.-based firms, securing a much larger share of their financing via bank loans. The second difference lies in the relationship between firms and their equity investors. Japanese and German investors are predominantly corporate entities who tend to hold their shares for long periods of time and work with the company to find solutions to problems in times of trouble. In Germany these "stable shareholders" are primarily the large universal banks; in Japan they are financial and nonfinancial companies linked together via an assortment of economic and social ties. Patient capital permits corporate managers a relatively long time horizon in making investment decisions and other strategic choices.

The U.S. financial system, by contrast, more closely approximates the textbook model of a decentralized capital market. Ownership of firms is seldom concentrated in the hands of large investors who might prioritize long-term success and stability. Instead, companies are dependent upon a multitude of owners with small shareholdings who tend to focus on near-term returns. Over 50% of all U.S. corporate stock is owned by institutional investors (pension funds, insurance companies, and so on), whose holdings are diversified across hundreds of firms and traded frequently (Porter 1992, p. 26). Stock turnover (the volume of traded shares as a percentage of total listed shares) on the New York Stock Exchange amounts to nearly two-thirds during the course of a year. The U.S. system is characterized by "exit-based" relationships, as opposed to the "voice-based" relationships obtaining in Germany, Japan, and a number of other countries.

According to the convergence thesis, these differences should diminish considerably as financial integration opens up the Japanese and German financial systems, pushing them closer to the decentralized U.S.-style capital market. In Japan there has indeed been a gradual shift toward greater use of equity financing. But the voice-based nature of equity relationships themselves seems not to have diminished. In fact, in many instances the banks who formerly acted as sources of debt financing have become key stable equity holders. Michael Gerlach (1992, pp. 16–17) describes the recent developments:

> Equity-based financing continues to be provided largely by the same financial institutions as the debt capital that it is replacing.... This gradual change in financing methods might have great significance if the financial institutions behaved quite differently as purchasers of securities than they do as financial lenders – for example, by becoming unstable stock market investors rather than stable lead banks. However ... equity ties among financial and nonfinancial companies, much like debt ties, continue to be structured in long-term relationships.

Indeed, Gerlach's careful study finds that stable shareholdings as a percentage of total shareholdings *increased* in Japan during the period 1969–86 (p. 76). For Germany the story is similar; recent studies suggest no marked change in the nature of relations between firms and their equity investors (Porter 1992; Jacobs 1991; Office of Technology Assessment 1990a, chap. 3). In the meantime, the U.S. financial system has become, if anything, increasingly short-term oriented. The average holding period of stocks in the United States declined from more than seven years in 1960 to two years by the early 1990s (Porter 1992, p. 42).

Relations Among Firms

Four types of interfirm relationships are of interest: purchaser-supplier relations, business groups, alliances among competitors, and formal business associations. Recent trends indicate some convergence in alliances among competitors and perhaps in purchaser-supplier relations, but not in the form or extent of business groupings and formal associations.

Consider purchaser-supplier relations first. At one extreme lies the exit-oriented strategy pursued by, for example, the three U.S. auto manufacturers. These firms' standard relationship with suppliers has traditionally been short-term, arms-length, adversarial, and based largely on price considerations. The problem with this type of arrangement is that, because there is no guarantee of future transactions, it discourages communication between purchasers and suppliers and among suppliers themselves and deters suppliers from making large-scale or asset-specific investments. Japanese automakers, by contrast, utilize a voice-based approach, centered around a commitment by the purchaser to work with suppliers over the long term. In return, the automakers insist upon close communication with their supplier firms and among suppliers, and require that suppliers steadily reduce costs. Suppliers readily comply, knowing that the sharing of information poses no direct threat to their own success, and that the relationship will not be severed just after they make a large investment to improve productivity (Womack, Jones, and Roos 1990, chap. 6; Helper 1991a, 1991c; Asanuma 1985; Cusumano and Takeishi 1991).

Recent reports suggest two potential signs of convergence. First, some Japanese firms are said to be increasing their use of foreign suppliers, in some cases at the expense of long-time domestic partners (*Business Week* 1994a). Frequently this is a response to pressure from the governments of countries, such as the United States, in which Japanese firms have set up assembly plants. Second, over the past decade the three major American car manufacturers and large firms in a variety of other industries have begun to shift their supplier relationships toward the Japanese type. Some supplier firms have been given long-term contracts, and exchange of information and direct supplier participation in the design process are now more common. To this point, however, the changes have been partial and halting, and it is unclear whether these firms are committed to making a genuine shift (Helper 1991b, 1991c; *Wall Street Journal* 1992b).

A second type of interfirm relationship is business groups, in which firms are linked through cross-ownership and/or some sort of long-term mutual obligation. Many large Japanese firms, including half of the largest 200 industrial corporations, are members of a *keiretsu* or similar business group (Gerlach 1992, p. 85). Although some firms in Europe have close links with other companies, the Japanese *keiretsu* are a unique phenomenon among the advanced industrial economies. While there is periodic speculation that the ties among Japanese firms in business groups are weakening, careful studies suggest otherwise (Gerlach 1992). Interestingly, substantial variation exists even among the principal East Asian economies in the structure of business groups. The Japanese *keiretsu* feature extensive cross-ownership between both large and small firms and financial institutions, and in many cases strong vertical links among independent companies. By contrast, the Korean *chaebol* are large vertically-integrated conglomerates, while Taiwanese groups consist of familial networks of small firms in different business sectors (Orru, Biggart, and Hamilton 1991).

A third key type of interfirm relationship is between competing companies. Once again there is a stark contrast between Japanese, and here also European, firms versus those based in the United States, the United Kingdom, Canada, Australia, and New Zealand (Hollingsworth, Schmitter, and Streeck 1994; Dore 1986; Campbell, Hollingsworth, and Lindberg 1991). In the former, competing firms frequently form alliances to cooperate in conducting research or providing employee training. Japanese firms in declining sectors also at times have formed "recession cartels" to reduce capacity in order to facilitate greater competitiveness or an orderly transition out of the industry. Competing companies in the Anglo economies, by contrast, have generally been highly individualistic. While oligopolistic price-setting behavior has been a recurrent feature of the U.S. steel and auto industries, formal alliances for other purposes have been rare.

However, that trend appears to be changing. For years, strong antitrust laws in the United States deterred R&D collaboration among competing firms. In 1984 Congress passed the National Cooperative Research Act, which loosened the restrictions on cooperative research. Since then, joint R&D ventures have occurred with greater frequency. Alliances between electronics companies and among auto manufacturers are pervasive, and in some cases include ownership ties. The list of corporate alliances within and across borders has grown by leaps and bounds in recent years

(Harrison 1994, chaps. 7–8; *Business Week* 1993c, 1994c; *Automotive Industries* 1992; Angel 1994, chap. 5). This is one area of interfirm relationships, then, in which genuine convergence is observable.

Will the trend continue? That is unclear. The recent surge in alliance formation is surely in part a fad. As one observer has remarked, "Unsure of what to do, many firms simply follow the herd, and in recent years the stampede has been towards the alliance" (Emmott 1993, p. 16). There is a clear economic logic to alliances among competitors. By pooling financial resources and discouraging free riders they can reduce innovation time, enable the exploitation of complementary technologies, increase access to markets, and facilitate skill formation. Yet there are also obvious drawbacks, chief among which is the partial loss of control over ideas or other assets. Because of the risks involved, it is particularly difficult to form large multifirm consortiums. It appears that a key to getting such large-scale alliances going lies in incentives and/or encouragement by either a strong industry association or the state. Hence we may continue to observe substantial differences between those countries with strong business associations and/or an interventionist state and those featuring weak business organization and a laissez-faire government orientation. It is noteworthy that with a few exceptions, such as Sematech and the Microelectronics Computer Corporation, virtually all alliances among U.S.-based companies in recent years involve just two or three companies. Japan and Germany, by contrast, are home to a variety of consortiums involving large numbers of firms.

This brings us to a final issue of interest in the area of interfirm relations: formal business associations. As with labor organization, there has long been, and continues to be, substantial variation among industrialized economies in the degree of business association. This is true within sectors, but it is most glaring in the strength and encompassingness of national business federations. In some cases – such as Austria, Sweden, Germany, Japan, and others – a national federation represents a large share of the country's firms and has substantial authority to speak and negotiate on their behalf. In others – the United States, Canada, and Australia, for example – federations are much less representative and centralized (Coleman and Grant 1988; Windmuller and Gladstone 1984).

Economic Performance

For government policies and institutional structures, the convergence thesis receives only lukewarm support. What about economic performance outcomes? Table 7 displays data for four performance indicators: productivity growth, unemployment, inflation, and trade balances.

The convergence thesis predicts that as firms around the globe come to have access to the same technologies, levels of productivity should converge. As an abundance of recent research has shown, that has indeed been the case for the industrialized countries throughout much of the post-World War II period (e.g., Baumol, Nelson, and Wolff 1994a; Dowrick and Nguyen 1989; Barro and Sala-i-Martin 1992). To the extent that technology is the driving force behind this convergence, it can occur, and seems to have done so, without nations converging in their economic policies or institutional arrangements.

As laggard countries catch up to the leaders – that is, as the gap in productivity levels diminishes – rates of productivity growth should also converge. But judging from the data in Table 7, this does not appear to have happened. Productivity growth diverged considerably in the immediate post-1973 years compared to the last decade of the postwar boom, then returned to something like the earlier degree of variation in the 1980s and early 1990s. The mid-to-late 1970s is best viewed as an exception to the normal course of events. This was a period when all industrialized economies faced sudden, severe shocks in the form of the oil price increases, wage explosions, and international monetary instability. Though growth rates declined in all nations (except Norway, which benefited from the discovery of North Sea oil), some economies weathered the storm better than others in the short run. Given these considerations, there is no indication of convergence in rates of productivity growth over the period 1960–94.

Unemployment conforms more closely to convergence predictions. The coefficient of variation for the 16 nations with available data declined by half between 1960–73 and 1990–94. Unemployment has increased everywhere since the early 1970s, but it has risen most sharply in countries that during the boom period were able

46   L. Kenworthy

Table 7 Convergence in economic performance?

	Productivity growth (%)				Unemployment (%)			
	1960–73	1974–79	1980–89	1990–94	1960–73	1974–79	1980–89	1990–94
Australia	2.5	1.8	0.6	1.9	2.0	5.0	7.5	9.6
Austria	5.0	2.2	1.1	0.9	1.7	1.7	3.3	3.8
Belgium	4.3	2.2	2.0	2.0	2.2	5.7	11.1	10.6
Canada	2.6	1.3	1.2	0.9	5.0	7.2	9.3	10.3
Denmark	3.0	1.0	1.2	2.4	1.3	5.1	8.0	11.1
Finland	4.7	1.4	2.8	2.2	2.0	4.4	4.9	12.1
France	4.7	2.4	2.1	0.9	2.0	4.5	9.0	10.5
Germany	4.1	2.7	1.4	2.2	0.8	3.4	6.8	7.8
Italy	5.8	2.8	2.0	2.3	5.3	6.6	9.9	11.0
Japan	8.1	2.9	2.8	1.0	1.3	1.9	2.5	2.4
Netherlands	4.0	2.2	-0.5	0.9	1.1	4.9	9.8	6.2
New Zealand	1.8	-0.9	1.4	0.9	0.2	0.8	4.8	9.2
Norway	3.4	2.7	2.0	3.2	1.3	1.8	2.8	5.6
Sweden	3.5	0.5	1.4	2.3	1.9	1.9	2.5	5.2
Switzerland	2.9	0.6	0.8	1.3	na	na	na	na
United Kingdom	2.8	1.3	1.9	1.7	1.9	4.2	9.5	8.7
United States	1.9	0.0	0.8	1.2	4.8	6.7	7.2	6.5
Average	3.8	1.6	1.5	1.7	2.2	4.1	6.8	8.2
Standard deviation	1.6	1.1	0.8	0.7	1.5	2.0	3.0	2.9
Coefficient of variation	0.42	0.69	0.53	0.41	0.68	0.49	0.44	0.35

(Continued)

Table 7   *(Continued)*

	Inflation (%)				Trade balance as a share of GDP (%)			
	1960–73	1974–79	1980–89	1990–94	1960–73	1974–79	1980–89	1990–94
Australia	3.5	12.1	8.4	2.9	-0.3	-0.5	-1.9	-0.6
Austria	4.2	6.3	3.8	3.4	0.2	-0.7	0.3	0.8
Belgium	3.6	8.4	4.8	2.8	0.5	-0.3	1.5	3.9
Canada	3.3	9.2	6.5	2.8	0.6	-0.1	1.8	-0.5
Denmark	6.2	10.8	6.9	2.1	-1.6	-2.9	1.2	6.4
Finland	5.7	12.8	7.3	3.3	-0.7	-0.7	0.6	2.2
France	4.6	10.7	7.3	2.6	0.7	0.3	-0.2	1.2
Germany	3.4	4.7	2.9	3.3	-1.2	-1.7	-1.8	0.2
Italy	3.9	16.7	11.2	5.5	0.7	-0.2	-0.3	1.6
Japan	6.2	9.9	2.5	2.0	0.2	0.4	1.9	1.9
Netherlands	4.9	7.2	2.8	2.9	0.1	1.8	3.6	4.8
New Zealand	4.8	13.8	11.8	2.6	-1.0	-4.0	-1.0	2.2
Norway	5.1	8.7	8.3	2.7	0.2	-4.7	4.3	7.3
Sweden	4.7	9.8	7.9	5.8	-1.1	-0.7	1.2	2.3
Switzerland	4.2	4.0	3.3	3.9	0.2	1.5	-0.2	3.0
United Kingdom	5.1	15.6	7.4	4.6	-0.5	-0.9	-0.1	-1.6
United States	3.2	8.5	5.5	3.6	0.4	-0.5	-2.0	-1.1

(Continued)

48   *L. Kenworthy*

Table 7   *(Continued)*

	Inflation (%)			Trade balance as a share of GDP (%)			
	1960–73	*1974–79*	*1980–89*	*1990–94*	*1960–73*	*1974–79*	*1980–89*	*1990–94*
Average	4.5	10.0	6.4	3.3	−0.2	−0.8	0.5	2.0
Standard deviation	1.0	3.5	2.8	1.1	0.7	1.7	1.8	2.5
Coefficient of variation	0.22	0.35	0.44	0.33	–	–	–	–

na = not available
Sources: OECD 1995a, Tables 3.7, 2.15, 8.11, and 6.14, supplemented by earlier editions of OECD, *Historical Statistics*; OECD 1995b, Annex Tables 1, 16, 20, and 21; OECD 1996

to hold joblessness to a low level. Hence, most of the former low unemployment countries have caught up with and in some cases – such as Australia, Belgium, Denmark, France, The Netherlands, and the United Kingdom – surpassed the others. This development owes partly to structural forces, including the deflationary bias, and partly to policy choices (Therborn 1986; Korpi 1991). By the 1980s the group of nations able to maintain low rates of joblessness had dwindled to Austria, Japan, Norway, Sweden, and perhaps Switzerland, and by the early 1990s only Japan and Austria were left.

Inflation is the performance indicator for which convergence forces are widely expected to be strongest. Financial markets, particularly those for national currencies, are the most highly integrated of any. And inflation, in combination with domestic interest rates, is commonly used as the basis upon which currency investment decisions are made. Consistent with these expectations, the average rate of inflation in the industrialized nations has declined sharply and steadily since the late 1970s. Interestingly, however, the coefficients of variation in Table 7 show an increase in variability during the 1980s. And even during the recession of the early 1990s, the degree of spread was about the same as that in the late 1970s.

Inflation shot up in many countries in the immediate post-1973 years, in some cases quadrupling in the space of a few years. While all of the industrialized countries experienced a substantial rise in prices, some were far more successful than others in limiting the extent of the damage. Austria, Germany, and Switzerland proved especially successful, while nations such as Australia, New Zealand, Finland, Italy, and the United Kingdom suffered extremely high rates of inflation during the mid-to-late 1970s. During the 1980s inflation fell in all countries. Most managed to hold price increases to a moderate level, and some, such as Germany, the Netherlands, and Japan, nearly brought them to a halt. Inflation remained fairly high in a number of nations, however, so the spread between countries widened. In the 1980s industrialized economies split into two groups: one that placed price stability above all other policy priorities and another in which it was merely one economic goal among many. The former group was headed by Germany and included several other nations with currencies linked to the deutschmark: Belgium, Denmark, and the Netherlands. The United

Kingdom also belongs in this group, though it was less successful at achieving low inflation. Among those for which inflation was not the top policy priority, some, including Austria and Japan, nevertheless managed to hold price rises in check, while others had less success.

By the early 1990s the average inflation rate for the 17 countries had fallen to 3.3%, down from an average of 10% in the late 1970s and 6.4% in the 1980s. The degree of variability also appears to have declined somewhat compared to the 1980s. The early 1990s were recession years, however, so it is difficult at this point to tell whether these developments represent real convergence or not.

The final performance indicator shown in Table 7 is trade balances. As capital and products flow more freely across national borders, the convergence thesis predicts a disappearance of sustained trade imbalances. Fiscal and monetary policies on the demand side and productive capacities on the supply side should become increasingly similar everywhere. More importantly, with floating exchange rates a trade imbalance should be quickly rectified via adjustments in the value of the currency. Yet the standard deviations suggest, on the contrary, heightened dispersion in trade balances over the past two decades.

What accounts for this development? Although it established fixed exchange rates, the Bretton Woods system was designed to avoid prolonged trade imbalances between countries. A nation with a sustained trade deficit generally had its currency devalued against the dollar (through a formal agreement) until its balance of payments more or less evened out. As the data in Table 7 indicate, the system functioned effectively in this regard. Most of the 17 countries averaged very small trade surpluses or deficits during the 1960–73 period. With the abandonment of fixed exchange rates in 1973 there was no longer a formal mechanism promoting trade balance. It was hoped that floating exchange rates would do the trick, but currency movements came to respond more to inflation than to trade figures. Furthermore, currencies were fixed for those nations participating in the European Monetary System after 1979, and unlike Bretton Woods the aim here was to stabilize currency values rather than trade balances. It is not surprising, therefore, that there has been a larger spread in trade balances since the early 1970s than before.

On the whole, then, productivity levels and unemployment rates are the only two performance indicators for which genuine convergence across nations appears clear. Inflation rates may also be converging, though it is too soon yet too tell. There has been little or no homogenization in rates of productivity growth or in trade balances.

Concluding Remarks

Orthodox economic theory has long assumed that globalization would erode national differences in economic institutions, policies, and performance outcomes. With the dramatic growth of trade, transnational production, and financial integration over the past three decades, this expectation of convergence has gained increasing currency among economic analysts and commentators. Yet, at least through the early 1990s, the world's industrialized economies have exhibited less convergence than seems to be commonly expected.[13]

One indicator of this comes from the quantitative data shown in Tables 2 through 7 above. In these tables there are 52 instances in which it is possible to compare coefficients of variation for a variable between two time periods and for which the convergence thesis predicts homogenization. Of these, in only six cases is the trend in the direction predicted by the convergence thesis (namely, a smaller coefficient of variation in the later period) *and* the difference statistically significant by conventional standards.[14]

---

[13] The same appears to be true of developing nations. See Gereffi (1990).

[14] The 17 nations examined here constitute a population, rather than a sample. Tests of statistical significance are useful, nevertheless, to give us an idea of the likelihood that a difference between the coefficients of variation for two time periods is simply a result of chance. To assess this probability, I used a resampling with replacement technique to generate a sample distribution of coefficients of variation for each two-period comparison. This enables a determination of the probability that the observed difference between the coefficients in two time periods could occur randomly. (For a discussion of the general logic of this "bootstrapping" technique, see Mooney and Duval 1993.) For each two-period comparison, 1,000 resamples were drawn to generate the distribution.

The six instances in which there is less than a 10% probability ($p < 0.10$, one-tailed test) that the difference between coefficients is due to chance are: nominal long-term interest rates, 1980–89 vs. 1990–93; social-welfare transfers, 1960–73 vs. 1990–93; productivity growth, 1974–79 vs. 1990–94; unemployment, 1960–73 vs. 1974–79, 1960–73 vs. 1980–89, and 1960–73 vs. 1990–94.

There are, it would seem, two reasons why there has been only limited convergence: (1) the extent of globalization itself has been limited, and (2) globalization's convergence-generating effects are limited. Despite the considerable increases in economic integration in recent decades, we are still far from living in a truly global economy (Hirst and Thompson 1996). As integration proceeds further, I suspect we will see greater convergence than has occurred thus far. That will be especially true for monetary policy if the nations of Europe carry through with their plan for full monetary integration and a single currency. At the same time, however, the degree of homogenization will likely continue to be more limited than some expect. There may continue to be occasional dramatic instances of governments bowing to transnational forces, as with French fiscal policy in the early 1980s. But there will also continue to be space for substantial variation in national policies and institutional arrangements, and hence in performance results. Markets allow multiple structures and practices to survive, and institutional differences generate considerable variety in preferences, choices, and capacities.

In addition, it is not inconceivable that the process of increasing globalization could slow considerably, come to a halt, or even be partially reversed. As several observers have recently noted, product and financial markets are currently no more integrated now than they were prior to World War I (Gordon 1988; Zevin 1992; Woodall 1995). Internationalization increased dramatically among industrialized economies from 1850 to 1913, but then plummeted in the 1920s and 1930s. The post-World War II increases have only managed to restore the degree of integration to its earlier levels. Furthermore, although trade (as a share of GDP) expanded at a rapid clip between 1945 and 1973, it has not increased at all since then. Formal barriers to trade have continued to fall in most industrialized nations, but many have been replaced by informal barriers (Mansfield and Busch 1995).[15] And some knowledgeable

---

[15] In the United States, for instance, the share of imports subject to quotas or other forms of protection increased from 8% in 1975 to 18% in 1992 (Barnet and Cavanaugh 1994, p. 176).

observers contend that national financial markets are by now fully integrated, suggesting that convergence pressures from this source may have reached their peak (Frankel 1991). If political or other developments do conspire to impede further globalization, the persistence of substantial variation across national economies is a virtual certainty.

References

Alchian, Armen A. (1950) "Uncertainty, evolution, and economic theory." *Journal of Political Economy* 58, 211–21.

Anchordoguy, Marie. (1988) "Mastering the market: Japanese government targeting of the computer industry." *International Organization* 42, 509–43.

Andrews, David M. (1994) "Capital mobility and state autonomy: toward a structural theory of international monetary relations." *International Studies Quarterly* 38, 193–218.

Angel, David P. (1994) *Restructuring for Innovation: The Remaking of the U.S. Semiconductor Industry*. New York: Guilford Press.

Applebaum, Eileen and Rosemary Batt. (1994) *The New American Workplace*. Ithaca, NY: ILR Press.

Asanuma, Banri. (1985) "The organization of parts purchases in the Japanese automotive industry." *Japanese Economic Studies* 13, 4, 32–53.

Automotive Industries. (1992) "Global joint ventures and affiliations for 1992." February.

Barnet, Richard J. and John Cavanagh. (1994) *Global Dreams: Imperial Corporations and the New World Order*. New York: Touchstone.

Barro, Robert J. and Xavier Sala-i-Martin. (1992) "Convergence." *Journal of Political Economy* 100, 223–51.

Baumol, William J., Sue Anne Batey Blackman, and Edward N. Wolff. (1989) *Productivity and American Leadership: The Long View*. Cambridge, MA: MIT Press.

Baumol, William J., Richard R. Nelson, and Edward N. Wolff, eds. (1994a) *Convergence of Productivity*. New York: Oxford University Press.

Baumol, William J., Richard R. Nelson, and Edward N. Wolff. (1994b) "Introduction: the convergence of productivity, its significance, and its varied connotations." In Baumol, Nelson, and Wolff (1994a).

Berglof, Erik. (1990) "Capital structure as a mechanism of control: a comparison of financial systems." In *The Firm as a Nexus of Treaties*, eds. Masahiko Aoki, Bo Gustafsson, and Oliver E. Williamson. London: Sage.

Bergsten, C. Fred. (1993) "The rationale for a rosy view: what a global economy will look like." *The Economist*, 11 September, 57–62.

Best, Michael H. (1990) *The New Competition: Institutions of Industrial Restructuring*. Cambridge, MA: Harvard University Press.

Blanchflower, David G. and Richard B. Freeman. (1990) "Going different ways: unionism in the U.S. and other advanced OECD countries." Working Paper 3342, National Bureau of Economic Research. Cambridge, MA.

Blinder, Alan S., ed. (1990) *Paying for Productivity*. Washington, DC: Brookings Institution.

Borrus, Michael, James E. Millstein, and John Zysman. (1983) "Trade and development in the semiconductor industry: Japanese challenge and American response." In *American Industry in International Competition*, eds. John Zysman and Laura Tyson. Ithaca, NY: Cornell University Press.

Bryant, Ralph C. (1987) *International Financial Intermediation*. Washington, DC: Brookings Institution.

Business Week. (1990) "The stateless corporation." 14 May, 98–105.

— (1993a) "Don't play games with the dollar." 30 August, 94.

— (1993b) "The global investor." 11 October, 120–26.

— (1993c) "The virtual corporation." 8 February, 98–102.

— (1994a) "Doing the unthinkable: Japan Inc.'s suppliers gasp as it buys abroad." 10 January, 52–53.

— (1994b) "The second year: Clinton weaves a security blanket for America." 24 January, 68–74.

— (1994c) "What's the word in the lab? Collaborate." 27 June, 78–80.

Cameron, David R. (1978) "The expansion of the public economy: a comparative analysis." *American Political Science Review* 72, 1243–61.

Campbell, John L, J. Rogers Hollingsworth, and Leon N. Lindberg, eds. (1991) *The Governance of the American Economy*. Cambridge, UK: Cambridge University Press.

Coleman, William and Wyn Grant. (1988) "The organizational cohesion and political access of business: a study of comprehensive associations." *European Journal of Political Research* 16, 467–87.

Commission on the Skills of the American Workforce. (1990) America's *Choice: High Skills or Low Wages!* Rochester: National Center on Education and the Economy.

Cosh, Andrew D., Alan Hughes, and Ajit Singh. (1992) "Openness, financial innovation, changing patterns of ownership, and the structure of financial markets." In *Financial Openness and National Autonomy*, eds. Tariq Banuri and Juliet B. Schor. Oxford: Clarendon Press.

Cusumano, Michael A. and Akira Takeishi. (1991) "Supplier relations and management: a survey of Japanese, Japanese-transplant, and U.S. auto plants." *Strategic Management Journal* 12, 563–88.

Donahue, Hugh Carter. (1989) "Choosing the TV of the future." *Technology Review*, April, 31–40.

Dore, Ronald. (1986) *Flexible Rigidities*. Stanford, CA: Stanford University Press.

— (1989) "Where we are now: musings of an evolutionist." *Work, Employment and Society* 3, 425–46.

Dowrick, Steve and Duc-Tho Nguyen. (1989) "OECD comparative economic growth 1950-85: catch-up and convergence." *American Economic Review* 79, 1010–30.

Eads, George C. and Kozo Yamamura. (1987) "The future of industrial policy." In *The Political Economy of Japan, vol. 1: The Domestic Transformation*, eds. Kozo Yamamura and Yasukichi Yasuba. Stanford, CA: Stanford University Press.

Eatwell, John. (1993) "The global money trap." *The American Prospect*, Winter, 118–26.

The Economist. (1993a) "The Rockies horror show." 28 August, 65.

— (1993b) "Storming the Bastille." 17 July, 69–70.

— (1995a) "Caught in the debt trap." 1 April, 59–60.

— (1995b) "Ecu-sounder." 8 April, 45.

— (1995c) "Put your factory here, please." 10 June, 70.

Eisinger, Peter K. (1988) *The Rise of the Entrepreneurial State.* Madison: University of Wisconsin Press.

Ellsworth, Richard R. (1985) "Capital markets and competitive decline." *Harvard Business Review*, September–October, 171–83.

Emmott, Bill. (1993) "A survey of multinationals." *The Economist*, 27 March, 1–20.

Esping-Andersen, Gosta. (1990) *The Three Worlds of Welfare Capitalism.* Princeton, NJ: Princeton University Press.

European Industrial Relations Review. (1981) "Employee board-level representation in eight countries." No. 84, 20–25.

Feldstein, Martin. (1995) "Global capital flows: too little, not too much." *The Economist*, 24 June, 72–73.

Ferner, Anthony and Richard Hyman, eds. (1992) *Industrial Relations in the New Europe.* Oxford: Blackwell.

Fortune. (1991) "The thaw in Washington." Special issue on "The New American Century."

Frankel, Jeffrey A. (1991) "Quantifying international capital mobility in the 1980s." In *National Saving and Economic Performance*, eds. B. Douglas Bernheim and John B. Shoven. Chicago: University of Chicago Press.

Fransman, Martin. (1995) "Is national technology policy obsolete in a globalised world? The Japanese response." *Cambridge Journal of Economics* 19, 95–119.

Frieden, Jeffry A. (1991) "Invested interests: the politics of national economic policies in a world of global finance." *International Organization* 45, 425–51.

Garrett, Geoffrey. (1995) "Capital mobility, trade, and the domestic politics of economic policy." *International Organization* 49, 657–87.

Garrett, Geoffrey and Peter Lange. (1991) "Political responses to interdependence: What's left for the left?" *International Organization* 45, 541–64.

— (1995) "Internationalization, institutions, and political change." *International Organization* 49, 627–55.

Garrett, Geoffrey and Deborah Mitchell. (1995) "Globalization and the welfare state: income transfers in the industrial democracies, 1965–1990." Unpublished typescript.

Gereffi, Gary. (1990) "International economics and domestic policies." In *Economy and Society: Overviews in Economic Sociology*, eds. Alberto Martinelli and Neil J. Smelser. London: Sage.

Gerlach, Michael L. (1992) *Alliance Capitalism: The Social Organization of Japanese Business*. Berkeley: University of California Press.

Gerschenkron, Alexander. (1952) "Economic backwardness in historical perspective." In *The Progress of Underdeveloped Countries*, ed. Burt Hoselitz. Chicago: University of Chicago Press.

Glasgall, William. (1993) "Is megabyte finance megatrouble?" *Business Week*, 26 April, 14.

Golden, Miriam. (1993) "The dynamics of trade unionism and national economic performance." *American Political Science Review* 87, 439–54.

Goldstein, Morris, Donald J. Mathieson, and Timothy Lane. (1991) "Determinants and systematic consequences of international capital flows." In *Determinants and Systematic Consequences of International Capital Flows*, Occasional Paper 77. Washington, DC: International Monetary Fund.

Goodman, John B. (1992) *Monetary Sovereignty: The Politics of Central Banking in Western Europe*. Ithaca, NY: Cornell University Press.

Goodman, John B. and Louis W. Pauly. (1993) "The obsolescence of capital controls? Economic management in an age of global markets." *World Politics* 46, 50–82.

Gordon, David M. (1988) "The global economy: new edifice or crumbling foundation?" *New Left Review*, no. 168, 24–64.

Gourevitch, Peter. (1986) *Politics in Hard Times*. Ithaca, NY: Cornell University Press.

Graham, Otis L., Jr. (1992) *Losing Time: The Industrial Policy Debate*. Cambridge, MA: Harvard University Press.

Hall, Peter A. (1986) *Governing the Economy: The Politics of State Intervention in Britain and France*. New York: Oxford University Press.

Harris, Robert G. (1989) "Telecommunications policy in Japan: lessons for the U.S." *California Management Review*, Spring, 113–31.

Harrison, Bennett. (1994) *Lean and Mean: The Changing Landscape of Corporate Power in the Age of Flexibility*. New York: Basic.

Helper, Susan. (1991a) "An exit-voice analysis of supplier relations." In *Morality, Rationality, and Efficiency: New Perspectives on Socio-Economics*, ed. Richard M. Coughlin. Armonk, NY: M. E. Sharpe.

— (1991b) "How much has really changed between U.S. automakers and their suppliers?" *Sloan Management Review*, Summer, 15–28.

— (1991c) "Strategy and irreversibility in supplier relations: the case of the U.S. automobile industry." *Business History Review* 65, 781–824.

Hibbs, D. (1977) "Political parties and macroeconomic policy." *American Political Science Review* 71, 1467–87.

Hicks, Alexander M. and Duane H. Swank. (1992) "Politics, institutions, and welfare spending in industrialized democracies, 1960–82." *American Political Science Review* 86, 658–74.

Hirst, Paul and Grahame Thompson. (1996) *Globalization in Question*. Cambridge, UK: Polity Press.

Hodder, James E. (1988) "Corporate capital structure in the United States and Japan: financial intermediation and implications of financial deregulation." In *Government Policy Towards Industry in the United States and Japan*, ed. John B. Shoven. Cambridge, UK: Cambridge University Press.

Hollingsworth, J. Rogers, Philippe C. Schmitter, and Wolfgang Streeck, eds. (1994) *Governing Capitalist Economies: Performance and Control of Economic Sectors*. New York: Oxford University Press.

Hollingsworth, J. Rogers and Wolfgang Streeck. (1994) "Countries and sectors: concluding remarks on performance, convergence, and competitiveness." In *Governing Capitalist Economies: Performance and Control of Economic Sectors*, eds. J. Rogers Hollingsworth, Philippe C. Schmitter, and Wolfgang Streeck. New York: Oxford University Press.

IMF (International Monetary Fund). (1990, 1992) *International Financial Statistics Yearbook*. Washington, DC: IMF.

Jackman, Richard. (1990) "Wage formation in the Nordic countries viewed from an international perspective." In *Wage Formation and Macroeconomic Policy in the Nordic Countries*, ed. Lars Calmfors. Oxford: Oxford University Press.

Jacobs, Michael T. (1991) *Short-Term America*. Boston: Harvard Business School Press.

Kamerman, Sheila B. and Alfred J. Kahn. (1995) *Starting Right: How America Neglects Its Youngest Children and What We Can Do about It*. New York: Oxford University Press.

Katzenstein, Peter J. (1985) *Small States in World Markets*. Ithaca, NY: Cornell University Press.

Kenworthy, Lane. (1995) *In Search of National Economic Success: Balancing Competition and Cooperation*. Thousand Oaks, CA: Sage.

— (1996) "Have the U.S. states converged? Constraints and opportunities of economic integration." Typescript. Department of Sociology, East Carolina University.

Kikkawa, Mototada. (1983) "Shipbuilding, motor cars, and semiconductors: the diminishing role of industrial policy in Japan." In *Europe's Industries: Public and Private Strategies for Change*, eds. Geoffrey Shepherd, Francois Duchene, and Christopher Saunders. Ithaca, NY: Cornell University Press.

Koechlin, Timothy. (1995) "The globalization of investment." *Contemporary Economic Policy* 13, 92–100.

Korpi, Walter. (1991) "Political and economic explanations for unemployment: a cross-national and long-term analysis." *British Journal of Political Science* 21, 315–48.

Kurzer, Paulette. (1991) "Unemployment in open economies: the impact of trade, finance, and European integration." *Comparative Political Studies* 24, 3–30.

Lange, Peter, Michael Wallerstein, and Miriam Golden. (1995) "The end of corporatism? Wage setting in the Nordic and Germanic countries." In *The Workers of Nations*, ed. Sanford Jacoby. New York: Oxford University Press.

Lash, Scott and John Urry. (1987) *The End of Organized Capitalism*. Madison: University of Wisconsin Press.

Levine, David I and Laura D'Andrea Tyson. (1990) "Participation, productivity, and the firm's environment." In *Paying for Productivity*, ed. Alan S. Blinder. Washington, DC: Brookings Institution.

Lincoln, James R. and Arne L. Kalleberg. (1990) *Culture, Control, and Commitment.* Cambridge, UK: Cambridge University Press.

Lindbeck, Assar. (1994) "The welfare state and the employment problem." *American Economic Review* 82 (Papers and Proceedings), 71–75.

Locke, Richard and Thomas Kochan. (1995) "Conclusion: The transformation of industrial relations? A cross-national review of the evidence." In *Employment Relations in a Changing World Economy*, eds. Richard Locke, Thomas Kochan, and Michael Piore. Cambridge, MA: MIT Press.

Lodge, G.C. and E.F. Vogel, eds. (1987) *Ideology and National Competitiveness.* Boston: Harvard Business School Press.

Lynch, Lisa M. (1993) *Strategies for Workplace Training: Lessons from Abroad.* Washington, DC: Economic Policy Institute.

Mansfield, Edward D. and Marc L. Busch. (1995) "The political economy of nontariff barriers: a cross-national analysis." *International Organization* 49, 723–49.

March, James G. (1982) "Theories of choice and making decisions." *Society*, November-December, 29–39.

Markusen, Ann R. (1991) *The Rise of the Gunbelt: The Military Remapping of Industrial America.* New York: Oxford University Press.

Mooney, Christopher Z. and Robert D. Duval (1993) *Bootstrapping: A Nonparametric Approach to Statistical Inference.* Newbury Park, CA: Sage.

Nelson, Richard R. and Gavin Wright. (1992) "The rise and fall of American technological leadership: the postwar era in historical perspective." *Journal of Economic Literature* 30, 1931–64.

Nakamura, Keisuke and Michio Nitta. (1995) "Developments in industrial relations and human resource practices in Japan." In *Employment Relations in a Changing World Economy*, eds. Richard Locke, Thomas Kochan, and Michael Piore. Cambridge, MA: MIT Press.

North, Douglass C. (1990) *Institutions, Institutional Change, and Economic Performance.* Cambridge, UK: Cambridge University Press.

Notermans, Ton. (1993) "The abdication from national policy autonomy: why the macroeconomic policy regime has become so unfavorable to labor." *Politics and Society* 21, 133-67.

OECD (Organization for Economic Cooperation and Development). (1991) *National Accounts: Main Aggregates, 1960–1990*, vol. 1. Paris: OECD.

— (1993) "Enterprise tenure, labour turnover and skill training." In *Employment Outlook*, July. Paris: OECD.

— (1994a) "Collective bargaining: levels and coverage." In *Employment Outlook*, July. Paris: OECD.

— (1994b) *Main Economic Indicators*, December. Paris: OECD.

— (1995a) *Historical Statistics, 1960–1993*. Paris: OECD.

— (1995b) *OECD Economic Outlook*, no. 58, December. Paris: OECD.

— (1996) *National Accounts: Main Aggregates*, 1960–1994, vol. 1. Paris: OECD.

Offe, Claus. (1985) *Disorganized Capitalism*. Cambridge, MA: MIT Press.

Office of Technology Assessment, U.S. Congress. (1990a) *Making Things Better: Competing in Manufacturing*. Washington, DC: Government Printing Office.

— (1990b) *Worker Training: Competing in the New International Economy*. Washington, DC: Government Printing Office.

Olson, Mancur. (1982) *The Rise and Decline of Nations*. New Haven, CT: Yale University Press.

Orru, Marco, Nicole Woolsey Biggart, and Gary G. Hamilton. (1991) "Organizational isomorphism in East Asia." In *The New Institutionalism in Organizational Analysis*, eds. Walter W. Powell and Paul J. DiMaggio. Chicago: University of Chicago Press.

Osborne, David. (1987) *Economic Competitiveness: The States Take the Lead*. Washington, DC: Economic Policy Institute.

Overbye, Einar. (1994) "Convergence in policy outcomes: social security systems in perspective." *Journal of Public Policy* 14, 147–74.

Patrick, Hugh. (1986) "Japanese high technology industrial policy in comparative context." In *Japan's High Technology Industries*, ed. Hugh Patrick. Seattle: University of Washington Press, 1986.

Pennar, Karen. (1995) "Is the nation-state obsolete in a global economy?" *Business Week*, 17 July, 80–81.

Pfaller, A., I. Gough, and G. Therborn, eds. (1991) *Can the Welfare State Compete?* London: Macmillan.

Porter, Michael E. (1992) *Capital Choices: Changing the Way America Invests in Industry*. Washington, DC: Council on Competitiveness.

Powell, Walter W. and Paul J. DiMaggio, eds. (1991) *The New Institutionalism in Organizational Analysis*. Chicago: University of Chicago Press.

Reich, Robert B. ([1991] 1992) *The Work of Nations*. New York: Vintage.

Rogers, Joel. (1990) "Divide and conquer: further 'reflections on the distinctive character of American labor laws.'" *Wisconsin Law Review* 1990, 1–147.

Rogers, Joel and Wolfgang Streeck. (1994) "Workplace representation overseas: the works councils story." In *Working Under Different Rules*, ed. Richard B. Freeman. New York: Russell Sage Foundation.

Rogers, Joel and Wolfgang Streeck, eds. (1995) *Works Councils: Consultation, Representation, and Cooperation in Industrial Relations*. Chicago: University of Chicago Press.

Rutter, John W. (1990) "Recent trends in international direct investment and the implications for U.S. business." In U.S. Department of Commerce, *1990 U.S. Industrial Outlook*. Washington, DC: Government Printing Office.

Samuels, Richard J. and Benjamin C. Whipple. (1989) "The FSX and Japan's strategy for aerospace." *Technology Review*, October, 43–51.

Saxonhouse, Gary R. (1983) "What is all this about "industrial targeting' in Japan?" *World Economy* 6, 253–73.

Scharpf, Fritz W. ([1987] 1991) *Crisis and Choice in European Social Democracy*. Ithaca, NY: Cornell University Press.

Simon, Herbert A. (1976) "From substantive to procedural rationality." In *Method and Appraisal in Economics*, ed. Spiro J. Latsis. Cambridge, UK: Cambridge University Press.

Steinmo, Sven. (1994) "The end of redistribution? International pressures and domestic tax policy choices." *Challenge*, November–December, 9–17.

Stephens, John D. (1994) "The Scandinavian welfare states: development and crisis." Paper presented at the World Congress of Sociology, Bielefeld, Germany.

Stephens, John D., Evelyne Huber, and Leonard Ray. (1994) "The welfare state in hard times." Paper presented at the American Political Science Association annual meeting, New York.

Stewart, Michael. (1983) *The Age of Interdependence: Economic Policy in a Shrinking World*. Cambridge, MA: MIT Press.

Streeck, Wolfgang. (1984) "Neo-corporatist industrial relations and the economic crisis in West Germany." In *Order and Conflict in Contemporary Capitalism*, ed. John H. Goldthorpe. Oxford: Clarendon Press.

— (1995) "Lean production in the German automobile industry? A test case for convergence theory." In *Domestic Institutions and International Trade*, eds. Suzanne Berger and Ronald Dore. Ithaca, NY: Cornell University Press.

Therborn, Goran. (1986) *Why Some Peoples Are More Unemployed Than Others*. London: Verso.

Totterdill, Peter. (1989) "Local economic strategies as industrial policy: a critical review of British developments in the 1980s." *Economy and Society* 18, 478–526.

Wall Street Journal. (1992a) "Answers to commonly asked questions about currency trading in a wild week." 17 September.

— (1992b) "Detroit's new strategy to beat back Japanese is to copy their ideas." 1 October.

Webb, Michael C. (1991) "International economic structures, government interests, and international coordination of macroeconomic adjustment policies." *International Organization* 45, 311–42.

Weir, Margaret and Theda Skocpol. (1985) "State structures and the possibilities for "Keynesian" responses to the Great Depression in Sweden, Britain, and the United States." In *Bringing the State Back In*, eds. Peter B. Evans, Dietrich Rueschemeyer, and Theda Skocpol. Cambridge, UK: Cambridge University Press.

Wellons, Philip A. (1985) "Competitiveness in the world economy: the role of the U.S. financial system." In *U.S. Competitiveness in the World Economy*, eds. Bruce R. Scott and George C. Lodge. Boston: Harvard Business School Press.

Whitely, Paul F. (1987) "The monetarist experiments in the United States and the United Kingdom: policy responses to stagflation." In *Coping with the Economic Crisis*, eds. Hans Keman, Heikki Paloheimo, and Paul F. Whiteley. London: Sage.

Williamson, Oliver E. (1981) "The economics of organization: the transaction cost approach." *American Journal of Sociology* 87, 548–77.

Windmuller, John P. and Alan Gladstone, eds. (1984) *Employers Associations and Industrial Relations*. Oxford: Clarendon Press.

Windolf, Paul. (1989) "Productivity coalitions and the future of European corporatism." *Industrial Relations* 28, 1–20.

Womack, James P., Daniel T. Jones, and Daniel Roos. (1990) *The Machine That Changed the World*. New York: Rawson Associates.

Woodall, Pam. (1995) "A survey of the world economy." *The Economist*, 7 October, 1–38.

Yamamura, Kozo. (1986) "Caveat emptor: the industrial policy of Japan." In *Strategic Trade Policy and the New International Economics*, ed. Paul R. Krugman. Cambridge, MA: MIT Press.

Yoshikawa, Akihiro. (1987) "The Japanese challenge in biotechnology: industrial policy." Working Paper 29, Berkeley Roundtable on the International Economy. Berkeley, CA.

Zevin, Robert. (1992) "Are world financial markets more open? If so, why and with what effects?" In *Financial Openness and National Autonomy*, eds. Tariq Banuri and Juliet B. Schor. Oxford: Clarendon Press.

Zysman, John. (1983) *Governments, Markets, and Growth*. Ithaca, NY: Cornell University Press.

[8]

THE STRATEGIC BEHAVIOR OF MNCs

HAVING SURVEYED the national systems of internal governance, financing, innovation, and investment within which the majority of the world's leading MNCs were originally grounded, we return to the questions that opened this volume. In the midst of markets now widely perceived to be fundamentally global, we ask in this chapter whether multinational firms are now truly losing their national moorings. More precisely, in their most crucial strategies and operations, we ask whether patterns of convergence are now emerging, patterns that herald the emergence of a global corporate economy. This chapter seeks answers in the two strategic areas at the core of the multinational corporation: strategies for creating and managing technological innovation, and the intimately linked strategies of foreign direct investment and intrafirm trade.

TECHNOLOGY AND COMMERCE

Many observers have noted that MNCs have in recent years increased the cross-border development and transfer of technical knowledge and technological assets.[1] The term *globalization*, in this sense, is often used to suggest that national technology bases are by virtue of that expansion becoming more integrated and interdependent.[2] Generally speaking, and certainly in sectors like pharmaceuticals, that integration is obvious. But it is also neither new nor particularly profound. As long as MNCs have been able to establish themselves in diverse markets, a degree of technological integration has always occurred. The key questions concern the relative magnitude and significance of any recent changes in this process. Has a threshold been crossed in the fundamental integration of national systems of innovation? Is a global technology base emerging?

The evidence presented below suggests not. The recent rapid growth in FDI has certainly expanded the local presence of foreign corporations, and with that has come growth in overseas R&D and increasingly dense channels for technology transfer across national borders. Yet the magnitude of this trend remains quite small relative to the national innovative activities of the world's leading MNCs. Those firms, moreover, continue to innovate as well as acquire and transfer new knowledge in distinct ways. Across the world's leading MNCs, and especially across American, German, and Japanese MNCs, distinctly national patterns can be seen in the three principal mechanisms through which MNCs extend technology across national borders: first, through overseas R&D activities; second, through the direct sale of technology in the form of intellectual property (in exchange for royalties and license fees); and third, through strategic technology alliances between firms.[3]

The Location and Intensity of Corporate Research and Development

Historically, R&D has been the last aspect of corporate activity to take on a multinational dimension. The economies of scale associated with research activities naturally tend to favor centralization, but that is not the end of the story. As firms establish foreign production capabilities, they in fact often decentralize selective elements of their R&D. In addition to supporting local production facilities, firms will move R&D abroad for a variety of reasons: to acquire foreign technology; to customize products for local markets; to stay abreast of technological developments; to gain access to foreign R&D resources, such as universities, public and private laboratory facilities, and scientists and engineers; to assist the parent company in meeting foreign regulations and product standards; and to gain cost efficiencies. Consequently, as production and commerce increasingly cross national borders, R&D might likewise be expected to exhibit a more global character.

Close observers of this process differ, however, in their diagnoses of its extent and nature. Some note that major MNCs are expanding their core R&D activities across national borders at unprecedented rates.[4] Foreign acquisitions often are aimed at gaining access to technology and other R&D resources that already are established in particular markets, such as biotechnology in the United States. In the United States, Germany, and the United Kingdom, foreign firms "are spending substantial sums on R&D, mainly for local markets though increasingly for global ones, reflecting new strategies in R&D intensive industries."[5] Other studies note that while R&D has indeed become more mobile, MNCs move R&D abroad far more slowly than production, sourcing, marketing, and other business activities.[6] Others contend that firms are responding to global competition by watching R&D activities closely and striving to retain centralized control.[7] Still others agree that MNCs conduct relatively little R&D outside the home country, but note that the strategies and policies of MNCs affect the way R&D is owned, organized, and located.[8]

Our own analysis notes the recent growth in the overseas R&D activities of foreign affiliates. Beneath that observation, however, it focuses on the distribution of R&D within multinational firms and shows that corporate R&D remains highly centralized in home markets. It also demonstrates that both the level and intensity of R&D conducted by MNCs outside their home markets varies markedly along national lines.[9] We suspect, moreover, that more than economic factors are needed to explain this variance.

R&D WITHIN MULTINATIONAL FIRMS

Although the aggregate volume of overseas R&D by corporate affiliates has increased substantially in recent years, it is still a relatively small fraction of total corporate R&D. The domestic and overseas R&D conducted by U.S.-based MNCs since the early 1980s illustrates both of these points (Figure 5.1. Distribution of R&D Expenditures within U.S.-based MNCs). Between 1982 and 1994, total R&D expenditures by U.S. multinational corporate parents increased an average of 12 percent per year, from $38.2 billion to $91.1 billion. During the same period, R&D spending by affiliates of U.S. MNCs grew at a faster rate of 18 percent per year, rising from $3.6 billion to $12.1 billion.[10] The accelerating growth of R&D by affiliates indicates that R&D has become more international in scope. At the same time, however, the proportion of total multinational corporate R&D conducted by affiliates remains relatively small—in 1994, the R&D conducted by majority-owned affiliates comprised 12 percent of the total R&D expenditures of U.S. MNCs, up slightly from 9 percent in 1982.[11] By comparison, in 1994 majority-owned foreign affiliates of U.S. MNCs accounted for 30 percent of net income, 24 percent of total MNC capital expenditures, and 23 percent of all employment.[12] Although no comparable data exists for European and Japanese MNCs, our interviews suggest that they conduct overseas similar if not smaller percentages of their R&D than do U.S. firms.[13]

Like the aggregate level of R&D spending, the R&D intensity of foreign affiliates tends to be substantially lower than that of parent groups.[14] For example, the R&D intensity of U.S. multinational corporate parent groups in 1994 was 2.3 percent, compared with 0.8 percent for their majority-owned foreign affiliates.[15] With the exception of foreign affiliates in the United States, the R&D intensity of foreign affiliates in most countries tends to be lower than or at best equivalent to the average for all manufacturing firms in the host country.[16] However, as with the volume of R&D spending, the R&D intensity of foreign affiliates has been increasing at a faster rate than that of MNC parent

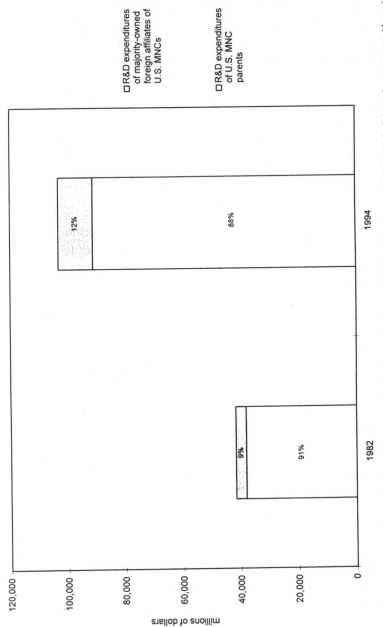

Figure 5.1. Distribution of R&D Expenditures within U.S.-based MNCs. *Data source:* BEA, *U.S. Direct Investment Abroad: 1994 Benchmark Survey* (January 1997): tables II.R 1, III.I 2; BEA, *Survey of Current Business* (June 1995): table 5, p. 36.

groups. For example, between 1982 and 1994 the annual growth rate in the R&D intensity of majority-owned foreign affiliates of U.S. MNCs averaged 10 percent, compared with 3 percent for their parent groups.[17]

Although low in absolute terms, the relatively rapid growth in overseas R&D by foreign affiliates does represent a gradual globalization of R&D. However, it is difficult to assess the significance of this trend, due to the lack of data regarding the technological and strategic contribution of the R&D conducted by foreign affiliates to the global competitiveness of MNCs.[18] Apparently, much of the growth in the R&D intensity of both foreign affiliates in the United States and U.S. affiliates abroad can be attributed to overseas acquisitions and/or joint ventures, and consequently may not represent a transfer of R&D operations from the home country to foreign markets.[19] The most challenging analytical task is to determine whether the R&D conducted by foreign affiliates contributes to the core technological competencies of the parent firms, or whether it contributes primarily to the affiliates' local process technology and product adaptation requirements.

Over time and across countries, the most significant reasons for conducting R&D in foreign markets are to customize products to accommodate local market conditions, improve foreign production processes, take advantage of local research competencies, assist parent companies in procurement, and keep abreast of competitors' technological and overall business strategies.[20] Firms usually take a long time to establish complex overseas R&D operations that fully support local production facilities. In the electronics industry—one of the most internationalized in terms of R&D as well as production—firms require at least a decade to establish an overseas research facility that can closely support affiliate manufacturing operations. For example, Philips Electronics NV has maintained a U.S. research facility at Briarcliff Manor, New York, for over two decades. The facility now accounts for approximately 15 percent of all corporate research activity, and is an integral part of Philips' laboratory network. The company maintains four laboratories in Europe—the central lab at corporate headquarters in Eindhoven, Netherlands, plus smaller facilities in France, Germany, and England. While each of the foreign facilities has its own technological capabilities and its own mix of research programs, most basic research continues to be conducted in Eindhoven. The U.S. facility focuses mostly on supporting Philips' substantial U.S. manufacturing facilities.[21]

Fully integrated affiliates that conduct independent product R&D are relatively rare, even for the largest and oldest MNCs. For instance, Siemens has a laboratory in Princeton, New Jersey, that conducts independent R&D in imaging, software engineering, multimedia, and learning systems. Much of this work involves missions tied to the central corporation, not just its U.S. divisions. At the same time, however, the Princeton facility's budget is only $21.8 million, less than 5 percent of Siemens' total R&D budget.[22] Similarly, Ford Motor Company, after many years of foreign production in Europe and elsewhere, only recently began to establish a single operating unit, Ford Automotive Operations, that would oversee five vehicle program centers, each with worldwide responsibilities for the development and production of independent product lines.[23]

In short, R&D moves overseas much more slowly than production, sourcing, and other business activities. Production facilities often can be established quickly and moved quickly, as market conditions change. By comparison, R&D facilities typically take a long time to set up and, once established, are relatively difficult to move.[24] Yet even in industries with extensive global production and sourcing networks as well as high R&D intensity levels—such as electronics, computers, and pharmaceuticals—R&D across the advanced industrial states remains fairly centralized. For instance, pharmaceutical firms conduct very little basic research and clinical evaluation outside of the home country,[25] and R&D in the computer industry is among the most highly centralized (a fact some analysts ascribe to domestic support programs that favor local firms).[26] The pattern is much the same in less R&D-intensive industries, especially those where core product technology varies little across national markets. For example, R&D in the auto industry remains relatively centralized, although design customization often is conducted locally.[27]

In general, most MNCs centralize core research and product development in the home market, while research oriented toward customization and foreign production support is gradually conducted locally as affiliates become more deeply integrated into foreign markets.[28] Indeed, many multinational firms have become more deeply integrated into local markets over time, which accounts in part for the rapid rate of increase in R&D conducted by foreign affiliates. Nevertheless, foreign affiliates that do conduct R&D abroad tend to do so at different levels and for different purposes.

R&D BY FOREIGN AFFILIATES IN THE UNITED STATES

Over the last decade, R&D spending by foreign affiliates in the United States has increased substantially. In 1980, foreign MNCs operating in the country spent $3.2 billion in real terms on R&D, equivalent to 6.4 percent of all R&D funded by U.S. businesses. By 1994 that level had risen to $14.9 billion, equivalent to 16 percent of all corporate

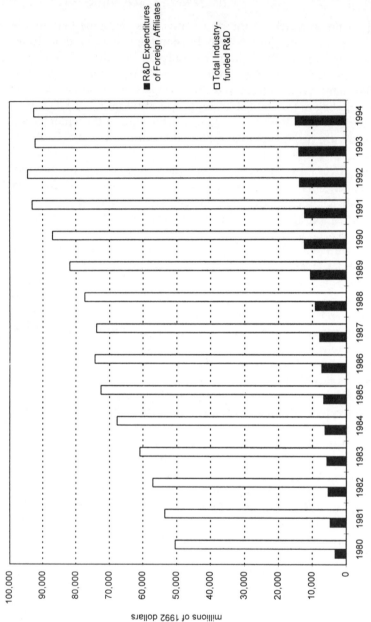

Figure 5.2. R&D Expenditures of Foreign Affiliates in the U.S. and All U.S. Firms. *Data source: BEA, Survey of Current Business (May 1995): table 6, p. 62; and BEA, Foreign Direct Investment in the U.S.: Preliminary Estimates, 1994; NSF, National Patterns of Research and Development Resources: 1995: tables B–6, B–9, and B–12.*

TABLE 5.1
R&D Expenditures of Foreign Affiliates in the U.S. by Country of Origin

	Japan	Germany	France	U.K.
R&D expenditures in 1994 (in billions of constant 1992 dollars)	$1.9	$2.3	$1.3	$2.4
Average percent of total R&D expenditures by all foreign affiliates in the U.S., 1983–1994	9.4%	15.1%	7.1%	15.5%
Average annual growth rate, 1983–1994	65.6%	17.2%	31.8%	19.0%

Source: Bureau of Economic Analysis, *Foreign Direct Investment in the U.S.: 1994* (Washington, D.C.: U.S. Government Printing Office, 1996): table I-6.

R&D funding that year (Figure 5.2. R&D Expenditures of Foreign Affiliates in the U.S. and All U.S. Firms).[29] Although small relative to total R&D funding by U.S. firms—$92.6 billion in 1994—the rate of increase in R&D spending by foreign affiliates has been much more rapid than that of total U.S. business R&D. Between 1980 and 1994, R&D expenditures by foreign affiliates in the United States grew at an average annual rate of 26 percent, compared to 6 percent for R&D funding by all U.S. firms.[30]

Firms based in each of the major advanced industrial nations contributed to the rapid increase in total affiliate R&D during the 1980s and early 1990s (Table 5.1. R&D Expenditures of Foreign Affiliates in the U.S., by Country of Origin). During that period, U.K. and German affiliates consistently outspent French and Japanese affiliates in absolute terms, each accounting for approximately 15 percent of all R&D conducted by foreign affiliates in the United States.[31] Although average annual increases in affiliate R&D spending were strong across all countries, French and Japanese affiliates expanded their R&D spending particularly quickly, especially after 1987.

Over 80 percent of the R&D conducted by foreign affiliates in the United States has been in manufacturing industries, most of which is concentrated in three sectors—in 1994, 29 percent of all R&D by affiliates was in pharmaceuticals, while 17 percent was in electronic equipment and 13 percent in industrial chemicals.[32] The most rapid rate of growth has been in the pharmaceutical sector, where foreign affiliates increased their R&D spending from $716 million in 1985 to $4.3 billion in 1994 (in constant 1992 dollars)—a stunning average annual increase of 56 percent (Figure 5.3. R&D Expenditures of Foreign Affiliates in the U.S., by Industry). Indeed, the growth of foreign R&D in the pharmaceutical sector accounts for over one third of the total increase in R&D

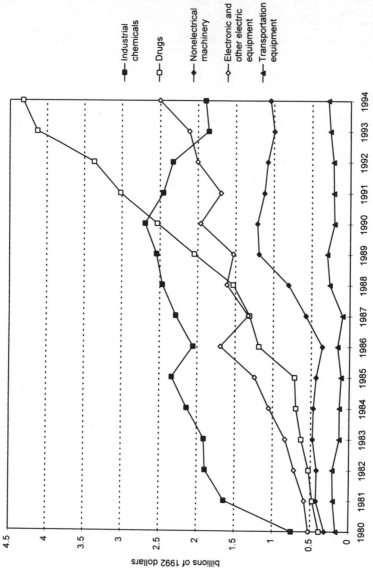

Figure 5.3. R&D Expenditures of Foreign Affiliates in the U.S., by Industry. *Data source:* BEA, *Foreign Direct Investment in the U.S.: Preliminary Estimates, 1994* (July: 1996) table J–6; and prior annual surveys.

conducted in the United States by foreign firms from 1980 to 1994. R&D spending by foreign affiliates has also grown significantly in industrial chemicals and machinery, again with fastest growth rates taking place in the late 1980s.

With only a few notable exceptions, such as NEC's laboratory in Princeton, most industrial laboratories run by foreign affiliates in the United States have been established not through new investment dedicated to R&D activities per se but rather through the merger and acquisition (M&A) strategies of foreign firms.[33] The rapid increase in R&D by foreign affiliates began in the late 1980s, corresponding to a very active period of M&A activity by foreign investors. Between 1986 and 1988, the value of foreign acquisitions in the United States jumped from $31.5 billion to $64.9 billion, and remained quite high during 1988–90.[34] The correspondence between this period of high acquisition activity and the rise in R&D spending by foreign affiliates after 1986 implies that part of the increase in affiliate R&D was due to acquisitions of U.S. research facilities, as opposed to the transfer of R&D activities from the home market to existing affiliates in the United States.[35] No sector illustrates this relationship better than pharmaceuticals, where the unusually high average annual growth rate in R&D by foreign affiliates—56 percent—corresponds to an even more remarkable average annual growth in direct investment of 106 percent (much of it related to the enormous amount of M&A as well as alliance activity in the industry during this period).[36]

Whether established through acquisition or direct establishment, foreign affiliates in the U.S. vary systematically in their levels of R&D per unit of sales, as seen in Figure 5.4 (R&D Intensity of Foreign Affiliates in the U.S.). Much of the difference in aggregate R&D intensity levels appears to be consistent with the sectoral distribution of foreign direct investment in the United States (FDIUS) by individual countries. For instance, the R&D intensity of European affiliates is above the average for all affiliates, which reflects in part the relatively high percentage of European FDIUS that is directed to R&D-intensive manufacturing sectors. In particular, German affiliates in the United States regularly have the highest R&D intensity level, as is consistent with the concentration of German affiliates in R&D-intensive manufacturing industries—in 1994, for instance, 38 percent of German FDIUS was in chemicals and allied products and industrial machinery (combined).[37] By comparison, the low R&D intensity of Japanese affiliates in the United States reflects in part the relatively low percentage of Japanese FDIUS directed to R&D-intensive manufacturing industries. In 1994, only 19 percent of Japan's FDIUS was in manufacturing industries altogether (and only 9

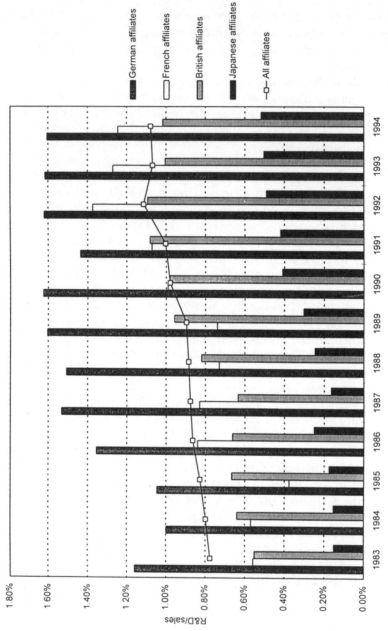

Figure 5.4. R&D Intensity of Foreign Affiliates in the U.S. *Data source:* BEA, *Foreign Direct Investment in the U.S.: Preliminary Estimates, 1994* (July 1996): tables E–8, J–6; and prior annual surveys.

percent in chemicals and industrial machinery), while 34 percent was in wholesale trade.[38]

Although the national variation in aggregate R&D intensity levels is consistent with the sectoral composition of FDIUS, a comparison of R&D intensities within sectors points toward another factor—consistent variation in the R&D strategies of MNCs along national lines. As Figure 5.5 (R&D Intensity of Foreign Affiliates in the United States, by Sector and by Country) shows, the R&D intensity levels of foreign affiliates in the United States vary significantly within as well as across sectors. In 1994, the average R&D intensity for all foreign affiliates in U.S. manufacturing industries was 2.6 percent. German affiliates in manufacturing industries were well above that average (at 3.5 percent), while French and U.K. affiliates were slightly above the average (at 2.8 and 2.7 percent, respectively). Japanese affiliates were well below average (at 1.1 percent). This pattern generally holds across the major industrial sectors: German, French, and U.K. affiliates share the highest R&D intensity levels across chemicals and allied products, metals, transportation, and instruments, while Japanese affiliates consistently have the lowest R&D intensity level (with the partial exception of machinery, where the R&D intensity of U.K. affiliates is lower).

In short, foreign affiliates operating in the United States have increased their R&D spending relatively quickly over the last 15 years, particularly in the pharmaceutical sector. In absolute terms, most of the R&D conducted by foreign affiliates is concentrated in pharmaceuticals, electrical and electronic machinery, and industrial chemicals. In general, affiliates of German MNCs have the highest R&D intensity levels in the United States, while affiliates of Japanese MNCs have the lowest. This difference appears to be consistent with the relative concentration of direct investment in R&D-intensive industries. However, consistent variation in the R&D intensity of German, Japanese, and other foreign affiliates operating in the same industry indicates that multinational firms based in different states tend to pursue distinct R&D strategies.

R&D BY U.S. AFFILIATES IN FOREIGN MARKETS

Like the R&D activity of foreign affiliates in the United States, the overseas R&D by affiliates of U.S. MNCs has increased steadily over time. Between 1989 and 1994, R&D expenditures by majority-owned foreign affiliates of U.S. MNCs increased by an average annual rate of 9 percent (from $7.9 billion to $11.5 billion, in real terms)—far slower than the growth rate of R&D spending by foreign affiliates in the United States

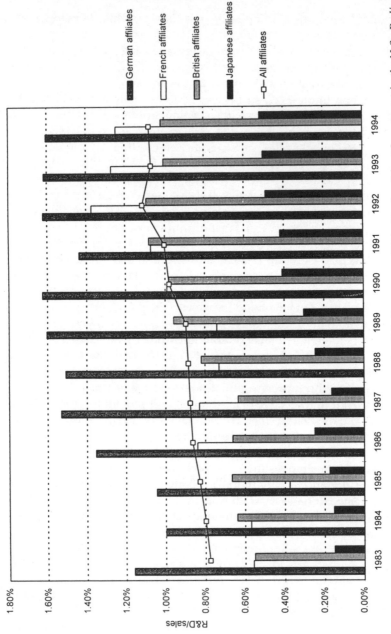

Figure 5.4. R&D Intensity of Foreign Affiliates in the U.S. *Data source:* BEA, *Foreign Direct Investment in the U.S.: Preliminary Estimates, 1994* (July 1996): tables E–8, J–6; and prior annual surveys.

THE STRATEGIC BEHAVIOR OF MNCs   97

TABLE 5.2
R&D Expenditures of U.S. Affiliates in Foreign Markets: Growth Rates and
Distribution across Countries

	Japan	Germany	France	U.K.
R&D expenditures in 1994 (in billions of constant 1992 dollars)	$1.1	$2.7	$1.3	$2.1
Average percent of total R&D expenditures by U.S. affiliates in all foreign markets, 1989–1994	7.0%	24.1%	9.3%	18.3%
Average annual growth rate, 1989–1994	19.4%	12.1%	22.6%	2.3%

Source: Bureau of Economic Analysis, *U.S. Direct Investment Abroad* (Washington, D.C.: U.S. Government Printing Office, 1997): table III.I 3.
Note: Data expressed in constant 1992 dollars. R&D data for U.S. affiliates in foreign markets are not available prior to 1989.

(26 percent), but faster than the real growth of R&D spending by all U.S. firms over the same period (6 percent).[39]

The distribution of R&D expenditures by U.S. affiliates across countries mirrors the relative level of R&D spending by foreign affiliates in the United States. R&D by U.S. affiliates is concentrated in Germany and to a lesser extent the United Kingdom, with comparatively little R&D in France and Japan (Table 5.2. R&D Expenditures of U.S. Affiliates in Foreign Markets: Growth Rates and Distribution across Countries). Between 1989 and 1994, U.S. affiliates on average spent $2.3 billion per year in Germany (24 percent of the total real R&D spending by U.S. affiliates in all foreign markets) and $1.9 billion per year in the United Kingdom (18 percent of the total), compared with $952 million (9 percent) in France and $716 million (7 percent) in Japan.

Most of the overseas R&D conducted by U.S. affiliates is in manufacturing industries. In 1994, manufacturing firms accounted for 84 percent of all R&D spending by U.S. affiliates in foreign markets, a level equivalent to that of foreign affiliates in the United States.[40] Also like their counterparts in the United States, a large percentage of the overseas R&D conducted by U.S. affiliates is concentrated in the pharmaceutical industry, which accounted for 17 percent of all foreign R&D by U.S. affiliates between 1989 and 1994. The industrial machinery sector accounts for an equivalent share of overseas R&D by U.S. firms. These two industries also display the strongest average annual real growth rates in affiliate R&D spending—16 and 25 percent, respectively. Quite unlike R&D by foreign affiliates in the U.S., however, the transportation equipment sector accounts for nearly a quarter of

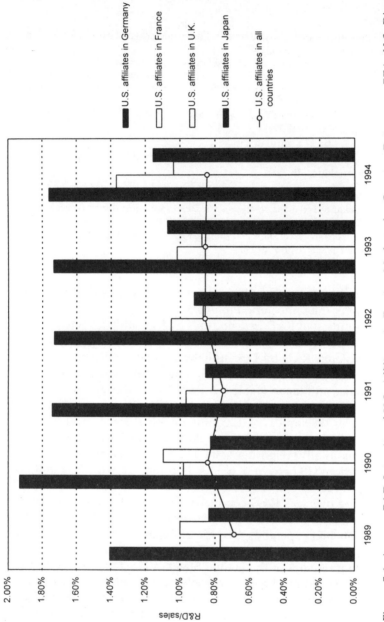

Figure 5.6. Average R&D Intensity of U.S. Affiliates in Foreign Markets, by Country. *Data source: BEA, U.S. Direct Investment Abroad: 1994 Benchmark Survey (January 1997): tables III.I 3.; III.E 3.*

TABLE 5.3
R&D Expenditures of U.S. Affiliates in Foreign Markets, by Sector and by Country, 1994

	Japan	Germany	France	U.K.
All industries ($ million)	$1,123	$2,808	$1,357	$2,179
Chemicals & allied products (% of all R&D by U.S. affiliates within country)	$397 (35%)	$296 (11%)	$543 (40%)	$616 (28%)
Primary & fabricated metals	$10 (1%)	$23 (1%)	$6 (0.5%)	$25 (1%)
Industrial machinery & equipment	$77 (7%)	$530 (19%)	$202 (15%)	$433 (20%)
Electronic & electric equipment	$136 (12%)	$128 (5%)	$41* (3%)	$46* (2%)
Transportation equipment	$6 (1%)	$1,435 (51%)	$27* (2%)	$383* (18%)
Wholesale trade	$307 (27%)	$87 (3%)	$120 (9%)	$120 (6%)

Source: Bureau of Economic Analysis, *U.S. Direct Investment Abroad: 1994* (Washington, D.C.: U.S. Government Printing Office, 1997): table III.I 3.

Note: Expenditure data expressed in millions of current dollars. (An asterisk represents 1993 data. 1994 data not available for these sectors.)

overseas R&D conducted by U.S. affiliates, although the average annual growth rate of R&D spending has been comparatively slow since 1989 (about 8 percent).[41]

Viewed across countries, the aggregate R&D intensity of U.S. affiliates is relatively similar but for one exception: Germany. As Figure 5.6 shows (Average R&D Intensity of U.S. Affiliates in Foreign Markets, by Country), the R&D intensity of U.S. affiliates in France, the United Kingdom, and Japan is within a narrow range, close to the average R&D intensity for U.S. affiliates in all markets. U.S. affiliates in Germany, however, consistently display substantially higher aggregate R&D intensity levels.

This pattern conforms in part to differences in the concentration of R&D by U.S. affiliates in R&D-intensive manufacturing industries. In 1994, fully 86 percent of all R&D expenditures by U.S. affiliates in Germany was concentrated in four R&D-intensive sectors—transportation equipment, chemicals and allied products, electronic and other electric equipment, and industrial machinery (Table 5.3. R&D Expenditures of U.S. Affiliates in Foreign Markets, by Sector and by Country). The equivalent concentration levels for U.S. affiliates in France and the United Kingdom was approximately 72 and 70 percent, respectively.[42]

100   CHAPTER 5

Surprisingly (since the average R&D intensity of U.S. affiliates in Japan is close to or higher than those in France or the United Kingdom), only 55 percent of the R&D expenditures by U.S. affiliates in Japan is concentrated in these four sectors. In Japan, unlike all European countries, the largest share of R&D by U.S. affiliates takes place in the wholesale trade sector, where U.S. affiliates spend over four times the level that they do in the German and U.K. wholesale trade sectors.

Variation in the sectoral distribution of R&D only partially explains cross-national differences in the R&D intensity of U.S. affiliates. When viewed across industries in the same country, additional variation in the R&D intensity of U.S. affiliates suggests that local investment and technological circumstances may be a factor as well. As Figure 5.7 (R&D Intensity of U.S. Affiliates in Foreign Markets, by Industry and by Country) illustrates, the R&D intensity of U.S. affiliates operating in the same sector often varies substantially across countries. In most major manufacturing sectors, the R&D intensity of U.S. affiliates operating in Japan is noticeably higher than affiliates operating in Germany, France, or the United Kingdom. In the transportation equipment and industrial machinery industries, the R&D intensity of U.S. affiliates in Germany is particularly high. And in the category of wholesale trade, which typically is among the least R&D intensive sectors, the R&D intensity of U.S. affiliates in Japan is approximately four times that of U.S. affiliates in Germany, France, or the United Kingdom.

In sum, the R&D activities of both foreign affiliates in the United States and U.S. affiliates abroad have increased significantly in recent years, but the scope and intensity of that activity varies by sector as well as by country.

By sector, the highest levels of foreign R&D conducted by MNCs are in pharmaceuticals, chemicals, electronic equipment, and, for U.S. MNCs, transportation equipment. More than any other sector, rapid growth in overseas R&D in pharmaceuticals accounts for a large share of the increase in foreign R&D by MNCs—particularly by foreign affiliates operating in the United States.

By country, the magnitude and intensity of R&D activity is the highest between the United States and Germany, in both directions and across most sectors. The magnitude and intensity of R&D activity between the United States and Japan is the lowest in terms of Japanese affiliates in the United States. By contrast, U.S. affiliates in Japan have R&D intensity levels similar to or greater than those of U.S. affiliates in France, the United Kingdom, and, in some sectors, Germany. Generally, the magnitude and intensity of R&D activity is relatively similar between the United States and both France and the United Kingdom, in each direction. However, there are noticeably different

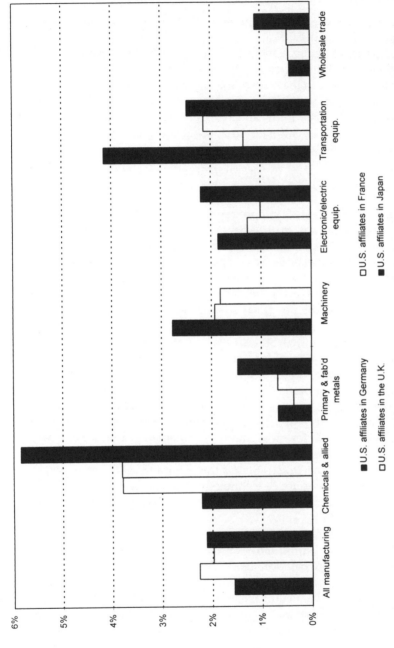

Figure 5.7. R&D Intensity of U.S. Affiliates in Foreign Markets, by Industry and by Country. *Data source: BEA, U.S. Direct Investment Abroad: 1994 Benchmark Survey* (January 1997): tables III.I 3.; III.E 3. *Note:* 1993 data for U.K. and France in electronic, electric equipment; transportation equipment (1994 data not available).

R&D intensity levels between French and U.K. affiliates operating in different U.S. industries.

These patterns can be viewed against other measures of the technology development strategies of MNCs, such as the direct sale or purchase of technology in the form of intellectual property. As described in the next section, trends in technology trade are consistent with the centralization of R&D by MNCs, and also point to additional variations in the tendency of foreign affiliates to develop and/or acquire technology in foreign markets.

Technology Trade

Beyond overt corporate R&D programs, technology can be transferred across national borders in different forms and through various mechanisms, many of which are difficult to measure. The best available quantitative indicator of technology exchange is the volume and direction of international royalty and license fee transactions.[43] Sales of intellectual property represent exports on the services account, and purchases represent imports; the net of sales less purchases constitutes the technology trade balance.

Outside of the United States, few countries have had a positive technology trade balance. In fact, with the exception of the United Kingdom until 1986, no other large OECD country has had a positive balance.[44] Figure 5.8 (Ratio of Technology Exports to Imports, by Country) shows the ratio of sales to purchases for the United States, Japan, France, Germany, and the United Kingdom. Throughout the 1980s and early 1990s, the ratio for most countries remained just under one, with the exception of the United Kingdom during the early 1980s. In other words, except for the United States, the major OECD countries export roughly the same amount of technology that they import. By contrast, U.S. technology exports have consistently outweighed imports by a substantial margin.[45]

Until the mid-1980s, many U.S. corporations did not treat their intellectual property as a productive asset—in fact, few corporations even included it on their balance sheets. Throughout the 1980s, however, U.S. companies gradually recognized and harnessed the financial power of their intellectual property. Sales of U.S. intellectual property increased steadily from $8.1 billion in 1986 to $27 billion by 1995.[46] Imports of intellectual property also increased, but remained at a substantially lower volume—over the same period, intellectual property imports increased from $1.4 to $6.3 billion. As a result, the technology trade balance remained decidedly positive, rising from a surplus of $6.7 billion in 1986 to $20.6 billion in 1995.

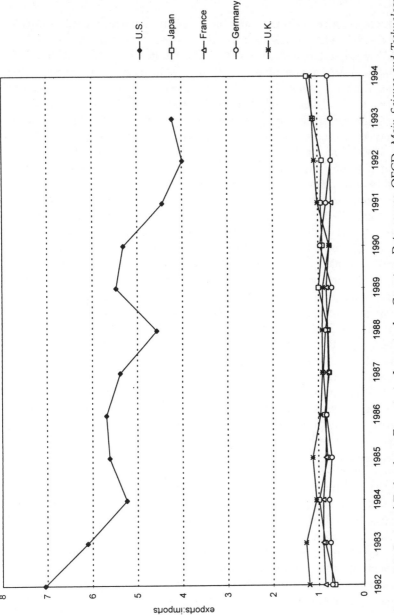

Figure 5.8. Ratio of Technology Exports to Imports, by Country. *Data source:* OECD, *Main Science and Technology Indicators:* 1995 no. 1; 1994 no. 1: table 82.

The unusually large U.S. surplus in technology trade could indicate that the U.S. technology base is very robust, producing valuable and highly marketable knowledge that contributes positively to the U.S. trade balance. On the other hand, the technology trade surplus also could indicate a relatively low willingness or ability of U.S. firms to import foreign technology.[47] Both interpretations may be correct, at least in part. Further analysis of the direction and composition of technology trade indicates that much of the volume of technology trade remains within multinational corporate networks, although firms vary along national lines in their tendency to trade technology within or outside of multinational corporate networks.

In terms of direction, Figures 5.9 (MNCs and U.S. Technology Exports) and 5.10 (MNCs and U.S. Technology Imports) indicate that a large percentage of both U.S. technology exports and imports is associated with MNCs. Between 1986 and 1994, U.S. MNCs and U.S. affiliates of foreign MNCs together sold 79 percent of all technology exports and bought 68 percent of all technology imports. However, U.S. MNCs sell virtually all of the MNC technology exports (Figure 5.9), while U.S. affiliates of foreign MNCs purchase most of the MNC technology imports (Figure 5.10). Between 1986 and 1994, 96 percent of all MNC technology exports was sold by U.S. MNCs to their foreign affiliates, while 4 percent was sold by affiliates in the United States to their foreign parents. The obverse pattern holds for imports: 8 percent of all MNC technology imports was purchased by U.S. MNCs from their foreign affiliates, while U.S. affiliates purchased 92 percent of all technology imports from their foreign parents.[48] In short, technology trade not only is dominated by MNCs, but also flows from parent firms to their foreign affiliates.[49]

These figures also illustrate the strong growth in both technology exports and imports since the mid-1980s, trends that can be linked to FDI flows during the same period. Between 1986 and 1994, technology exports from U.S. MNCs to their foreign affiliates increased at an average annual rate of 22 percent, which corresponds to the growth in U.S. direct investment abroad during this period. Similarly, during the same period, imports by U.S. affiliates from their foreign parents increased at an annual rate of 44 percent, corresponding to the rapid increase in FDI in the United States during the late 1980s.[50] Moreover, the geographical distribution of technology trade tends to conform to the geographical distribution of investment: in 1994, for instance, 44 percent of all U.S. technology exports were received by U.S. affiliates in Europe, while 11 percent were received by U.S. affiliates in Japan; likewise, 46 percent of all U.S. technology imports were by

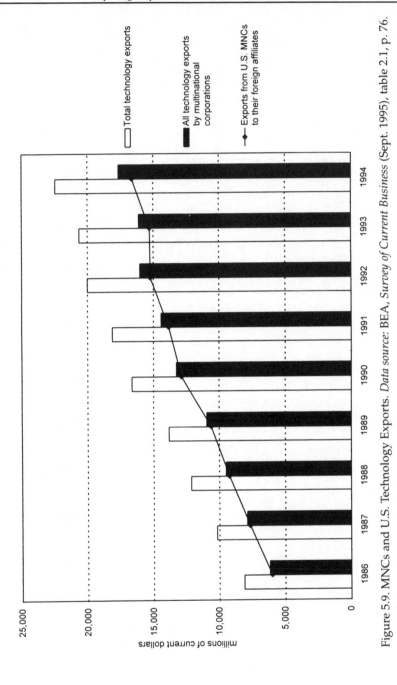

Figure 5.9. MNCs and U.S. Technology Exports. *Data source:* BEA, *Survey of Current Business* (Sept. 1995), table 2.1, p. 76.

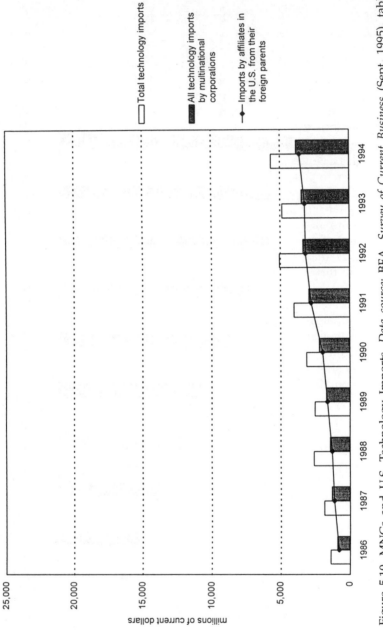

Figure 5.10. MNCs and U.S. Technology Imports. _Data source:_ BEA, _Survey of Current Business_ (Sept. 1995), table 2.1, p. 76.

U.S. affiliates of European firms, while 13 percent were by U.S. affiliates of Japanese firms.[51]

In essence, technology export and import patterns indicate that cross-border technology flows certainly have increased over time, yet those flows consistently have stayed within multinational corporate networks. In addition, the data imply that technology typically is developed in the home market operations of MNCs and gradually extends abroad in the wake of foreign direct investment.[52] In this respect, the technology trade data are consistent with the R&D data, which indicate that technology development remains relatively centralized in the home market operations of MNCs.

In terms of composition, unaffiliated technology trade patterns indicate that there are significant variances in the propensity of firms based in different nations to trade technology within or outside of multinational corporate networks. Unaffiliated or arms-length technology trade takes place among firms that have no economic relationship other than through the market. Since unaffiliated technology transactions take place through market-based bargaining, they reflect the market value of technology more accurately than trade among firms within multinational corporate networks. Moreover, unaffiliated transactions imply less control by the originator and more control by the purchaser. Consequently, cross-national differences in technology acquisition strategies should apply in the propensity of firms based in different states to purchase technology from unaffiliated sources.

The data on unaffiliated technology trade reveal that Japanese firms buy an unusually large percentage of U.S. technology through arms-length transactions. In 1994, 39 percent of all U.S. technology sales to Japan were purchased through arms-length transactions, compared to 12 percent of all U.S. technology sales to Europe and even lower percentages for firms in the larger European countries—13 percent for Germany, 12 percent for the United Kingdom, and 11 percent for France.[53] Consequently, since unaffiliated transactions impart a higher degree of control to the purchaser, Japanese firms retain greater control over the technology they purchase from the United States than do European firms.

Most of the unaffiliated U.S. technology exports are of industrial process technology. Between 1987 and 1994, industrial process technology accounted for 65 percent of unaffiliated U.S. technology exports. This subset of technology trade is particularly critical to commercial competitiveness, given the direct bearing of industrial process technology on production costs and productivity. Consequently, trends in the unaffiliated sale of industrial process technology provide an important

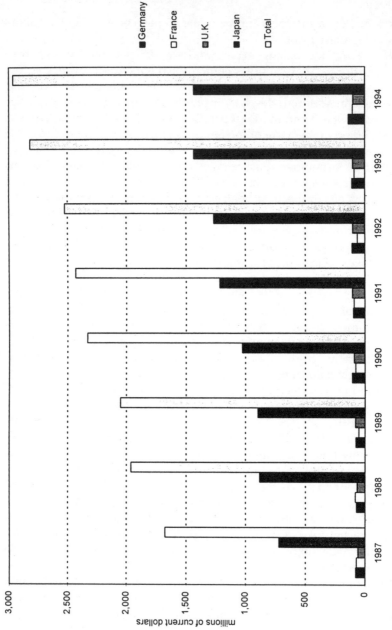

Figure 5.11. U.S. Exports of Industrial Process Technology to Unaffiliated Firms, by Country. *Data source:* BEA, *Survey of Current Business* (Sept. 1995), table 2.1, p. 76; (Sept. 1994); (Sept. 1993).

indicator of the near-term competitive strategies of MNCs across the advanced industrial states.

As with total technology trade, unaffiliated U.S. exports of industrial process technology have consistently outweighed U.S. imports, resulting in an average annual surplus of $1.6 billion between 1987 and 1994. Japan is the largest consumer of unaffiliated U.S. industrial process technology—in 1994, U.S. exports to Japan accounted for 48 percent ($1.4 billion) of all industrial process technology exports, compared with 5 percent for Germany, 3 percent for the United Kingdom, and 24 percent for Europe as a whole (Figure 5.11. U.S. Exports of Industrial Process Technology to Unaffiliated Firms, by Country). This same pattern has been consistent throughout the 1980s and 1990s.

The large percentage of unaffiliated industrial process technology purchased by Japanese firms is further reflected in the sources of the U.S. trade surplus in unaffiliated industrial process technology trade. As shown in Figure 5.12 (U.S. Trade Balance among Unaffiliated Firms in Industrial Process Technology, by Country), Japan consistently accounts for the bulk of this surplus: between 1987 and 1994, Japan's average annual surplus accounted for 60 percent of the total U.S. surplus in arms-length trading of industrial process technology. During this period, Japan ran average annual surpluses with the United States of $764 million, compared with $27 million for all of Europe combined. The only countries with which the United States has had a trade deficit in unaffiliated industrial process knowledge have been the United Kingdom and Germany, averaging -$18 million and -$45 million per year respectively from 1987 through 1994.

In sum, U.S. technology trade data reveal two important patterns in the international exchange of technology. First, most of the formal cross-border exchange of technology takes place within multinational corporate networks—in particular, most of the technology flows from parents to their affiliates. Like the distribution of R&D within multinational corporate networks, this pattern implies that the development of new technology remains centralized in the home market operations of MNCs. Second, there are notable differences in the tendency of firms based in different nations to acquire technology through unaffiliated channels. In particular, Japanese firms purchase far more U.S. technology through arms-length transactions than do European firms—in fact, the total U.S. surplus in the unaffiliated trade of industrial process knowledge is due largely to surpluses with Japan, while the United States has been a net importer of U.K. and German industrial process knowledge. This pattern is consistent with other comparative analyses showing that Japanese firms have a greater tendency to

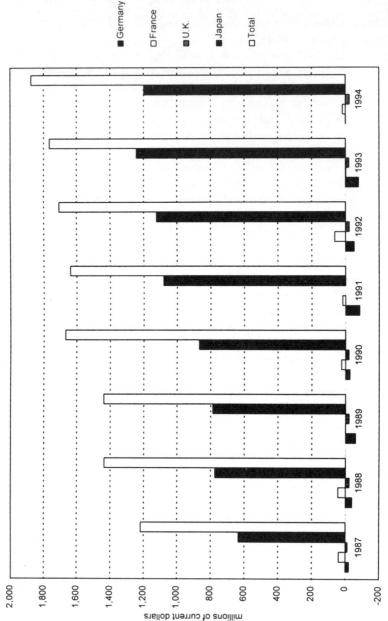

Figure 5.12. U.S. Trade Balance among Unaffiliated Firms in Industrial Process Technology, by Country. *Data source:* BEA, *Survey of Current Business* (Sept. 1995), table 2.1, p. 76; (Sept. 1994); (Sept. 1993).

acquire foreign technology through direct purchases than do U.S. and European firms.[54]

Although both the R&D and technology trade data indicate that technology development remains relatively centralized, technology can be globalized through other mechanisms such as international strategic alliances and related forms of intercorporate cooperation designed to spread investment costs and gain access to a wider range of technologies. Interfirm alliances and joint ventures in R&D and product development have become increasingly common, particularly in information technologies and biotechnology. At the same time, however, the density of alliances among U.S., European, and Japanese firms varies considerably.

International Technology Alliances[55]

Corporations can cooperate on technology development through a variety of mechanisms, some of which imply clear directions of technology flow either out of or into a national base. In the 1970s, the most common form of international technology collaboration was through joint ventures and research corporations, where firms shared equity ownership (and corresponding profits and losses) in a separate and distinct corporate entity. By the late 1980s, joint equity collaboration was eclipsed by non-equity alliances, in which firms forgo formal equity linkages and directly organize joint R&D activities to reduce the cost and risk of pursuing related innovations.[56] Whether through direct or indirect linkages, alliances tend not to displace but to complement firms' internal research activities, and generally work best between firms that have different but complementary technological assets.[57]

Technology alliances began to grow substantially during the late 1980s and continue to do so today.[58] Contemporary economic and technological conditions provide a variety of incentives for firms to engage in international technology alliances.[59] Many firms use alliance strategies to reduce rapidly rising R&D costs and associated risks, particularly in sectors with increasingly capital-intensive scientific and technological disciplines, shorter innovation to commercialization periods, accelerated product life cycles, and a rapid diffusion of technology across competing firms. In addition, many firms use alliances to better monitor and retain access to a wider array of technological and scientific developments, which is increasingly important as product and process technologies become more complex and geographically dispersed. Moreover, alliances can generate new business opportunities, improve access to foreign markets, and reduce time to market.

Alliances are most common in high-technology industries. Most alliances in fact are concentrated in a few industries, particularly information technologies, biotechnology, and new materials.[60] Alliances in information technologies have grown far faster than in any other area, owing in part to the rapid growth of information technology (IT) industries generally as well as the overlapping nature of technological developments in computer software and hardware, telecommunications, industrial automation, and microelectronics. Alliances also are quite common in biotechnology, largely because of the unique division of labor between small, specialized biotechnology firms and large pharmaceutical and agro-chemical firms: the latter are attracted to the specialized research capabilities of dedicated biotechnology companies, which in turn are attracted to the financial depth, production capacity, and marketing capabilities of diversified pharmaceutical and agro-chemical firms. Alliances are also fairly common in new materials, in part because of the concentrated costs of R&D in new materials and the relative dispersion within and across industries of technological advances in this area.

Between 1980 and 1994, there were over 2,800 technology alliances among U.S., European, and Japanese firms in information technology industries. Over the same period, there were less than half as many alliances in biotechnology (approximately 1,300), and considerably fewer in new materials (approximately 560).[61] Figure 5.13 (Distribution of Technology Alliances between Economic Regions, by Technology) conveys the relative magnitude of alliances in these three sectors from 1980 to 1994.

Figure 5.13 also indicates that technology alliance formation varies considerably across countries. In new materials, biotechnology, and especially information technologies, the largest number of alliances occurred between U.S. firms and other U.S. firms—not foreign firms. Information technology alliances among U.S. firms have grown steadily since the early 1980s, and account for 37 percent of all alliances in this area from 1980 to 1994. In 1994 alone, IT alliances among U.S. firms accounted for 56 percent of the total. Similarly, alliances among U.S. firms account for nearly 40 percent of all biotechnology alliances over the period. Intra-U.S. alliances in these two technologies account for most of the recent growth in strategic technology alliances among U.S., European, and Japanese firms.

Across each of the three technologies, the second most frequent alliance combination has been between U.S. and European firms. In information technologies, alliances between U.S. and European firms have accounted for 22 percent of all alliances in this category between 1980 and 1994, although the growth of IT alliances among U.S. firms has far

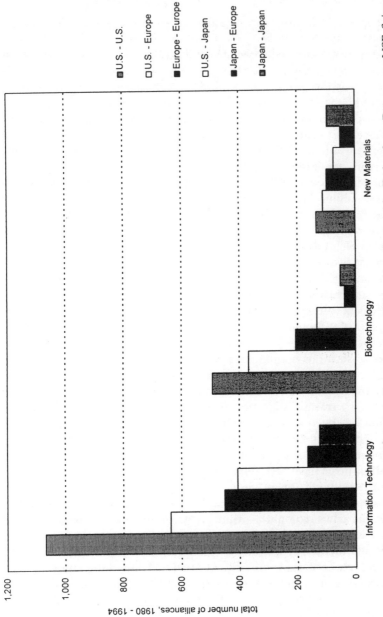

Figure 5.13. Distribution of Technology Alliances between Economic Regions, by Technology. *Data source: NSF, Science and Engineering Indicators* (1996): 158.

outstripped U.S.-European IT alliances since the mid-1980s. Biotechnology alliances have been more evenly distributed. Since 1989, biotechnology alliances between U.S. and European firms have been close to and occasionally greater than the number of alliances among U.S. firms. Over the entire time period, biotechnology alliances between U.S. and European firms accounted for 28 percent of the total.

In each technology, intraregional alliances among European firms represent the third most frequent alliance combination. Intraregional European alliances in each of the three technologies peaked in the late 1980s, most likely a product of strategic maneuvering prior to the European Union's 1992 market liberalization. Of all alliance combinations involving Japanese firms, the most frequent have been with U.S. firms in information technologies. In other technologies and other alliance combinations, however, Japanese firms are the least likely to engage in technology alliances, whether with U.S., European, or other Japanese firms.

In short, given a variety of technological and market pressures, firms have been turning to alliance strategies to reduce R&D costs, spread product development risks, and maintain access to a relatively broad portfolio of technologies and market opportunities while focusing their internal R&D efforts on core competencies. However, firms based in different states have different tendencies to form alliances, and tend to favor some technologies more than others. Most of the technology alliances over time and across technologies have involved U.S. firms and other U.S. firms. Of all combinations, the fastest growth in alliance formation has been among U.S. firms in information technology industries. Alliances between U.S. and European firms also have been quite frequent, particularly in biotechnology. By contrast, alliances involving Japanese firms have been relatively infrequent, with the exception of IT alliances with U.S. firms.

These variations in the tendency to use technology alliances complement the cross-national portrait of multinational corporate behavior that emerges from R&D and technology trade patterns. In the broadest view, the picture of technology development by multinational firms appears concentrated, not diffuse: most of the R&D conducted by MNCs takes place in the home market, and most international technology trade flows from parents to their affiliates. The fact that technology alliances are most frequent among U.S. firms is consistent with this central pattern.

On the periphery, much more variation appears. Sectoral detail indicates that the global spread of technology is far more extensive in some industries than others. The highest levels of foreign R&D conducted by MNCs are in pharmaceuticals, chemicals, electronic equipment, and, for U.S. MNCs, transportation equipment. More than any other sector, pharmaceuticals presents the clearest view of the diffusion of corporate R&D operations, showing both rapid growth and a large share of total R&D by foreign affiliates—particularly those operating in the United States. The concentration of international technology alliances in biotechnology and information technologies adds further resolution to this picture.

Country detail reveals even more variation. Generally, the R&D intensity of U.S. affiliates in different foreign markets varies less than the R&D intensity of different foreign affiliates in the United States. German affiliates have both the highest R&D expenditures and the highest R&D intensity of all foreign affiliates in the United States, while Japanese affiliates in the United States have the lowest levels in both respects. The magnitude of R&D is relatively similar for French and U.K. affiliates, although there are noticeably different R&D intensity levels between French and U.K. affiliates operating in different U.S. industries. By contrast, U.S. affiliates in Japan have R&D intensity levels similar to or greater than those of U.S. affiliates in France, the United Kingdom, and, in some sectors, Germany. Technology trade flows add further depth to this pattern. Japanese firms purchase far more U.S. technology through arms-length transactions than do European firms—in fact, the U.S. maintains a large export surplus in unaffiliated industrial process knowledge with Japan, while the United States has been a net importer of U.K. and German industrial process knowledge. Again, the distribution of technology alliances provides complementary color: alliances involving Japanese firms are infrequent, while alliances involving European and especially U.S. firms are common.

In sum, MNCs based in different states and operating in different sectors internationalize their technology development functions in different ways and to different degrees. The nature and identity of the base itself are mirrored in ultimate corporate behavior. As the following section demonstrates, such cross-national variations in foreign technology development strategies are similar in nature to cross-national variations in corporate investment, trade, and local production.

DIRECT INVESTMENT AND INTRAFIRM TRADE

Are the national patterns observed in the research and development activities of today's leading MNCs matched in other key areas of corporate strategy? This section compares the operations of MNCs along three closely related dimensions: the composition of direct investment, the volume and direction of intrafirm trade, and the domestic content of production by foreign affiliates. These indicators measure the types of industries in which MNCs operate outside their home markets, the degree to which they trade within or outside of their own internal networks, and the extent to which their foreign operations are integrated with host markets.

The evidence along each of these dimensions suggests that leading MNCs tend to pursue distinct operational styles in foreign markets and that these styles vary along national lines. U.S. MNCs represent one style, operating largely in foreign manufacturing and financial sectors, using intrafirm trade (IFT) channels relatively moderately, and displaying a comparatively high degree of integration in local markets. Japanese MNCs represent quite a different style, operating largely in foreign wholesale trade sectors, using IFT extensively, and displaying a comparatively low level of integration in local markets. If U.S. and Japanese MNCs can thereby be depicted at opposite ends on a spectrum of corporate behavior, German MNCs may be placed between the midpoint of that spectrum and the Japanese end. In addition, the evidence also suggests that French and British MNCs could be placed between the midpoint and the U.S. end of the spectrum (with British MNCs quite close to U.S. MNCs).

The Composition of Direct Investment[62]

The volume of FDI flows among advanced industrial states often varies substantially, in ways that tend to reflect different national approaches to inward direct investment. The largest variation is the relatively low level of direct investment in Japan, particularly in comparison to very high levels of outward investment by Japanese MNCs. For instance, although the ratio has declined slightly over time, in 1995 the volume of Japanese direct investment in the United States was almost three times the size of U.S. direct investment in Japan—$108.5 billion to $39.2 billion, respectively. This pattern reflects historically rooted structures in Japan's political economy, which tend to inhibit inward investment.[63]

As the evidence in this section illustrates, national patterns of direct investment differ not only in volume but also in composition, suggesting that both the home and host economies play a significant role in shaping FDI.

Figures 5.14 (Germany's Direct Investment Position in the U.S., by Sector) and 5.15 (Japan's Direct Investment Position in the U.S., by Sector) illustrate the composition of direct investment by German and Japanese MNCs in the United States.[64] In both cases, direct investment in the United States has increased over time, although at different rates:

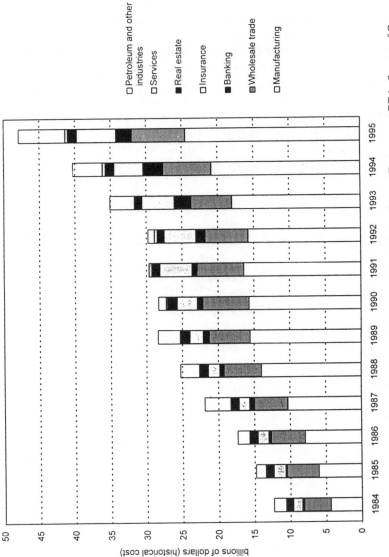

Figure 5.14. Germany's Direct Investment Position in the U.S., by Sector. *Data source:* BEA, *Survey of Current Business,* "Foreign Direct Investment in the United States: Detail on Historical Cost Position" (annual series): table 10.

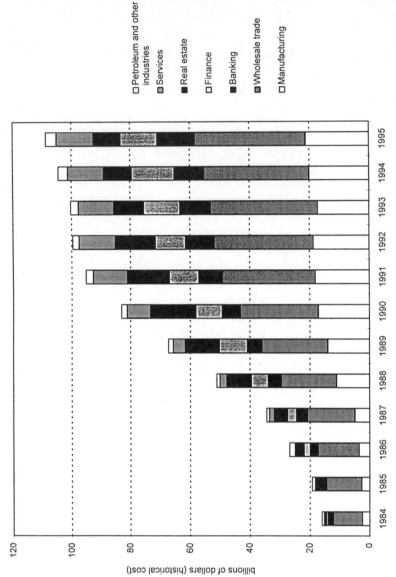

Figure 5.15. Japan's Direct Investment Position in the U.S., by Sector. *Data source:* BEA, *Survey of Current Business,* "Foreign Direct Investment in the U.S.: Detail on Historical Cost Position" (annual series): table 10.

German direct investment in the United States rose from $12.3 billion in 1984 to $47.9 billion in 1995, while Japanese direct investment increased very rapidly, from $16.0 billion to $108.6 billion (nearly twice the magnitude of German direct investment).[65] At the same time, direct investment from each nation has been placed in different segments of the U.S. economy.

Over the 1984–1995 period, half of all German direct investment in the United States was in manufacturing industries, slightly higher than the average for all European countries (43 percent). A sizable portion—22 percent—of German direct investment has gone into the U.S. wholesale trade sector, compared to just 9 percent for all European countries. As with other European countries, most other sectors account for fairly small shares of German direct investment in the United States.

By comparison, over the same period only 18 percent of Japanese direct investment in the United States was located in manufacturing industries. The wholesale trade sector consistently accounts for the largest share of Japan's direct investment—on average, 41 percent from 1984 to 1995. Compared to German and other European investors, fairly large shares of Japanese direct investment also have gone into banking (10 percent) and services (9 percent).

The composition of foreign direct investment flowing from the United States to both Germany and Japan also differs, but far less substantially than for foreign investment in the United States (Figure 5.16. U.S. Direct Investment Position in Germany, by Sector; and Figure 5.17. U.S. Direct Investment Position in Japan, by Sector). Over the 1984–1995 period, 60 percent of U.S. direct investment in Germany was in manufacturing industries, higher than the average for all European countries (40 percent).[66] Only 6 percent of U.S. direct investment went to Germany's wholesale trade sector, lower than the average for all European countries (12 percent). The composition of U.S. direct investment in Japan is close to the average for U.S. investment in Europe: 47 percent in manufacturing, and 18 percent in wholesale trade. Also, unlike German or Japanese investment in the United States, a substantial portion of U.S. direct investment abroad goes into the financial sector: finance accounts for 25 percent of U.S. direct investment in Europe, 12 percent in Germany, and 11 percent in Japan.

In short, the composition of direct investment flows across the Triad varies markedly. In general, there is far more variation in FDI in the United States than United States investment abroad. Japanese direct investment in the United States is unusually concentrated in the wholesale trade sector. Far more of German investment flows to U.S. manufacturing industries, although wholesale trade also accounts for a large

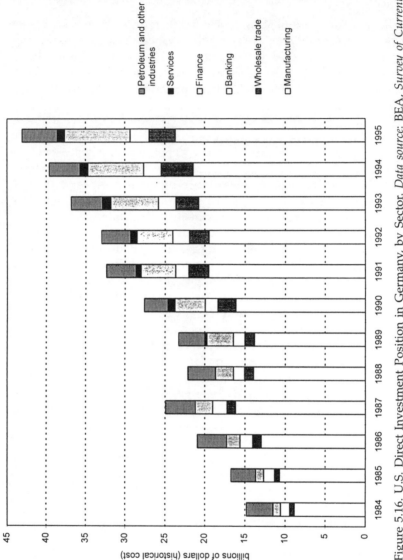

Figure 5.16. U.S. Direct Investment Position in Germany, by Sector. *Data source*: BEA, *Survey of Current Business*, "U.S. Direct Investment Abroad: Detail on Historical Cost Position" (annual series): table 11.

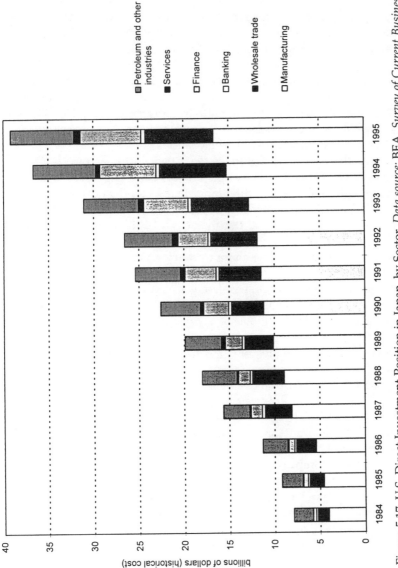

Figure 5.17. U.S. Direct Investment Position in Japan, by Sector. *Data source:* BEA, *Survey of Current Business,* "U.S. Direct Investment Abroad: Detail on Historical Cost Position" (annual series): table 11.

share. By comparison, European MNCs as a whole invest in U.S. manu-facturing industries at levels comparable to German MNCs, but direct substantially less investment to the U.S. wholesale trade sector.

U.S. direct investment abroad is distinctive primarily by virtue of the large fraction that goes into the finance sector. In addition, U.S. direct investment in Germany is concentrated in manufacturing industries, while the share directed to wholesale trade is relatively small. Other-wise, the composition of U.S. direct investment in Europe as a whole, in Germany, and in Japan is relatively similar.

The fact that U.S. outward investment varies little across countries, while direct investment in the United States varies significantly across countries, suggests that multinational firms based in different states tend to engage foreign markets in distinct ways. At one end of the spectrum, U.S. MNCs place the majority of their direct investment abroad in manufacturing industries, comparatively little in wholesale trade, and a relatively large share in finance. At the other end of the spectrum, Japanese MNCs place the majority of their direct investment in wholesale trade, and comparatively little in manufacturing indus-tries. German firms combine elements of both U.S. and Japanese styles of direct investment, with the majority in manufacturing industries but a large share in wholesale trade as well. Other European investors are closer to the U.S. model, with a considerably lower share in whole-sale trade.

The sectoral distribution of direct investment is particularly signifi-cant because of its implications for the operational style of affiliates in foreign markets. By design, foreign affiliates in the wholesale trade sec-tor import very large shares of their total output, as they primarily import finished goods for resale. Affiliates in manufacturing industries may or may not import large shares of their total output, as they can procure intermediate inputs (ranging from manufactured components to commodity-type bulk materials) through local suppliers.

Given the sectoral distribution of direct investment, this basic differ-ence between wholesale trade and manufacturing industries implies that affiliates of Japanese MNCs, in the aggregate, are less likely than Europe and U.S.-based MNCs to be deeply integrated in local markets. Foreign affiliates of U.S. firms are more likely to be integrated in local markets. Affiliates of German MNCs are likely to represent a midpoint on this spectrum.

These expectations are borne out by national variations in the trade flows associated with MNCs. Data on trade among affiliated firms—that is, intrafirm trade—are largely consistent with cross-national dif-ferences in the composition of investment.

Intrafirm Trade

Intrafirm trade (IFT) represents cross-border transactions between affiliated units of MNCs. In the United States, the volume of intrafirm trade represents a substantial share of total merchandise trade: in 1994, IFT accounted for more than one third of all merchandise exports and over two fifths of all merchandise imports.[67]

Like many domestic firms, foreign affiliates in different markets import and export a mix of finished and intermediate goods, depending upon their production and marketing strategies, price differentials, and a variety of additional factors internal and external to the firm. However, IFT data indicate that affiliates based in different states use IFT to different degrees, in part reflecting differences in the composition of direct investment.

Figures 5.18 (The Volume of Intrafirm Trade: Germany and the U.S.) and 5.19 (The Volume of Intrafirm Trade: Japan and the U.S.) represent the volume of IFT between the United States and both Germany and Japan (respectively), relative to the total volume of merchandise trade in each bilateral relationship.[68] Together, the two figures illustrate that IFT accounts for a larger percentage of total merchandise trade between the United States and Japan. Between 1983 and 1994, IFT has averaged 72 percent of total merchandise trade between the United States and Japan, compared to 55 percent for U.S.-German trade. In both instances, the IFT share of total trade has increased over time: IFT between the United States and Germany increased from 52 percent of all merchandise trade in 1983 to 63 percent in 1994, while IFT between Japan and the United States increased from 68 percent to 77 percent. While U.S.-German IFT is lower than U.S.-Japan IFT, it is higher than the average for U.S. trade with all Europe generally: from 1983 to 1994, IFT accounted for 51 percent of all merchandise trade between the United States and Europe.[69]

Figures 5.18 and 5.19 also indicate that IFT within U.S. firms represents a relatively small share of total IFT within each bilateral trade relationship. In U.S.-Japan trade, IFT among Japanese MNCs accounts for 92 percent of all bilateral IFT. In U.S.-German trade, IFT among German MNCs accounts for 71 percent of all IFT. By comparison, IFT among European MNCs accounts for 57 percent of all IFT between the United States and Europe.

Further detail on the direction of trade within MNCs indicates that IFT, in all cases, flows primarily from parents to their foreign affiliates. Figures 5.20 (The Direction of Intrafirm Trade: Germany and the U.S.) and 5.21 (The Direction of Intrafirm Trade: Japan and the U.S.) portray

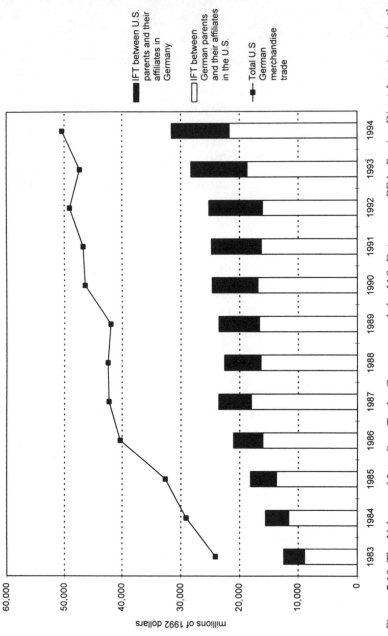

Figure 5.18. The Volume of Intrafirm Trade: Germany and the U.S. *Data source:* BEA, *Foreign Direct Investment in the U.S.* (annual series); BEA, *U.S. Direct Investment Abroad* (annual series); BEA, *Survey of Current Business* (June 1995).

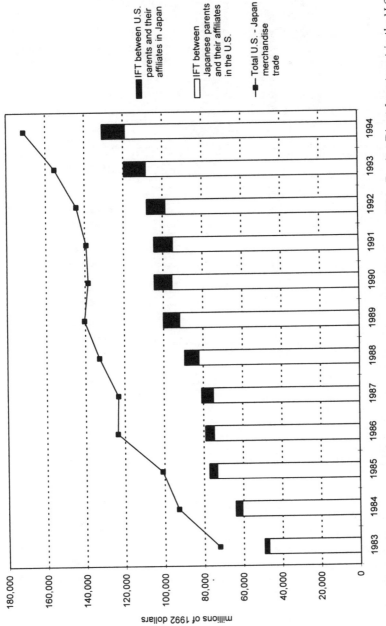

Figure 5.19. The Volume of Intrafirm Trade: Japan and the U.S. *Data source:* BEA, *Foreign Direct Investment in the U.S.* (annual series); BEA, *U.S. Direct Investment Abroad* (annual series); BEA, *Survey of Current Business* (June 1995).

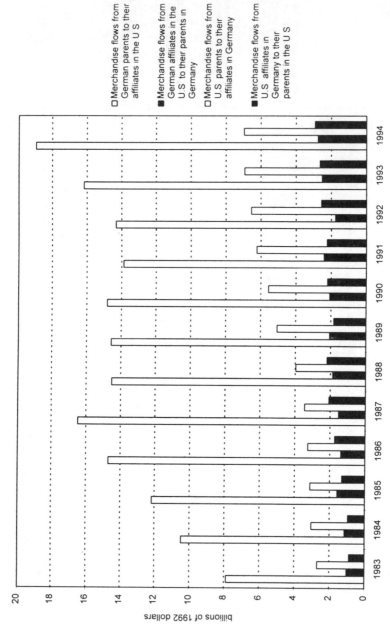

Figure 5.20. The Direction of Intrafirm Trade: Germany and the U.S. *Data source*: BEA, *U.S. Direct Investment Abroad*, (annual series): table III.H 1; and prior annual surveys; BEA, *Foreign Direct Investment in the U.S.*, (annual series): table H2.

IFT flows in each of four possible directions for U.S. trade with Japan and Germany: from parent to affiliate, and vice versa, for each country. In all cases, trade flows from multinational corporate parent groups to their foreign affiliates outweigh flows from foreign affiliates to their parent groups, suggesting that outward direct investment consistently creates trade. However, the relative magnitude character of IFT varies considerably across MNCs based in different states.

Most of the total IFT between the United States and both Japan and Germany flows from the foreign parent group to affiliates in the United States. Merchandise flows from German multinational corporate parents to their affiliates in the United States are approximately twice the size of flows from U.S. parents to their affiliates in Germany, while merchandise flows from affiliates to parents are similarly low in both directions (Figure 5.20). In the case of U.S.-Japan trade, merchandise trade flows from Japanese parents to their affiliates in the United States far outweigh any other IFT flow (Figure 5.21). In addition, unlike the U.S.-German trade relationship, IFT from Japanese affiliates in the United States to their foreign parents is over three times the volume of trade flows from U.S. parents to their affiliates in Japan.

These cross-national variations in the volume and direction of IFT are consistent with variations in the volume and composition of direct investment. Japanese direct investment in the United States is three times the size of U.S. direct investment in Japan. It is also far more concentrated in the wholesale trade sector, which characteristically involves a large share of finished goods imports. These direct investment patterns are consistent with the very large share of total U.S.-Japan trade that flows from Japanese parents to their affiliates in the United States. A similar but less stark pattern exists in the investment and trading relationship between the United States and Germany. German direct investment in the United States is about the same size as U.S. investment in Germany, although a larger share of it is in wholesale trade. In line with this investment pattern, more IFT flows from German parents to their affiliates in the United States than vice versa, while IFT flowing from affiliates to parents is similar in both directions.

In short, cross-national variation in the basic sectoral composition of direct investment provide some basis for understanding the net tendency of affiliates from individual countries to trade within or outside of multinational corporate networks. In general, overseas investment by U.S., German, and Japanese MNCs creates trade, through IFT flows from parents to affiliates. But U.S. MNCs invest abroad in ways that tend to create less IFT than either German or especially Japanese

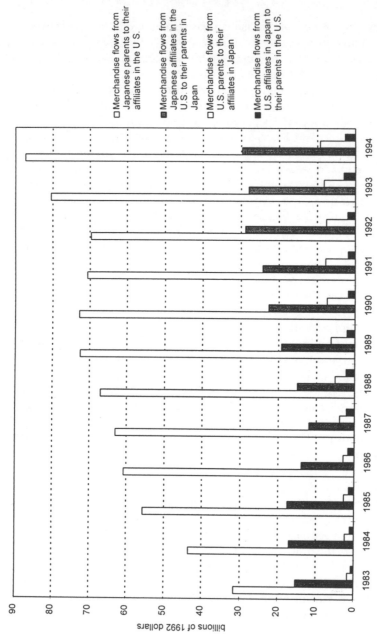

Figure 5.21. The Direction of Intrafirm Trade: Japan and the U.S. *Data source:* BEA, *Foreign Direct Investment in the U.S.* (annual series); BEA, *U.S. Direct Investment Abroad* (annual series); BEA, *Survey of Current Business* (June 1995).

MNCs, both of which invest abroad in ways that tend to foster particularly high levels of IFT.

Further data on the intended use of intrafirm trade provide additional evidence that MNCs based in different states engage foreign markets in distinctive ways. IFT flows from parents to their foreign affiliates generally fall into two categories, goods for resale without further manufacture (typically, finished goods) and goods for further manufacture (typically, intermediate goods). The mix of these two types of goods provides an approximate measure of the degree to which affiliates are integrated in local markets: the higher the share of imports for further manufacture, the more likely that the affiliate is adding value through local production.

Table 5.4 (Intrafirm Trade of Foreign Affiliates in the U.S. and U.S. Affiliates Abroad, by Intended Use) presents data describing how affiliates from different countries use goods received from their foreign parent group. Of foreign affiliates in the United States, the share of imports used for further manufacture is lowest among Japanese and German affiliates, and highest among French and U.K. affiliates. Of the different foreign markets in which U.S. affiliates operate, the share of imports used for further manufacture is lowest in Japan, highest in the United Kingdom, and relatively similar for Germany and France. Moreover, in all cases, a considerably higher share of the goods sent from U.S. parents to their foreign affiliates is used for further manufacture in each country than is the case for the corresponding foreign MNCs operating in the U.S. market. This suggests that U.S. affiliates are more likely to add value in foreign markets than MNCs based in the United Kingdom, France, Germany, or Japan, collectively as well as individually.

These patterns are consistent with the basic composition of direct investment by affiliates operating in each market. Other factors, however, may play a role as well. For instance, variation in the share of IFT goods used for further manufacture between U.S. affiliates in Japan and U.S. affiliates in the United Kingdom could reflect the relative ease of production for U.S. MNCs in the United Kingdom because of commonalities of language and culture, standards, legal and regulatory systems, and other business climate factors. The variation also seems associated with the fact that the United Kingdom has traditionally been far more accommodating of inward investment than Japan.

In addition, variation in the use of IFT among different foreign affiliates operating in the relatively open U.S. market is consistent with cross-national variation in the sectoral composition of investment. IFT patterns could, however, also reflect cross-national differences in how foreign affiliates pursue local production. Differentiating these two

130   CHAPTER 5

TABLE 5.4
Intrafirm Trade of Foreign Affiliates in the U.S. and U.S. Affiliates Abroad, by Intended Use

	Japan	Germany	France	U.K.	All countries
Imports of foreign affiliates in the U.S., from their foreign parent group (1992):					
Goods for resale without further manufacture, as a percent of total imported from foreign parent group	79	81	60	55	74
Goods for further manufacture, as a percent of total imported from foreign parent group	21	19	40	45	25
Exports to U.S. affiliates in foreign markets, from their U.S. parent group (1994):					
Goods for resale without further manufacture, as a percent of total exported by U.S. parent group	72	53	48	32	46
Goods for further manufacture, as a percent of total exported by U.S. parent group	28	43	49	67	52

Source: Bureau of Economic Analysis, *Foreign Direct Investment in the U.S.: 1992* (Washington, D.C.: U.S. Government Printing Office, 1994) table G-36; Bureau of Economic Analysis, *U.S. Direct Investment Abroad: 1994* (Washington, D.C.: U.S. Government Printing Office, 1997) table III.H 14.

Note: The two categories, goods for resale and goods for further manufacture, may not equal 100 percent due to the small fraction of intrafirm trade that consists of capital equipment.

factors requires observations of different affiliates operating within the same industry in the same foreign country. Domestic content data provide this degree of discrimination, and ultimately suggests that MNCs in different countries do indeed pursue different production strategies in foreign markets.

Domestic Content

The 1994 Benchmark Survey on Foreign Direct Investment in the United States, conducted by the Bureau of Economic Analysis of the U.S. Department of Commerce, provides detail on the imports of foreign affiliates by intended use. Such data allow observations of national differences across affiliates that otherwise appear very similar: they all operate in manufacturing industries and report high shares of goods intended for further manufacture. From this particular class of affiliates, one can observe whether affiliates based in different nations differ in their tendency to use local versus imported inputs for their U.S. production operations.[70]

Recent analyses of this class of affiliates provide findings quite similar to those reached in earlier sections of this chapter: foreign affiliates based in the United Kingdom have higher levels of domestic content across U.S. manufacturing industries, while foreign affiliates based in Germany and, to a greater extent, Japan, have considerably lower levels of domestic content.[71] In other words, affiliates based in the United Kingdom are more likely to be deeply integrated in the U.S. economy than are affiliates based in Germany. Japanese affiliates are least likely to be integrated.

Across all affiliates in all U.S. industries, the domestic content of production is slightly less than the estimated level for all firms—89 and 93 percent, respectively.[72] Across industries, domestic content tends to be lowest in machinery-intensive industries that have large amounts of manufactured intermediate goods, including construction, mining, and materials handling machinery; computer and office equipment; household audio and video; communications equipment; electronic components and accessories; and motor vehicles and equipment.

At the same time, domestic content rates in each of these industries vary across foreign affiliates based in different states. For instance, German-owned affiliates in the United States in nonelectrical machinery have a domestic content level of 79 percent, their British counterparts register a 95 percent level, while Japanese affiliates have a domestic content rate of 87 percent. In instruments and related products, 88 percent of production by German-owned affiliates is domestic content, French-owned affiliates register 95 percent, British-owned affiliates 97 percent, and Japanese affiliates 82 percent. In the electrical and electronic equipment sector, the domestic content for German-owned firms is 69 percent, while it is 96 percent for their French counterparts and 89 percent for Japanese affiliates.

Otherwise, in the construction, mining, and related machinery sector, the domestic content for Japanese-owned affiliates as a percentage of total output was 55 percent, compared to an average for all foreign affiliates of 89 percent. In computer and office equipment, the domestic content level for Japanese affiliates is 56 percent, compared to an average of 90 percent. In motor vehicles and equipment, the domestic content figure for Japanese affiliates was 63 percent, compared to 86 percent for other foreign affiliates.

Comparable domestic content data are not available for U.S. affiliates operating in foreign markets. However, the data on IFT exports by intended use (Table 5.4), which show comparatively high levels of exports for further manufacture, suggests that U.S. firms are likely to use local inputs more extensively than most foreign affiliates in the United States. Moreover, general domestic content data for all U.S. firms operating abroad, in all industries, show an average local content rate of 91 percent. The domestic content of U.S. affiliates is slightly higher in Europe (95 percent) than in Asia and the Pacific (90 percent), largely because of different levels of imports in the wholesale trade sector.[73]

In sum, there are consistent cross-national variations in the level and composition of direct investment, the degree to which MNCs maintain trade within their own corporate networks, and the extent to which foreign affiliates are integrated with local markets. Generally, U.S. MNCs are most likely to be located in manufacturing and service industries, to have comparatively low levels of IFT, and to be relatively well integrated within local markets. Japanese MNCs are most likely to be located in wholesale trade, to have comparatively high levels of IFT, and to be more independent from local markets. European MNCs generally represent different combinations of these two models, with German MNCs being closer in form to the Japanese style, and both French and U.K. MNCs being closer in form to the U.S. style.

These variations correspond to different strategies through which MNCs invest and produce in foreign markets, as well as to the relative openness of host economies to inward investment. We do not doubt the relevance of other factors, such as fundamental macroeconomic variables (for instance, the impact of different national savings rates on international trade and investment flows).[74] But the evidence surveyed in this chapter strongly suggests that there are inherent and enduring structural factors that profoundly influence the location decisions and operating styles of MNCs.

Such a conclusion could be tested further through a similar analysis of investment and trading patterns between Japan and the European Union. Unfortunately, data comparable to that considered in this chapter do not exist for this leg of the Triad. Anecdotal evidence, however, indicates that the patterns would be similar. Our own interviews with European corporate executives and officials of the Commission of the European Communities conducted in 1992 and 1993 suggested that similar structural imbalances in investment and IFT exist between many European countries and Japan.[75] In addition, in some key areas, such as automobiles in Germany, Japanese imports peaked at a much lower level than they did in the United States and stayed at that level despite the rising relative competitiveness of Japanese industry over time. Not only do the strategies of MNCs appear to vary by nationality when it comes to the investment and IFT, but states also appear to manage their own associated bilateral relations differently and with different results.

Together, national variations in MNC investment, trade, and local production patterns are consistent with the evidence presented on MNC innovation, technology trade, and international strategic alliances. Although both innovation and trade remain centralized in most MNCs, the degree of that centralization generally varies by corporate nationality. U.S. and U.K. firms tend to be more integrated with the foreign economies in which they operate, while German and especially Japanese MNCs tend to retain large shares of their innovation and trading operations within their own networks. These variations partly reflect the orientation and competencies of the foreign systems in which they operate, but taken together they seem mainly related to the structure and character of the national systems in which they are based.

INTERACTION OF CORPORATE INVESTMENT, TRADE AND INNOVATION

In light of the above findings, it is important to note that national innovation systems are not entirely independent, nor are they static. Elements of some systems were explicitly modeled on others, and there are numerous interdependencies and linkages across systems.[76] In addition, national systems exhibit different capacities to learn and adapt to changing technological and economic conditions.[77] Indeed, linkages across innovation systems are likely to deepen over time, as technology and industry spread across national borders. Higher rates of external patenting, more rapid diffusion of technology across borders, increasing rates of overseas R&D activity, and other trends such as the increasing prevalence of international technology alliances all point toward the increasing openness of many national technology bases. MNCs are typically at the heart of that process of opening.

In fact, MNCs may be diffusing technology more extensively through their overseas production facilities than can be captured by such measures as foreign R&D, technology trade, and strategic technology alliances. Some analysts have argued, for instance, that tacit knowledge—that is, technical knowledge and know-how embodied in both people and organizations—can be central to successful technology development, commercialization, and production (although in ways that are intrinsically difficult to measure and evaluate).[78] In addition, technology also can be transferred abroad in the form of goods themselves.[79] Given their extensive international production and sourcing networks, MNCs are particularly likely to transfer technology abroad in the form of people, organizational assets, and intermediate goods.

If MNCs were thoroughly and relentlessly integrating national innovation systems through the systematic diffusion of technology abroad, however, it would register in the overseas R&D data as well as the technology trade data. By these and related measures, MNCs still retain the bulk of their innovative capabilities in their home markets, and technology that does flow overseas tends to stay within multinational networks as it moves from parent firms to their foreign affiliates. Again, inside the corporation—where the vast majority of commercially significant innovation takes place—R&D remains relatively centralized.[80] Overseas R&D by affiliates appears quite limited when compared to both the R&D activities of the parent group and the more extensive global spread of production and sourcing, while the R&D that does move overseas tends to be associated with product customization and local production processes. Only very rarely do companies transfer basic research functions to foreign markets.[81]

The tendency of MNCs to move R&D overseas in a measured fashion, mainly through their foreign direct investment and local production, suggests to some an R&D life cycle analogous to the life cycle of foreign direct investment.[82] According to such a model, firms in the early stages of overseas production will tend to use product and process technology developed in the home market; as overseas production units become more established, local R&D activities emerge to customize products in accordance with local market conditions and, eventually, to support affiliate production operations. In advanced stages, as affiliates become deeply integrated into local economies, they may undertake more substantial forms of R&D to develop products exclusively for the local market. In fact, however, few firms reach such stages.

If an R&D life cycle were the rule rather than the exception, one would expect overseas R&D to be more pronounced for European affiliates in the United States than for their Japanese counterparts, and relatively similar for U.S. affiliates in Europe and Japan. The evidence is consistent with this expectation. Both the magnitude and intensity of R&D conducted by German, French, and U.K. affiliates in the United States is substantially higher than R&D by Japanese affiliates. Studies of Japanese investment in Europe indicate that Japanese affiliates conduct substantially less R&D there than do U.S. affiliates.[83] In addition, the average intensity (but not the magnitude) of R&D is relatively similar for U.S. affiliates operating in different sectors in France, the United Kingdom, and Japan. But these observations more plausibly reflect differences in the composition of foreign direct investment, not life cycles. By this account, the difference in average R&D intensities between European and Japanese affiliates in the United States is related to the comparatively large percentage of European investment in technology-intensive manufacturing sectors, that is, sectors with far more R&D per unit of sales than other areas of FDI. Furthermore, such observations are consistent with the idea that MNCs conduct R&D overseas as one among a number of possible means of acquiring technology in foreign markets.

Altogether, the evidence considered in this chapter suggests that variations in the foreign technology development practices of MNCs are not a straightforward function of investment composition or life-cycle effects. Sectoral variations in the R&D intensity of foreign affiliates in the United States suggest that investment composition does not explain MNC behavior. In each of the major manufacturing sectors, either German, British, or French affiliates have the highest R&D intensities, while Japanese affiliates consistently have the lowest. In addition, variations in technology trade as well as strategic technology alliances indicate that firms based in different nations use very different methods for gaining access to foreign technology. Compared to European firms, Japanese firms tend to acquire U.S. technology through unaffiliated channels; they also tend to avoid international technology alliances. These measures, along with the relatively low level of R&D by Japanese affiliates in the United States, support the contention that Japanese MNCs pursue far more centralized technology development strategies than their European counterparts.

It is true that the degree to which R&D is centralized or decentralized often conforms to the particular characteristics of individual technologies and markets. For instance, one of the reasons pharmaceutical companies conduct R&D overseas is to accommodate different national regulatory standards and practices.[84] In the consumer electronics industry, firms often conduct R&D abroad to keep in touch with leading-edge technological developments as well as to adapt technologies to local standards, such as different voltages or broadcasting systems.[85] In the automotive industry, the uniform nature of core technologies tends to encourage centralized R&D, even though production has become highly decentralized.[86] In the semiconductor industry, moreover, the high R&D component of new product costs leads firms from different countries to collaborate on next-generation product development.[87]

At the same time, however, MNCs from different locations do respond to such industry characteristics in unique ways. For instance, in the pharmaceutical industry, U.S. firms have set up more secondary R&D facilities than MNCs based elsewhere. European pharmaceutical firms tend to locate their secondary R&D facilities in the United States, while Japanese pharmaceutical firms have very little exposure in foreign markets.[88] In the consumer electronics industry, Japanese firms conduct the bulk of their R&D at home, unlike European firms.[89] And in the automotive industry, U.S. firms have long had independent operations in Europe that conduct advanced R&D work. By contrast, Japanese auto producers have only recently begun to establish local technological support operations for their foreign assembly plants.[90]

Only the passage of time will fully reveal the impact of life-cycle effects on the distinctive technology acquisition style of Japanese MNCs. But if the length of investment is a powerful explanatory factor in itself, then one would expect the R&D intensity of U.S. affiliates to be relatively similar in most European economies, and perhaps slightly lower in Japan. To the contrary, the R&D intensity of U.S. affiliates in Germany actually is far higher than in other countries, and in many individual sectors the R&D intensity of U.S. affiliates operating in Japan is noticeably higher than affiliates operating in France, the United Kingdom, and in some cases Germany as well.

The fact that U.S. affiliates operating in the same sector have different R&D intensities in different foreign markets suggests that the technological orientation of national innovation systems very likely has a significant bearing on the location and level of technology development by foreign affiliates. Indeed, the R&D intensity of U.S. affiliates in Germany and Japan is unusually high in precisely those scale-intensive, medium-technology sectors that those nations specialize in— transportation equipment, and electronic and other electric equipment. Similarly, the level and intensity of R&D by foreign affiliates in the United States is most pronounced in the pharmaceutical sector, which accounts for a large and rapidly growing share of the nation's scientific and technological resources.

Cross-national variations in the foreign technology development strategies of MNCs are consistent with broader patterns in overseas investment, trading, and production styles. Generally, U.S. MNCs invest abroad primarily in manufacturing industries, and do so in a way that involves deeper levels of integration with the local economy. Japanese MNCs invest far more in wholesale trade, and tend to pursue strategies that involve high degrees of IFT and comparatively low levels of local market integration. German firms represent a hybrid case, investing heavily in manufacturing as well as wholesale trade operations, trading relatively heavily through IFT, and integrating with local markets at comparatively modest levels.

National innovation systems and national investment styles convey different degrees of attractiveness and different degrees of access to foreign MNCs. The degree of attractiveness is partly a function of nationally distinctive resources, as well as of the fundamental governing and financial structures embedded within firms. The degree of access is itself partly a function of the structure of the national political and economic system. Among other things, that structure conditions the extent to which science and technology resources are centralized within firms or dispersed more broadly. The next and last chapter of this book summarizes such linkages between national structural context and MNC behavior and sketches analytical and policy implications.

Notes to this chapter on page 308

1. See, for instance, Donald H. Dalton and Manuel G. Serapio, *Globalizing Industrial Research and Development* (Washington, D.C.: U.S. Department of Commerce, 1995); "Technology and Globalization," in OECD, *Technology and the Economy: The Key Relationships* (Paris: OECD, 1992) pp. 209–36. For an extended analysis with particular reference to MNCs, see O. Granstrand, L. Håkanson, and S. Sjölander, *Technology Management and International Business: Internationalization of R&D and Technology* (New York: John Wiley & Sons, 1992).

2. See David C. Mowery, *Science and Technology Policy in Interdependent Economies* (Boston: Kluwer Academic Publishers, 1994).

3. The increased frequency of offshore R&D and the increased frequency of international technology alliances have been associated with the rise of "technoglobalism" during the 1980s. See OECD, Economic Analysis and Statistics Division, *The Performance of Foreign Affiliates in OECD Countries* (Paris: OECD, 1994) p. 49. For a broader discussion, see Sylvia Ostry and Richard Nelson, *Technonationalism and Technoglobalism* (Washington, D.C.: Brookings, 1995).

4. See, for example, Dalton and Serapio, *Globalizing Industrial Research and Development*.

5. G. Vickery, "Global Industries and National Policies," *OECD Observer*, vol. 179 (December 1992/January 1993) pp. 11–14. Smaller countries with limited domestic R&D resources (e.g., Sweden, Netherlands, and Switzerland) tend to locate even more R&D abroad, often as a means of tapping foreign technological resources.

6. J. A. Cantwell, *Technological Innovation and Multinational Corporations* (Oxford: Basil Blackwell, 1989).

7. P. Patel and K. Pavitt, "Large Firms in the Production of the World's Technology: An Important Case of 'Non-Globalization,'" *Journal of International Business Studies* (First Quarter, 1991) pp. 1–21.

8. J. H. Dunning, "Multinational Enterprises and the Globalization of Innovatory Capacity," *Research Policy*, vol. 23, no. 1 (January 1994) pp. 67–88.

9. It would be preferable to compare all the permutations of R&D conducted by U.S., European, and Japanese MNCs in each others' markets. Unfortunately, apart from the United States, there are few sources of country data that distinguish the R&D activities of foreign affiliates from those of parent firms and all domestic businesses. Consequently, the analysis of MNC R&D in this chapter is limited primarily to comparisons of foreign affiliates in the United States and U.S. affiliates in foreign markets.

10. U.S. Department of Commerce, Bureau of Economic Analysis, *U.S. Direct Investment Abroad: 1994 Benchmark Survey* (Washington, D.C., January 1997) tables II.R 1, III.I 2; U.S. Department of Commerce, Bureau of Economic Analysis, *Survey of Current Business* (Washington, D.C., June 1995) table 5, p. 36. Data expressed in billions of current dollars.

11. U.S. Department of Commerce, Bureau of Economic Analysis, *U.S. Direct Investment Abroad: 1994 Benchmark Survey* (Washington, D.C., January 1997) tables II.R 1, III.I 2. The percentage of total MNC R&D conducted by majority-owned affiliates varies somewhat by sector; in 1994 it ranged from 17 percent in food and kindred products to 6 percent in electric and electronic equipment.

12. U.S. Department of Commerce, Bureau of Economic Analysis, *U.S. Direct Investment Abroad: 1994 Benchmark Survey* (Washington, D.C., January 1997)

tables II.R 1, III.I 2, II.K 1, III.E 1, III.D 6, III.G 1.

13. U.S. Congress, Office of Technology Assessment, *Multinationals and the U.S. Technology Base*, pp. 85–90.

14. This chapter uses the conventional definition of R&D intensity: the ratio of R&D expenditures to sales.

15. U.S. Department of Commerce, Bureau of Economic Analysis, *Survey of Current Business* (June 1995), table 1/p. 32; table 5/p. 36.

16. The average R&D intensity of foreign affiliates in the United States is unusually high due to the concentration of foreign direct investment in high R&D intensity sectors, principally pharmaceuticals, chemicals, and mechanical engineering. For different reasons, foreign affiliates in Ireland and Australia also have higher average R&D intensities than domestic firms. OECD, Economic Analysis and Statistics Division, *The Performance of Foreign Affiliates in OECD Countries* (Paris: OECD, 1994) pp. 64–65.

17. U.S. Department of Commerce, Bureau of Economic Analysis, *U.S. Direct Investment Abroad: 1994 Benchmark Survey* (Washington, D.C.: January 1997) tables II.R 1, III.I 2, II.K 1, III.A 2.

18. OECD, Economic Analysis and Statistics Division, *The Performance of Foreign Affiliates in OECD Countries* (1994) pp. 61–76.

19. For data and analysis of U.S. MNCs, see U.S. Department of Commerce, Bureau of Economic Analysis, *Survey of Current Business* (June 1995) pp. 31–51. For an analysis of foreign affiliates in the United States, see U.S. Department of Commerce, *Foreign Direct Investment in the United States: An Update* (Washington, D.C.: U.S. Government Printing Office, 1995).

20. See Robert Pearce and Marina Papanastassiou, "R&D Networks and Innovation: Decentralised Product Development in Multinational Enterprises," *R&D Management*, vol. 26, no. 4 (October 1996) pp. 315–33; Donald H. Dalton and Manuel G. Serapio, *Globalizing Industrial Research and Development* (Washington, D.C.: U.S. Department of Commerce, 1995) pp. 23–26; U.S. Department of Commerce, Technology Administration, Japan Technology Program, *U.S. Research Facilities of Foreign Companies*, prepared by D. H. Dalton and M. G. Serapio, NTIS Pub. No. 93–134328 (Washington, D.C.: January 1993); U.S. Department of Commerce, Technology Administration and the Japan–U.S. Friendship Commission, *Japan–U.S. Direct R&D Investments in the Electronics Industries*, prepared by M. G. Serapio, NTIS Pub. No. 94–127974 (Washington, D.C.: 1994); OECD, Economic Analysis and Statistics Division, *Performance of Foreign Affiliates in OECD Countries* (Paris: OECD, 1994).

21. On Philips' R&D operations, see Philips Electronics NV, *Annual Report 1993* (Eindhoven, The Netherlands, 1994); Philips Electronics NV, "Electronics for People," corporate brochure (Eindhoven, The Netherlands, 1993) p. 13; Philips Research, "Philips Research: A Gateway to the Future," corporate brochure (Eindhoven, The Netherlands, 1993).

22. Presentation by Knut Merten, Siemens Inc., at the National Academy of Sciences, May 30, 1995.

23. Kevin Done, "Tomorrow, the World," *Financial Times*, Apr. 22, 1994, p. 15.

24. The relative ease of establishing R&D operations varies across industries that specialize in different scientific and technological disciplines, given variations in the degree of capital intensity and the types of linkages to production facilities characteristic of different disciplines.

25. OECD, "Globalization in the Pharmaceutical Industry," draft manuscript (March 10, 1993) table 4/p. 9, p. 42.

26. OECD, "Globalization of Industrial Activities: Sector Case Study of Globalization in the Computer Industry," draft paper (September 27, 1993) p. 11.

27. P. Patel and K. Pavitt, "Large Firms in the Production of the World's Technology: An Important Case of 'Non-Globalization" *Journal of International Business Studies* (First Quarter, 1991) pp. 1–21; R. Miller, "Global R&D Networks and Large-Scale Innovations: The Case of the Automobile Industry," *Research Policy*, vol. 23, no. 3 (May 1993) pp. 27–46. Although the R&D intensity of the automotive industry is low relative to electronics, computers, and pharmaceuticals, it has been increasing over time and is well above the national average for manufacturing industries. OECD, "Globalization of Industrial Activities: Sector Case Study of Globalization in the Automobile Industry," (draft paper, June 16, 1993) p. 10.

28. Patent evidence also supports the conclusion that corporations retain most of their technology development functions in the home market. See P. Patel and K. Pavitt, "Large Firms in the Production of the World's Technology." Similar findings also were reached for British firms; see J. A. Cantwell and C. Hodson, "Global R&D and British Competitiveness," in M. C. Casson, ed., *Global Research Strategy and International Competitiveness* (Oxford: Basil Blackwell, 1991).

29. Data expressed in constant 1992 dollars. Data on R&D spending by foreign affiliates from U.S. Department of Commerce, Bureau of Economic Analysis, *Survey of Current Business* (May 1995) table 6/p. 62, and U.S. Department of Commerce, Bureau of Economic Analysis, *Foreign Direct Investment in the United States*, (annual surveys). Data on total U.S. industry-funded R&D from National Science Foundation, *National Patterns of R&D Resources–1995*, table B3.

30. Ibid.

31. In 1994, Swiss firms also accounted for a substantial share of R&D spending by foreign affiliates in the United States, spending $2.3 billion, or 15.4% of the total. Approximately half of Swiss affiliate R&D spending was in the pharmaceutical sector. Source: U.S. Department of Commerce, Bureau of Economic Analysis, *Foreign Direct Investment in the U.S.: Preliminary Estimates, 1994,* July 1996, table I-6. (Data expressed in constant 1992 dollars.)

32. Ibid.

33. H. Fusfeld, *Industry's Future: Changing Patterns of Industrial Research* (Washington, D.C.: Industrial Research Institute, 1994).

34. See OTA, *Multinationals and the National Interest*, figure 5–8.

35. For supporting analyses, see Dalton and Serapio, *Globalizing Industrial Research and Development*; OECD, *Performance of Foreign Affiliates*, 1994, p. 50; U.S. Department of Commerce, Bureau of Economic Analysis, *Foreign Direct Investment in the United States: An Update*, 1994, p. 70; H. Fusfeld, *Industry's Future: Changing Patterns of Industrial Research.*

36. FDI in the pharmaceutical sector increased from $2.4 billion in 1985 to $25.5 billion in 1994. In 1995, direct investment in this sector jumped another 33%, to reach $33.9 billion. U.S. Department of Commerce, Bureau of Economic Analysis, *Survey of Current Business*, September 1996, July 1995, August 1994, and July 1993.

37. Data source: U.S. Department of Commerce, Bureau of Economic Analysis, *Survey of Current Business*, September 1996, table 10.3, p. 77. See pages

116–22 in this volume for a complete analysis of national variations in the composition of direct investment.

38. Ibid.

39. U.S. Department of Commerce, Bureau of Economic Analysis, *U.S. Direct Investment Abroad*, annual series, tables III.I 3 and III.E 3; U.S. Department of Commerce, Bureau of Economic Analysis, *Survey of Current Business*, June 1995, table 11.2, pp. 44–45. Data expressed in constant 1992 dollars. Data on overseas R&D expenditures by U.S. firms are available only since 1989.

40. U.S. Department of Commerce, Bureau of Economic Analysis, *U.S. Direct Investment Abroad: Benchmark Survey, Preliminary 1994 Estimates*, January 1997, table III.R 2; and prior annual surveys; U.S. Department of Commerce, Bureau of Economic Analysis, *Survey of Current Business*, June 1995, table 11.2, p. 45.

41. Ibid.

42. These percentages for France and the United Kingdom represent 1993 data (because of missing sectoral detail, 1994 data cannot be used).

43. There are four limitations to using royalty and license fee transactions as a proxy for technology trade. First, the available U.S. data for royalties and license fees include transactions of all forms of intellectual property, e.g., they combine industrial process technology along with other forms of intellectual property, such as copyrights, trademarks, franchises, and rights to broadcast live events. (Bureau of Economic Analysis provides data on industrial process technology only for unaffiliated or arms-length transactions; for a discussion of these transactions see the following pages.) Second, it is difficult to measure intellectual property traded between affiliated firms, since the value of affiliated transactions is not always determined on the open market. Although MNCs dispute the contention, many observers believe that both U.S. and foreign MNCs adjust intellectual property fees to shift costs from their firms in low-tax regions to those in high-tax regions, thereby lowering their net tax obligations. Third, the data do not differentiate royalty and license fees associated with new technology from those associated with old technology transactions; as a consequence, for example, a large portion of U.S. technology exports in any given year may not represent new technology leaving the country but, instead, may represent continued financial transactions from technology transferred in prior years. Fourth, technology also can be transferred through a variety of channels that are not captured by this or any other reliable measure—for instance, technology can be transferred through the exchange of technologically intensive goods, depending on how the purchaser utilizes those goods. Notwithstanding these four limitations, analysts commonly use intellectual property transactions as a proxy for technology transfer by MNCs.

44. OECD Economics Analysis and Statistics Division Database, *Main Science and Technology Indicators*, no. 1, 1995, table 82.

45. This observation holds insofar as intellectual property transactions represent technology trade per se (see endnote 43). The validity of this indicator is somewhat stronger for OECD data on technology trade than for Bureau of Economic Analysis data on intellectual property transactions, due to slight measurement differences. The available Bureau of Economic Analysis measure covers all intellectual property transactions, which includes patents for industrial process technology along with copyrights, trademarks, franchises, rights to broadcast live events, and other intangible property rights. The OECD measure is more tightly focused on technology trade per se, covering patents,

licenses, trademarks, designs, know-how, and closely related technical services for industrial R&D. For the purposes of this analysis, the difference in the two measurements is not significant. This chapter uses OECD data for broad international comparisons of technology trade, and Bureau of Economic Analysis data for more detailed analysis of technology trade patterns specific to the United States.

46. Owing to the lack of an appropriate price index for intellectual property transactions, this chapter presents the data on technology trade in current dollars.

47. See M. E. Mogee, "Inward International Licensing by U.S.-Based Firms: Trends and Implications," *The Journal of Technology Transfer*, vol. 16, no. 2 (Spring 1991) pp. 14–19.

48. U.S. Department of Commerce, Bureau of Economic Analysis, *Survey of Current Business*, September 1995, table 2, p. 76; see also tables 4.1–4.4.

49. This conclusion holds to the extent that intellectual property transactions represent technology trade; see endnote 43 regarding measurement qualifications.

50. See chapter 4 for a description of FDI trends in the United States. For data and supporting analysis of the relationship between FDI and technology trade flows, see U.S. Department of Commerce, Bureau of Economic Analysis, *Survey of Current Business*, September 1993, table 4.4, p. 132; and U.S. Department of Commerce, Bureau of Economic Analysis, "U.S. International Sales and Purchases of Private Services," *Survey of Current Business*, 1992, p. 85.

51. U.S. Department of Commerce, Bureau of Economic Analysis, *Survey of Current Business*, September 1995, p. 82.

52. Data on technology trade between Japan and Europe could provide confirming evidence of this observation. As with affiliate R&D data, however, comparable affiliate technology trade data is not available for the European-Japanese relationship.

53. Importing patterns by U.S. affiliates of foreign firms are more mixed. In 1994, 65% of total U.S. technology imports from Europe were from European MNCs to their U.S. affiliates, although there were some variations among the large European countries—78% from the United Kingdom, 70% from Germany, and just 55% from France. Of all 1994 U.S. technology imports from Japan, 73% were purchased by the U.S. affiliates of Japanese MNCs. U.S. Department of Commerce, Bureau of Economic Analysis, *Survey of Current Business*, September 1995, p. 82.

54. OECD, Economic Analysis and Statistics Division, *Performance of Foreign Affiliates in OECD Countries* (Paris: OECD, 1994). On Japan's general orientation toward a strategy of technology acquisition, see Samuels, "Rich Nation, Strong Army."

55. Analysts frequently use different terms to describe technological collaboration among firms. There are important distinctions in the literature between short-term tactical alliances and relatively-longer-term strategic alliances, as well as between alliances used to develop and/or diffuse technology and those used to gain market access and pursue other nontechnological goals. For simplicity, this chapter uses a single term—international technology alliances—to describe any interfirm collaboration (equity or non-equity) that includes arrangements for joint research and/or technology transfer. For more general

discussion of international alliances, see OTA, *Multinationals and the National Interest*, ch. 5.

56. In general terms, joint ventures are more common among firms seeking to improve their long-term market position, while technology alliances are more common when firms are pursuing more immediate technological achievements. See J. Hagedoorn, "Understanding the Rationale of Strategic Technology Partnering: Interorganizational Modes of Cooperation and Sectoral Differences," *Strategic Management Journal*, vol. 14 (1993) p. 371.

57. National Science Board, *Science and Engineering Indicators–1993* (Washington, D.C.: U.S. Government Printing Office, 1993) p. 122; and D. C. Mowery, "International Collaborative Ventures and U.S. Firms' Technology Strategies," in Granstrand, Håkanson, and Sjölander, *Technology Management and International Business* (New York: John Wiley, 1992) pp. 224–29.

58. See National Science Board, *Science and Engineering Indicators–1996* (Washington, D.C.: U.S. Government Printing Office, 1996) p. 43–44; and National Science Board, *Science and Engineering Indicators–1993* (Washington, D.C.: U.S. Government Printing Office, 1993) p. 123. The data cited in this source are drawn from the Maastricht Economic Research Institute's MERIT/CATI database, which covers only interfirm agreements that involve technology transfer or joint research.

59. See Hagedoorn, "Understanding the Rationale of Strategic Technology Partnering."

60. National Science Board, *Science and Engineering Indicators–1996* (Washington, D.C.: U.S. Government Printing Office, 1996) pp. 43–44; Lynn K. Mytelka and Michael Delapierre, "Strategic Partnerships, Knowledge-Based Networked Oligopolies, and the State" (manuscript, August 26, 1996).

61. National Science Board, *Science and Engineering Indicators–1996* (Washington, D.C.: U.S. Government Printing Office, 1996) appendix table 4–38. The data cited in this source are drawn from the Maastricht Economic Research Institute's MERIT/CATI database, which, although not comprehensive, is the best available source of quantitative data on interfirm technology alliances. All of the quantitative evidence cited in this section is from this data source.

62. Foreign direct investment is not easy to measure. The method most widely used is the "historical cost" approach, which calculates the value of FDI by focusing on the initial cost of any investment but largely understates its current value. It is also subject to distortion as a result of currency fluctuations. A principal alternative is the "stock" method of evaluation which calculates the value of initial investments according to their current values. Current values, however, can only be calculated in the broadest sense. A third approach adjusts for "replacement costs." This market-value method largely replicates the second method but tends to focus less on share price indices and more on price indices for investment goods. It has two major deficiencies. First, the current value of many direct investments has little to do with the replacement cost of the actual capital, much of which may be outdated. Second, the value of an investment may have less to do with the market value of the physical capital than with the value of intangible assets such as skills, knowledge, or goodwill. Critics suggest that the historical cost approach understates European investment in the United States and overstates more recent Japanese investment. In fact, the vast majority of FDI within the Triad occurred in the 1980s. For a

detailed discussion of how this influences the U.S. position, see Robert Eisner and Paul J. Pieper, "The World's Greatest Debtor Nation?," *North American Review of Economics and Finance,* vol. 1, no. 1 (1990) pp. 9–32.

63. By nature, these features resist change. Many managers of U.S.-based MNCs, for instance, contend that U.S. governmental efforts to overcome the private and public sector barriers to inward investment in Japan have achieved only limited success in making the Japanese domestic market more receptive to foreign investors. Sources: Confidential interviews with MNC executives and government officials conducted by the authors in 1993 and 1994 in Japan and the United States. See also The American Chamber of Commerce in Japan, *The United States–Japan White Paper 1993* (Tokyo: American Chamber of Commerce in Japan, 1993) pp. 30–34, 49–50, 64–68, 90–92; Office of the United States Trade Representative, *1993 National Trade Estimate Report on Foreign Trade Barriers* (Washington, D.C.: GPO, 1993) pp. 79–94, 143–170; Ad-Hoc Committee on Foreign Direct Investment in Japan, *Improvement of the Investment Climate and Promotion of Foreign Direct Investment into Japan* (Tokyo: Keidanren/Committee on International Industrial Cooperation and Committee on Foreign Affiliated Corporations, 1992); and The House Wednesday Group, *Beyond Revisionism: Towards a New U.S.–Japan Policy for the Post–Cold War Era* (Washington, D.C.: March 1993).

64. Due to accounting methods, it is difficult to identify precisely the sectoral allocation of direct investment. The BEA categorizes firms based on the sectoral location of final sales; the sector with the largest share of final sales represents the firm's entire sector of operation. In diversified affiliates, this categorization method can obscure other sectors in which the affiliate operates at a significant level. Largely for this reason, the analysis in this chapter focuses on major industrial groupings. Even at this level, however, the categorization rules can partially mischaracterize the sectoral distribution of direct investment.

65. U.S. Department of Commerce, Bureau of Economic Analysis, *U.S. Direct Investment Abroad,* annual series; U.S. Commerce Department, *Survey of Current Business,* annual series; U.S. Department of Commerce, Bureau of Economic Analysis, *Foreign Direct Investment in the United States,* annual series.

66. See U.S. Commerce Department, Bureau of Economic Analysis, *Foreign Direct Investment in the United States,* annual series; and U.S. Commerce Department, Bureau of Economic Analysis, *Survey of Current Business,* August 1987– August 1996.

67. BEA, "U.S. Intrafirm Trade in Goods," *Survey of Current Business,* February 1997, p. 23.

68. IFT data is not available for trade in services.

69. All IFT figures cited in this section were compiled from U.S. Department of Commerce, Bureau of Economic Analysis, *Foreign Direct Investment in the United States,* annual series, table G-4 (1983–1986) and table G-2 (1987–1994); U.S. Department of Commerce, Bureau of Economic Analysis, *U.S. Direct Investment Abroad: Operations of U.S. Parent Companies and their Foreign Affiliates: Preliminary 1994 Estimates,* and prior annual surveys, tables 50 (1983–1988) and III.H.I (1989–1994); U.S. Department of Commerce, Bureau of Economic Analysis, *Survey of Current Business* 72(6), June 1992, table 2, pp. 88–90; 73(3), March 1993, table 2, pp. 90–91; 74(3), March 1994, table 2, pp. 68–69.

70. Undifferentiated domestic content data does not allow one to see

whether the low domestic content rates are due to intermediate goods sourcing practices or to high finished goods imported through the affiliates' secondary activities in wholesale trade.

71. William J. Zeile, "Imported Inputs and the Domestic Content of Production by Foreign-Owned Manufacturing Affiliates in the United States" (unpublished paper presented at the NBER Conference on Geography and Ownership as Bases for Economic Accounting, December 6, 1995, pp. 14–15).

72. Ibid, p. 9.

73. BEA, *Survey of Current Business* (February 1994) table 9, p. 55.

74. See Edward Graham and Paul Krugman, *Foreign Direct Investment in the United States*, 3rd edition (Washington, D.C.: Institute of International Economics, 1995) pp. 35–55.

75. See OTA, *Multinationals and the U.S. Technology Base.*

76. See Nelson, ed., *National Innovation Systems*; and David C. Mowery, *Science and Technology Policy in Interdependent Economies*; and Jorge Niosi and Bertrand Bellon, "The Global Interdependence of National Innovation Systems," *Technology in Society*, vol. 16, no. 2 (1994) pp. 173–197.

77. See Lundvall, *National Systems of Innovation.*

78. Alic, "Technical Knowledge and Technology Diffusion."

79. See OECD, DSTI, "Embodied Technology Diffusion: An Empirical Analysis for 10 OECD Countries," *STI Working Papers* 1996/1 (Paris: OECD, 1996).

80. In most countries and in most sectors, the corporate research lab has been and remains the largest and most significant location of technological innovation. See Nelson, ed., *National Innovation Systems*. Of course, the innovative capabilities and activities of firms are shaped by numerous factors external to the firm, including the educational infrastructure as well as direct and indirect forms of governmental support.

81. One exception to this tendency is biotechnology, where a number of European and Japanese MNCs have close basic research contacts and often ownership arrangements with many small U.S. biotechnology firms.

82. For an analysis, see OTA, *Multinationals and the U.S. Technology Base*; see also Raymond Vernon, "International Investment and International Trade in the Product Cycle," *Quarterly Journal of Economics*, vol. 80, no. 2 (1996) pp. 190–207; J. H. Dunning, *Multinational Enterprises and the Global Economy* (Reading, Mass: Addison-Wesley, 1993); J. H. Dunning, *Japanese Participation in British Industry* (London: Croom Helm, 1986); and J. Hennert, *A Theory of Multinational Enterprise* (Ann Arbor: University of Michigan Press, 1985).

83. M. Gittelman and E. Graham, "The Performance and Structure of Japanese Affiliates in the European Community," in M. Mason and D. Encarnation, *Does Ownership Matter? Japanese Multinationals in Europe* (Oxford: Clarendon Press, 1994) pp. 154–55.

84. OECD, "Globalization in the Pharmaceutical Industry," draft paper (March 10, 1993) p. 9.

85. D. E. Westney, "Cross-Pacific Internationalization of R&D by U.S. and Japanese Firms," *R&D Management*, vol. 23, no. 2 (1993) pp. 171–81; OECD, "Globalization of Industrial Activities: Sector Case Study of Globalization in the Consumer Electronics Sector" (draft paper dated November 9, 1993) p. 17.

86. R. Miller, "Global R&D Networks and Large-Scale Innovations: The Case of the Automobile Industry," *Research Policy*, vol. 23, no. 3 (May 1993) pp. 27–

46. See also P. Patel and K. Pavitt, "Large Firms in the Production of the World's Technology: An Important Case of 'Non-Globalization,' " *Journal of International Business Studies* (First Quarter, 1991) pp. 1–21.

87. The semiconductor chip development alliance between IBM, Siemens, and Toshiba is frequently cited in this regard.

88. OECD, "Globalization in the Pharmaceutical Industry," pp. 9, 39. In 1989, Japanese pharmaceutical firms commanded only 1.1% of the U.S. market, while European firms commanded 26.7% of U.S. market share. The pattern in Europe is similar: Japanese firms have a very low market presence, while U.S. pharmaceutical firms command from 18% (in Germany) to 33% (in the U.K.).

89. OECD, "Globalization of Industrial Activities: Sector Case Study of Globalization in the Consumer Electronics Sector," p. 17.

90. "Much of their activity is in component testing, procurement and process development, but more substantial product development is slowly gathering pace—the Honda Accord in the United States and the Nissan Primera in the United Kingdom had substantial local design inputs." OECD, "Globalization of Industrial Activities: Sector Case Study of Globalization in the Automobile Industry," (draft paper June 16, 1993) p. 27.

[9]

Review of International Political Economy 5:3 Autumn 1998: 445–481

Internationalization and varieties of capitalism: the limited effects of cross-national coordination of economic activities on the nature of business systems

Richard Whitley

Manchester Business School, University of Manchester

ABSTRACT

The increasing internationalization of economic activities in the late twentieth century has encouraged the belief that a new form of cross-national economic organization is becoming established and replacing existing forms of capitalism. Both the intensification of international competition and growth of managerial coordination across borders are seen as generating the convergence of currently separate business systems. However, the extent of such internationalization is less than often claimed, especially when compared to the late nineteenth century, and the processes by which it will lead to such convergence remain obscure. Since the different varieties of capitalist economic organization in Europe, Asia and the Americas developed over some time interdependently with dominant societal institutions, the ways in which they change as a result of internationalization are path dependent and reflect their historical legacies as well as current institutional linkages. Qualitative changes in central business system characteristics, such as ownership relations, non-ownership coordination and employment policies, are therefore unlikely to be rapid or to result solely from internationalization. Furthermore, the ways in which firms from different business systems internationalize reflect their varied natures and strategies which are unlikely to alter greatly unless key institutions alter. If multinational firms do develop different characteristics from national competitors, their impact on their domestic and host business systems will likewise depend on a number of strong conditions. Similarly, the establishment of a distinctive and dominant 'global' business system is only likely in very restrictive circumstances.

KEYWORDS

Internationalization; business systems; multinationals; societal institutions.

ARTICLES

INTRODUCTION

The growing interdependence of most industrialized economies and increasing managerial coordination of economic activities across national boundaries over the past five decades have encouraged claims that capitalism was becoming – or has become – 'globalized' and that national differences in patterns of economic organization were declining in significance. While much of the 'globaloney' literature (Emmott, 1992) is rather vague about what globalization actually means and what evidence there is to support these sorts of claims, a common thread in many discussions concerns the growth of multinational firms which organize production and exchange across many countries and continents and are thereby seen as new, non-national kinds of economic actors which behave differently from more nationally based competitors (cf. Hu, 1992).

Together with the growth of international capital markets, this increasing international managerial control of economic activities has been heralded as leading to a 'borderless' world in which national boundaries and the states controlling them have less significance in terms of economic decision making and development than 'transnational' business elites and financial markets. Within Europe, such claims have, of course, been accentuated by the expansion of the European Union, moves to a single European market, and related efforts to standardize the 'rules of the game' governing economic competition. Some authors have viewed these changes as intensifying the establishment of sectoral economic coordination and control systems on an international scale and the concomitant decline of national and regional ones (e.g. Hellgren and Melin, 1992; Rasanen and Whipp, 1992). Others have heralded the development of 'global commodity chains' as new kinds of global economic coordination and control systems (e.g. Gereffi, 1995a, 1995b; cf. Whitley, 1996b). In general, such 'globalization' is seen as diminishing the significance of different kinds of national and regional forms of economic organization in favour of a new cross-national form of capitalism that is in the process of replacing them by virtue of its superior efficiency.

Over the last few years a number of contributions have pointed out the limitations of much globalization rhetoric and the limited extent of many of the developments discussed (e.g. Hirst and Thompson, 1996; Kenworthy, 1997). The internationalization of trade and investment flows has not, in many instances, exceeded those common before 1914 and, in any case, most international, let alone intercontinental, direct investment has been dwarfed by domestic investment over the past decade or so (Koechlin, 1995). Similarly, cross-national ownership of corporate bonds and equities remains limited despite the growth of Eurocurrency markets and foreign exchange dealings. Overall, as

INTERNATIONALIZATION AND BUSINESS SYSTEMS

The Economist (1997b) has recently concluded, global capital markets do not yet exist.

More significantly, though, the ways in which the increasing internationalization of competition and of economic coordination necessarily generate qualitative changes in established forms of economic organization, let alone lead to a new form of capitalism dominating them, remain unclear. Many proponents of the globalization thesis seem to adhere to a form of economic functionalism which assumes that market competition inevitably replaces inefficient economic systems by more efficient ones, and that global competition will produce a new transnational system which will outcompete the many current varieties of capitalism. As is the case with much work in economics, these processes are typically assumed to take place irrespective of their institutional contexts by hypostatizing some absolute market system that inexorably generates efficient outcomes.

Since, however, the organization and operation of markets, not to mention the nature and behaviour of firms, vary so much across societies and regions because of significant differences between states, financial systems, labour market institutions, etc., it seems odd to believe that the characteristics of cross-border competition, markets and firms are immune to their geopolitical and institutional environments (Boyer and Hollingsworth, 1997; Hollingsworth and Streeck, 1994; Orru *et al.*, 1997; Whitley, 1992b; Whitley and Kristensen, 1996, 1997). The institutional embeddedness of production and exchange systems means that any new 'global' competitive system would reflect the national, regional and international institutional arrangements in which it emerged, and be structured by conflicts and competition between existing economic systems and their leading actors for control over its defining norms and characteristics.

Just as the 'national' German system of economic organization emerged from competing regional 'industrial orders' (Herrigel, 1996), so too any distinctive transnational system of economic coordination and control would bear the marks of conflicts between opposing conceptions of capitalism and their allied institutional arrangements and interest groups. Rather than simply assume that abstract 'market forces' will inevitably produce a new international form of economic organization, then, the advocates of the globalization thesis need to clarify three key points: first, how such new global systems differ from existing forms of economic organization; second, the ways in which these novel characteristics developed and became established as a distinct system of economic coordination and control; third, the conditions in which and processes by which they are going to dominate currently established ones.

While, then, the growth of international trade, foreign direct investment (FDI) and expansion of international capital markets have been

447

considerable since the 1950s (Dicken, 1992), their implications for existing forms of capitalism are by no means as straightforward as some would have us believe. In particular, the ways in which different types of internationalization of economic activities affect the many varieties of capitalism, and especially the nature and behaviour of leading firms in them, need to be explored rather more systematically. To assess whether increasing cross-national coordination of economic activities does indeed alter the ways that different market economies are organized, we need to be clear about the central differences between forms of economic organization and how they are likely to be affected by internationalization. This requires the identification of: (a) the key characteristics of established forms of capitalism that might be affected by internationalization and their links to particular features of their institutional environments; (b) the major ways in which, and extent to which, the international coordination and control of economic activities through authority relations has taken place; (c) the conditions in which such internationalization could be expected to change the nature of firms and of domestic and host business systems, and to lead to the establishment of distinctive 'global' systems of economic organization.

In this article I outline a way of dealing with these issues drawing on the comparative business systems framework for describing and explaining differences in the organization of market economies. This framework identifies the key characteristics of economic coordination and control systems that together constitute distinctive business systems and vary interdependently with particular features of societal institutions and forms of interest organization (Whitley, 1992b; Whitley and Kristensen, 1996, 1997). If internationalization is to affect established systems of economic organization significantly, it will modify these characteristics substantially. In the next section of this article I summarize the central characteristics of business systems as distinctive ways of structuring market economies to highlight their wide-ranging and long-term nature. These characteristics typically developed during industrialization and are often reproduced by the dominant societal institutions and forms of interest representation that became established during the conflicts that occurred at that time.

The level of social organization most commonly associated with the establishment and reproduction of distinctive business systems and hence the nature of business system boundaries will be outlined in the subsequent section, together with the key linkages between institutional features and business system characteristics. The next part of the article focuses on the major modes of internationalization of economic activities in the late twentieth century, and the extent to which they have occurred since the end of the Second World War. Lastly, the conditions in which these forms of internationalization are likely to lead to significant

INTERNATIONALIZATION AND BUSINESS SYSTEMS

qualitative changes in internationalizing firms, their domestic business systems and host economy characteristics are specified, together with the circumstances in which distinctive cross-national systems of economic coordination and control could become established.

CENTRAL CHARACTERISTICS OF BUSINESS SYSTEMS

In very broad terms, market economies can be compared as different kinds of systems of economic organization according to the prevalent ways in which economic activities and relationships are coordinated and controlled. Business systems, in this view, are distinctive ways of structuring economic activities with different kinds of actors following contrasting priorities and logics. They therefore vary in the sorts of activities and resources that are integrated, how they are coordinated and controlled, the nature of controlling groups and how they compete and cooperate.

The Marshallian industrial district, for example, is composed of small, owner-controlled, narrowly specialized actors whose activities are mostly coordinated through short-term market contracting (Langlois and Robertson, 1995). The post-war Japanese economy, in contrast, has been dominated by large insider-controlled corporations with extensive obligational networks between suppliers and customers and significant cross-ownership ties between members of horizontally diversified business groups (e.g. Gerlach, 1992; Westney, 1996). In many respects this represents the most highly organized post-war economy in terms of the extent of non-spot market-based coordination of economic activities, and the behaviour of its 'firms' and various groups or networks has, of course, followed quite different rationalities to that of industrial district members or US diversified corporations.

The degree and form of non-spot market-based economic coordination and control are, then, major differentiating characteristics of market economies. They can be compared on a number of dimensions dealing with ownership relations and ownership-based integration of economic activities, non-ownership-based coordination processes, competitor relations and employment relations. These are central aspects of economic organization which vary in their closeness to *ad hoc*, short-term and price-based market contracting and are connected to differences in the nature of 'firms' – understood here as economic actors under unified, common ownership – and their strategic choices.

Ownership, for example, can be exercised directly over economic activities and resources as in the owner-managed firm, or may delegate such control to trusted agents with varying degrees of interdependence and commitment. It may also integrate whole production chains through formal authority systems or be much more narrowly specialized. Similarly,

ARTICLES

inter-firm relations can be dominated by *ad hoc*, one-off, anonymous and adversarial bargains, as in much pure market contracting, or by more repeated, particularistic and cooperative connections, as in obligational contracting (Dore, 1986; Sako, 1992).

Competitor relations may likewise be almost entirely adversarial and zero-sum, or may in contrast encompass collaboration over a number of issues such as R&D, training and union negotiations. Finally, employer–employee relations can vary considerably between the sort of adversarial zero-sum conflicts typical of early industrialization in many societies and the more institutionalized forms of cooperation represented by Germany's Co-Determination Acts, and large firm–core workers interdependences in post-war Japan.

Such comparisons highlight the unusual nature of the 'pure' market system in which individual owner-managed firms are horizontally and vertically specialized and engage in essentially adversarial competition, and the considerable variety of types of economic organization which are possible. In practice, of course, the societal institutions which encourage particular kinds of competitor relations are also likely to encourage similar kinds of connections between elements of production chains, so that the number of highly distinctive business systems that do become established and reproduced over many decades is rather less than the combinatorially possible number. These business systems can be compared and contrasted in terms of the nine central characteristics summarized in Table 1.

Considering first ownership relations, an important dimension for distinguishing economies concerns the closeness of owners' involvement in managing economic resources and activities. There are three major

Table 1   Key characteristics of business systems

A. *Ownership relations*
1 Primary means of owner control (direct, alliance, market contracting)
2 Extent to which unified ownership is associated with systematic managerial integration of economic activities
3 Extent of ownership integration of production chains
4 Extent of ownership integration across sectors

B. *Non-ownership coordination*
1 Extent of alliance coordination of production chains
2 Extent of collaboration between competitors
3 Extent of alliance coordination across sectors

C. *Employment relations and work management*
1 Employer–employee interdependence
2 Delegation to, and trust of, employees (Taylorism, task performance discretion, task organization discretion)

INTERNATIONALIZATION AND BUSINESS SYSTEMS

types of relationship here: direct control, delegated but committed control, and arm's length portfolio control. Owner managers of family businesses – whether artisanal elements of industrial districts or the massive Korean conglomerates (*chaebol*) – typify direct control. Bank and allied companies' ownership of some shares in Germany and Japan exemplify the second type of 'alliance' ownership, while the Anglo-Saxon pattern of institutional portfolio investment demonstrates the arm's length, 'market' type of owner control.

A second aspect of ownership relations concerns the extent to which unified ownership typically implies managerial integration and control of economic activities. Holding companies in Europe, for instance, often own a wide diversity of subsidiaries that have little in common with each other and exhibit a low degree of economic complementarity (Iterson, 1996; Kurgen-van Hentenryk, 1997; Mayer and Whittington, 1996). Similarly, many large British companies manage their operating companies as discrete stand-alone units through predominantly financial procedures, rather than as integrated administrative systems, whether these are highly diversified or not (Horowitz, 1980). Most of the large Korean *chaebol*, on the other hand, are quite diversified but also exhibit considerable central managerial control and integration, at least of managerial personnel and procedures (Amsden, 1989; Janelli, 1993).

As these examples indicate, unified ownership units also vary greatly in the range and type of activities they control. Two further dimensions for comparing business systems, then, concern the extent to which unified and common ownership entities control and integrate substantial parts of production chains in a number of sectors – as opposed to being largely vertically disintegrated – and the degree of horizontally diverse activities integrated through common ownership. The largest *chaebol* in Korea are both vertically and horizontally diversified, but the smaller ones tend to focus on vertical integration rather than unrelated diversification (Fields, 1995), while many large German firms are quite vertically integrated but usually remain active within technologically and/or market-related boundaries (Feldenkirchen, 1997; Herrigel, 1996). Chinese family businesses have been characterized as pursuing opportunistic diversification which is typically horizontal, although backward integration from retailing and distribution to manufacturing in light consumer goods industries is quite a common pattern of development (Hamilton, 1997; Hamilton and Kao, 1990; Redding, 1990; Wong, 1988).

Moving on to consider relationships between ownership units, three types can be distinguished. There are, first, those between members of a production chain; second, between competitors in the same industry; and, third, between firms in different sectors. In each case, the broad comparison is between zero-sum, adversarial contracting and competition, on

ARTICLES

the one hand, and more cooperative, long-term and mutually committed relationships between partners and competitors, on the other hand. Production chains, for example, may be quite fragmented in ownership terms, but exhibit strong networks of obligational contracting between relatively stable suppliers and customers – sometimes of course with limited exchanges of shares as in Japan. Similarly, competitors may compete fiercely for customers and yet collaborate over the introduction of new technologies, employment policies and state lobbying through various formal associations and alliances, as numerous studies have shown (Campbell *et al.*, 1991; Hollingsworth *et al.*, 1994). They may also form production and profit-pooling federations and interest groups as in Germany and some other European countries (Daems, 1983; Herrigel, 1996).

Third, firms may develop alliances across sectors, of varying stability, scope and depth, to enter new markets, reduce the risks of specialization or acquire new technologies. Occasionally these may involve long-term exchanges of equity, as in the Japanese inter-market groups (Gerlach, 1992), but more commonly they take the form of joint ventures and partnerships focused on fairly specific activities. Inter-sectoral business groups therefore differ considerably in the range of activities they carry out jointly, the extent and longevity of their collaboration, and the variety of linkages between members, with the Japanese *kigyo shudan* at one extreme and short-term, opportunistic, narrowly based alliances at the other.

In comparing market economies, the crucial issue here is the extent to which economic activities are consciously and repeatedly coordinated across sectors by these sorts of horizontally diversified business groups. The existence of some such groups in Taiwan, for instance, does not seem to imply a high level of this form of coordination because they tend to be quite narrowly focused, based on personal rather than long-term organizational commitments, and do not dominate the economy to the extent that their Japanese counterparts do (Hamilton, 1997; Numazaki, 1992).

These variations in non-ownership forms of economic coordination and control are linked to differences in ownership relations. For example, direct owner control of managerial decisions will often limit the scope and depth of collaboration with competitors because of the strong sense of personal identity with the enterprise and reluctance to share information or control, especially in cultures where trust in formal institutions is low. Similarly, market forms of owner control are unlikely to encourage inter-firm alliances and cooperation since they are typically associated with capital market-based financial systems that develop strong markets in corporate control and hence unstable owner–firm connections. Establishing long-term and wide-ranging alliances with

INTERNATIONALIZATION AND BUSINESS SYSTEMS

business partners is riskier and more difficult in this situation than in economies where owners are more committed to the future of particular enterprises. Relatedly, since alliance- and ownership-based modes of coordination and control are functionally equivalent in many circumstances, the dominance of large, diversified firms tends to prevent the development of alliances within and across production chains.

Considering finally employer–employee relations and work systems, the major contrast is between those societies encouraging reliance on external labour markets in managing the bulk of the labour force and those encouraging more commitment and mutual investment in organizational capabilities. Organization-based employment systems, such as those institutionalized in many large Japanese firms in the 1960s and 1970s, represent perhaps the greatest extent of mutual dependence between employers and the bulk of the workforce, while the Anglo-Saxon pattern of 'flexible' external labour markets and high rates of employment change represents the other extreme of this dimension (Dore, 1973; Whittaker, 1990). Intermediate employment systems combine greater mobility among manual workers than is common in large Japanese firms with considerable employer and employee investment in skill development and improvement and de facto, if not formally agreed, long-term commitments by both parties. The German and some Scandinavian business systems perhaps come closest to this combination.

Work systems can be distinguished primarily in terms of the discretion and trust employers grant to the bulk of the workforce in organizing and carrying out tasks. The pure case of 'scientific management' removes all discretion from manual workers and fragments tasks to simplify them for unskilled and easily replaced employees. 'Responsible autonomy' strategies, on the other hand, trust manual workers to carry out tasks with more discretion and independence from managers. This autonomy, though, need not extend to questions of work organization and task definition. Few Japanese companies, for example, and even fewer Korean or Taiwanese ones, delegate the selection and organization of tasks to manual workers, while being keen to involve them in problem-solving activities, and many grant considerable discretion over task performance. In many Danish and German firms, and firms in some other European countries, on the other hand, employees have substantial influence on work organization decisions, both formally and informally, particularly skilled workers (Kristensen, 1992, 1997).

Employment strategies and work systems are interrelated in that it is difficult to envisage a firm pursuing a radically Taylorist system of work organization and control at the same time as seeking long-term commitments from the manual workers and investing in their skill development. Taylorism and market-based employment systems would, then, seem to be highly consonant. However, it clearly is possible to combine considerable fluidity in external labour markets with reliance on highly skilled workers who exercise high levels of discretion over work performance, as Kristensen's (1997) accounts of Danish work systems and many Anglo-Saxon professional service firms illustrate. High mutual commitment employment systems, on the other hand, encourage firm-specific skill development, functional flexibility and delegation of task performance autonomy to most manual workers, but not necessarily decisions over task structure and allocation.

This summary of key business system characteristics emphasizes their general and relatively long-term nature. This implies they do not change very quickly or in response to the behaviour of individual firms. Significant change in these characteristics clearly involves considerable restructuring of economic relationships and typically requires substantial institutional reforms of the kind associated with the Allied occupations of Germany and Japan after the Second World War or the transformations of the former state-socialist societies. Even in these cases, substantial continuities in many aspects of economic organization remain (Clark, 1979; Herrigel, 1996; Whitley, 1992a, 1997; Whitley and Czaban, 1998). Internationalizing operations, *per se*, is not then likely to result in radical changes in these sorts of characteristics overnight.

THE BOUNDARIES OF BUSINESS SYSTEMS AND ASSOCIATED INSTITUTIONS

So far I have talked mostly of market economies and business systems rather than of countries and national economies. In principle, distinctive systems of economic organization arise wherever key associated institutions are both mutually reinforcing and distinctive from other ones. However, given the importance of state-based legal systems for defining and enforcing private property rights in many capitalist economies, the role of the state in maintaining public order, structuring interest groups and the conventions governing their competition and collaboration, regulating financial systems and organizing skill development and control, it is not surprising that many distinctive characteristics of business systems are nationally specific.

Even where distinctive norms and values that affect business behaviour are reproduced by families and ethnic communities which are both subnational and international, as in the case of the overseas Chinese and many migrant communities, the significance of these for systems of economic organization depends on the structures and policies of states and political economies more generally. This is because states determine how effective are the legal and educational systems, and hence the role of the formal institutions governing many important aspects of economic coordination, as well as greatly influencing the formation of interest

INTERNATIONALIZATION AND BUSINESS SYSTEMS

groups and modes of conflict resolution. For example, the organization and actions of owners, managerial elites and other groups of manual and non-manual workers have been, and remain, highly nationally distinct and primarily focused on national arenas of competition for resources and legitimacy (Whitley, 1997).

If, however, these groups were primarily organized regionally, or internationally, and the major institutions governing their formation, competition and collaboration were also regionally, or internationally, distinctive and cohesive at those levels of social organization, then they would constitute distinct sub- or international systems of economic organization. In the case of the post-war, or perhaps post-1960s, Italian industrial districts, for example, it is debatable whether the key political, financial and labour institutions in north-east and central Italy are suffi-ciently cohesive, separate and distinct from those in the rest of Italy to constitute a quite different unit of socioeconomic organization which can be contrasted with, say, that established in north-west Italy or the Mezzogiorno.

While regional differences clearly are important and have encouraged considerable variations in patterns of economic organization across parts of Italy, it is difficult to understand the development of these industrial districts without taking account of the development of the Italian state and banking system, or the changes that occurred in the large firms of Milan and Turin in the post-war period (Weiss, 1988). The interdepen-dences between both local economic actors and local institutions and those in other regions and at the national level are too strong and signif-icant to classify these industrial districts as a separate and distinctive business system. On the other hand, they do constitute an important and distinctive part of the post-war Italian business system, just as the small firms of Jutland constitute a significant – and arguably defining – component of 'the' Danish system (Kristensen, 1992, 1997).

These examples highlight the need to identify the dominant role of insti-tutions at each level of analysis. Where regional governments, financial institutions, skill development and control systems and broad cultural norms and values are distinct from national ones and able to exert consid-erable discretion in the economic sphere, we would expect distinctive kinds of economic organization to become established at the regional level. Herrigel (1993, 1994, 1996), for instance, claims that the 'decen-tralised industrial order' which developed in Baden-Württemberg, Sax-ony and elsewhere in Germany was quite different from the 'autarkic' industrial order characteristic of the Ruhr and other regions because of contrasting pre-industrial legacies and institutional arrangements during and after industrialization.

He also emphasizes the importance of the conflicts between these forms of industrial order and their associated interest groups for the

455

development of the German state and its policies in the late nineteenth and early twentieth centuries. The 'national' German industrial order was constructed, in his view, from the struggles of two quite distinct regional ones with their own pattern of institutional arrangements and agencies. As in Italy, particular patterns of industrialization and state development resulted in considerable regional differences in economic organization and in the ways that firms and economic networks were, and are, linked to regional state agencies, banks, unions and educational and research institutions. The continued strength and interconnectedness of regional economies and governing institutions in Germany prevented the establishment of a single industrial order across the whole country, in contrast to other political economies where the national state and related institutions became established as the dominant forces structuring economic relationships.

For example, the dominant role of the London commercial and merchant banks at the end of the nineteenth century, at the expense of the provincial banks which had developed closer ties to industrial companies, represented such a centralization and standardization of the financial environment of British firms (Ingham, 1984). Similarly, the dominating role played by the central state in most successful industrialization processes outside Europe and North America, usually in the absence of significant local or regional governments or associations, has meant that business systems are more national than regional in the late twentieth century.

The national boundedness of distinctive systems of economic organization is, then, historically contingent and variable. Distinctive and cohesive kinds of business system can become established and reproduced at regional, national and international levels of socioeconomic organization depending on the strength and integration of the actors and institutions involved at each level. If, for example, owners, managers, unions and other organized groups became structured at a European level, together with the emergence of a European state that dominated national and regional political systems and established standardized labour and financial systems across Europe, we would expect nationally distinct business systems to become less significant than the emerging European form of economic organization.

Such a novel system would, of course, bear the marks of the struggles between national groupings, agencies and institutional arrangements, just as national and regional business systems currently reflect the historical processes that led to their establishment. Both the characteristics of any pan-European business system and the features of its institutional context, as well as the ways in which political, financial and labour systems at the European level are related to the system of economic organization, would emerge from an extensive series of competitive

456

INTERNATIONALIZATION AND BUSINESS SYSTEMS

conflicts between existing ones and the rationalities they exemplify and reproduce.

The key institutions affecting business system characteristics concern the organization and conditions governing the availability of capital and labour power, the governance of economic exchanges and the organization of competing interests (Whitley, 1992b). In particular, variations in the nature and policies of the state, the financial system, the education and training systems and prevalent norms and values have helped to structure qualitative differences between business systems. The dominance and involvement of the state in economic development, the strength and incorporation of interest groupings and the extent of market regulation, together with the nature of the financial system, the strength and organization of the public training system, and dominant beliefs about trust, authority and loyalty all affect the ways in which economic activities are organized in a society. On the basis of previous work in Asia and Europe (see, for example, Kristensen, 1996, 1997; Whitley, 1992a, 1992b, 1996a, 1997), the main interdependences between these institutional factors and business system characteristics are summarized in Table 2.

It can readily be seen that major variations in most of these are also variations across countries. Strong intermediary associations in Germany and some other central European states, for example, can be contrasted with the much weaker ones found in France for most of the post-1789 period. Similar contrasts can be drawn between Japan, on the one hand, and most other East Asian states. Many business systems with distinctive characteristics linked to most of these institutional features are, then, found in particular nation-states, although not all states exhibit distinctive business systems. Where many of these features are similar across national boundaries, as in the financial systems of Britain and the USA, the interdependent business system characteristics will also be similar.

While highly distinctive and integrated business systems often develop within national boundaries, because dominant institutions are usually more cohesive and specific at the national level, especially where a highly centralized state has dominated the industrialization process, business system characteristics are also common across countries and may, as we have seen, also vary within them. The significance of internationalization for business system characteristics depends, then, on how national boundaries are connected to institutional differences and the organization of interest groups. It also of course depends on the mode and degree of internationalization that will now be discussed in more detail.

Table 2   Connections between institutional features and business system characteristics

Institutional features	Business system characteristics									
	Strong owner controlled	Market owner control	Low managerial integration	High vertical integration	High ownership diversification	Low alliance vertical integration	High competitor collaboration	Low alliance horizontal integration	High employer–employee inter-dependency	High delegation to workers
A. State characteristics										
Dominant, risk-sharing state	+	–		+		+	–	+		
Antagonistic to intermediaries						+	–	+	–	
Formal regulation of markets			–		–		+		+	
B. Financial system										
Credit based		–		+	–	+	+	+	+	
Capital market based	–	+	–		+		–	–	–	
C. Skill development and control system										
Strong public collaborative training system					–		+		+	+
Strong unions				+					+	+
Strong academic stratification of labour markets									–	–
Strong skill-based groupings			+				–		–	+
D. Trust and authority										
Low trust in formal institutions	+	–	–			+	–	+	–	–
Paternalist authority relations	+	–	–							–
Communitarian formal authority relations			–		–				+	+

INTERNATIONALIZATION AND BUSINESS SYSTEMS

MODES AND DEGREES OF INTERNATIONALIZATION

The growing internationalization of economic activities is often seen as composed of three interconnected phenomena that have major consequences for existing forms of capitalism. First, the increase in international trade and competition from foreign exporters is considered likely to threaten many domestic ways of organizing economic activities. Second, the expansion of managerial coordination and control across national boundaries in multinational firms is viewed as changing both the nature of those firms and, by extension, that of the business system they developed within, as well as the characteristics of the host economies they invest in. Similar but weaker consequences could presumably be expected from the cross-national alliances and networks that have developed over the past decade or so. Third, the 'globalization' of capital markets has both reduced large firms' dependence on domestic financial institutions – and so might encourage some change in their strategic preferences and choices – and internationalized their ownership so that previous patterns and priorities may shift. In particular, such changes in the ownership and control of shareholdings might be expected to affect dominant criteria of performance assessment in business systems – for example, towards more profit-focused priorities.

International trade and competition

Considering first the increase in international trade and competition since the 1950s, it is important to note that this is still lower as a proportion of GDP in many countries than it was in 1913 and has not increased greatly in the past two decades in a number of OECD countries (Hirst and Thompson, 1996; Kenworthy, 1997). In fact, the average proportion of exports and imports in GDP between 1974–9 and 1990–4 has fallen in the UK, Norway, Japan, Italy and Finland, and risen by less than 5 per cent in Australia, Canada, Denmark, France, Germany, the Netherlands, New Zealand, Sweden, Switzerland and the USA. Overall trade dependence is much greater in the industrializing countries of East Asia and the Middle East than in much of Europe or North America. Further more, much of the growth in the external trade of these countries has occurred within their geographical regions, especially North America and Europe. While, then, the openness of most OECD economies has grown significantly since the war, it has certainly not resulted in their becoming dominated by imports and exports, and indeed most remain little more or, indeed, less, dependent on external trade than they were before 1914.

The effects of such increasing international trade on business system characteristics, such as ownership relations and employment policies,

ARTICLES

seem likely to be limited when it is primarily conducted through spot market, short-term transactions. While increasing domestic competition from imports may encourage firms to change products, cut costs and search for new markets, the ways in which they adapt will reflect the overall characteristics of their business system and their roles within it. It could also intensify firms' willingness to look for and introduce technological and organizational innovations, especially from abroad, but such innovations were, and are, introduced in quite protectionist environments, as in the case of Japanese companies seeking to transfer 'Fordist' principles of production organization in the 1930s.

The search for the 'best practices' of foreign economies to transfer to domestic ones, moreover, is often based on serious misunderstandings of actual managerial practices. Additionally, idealized procedures and practices are usually transformed considerably when they are introduced in the domestic economy (Boyer and Hollingsworth, 1997; Hollingsworth and Streeck, 1994). There is no particular reason, then, to expect growing international competition, *per se*, to lead to radical business system change, let alone that it will do so in a single direction.

Where trading relations are more stable and perhaps based on longer-term alliances between specific firms, we might expect some to adopt novel procedures and practices. However, the impact of this on domestic business systems is likely to be limited unless: (a) a large number of leading firms engage in such alliances; (b) they form a major part of their activities for some considerable time; (c) such alliances are mostly with partners from the same kind of foreign business system; and (d) the practices being changed are not closely connected to powerful domestic agencies and institutions. These conditions are, I suggest, not going to be realized together very often.

Furthermore, the capacity of dominant firms to develop such international alliances effectively itself depends on their previous success in doing so within countries, which in turn depends on the nature of the business system they are part of. Similar points apply to the sorts of firms they are successful in linking with, so that cross-national alliances will develop and be more effective when partners are both from business systems which already are characterized by substantial inter-firm connections. This point highlights the dependence of different forms of international coordination on existing, typically national, patterns of economic organization. It follows from this that expanding international trading links to longer-term alliances is unlikely to alter domestic business systems significantly. Overall, then, both the extent and impact of trade internationalization and intensifying competition are less than is often thought, and are unlikely to result in radical changes to established business system characteristics.

INTERNATIONALIZATION AND BUSINESS SYSTEMS

Cross-national coordination and control

The growth of multinational firms (MNCs) coordinating economic activities across national borders since the war has been seen by many as heralding major changes in economic organization and markets, as well as leading to the creation of a distinctive 'global' system of economic coordination and control. Particularly in the 1980s, the rate of FDI grew quite dramatically, at an average annual rate of 34 per cent between 1983 and 1990 compared to annual global trade increases of 9 per cent in that period. However, it fell slightly in 1992 and 1993, and still forms a small proportion of total investment in many countries. Between 1985 and 1991, for example, the average annual rate of overseas direct investment as a percentage of total investment was only 5 per cent in the USA, 7 per cent in Japan, Germany and France, and 17 per cent in the UK (Hirst and Thompson, 1996). Again, the total stock of foreign investment of most richer countries as a proportion of GDP was less in 1996 than in 1914, and only amounted to 6 per cent of their total domestic investment in 1996 (*The Economist*, 1997a). While, then, the growth of FDI since the 1960s has been quite considerable, its overall significance is still limited.

Similarly, although the percentage of firms' sales and assets located outside their native frontiers has increased in the last few decades, the bulk of these remain in the home region. Leading MNC manufacturers from the Netherlands, for example, sell only 12 per cent of their turnover to domestic customers, but another 50 per cent goes to West European ones. Similarly, French MNCs in 1992–3 made less than half of their total sales to domestic customers but a further 31 per cent went to European ones. Even the British made 65 per cent of their total sales to European customers as a whole. As might be expected, Japanese and US MNCs were even more focused on domestic customers at 75 per cent and 64 per cent respectively (Hirst and Thompson, 1996).

Comparable results were found for the locations of leading MNCs' assets. According to Hirst and Thompson (1996: 90–6), 54 per cent of large French firms' assets were in France in 1992–3, with a further 31 per cent in the rest of Europe, 39 per cent of equivalent British firms' assets were similarly in the UK and a further 23 per cent were elsewhere in Europe. Again, the vast bulk of US and Japanese firms' assets were situated within their national boundaries. Although, then, some increase in foreign sales and foreign investment of assets has undoubtedly taken place, its extent and importance are considerably less than is often claimed by advocates of globalization. Additionally, as we shall see, the consequences of such cross-national coordination of economic activities for the nature of firms and business systems are also less radical than is sometimes suggested.

461

Internationalization of capital markets

As mentioned above, one of the most marked aspects of economic internationalization in the last few decades has been the growth in cross-border capital flows and currency trading as many countries have liberalized exchange controls. Not only has the total stock of international bank lending grown from $265 billion in 1975 to $4,200 billion in 1994, but the annual amount of capital raised through issuing bonds and equities on international capital markets grew from $36.2 billion in 1976–80 to $521.7 billion in 1993 (Hirst and Thompson, 1996: 40; Kenworthy, 1997). Foreign exchange transactions have also grown dramatically, from around $15 billion a day in 1973 to nearly $1,300 billion a day in 1994/5.

However, these high growth rates should not obscure the fact that the international financial system still remains less integrated than it was before 1914 in many important aspects. For example, the overwhelming majority of the shares quoted on the world's stock markets are still held in domestic securities and leading fund managers in Europe and the USA had only 11.4 per cent of their holdings in foreign assets in 1991. American investors, for instance, remained overwhelmingly committed to domestic securities, which accounted for 94 per cent of the value of the US exchanges (Hirst and Thompson, 1996: 37; Kenworthy, 1997). Furthermore, as *The Economist* (1997b) has recently pointed out, real bond yields continue to diverge considerably across countries, national savings and investment rates are still highly correlated and capital mobility in the 1990s remains lower than in the thirty-year period before 1914. There is no single global interest rate and no integrated capital market across the world. While, then, international financial flows have grown considerably since the 1950s, their overall importance is much less than the enthusiasts of global capital markets have claimed, and remains lower than in the gold standard period.

In sum, the recent growth in international trade, investment and financial flows forms a strong contrast with the immediate post-war decades, and even more so with the inter-war period. It does not, though, herald a radical break with all previous periods of capitalism, and can indeed be seen as a return to many aspects of the pre-1914 situation. Furthermore, it is important to note that it resulted from national decisions to deregulate financial systems and delegate substantial powers to international agencies such as GATT and the WTO, as well as to the European Commission. Although facilitated by reductions in communications and transport costs, it was these political choices that enabled this growth in internationalization to develop and, as we saw during the slump, such decisions can be reversed, as Hirst and Thompson (1996), among others, have emphasized.

462

INTERNATIONALIZATION AND BUSINESS SYSTEMS

Additionally, the nation-state remains the primary focus of political loyalties and battles, as well as the dominant regulating and policing agency. Cross-border economic flows and coordination processes depend overwhelmingly on national state legal systems, enforcement mechanisms and institutional arrangements to manage risks and uncertainty sufficiently to enable strategic decisions to be made, as has recently been highlighted by the role of the USA and other states in the management of the Pacific-Asian financial crises. Internationalization, then, remains highly interdependent with national agencies' and institutions' structures and actions. As a result, its effects on established systems of economic organization and firms are greatly guided and limited by variations in these national institutions, as I will now discuss.

CONSEQUENCES OF INTERNATIONALIZATION FOR BUSINESS SYSTEMS AND FIRMS

The growing internationalization of economic activities is often thought to result in major changes to existing forms of capitalism in three ways: first, by changing the nature and behaviour of firms that engage in large-scale international coordination and control, which in turn could transform the characteristics of their home business system; second, by inward foreign direct investment and capital market internationalization altering current rules of the competitive game and the nature of firms, and introducing more 'efficient' practices; third, by generating a new supra-national level of economic organization and competition which in time will come to dominate national and regional ones. These do, of course, overlap and interact, but it is useful to separate them analytically for purposes of discussion.

Accordingly, I first consider the factors effecting the transformation of multinational firms into qualitatively different kinds of companies in terms of their ownership structures, dominant strategies and competences from their domestically based national competitors by virtue of their cross-border operations. The conditions in which such changes could impinge upon their domestic business systems will also be examined here. Next, I consider how the growing internationalization of trade, investment and capital might affect host business system norms and characteristics. Third, the likelihood of a separate and distinct international system of economic organization becoming established and dominating national ones will be discussed.

The effects of internationalization on MNCs and their domestic business systems

The expansion of firms into foreign locations and markets could affect their governance structures and capabilities in four major ways. First, it

ARTICLES

might enable top managers to develop greater autonomy from domestic pressure groups, especially state agencies, banks and other shareowner/controllers and unions. Second, it might similarly increase their distance from domestic business partners as MNCs find new ones abroad. Third, such autonomy from domestic pressures could lead to changes in dominant objectives as managers have to deal with more varied interest groups from different societies with contrasting priorities. This greater variety of 'stakeholders' and interests in turn may well encourage increased organizational complexity as MNCs attempt to manage conflicting expectations by establishing special groups to deal with them.

Finally, the growth of business units in geographically and institutionally diverse environments could decrease organizational cohesion and integration, which in turn might reduce the ability of firms to develop distinctive innovative strategies through continuous collective learning. Just as market and technological diversification can limit the continuing improvement of distinctive organizational competences, so too the diversification of operations and units across societal contexts may restrict MNCs' innovative abilities. Insofar as they do focus on such 'entrepreneurial' organizational strategies in their domestic contexts, large-scale internationalization will encourage either substantial reorganization or separation of this domestic capability from most foreign subsidiaries, as is arguably the case in many Japanese MNCs.

The extent to which these consequences are likely to follow from outward FDI depends on six factors. First, the size of such foreign investments and operations relative to domestic ones clearly affects their impact on firm structures and strategies. For instance, Dutch firms which located on average 20 per cent of their total investments in 1985–91 abroad are, on the whole, more likely to be influenced by their internationalization than, say, US (5 per cent) or Japanese ones (7 per cent) (Kenworthy, 1997). To deal with a significantly more varied environment, they may restructure their organization and take more account of different interest groups than their less internationalized competitors.

Second, and more significant than the relative amount of foreign assets, is the nature of their location, specifically their concentration in a particular kind of business system. Other things being equal, the more a company's key assets and activities are located in a distinctive and different environment from its domestic one, the more likely it will adapt its structures and strategies to the prevalent pattern in that type of business system. If, for example, some large Japanese firms located over 50 per cent of their core assets and activities in Anglo-Saxon economies, we might reasonably expect them to develop in more Anglo-Saxon than Japanese ways. So far, though, this degree of outward concentration does not seem to have happened in most countries. Indeed, there appears to be considerable evidence that large firms investing abroad

INTERNATIONALIZATION AND BUSINESS SYSTEMS

tend to be more committed to countries that share key institutions with their home society than to those that are strongly contrasting (Koechlin, 1995).

Third, the effects of outward FDI on a firm's characteristics are more likely to be visible when it is investing a large proportion of its resources in more technologically advanced and wealthier markets, not least because of the greater power of dominant interest groups and institutions in these economies and their overall significance in the world economy. Japanese, Korean and Taiwanese investment in China, parts of South-East Asia and Eastern Europe, for instance, is less likely to affect firms' general policies and practices than large-scale investments in Western Europe and North America. Rather, such relocation of facilities and activities in relatively less industrialized economies may result in the generalization of domestic business system characteristics to the host economies.

Fourth, firms are going to be more affected by large-scale foreign investment when it is concentrated in economies with strong, cohesive business systems closely linked to integrated institutions than when host business systems and institutions are weakly structured and poorly integrated. This will be especially so if their domestic business system is relatively fragmented and dominant institutions are as much contradictory as mutually reinforcing in their implications for economic relations. British investors in Japan, for example, are more likely to adapt to the local way of managing the workforce and supplier relation than are Japanese firms in Britain. Similarly, foreign firms investing in Germany have to adapt to the highly institutionalized training system and consultation procedures since these are quite standardized, legally regulated and enforced.

This also affects the kinds of changes that are made by MNCs in their foreign operations. Practices that are most closely linked to strong local agencies and institutions are most likely to be implemented by foreign firms. The New Economic Policy in Malaysia, for instance, had more effect on foreign investors' managerial practices than many other features of the Malaysian political economy because it was a central focus of the state's development plans and affected state–business relations in a wide variety of ways. This does not, though, mean that such changes will be 'repatriated' to their domestic economies, or even transferred to other subsidiaries.

The extent to which such local adaptation influences firm behaviour more generally depends on the factors listed above together with, fifth, the dominant way in which foreign subsidiaries are integrated into the parent organizations. The more managerially integrated into the whole firm are foreign operations, the more likely are changes in these to affect the domestic enterprise and, of course, the less easy will it be to implement

465

ARTICLES

them. Where multinational firms are organized as holding companies with foreign subsidiaries primarily controlled through financial targets and results and granted substantial operating autonomy, they are likely to display considerable local variety of managerial practices but these will have only limited effects on the domestic organization. Kristensen's (1994) account of how a Danish subsidiary was able to preserve considerable autonomy after being taken over, for example, at least partly reflects the financially oriented control systems of its new British parent. More integrated and centrally controlled enterprises, on the other hand, are less likely to tolerate wide fluctuations in procedures and choices but once innovations are accepted in one subsidiary they may well be generalized throughout the organization.

British firms, for example, have invested more in foreign facilities than have German ones for much of the twentieth century, and have also tended to rely on financial controls while granting subsidiaries substantial discretion on how they achieve general targets. German firms have, in general, preferred to export from their domestic facilities and integrate operations more closely. However, when some of these recently invested abroad in new 'lean production' factories – partly because they considered it would be too difficult to do so directly in 'Standort Deutschland' – this was intended to serve as a model for restructuring their domestic production system, and so here foreign innovation is likely to result in some changes to the basic organization (cf. Mueller and Loveridge, 1997).

Such repatriation of novel practices from foreign subsidiaries is, finally, dependent on their interdependence with central characteristics of the domestic business system and dominant institutions. Many Japanese firms, for instance, have had to adapt some of their employment and labour management strategies to local conditions, especially on brownfield sites (Botti, 1995; Sharpe, 1997), but it is most unlikely that these modifications will be transferred back to their domestic operations given the central role of their labour management policies in their overall development and business system, not to mention the active involvement of the state in limiting enforced redundancies. Similarly, British and US firms operating in Germany would find it difficult to implement local training and work system practices in their domestic operations, given the very different institutional environment they face at home – although their experience may, of course, encourage them to try to change that environment.

In summary, then, internationalizing firms seem unlikely to change their key attributes and practices substantially unless: (a) foreign operations, assets and profits constitute a large proportion of the total; (b) they are concentrated in a different kind of business system which (c) is more developed than the domestic one; and (d) is more cohesive

466

INTERNATIONALIZATION AND BUSINESS SYSTEMS

and linked to strong, more integrated institutions than the domestic one; (e) they integrate foreign subsidiaries closely to domestic operations; and (f) these attributes are not highly interdependent with strong domestic agencies and institutions. Similar conditions apply to the likelihood of less integrated forms of international coordination such as alliances and federations affecting key characteristics of firms. These conditions are not all realized together in many cases and so the extent of radical organizational changes as a direct result of outward FDI seems rather less than is sometimes suggested.

Turning next to consider how the changing characteristics of internationalizing firms might affect the distinctive nature of their domestic business systems as summarized by the dimensions outlined earlier, these are significantly affected by many of the factors just discussed. Three broad sets of influences are particularly critical. First, the number and centrality of the firms and sectors involved for the domestic economy, as well as the degree to which they have changed, are clearly critical to any qualitative change in business system characteristics. Major changes in, say, the degree of ownership-based vertical integration of the largest Finnish forest sector firms would imply much more significant shifts in the organization of the Finnish economy than growing foreign investments of smaller firms in light industry or their increasing exposure to international capital markets (Lilja and Tainio, 1996).

Second, because business system change implies a reorganization of economic coordination and control relations, it involves the restructuring of interest groups outside as well as inside the firms concerned, and often a reshaping of sectoral strengths. Thus, significant institutional shifts and changes in dominance relations between major social groupings are typically associated with qualitative changes in key business system characteristics, such as ownership relationships or competitor cooperation. For internationalizing firms to effect such shifts in the organization of their domestic economy, then, they would have to be allied to powerful groups and interests.

Business systems dominated by export-oriented manufacturing industry, for example, may begin to change as a result of outward FDI and reliance on foreign capital markets if the owners and managers involved become detached from their domestic alliances and create international ones at the same time as previously dominant allies in the state and economy begin to lose ground to new groups based on, say, financial services and domestically focused industries. In the absence of such sectoral and interest group shifts that would usually be associated with significant institutional developments, business system changes are unlikely to be very substantial.

Third, any important shifts in economic organization, whether due to internationalization or not, also imply some change in associated

ARTICLES

institutions which is less probable where those institutions are strongly established and highly integrated. Changes to firms' skill development practices and labour strategies in Germany, for example, are much more difficult to implement than in Britain because the German training system is more standardized and regulated throughout the economy than is its British equivalent. Strong and cohesive institutions are even more likely to limit any changes introduced by internationalizing firms where they are linked to quite different kinds of institutions and patterns of economic organization.

The labour management innovations achieved by Mercedes and BMW in the USA, for instance, are likely to be considerably modified when they attempt to repatriate them to the domestic economy, and their overall impact on 'the' German production system will be considerably restricted by the established institutional order (cf. Mueller and Loveridge, 1997). In contrast, business system characteristics linked to peripheral, weakly integrated institutions and groups are more susceptible to change as a result of internationalization by powerful firms and sectors, especially if those firms are supported by state agencies.

In summary, then, significant change in the dominant system of economic organization in a particular region or country as a result of firms' outward FDI depends on a number of quite demanding conditions being met. The firms concerned have: (a) to be substantial and central to the business system; (b) to have qualitatively changed major attributes and strategies; (c) to have close ties to major interest groups which also seek change in the prevalent system; and (d) also to be linked to institutional agencies and governance structures that do not prevent significant changes and/or are weakly integrated with the current institutional order.

The effects of inward FDI and capital market internationalization on business systems

The likelihood that inward foreign investment and control of economic activities, and the internationalization of financial flows, will significantly change business system characteristics is similarly structured by the strength and cohesion of host economy institutions and their closeness to particular characteristics of the economic coordination and control system. Considering first the impact of inward FDI on host business systems, the overall weight and relative significance of FDI is obviously a critical factor. Where foreign firms dominate an economy it is unlikely to develop its own distinctive patterns of economic coordination and control. Additionally, though, the concentration of such FDI from a particular kind of business system will affect how much influence it has on an economy.

INTERNATIONALIZATION AND BUSINESS SYSTEMS

If, for example, the bulk of the total stock of manufacturing investment in a country was owned and/or controlled by foreign firms from the same type of business system, such as the Anglo-Saxon one, we would expect the host economy to display similar sorts of economic organization characteristics to those prevalent in the home economies of such firms. While high levels of FDI from a single type of business system are not a common occurrence in industrialized economies, the Australian economy may form an example of this phenomenon (Marceau, 1992). In this case, of course, the colonial legacy has resulted in many of the key domestic institutions being 'Anglo-Saxon', so that the influence of inward FDI on its own is difficult to distinguish. More common in the late twentieth century is inward FDI from a number of different kinds of business system so that no single type dominates, together with substantial domestic ownership and control of economic activities. The extent to which foreign firms have qualitatively changed established host business system characteristics in these circumstances is limited. In industrializing countries, however, their impact may be more marked, especially when MNCs are predominantly from a single type of business system.

Third, the more dependent are foreign firms on domestic organizations and agencies, both within and across sectors, the less likely are they to change prevalent patterns of behaviour. Japanese firms linked to Japanese suppliers and financed by Japanese banks, for instance, are more independent from local practices than those from other countries which rely more on host economy companies. Such Japanese firms are therefore more able to maintain distinctive practices which deviate substantially from those current in the local business system than, say, US ones which become more interdependent with local organizations. So Japanese car manufacturers have maintained many of their distinctive linkages with suppliers, customers and some competitors in the USA and UK, whereas most foreign investors in Japan have adapted their patterns of inter-firm connections to the prevailing norms there.

Such change depends also, fourth, on the overall integration and cohesion of the local form of economic organization and associated institutions. This factor helps to explain why much Japanese investment in the UK has had more impact in the particular sectors where it has been concentrated, mostly cars and electronics, than has British investment in Japan. As well as the level and sectoral concentration of the latter being less – and of course the overall level of inward FDI to Japan has been minuscule relative to GDP at 0.4 per cent in 1994 (UNCTAD, 1996: 262) – the sheer strength and cohesion of the host business system and allied institutions greatly restricts the effects of foreign investment in Japan.

469

ARTICLES

Relatedly, the impact of any change introduced by outside enterprises depends on, fifth, the strength of the sector and its centrality to the economy, as well as on the strength of the particular institutions connected to different spheres of activity. Japanese manufacturing firms, for example, have probably been able to have more influence on British industrial companies than their counterparts in financial services because of the dominant role of the latter sector in the British economy and its closer ties to political and bureaucratic elites. Similarly, their effects on labour and production management in Britain have been more marked than on financial and ownership issues, and probably more so than in other parts of Europe, as a result of the weakened position of the unions and decline of the manufacturing sector in general.

It should be noted, however, that the evidence for wholesale 'Japanization' – however that may be interpreted – of the British and other economies is extremely limited, as many authors have pointed out (e.g. Elger and Smith, 1994; Stewart, 1996; Strange, 1993). Even in the former state-socialist societies of Eastern Europe the impact of foreign multinationals on factory organization and labour management has been limited by local unions and quite strong norms governing managerial behaviour (Czaban and Whitley, 1998; Globokar, 1997; Mako and Novoszath, 1995).

In sum, significant shifts in business system characteristics as a result of foreign firms controlling economic resources and activities in an economy depend on those firms' investments being large relative to domestic ones, being predominantly from one kind of business system, and remaining substantially independent of local organizations and agencies. In addition, they are more likely to occur in sectors that are peripheral to dominant interest groups and institutions and/or in business systems that are quite fragmented with relatively weakly integrated institutions.

Considering next the effects of internationalizing financial flows on business system characteristics, these again depend on the relative importance of external capital and owners on domestic investments and firms, as well as the sorts of business systems these foreign owners come from and the conditions on which they take stakes in companies. If, for instance, most of the leading firms in credit-based financial systems were to raise the bulk of their external finance from international capital markets instead of relying on their usual business partners, and subsequently disengaged themselves from the banks in other ways, this could have quite significant effects on the strategies of these firms and on their domestic business system. Since these international markets are typically 'Anglo-Saxon' in their governance norms and priorities, we could expect a general move to market-based relations between large shareholders and individual firms, more adversarial relations between firms

470

INTERNATIONALIZATION AND BUSINESS SYSTEMS

and between employers and employees and more emphasis on profits than growth goals.

This sort of change implies considerable shifts in established institutional arrangements, as well as in the relative influence and ability to control key resources of interest groups and organizations. It therefore seems unlikely to occur without substantial debate and conflict. Both competing groups within the firms concerned and their financial partners, as well as those elsewhere in the economy and society more broadly, can be expected to play an important role in dealing with changing financial structures and relationships, and it is by no means clear that the recent growth in international capital market funding will continue through the next recession, or that it will constitute the dominant source of new investment funds in most economies. The more pension fund managers and other institutional shareholders pursue 'Anglo-Saxon' notions of transparency, shareholder value and appropriate dividend payout ratios in continental Europe and East Asia, the more resistance can be expected from managerial elites anxious to preserve their autonomy and independence from both banks and shareholders.

It does not require a particularly cynical turn of mind to see the adoption of capital market funding and globalization rhetoric by some European business leaders as weapons in their struggles to impose their goals and priorities on governments and 'social partners' within firms and across economies (cf. Hirst and Thompson, 1996: 1–7). Depending on the balance of groups and forces in particular economies, such attempts will be more or less successful, as the contrast between, say, the Netherlands and France in the mid-1990s indicates. In terms of qualitative changes in business system characteristics, though, the expansion of corporate fund raising from international capital markets seems unlikely to lead to substantial shifts without other changes occurring in dominant institutions and social groupings.

Considering finally the possible consequence of growing foreign ownership through international equity ownership – as distinct from foreign firm ownership and control – these obviously depend on similar factors to those already discussed. The more shares of firms in one economy are owned by investors from a different kind of business system, the more we would expect those firms to begin to change key characteristics and strategic priorities. This would depend, though, on the overall distribution of share ownership in each firm and the prevalent nature of the financial system in that economy.

If, for example, a firm has substantial domestic shareholders and foreign shareholders are relatively fragmented, managers' responsiveness to alien shareholder preferences will be limited, particularly if there is only a weak market for corporate control so that declining share prices

ARTICLES

do not usually generate hostile take-over bids. Relatedly, the effects of increasing foreign portfolio investment in a country are strongly mediated by the nature of its financial system. The more it generates close interdependence between investors and firms, the less likely are foreign shareholders to be able to impose their performance standards by threatening to sell their stakes.

More generally, the role of foreign portfolio investment depends on the overall role of the firms concerned in a particular business system and their connections to powerful agencies and groups. The responsiveness of Finnish paper firms to increasing overseas shareholding, for example, is likely to be less marked in the event of conflicts with managers than it might be for those less central to the economy and less integrated with the political and financial systems (Tainio, 1997). In general, of course, the more cohesive and integrated are key institutions in a society, the less likely is foreign portfolio investment to affect business system characteristics significantly, as the behaviour of the Japanese business system in the 1990s indicates. Even in the transforming societies of Eastern Europe, the effects of such investment on, say, labour management strategies have been less marked than some might have expected (Czaban and Whitley, 1998; Whitley *et al.*, 1997).

In sum, the growth of foreign portfolio investment in an economy need not, on its own, result in significant shifts in firm governance and behaviour. Even if it was on such a large scale, and so concentrated, as to alter the priorities and choices of some firms' dominant coalitions, this would not imply the qualitative change of a particular business system. That would require a reorganization of central institutional structures and relationships, as well as a restructuring of interest group relations and, perhaps, of their constitution and organization. Particular characteristics of a business system could, though, be affected by such substantial transfers of ownership if they were: (a) weakly standardized and regulated across the whole economic order; (b) relatively poorly integrated with other aspects of the business system; and (c) linked to rather peripheral groups and institutions in the wider society.

The establishment of new cross-national business systems

The growth of cross-border coordination and control of economic activities by managerial hierarchies and of competition between firms on a worldwide scale has led to suggestions that a new kind of international system of economic organization is becoming established. This system is dominated by distinctive 'transnational' (Bartlett and Ghoshal, 1989) MNCs that have considerable autonomy from national institutions and agencies and are able to pursue competitive strategies on a global rather than a national or regional basis. Such firms develop characteristics that

INTERNATIONALIZATION AND BUSINESS SYSTEMS

are more similar to each other than to those of their domestic competitors, and their strategies are also focused more on each other's resources and actions than those of domestic firms.

Relatedly, Gereffi (1995a, 1995b) and his colleagues have seen the development of consumer-driven 'global commodity chains' as heralding a new form of international economic integration. These sorts of suggestions are often made rather informally and the exact nature of such distinctively 'global' systems of economic organization remains unclear. However, it is worth while briefly considering the issues involved in distinctive and separate business systems becoming established at the international level because they highlight the strong conditions required, especially if they were to dominate existing national ones to the extent of determining their performance and key characteristics.

Before examining the conditions required for such distinctive cross-national business systems to develop, it is important to distinguish these new kinds of international economic organization from the rather more likely extension of existing systems of economic coordination to new geographical and institutional locations. The generalization of dominant business systems – such as the 'Fordist' one in the USA – over new territories through FDI and/or capital market internationalization does not really herald the creation of a separate and distinctive cross-national business system, but rather the domination of an existing national or regional one over other economies. The growth of US FDI and the expanding influence of the predominantly Anglo-Saxon capital markets in the post-war period indicated not the emergence of a new kind of 'global' business system with its own actors and rules of the game, but, rather, the internationalization of the US business system. The continued significance of different kinds of business systems in Europe and Asia despite the dominant role of the US economy in the post-war period demonstrates the limited changes induced by these developments, for the reasons outlined above.

For a new kind of business system, that is genuinely different from existing national ones, to become established at the international level, three requirements have to be met. First, it has to combine a particular set of characteristics that differ significantly from those of established business systems. This means that the structure of international ownership relations, the ways that MNCs deal with each other and the nature of their employment relations are together organized in distinctive ways across national boundaries. It also implies that different kinds of international firms become established, exhibiting particular governance and capability characteristics which differ from those of domestic competitors because they coordinate cross-national operations. These novel characteristics of cross-national firms would become increasingly uniform as such a new kind of international business system developed.

ARTICLES

Second, such patterns would have to be fairly well established and stable so that, say, distinctive ownership relations or supplier–customer connections do not change rapidly, and international cooperative/competitive behaviours remain similar over business cycles. Distinctive governance structures and organization of international linkages need to be reproduced over some time if such a cross-national system of economic coordination is to be considered well established. It is not at all clear that either producer- or consumer-driven global commodity chains meet these conditions. Rather they – the consumer-driven chains especially – seem to be characterized by short-term arm's length contractual relationships. They are also constituted by quite varied kinds of firms whose characteristics reflect their domestic business systems more than any distinctive international one.

Third, the establishment of a separate and different kind of economic coordination and control system at the international level implies the concomitant emergence of distinctive and powerful international agencies, institutions and interest groups. For new rules of the game and ways of organizing economic activities to become institutionalized cross-nationally, new institutional arrangements have to develop to support and reinforce them. This, in turn, implies that existing, largely national, agencies and groups either become more involved in international competition, cooperation and conflicts, and/or delegate some of their powers and interests to international organizations and arenas. This has already happened to some extent in the areas of trade policies and financial intermediation, as well as politically and juridically in the case of Europe.

Such internationalization of agencies and institutions, however, typically involves considerable competition for control over their form, remit and resources between national groups and interests, just as the establishment of national state agencies and political arenas did. This competition is not only a matter of personal and group aggrandizement, but also involves conflicts between different conceptions of how agencies and institutions should be organized and evaluated and economic activities structured. The nature and behaviour of the European Commission, for example, reflect the dominant groups involved in its establishment and subsequent development, just as many aspects of the IMF and World Bank reflect the assumptions and interests of elite groups in the dominant post-war economies, especially the USA (Taylor, 1997; Ross, 1995).

Furthermore, the autonomy of such agencies from national ones, and their ability to initiate programmes and implement new kinds of cross-national rules of the game, fluctuate considerably as the recent history of the European Union demonstrates. The single European market has by no means resulted in standardized norms and rules governing

INTERNATIONALIZATION AND BUSINESS SYSTEMS

economic activities across Europe, let alone the emergence of distinctly 'European' firms which operate quite differently from national ones (Whitley and Kristensen, 1996). Indeed, the limited significance of both pan-European institutions and agencies, on the one hand, and European-level systems of economic organization, on the other hand, despite the existence of the European Economic Community and its successors for more than forty years, reveals the tenacity of national institutional arrangements and national business systems.

Similar points are involved in considering whether and how distinctive cross-national business systems – once they have developed – could dominate national ones to the extent of determining the prevalent rules of the game. Such domination would imply that: (a) the worldwide institutions and agencies associated with such business systems dominate national and regional systems; (b) that global competition between transnationals dominates competition at other levels; and (c) transnational firms are able to dominate largely national or regional ones because of their 'global' operations and resources. As the European example suggests, the first phenomenon is unlikely to occur quickly or to be widespread. It clearly depends on the cohesion and strength of host economy institutions and the willingness of state agencies to accept the authority of supra-national organizations.

The second point assumes that world markets are dominated by oligopolies which increasingly compete with each other across national economies, rather than with more nationally focused firms. However, the number of industries where such global dominance by a small number of firms has developed is still quite small, and competitive strategies remain national and regional in many sectors. Despite the growth of very large multinational firms in the white goods industry, for example, markets and competitive advantages remain quite specific to particular territories (Baden-Fuller and Stopford, 1991).

Similarly, the dominance of MNCs assumes that sheer size and the advantages of combining operations across countries outweigh the costs of managerial coordination of activities across institutional contexts. However, the increasing demands for flexibility in production methods and product lines coupled with the difficulties involved in generating collective continuous learning and improvement in diversified enterprises suggest that MNCs are more likely to be at a disadvantage compared to more focused organizations. Overall, then, it seems unlikely that distinctive, separate and stable cross-national business systems will become established, and will dominate existing, strongly institutionalized ones, unless much greater changes take place in national and regional institutions and firms.

CONCLUSIONS

This discussion highlights five major points about the impact of internationalization of economic coordination and control on established varieties of capitalism. First, the conditions required for significant changes to take place in the nature and behaviour of firms as a result of expansion of their operations abroad are so stringent that present patterns of internationalization are unlikely to generate step changes in the characteristics and strategies of leading firms in most economies. This is not to say that firms never alter when they internationalize – simply dealing with more diverse environments is likely to encourage some differentiation of structures and procedures – but to emphasize that they are unlikely to change their central characteristics so radically that they become different kinds of economic actors. Thus, modifying some labour management practices in some foreign subsidiaries or developing closer supplier links in Japan does not, in this view, signify significant change in the control and strategies of, for instance, US corporations.

Second, even where some firms do develop differently because of their concentration of assets and activities abroad, and such changes are not, of course, likely to be only a result of internationalization, this need not, and often will not, herald qualitative change in the nature of the domestic business system. In terms of the framework present here, significant business system change implies substantial shifts in ownership relations, the division of organizational labour, the level and/or type of non-ownership coordination processes and/or employment and labour management relations. Such changes are, then, large scale and far reaching, requiring considerable institutional restructuring and realignment of major societal interests. They are unlikely to develop simply as a consequence of internationalization, or to occur within one or two decades. The significant but limited consequences of the institutional reforms imposed by the Allied occupation of Germany and Japan for the organization of those economies demonstrate the incremental and path-dependent nature of system change in industrial societies, as do the current transformations of the former state-socialist countries of Eastern Europe.

Third, the impact of inward FDI and capital market internationalization on a host business system is mediated by local institutions and agencies. It is therefore unlikely that significant changes in core characteristics of industrialized societies will follow at all quickly, even where the investment is concentrated in one or two sectors and is dominated by firms from a particular business system. The more cohesive is the host business system and its associated institutions, the less likely is that system to change just as a result of foreign firms developing a

476

INTERNATIONALIZATION AND BUSINESS SYSTEMS

significant presence within it. Even in industrializing countries where a particular system of capitalist organization is in the process of being established, foreign investment does not necessarily determine the shape of the emergent economy, especially where the state plays a dominating role in organizing economic development and effectively controls the degree and nature of that investment.

Fourth, the globalization of capital markets likewise has had only limited effects on systems of economic coordination and control. Some large firms have increased their financial autonomy from domestic intermediaries, but the overall functioning of credit-based financial systems does not seem to have changed greatly as a result of such growing independence. In particular, the considerable lock-in and mutual interdependence between large firms and banks in such economies have not yet been transformed into 'Anglo-Saxon' forms of ownership organization and control. Given the major changes in related institutions and dominance relationships which such a shift would imply in most continental European and Asian economies, it seems unlikely to occur just as a result of capital market expansion and internationalization.

Finally, the internationalization of managerial coordination and of capital markets has increased competition between predominantly national business systems and their associated institutions, rather than establishing a radically new cross-national system of economic coordination and control. As firms, states and interest groups become more focused on international integration and competition, they seek to influence and control the emerging international norms governing the constitution of economic actors and the ways that their performance is evaluated and rewarded. Insofar as there are such emergent international 'industrial orders', to use Herrigel's (1994) term, they will reflect this competition and their characteristics will be strongly influenced by those of the leading economies, rather than by the logic of an institutionally disembodied, idealized market.

REFERENCES

Amsden, Alice H. (1989) *Asia's Next Giant*, Oxford: Oxford University Press.

Baden-Fuller, Charles W. F. and Stopford, John M. (1991) 'Globalisation frustrated: the case of white goods', *Strategic Management Journal* 12: 493–507.

Bartlett, C. and Ghoshal, Sumantra (1989) *Managing across Borders*, London: Hutchinson.

Bauer, Michael and Cohen, Elie (1981) *Qui gouverne les groupes industriels?*, Paris: Seuil.

Botti, Hope (1995) 'Misunderstandings: a Japanese transplant in Italy strives for lean production', *Organization* 2: 55–86.

Boyer, Robert and Hollingsworth, J. Rogers (1997) 'From national embeddedness to spatial and institutional nestedness', in J. R. Hollingsworth and R. Boyer (eds) *Contemporary Capitalism*, Cambridge: Cambridge University Press.

ARTICLES

Campbell, J. L., Hollingsworth, J. Rogers and Lindberg, Leon N. (eds) (1991) *Governance of the American Economy*, Cambridge: Cambridge University Press.

Clark, Rodney (1979) *The Japanese Company*, Newhaven, Conn.: Yale University Press.

Czaban, Laszlo and Whitley, Richard (1998) 'The transformation of work systems in emergent capitalism: the case of Hungary', *Work, Employment and Society* 12: 47–72.

Daems, Herman (1983) 'The determinants of the hierarchical organization of industry', in Arthur Francis, Jeremy Turk and Paul Willman (eds) *Power, Efficiency and Institutions*, London: Heinemann.

Dicken, Peter (1992) *Global Shift*, London: Paul Chapman Publishing.

Dore, Ronald P. (1973) *British Factory – Japanese Factory*, London: Allen & Unwin.

—— (1986) *Flexible Rigidities*, Stanford, Calif.: Stanford University Press.

Economist, The (1997a) 'One world?', 18 October, pp. 134–5.

—— (1997b) 'Capital goes global', 25 October, pp. 139–40.

Elger, Tony and Smith, Chris (1994) *Global Japanisation?*, London: Routledge.

Emmott, Brian (1992) *Japan's Global Reach: the Influences, Strategies and Weaknesses of Japan's Multinational Companies*, London: Century.

Enright, M. J., Scott, E. E. and Dodwell, D. (1997) *The Hong Kong Advantage*, Hong Kong: Oxford University Press.

Feldenkirchen, W. (1997) 'Business groups in the German electrical industry', in T. Shiba and M. Shimotani (eds) *Beyond the Firm*, Oxford: Oxford University Press.

Fields, Karl J. (1995) *Enterprise and the State in Korea and Taiwan*, Ithaca, NY: Cornell University Press.

Gereffi, Gary (1995a) 'Global commodity chains and Third World development', paper presented to ILO Forum on Labour in a Changing World Economy, Bangkok, 23–26 January.

—— (1995b) 'Contending paradigms for cross-regional comparison: development strategies and commodity chains in East Asia and Latin America', in P. H. Smith (ed.) *Latin America in Comparative Perspective*, Boulder, Colo.: Westview.

Gerlach, Michael (1992) *Alliance Capitalism*, Berkeley, Calif.: University of California Press.

Globokar, Terese (1997) 'Eastern Europe meets West: an empirical study on French management in a Slovenia plant', in S. Sackmann (ed.) *Cultural Complexity in Organizations*, London: Sage.

Hamilton, Gary (1997) 'Organization and market processes in Taiwan's capitalist economy', in M. Orru, N. W. Biggart and G. Hamilton, *The Economic Organization of East Asian Capitalism*, Thousand Oaks, Calif.: Sage, pp. 237–93.

Hamilton, Gary and Kao, Cheng-Shu (1990) 'The institutional foundation of Chinese business: the family firm in Taiwan', *Comparative Social Research* 12: 95–112.

Hellgren, Bo and Melin, Leif (1992) 'Business systems, industrial wisdom and corporate strategies: the case of the pulp and paper industry', in Richard Whitley (ed.) *European Business Systems: Firms and Markets in their National Contexts*, London: Sage.

Herrigel, Gary (1993) 'Large firms, small firms and the governance of flexible specialisation', in B. Kogut (ed.) *Country Competitiveness*, Oxford: Oxford University Press.

—— (1994) 'Industry as a form of order', in J. Rogers Hollingsworth, P. Schmitter and W. Streeck (eds) *Governing Capitalist Economies*, Oxford: Oxford University Press.

478

INTERNATIONALIZATION AND BUSINESS SYSTEMS

—— (1996) *Industrial Constructions: the Sources of German Industrial Power*, Cambridge: Cambridge University Press.

Hirst, Paul and Thompson, Grahame (1996) *Globalization in Question*, Oxford: Polity Press.

Hollingsworth, J. Rogers and Streeck, Wolfgang (1994) 'Counties and sectors: concluding remarks on performance, convergence and competitiveness', in J. Rogers Hollingsworth, P. Schmitter and W. Streeck (eds) *Governing Capitalist Economies*, Oxford: Oxford University Press.

Hollingsworth, J. Rogers, Schmitter, Philippe and Streeck, Wolfgang (eds) (1994) *Governing Capitalist Economies*, Oxford: Oxford University Press.

Horowitz, J. H. (1980) *Top Management Control in Europe*, London: Macmillan.

Hu, Yao-Su (1992) 'Global firms are national firms with international operations', *California Management Review* 34: 107–26.

Ingham, Geoffrey (1984) *Capitalism Divided? The City and Industry in British Social Development*, London: Macmillan.

Iterson, A. van (1996) 'Institutions and types of firm in Belgium: regional and sector variations', in Richard Whitley and P. H. Kristensen (eds) *The Changing European Firm: Limits to Convergence*, London: Routledge.

Janelli, R. L. (1993) *Making Capitalism: the Social and Cultural Construction of a South Korean Conglomerate*, Stanford, Calif.: Stanford University Press.

Kenworthy, L. (1997) 'Globalization and economic convergence', *Competition and Change* 2: 1–64.

Koechlin, T. (1995) 'The globalization of investment', *Contemporary Economic Policy* 13: 92–100.

Kristensen, Peer Hull (1992) 'Strategies against structure: institutions and economic organization in Denmark', in Richard Whitley (ed.) *European Business Systems: Firms and Markets in Their National Contexts*, London: Sage.

—— (1994) 'Strategies in a volatile world', *Economy and Society* 23: 305–34.

—— (1996) 'On the constitution of economic actors in Denmark: interacting skill containers and project coordinators', in Richard Whitley and Peer Hull Kristensen (eds) *The Changing European Firm: Limits to Convergence*, London: Routledge, pp. 118–58.

—— (1997) 'National systems of governance and managerial strategies in the evolution of work systems: Britain, Germany and Denmark compared', in Richard Whitley and Peer Hull Kristensen (eds) *Governance at Work: the Social Regulation of Economic Relations*, Oxford: Oxford University Press.

Kurgen-van Hentenryk, G. (1997) 'Structure and strategy of Belgian business groups', in T. Shiba and M. Shimotani (eds) *Beyond the Firm*, Oxford: Oxford University Press.

Langlois, R. N. and Robertson, P. L. (1995) *Firms, Markets and Economic Change*, London: Routledge.

Lilja, Kari and Tainio, Risto (1996) 'The nature of the typical Finnish firm', in Richard Whitley and Peer Hull Kristensen (eds) *The Changing European Firm: Limits to Convergence*, London: Routledge.

Mako, Csaba and Novaszath, P. (1995) 'Employment relations in multinational companies: the Hungarian case', in Eckhardt Dittrich, Gert Schmidt and Richard Whitley (eds) *Industrial Transformation in Europe*, London: Sage.

Marceau, Jane (1992) 'Small country business systems: Australia, Denmark and Finland compared', in Richard Whitley (ed.) *European Business Systems: Firms and Markets in Their National Contexts*, London: Sage.

Mayer, Michael and Whittington, Richard (1996) 'The survival of the European holding company: institutional choice and contingency', in Richard Whitley

ARTICLES

and Peer Hull Kristensen (eds) *The Changing European Firm: Limits to Convergence*, London: Routledge.

Mueller, Frank and Loveridge, Ray (1997) 'Institutional, sectoral and corporate dynamics in the creation of global supply chains', in Richard Whitley and Peer Hull Kristensen (eds) *Governance at Work: the Social Regulation of Economic Relations*, Oxford: Oxford University Press.

Numazaki, I. (1992) 'Networks and partnerships: the social organization of the Chinese business elite in Taiwan', unpublished Ph.D. thesis, Department of Anthropology, Michigan State University.

Orru, Marco, Biggart, Nicole Wolsely and Hamilton, Gary (1997) *The Economic Organization of East Asian Capitalism*, Thousand Oaks, Calif.: Sage.

Rasanen, Keijo and Whipp, Richard (1992) 'National business: a sector perspective', in Richard Whitley (ed.) *European Business Systems: Firms and Markets in Their National Contexts*, London: Sage.

Redding, S. Gordon (1990) *The Spirit of Chinese Capitalism*, Berlin: de Gruyter.

Ross, George (1995) *Jacques Delors and European Integration*, Oxford: Polity Press.

Sako, Mari (1992) *Prices, Quality and Trust*, Cambridge: Cambridge University Press.

Sharpe, Diana (1997) 'Compromise solutions: a Japanese multinational comes to the UK?', in Richard Whitley and Peer Hull Kristensen (eds) *Governance at Work: the Social Regulation of Economic Relations*, Oxford: Oxford University Press.

Stewart, Paul (ed.) (1996) *Beyond Japanese Management*, special issue of *Asia Pacific Business Review* 2 (4): 1–204.

Strange, Roger (1993) *Japanese Manufacturing Investment in Europe*, London: Routledge.

Tainio, Risto (1997) 'Does foreign ownership matter? Organizational responses to ownership changes in Finnish companies', paper presented to the 13th EGOS Colloquium, Budapest, 2–5 July.

Taylor, Lance (1997) 'The revival of the liberal creed – the IMF and the World Bank in a globalized economy', *World Development* 25: 145–52.

UNCTAD (1996) *World Investment Report 1996*, New York and Geneva: United Nations.

Weiss, Linda (1988) *Creating Capitalism. The State and Small Business Since 1945*, Oxford: Blackwell.

Westney, Eleanor (1996) 'The Japanese business system: key features and prospects for changes', *Journal of Asian Business* 12: 21–50.

Whitley, Richard (1992a) *Business Systems in East Asia: Firms, Markets and Societies*, London: Sage.

—— (1992b) 'Societies, firms and markets: the social structuring of business systems', in Richard Whitley (ed.) *European Business Systems: Firms and Markets in Their National Contexts*, London: Sage.

—— (1996a) 'The social construction of economic actors: institutions and types of firm in Europe and other market economies', in Richard Whitley and Peer Hull Kristensen (eds) *The Changing European Firm: Limits to Convergence*, London: Routledge, pp. 39–66.

—— (1996b) 'Business systems and global commodity chains: competing or complementary forms of economic organization?', *Competition and Change* 1: 411–25.

—— (1997) 'The social regulation of work systems; institutions, interest groups and varieties of work organization in capitalist societies', in Richard Whitley and Peer Hull Kristensen (eds) *Governance at Work: the Social Regulation of Economic Relations*, Oxford: Oxford University Press.

INTERNATIONALIZATION AND BUSINESS SYSTEMS

Whitley, Richard and Czaban, Laszlo (1998) 'Institutional transformation and enterprise change in an emergent capitalist economy: the case of Hungary', *Organization Studies* 19: 259–80.

Whitley, Richard and Kristensen, Peer Hull (eds) (1996) *The Changing European Firm*, London: Routledge.

—— (eds) (1997) *Governance at Work: the Social Regulation of Economic Relations*, Oxford: Oxford University Press.

Whitley, Richard, Henderson, Jeffrey and Czaban, Laszlo (1997) 'Ownership, control and the management of labour in an emergent capitalist economy: the case of Hungary', *Organization* 4(1): 75–98.

Whittaker, D. H. (1990) *Managing Innovation*, Cambridge: Cambridge University Press.

Wong, S.-L. (1988) 'The applicability of Asian family values to other sociocultural settings', in P. L. Berger and H.-H. M. Hsiao (eds) *In Search of an East Asian Development Model*, New Brunswick, NJ: Transaction Books.

[10]

Strategic Fit and the Societal Effect: Interpreting Cross-National Comparisons of Technology, Organization and Human Resources*

Arndt Sorge

Abstract

Arndt Sorge
Department of
Business
Administration.
University of
Limburg.
Maastricht, The
Netherlands

The neo-contingency framework, responding to criticism against previous contingency thinking, appears to be potentially capable of serving as a basis for interpreting research in the tradition of the societal effect approach. This hypothesis is further developed using existing literature. The hypothesis is then examined by looking at the results of various cross-national comparisons of the organizational, human resources and strategic contexts of technical change in manufacturing. This leads to a reflection on the underlying factors influencing competitive advantage in national sectors or industries, and to a proposal on how distinct and different theoretical approaches can be conceived to be related to one another.

Introduction

According to the dictum of a dialectical thinker, which can probably be traced back to Huckleberry Finn (Reitzug 1989), there are always two kinds of people: those who think that there are always two kinds of people and those who don't. Let us pretend that there are always two kinds of organization theorists: universalists and contingency theorists. The former think that organizing is governed by universal principles, and the latter that it is specific to the task environment which an organization confronts. Universalists often believe in one best way. They include such figures as Taylor, Weber, Fayol, but also authors of a different persuasion such as Argyris (1972) or the socio-technical school, with its idea of joint maximization of task and social systems. Contingency theorists believe that the best way is always specific to the nature of a task and the task environment (Thompson 1967).

The essence of the contingency approach might now be formulated in the language of population ecology, following authors such as Aldrich (1979), in this way: societies or economies will be populated by those organizational forms and practices which correspond most closely to the task environments prevailing in respective niches. This implies that organizational forms and practices will emerge and mutate, in line with properties of the task environment. The underlying idea is that actors will try to work towards a 'fit' between conditions in an environmental niche and organization forms and practices. This will be the case to the extent that

Organization
Studies
1991, 12/2:
161–190
© 1991 EGOS
0170–8406/91
0012–0007 $2.00

their behaviour is governed by a selection mechanism such as competitive pressure. The degree of fit is considered to be essential for performance. It may be measured in different ways but implies, at least, the survival, growth or multiplication of organizational units which have a particular form.

Working towards a fit between the properties of a niche and organizational forms and practices may then be called establishing a successful generic strategy. This may happen in a deliberate or an emergent way. According to Miles and Snow (1978), it may be governed by further environmental selection (survival of those with the most fit), by a more judicious selection and construction of niches by actors, or by a more active adaptation of organization forms and practices. A combination of these mechanisms may take place. The neo-contingency approach has tried to counter a great deal of the earlier criticism against contingency thinking, but in its revised form, it approximates with Miles and Snow's summary, above.

In particular, such an approach responded to criticism from, for instance, Schreyögg (1980), by abandoning some earlier deterministic concepts. Out has gone the idea that environment and context determine organization unidirectionally, and in came the concept of a reciprocal conditioning between organization, context and environment. This allowed, at least implicitly, a great deal of constructivistic and interactionist theory-building, despite demonstrative saber-rattling in that direction (Donaldson 1985). By using, in particular, the concepts of (a) institutionally, culturally or idiosyncratically influenced, functionally equivalent solutions (Child 1972), and (b) business policy or generic strategy-making, a hard core of contingency theory has thus been purified, fortified and made more accessible to countervailing approaches.

Some of the criticism against the previous, more deterministic strand of contingency theory came from the 'Aix Group' (Rose 1985), which had posited the 'societal effect approach' (Maurice et al. 1982; Maurice et al. 1980). By means of cross-national comparisons of organizational units which were fairly identical with regard to acknowledged contingencies, this Group has identified quite a large cross-national variety of organizational forms and practices which though unrelated to task context or performance differences, is very closely bound to institutionalized human resources (education, training, work careers), social stratification and industrial relations.

The pioneering study of this Group had suggested that the cross-national variety found at that time between Germany and France, was apparently linked with the different qualitative and quantitative strengths of economic sectors in the two societies (Maurice et al. 1977: 764). In terms of concepts used in this paper, the argument was that the development of societally specific, institutionalized populations of organizational forms and practices, was intimately linked with the pre-eminence of particular economic niches (types of markets and overall sector-specific tasks). From the Aix study therefore, an idea emerges which is reminiscent of neo-contingency thinking i.e. that the *espace d'organisation* (organization forms and practices), *espace de qualification* (human resources) and *espace industriel* (industrial structure and organization) of a society are interdependent.

Framework and Earlier Findings

The introduction suggests a central hypothesis, which will be examined and tested in this paper. It can be formulated as follows: the societal effect approach is best conceived as a special case of the evolved neo-contingency framework. *Societal differences in organizing and generating human resources, and the pursuit of different business strategies, are reciprocally related. An economy and society becomes populated by specific institutionalized organizational and human resource forms and practices, because economic niches and business strategies are different, and vice versa.* The argument implies that economies and societies develop Ricardian comparative advantage on the basis of institutionalized organization and human resource patterns. This comparative advantage resides in the fit between institutionalized patterns and the requirements arising from specific niches.

The present argument is to refer to manufacturing organization in general. Insofar as competitiveness is concerned, it pertains, in particular, to industries which are internationally competive. It might be developed in a different way for service sectors, and it could be amplified in order to be valid with regard to basic societal mechanisms which are not sector or industry specific. However, there is insufficient space for that here.

This is therefore an attempt to analyze what Porter has termed in his recent work (Porter 1990) the 'competitive advantage of nations', but to do it in a way which is more specific, restricted to fewer countries, related to the organization and human resource literature in greater detail, and informed by matched comparisons of cases. Let us see how the overall argument can be analytically decomposed, derived in more specific form from previous findings, and how it can be tested.

What is needed is, first, a concept that relates cross-national institutionalized differences to business strategies and organizational forms, in more concrete terms. Second, there is a need for a body of findings to test propositions. The concept will subsequently be developed in this section of the paper. The overall hypothesis and its ramifications will be examined on the basis of recent cross-national comparisons:

- a comparison of the introduction of CNC (computer numerically controlled) machine-tools in Great Britain and West Germany (Sorge et al. 1983; Sorge 1985);
- a comparison of the introduction of microelectronics into manufactured products in Great Britain and the Federal Republic of Germany (Campbell, Sorge and Warner 1989);

- the recent evolution of the machine-tool manufacturing industries in France and West Germany (Maurice and Sorge 1989);
- related comparisons of other authors, such as S. J. Prais and colleagues (Prais et al. 1989; Steedman and Wagner 1987, 1989), Streeck (1985), Cox and Kriegbaum (1980), Northcott et al. (1985).

To link up cross-national and business strategy related organizational variety, let us first define a concept of competitive advantage. Porter (1980, 1983) has distinguished between cost leadership, differentiation and focus as alternative and often mutually exclusive sources of competitiveness. Whilst this approach has found much interest and is quite well linked with a marketing perspective, it cannot be translated as easily into clear-cut production organization and human resources terms. A company which differentiates its products from those of competing firms by advertizing and creating a marketing image, may not be much different from them in terms of development, production engineering and organization. It may not differ from a focus strategy firm, either, which specializes in a particular market segment or niche, except if its relative market share is different. There is a need to translate primarily marketing-orientated concepts more clearly into terms which are meaningful with respect to the way a company organizes operations. At the same time, the industry must not be neglected as a level of analysis; Bamberger (1989) has shown that strategy differences are closely linked to industry sector contexts.

It is useful to retain, as elementary alternative parameters of competition, product cost and product quality, and to focus on these more single-mindedly than did Porter. Lower costs are a result of efficiency strategies by which the value of output related to inputs is increased through increasing the shear volume of identical products. Product quality is based on qualitative competitiveness strategies; in this case, the competitive edge is due to higher value added and a higher selling price for individual products. Whilst this may be due to monopolistic behaviour, the only strategies considered here are those that are also facilitated by development and design related product differentiation. This implies monopolistic competition as a market form, and this market form may in turn be brought about by enterprise product strategies.

The concepts, of cost and price related efficiency and qualitative effectiveness strategies, have been used in an Anglo–German comparison by Cox and Kriegbaum (1980). Cost efficiency is likely to be associated with economies of scale and hence market share or, more generally, volume of output. This has, through the central organizational concept of size, a clear link with the organization and human resources literature (Sorge 1989). Things are probably more difficult regarding the general notion of product quality. We have put forward the distinction between volume of output and differentiation of output, the latter implying the degree of customization, to organize central product and production contingencies and strategies, linked with specific human resources arrangements and policies (Sorge and Streeck 1988). The explanatory potential of this typology and further relationships are explored by Sorge (1989).

In Porter's terms, customization or differentiation of a product range is equivalent to a specific mode of his definition of differentiation, plus a differentiated focus strategy. The specificity consists of a flexible development and production apparatus. Differentiation purely based on price, product quality or market image is not a necessary part of this more specific concept.

From here, it is easier to build a bridge over to central concepts and findings in the organization and industrial sociology literature. A greater degree of product differentiation in the form of customization implies, in Perrow's (1971: 83) terms, 'more exceptions'. This is one important dimension of 'non-routineness', which is one dimension in an overall notion of task uncertainty. With higher product differentiation, there is also likely to be a greater amount of organismic rather than mechanistic organization (de Sitter 1986; den Hertog and van Diepen 1988).

The argument is in the tradition of organization theory (Thompson 1967), the origins of contingency approaches (Burns and Stalker 1961), the socio-technical school (Trist 1981) and the organizational learning literature (Argyris and Schön 1978), although it does not necessarily see the choice of organic organization as contingent upon a particular business strategy. It is clear, though, that the economic advantage of this form of organizing is linked with a more rapid rate of product innovation and other forms of output differentiation (Trist 1981).

The organizational and human resources implications of the organismic variant, as opposed to the mechanistic which is seen to fit stable, task-certain, product-homogeneous and therefore often large-scale or mass production environments, may now be shortly described as follows.

– Organizational boundaries and formal and hierarchical coordination mechanisms are softened and complemented by informal and professional modes of coordination (van de Ven et al. 1976).
– Sets of skills and knowledge specific to sub-units and jobs overlap rather than being set apart; the organization is more holographic in this respect than when characterized by a strict division of labour (Morgan 1986: 97).
– Recruitment, training and career mobility serve to create richer professional role sets as well as bridging lateral and vertical distances between jobs, departments and levels.

Such inter-linked differences in product and market strategies, organization and human resources patterns can be related to findings of cross-national comparisons. To cover the countries to be discussed here, I will summarize some findings from Lane (1989), Maurice et al. (1982), Maurice et al. (1980) and Sorge and Warner (1986). In general, these have not dealt directly with product and market-related strategies of enterprises. On the basis of organization and human resources results, however, one may hypothesize a fit between types of product markets and strategies on the one hand, and societal organization and human resource structures on the other. The argument thus relates institution-alized — i.e. relatively task-unspecific — societal patterns to task-specific organization forms as presented by Woodward (1965), one of the founders of the contingency approach, and Mintzberg (1983), who pro-vided a major analytical overview and typology.

The German style of organizing and creating human resources gives the impression of being strongly characterized by blurred organization boundaries; less segmentation; fewer line-staff; management–execution, technical work–shop-floor work and generalism–specialism distinctions. It might be described, in Mintzberg's terms, as a mixture of a professional bureaucracy and an adhocracy, with some affinity towards the simple structure, notably that of small-scale craft production. It seems to embody the structures which can be found in many societies in medium-sized investment-goods engineering firms — notably in mechanical engineering — which has a large operating core, a craft worker base and worker-technician/engineer work role and career continuity, as pillars of the enterprise's competitiveness. This structure appears to be generalized beyond the product-market segments, where it might be thought to apply according to a neo-contingency framework. As it is generalized, such a societal pattern would suggest that a premium is placed on the explora-tion of corresponding product markets and the relative growth of such sectors in the economy.

The French type of organization may be characterized by greater hier-archical and lateral segmentation. It de-emphasizes craft training and craft worker role-sets, using career progression and the combination of school and college education with job-specific training in the enterprise as more important mechanisms of generating competence. Distinctions between generalist engineering and management on the one hand and specialists on the other, and between strata of engineers, technicians and workers, are more in evidence. There is greater and more refined dif-ferentiation between management, conception, design or planning, and execution. The society and enterprise policies appear to promote organizational, career pattern and human resources arrangements which are typically found in large-scale, mass and continuous process produc-tion. French patterns are also similar to those found in 'high-technology' and highly concentrated industries with large units, such as aerospace, sophisticated armaments or consumer and telecommunications electronics.

In Mintzberg's terms, one is dealing with a mixture of the machine and the professional bureaucracies. This pattern seems to be generalized above and beyond the product-market situation to which, under neo-contingency theory, it would specifically apply. This appears to go hand-in-hand with the dominance of large-batch, mass and continuous process production firms, plus highly complex enterprises making sophisticated products which are dependent on, and interact with, the government and its machine or with professional bureaucracies. The societal generaliza-tion of such organization, human resource and dependency patterns can be interpreted as favouring the deployment of corresponding markets, product strategies and industrial sectors.

The British organization is somewhat more equivocal. It is rather pluri-central, in addition to being segmented. Functional segmentation between production and maintenance, management and engineering, supervision and technical work is pronounced. The management hierarchy is less technical and more subject to financial controls. There are 'pockets' of specialized professionalism in maintenance, production engineering, production control, etc., but these are more detached and occupationally less part of an overall controlling set-up. The latter may probably be characterized as a general management hierarchy orientated by general financial success criteria.

The historical strength of craft work forces, worker-engineer professional continuity, autonomy of craftsmen and professional rather than bureaucratic modes of control, make British patterns appear to be more similar to German ones than do the French arrangements. Craft and apprenticeship are more of a historical legacy in Britain, but their relative importance has dwindled. Technician and engineering professions have detached themselves from worker training and experience to a greater extent. The craft base in direct production, and its extension into planning and technical functions, has become eroded. More stratified categories of engineers and technicians have taken its place, imposed on routinized or 'diluted skills' in direct production. A greater vertical and lateral professional segmentation has taken place.

Again, we notice a mixture of machine and professional bureaucracy elements, but the mixture is different from that in the French case, notably in that contrasted arrangements exist side by side.

Hence, the choice of the matching product-market situation is not straightforward. Again, it points more in the direction of large-scale and continuous-process production types as well as 'high-tech' industries. This is because of the greater weight and detachment of differentiated technical and administrative components in relation to execution or production components in the organization. Steedman and Wagner (1987, 1989) have shown, for the furniture and the garments industries, that the organization and human resources differences found between Britain and Germany match product strategy differences, with more standardized, lower priced, mass-produced products prevailing in Britain.

It should also be mentioned that the divisionalized form appears to be more prevalent in Britain. A possible reason for this is to permit a simultaneous focus on products and financial and commercial control in otherwise less product-centred enterprises. This came out of our earlier more general Anglo–German comparison (Sorge and Warner 1986). It also fits the finding of Horovitz (1978) that enterprise management is conceived more in financial terms in Britain. This can be seen to require the definition of quasi-independent business units in accounting terms and, therefore, divisions or organizational forms closely akin to divisions. It is again conceivable that generalized societal patterns in Britain encourage product strategies and industrial sectors to evolve in the direction of large-batch, mass and continuous process production firms, concentrated divisionalized conglomerates and 'high-tech' firms in electronics or aerospace.

It is convenient to visualize some of the affinities summarized here, by developing a scheme presented in Sorge and Streeck (1988: 30). We had pictured four manufacturing types as a result of crossing dichotomized types (small and large) of two dimensions: volume of output (related to organizational size) and differentiation/variation of output. The scheme is presented, in modified form, in Diagram 1. This shows societally significant organizational types in the boxes defined by task contingency and strategy types, thereby hypothesizing an elective affinity or correspondence between universal task-and-volume related patterns on the one hand, and societally specific patterns on the other. The latter are entered in the four-fold table depicting central task contingencies, roughly at the place to which they correspond according to the logic of contingency theory.

The nature of the affinities is not precise enough, though, to suggest a one-to-one match between organizational variety linked to business strategies and markets, and that variety which is due to the societal effect. The German mode is definitely not the only or best mode of operating within the respective product market segment, for instance, and the mass or the continuous process mode is not identical with French-style practices. The principle of functional equivalence, of different socio-organizational arrangements with regard to overall business and organizational goals (Child 1972), still appears pertinent. However, the above discussion also points to the limits of the functional equivalents perspective. Arrangements that are institutionalized and therefore transcend a functional purpose (Berger and Luckmann 1971: 72), have an affinity, nevertheless, with tasks, markets and overall strategies. The question of to what extent, and where, an institutionalized arrangement is not functionally neutral, is fairly open.

Comparisons with a longitudinal element are useful in order to estimate the tightness of such relations. Since the mentioned affinities are likely to come out in the process of a quasi-Darwinian selection in the intensifying international division of labour, over-time analysis is a good test. Empirical study results which will be referred to, are evaluated in order to test, as far as possible, hypotheses against evolutions over time. The point of departure is what we have called 'elective affinity' (Sorge and Streeck 1988: 27), i.e. reciprocal interdependence rather than one-way determinism, in line with the evolved neo-contingency approach.

Comparative Tendencies in Britain and West Germany

In an earlier study, we investigated the organizational and human resource circumstances around the introduction and use of CNC (com-

Diagram 1. Organizational Task Contingencies and Societal Patterns

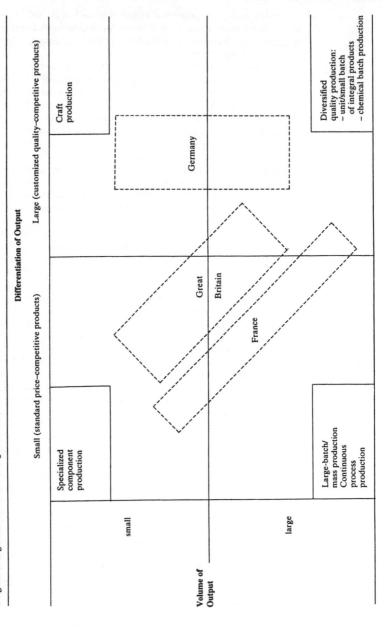

puter numerically controlled) machine tools in Britain and West Germany. The results of this comparison can be interpreted, rather smoothly, in terms of the framework posited here. When size and technology were controlled for by matching pairs of plants, the British firms showed the followed characteristics:

– a larger and organizationally, as well as occupationally, more differentiated superstructure of technical and administrative staffs and management ladders,
– a greater differentiation of worker and technician apprenticeships and careers,
– fewer fully apprenticed workers as part of the production workforce and more semi-skilled workers,
– a lesser inclination to explore or use shop-floor programming of CNC machines (Sorge et al. 1983).

The interpretation of these findings seemed to be quite straightforward. The British firms, relatively more geared for large-batch and mass or process production, de-emphasized the links between worker and technician careers, and detached technician, engineering and planning functions from the shop floor. Hence, there was more of a power struggle around the appropriation of programming tasks, in which technicians had the upper hand. Shop-floor programming, on the other hand, attracted less interest. We did not develop, to any extent, at this time, the finding that these cross-national differences were most pronounced between the respective larger plants with small-batch production in the two countries. We tended to consider this as accidental. It did not seem to clearly contradict or qualify the overall explanation of differences.

We concluded that Germany seemed better set to pursue differentiated quality and craft production than Britain, and to maintain its manufacturing industry in a setting where a differentiation of product markets could be observed. Organization and human resources in German manufacturing conceivably made it easier or 'more natural' to engage in differentiated quality or craft production, thus enabling firms to develop strategies that were more in line with pervasive shifts in product markets. This interpretation was confirmed by more massive de-industrialization in Britain and the crumbling of its Midlands and Northern traditional industrial base. Particularly evident was the virtual disappearance of a domestically owned machine-tool industry, a sector noted for its strong machining craft tradition in both production and development departments.

The interpretation was supported by authors writing about the machine-tool industry, such as Daley and Jones (1980). Strong confirmation also came from Steedman and Wagner (1987, 1989) with regard to the furniture and garment industries, who showed that greater frequency and intensity of worker and foreman training in Germany coincided with a stronger position in the more differentiated, high value-added and quality-conscious segments of the market. The British firms had become focused on staple, mass-produced goods where the selling price was the

primary competition parameter. The interpretation was further supported by the Study of Cox and Kriegbaum (1980). This study demonstrated, by a longitudinal comparison of several British and German
manufacturing sectors (mechanical engineering, motor vehicles, chemicals, textiles) at a more aggregate level, that the British sectors had
manoeuvred themselves, through lower investment, into a downward
spiral. By investing into more price-sensitive segments, offering less value
added, their capability to invest out of retained profits was also
reduced.

Another powerful confirmation came from an international study on the
automobile industry. This showed that the German industry had taken a
more favourable course, in terms of competitiveness and employment,
than many other national automobile industries. It aimed at the less
price-sensitive, more differentiated and quality-conscious up-market segments, and at the same time developed production flexibility and shop-
floor skills in addition to more organic work organization concepts
(Streeck 1985). Once again, it appeared that there was a good fit of a
particular product-market strategy with its corresponding societal
organization and human resources profile. The latter profile made it
possible for companies in the industry to move towards corresponding
product strategies and adapt to, or actively pre-empt, general market
developments where the price-sensitive mass-production segments were
increasingly being captured by Japanese producers, who not only competed on price but also on finish and reliability.

The fit was so tempting that we left aside the fact that the automobile
industry lends itself more to a machine bureaucracy. Using international
comparisons (Sorge and Streeck 1988), this is different from the professional bureaucracy and affinity with simple structures found in Germany. We also did not fully consider the fact that, in the Cox and
Kriegbaum study, the most striking differences between Britain and Germany had not been found in mechanical engineering, i.e. the sector to
which societal profiles in Germany appeared best adapted, according to
the neo-contingency approach. It was the automobile industry which,
according to Cox and Kriegbaum (1980: 6), showed the most strikingly
different evolutions of performance between the two countries.

At the time, we stressed an interpretation which held that the relative
success of a firm and of a national sector was primarily due to the extent
to which they were able to approximate an 'ideal' organization and
human resources profile, given a particular product market strategy. The
embeddedness of a firm and of a national sector in societal arrangements
were held to be closer to that 'ideal' profile. Feeling rather comfortable
with that interpretation, we disregarded some loopholes and cracks that
emerged. Should it not have been the mechanical engineering industry in
Germany which ought to have shown the most spectacular relative success? If it did not, why was this so? These reflections shed doubt on an
ideal match between sectoral or company and societal profiles.

The next Anglo–German comparison to be discussed was somewhat different but again, it did not seriously rattle the underlying interpretation presented so far. After working on CNC machines, i.e. a process innovation, we concentrated on product applications of microelectronics, where microelectronics entered into the products of companies rather than into tools and process equipment. We also looked at process changes, but in the context of product applications of microelectronics. This involved a change of interest and concepts, insofar as the earlier comparisons had been focused on characteristics and transformation of process technology, which also figures more prominently in the organizational literature. Arguably, process characteristics are more immediately related to work organization and human resources. In a way, they can be interpreted as an intermediate variable between a unit's product characteristics and work organization and human resources arrangements.

Our research design had also evolved in the meantime. Previously, the possible link between sectoral and organization level comparisons had not been so central. The case studies, however, were few in number, quite intensive and selected to match in pairs as closely as possible. In the more recent study, a research design seemed attractive, which reflected the spread of potentially different product types and strategies in the two countries. This allowed for the possibility that products, product ranges and forward or backward integration differences between organizations in different societies are not simply haphazard flaws that ruin a perfect matching of plants.

The potentially systematic nature of these differences made it necessary to look at product strategies and product development as something internal to the working-out of societal differences, rather than as a factor to be held constant by perfect matching. In consequence, we moved from pair-matching towards studying a larger number of cases. The cases selected were those which were more quantitatively representative of the respective populations of companies that applied microelectronics in their products, and which emerged through an approximation of quota sampling.

Research results have recently been published elsewhere (Campbell et al. 1989), so that a more detailed description is not appropriate. The results of the German study have also been published in book form (Beuschel et al. 1988). I will only review some central findings which need to be underlined in the present argument. First, it could be generally seen that the evolution of work competence requirements and organization characteristics happened in a rather parallel fashion in the two national sets of companies compared. There was a general tendency to emphasize the integration or intertwining of software, electronics and the application of specific knowledge and experience, and the increasing importance of organic links between companies with more differentiated product and competence domains. This finding is worth stressing since it has implications for competence development in all kinds of education and training institutions. This is not so surprising, in view of the increasing diffusion of electronics into all manner of products and contexts of utilization, the functional intertwining of electronic and other techniques and the growing importance of interface technology (sensors, actuators, etc.).

Second, the nature and function of a product as well as product strategies, in the sense of the extent and qualitative nature of forward integration into electronic component development and production, turned out to be a good explanation for competence requirements and bottlenecks arising in both countries. This reinforced the impression, which underlies the present paper, that product strategy and organizational phenomena are closely linked. However, the link between competence requirements and their evolution on the one hand, and product strategy on the other, was much closer than between competence requirements and the human resource development activities pursued. Companies met their perceived competence needs through different training and recruitment measures, and such patterns varied in similar ways within the two countries as well as being systematically different between Britain and Germany.

Thus, when product strategies were 'controlled for' — not statistically but in tabular form —, tendencies in the evolution of competence requirements appeared to be similar in the two countries. The evolution of measures to develop human competence was less similar. This was largely under the influence of societally different systems of education, training and labour markets. On the other hand, and this is the third central finding to be mentioned here, the cross-national differences in sectoral strengths — quantitatively and qualitatively —, in sectoral application rates of microelectronics, in product strategies and in recruitment and training policies, were in a harmony that we had not initially expected at the time. Here is a possible explanation.

The British economy features larger electronics, office equipment and computing, military technology and telecommunications sectors than in Germany. High performers by international comparison are concentrated in these sectors. Mechanical engineering and metal-working, however, have weaknened more than in West Germany (Auer 1988). In Britain, the product strategy differences between 'core' electronic producers (electronics, telecommunications, computing and office equipment goods) and manufacturers making products with a more pronounced physical extension and function (moving, treating or processing of physical objects or persons) are quite strong. The latter integrate electronics development and production much less, except in the armaments and aircraft industries.

On the recruitment and training side, the British manufacturers met competence needs by focusing almost exclusively on university graduates and technicians in recruitment, basic and further training. Worker craftsmen in electronics and electrical trades were hardly mentioned, as if electronics was outside their domain anyway. The central element in the training and recruitment policy was to have good contacts with a university or polytechnic. Relative elitism and product unspecificity thus played a larger part at the stage of recruitment for the first job, although 'poaching' experienced engineers and technicians also played an important part.

The picture was different for Germany in all respects. This country has, quantitatively and qualitatively, stronger sectors of mechanical engineering and automobile manufacture than Britain, where a larger craft worker force and continuity of skills and knowledge from workers to technicians and engineers are more prevalent. Application rates of microelectronics in mechanical engineering products are much higher in Germany than in other countries (Northcott et al. 1985). It seems to be a society that thrives more than others on modernizing its 'traditional' industrial sectors by injecting new techniques and emphasizing the customized and high quality ends of these sectors.

Hence, not only is the rate of application of microelectronics less different between electrical and mechanical engineering in Germany, but also the product strategies between these sectors. It is common for German companies outside the core electronics industries to integrate backwards into electronics development and production more than their British counterparts. They encounter fewer obstacles because the status and competence of electronic and mechanical engineers and technicians is on a similar level, and because of the strong presence of a more practically oriented tier of higher education (*Fachhochschulen*).

Although noticeable problems exist in Germany, too, companies appear to smoothen the professional and status gap between electronic, software and other engineers more easily. German electrical and electronic engineers have traditionally had training in elementary metal-working and mechanical design. This not only has implications for the professional habitus of the groups, but also for product strategy and personnel development in companies. Electronics and software are technically made to blend into mainly non-electronic or not primarily information-processing products. This must be seen as being related to the social construction of professions and occupations, which makes workers, foremen, technicians and engineers, as well as application, electronics and software specialists, blend into each other.

The human resource development policies of the German companies also featured a greater involvement with craft worker training in electronics. It showed in the upgrading of their skills and knowledge, advancement to technician roles, and their substitution for, or cooperation with, engineers in design and development functions. The international comparison was quite illuminating in this respect. Whereas we thought, on the basis of the German study by itself, that the German companies might have made life easier for themselves by recruiting, training and promoting more craftsmen, in order to alleviate shortages of engineers and to inject more product and production-related experience, their efforts in this respect stood out against the British companies.

To sum up the comparison, it may be said that the German companies produced more mundane and 'traditional industry' types of goods, but they were thriving on the modernization of these products and the customization of the product range. This implied a more intensive involvement with electronics, although mostly not at a high level of sophistication in semiconductor technology. This was helped by a more cohesive technical and engineering culture, less divided by specialism and the extent of practical or scientific orientation. The British companies were more likely to be in 'high-tech' sectors, show remarkable product strategy differences between mundane and 'high-tech' producers and feature lateral and hierarchical working culture differentiation. This is probably a feature of such sectors everywhere, when compared with other sectors in the same society. Thus, we found phenomena which may briefly be labelled as de-industrialization and sectoral shifts for Britain, and modernization of traditional industry for Germany.

Again, we tended to underline the power of a neo-contingency framework in the explanation: those sectors will thrive in a society, whose 'ideal' professional and organizational profiles are approximated most closely by the institutions prevailing in the wider society. The approximation of the sectoral, task-related profile is related to the comparative advantages of the sector concerned, and to the economy being populated by the corresponding organizational forms, human resources and business strategies. A shift towards electronics and data processing equipment industries is, structurally, noticeable in both Britain and Germany, of course. From the point of view of production, productivity and employment, this has been a boom industry in both countries for some time. We are not saying, however, that a sector should decline relative to total employment in one country as it expands in another one.

Whereas electronics and data processing have been favoured by economic and technical tides in many countries (CEPII 1980), the position of these, relative to other sectors, have been different between countries. In Germany, during the period 1977–1985, data processing and office equipment had an above-average employment performance, with a 7.7 percent increase. However, this performance is second to that of the German automobile industry which increased employment over that period by 8.2 percent. Moreover, throughout the boom period, the import–export performance of the data processing industy deteriorated, leading to a 38 percent import surplus in 1985, whereas exports equalled imports in 1970.

Similarly, electronics imports in West Germany have caught up on exports. In 1970, exports stood at twice the value of imports, and in 1985, at 1.4 of the value of imports (all cited figures from Jeske and Kohlmeyer 1987). The performance is much worse if electronic components, as distinct from larger sets and equipment, are concerned. Germany seems to have more success in the application and adaptation of electronics than in component design and production, both within the electronics sectors, and particularly outside it and the data processing industries.

Although it is an anecdotal piece of evidence, it is interesting to note that the most successful larger firm in terms of output and employment expansion in these two sectors (Nixdorf) is distinctive for modularized computer applications to fit market niches, rather than for mass markets or high tech components. More recently, even this firm got into difficulties and was taken over by Siemens, which is stronger in the application of electronics to investment goods. Elsewhere in Germany, consumer electronics firms have increasingly been taken over by Japanese, French and Dutch multinationals.

A detailed analysis for Britain is not possible here. The fast decline of many metalworking sectors is obvious (Auer 1988), whilst services and electronics, data processing equipment, aviation and defence related industries achieved a much greater relative importance than in Germany. The temptation was thus great to highlight parallel developments at the sectoral, company and plant levels, and to interpret parallels as being due to the affinity — or conflict — between societal institutional and sectoral, task and market-related patterns.

The electronics and data processing equipment industries are distinctive for having higher percentages of engineers in the work force, fewer craft workers, more semi-skilled operatives and a rather more broken professional continuity from workers to technicians and engineers, than in mechanical engineering. These were not the sectors in which Germany would be presumed to enjoy a comparative advantage, but this would increasingly be the case for Britain.

Much as in the previous comparisons, we attributed less weight to the finding that the product strategy related differences were clearly larger between Britain and Germany, for products whose central function was not to process signals and information but to move, treat or process people or physical objects. The strategy differences between the countries were less pronounced for the electrical, electronic and information technology industries. This finding slipped through the neo-contingency framework; it was neither explained by it, nor did it appear to go against it. A more striking falsification occurred in the following comparison, where we had probably expected it least of all.

Manufacturing Machine-Tools in France and West Germany

At the start of the comparison, things appeared to be rather simple. The machine-tools producing industry can, in most countries, be safely expected to retain more artisanal or craft features than other sectors in manufacturing: more craft workers; the importance of a link-up of production and development or design experience; greater professional continuity from workers to technicians and engineers; more customized development and production rather than large-batch or mass markets. Indeed, it is an industry in which Germany has had a very strong position since the turn of the century. It has also held this position reasonably well under the Japanese onslaught after the middle of the 1970s. It appears obvious to suggest that this is due to the near-perfect affinity of this profile with that of organization, business strategy and human resources practices in German society at large.

The French machine-tool industry, however, has 'always' been weaker. Although it expanded more rapidly in the post-war period up to 1975, than the German sector, it suffered a much more serious decline thereafter and well into the 1980s. The German industry only declined from 125,000 employees in 1970 to 93,000 in 1987. The decline was not monotonic; there were periods of increasing and decreasing employment. The French industry, on the other hand, was more than halved, from 27,000 employees in 1974 down to 11,000 in 1988.

One might have suggested, again seemingly obviously, that the greater French post-war expansion in the machine-tool industry was due to the heyday of mass production in that period, and that subsequent decline resulted from the lesser ability to exploit the more differentiated emerging markets, to which application of microelectronics in machine-tool control systems (CNC controls) appeared to open up better access. The first part of this explanation is probably correct. The second part appeared quite plausible, too. This would have required the French industry to have had more specialized product ranges, less flexible production systems, lower craft worker shares and a more broken continuity between professions than German firms, in order to be less prepared for diversified quality production.

However, surprisingly, on a number of counts, quite the opposite was true. For a detailed account, the reader is referred to Maurice and Sorge (1989) whose results and interpretation underlie the following discussion. I can only underline some essentials here. It is the French machine-tool industry which, until today, has had consistently higher percentages of craft workers, fewer semi-skilled workers and engineers and, to match, less specialized production and smaller production runs. It appeared that, on all these counts, the differences between French and German machine-tool producers were diametrically opposed when compared with contrasts between French and German firms more generally, as referred to in the introduction.

Thus, the posited relationship between organization, human resources and business strategy arrangements seemed to hold up, but things were simply the other way round in the machine-tool industry. It appeared as if a clearly more artisanal part of mechanical engineering had done increasingly well in Germany, of late, although its business policy and social structure was less artisanal. On the other hand, the more artisanally structured industry in France was much less successful, and this happened at a time during which observers frequently noted a resurgence of differentiated markets, needs for production flexibility and a craft worker renaissance. These findings appeared hard, despite omnipresent matching and data interpretation problems. At first sight, it appeared impossible to make them compatible with the explanatory framework posited here.

However, results did not point in this direction on all counts. Professional careers in the French firms, more than in Germany, appeared to be segmented between production and design and development departments. Similarly, the physical distance between headquarter and development functions on the one hand and production facilities on the other was greater in an important case investigated by colleagues in France (Maurice et al. 1986). This is more in line with the earlier findings in the Franco–German comparison by the Aix Group (Maurice et al. 1982, 1977). It was also clear that the higher percentages of engineers in the German machine-tool industry were not largely due to a greater employment of engineers in production installations, which had been the core of the earlier Aix comparison. The German firms had very much larger engineer-intensive product development departments, and this explained most of the difference.

Even allowing for such a finding, which fitted earlier, more generally comparative, results better, the picture was highly bewildering, as were the findings of other studies. Perrin and Réal (1976), for instance, had been struck by the observation that machine-tool manufacture in France appeared less industrialized, less specialized by type of machine, more customized according to individual requirements, and was carried out in significantly smaller enterprise and production units, on average, than in Germany. Why, therefore, should the French industry not have done particularly well in an age of 'flexible specialization' (Piore and Sabel 1984)?

It would have been possible to explain away the fact that the Franco–German comparison came out the other way round in the machine-tool industry, in relation to the comparison of industrial work at large. That might have been a fluke result in a deviant industry. It was not possible to explain away the fact that the more artisanal industry should have done badly at a moment when one would have predicted that it should have been doing better than the German industry.

First, there appeared to be no such thing as a societal approximation of conditions supposedly ideal for a particular industry. This lesson might have been read out of the earlier comparisons where the identification of an ideal profile could only be done at the cost of some ambiguity, and where some deviant results were neglected. This last comparison gives much greater weight to the existing doubts. Whereas the structure of the workforce and business strategy in the French machine-tool industry were more artisanal, the continuity of professional careers between production and design made the German industry appear more artisanal. This might have led to the conclusion that there were separate dimensions to work organization, business strategy and human resources concepts, and that it was not possible to link these and sectoral evolutions to the extent believed earlier on.

Before dropping the more general hypothesis of a link entirely, we examined evolutions in the inudustry in greater detail. This furnished the second lesson, and it went roughly as follows. The fact that the, in many respects, less artisanal Germany machine-tool industry prospered in a period of differentiated quality production, in spite of being located in a society whose manufacturing industry is more craft-based than most, is no accident. Nor is the lack of success of the strongly artisanal French machine-tool industry during the same period. It was trying to function in a society where large batch or process production logics prevail. The German industry is thus relatively closer to the dominant societal arrangements, whereas the French industry has almost the opposite characteristics to those applying in its societal context.

The crux of the problem is that machine-tool producers tend to adopt strategies, organization and human resource policies which are almost the opposite of those of their clients. German producers face a multitude of clients in mechanical engineering who ask for flexible standard machines, and such clients are singled out both at home and abroad. French producers, on the other hand, face a multitude of clients who are traditionally more wont to require single-purpose or dedicated machines, so that they themselves are forced to be more artisanal in order to manufacture to individual specification.

This explanation seemed to pull together a number of diverse findings. The artisanal character of work in French machine-tool firms could be reconciled with the insight that a different logic prevailed in French manufacturing at large, in that special-purpose machines were made for mass production. The machines were more client-specific, precisely because the clients used them in a mass production context. As one would expect, customization varies with the special purpose nature of machines, and special purpose machines are the obvious solution to mass production problems. Yet, the distance between client and producer profiles is different in the two countries. In Germany, a more industrialized population in a basically artisanal industry, faces a client population with more artisanal traits; in France, a very artisanal population in an artisanal producer industry caters for a very industrial user population, so that the clash is more striking.

Technically, the most outstanding innovation during the period in which the French industry declined and the German one roughly managed to hold its own, was the application of CNC controls. Now, the German firms had apparently been more accustomed to making universal lathes, milling machines, etc., which the client could flexibly use in an 'ordinary' workshop context without much previous automation, use of earlier NC generations or elaborate and functionally separate work planning offices. The recent interests of a number of large-plant users of CNC machines with an existing planning bureaucracy, which entered into development specifications in machine-tool producing firms, were similar to the interests of new small-plant adoptors of CNC, at least more so than in France.

Here again, it is the relative uniformity of socially interpreted task requirements, the intertwining of craft and bureaucratic regimes, which counts in Germany, and which sets it apart from France. Hence, the German firms went in for a strategy where they tried to fit numerical control into machines in a more novel way, stressing the handiness and ease of manipulation of CNC on the shop floor. This appeared more appropriate, both in view of absent or weak production planning departments with many clients at home, who were perceived as a large pool of potential new users of NC machinery, and also of large-plant users with previous NC experience. The German machine-tool makers thus went into development of control systems more frequently than they had done in the past. In this way, they were more able to use their own knowledge and ideas about machining work to design novel control systems requiring less planning bureaucracy, and integrate these with machines from a user-oriented point of view, particularly a workshop point of view.

This would not have been so easy, had the German firms not had stronger contacts with technical universities and contract research institutes, and had they not been larger than French firms. The more systematic interpenetration of craft and artisanal backgrounds with technological engineering in Germany (Sorge 1985) meant that academic research and development was also more readily on tap for machine-tool producers. The decisive difference is therefore not simply that engineering is more craft-like in Germany, but rather that there is more reciprocal intertwining of the craft and technological elements. In the French case, it is not that there is an absence of craft tradition and presence — quite the opposite, as we have seen. The determining characteristic is that there is less interpenetration of the craft and technological elements, within education and training patterns, careers and work role sets.

The common denominator of all these arguments is that a manufacturing logic which is more artisanal and less 'industrial', is stabilized by its cross-fertilization with the opposed industrial and technological principles and methods, not by being separated from them. The long-term stability of the German machine-tool industry is the result of what almost appears to be a move against task-related contingencies, by trying to combine industrialization of machine-tool manufacturing with highly craft-infused engineering functions. Similarly, the French machine-tool industry was weakened, not by the weakness of craft elements *per se* but by its separation from the societal pattern of engineering work and education.

The German machine-tool makers essentially lost markets and employment before 1976, i.e. before the advent of CNC technology. The latter helped to stabilize the industry after a crisis, although the introduction of CNC was far from smooth. Quite the opposite holds for France, where employment and market losses, as well as take-overs and bankruptcies, happened above all after 1981, as a result of a more problematical conversion to new markets and techniques.

Whilst machine-tool producers in France had strong craft forces frequently working under conditions of responsible autonomy, the orientation of firms was more frequently directed at clients whose markets were more stable and uniform, requiring purpose-specific machinery, or clients with more polarized work organization and human resource concepts. Here, too, the artisanal form stabilized at the producers, partly due to opposite concepts prevailing with the clients, i.e. more polarized responsibilities and industrialized methods. No decisive reorientation of previous NC controls was carried out. This meant less involvement of machine-tool makers with CNC development. There were also cases of failing involvement, which was probably also due to the smaller size of the enterprises.

Although it may seem paradoxical at first, the craft-based and more artisanal character of work in German manufacturing in general, was stabilized by cross-referencing with a more industrialized machine-tool industry. Similarly, the more industrial, large batch and process industry context in French manufacturing stabilized the artisanal traits of French machine-tool producers in the post-war period. When this stabilizing element was weakened, so were the artisanal characteristics of the industry. The decisive weakness, we suggest, was that organization, business strategy and human resource patterns of the machine-tool industry in France were more remote from the respective patterns in the society and economy-at-large.

Conversely, the strength of the German industry, relative to that of France, has been that it is closer to a societal regime which allowed forward integration into control system development through cross-fertilization with research institutes and the electronics industry. It avoided having a passive dependency on these, and did not waste effort in searching for new customers and markets with a new CNC product strategy. However, this was a variant on the more traditional theme of producing flexible high-quality universal machines of a specific type.

Another complementary and suggestive finding was that the structural stability of the German industry throughout the transformation of technology and markets was rather great. There were only small changes in the composition of the work force, in average plant and company size, industrial concentration and forms of dependency and ownership. The French industry shows significant changes on all these counts, with moves to even lower plant size and they were already half that of the German companies, and higher concentration and dependency on industrial groups, frequently foreign competitors. There was also a strong increase in the numbers of technicians and engineers with more substantial education. As the French machine-tool industry declined, shrunk and was transformed, it seemed to stabilize itself in a more French way: introduction of new technology by rupture rather than by continuous change, a more high-tech product portfolio, more ruptures in professional career patterns, investment into high-calibre staff.

It is seemingly paradoxical that the German industry should have operated an earlier and more sudden conversion of product technology, by making very few structural changes on most counts. In fact, this is well explained by the approach which emerges here. These were changes which were in harmony with what now appears to be specific for machine-tool manufacturing in this country: intertwining artisanal and industrial modes of operation and job properties. In France, structural ruptures were apparently needed to bring about change since the distance between characteristics of machine-tool manufacture and manufacturing industry in general had become so large. On the whole, the continuity of French manufacturing seems to rest on the necessity of structural breaks and intertemporal ruptures every now and then, whereas in Germany, the capacity to generate changes in company strategies appears to go hand in hand with a high degree of structural stability.

In a nutshell, the lesson learnt from this comparison means that the recent quantitative success of a machine-tool industry reflects the extent to which the societally specific qualitative properties of a national sector are closer to, and articulated with, the qualitative features of wider societal arrangements and policies. It seems to be this relationship which counts, rather than the relationship of a national sector's properties to those of a supposedly universal or ideal pattern in the respective industry. The success of an industry appears to depend, therefore, on its characteristic infusion with elements that deviate from a supposed ideal.

It is tempting to generalize that performance is the result of innovatively combining supposedly conflicting task contingencies, and combining these with matching organization and human resource policies. To the extent that this is tenable, the machine-tool comparison may not be an isolated example. Other examples, from the French food industry to the Japanese motor industry, surely attest to combinations of opposed strategic elements, such as price competitiveness *and* quality of the product, economies of scale *and* of scope, as a basis of success. This interpretation helps to see the example of machine-tools in France and West Germany, not as an aberration within a generally valid pattern, but as a case that helps the interpretation of other comparisons. This can be developed in the following section.

Interpretation and Conclusions

Through the build-up of the argument from one section of the paper, and from one cross-national comparison, to another, it is hoped that the general treatment of societal differences in relation to company and sectoral performance can be gradually improved. The point of departure was to picture company and industry performance as a result of the extent to which organization, business strategy and human resources arrangements enabled a company or industry to approximate an ideal profile, which was thought to be characteristic of the type of operation or organizational task concerned. It was shown that, allowing for some loopholes and ambiguity, this neo-contingency framework worked reasonably well. Performance in the sense of the relative strength of a sector could thus be explained by closeness of fit

– within an ensemble of business policy, organization and human resources patterns identified as ideal, given a particular task contingency specific to an industry,

– and between this ideal profile and an actual company or industry profile which was seen to be conditioned by relatively task-unspecific patterns in the respective society.

This framework got into more serious difficulty, though, in a case where one might have assumed that it was eminently able to account for Franco–German differences — in the evolution of machine-tool manufacturing. This led to a modification of the approach. In the light of the last comparison, performance appeared to be dependent on the closeness of an industry profile to a societal profile, in terms of strategy, work organization and human resources, and on how intensively a specific set of organizations was linked with its economic and institutional environment. It also became clear that industry and societal profiles are likely to influence each other, so that any given company or industry profile is always subject to a societal effect. This is different from the effect being due to general task contingencies.

In the course of this 'societalization' — for want of a nicer word —, ideal profiles are blurred, just like the value of the neo-contingency approach. As it turns out, the societal effect cannot be reduced to a specific instance of the neo-contingency framework. It is very important for the survival and success of organization forms and human resource profiles in firms and sectors, that these are close to societal norms and articulated with institutions in the organizational environment. In that respect, consideration of goodness-of-fit in neo-contingency terms (with regard to generally defined task contingencies) gives way to looking at goodness-of-fit in societal terms, denoting the fit between specific and societal regimes. Clark (1987: ch. 1) had suggested that one finds a variety of patterns in societies, rather than a single one. This is certainly confirmed here, and is important to remember. At the same time, it also appears that dominant patterns exist within such a band of variety. The farther away variable regimes are from the mean or modal regime, the greater the tendency seems to be for such regimes to be weakened.

Now, this view is not purely relativistic, as one might think at first. It has a more abstract universalistic element, in that performance is explained by the institutional ability to reconcile conflicting contingencies. The last comparison illustrates quite well that the success of a particular business strategy rests on its own impurity, i.e. on the selective combination of opposing contingent task requirements. In this specific case, the relative success of the German machine-tool makers was due to a combination of productivity, product quality and innovation policies, of flexible specialization and economy of scale motives, and of artisanal and industrial modes of work.

This argument makes the transition from a contingency to an interactionist approach clear. Just as, in Weick's (1969) terms, higher-order motives and goals are 'enacted' by trying out concrete forms of action, business

strategies and organizational and human resource patterns are also specified and enacted to form a coherent whole, despite loose coupling
between them. Now, the performance value of an enactment appears not
to lie in it striking a near-ideal match, based on specific and pure contingencies and strategies. It seems instead to be based on the specific
combination of distinct and contrasting business strategy elements, both
with each other and with loosely coupled organization and human
resources patterns, that facilitate the combination of these distinct
elements.

Rather than assuming that firms striving for performance get 'stuck in the
middle' between alternative strategies and have to purify a strategic
choice, the present argument thus makes the point that success very much
resides in the ability to combine, albeit selectively, distinct alternatives.
Such alternatives to be combined may be, for instance,

– cost leadership *and* differentiation of the product range,
– production efficiency *and* product quality,
– flexibility *and* productivity improvement,
– economies of scale *and* of scope,
– mechanistic and organismic forms.

Wider societal arrangements have an important function within this
framework. Through providing relatively problem-unspecific institutions
in the widest sense (Berger and Luckmann 1971), 'normal' practices and
implicit mental definitions, they allow actors to combine seemingly contradictory or conflicting elements. They make them work out effective
compromises between distinct and opposed elements such as those mentioned above, and they may even reduce the trade-off between them.
Successful patterns are those which make the combination or speedy
adaptation of countervailing strategies feasible.

The argument is therefore not only more interactionist but also more
universalistic than contingency theory. It does not associate the 'one best
way' with very specific organizational forms and practices. It does point
out, however, that, in a very general way, performance seems to be due,
not to the match between specific task contingencies, strategies, organization and human resources, but to the capacity to link up distinct and even
opposed task contingencies and strategy elements. In that respect, the
societal effect approach is somewhat more universalistic, in the same
way, as is the recent organizational excellence literature (Peters and
Waterman 1982). As Lammers (1986) showed, this also reverted against
contingency theory by pointing out universal conditions for excellence,
which do not imply adaptation to task specific contingencies as a necessary condition of success.

This analysis sheds a different light on the earlier comparisons described
here, and it allows a more refined interpretation. The demise of the
British machine-tool industry analyzed by Daley and Jones (1980) is
probably not due to the underrepresentation and neglect of skilled workers in that industry, but to an increasing split between shop-floor occupation and technician apprenticeship, between engineering education and

worker skills in the society-at-large, and the ensuing distance between industry-specific and general patterns.

Similarly, the relative success of the West German automobile industry in Europe, of late, appears to be due to the fact that a combination of efficiency and diversified quality production strategies was permitted. This was achieved by means of a strong mutual infusion of artisanal and industrial modes of operation and professional habitus, rather than by trying to achieve a best fit with task contingencies applying to the automobile industry everywhere. This can help explain why it was the automobile industry that was more significantly successful in an age of increasing flexible specialization in Germany, compared to machine manufacturing — the all-time star of flexible specialization in most societies.

In the same way, one can explain why our CNC comparison of Britain and West Germany showed the most striking differences in the large company – small batch bracket. The more pervasive link of craft principles and industrial rationality in Germany allows, above all, the larger plants to be more flexible. This is so because the competitive advantage of such a link goes to a type of enterprise whose competitors in another economy are more weakened by a general societal regime that distinguishes between flexible plants — the small ones — and less flexible but more productive plants — the large ones. Hence, the contrast between Germany and Britain with regard to CNC use is probably not primarily that this happens less flexibly in Britain across the board, but that flexible and bureaucractic forms are more distinct.

The same basic argument also lends itself to a better explanation of Anglo–German differences in product applications of electronics than by invoking closeness of fit between product strategies and organization and human resources practices. In Germany, the affinity between sectoral and general patterns is greater in applications industries generally, and specifically outside the electronics and data processing/office equipment industries. A comparative advantage accrues to such sectors, and it occurs as product strategies are transformed through backward integration into electronics design and/or production.

A different comparative advantage is generated for Britain. Segmented engineering cultures in the society, with greater status differences, favour a focus on more specialized electronics and data-processing. Applications are also present in which industrial group size and the professional status of other specialists (e.g. aeronautical engineers) presumably make technical, occupational and organizational integration easier.

There are probably many more examples. Whether one looks at Japanese motor cars, Italian shoes, French dairy products, or American passenger aircraft, their competitive advantage seems to be based on elements of cost leadership and differentiation, economies of scale and of scope. A reviewer of the manuscript suggested that the picture may change after 1993 under changing conditions of a European market. My own view is that this will not be the case. Manufacturing in the European Communi-

ties already takes place in very internationally open markets. Harmonization of the institutional factors addressed here has not occurred on the
whole, despite the fact that economic integration of manufacturing
markets has already made the most important advances. It is more likely
that, under intensified competition, societal specialization along the lines
of institutionally founded competitive advantages will increase, and so
will the institutional distinctiveness of societies.

It may happen, as the reviewer also suggested, that regionally based
competititve advantage becomes more important. This can also be
related to the present framework by adding another level of analysis. For
instance, the vocational education and training system in Alsace — a
French region — has traditionally shown 'German' traits such as higher
status of apprenticeship in workplaces, which softens the differences
occasioned by that famous border along part of the Rhine river. It would
be far-fetched, though, to suggest that Alsace and Baden show more
similar societal patterns than, say, Alsace and Rhône-Alpes. It may, of
course, happen that regional patterns become more specific, in line with
regional sectoral, economic–structural or business strategy distinctiveness. That would be a variant, on the neo-contingency side of the argument which is tested here, namely that there is a relation between
institutional and business strategy and sectoral patterns. However, one
would also think that such emerging or reasserted differences do not
remove existing societal ones. The interaction of national–societal and
regional factors may increase the overall breadth and differentiation of
economic and institutional variety.

In essence, the theoretical conclusion can be summarized in the following
way:

1. Performance in an industry or sector is due to a correspondence
between an industry, sector or company specific profile and the societal
profile, rather than correspondence between a supposedly ideal profile
and the societal profile.

2. The interaction between societal and industry profiles implies enactment and continuous re-enactment, which includes innovation and
change of business strategy, organization and human resources.

So far, the initial hypothesis of the paper is therefore rejected. The
societal effect approach cannot be subsumed under the neo-contingency
framework. The former helps to explain phenomena with which the latter
has greater difficulty. This is not to say that the neo-contingency approach
can be thrown out whole-sale. Throughout, it should have become clear
that generic strategies, organization and human resources are reciprocally
related, even in the case of machine-tools in France and Germany. Even
if strategies and task contingencies have to be depicted differently from
on-going typologies, and even if the organization and human resources
patterns attached to these are subject to a societal effect, the fact still
remains that a basic contingency argument is inevitable. Wherever a
correspondence between markets, strategies, organization and human
resources is postulated or recognized, the argument which makes this

explicit is potentially or even necessarily of a neo-contingency type.

One might then say that the societal effect approach, although different from neo-contingency thinking, leads back to it. The fit between sectoral and societal regimes has a more extended explanatory power if the sectoral regime is not purely institutional, but can be related to the task environment prevailing in an industry. Only in that way can the gap between the notions of institutional regimes and task environments be bridged, thus making an explanation of societal competitive advantage possible.

This means that a theory about which organizational types and human resource arrangements fit which business strategies and task contingencies, is indeed called for. However, greater attention has to be given to combinations of different and opposed strategy elements and task contingencies, and to corresponding combinations of different organization and human resource arrangements. It does not appear sensible to deny a systematic link between the generation of tasks and business strategies on the one hand and organization and human resources on the other. Much as a contingency approach runs counter to universalistic theory and the societal effect in particular, it does supply an important functional baseline argument. One does not simply leave the baseline, as a countervailing argument is developed. Developing the counter-argument appears to bounce one back to the baseline, but the baseline has to be developed further, thus undoubtedly stimulating a new countervailing argument. An interactionist approach is probably best suited to integrate such conflicting approaches. One might even argue that it is designed to do precisely this and to provide an overarching theory which combines conflicting approaches and paradigms, in the way Morgan (1986) does, for example.

A third, metatheoretical conclusion would thus be that the application of one paradigm demands, in the final consequence, the application of its logical or methodological opposite, in order to make a more exhaustive explanation of the subject matter possible. Some would call this dialectics, other eclecticism, and some post-modernism (Cooper 1989). It seems important to note that the development and application of one paradigm in research and theory-building, leads on to its opposite. This is a firm plea in favour of heterodoxy rather than the drive to establish one orthodoxy by fighting another. Huck Finn probably would have agreed.

Note

*This paper was discussed in Group 5 of the EGOS Colloquium 1989 in Berlin. I am very grateful to group members for constructive comments and suggestions, notably Ali Dastmalchian and Bengt Stymne. As always, discussions with Marc Maurice and Wolfgang Streeck were even more suggestive than my own citations indicate. The two anonymous reviewers and O.S. have helped me very much to improve the first draft.

188   Arndt Sorge

References

Aldrich, Howard E.
1979 *Organizations and environments.*
      Englewood Cliffs: Prentice-Hall.

Argyris, Chris
1972 *The applicability of organizational
      sociology.* Cambridge (U.K.): Cam-
      bridge University Press.

Argyris, Chris, and Donald A. Schön
1978 *Organizational learning. A theory of
      action perspective.* Reading, Ma.:
      Addison-Wesley.

Auer, Peter
1988 'Neue Technik Qualifikation und
      Beschäftigung: ein deutsch-briti-
      scher Vergleich'. *Internationale
      Chronik zur Arbeitsmarktpolitik* 34:
      1–4.

Bamberger, Ingolf
1989 'Developing competitive advantage
      in small and medium-sized firms'.
      Long Range Planning 22: 80–88.

Berger, Peter A., and Thomas Luckmann
1971 *The social construction of reality. A
      treatise in the sociology of know-
      ledge.* Harmondsworth: Penguin.

Beuschel, Werner, Sabine Gensior, and
Arndt Sorge
1988 *Mikroelektronik. Qualifikation und
      Produktinnovation. Ergebnisse von
      Fallstudien.* Berlin: Edition Sigma.

Burns, Tom, and G. M. Stalker
1961 *The management of innovation.*
      London: Tavistock.

Campbell, Adrian, Arndt Sorge, and
Malcolm Warner
1989 *Microelectronic product applications
      in Great Britain and West Germany.
      Strategies, competence and training.*
      Aldershot (U.K.): Gower.

CEPII (Centre d'Etudes Prospectives et
d'Informations Internationales)
1980 'Spécialisation et adaptation face à
      la crise'. *Economie Prospective
      Internationale* Nr. 1. Paris: La
      Documentation Française.

Child, John
1972 'Organizational structure, environ-
      ment and performance: The role of
      strategic choice'. *Sociology* 6: 1–22.

Clark, Peter
1987 *Anglo–American Innovation.* Berlin:
      Walter de Gruyter.

Cooper, Robert
1989 'Modernism, post-modernism and
      organizational analysis 3: The con-
      tribution of Jacques Derrida'.
      Organization Studies 10/4: 479–502.

Cox, Joan G., and Herbert Kriegbaum
1980 *Growth, innovation and employ-
      ment: An Anglo–German com-
      parison.* London: Anglo–German
      Foundation for the Study of
      Industrial Society.

Daley, Anne, and Daniel T. Jones
1980 'The machine-tool industry in
      Britain, Germany and the United
      States'. *National Institute Economic
      Review* 92: 53–63.

Donaldson, Lex
1985 *In defence of organization theory. A
      reply to the critics.* Cambridge
      (U.K.): Cambridge University
      Press.

den Hertog, J. Friso, and S. J. B. van
Diepen
1988 Technological innovation and
      organizational learning. Milano:
      Paper for ISO Conference.

Horovitz, Jacques H.
1978 'Management control in France,
      Great Britain and Germany'. *Col-
      umbia Journal of World Business*
      (Summer): 16–22.

Jeske, Harald, and Klaus Kohlmeyer
1987 Branchenstatistiken über die Haupt-
      anwendungsgebiete der Mikroelek-
      tronik. Berlin: Paper for
      Wissenschaftszentrum Berlin
      (AMB).

Lammers, Cornelis
1986 'De excellente onderneming als
      organisatiemodel'. *Harvard Hol-
      land Review* 8: 18–27.

Lane, Christel
1989 *Management and labour in Europe.
      The industrial enterprise in Ger-
      many, Britain and France.* Alder-
      shot: Edward Elgar.

Maurice, Marc, François Sellier, and Jean-Jacques Silvestre
1977 *La production de la hiérarchie dans l'entreprise. Recherche d'un effet sociétal.* Aix-en-Provence: Laboratoire d'économie et de sociologie du travail, research report.

Maurice, Marc, François Sellier, and Jean-Jacques Silvestre
1982 *Politique d'éducation et organisation industrielle en France et en Allemagne. Essai d'analyse sociétale.* Paris: Presses Universitaires de France.

Maurice, Marc, François Eyraud, Alain d'Iribarne, and Frédérique Rychener
1986 *Des entreprises en mutation dans la crise. Apprentissage des technologies flexibles et émergence de nouveaux acteurs.* Aix-en-Provence: Laboratoire d'économie et de sociologie du travail, research report.

Maurice, Marc, and Arndt Sorge
1989 *Dynamique industrielle et capacité d'innovation de l'industrie de la machine-outil en France et en RFA.* Aix-en-Provence: Laboratoire d'économie et de sociologie du travail, document 89-1.

Maurice, Marc, Arndt Sorge, and Malcolm Warner
1980 'Societal differences in organizing manufacturing units. A comparison of France, West Germany and Great Britain'. *Organization Studies* 1/1: 59–86.

Miles, Raymond E., and Charles C. Snow
1978 *Organizational structure, strategy and process.* New York: McGraw-Hill.

Mintzberg, Henry
1983 *Structure in fives. Designing effective organizations.* Englewood Cliffs: Prentice Hall.

Morgan, Gareth
1986 *Images of organization.* Beverly Hills: Sage.

Northcott, Jim, Werner Knetsch, Bérengère de Lestapis, and Petra Rogers
1985 *Microelectronics in industry. An international comparison: Britain, Germany and France.* London: Policy Studies Institute.

Perrin, Jacques, and Bernard Réal
1976 *L'industrie des biens d'équipements mécanique et l'engineering en France et en Allemagne de l'Ouest,* Vol. 2. Grenoble: Institut de recherche économique et de planification, research report.

Perrow, Charles
1971 *Organizational analysis. A sociological view.* London: Tavistock.

Peters, Thomas J., and Robert H. Waterman
1982 *In search of excellence. Lessons from America's best run companies.* New York: Harper and Row.

Piore, Michael, and Charles Sabel
1984 *The new industrial divide.* New York: Basic Books.

Porter, Michael E.
1980 *Competitive strategy.* New York: The Free Press.

Porter, Michael E.
1983 *Competitive advantage.* New York: The Free Press.

Porter, Michael E.
1990 *The competitive advantage of nations.* New York: The Free Press.

Prais, S. J., Valerie Jarvis, and Karin Wagner
1989 'Productivity and vocational skills in services in Britain and Germany: Hotels'. *National Institute Economic Review* 89/4: 52–74.

Reitzug, Ulrich C.
1989 'Huck Finn revisited: A 19th century look at 20th century organization theory'. *Organization Studies* 10/2: 145–148.

Rose, Michael
1985 'Universalism, culturalism and the Aix Group'. *European Sociological Review* 1: 65–83.

Schreyögg, Georg
1980 'Contingency and choice in organization theory'. *Organization Studies* 1: 305–326.

de Sitter, L. Ulbo, (editor)
1986 *Het flexibele bedrijf.* Deventer: Kluwer.

Sorge, Arndt
1985 *Informationstechnik und Arbeit im
      sozialen Prozess. Arbeitsorganisa-
      tion, Qualifikation und Produk-
      tivkraftentwicklung.* Frankfurt a.M.:
      Campus.

Sorge, Arndt
1989 'An essay on technical change: Its
      dimensions and social and strategic
      context'. *Organization Studies* 10/1:
      25–46.

Sorge, Arndt, Gert Hartmann, Malcolm
Warner, and Ian Nicholas
1983 *Microelectronics and manpower in
      manufacturing. Applications of
      computer numerical control in Great
      Britain and West Germany.* Alder-
      shot (U.K.): Gower.

Sorge, Arndt, and Wolfgang Streeck
1988 'Industrial relations and technical
      change: The case for an extended
      perspective' in *New technology and
      industrial relations.* R. Hyman and
      W. Streeck (eds.), 19–47. Oxford:
      Blackwell.

Sorge, Arndt, and Malcolm Warner
1986 *Comparative factory organisation.
      An Anglo-German comparison of
      management and manpower in
      manufacturing.* Aldershot (U.K.):
      Gower.

Steedman, Hilary, and Karin Wagner
1987 'A second look at productivity,
      machinery and skills in Britain and
      Germany'. *National Institute Econ-
      omic Review* 87/4: 84–95.

Steedman, Hilary, and Karin Wagner
1989 'Productivity, machinery and skills:
      Clothing manufacture in Britain and
      West Germany'. *National Institute
      Economic Review* 89/2: 41–57.

Streeck, Wolfgang
1985 'Introduction: Industrial relations,
      technical change and economic
      restructuring' in *Industrial relations
      and technical change in the British,
      Italian and German automobile
      industries: three case studies.* W.
      Streeck   (ed.).   Wissenschafts-
      zentrum Berlin für Sozialforschung:
      Discussion Paper IIM/LMP 85–5.

Trist, Eric
1981 *The evolution of socio-technical
      systems. A conceptual framework
      and an action research program.*
      Toronto: Ontario Ministry of
      Labour.

Thompson, James, D.
1967 *Organizations in action.* New York:
      McGraw-Hill

van de Ven, Andrew H., Andre Delbecq,
and Richard Koenig
1976 'Determinants   of   coordination
      modes   within   organizations'.
      American Sociological Review 41:
      322–338.

Weick, Karl
1979 *The social psychology of organizing.*
      Reading, Ma.: Addison-Wesley.

Woodward, Joan
1965 *Industrial organization: Theory and
      practice.* Oxford: Oxford University
      Press.

[11]

Countries and Sectors

Concluding Remarks on Performance,
Convergence, and Competitiveness

*J. Rogers Hollingsworth
and Wolfgang Streeck*

O UR concluding chapter will attempt to draw together some of the insights of the sectoral case studies in this volume and place them in comparative perspective. We will begin by exploring the *relationship between sectoral and national factors* in the creation of industrial order, examining how they account for the diversity in economic governance regimes that the chapters in this book have uncovered. Next, we will turn to the differences in the *institutionalized performance standards* and in the actual economic *performance* of sectors and their governance regimes, and their relationship to the increasing *internationalization* of sectoral economies. Following this, we will discuss the prospects for *institutional convergence under competitive pressures in international markets*. In particular, we will address the possibility that internationalization may amount to *deregulation* of sectoral regimes, with national or local governance mechanisms being increasingly superseded by an institutionally "thin," neoclassical order governing the "world market."

The Character of Industrial Regimes: Country and Sector

Markets and corporate hierarchies, the two core institutions of both capitalism and economic theory, are but *elements of larger systems of social-industrial order* that also include, at a minimum, *communities* of shared cultural identity. *associations* representing common structurally based interests, and *state agencies* protecting and creating socially generated obligations and exercising public power with the ultimate backing of legitimate force (Streeck and Schmitter. 1985; Campbell, Hollingsworth, and Lindberg, 1991). Regimes of economic governance differ in the way in which these, and possibly other, elements are configured—in particular, the way in which market and corporate hierarchy relations are embedded in community structures, moderated by associational bargains, and conceded, protected, facilitated, promoted, subsidized, privileged.

270

prescribed, or, for that matter, outlawed by the state. The resulting institutional configuration governs economic transactions by, among other things, generating and sanctioning motivations for gainful exchange, setting prices, standardizing products, providing and maintaining durable relations between traders, enforcing contracts, ensuring hierarchical compliance, arranging for cooperation in the face of competition, and extracting contributions to the generation and maintenance of collective resources without which the rational pursuit of self-interest would be self-defeating or yield less than optimal results.

Regimes of economic governance vary with *spatial-territorial location* as well as between *functional-economic sectors*. Variation by territory occurs because social institutions are rooted in local, regional, or national political communities and their shared beliefs, experiences, and traditions. While localities and regions always were, and continue to be, important bases for distinctive institutional orders (Sabel, 1989), comparative social research has focused primarily on the *nation* as its principal unit of analysis. This is because in the modern period, crucial resources for institution-building—especially formal law and physical force—have come to be vested in the nation-state. Typically, as regimes of economic governance are configured and reconfigured, actors advance their interests by having recourse to "power resources" (Korpi, 1978) derived from their participation in national politics, from nationally shared cultural values, and from already existing nationally sanctioned institutional constraints and opportunities.

In addition, regimes of governance are shaped by *sectoral properties*, in particular the contingencies of *technology* on the one hand and *products and product markets* on the other. Products may be customized (printed circuit boards, ships) or standardized (television sets, steel); they may be homogeneous (milk) or heterogeneous (fine chemicals); perishable (milk) or easy to keep (steel), and so forth. Similarly, acquiring up-to-date technology may require large and lumpy investment in some sectors (automobiles, chemicals) and relatively little in others (machine tools). Also, technologies may be operated by unskilled (printed circuit board) or skilled labor (shipbuilding), or by manual (steel) or nonmanual workers (securities). It is important to note that all of these conditions may change, and that much of what happens in the politics of industrial sectors has to do with adjustment of governance structures to such changes.

A sector's technological and economic contingencies influence its *industrial organization*. By defining the pertinent economies of scale and scope—the extent to which newcomers face barriers to access, the trade-offs that firms confront between capital and labor intensity, the requisite composition of their labor force, etc., technological and market conditions affect, among other things, an industry's rate of concentration, the vertical integration of its member firms, the scope of their product range, and the extent to which they may rely on internal labor markets. Unlike what transaction cost economics and much of mainstream organization theory suggest, however, industrial organization in the technical sense of a specific combination between corporate hierarchies and market exchanges is only part of a sector's regime of governance. Technology and economics also affect the inclination and ability of capital and labor in a sector to engage in associative action, separately or together; the extent to which firms and workers may benefit from involvement in dense, communal "networks" of privileged, preferential trading relations; and their interests and capacities in relation to the state and the public sphere in general.

While identical technologies and market conditions do make for similarities in the industrial organization and the governance of sectors across countries, historically they have left room for significant national differences. *Just as sectoral differences in technology and market conditions give rise to differences in industrial order within countries, national differences produce different governance regimes within sectors* (Campbell, Hollingsworth, and Lindberg, 1991; Aoki, 1988). A important example is the different organization of the financial sector in the Anglo-American countries (Coleman, this volume) and, for example, Germany and Japan with their universal bank systems. Also, vertical integration and contracting practices in the printed circuit board industries of Japan and the United Kingdom differ regardless of basically identical technologies and market conditions (Sako, this volume); and the role of the state, the influence of shareholders, and the significance of market pressures in the governance of the Japanese steel industry are quite unlike what they are in the United States (O'Brien, this volume).

Similarly, while American machine tools are, or used to be, produced by large vertically integrated firms, German machine-tool producers are typically small or medium-sized (Herrigel, this volume); and German chemical firms tend to be more research-intensive than their competitors, their product range being more differentiated (Grant and Paterson, this volume).

Differences in governance within sectors are often recognizable as national differences in that they follow a similar logic across sectors. To this extent, they can be traced back to contextual, or "societal" (Maurice, Sellier, and Silvestre, 1984), effects that modify the impact of sectoral contingencies—just as these modify the sectoral manifestation of national properties. The impact of the national context makes itself felt in at least three ways:

1. Through *identical rules of behavior* created and enforced at national level that penetrate all sectors of a national economy regardless of technical and economic conditions. An example would be a country's antitrust law, or the influence national company law grants to shareholders over the operation of a business (Cornish, 1979; Bork, 1978; see the contrast among the American case and the Japanese, German, and Swedish cases, as documented in various chapters in this volume).

2. Through *identical factual conditions* facing all economic actors in a given country. Such conditions may be created by distinct nationwide institutions that affect, for example, the procurement of vital production inputs for all economic sectors. Thus, national differences in the organization of capital markets—as among the United States, Japan, and Germany—may require or generate nationally typical cross-sectoral practices in the governance of financial transactions. Similarly, nationwide systems of general and, perhaps more important, vocational education create similar constraints and opportunities for employers in all sectors of a national economy—see, for example, the role of the German vocational training system in automobiles, chemicals, and machine tools (Dankbaar; Grant and Paterson; Herrigel, this volume). A third example would be a national pattern of craft trade unionism standing in the way of long-term job tenure with high internal labor market flexibility.

3. Through *identical cultural and political resources* defining the constraints and opportunities under which individual and collective actors operate. Such resources determine, among other things, the extent of "trust" on which actors can draw; the degree to which socially imposed obligations can be invoked to regulate economic transactions; the acceptability and feasibility of formalization of exchange relationships; a governance regime's preference and capacity for standardization of transactions, and so forth.

The material in this volume allows us to identify a number of national differences that seem to generate consistent *cross-national variations* in the governance of sectors:

1. The degree and mode of *state intervention* in a sector seems to be determined almost exclusively by national factors, with only marginal impact of sectoral technologies and economics. There are some indications that sectors with small firms (see the chapters on the dairy, printed circuit board, and machine-tool industries in this volume) may attract direct state intervention more regularly than sectors with large, internationalized firms, like automobiles[1] and chemicals. A counter example, of course, is offered by shipbuilding, which in Japan, Germany, and Sweden received strong state support long before the "socially compatible" and heavily subsidized "management of decline" in the 1970s and 1980s (Stråth, this volume).[2] In any case, however, differences among countries appear vastly more significant. The American state stands out as a vigilant enforcer of antitrust rules, intensely devoted to protecting, and indeed permanently re-creating, the "self-regulating" "free" market against associative collective action and communal networks (Campbell, Hollingsworth, and Lindberg, 1991; Hollingsworth, 1991). At the same time, especially but not exclusively where "national security" interests are at stake, it is also capable of deep and highly bureaucratic regulation. While the British state shares the basic American commitment to the moral primacy and economic superiority of "the market," formal-legal regulation, in the spirit of nineteenth-century liberalism, is generally eschewed (cf. Coleman on the securities industry, this volume).

At the other end of the spectrum, the French state is known to be extremely interventionist, and in the two French sectors that were studied for this volume (consumer electronics and the automobile industry), it certainly lived up to its reputation. But while its state-centeredness sets the French system apart from the two market-centered Anglo-Saxon countries, it shares especially with the United States a fundamental discomfort with collective action outside the state proper (Hayward, 1986; Suleiman, 1974; Keeler, 1987; Hall, 1986).

Germany and Japan, on the other hand, appear as *facilitating* or *enabling states* that contribute to economic governance by encouraging—and even compelling—sectoral interests to organize and govern themselves. What seems to distinguish these countries from the three others is the presence *between state and market* of institutional and organizational resources, underwritten by, but not necessarily incorporated in, the state, that provide their sectors with *additional facilities* to govern their transactions.[3] Indeed, while direct state intervention seems to play a larger role in Japan than in Germany—see O'Brien (this volume) on the Japanese steel industry—in both countries the presence of strong potential agents of intermediary self-regulation may make direct state intervention dispensable (Okimoto, 1989; Johnson, 1982; Johnson et al., 1989; Katzenstein, 1989). This would explain the apparent paradox that countries like the United States and Britain, for all their emphasis on free markets, periodically have to go through surprising bouts of etatism unthinkable in postwar Germany or, perhaps less so, Japan[4] (Atkinson and Coleman, 1989; Rabin, 1986).

2. Like state intervention, *trade associations* are most likely to play a prominent role in sectors with small firms.[5] Again, however, differences in the character of the national state appear of greater importance than do sectoral factors (Schneiberg and Hollingsworth, 1990). The trade association is a powerful player in the Japanese printed circuit board industry where it is backed and encouraged by an enabling state; in laissez-faire Britain, the association looks pathetic by comparison. In machine tools, the small firms that constitute the industry in Germany depend greatly on their association. In the United States, machine tool manufacturers are typically not small, and as one would expect, associations are much less developed and significant. Indeed, it could be argued on the basis of Herrigel's chapter that American machine tool companies are large (and specialized) precisely because the American antitrust regime has made it impossible for them to survive *as small* (and generalist) *firms*, so that it may in fact be the absence of associations that accounts for the pattern of industrial organization, rather than vice versa (see Hollingsworth, 1991).

Large companies are less likely to need associations than small ones since they may either be able to survive on their own or able to cooperate without the help of a formal organization (see the chapters on shipbuilding and consumer electronics, this volume). Again, however, the prevailing pattern of state activity modifies the impact of industrial organization. In the German chemical industry, the close historical links between firms and the public educational system have traditionally been operated through a strong industry federation. More recently, the German state's environmental policy activism—combined with a general inclination of German regulatory agencies to press industries into some form of negotiated self-regulation—seems to have confirmed the importance of that federation. Environmental policy is of much lower significance for the British state, and the chemical industry association is weak (Grant and Paterson, this volume; Allen, 1989).[6]

National patterns of industrial relations and collective bargaining also influence the position of associations, adding a further national characteristic to the composition of sectoral governance systems (Schneiberg and Hollingsworth, 1990). In no country does the automobile industry form strong trade associations: Firms are large and few in number to begin with; foreign ownership is frequent (Opel and Ford in Germany, Ford in the United Kingdom); and in some countries (France, the United Kingdom, to some extent Germany) part of the industry was for a long time owned by the government. Even Germany conforms to the general pattern in that the trade association of its automobile industry is one of the weakest of its manufacturing sector (Streeck, 1989). However, Germany does have centralized, industrywide collective bargaining and a large, inclusive industrial union representing not just the automotive but the entire metalworking industry. As a result, automakers are active and leading members in the general employer association of the metal sector.

Similarly, industrywide collective bargaining ultimately led to the merger of the German Chemical Industry Association with the sector's employer association. In Britain, by comparison, the final disintegration of decline of industrywide bargaining in the metalworking sector was brought about by the withdrawal of British Leyland from the sector's employer association (see the chapters by Grant and Paterson and by Dankbaar, this volume).

3. Trust-based preferential trading relations, in spite of the technocratic-mathematical connotations of the term that is now commonly applied to them, are the least tangible mechanisms of economic governance. Japanese sectors are always suspect of being wired with invisible "networks"; so are, to a lesser extent, German sectors. In a very general sense, any trading relation where the personal identity of the trading partner—and, in particular, favorable past experience with the partner's performance—plays a role seems to qualify as a network relationship.[7] It is important to note that experientially based information on a trader's good faith is not the same as a common culture; it can be used for calculating the risks and costs of a planned transaction regardless of the presence or absence of a shared value system or social identity. While the latter may well result from repeated satisfactory exchanges (Blau, 1964), it does not have to in order for a "network" to crystallize and reproduce.

"Networks," then, may or may not be underwritten by culturally shared value orientations. To the extent that they reflect no more than the transaction cost advantages of repeated dealings with certified bona fide traders, they are likely to be present even in the most anomic of societies,[8] if only as a statistical probability that traders will prefer to treat with traders with which they have successfully treated before. Technological and economic sectoral differences may more or less encourage this.

For example, while automobile or shipbuilding firms have traditionally never traded with one another, chemical companies always had to for both technical and economic reasons, and from early times, on a global scale. It is likely that the resulting "trust" relationships, and the opportunities offered by frequent interaction, account for the chemical industry's infamous ability to build national and international cartels (Grant and Paterson, this volume). Similarly, the technology of printed circuit board making allows for a high degree of customization, which encourages dense, preferential relations between producers and customers, in principle even in an "arms-length" country like Britain (Sako, this volume).

How much trust can actually be generated by successful commercial transactions, and how much networks can support customization, joint development, and reduction in costs is a different matter and depends on exogenous conditions.

One way in which networks can be made to work beyond what "weak ties" (Granovetter, 1973) between rational individuals can sustain is through *pre-existing cultural-communal bonds*, often associated with common ethnicity or a traditional social structure of informally enforced social obligations. Thus, in a country like Japan or in certain regional economies—see the already mythical "industrial districts" in Italy (Beccattini, 1990; Brusco, 1982)—it seems to be primarily through such mechanisms that network participants receive important additional reassurance reinforcing, validating, and sometimes substituting for information gathered through direct personal experience that trading partners will not defect; that "trust" will not be abused; and that conscientious performance of contractual obligations will not depend exclusively on the other side's shifting perception of self-interest.

Alternatively, market-generated and individually based (and even individually owned) trust my be reinforced and underwritten by formal and politically generated, as opposed to traditionally inherited, institutions like associatiohs, collective bargaining, and state regulation. *Reconstructing community through politics* may be the only way for societies that have irrevocably moved beyond traditionalism fully to exploit the transactional economies of networks. In such societies, networks of privileged trading are likely to be maintained and activated through purposely designed instruments of collective action—like associations or government agencies—which, in turn, tap into the integrative dynamics of successful exchanges to develop their own organizational capacities.

Empirical research is therefore more likely to find networks to be present and effective where there is also a facilitating state or association. Herrigel's analysis of the machine tool industry in Baden-Württemberg (this volume) is a case in point. Also pertinent is Coleman's study of the securities industry (this volume)—a sector that would appear to be a particularly privileged site for network governance given its need for "trust" and the close cultural bonds both among traders and between traders and their customers. Coleman shows, however, that the industry's growth during the twentieth century, with its accompanying and inevitable increase in the number and diversity of market participants, required a continuous upgrading of self-regulatory networks through formal associative action under continuous and growing, albeit indirect, government intervention. In the process, self-governance moved from a voluntary through a negotiated to, more recently, a legally mandated stage—with industry associations turning into "private-interest governments" (Streeck and Schmitter, 1985) utilizing but also mandating network-like relationships among firms so as to increase their effectiveness as self-regulatory mechanisms.[9]

Networks, then, especially where they work, are more than just networks. Tendencies at the microlevel of social exchange toward privileged trading with previous partners are universal and occur in all settings: markets, hierarchies, associations, communities, and states. But to contribute significantly to the governance of economic relations, privileged trading must be insured and reinforced by institutions, from contract law to trade unions, which often happen to be nationally based. Different countries may thus be more or less able to utilize the social cohesion, generated by repeated successful exchanges, for the construction of sectoral industrial orders; in the limiting case, they may consider emerging networks as possible threats to the free market or to political liberty and try to dismantle them under antitrust and conspiracy law. It is only if "embedded" in a favorable macroinstitutional context that the microdynamics of exchange between individual actors can contribute to the governance of economic sectors.

4. States, associations, and networks regulate *market* competition and support as well as circumscribe the functioning of corporate *hierarchies*. Hierarchies are more important in some sectors than in others, reflecting transaction cost advantages of vertical integration under certain economic and technological conditions. But within sectors, the extent to which actors are allowed to, or must, rely on hierarchical means of coordination differs greatly by country. An instructive example is the German machine tool industry, which appears to have found hierarchical coordination dispensable, given the rich availability of associative governance in its country.

Moreover, hierarchies function differently in different countries. The Japanese style of informal, diffuse, collective, group, or, again, network-based organizational decision making in large companies, and its difference from American "macho-management," has often been noted (Aoki, 1988). Less attention has been paid to the impact of co-determination on large German firms (see, however, the chapters by Dankbaar and Stråth, this volume), where hierarchical authority is both constrained and legitimated, not by informal understandings and cultural obligations, but by legally based participation rights of an associatively organized work force.[10]

As far as *markets* are concerned, relations between producers and their customers would seem to be generally more market like in sectors that produce consumer goods (automobiles, yogurt, television sets) than in sectors producing investment goods (shipbuilding, chemicals, and machine tools). Once again, however, national differences are pervasive. Relational, or obligational, contracting with customers and, for example, cooperation in product design occur more frequently in the Japanese printed circuit board and the German machine tool industries than in their respective British and American counterparts. Similarly, early successful efforts at product customization have enabled German auto manufacturers to produce tailor-made automobiles for individual consumers in a way quite unknown in the British or French markets.

More importantly, firms in different countries are exposed to different product market pressures, reflecting different ways in which markets are defined and circumscribed by other mechanisms of governance. As in the growth period of the Japanese steel industry or the transition period of the French consumer electronics industry (O'Brien and Cawson, this volume), state agencies may intervene to suspend the imperatives of short-term profitability in the pursuit of longer-term objectives like technological leadership, progress toward which is not properly indicated by current operating returns. As the chapters in this volume demonstrate, markets are not only social constructs but would as "pure" markets neither function nor exist.

For example, a frequent pattern seems to be that of sectoral trade associations defining the arenas and rules of competition among sectoral producers, often converting price competition into competition over quality or innovation (e.g., machine tools and chemicals in Germany, or printed circuit board and steel in Japan). Such collective definition of arenas of competition must not be confused with elimination of competition. The latter is as likely to be brought about by free markets themselves, with their tendency toward industrial concentration requiring from time to time a restoration of competition by political intervention—for example, through antitrust action or government support for small firms. Also, as Herrigel's study (this volume) shows, the alternative to associationally instituted quality competition is not necessarily unregulated competition. In the American case, it was a highly competitive market regime that eliminated "generalists" and favored large, vertically integrated producers with high economies of scale, ultimately replacing market relations along the production chain with hierarchical authority and creating a need for continued antitrust intervention by the state.

National differences are perhaps most pronounced in the governance of labor markets and employment relationships, and in the way in which "pure" markets are institutionally modified if the commodity at stake is labor power. Since comparative industrial relations is a relatively well-studied subject (Bean, 1985; Poole, 1986), the chapters in this volume focus primarily on other aspects of sectoral governance. Still, they do suggest that nationally different institutionalized constraints and opportunities for firms in labor markets may have important consequences for the behavior of firms in other arenas, including strategic decision making with respect to product markets and products.

As Stråth's chapter (this volume) illustrates, Japanese shipbuilding firms operated under a strong *labor constraint* that forced them to expand their presence in other markets and sectors, so as to be able to keep their commitment to lifetime employment for their core labor force. Rather than releasing "redundant" workers, Japanese firms retrained and redeployed them, thereby confirming and renewing the paternalistic bonds with their work forces that serve them so well in their labor process.

Similarly, institutionalized pressures on German automakers to upgrade the skill level of their employees and win the support of a strong works council seem to have significantly contributed to their strategic decision in the 1970s to move upmarket toward higher value-added, more innovative, and more customized production (Dankbaar, this volume; Streeck, 1989). These and other observations suggest that, as with government intervention and regulation, the "right" kind of labor constraint may serve to suspend or counterbalance managerial preferences for short-term allocative efficiency and profitability *in a way that ultimately contributes to a firm's international competitiveness.*

National-sectoral regimes of economic governance *evolve over time* and constitute *historically grown social facts* for each new generation of traders. At any given point, economic actors are confronted with a legacy of local social institutions that are not of their making; not subject to their choosing; not in principle amenable to contractual reordering; and whose functional and evolutionary logic is different from that of a market or a formal-organizational hierarchy. At the center of this logic is the ability of governance regimes to impose *socially constructed collective obligations* on individuals, if necessary against their resistance.[11] It is only in the limiting case of a completely "de-regulated" market regime—which interestingly constitutes the normal, and indeed the only theorizable, case in standard economics—that institutional constraints and obligations are entirely and timelessly at the disposal of market participants. At that stage, they arguably cease to be constraints and obligations—just as the order that generates them ceases to be one that exists outside of the shifting volitions of its members.

In the real world, the "givenness" of an industrial order is visible in its ability to *socialize* its subjects into distinctive identities. While individuals "belonging to" a particular order may undertake to remake it—for example, in line with perceived imperatives of efficiency and "economizing"—in doing so they are forced to observe its present modus operandi and the constraints it imposes on them (in other words, to accept its "path-dependency"). This implies a funda-mental paradox for actors who expect their interests to benefit from liberation of markets and hierarchies from the encumbrance of other social or political institutions. To transform an existing governance regime in the ideal image of neoclassical economics, actors have to acquire and deploy cultural, social, and political power resources of a more-than-just-economic kind. Also, if successfully instituted, the resulting new order would, in violation of its own basic principles, have to be continuously watched over and enforced by strong noneconomic mechanisms of governance, among them very likely a strong state.[12]

The omnipresence in economic action of logics other than those of markets and hierarchies is indicated by the fact that even multinational companies continue to retain local-national properties that make it easy to identify their "home base."[13] According to Michael Porter (1990), both the structure and the organizational culture of a multinational firm represent a product of an inter-action between sectoral contingencies and the institutional environment of its country of origin. Multinationalization does not diminish the importance of the latter, as illustrated by the distinctively "German" characteristics of organizations like Bayer Leverkusen, Hoechst, and BASF; the "Japanese" makeup of Honda, Toyota, Sony, Mitsubishi, and others; and the identifiable "Americanness" of companies like Ford of Europe. This seems to confirm the idea, implicit in the extended concept of economic governance put forward in this volume, that the markets-and-hierarchies logic of industrial organization is by itself not sufficiently instructive for economic actors to organize their transactions satisfactorily. To close the Gestalt of a "sector" or "firm" and to know how to "do business," traders must be able to draw on additional *social rather than economic* instructions. The persistence of national traits in multi-national enterprises thus tends to confirm the idea that *purely economically driven economic behavior is underdetermined*, leaving fundamental gaps in the orientations of actors that must be filled by rules generated and enforced by more-than-economic social institutions. In the present period, most such institu-tions are still nationally distinct.[14]

Industrial Order and Economic Performance in an
Internationalized Economy

Sectoral analysis within and across countries suggests that the relationship between institutional arrangements and economic performance is far more complex than the neoclassical economic literature indicates. To begin with, there are alternative *standards of good economic performance* that firms within sectors may adopt, and there is apparently no "natural" rank-order between them. The type of performance that companies seek differs not only from sector to sector within countries but also between countries within sectors. For example, Traxler and Unger (this volume) demonstrate that the relative priority of *allocative, dynamic, and distributional efficiency* varies substantially among the dairy industries of the United Kingdom, Germany, and Austria. Similarly, according to O'Brien (this volume), the performance of firms in the American steel industry is typically evaluated in terms of their profitability, while the most important performance criterion for Japanese steel firms was for a long time their advancement toward technological leadership and their share in the world market.[15]

The chapters in this volume suggest that countries have a tendency to favor "typical" performance standards across sectors. For example, while there is some sectoral variation in the type of economic performance that American companies pursue, large American manufacturing firms tend to place strong emphasis on allocative efficiency and to give high priority to maximizing short-term rates of return on capital invested. As a consequence, American corporations work to maintain an environment in which capital and labor have freedom to move between firms and sectors. Or, put the other way around, given the high mobility and the resulting "unreliability" of production factors in the American economy—which may reflect a nontraditional, highly modern type of social structure—the pursuit of short-term profitability at the expense of other possible economic objectives would appear to be a rational response of firms to their environment.

On the other hand, countries whose institutional arrangements reflect or impose communitarian and political obligations and commitments, resulting in lower factor mobility, tend to give less priority to short-term maximization of profit. For example, Japanese and German firms in a number of sectors—and indeed their sectoral governance arrangements *in toto*—often seem to be oriented toward maximizing the pursuit of what Leibenstein (1976, 1978) has called X-efficiency (see Sako, this volume). In contrast to allocative efficiency, however, there are no readily available quantifiable measures for X-efficiency. X-efficiency involves complex social processes leading to long-term improvement in the skill levels of employees, and to better communication among actors engaged in producing, processing, and consuming goods and services. Investments designed to enhance X-efficiency tend to improve product quality and innovativeness in product development, and to contribute to the ability of firms to shift from one product to another in response to changing marketing conditions. Lower factor mobility and, perhaps, lower productivity may thus coincide with higher process flexibility and product innovativeness.

National sectoral regimes can be conceived as institutionalized constraints and opportunities for companies strategically selecting their performance standards in line with what their environment permits, rewards, and forbids. Different industrial orders favor different performance standards,[16] which out of the wide range of possible economic objectives that a sectoral regime emphasizes—allocative efficiency, high employment, use of high-skilled as opposed to unskilled labor, high wages, an equitable distribution of returns, a high long-term share in the world market, etc.—is not a foregone conclusion. Unlike in the simple world of economics, there is in real economies no preestablished universal standard toward which economically rational actors will "economize." Performance standards are, and have to be, socially selected and may differ in time and space. In particular, even under capitalism, "profitability" as an objective of economic activity remains less than determinative and unable to instruct economic behavior unless supplemented by additional criteria establishing, for example, whether profits are to be sought in the short or in the long term; what, at a given point in the product and business cycle, can be regarded as an "adequate" level of profit; or how long and in what conditions profitability can, or has to, be neglected in pursuit of partly or temporally conflicting objectives.

Whether or not an industrial order can sustain its chosen performance standard depends not on the latter's intrinsic economic "rationality" but on the system's environment and external relations. Interestingly, it is on this fact that standard economics today seems to place its strongest hope for an unambiguous, "objective" criterion of economic performance. More specifically, the hope seems to be that global competition in an integrated world market will ultimately replace the variety of national definitions of good economic performance with a general standard of universal *competitiveness*. Economists may grudgingly have come to accept that a country may for a long time be able to hold on to a non-neoclassical, and less than "allocatively efficient," institutional order, presumably employing "politics" of all kinds to suspend the "economizing pressures" of "the market" at the cost of a reduction in overall welfare. However, as national sectors are no longer isolated from international competition, market forces may be expected eventually to undermine and destroy "artificial" regimes that try to distort the "laws" of the marketplace. Internationalization of sectors, by introducing *competition over the performance of performance standards*, would thus adjudicate—and indeed lay to rest once and for all—heretic claims that a unionized economy with a low wage spread, high wages, and high employment stability may be "efficient"; that government support for selected industries may contribute to economic growth; and that firms with co-determination of workers and long-term "captive" investors may perform better than firms with unmitigated managerial prerogative that operate in a highly flexible capital market.

Again, however, sociological and historical analysis raises a number of caveats. First, the world market is no less an "instituted," socially constructed, and politically contested order than are national markets. Only in the limiting case, if ever, will its institutional structure and operation follow strictly neoclassical prescriptions. Even to the extent that it does, this is not "naturally" so, but is the result of collective political choice among nations in the arena of international politics. Powerful countries may create trade regimes that favor their industries and firms by rewarding their strengths and neutralizing their weaknesses and even force competitor nations to reorganize their domestic institutions in the image of the "hegemonic" country. In this respect, the construction of international economic regimes for trade, investment, and production is exactly analogous to domestic regime building in that both, by defining the cultural, social, and political rules under which economic transactions may take place, determine which firms with which strategies and capacities will have competitive advantage over others (Keohane, 1984; Krasner, 1983; Ruggie, 1983; Haggard and Simmons, 1987; Keeley, 1990; Gilpin, 1987).

Second, even under an international free trade regime where national markets are easily accessible to nonnational traders, there is no guarantee that this will favor firms whose domestic systems of industrial order are primarily based on markets and corporate hierarchies (McKeown, 1983). Indeed, the chapters in this volume offer strong evidence that institutionally rich domestic regimes capable of overriding or supplementing the logic of markets and hierarchies may help "their" firms prevail over competitors based in institutionally impoverished, neoclassical, market and hierarchy-driven governance systems. Examples are the competitive advantages that German firms draw from the German vocational training system—under which their workplace-based training activities are to a large extent institutionally governed rather than market-driven (Streeck et al., 1987); the positive impact of co-determination on the ability of large German companies to run advanced human resource policies (Streeck, 1984); and the positive consequences of the institutional suspension of the profit motive in the Japanese steel industry for its competitiveness at the international level (O'Brien, this volume).[17]

Not all of a country's sectors compete and perform equally well internationally. Countries typically succeed in some sectors but not in all. At the same time, they rarely have isolated sectors that perform well at the global level. National success tends to occur with clusters of sectors that are complementary or similar to one another. Moreover, firms within successful sectors are often concentrated within specific regions of countries where they are covered by similar governance arrangements allowing them, among other things, to utilize similar skills and to rely on the same kind of educational and research institutions. Spatial proximity also enables companies to have rich communication with their competitors and feedback from their suppliers and customers (Porter, 1990). Whether or not a country excels in a particular sector seems to depend on whether its national (or regional) institutions define, favor, or prescribe performance criteria for firms that happen to match current requirements of success in international competition. The same criteria, if imposed on firms in other sectors whose international environment is different, may well be counterproductive. It is also possible that institutionalized performance criteria that enhance the competitiveness of a company in one period may, as environmental conditions change, detract from it in the next.

The often superior world market performance of firms governed by non-laissez-faire domestic institutional arrangements poses a puzzle for countries with market-driven economies as they attempt to design the world economy in the image of their own domestic practices.[18] In general, the effect of domestic institutions on the international performance of a company's sector or economy seems often paradoxical, difficult to predict, and unintended. For example, a demanding industrial relations and training regime that drives up the costs of labor may, as shown by the German case, increase rather than reduce the competitiveness of a national economy by forcing its firms into a pattern of quality-competitive and highly customized production.

Similarly, the presence of seven automobile producers in Japan, and of five in Germany, was for a long time regarded as a liability for the two industries in international competition; this was based on the assumption that fragmentation on the supply side would prevent companies from attaining necessary economies of scale. It was only in the 1970s that the fierce competition in the German and Japanese domestic automarkets and the diverse and "oversized" design capacities associated with industrial "fragmentation" were recognized as sources of international competitive advantage. Also, when after World War II the German machine tool industry re-created its traditional, quasi-artisanal structure and its long-standing arrangements of associational governance, there was no way of predicting that fragmentation of product markets and the emergence of microelectronics in the 1980s would turn a pattern of industrial organization and institutional governance inherited from the nineteenth century into a source of worldwide competitive advantage.

As noneconomic domestic institutions are increasingly recognized as important sources of success and failure in world markets, economic competition turns into social system competition, and competitive pressures for economic rationalization become pressures for general social change. A country whose system of industrial order—under given "terms of trade" (i.e., given institutionalized criteria of success and failure in the international "market")—provides firms in a particular sector with competitive advantage is likely to turn into a principal location for production in that sector.[19] As a result, its share in global sectoral output and capacity will increase. The country will also be able to retain its system or governance, including its preferred performance standards.

Conversely, a country whose industrial order disadvantages firms under given conditions of international competition will either experience sectoral deindustrialization,[20] or will have to rebuild its institutions and adjust its performance preferences. The latter will as a rule be accompanied by redistribution of political power and economic advantage, between as well as within sectors.[21] Competition between industrial orders may thus cut deeply into a country's social and political fabric[22] and may raise fundamental questions about the *democratic sovereignty* of political entities that cover a significantly smaller territory than the market in which their citizens must operate.[23]

Competition, Selection, Convergence

Economic functionalism would expect that under a given international trade regime, national systems of sectoral governance that create competitive disadvantage for the firms under their control[24] will be reconfigured on an institutional "model" of "best practice." There are, however, a number of reasons why such *convergence*[25] may fail to occur:

1. While some industrial orders may be capable of restructuring toward a given high-performance "model," others may not. To the extent that the evolution of an institutional configuration is *path-dependent*—that is, conditioned by its historically grown structure—the number of developmental trajectories on which a system can embark is limited. Inability to copy a more "efficient" mode of governance may condemn a country to permanent competitive disadvantage in specific sectors—unless it can develop a functionally equivalent arrangement (see below) that fits its existing structure and raises its sectoral performance to a competitive level. Without change, a country may face the prospect that certain productions that are disadvantaged by its mode of governance will move to other countries. For example, one may argue that the present labor market regime in the United States—with its erratic school-to-work transition, a widespread preference for narrowly specialized job definitions, on average very short job tenure, and an almost complete absence of systematic workplace-based training—is both deeply culturally rooted and therefore unchangeable, *and* incompatible with the requirements of advanced manufacturing. Assuming that this was the case, one would *ceteris paribus* expect the deindustrialization of the U.S. economy to continue.[26]

2. Convergence also fails to occur if sectors under noncompetitive modes of governance manage to reorient themselves toward a market niche whose performance requirements match their institutional endowment. To the extent that the new niche allows for a satisfactory level of output and investment, *specialization* may thus offer a viable *alternative to convergence*. If a country cannot give its firms the institutional support required to compete successfully for product quality and diversity, its industries may instead move downmarket toward price-competitive, standardized production. Conversely, firms that are forced to operate under a "rigid" high-wage labor market regime that is resistant to convergence on more "flexibility," lower wages, and a wider wage spread may as an alternative to emigration move upmarket so as to earn the margins they need to pay their expensive workers. The result may be very different modes of governance coexisting in different national divisions of the same sector.[27]

3. A country's "dominant coalition" may be willing to pay a price for the preservation of a noncompetitive industry by granting it *protection from foreign competition*. The price of protection is, of course, paid by consumers who are deprived of access to less expensive or superior products, and by producers in other sectors who may lose their export markets as a consequence of other countries' retaliation. Treating a sector as "infrastructure" (Traxler and Unger, this volume) and paying for its preservation is not necessarily against a country's general interest, even though this involves a less than optimally efficient allocation of resources and serves the special interest of sectoral producers. A prominent example of a sector whose state-sponsored industrial order shields it against competitive pressures—and that is for this purpose isolated from international convergence pressures—is European agriculture. It is arguable that even with complete convergence on the industrialized, market-driven "best practice" represented by, perhaps, the United States, European agriculture could never successfully compete with American agriculture. It is also arguable that given the unpredictability of international trade policy, tendencies to employ trade restrictions for political purposes, and wide currency fluctuations, high publicly administered and guaranteed prices of domestic produce may be a reasonable insurance premium for a country to pay. Convergence on a superior mode of governance may thus fail to come about in spite of strong market pressures for "economizing."

4. Even in a free-trade international environment, a less competitive country may avoid convergence on a best practice governance mode by *forcing its superior foreign competitors to converge on its own institutional pattern.* If domestic change—for whatever reasons—is not feasible, if specialization is impossible, and if the costs and opportunity costs of protectionism are unacceptable, then a country may employ its international power to intervene in a competitor's domestic structure so as to undo its institutional advantages or impose on it the same handicaps that it itself faces. If successful, the country may in this way protect its "way of life" from "unfair competition." *Reverse convergence* of this kind is not as infrequent as it might appear—take the successful effort of the post–New Deal United States after 1945 to install free trade unions and collective bargaining in other countries, especially Japan and Germany, in part to saddle them with the same social costs that America had to accept. A similar and more exclusively economically motivated case would be the current Structural Impediments Talks between the United States and Japan, in which the United States tries to persuade the Japanese government, among other things, to dismantle the *keiretsu* business networks and a range of capital market practices that may have been an important source of Japan competitive advantage.[28] Reverse convergence—or *convergence on second-best practice*—may be demanded as a precondition for "free trade" where access to the market of a larger country is made conditional on the smaller country accepting foreign intervention in what effectively ceases to be its "domestic affairs."[29]

5. Convergence on a universal pattern of "best practice" can also be avoided if a country manages to develop institutional arrangements that, while *structurally different* from the leading model, *perform equally well* under existing terms of international competition. Indeed *functional equivalence* may be more frequent than outright convergence since institutional arrangements, in order to be stable and efficient, have to "fit" their larger societal contexts, which differ by country. A functionally equivalent arrangement would not upset its institutional context as much as, perhaps, a structural transplant. At the same time, confidence in the capacity of different structures to produce equivalent economic outcomes seems to decline with internationalization and competition, as national arrangements that in the past were regarded as equivalent are increasingly discovered to have survived only under the protection of, now dissolving, institutional mechanisms of market segmentation.

For example, while for a time the "societal effect" theory associated with the Aix-en-Provence school of industrial sociology tended to treat different national patterns of work organization in manufacturing as equivalent, they now regard them as sources of competitive advantage and disadvantage (Maurice, Sellier, and Silvestre, 1982). Note that the development of functionally equivalent regime structures may in a given case be as impossible as convergence on best practice for the same reasons of institutional path-dependency. Note also that protectionism, specialization, and reverse convergence can be employed to avoid the need, not just for copying a leading model, but also for devising functionally equivalent solutions.

6. Another reason why convergence on a model configuration of markets, "networks," corporate hierarchies, associations, and state authority may not be empirically observable is that the reconfiguration of an institutional order in line with given economic performance requirements is likely to be a protracted process. While in standard economics adjustment occurs instantly and without delay, empirical analysis must allow for *historical time*. Above all, this is because social institutions are less economically accountable than, ideally, business. Since they serve a diversity of functions, their performance cannot be unambiguously judged; there is for an industrial order no equivalent to what profitability is for an individual firm. Also, under a less than competitive regime, some firms may still be doing well, giving rise to hopes that things may get better without fundamental change. And declining industrial performance can always be attributed to a large number of noninstitutional factors, such as the business cycle, macroeconomic mismanagement, or simple bad luck—which may further delay institutional reform.[30]

Institutional inertia and delayed adjustment may also result from the agonizing difficulty of the *strategic choices* that have to be made. In principle, a country whose institutions perform unsatisfactorily in a given sector can always try to change the rules of the international trade regime so that they better match its capabilities[31]; or it may try to isolate itself from international pressures by protectionism. Exploring these strategies and ruling them out will typically require time. But even when domestic institutional reform is accepted as inevitable, there still remains the choice between adaptation of the leading "model" or development of an indigenous functional equivalent. While the former may run up against formidable and unpredictable contextual constraints,[32] the result of the latter is uncertain. Given the long feedback time required for evaluating the effects of institutional reforms and the opportunities this creates for opponents of change and proponents of alternative strategies, institutional responses to governance deficits can be expected to be systematically, and not just contingently, long-drawn processes.

7. Best-practice convergence is further impeded by *uncertainty* as to what exactly "best practice" is. For example, there was always wide variation in "Fordist" production regimes not only between but even within countries— consider the different "corporate cultures" of Ford and General Motors. Similarly, the way different Japanese auto manufacturers organize production is far from identical, leaving those trying to adopt "the Japanese way" wondering what it is. Moreover, leading regimes may evolve over time, so that what is "best practice" may significantly change while others are trying to emulate it. Also, since the economic effects of institutional structures cannot be easily measured and decomposed, no one can say unambiguously how much of a difference quality circles really make, or whether enterprise unionism is a central or a peripheral element of the "Japanese mode of production." In other words, there is an endemic uncertainty as to which out of a number of more or less fluid institutional provisions that together constitute an industrial order are actually the ones responsible for a regime's superior performance.[33] This allows for claims and counterclaims by proponents of different institutional reforms that are typically not adjudicable within the time in which decisions have to be made.

8. Pressures for institutional convergence are also mediated by *shifting performance requirements*, making the "best-practice" point of convergence a *moving target of uncertain location.* In the historical time needed for performance pressures to move divergent sectoral-industrial orders toward convergence, the technological and economic conditions that would have favored one sectoral order over another may themselves change. Such change can be expected to proceed only slowly, gradually and inconspicuously, and to be fully understandable only with hindsight—which is another way of saying that institutional adjustment takes place in an historical setting where the horizon is open and all that can be said about the future is that it lies ahead.

Taking unpredictable shifts in the point of institutional equilibrium into account, even a simple economistic, "best-practice" model of competition-driven convergence would be fully compatible with high observed institutional diversity, where progress toward convergence would be continually reversed by surprising changes in its required direction. For example, while present economic and technological conditions seem to favor governance arrangements that engender and support highly diversified and quality-competitive production (Streeck, 1991), there is no guarantee that this will not give way at some later time to a situation that calls for some other, as yet unknown, producton pattern. The present capacity of institutionally embedded, or governed, "diversified quality producers" to outcompete "mass producers" by making smaller batches of more customized products at not excessively higher prices is, to an important extent, an offshoot of the discovery, some three decades ago, of microelectronic technology in the U.S. weapons and space program. That discovery was largely exogenous to the dynamics of institutional evolution at both the national and the international level (and in any case had the quite unanticipated consequence that it placed the very country where it occurred at a disadvantage relative to countries that had less successfully and less completely adapted to the performance requirements of mechanized mass production—countries whose "lagging" institutions happened to be more congenial to the new technology's potential to narrow the price differential between standardized and customized products). Just as no one would have predicted microelectronics elevating "outmoded," pre-Fordist production regimes to the place of "best practice," no one knows what today's ongoing and as yet hidden technological, economic, political, and institutional changes may imply for the direction of convergence pressures in the next several decades.

Taking seriously the inherent dynamic and constitutive unpredictability of performance criteria and institutional "best-practice" convergence points, the most important property of a competitive institutional system may be a *general capacity to respond to a wide variety of continuously shifting performance pressures.* "Best practice," in this sense, would be almost the opposite of structural adjustment and dedication to a historically dominant set of performance criteria. Rather, it would consist in the preservation of a *rich "requisite variety" of self-reorganizing responses to newly emerging opportunities and constraints.* The essence of such a system would consist of its observable configuration at any given point in time, not in the underlying *reflexive intelligence* that has created and may undo that configuration—that is, in what the system, in any of its contingent structural incorporations, is *not* (Streeck, 1991).

It is important to emphasize that under any given set of competitive performance pressures, core capacities of a high requisite variety governance regime are liable to appear expendable or "redundant." This is due, among other things, to the inevitable tendency of actors to take present contingent conditions as constant; develop apparently experience-tested orthodoxies; and "economize" by devoting all available resources to the most urgent task. For this reason, *an institutional system's reflexive intelligence is difficult to build and maintain if the system is governed exclusively by rational-economic considerations.* This holds even if the pressures that place a premium on reflexive intelligence are economic in kind. Ultimately, competitive superiority in an unpredictable and rapidly changing environment requires a *culturally rather than instrumentally* based "higher-order rationality" that prevents actors from being excessively "economistic"; that obliges them not to dedicate "redundant" resources irreversibly to specific purposes; and that makes them adhere to a *logic of efficient nonallocation.*

To the extent, then, that the competitive economic performance of institutional arrangements depends on their requisite variety, the problem of convergence would have to be fundamentally redefined. If best practice consists in "cultural" preservation of potential structural alternatives of as yet unknown use, the *economic performance of an institutional governance system would depend on its successful refusal to become totally controlled by economic performance criteria.*[34] The problem of competitive survival may therefore not at all be to converge on some contingent "best practice." Rather, it may be to ensure that noneconomic values and institutions ramain resistant against the "satanic mill" (Polanyi, 1944/1957) of market-driven economic-instrumental rationalization. The difficulty, of course, is that such resistance cannot be successfully mobilized *for economic purposes and from economic motivations alone.*

Internationalization of Governance?

One way in which cross-national convergence of sectoral governance may be advanced is by international or supranational regime formation in response to *internationalization of sectoral economies.* While internationalization usually refers to growth of *product markets* and *product market competition* beyond national boundaries, there are other distinct but equally important aspects of the process, such as the following:

1. internationalization of *products*, as in the case of the "world car" of the 1960s and 1970s;

2. internationalization of *supplier relations* and *production chains*, with firms engaging in "global sourcing" and entering in international "strategic alliances" in marketing, production, or research;

3. internationalization of *finance markets*, as a result of which firms may obtain credit globally and outside the purview of national regulatory agencies. Being able to move their capital rapidly from one nation to another, investors may drive up the price they extract from firms, labor, and national governments for their cooperation in "job creation";

4. internationalization of *labor markets* due to higher mobility of labor between countries, which may undermine the control of national unions and governments over labor standards;

5. internationalization of *industrial organization*, where large firms locate their subsidiaries worldwide and in the process become multinational enterprises whose "corporate culture" may or not begin to cut across national boundaries.

The different dimensions of internationalization do not necessarily develop concurrently. In both form and extent, internationalization may vary vastly between sectors and countries. National dairy industries seem to be almost entirely unaffected (Traxler and Unger, this volume)—or only indirectly in that growing competition in other sectors may cut the resources that national governments give to support low-productivity domestic agriculture.[35] By comparison, the chemical industry has been highly international from its inception (Grant and Paterson, this volume). Similarly, whereas printed circuit board production is still largely local (Sako, this volume), internationalization of the machine tool industry varies strongly among countries, with French or American producers exporting a much lower share of their product than, for example, Swiss, Swedish, and German producers (Herrigel, this volume).

Internationalization of product markets, products, production chains, factor markets, and industrial organization gives rise to "networks" of relations among sectoral actors across national borders. As these become sufficiently dense and stable, they may serve as a basis for an emerging international governance regime distinct from the national regimes preceding it. In the limiting—as it were, "federalist"—case, this new regime will eventually become strong enough to "harmonize," unify, supersede, and absorb its constituent national regimes, resulting in *integrated supranational governance* for the sector as a whole. Rather than market pressure or, as in older theories of "convergence," technology, the driving force behind this would be a new layer of (international) institutions obliging previously "sovereign" national systems, and the actors within them, to submit to uniform and more encompassing regulation.

This event, however, is far from predetermined. Most international regimes exist on top of strong and heterogenous national regimes that do not seem likely to wither away soon. Basically, this is because markets and hierarchies are easier to internationalize than other governance mechanisms, especially those associated with public power. While internationalization of markets and hierarchies can erode the *effective sovereignty* of national states over sectoral economies, it does not by itself restore at a higher level the authority historically vested in national governments and create supranational public institutions with the authority to set and enforce common standards. As a consequence, economic relations that have outgrown national regulation are typically internationally governed by private, market or network-like arrangements embedded in—and partly shaped by—complex and dynamic relations between fragmented national and weak international industrial orders. This is why internationalization and international regime formation are today so often associated with *deregulation* (i.e., with "freer," more "self-regulating" markets than were typically allowed to exist under national auspices).

As integration of sectoral markets and hierarchies is not necessarily accompanied by integration of other institutions, it is bound to complicate the study of sectoral regimes of economic governance. Instead of assuming as a matter of course that economic internationalization will ultimately somehow result in global regime consolidation, empirical analysis has to be attentive to a wide range of interaction effects between international and national regimes, as well as among the latter, affecting the way in which internationalized markets and hierarchies are embedded in sectoral institutional orders. Three types of interactions seem to be of particular importance (Streeck, 1992b):

1. *Horizontal interaction among diverse national regimes in an internationalized economy.* In most internationalized sectors, national regimes of governance continue to figure prominently as sources of competitive advantage and disadvantage for "their" firms in the international arena. Although the chemical industry is highly internationalized (Grant and Paterson, this volume), the German vocational training system and the close traditional links in Germany between the industry and the universities are still important determinants of competitive outcomes on a global scale. Similarly, the competitive position of firms in the globalized consumer electronics industry of the 1990s is significantly influenced by nationally specific factors like the Japanese social system of production and the capacity of French "industrial policy" in the 1980s to convert its "national" into a "European champion" (Cawson, this volume).

More generally, separate national industrial orders in internationalized sectors tend to be subject to what may be called *regime competition*. Very little is known about the dynamics of this. What seems clear, however, is that in addition to more or less successful efforts to emulate international models of "best practice," competition may as such fundamentally change the political capacities and the internal makeup of national governance.

For example, as economic internationalization enables producers and mobile production factors to move between regimes and pick the one most convenient to them, the balance of power inside national industrial orders may tilt against less mobile parties, making it difficult to sustain and enforce social obligations like high taxes or a mandate on employers to share their managerial prerogative with their work forces. In this way, regime competition may make regimes more voluntaristic and contractual—in other words, deregulate them. (This, essentially, is meant when internationalization is described as undermining the "sovereignty" of national systems.) Deregulation and emulation of best practice may not always be the same, or only after fundamental and potentially painful adjustment of domestic performance criteria or of the international rules of the game.[36]

2. *Upward delegation of governance from national regimes to an emergent international regime.* As sectors internationalize, national actors may find it to their advantage to overcome their fragmentation by reorganizing into integrated supranational actors and submitting to supranational rules and regulations. This process, too, is uneven and contradictory, and may have a wide range of outcomes. Private traders in commodities and corporate property rights seem to require not much more than an internationally compatible civil law to start building international markets and hierarchies. Community relations, by comparison, are less easy to transfer to an international level, although they may newly emerge from specialized networks of mutually beneficial trading relationships. Associations, to the extent that they require state facilitation for their full development, may also have difficulties developing governing properties in an international setting. As a result, emergent international regimes are likely to be dominated by private arrangements among large firms, as in the chemical, financial, or consumer electronics sectors (see the chapters by Grant and Paterson; Coleman; and Cawson, respectively, this volume), with a strong role for informal networks and relatively little associational intermediation.

A critical question in the construction of supranational governance concerns the role of states and statelike agencies. National states, in response to the pressures of regime competition and the "tyranny of external effects" resulting from economic internationalization under nationally fragmented governance, may try to defend their "sovereignty" by collective action through international organizations. However, limiting the functions of supranational governance to the protection of national governance is difficult. Building a capacity for public intervention at the supranational level to compensate for its erosion at the national level may require national states to submit themselves to the authority of a new supranational sovereign, thereby formalizing the very loss of sovereignty they are trying to reverse. National states may not be willing to pay that price, nor may they have to, as long as they can use their remaining sovereignty to resist absorption into a unified supranational order. The result may be unabated regime competition in the public sphere of internationalized sectors—or, more likely, an uneasy coexistence among competing national and international states and quasi-states, permanent haggling over jurisdiction, and continuous oscillation between nationalism and internationalism in sectors whose markets, corporate hierarchies, and private networks may be increasingly integrated and unified.

An outcome like this would appear especially likely under national governments that pursue economic deregulation as a policy objective in its own right, and may hope to use a deregulated international regime to advance their domestic agenda. From their perspective, the dialectics of *sacrificing sovereignty in order to restore it*[37] would seem to make particularly little sense as such sacrifice would contribute to an unwelcome reassertion of public control over private markets. As the policy of the Thatcher government on European integration has shown, insistence on national sovereignty in an internationalized economy can be an extremely effective instrument for the political creation of a "self-regulating" market—just as neoliberal disengagement of public policy from the economy may be at least as effective in protecting state sovereignty as its transfer from national to international governments.

Whatever the relative role of national and supranational governance in an internationalized sectoral economy, national governments will always try to ensure that international regimes are compatible with their domestic practices and thereby confer competitive advantage on firms based in their countries.[38] Sometimes countries can rely on sheer economic, political or military power to shape the international regime to their image and to the benefit of their corporations. But it seems also true that countries have *ceteris paribus* more influence on how internationalized sectors are governed if they prefer private over public regimes, and favor freedom for markets and hierarchies over political interference. As again the Thatcher experience has shown, all that these countries may have to do is stick to "negative politics" and refuse to contribute to supranational public institution-building.[39]

3. *Downward authoritative modification of national regimes by supranational governance.* International regimes may acquire the authority to homogenize the national regimes comprised by them.[40] While this is the purest form of institutionally *mandated* convergence, and ideally suited to contain regime competition, it presupposes the growth of a powerful statelike international organization—which may be unlikely as long as such growth is controlled by the nation-states affected by it. More frequent seems to be *imposed* convergence under a common regime administered by a hegemonic country. An example would be the successful effort of the United States in the postwar period to build a free-trade regime among democratically organized nation-states with similar labor-inclusive "settlements" between capital and a moderate labor movement modeled on the New Deal and ensuring that firms from all countries had approximately the same social costs to bear as American firms.[41] The breakdown of this regime was accompanied by rising diversity, especially in the 1970s and 1980s, among the industrial relations systems of the three leading trading nations—Germany, Japan, and the United States.

How much homogeneity among their constituent countries international regimes require is not well understood. Nor are the conditions under which an international order may radiate into the national orders covered by it and change them. To the extent that international economic regimes do acquire formal jurisdiction over national public policies, their authority tends to be limited to the opening of national borders for international trade. In some cases, what has been referred to as "market-making" may even involve a measure of hierarchical intervention in national systems, to rearrange their rules so as to make them compatible with those of other countries so as to facilitate traffic of products, production factors, and property rights across borders.

Beyond this, however, there appears to be no guarantee that international regimes will develop a capacity to "harmonize" national standards, overcome regime fragmentation, and contain regime competition. In fact, as we have pointed out, such fragmentation and competition may be preserved or instituted on purpose in order to promote convergence in a "liberal," free-market direction, perhaps even in the name of a desirable diversity of national political institutions.[42] Whether and to what extent the institutionalization of a "self-regulating" international market will nevertheless ultimately require national actors, and in particular national states, to cede growing chunks of authority and sovereignty to supranational authorities—whether, in other words, there actually is such a thing as a logic of "spillover" from economic to political integration (Haas, 1958; Lindberg and Scheingold, 1970)—is a question that is presently being explored in the politics of the European Community. Here, the struggle over the "Social Dimension of the Internal Market" is essentially about the problem of whether market-making is possible in the long term without state-building; whether the former may in fact be pursued in the service of the latter; how far international regime formation can advance under conditions of fragmented sovereignty and competing political authority; and what the economic and social consequences may be of a potential supersession of public national by private international governance.

While the jury on this is still out, earlier assumptions that an integrated European economy can only be a "mixed," "managed," or "bargained" economy with strong integrated public governance are no longer being taken for granted after the experience of the 1980s (Streeck and Schmitter, 1991). That experience shows, in short, that the absence of an affirmative state at the supranational level, *whatever dysfunctions it may also have*, offers the advantage to nationalist governments that it is relatively compatible with national state sovereignty vis-à-vis other states, and to conservative governments and their business clientele in particular that it is supportive of neoliberal projects of general political disengagement from the economy.

Moreover, it would seem that the beneficiaries of a primarily "negative" mode of integration and regime formation have not only the interest but also the political power effectively to arrest whatever spillover automatism may in addition be at work in internationalized sectors and economies. In such circumstances, it seems premature at best to base predictions of supranational institutional development on assumed "functional needs" for the effective deregulation of national regimes through internationalization to be compensated by supranational re-regulation. While national states are not generally faring well in an age of internationalization, under given conditions their role and status may be maximized if internationalized sectors are governed primarily by private networks and if states make it their sovereign policy to spin off control over domestic economies to the "free play of market forces."

In several of the chapters in this volume (Cawson; Coleman; Grant and Paterson; Traxler and Unger, among others), the European Community figures prominently as an example of an emerging agent of strong, statelike, supranational public governance. Assessments differ as to its actual and potential impact on both economic actors and national regimes, and on the difference it makes, or will eventually make, for economic governance. Even in the strongest possible case, however, it is important to remember that the jurisdiction of the European Community extends only to part of the world economy. Today's global economy links Western Europe, internally integrated or not, to many other areas, in particular Japan and the United States.

For the German chemical industry, for example, Europe is no more than a segment, albeit an important one, in an effectively global marketplace and production system (Grant and Paterson, this volume). The same holds even more for large European financial institutions.

Finally, whatever may happen in Europe itself, there is no indication at all that the larger relationships that make up the world economy will any time soon be brought under the purview of anything only faintly resembling a supranational government. Even if the European Community were to grow institutionally beyond any reasonable expectation, the coincidence of internationalization of economic relations with privatization of governance in networks and corporate hierarchies, and the attrition this is likely to cause on public capacities for the correction of markets and the domestication of hierarchies, will continue to be a core problem for the governance of advanced capitalism.

Notes

1. Where state ownership of key manufacturers in Europe—a holdover from the age of extended land wars (France, Germany) and from 1970s-style industrial-*cum*-social policy (Britain)—has either disappeared (in Britain and, for all practical purposes, in Germany) or is on its way out (France).

2. To the extent that the direct role of the state in large-firm sectors has declined in the past decade, this may have to do with declining "effective sovereignty" of national states in an internationalizing economy—a theme we will address in the last part of this chapter.

3. A sector in which the apparent reluctance of Anglo-American states to employ "corporatist" self-regulation for public purposes is overridden by sectoral contingencies is the securities industry (Coleman, this volume). Here, the presence of strong networks among a powerful elite (investment bankers), the high technical complexity of the trade, the need for judgment and discretion, and a compelling self-interest among market participants in projecting an image of trustworthiness to potential customers forced and allowed governments to leave regulation to collective action of the industry itself.

4. For example, mandatory incomes policies. France and the United States have since their formative periods (which, of course, took place simultaneously under the influence of similar political ideas) shared deep-seated suspecions against "factions" and organized intermediary powers. Compare today the very low level of unionization and the indistinct role of political parties in the two countries. Britain is a special case in that older traditions of collective action have survived and prospered there in a pattern of "collective *laissez-faire*," without ever organically connecting with the constitution

of the state. Apart from sectoral exceptions, intermediary organizations thus were never in a situation in which they could have been turned into resources of public policy.

5. See Traxler and Unger (this volume), who show that trade associations are well developed in the dairy industries of most countries. This includes Britain where the Milk Marketing Board stands out as a rare example of a genuinely corporatist arrangement in that country. Note, however, that the other type of industrial association, labor unions, tends to be much better organized in sectors with large firms.

6. It must be added, of course, that there are three large chemical companies in Germany and not just one; and that the number of small chemical firms is much larger in Germany.

7. In other words, any transaction that is only marginally more personal and "particularistic" than a spot market contract. This would appear to entail the danger of the concept becoming all-encompassing.

8. *Nota bene* that Macauley (1963) discovered preferential and "relational" contracting among, of all occupational groups, traveling salesmen in, of all countries, the United States—and *not* in Japan, the favorite place of the "network" industry.

9. That networks exist primarily inside other, more "classical" social formations should not come as a surprise. According to Granovetter (1985), networks are present in both markets and corporate hierarchies, making them work better by compensating for their respective shortcomings. In Granovetter's world (where there are neither states nor associations), markets and hierarchies actually seem to dissolve into "networks," and it is difficult to conceive of anything social that is *not* one.

10. Both Japanese and German corporate decision making has been described as taking an inordinately long time by American standards, while also often resulting in qualitatively better decisions (Aoki, 1988; Katzenstein, 1989; Streeck, 1984).

11. As Coleman (this volume) points out, to the extent that the "deregulations" of financial markets in the 1980s involved the construction of a new, globalized industrial order, it was inevitably accompanied by far-reaching re-regulation.

12. This is the theme of Andrew Gamble's book on Thatcherism. *The Free Economy and the State* (1988).

13. The only example in this volume of a multinational corporation that seems to be abandoning its home base may be the Britain chemical company ICI. But this apparent cosmopolitanism may itself be a national trait, given the historical footlooseness of British capital and the notorious inhospitability of the British institutional environment to manufacturing industry. Also, a move from Britain to the United States is not one over a very long distance.

14. This is not to say that a company could not try to construct a worldwide, nationally indistinct "corporate culture" or could not succeed at it. The important point is, however, that the result would have to be a "culture" (i.e., would have to be morally in addition to economically based). Whether this is possible without alignment to a localized social and political community is an interesting empirical question.

15. Also see the different performance criteria of firms in the securities industry, depending on whether they are investment banks only or universal banks. How the industry is organized, in turn, depends entirely on the national regulatory regime. To the extent that international regulation mandates a particular performance standard, it may create competitive disadvantages for companies from one country in relation to companies from another (Coleman, this volume).

16. A particularly good example is the securities industry (Coleman, this volume) where national regulatory regimes give different priority to such criteria as profitability

and high returns on the one hand, and prudence and long-term stability on the other (Coleman, this volume).

17. Also see the important advantages the French consumer electronics industry derived from a traditional, etatistic industrial policy in the 1980s. As Cawson (this volume) points out, comparing the French to the British case, it is largely because of deep government intervention that there still is a significant French presence in the sector. The case is particularly interesting since it demonstrates the potential effectiveness of nonmarket national governance in an industry undergoing rapid internationalization in a highly competitive world market.

18. See Coleman (this volume) on the "deregulation" of the international capital market, in the image of traditionally Anglo-American sectoral regimes, and the potential incompatibility of the emerging international regimes with French and German practices.

19. However, it will attract inward investment only to the extent that foreign companies feel confident about their ability to operate in the country's institutional environment. See the almost complete absence of Japanese manufacturing in Germany.

20. See the shipbuilding industries in Germany and Sweden, or the automobile and consumer electronics industry in Britain.

21. An example is the effective takeover of consumer electronics production (and, in part, of automobile production) in Britain by Japanese firms, with the attendant changes in government industrial policy and, very importantly, industrial relations.

22. For example, a national capital market regime that makes a country's banking system subservient to the government's industrial policy objectives may have to be "liberalized" and "deregulated," with potentially major political and social consequences, if under new international conditions it can no longer attract enough capital for successful performance (see Coleman, this volume).

23. We will return to this theme in the final section of this chapter.

24. That is, in a "free" world market, regimes of governance that detract from the allocative efficiency of companies.

25. *Nota bene* that in comparison to the 1950s and 1960s (see Kerr, et al., 1960), expectations of institutional "convergence" among industrial societies today are only rarely based on assumptions of common, endogenous evolutionary tendencies. Usually these were located in the constraints imposed on social organization by modern technology. Today, technological determinism seems to have been superseded by a form of economic determinism, reflecting the vastly increased expansion and integration of the world market.

26. For more examples of production emigrating from an unfavorable regime, see the decline of the British consumer electronics and automobile industries (Cawson and Dankbaar, this volume). Certain models of "best practice" may be more suitable than others to being emulated, and national systems seem to differ in their ability or willingness to "converge" on foreign practices. While Japanese "lean production" is claimed to be universally applicable (Womack, Jones, and Roos, 1990), there have been no attempts to re-create German work organization or co-determination outside Germany, probably bacause of the dependence of these factors on supportive societal institutions outside the individual plant or enterprise. Moreover, while the United States and Britain seem to find it easy to accommodate Japanese "transplants" and even remodel parts of their own social system of production in their perceived image (for a strong note of caution, however, see Milkman, 1991), the few Japanese plants in Germany are said to have extremely poor labor relations.

Performance, Convergence, and Competitiveness / **297**

27. Of course, as the products sold in the two market segments cease to compete with one another, we would eventually have to speak of two different sectors. While Hyundai and Daimler Benz are usually regarded as belonging to the same industry, they may in fact not really be competitors.

28. The Japanese response is to suggest upgrading American instead of downgrading Japanese competitiveness. Realization of their proposals, however (e.g., elimination of the federal deficit, a higher savings rate, better education, and a more long-term orientation of American firms), would appear to require institutional changes vastly beyond the reach of any American government.

29. The underlying general problem, of course, is that of the allowable range of domestic regime diversity for countries subject to a common international regime—in this case, one of "free trade." For more on this, see below.

30. This was what happened in British industrial relations from the early 1960s on, when the incompatibility of "free collective bargaining" under "voluntaristic" rules with the postwar political commitment to full employment and a basic social wage began to become visible. Reform was tried not before the early 1970s, only to be rejected under highly divisive domestic conflict.

31. This applies even to small countries that can attempt to mobilize majorities in international organizations in favor of their interests.

32. As, for example, the introduction of flexible job allocation and redeployment between direct and indirect production functions in an environment of powerful craft unionism.

33. This problem is not just a methodological one for studies like ours, but also, as it were, an ethnomethodological problem for practitioners in the real world.

34. In other words, greed does not pay, or greed alone is not enough.

35. Also, countries may be forced to open their agricultural product markets by threats of retaliation against revenue-generating export sectors.

36. The possibility of a regulatory "downward spiral" as a consequence of regime competition, and of a Gresham's law-type replacement of high performance by low performance regimes, has recently been discussed with respect to the European Community (Mayes, Hager, and Streeck, in press).

37. Or of sacrificing national for supranational sovereignty, or external sovereignty in relation to other states for internal sovereignty over the economy.

38. See the example, reported by Coleman (this volume), of the potentially negative effects of a deregulated—or only privately regulated—international securities market on countries with a universal bank system and more traditional prudential standards.

39. Another possibility is that a country may force accelerated internationalization and deregulation on an international scale by deregulating its own industry (see Coleman, this volume, on the securities sector).

40. Which is what is called "harmonization" in European Community jargon.

41. By comparison, the possible outcomes of the Structural Impediments Initiative for the American and Japanese political economies could be characterized as *negotiated convergence*.

42. See the recent rise in the European Community of the concept of "subsidiarity." In some interpretations, subsidiarity refers to a general principle to accomplish common policies through diverse national regimes, interfering with the latter only to the extent that they are unable to comply with—narrowly defined—common standards. However, subsidiarity is also invoked to legitimize abstention from supranational standard-setting and a policy of *laissez-faire* in relation to national standards.

References

Allen, Christopher S. (1989). "Political Consequences of Change: The Chemical Industry." In Peter Katzenstein (ed.), *Industry and Politics in West Germany: Toward the Third Republic* (pp. 157–84). Ithaca, N.Y.: Cornell University Press.

Aoki, Masahiko. (1988). *Information, Incentives and Bargaining in the Japanese Economy.* Cambridge: Cambridge University Press.

Atkinson, Michael, and William D. Coleman. (1989). "Strong States and Weak States: Sectoral Policy Networks in Advanced Capitalist Economics." *British Journal of Political Science*, 19, 47–65

Bean, Roy. (1985). *Comparative Industrial Relations: An Introduction to Cross-National Perspectives*, London: Croom Helm.

Becattini, Giacomo. (1990). "The Marshallian Industrial District as a Socio-Economic Notion." In Frank Pyke, Giacomo Becattini, and Werner Sengenberger (eds.), *Industrial Districts and Inter-firm Cooperation in Italy* (pp. 37–51). Geneva: International Institute for Labor Studies.

Blau, Peter M. (1964). *Exchange and Power in Social Life.* New York: John Wiley.

Bork, Robert H. (1978). *The Antitrust Paradox: A Policy at War with Itself.* New York: Basic Books.

Brusco, Sebastiano. (1982). "The Emilian Model: Production Decentralization and Social Integration." *Cambridge Journal of Economics*, 6, 167–84.

Campbell, John, Rogers Hollingsworth, and Leon Lindberg. (1991). *The Governance of the American Economy.* Cambridge and New York: Cambridge University Press.

Cornish, William R. (1979). "Legal Control over Cartels and Monopolization, 1880–1914: A Comparison." In Norbert Horn and Jürgen Kocka (eds.), *Law and the Formation of the Big Enterprises in the Nineteenth and Early Twentieth Centuries: Studies in the History of Industrialization in Germany, France, Great Britain and the United States* (pp. 280–303). Gottingen: Vandenhoeck and Ruprecht.

Gamble, Andrew. (1988). *The Free Economy and the State: The Politics of Thatcherism.* Durham, N.C.: Duke University Press.

Gilpin, Robert. (1987). *The Political Economy of Industrial Relations.* Princeton, N.J.: Princeton University Press.

Granovetter, Mark. (1973). "The Strength of Weak Ties." *American Journal of Sociology* 78, 1360–80.

Granovetter, Mark. (1985). "Economic Action and Social Structure: The Problem of Embeddedness." *American Journal of Sociology* 91, 481–510.

Hass, Ernst B. (1958). *The Uniting of Europe: Political, Social and Economic Forces 1950–1957.* London: Stevens and Son.

Haggard, Stephan, and Beth A. Simmons. (1987). "Theories of International Regimes." *International Organization*, 41, 491–517.

Hall, Peter A. (1986). *Governing the Economy: The Politics of State Intervention in Britain and France.* New York: Oxford University Press.

Hayward, Jack. (1986). *The State and the Market Economy: Industrial Patriotism and Economic Intervention in France.* Brighton, UK: Wheatsheaf Books.

Hollingsworth, J. Rogers. (1991). "Die Logik der Koordination des verabeitenden Gewerbes in Amerika." *Kölner Zeitschrift für Soziologie und Sozialpsychologie*, 43, 18–43.

Johnson, Chalmers. (1982). *MITI and the Japanese Miracle: The Growth of Industrial Policy, 1925–1975.* Stanford, Calif.: Stanford University Press.

Johnson, Chalmers et al. (eds.). (1989). *Politics and Productivity: The Real Story of Why Japan Works.* New York: Harper Business.

Katzenstein, Peter (ed.). (1989). *Industry and Politics in West Germany: Toward the Third Republic.* Ithaca, N.Y.: Cornell University Press.

Keeler, John S. (1987). *The Politics of Neocorporatism in France.* New York: Oxford University Press.

Keeley, James F. (1990). "The Latest Wave: A Critical Review of the Regime Literature." In David G. Haglund and Michael K. Hawes (eds.), *World Politics: Power, Interdependence and Dependence* (pp. 553–69). Toronto: Harcourt Brace Jovanovich.

Keohane, Robert O. (1984). *After Hegemony: Cooperation and Discord in the World Political Economy.* Princeton, N.J.: Princeton University Press.

Kerr, Clark, John T. Dunlop, Frederick Harbison, and C. A. Myers. (1960). *Industrialism and Industrial Man.* Cambridge, Mass.: Harvard University Press.

Korpi, Walter. (1978). *The Working Class Under Welfare Capitalism: Work, Unions and Politics in Sweden.* London: Routledge & Kegan Paul.

Krasner, Stephen D. (ed.). (1983). *International Regimes.* Ithaca, N.Y.: Cornell University Press.

Leibenstein, Harvey. (1976). *Beyond Economic Man: A New Foundation in Microeconomics.* Cambridge, Mass.: Harvard University Press.

Leibenstein, Harvey. (1978). *General X-Efficiency Theory and Economic Development.* New York: Oxford University Press.

Lindberg, Leon N., and Stewart A. Scheingold. (1970). *Europe's Would-Be Polity: Patterns of Change in the European Community,* Englewood Cliffs, N.J.: Prentice Hall.

Maurice, Marc, Francois Sellier, and Jean-Jacques Silvestre. (1982). *The Social Foundations of Industrial Power: A Comparison of France and Germany.* Cambridge, Mass.: MIT Press.

Maurice, Marc, Francois Sellier, and Jean-Jacques Silvestre. (1984). "Rules, Contexts and Actors: Observations Based on a Comparison Between France and West Germany." *British Journal of Industrial Relations,* 22, 346–63.

McKeown, Timothy. (1983). "Hegemonic Stability Theory and 19th-century Tariff Levels in Europe." *International Organization,* 37, 73–91.

Macauley, Stewart. (1963). "Non-Contractual Relations in Business: A Preliminary Study." *American Sociological Review,* 28(1), 55–67.

Mayes, David, Wolfgang Hager, and Wolfgang Streeck. (in press). *Public Interest and Market Pressures: Problems Posed by Europe 1992.* London: MacMillan.

Milkman, Ruth. (1991). *Japan's California Factories: Labor Relations and Economic Globalization.* Los Angeles: University of California, Institute of Industrial Relations.

Okimoto, Daniel I. (1989). *Between MITI and the Market: Japanese Industrial Policy for High Technology.* Stanford, Calif.: Stanford University Press.

Polanyi, Karl. (1957). *The Great Transformation: The Political and Economic Origins of Our Time.* Boston: Beacon Press. (Original work published 1944).

Poole, M. (1986). *Industrial Relations: Origins and Patterns of National Diversity.* London: Routledge & Keagan Paul.

Porter, Micheal E. (1990). *The Competitive Advantage of Nations.* New York: Free Press.

Rabin, Robert L. (1986). "Federal Regulation in Historical Perspective." *Stanford Law Review,* 38, 1189–1326.

Ruggie, John Gerard. (1983). "International Regimes, Transactions, and Change: Embedded Liberalism in the Postwar Economic Order." In Stephen Krasner (ed.), *International Regimes.* (pp. 423–88). Ithaca, N.Y.: Cornell University Press.

Sabel, Charles F. (1989). "Flexible Specialization and the Re-emergence of Regional Economies." In Paul Q. Hirst and Jonathan Zeitlin (eds.), *Reversing Industrial Decline: Industrial Structure and Policy in Britain and Her Competitors* (pp. 17–70). Oxford: Berg.

Scheniberg, Mark, and J. Rogers Hollingsworth. (1990). "Can Transaction Cost Economics Explain Trade Associations?" In Masahiko Aoki, Bo Gustaffason, and Oliver Williamson (eds.), *The Firm as a Nexus of Treaties* (pp. 199–232). London and Beverly Hills: Sage Publications.

Streeck, Wolfgang. (1984). "Co-Determination: The Fourth Decade." In B. Wilpert and A. Sorge (eds.), *International Perspectives on Organizational Democracy: International Yearbook of Organizational Democracy, Vol. 2* (pp. 391–422). London: John Wiley.

Streeck, Wolfgang. (1989). "Successful Adjustment to Turbulent Markets: The Automobile Industry." In Peter J. Katzenstein (ed.), *Industry and Politics in West Germany: Towards the Third Republic* (pp. 113–56). Ithaca, N.Y.: Cornell University Press.

Streeck, Wolfgang. (1991). "On the Institutional Conditions of Diversified Quality Production." In E. Matzner and W. Streeck (eds.), *Beyond Keynesianism: The Socio-Economics of Production and Employnent* (pp. 21–61). London: Edward Elgar.

Streeck, Wolfgang. (1992a). *Social Institutions and Economic Performance: Studies of Industrial Relations in Advanced Capitalist Economies.* London and Beverley Hills: Sage Publications.

Streeck, Wolfgang. (1992b). *European Social Policy: Between Market-Making and State-Building.* Unpublished manuscript.

Streeck, Wolfgang, Josef Hilbert, Karl-Heinz van Kevelaer, Friederike Maier, and Hajo Weber. (1987). *The Role of the Social Partners in Vocational Training and Further Training in the Federal Republic of Germany.* Berlin: European Centre for the Development of Vocational Training (CEDEFOP).

Streeck, Wolfgang, and Philippe C. Schmitter. (1985). "Community, Market, State—and Associations? The Prospective Contribution of Interest Governance to Social Order." In W. Streeck and P. Schmitter. (eds.), *Private Interest Government: Beyond Market and State.* Beverly Hills and London: Sage Publications.

Streeck, Wolfgang, and Philippe C. Schmitter. (1991). "From National Corporatism to Transnational Pluralism: Organized Interests in the Single European Market." *Politics and Society,* 19(2), 133–64.

Suleiman, Ezra N. (1974). *Politics, Power, and Bureaucracy in France: The Notaires and the State.* Princeton, N.J.: Princeton University Press.

Womack, James P., Daniel T. Jones, and Daniel Roos. (1990). *The Machine That Changed the World.* New York: Rawson Associates.

Zeitlin, Jonathan. (1992). "Industrial Districts and Local Regeneration: Overview and Comment." In F. Pyke and W. Sengenberger (eds), *Industrial Districts and Local Regeneration.* Geneva: International Institute for Labour Studies.

[12]

Institutional Adaptiveness, Technology Policy, and the Diffusion of New Business Models: The Case of German Biotechnology*

Steven Casper

Steven Casper
Judge Institute for
Management
Studies, Cambridge
University, UK

Abstract

The German economy has been widely seen as failing to develop the commercial innovation competencies necessary to compete in new technologies. Starting in the mid-1990s, the German government instituted a series of new technology policies designed to orchestrate the development of small entrepreneurial technology firms. These policies have fostered several hundred new high-technology start-ups in Germany. This development represents an interesting challenge to prevailing institutional theory, which tends to view the characteristics of organizations as strongly constrained by the orientation of a number of key national institutional frameworks. Focusing on biotechnology, this article examines the relative importance of national institutional frameworks as opposed to sector-specific policies that are presently pervasive in Germany. Analysis of the new firms demonstrates that Germany's new technology policies have facilitated important extensions within the business system that have, for the first time, allowed the systematic promotion of entrepreneurial technology companies. However, the dominant strategies of market specialization and company organizational patterns found within these companies have been strongly influenced by incentives and constraints created by long-established national institutional structures. Technology policy has, however, promoted institutional adaptiveness by providing opportunities for firms to experiment with or reconfigure elements of relatively stable national institutional frameworks to create new business practices.

Descriptors: institutional theory, national systems of innovation, biotechnology, varieties of capitalism, entrepreneurialism

Introduction

Throughout the 1980s and early 1990s, the German economy was widely seen as failing to develop the commercial innovation competencies necessary to compete in new technologies (Soskice 1997; Streeck 1996; Casper and Vitols 1997). In the mid-1990s, however, the German government introduced a series of new technology policies designed to orchestrate the development of small entrepreneurial firms. By the end of the 1990s these policies had fostered several hundred high-technology start-up firms in Germany, many of which are pursuing strategies that differ dramatically from those commonly associated with small- and medium-sized German firms. These developments pose an interesting challenge to prevailing institutional approaches to organization that tend to view the characteristics of

Organization
Studies
2000, 21/5
887–914
© 2000 EGOS
0170–8406/00
0021–0035 $3.00

organizations as strongly constrained by key national institutional frameworks. Focusing on biotechnology, this article examines the impact of institutions on the development of entrepreneurial technology firms in Germany and the United States, and by doing so, it attempts to construct an analytical framework that can better understand patterns of institutional adaptation within the economy.

The strong role of government technology policies in the creation of entrepreneurial technology firms in Germany gives empirical support for a new perspective on the role of institutions in the governance of the economy — what I call the 'resource orchestration' approach. It suggests that government policies can develop financial subsidies, alternative technology transfer mechanisms, and other resources to create customized institutional frameworks to support particular sectors. This view can be effectively contrasted with the 'varieties of capitalism' theoretical perspective, which suggests that differences in national institutional architectures create distinctive patterns of industrial specialization across the advanced industrial economies. According to this view, German institutional frameworks produce obstacles to firms in radically innovative industries, but help the organization of competencies needed for a variety of industries that rely on continuous process innovations and product improvements within sophisticated, but established technologies (Hollingsworth and Boyer 1997; Casper et. al. 1999).

By making comparisons with the United States, this paper examines how national institutional frameworks have combined with resources and incentives created by Germany's new technology policies to encourage particular strategies of commercial innovation by entrepreneurial biotechnology firms. Evidence suggests that German institutions strongly influence both the organizational structures and innovation strategies of Germany's new entrepreneurial firms. State technology policies do not allow firms to circumvent economy-wide institutions, tending instead to promote institutional adaptiveness by providing opportunities for firms to experiment with, or reconfigure elements of, relatively stable national institutional frameworks to create new business practices. Indeed, while German firms face severe organizational hurdles when attempting to develop many radically innovative product market strategies that can be successfully sustained within the US institutional environment, they may develop new business strategies in some high-technology segments that cannot easily be sustained by US firms.

The article contrasts a number of technological characteristics and related organizational dilemmas pervasive within two core segments of biotechnology, therapeutics and platform technologies. Industry specialization data reveal that German firms overwhelmingly specialize on the platform technology segment of biotechnology, while firms in the United States, though also present in the platform technology field, tend to dominate the therapeutics segment. Explaining this divergent pattern of specialization is the primary empirical concern of the paper. While firms in each of these segments are 'entrepreneurial' in the sense that most of them are small, technology oriented, and have rapid growth potential, important differences exist in a number of organizational dilemmas that they face. These include differences in the financial risks, employee motivational problems, and the orchestration of adequate human resources. I then assess how sector-specific technology policies interact with national institutional frameworks to influence the ability of firms in the two countries to resolve the organizational dilemmas underpinning the two market segments.

To establish these points, the article is structured around three empirical sections, followed by a conclusion. First, to frame the debate and introduce key concepts, I discuss competing institutional perspectives on the sources of organizational structures within technologically innovative commercial environments. Second, I analyze technological regime characteristics and related organizational dilemmas of the therapeutics and platform technology segments of biotechnology. By comparing these with the United States, the final empirical section examines how German institutional structures influence the orchestration of organizational structures within entrepreneurial firms, and in particular how technology policies work within long-standing institutional arrangements to create comparative institutional advantages in the platform technology segment, but not in therapeutics. The paper concludes with a discussion of the implications of this research for the comparative institutional theory of the firm and its environment.

Institutions and National Patterns of Innovation: Two Perspectives

The 'Varieties of Capitalism' Perspective

Institutionalist scholars within the comparative political economy and organizational studies fields argue that variations in economy-wide national institutional frameworks encourage the construction of different organizational patterns within the economy (Crouch and Streeck 1997; Hollingsworth and Boyer 1997; Whitley 1999; Soskice 1994). Varieties of capitalism proponents suggest that contrasting patterns of market regulation and forms of business coordination within the economy create incentives that lead to differences in the organization of company-level activities.

Germany is often characterized as a 'coordinated market economy' (Soskice 1994) underpinned by a regulatory private law system. Non-market forms of business coordination are facilitated by the embeddedness of large firms within networks of powerful trade and industry associations, as well as a similar, often legally mandated, organization of labour and other interest organizations within para-public institutions (Katzenstein 1987, 1989). Businesses and other social actors engage in these associations to create important non-market collective goods, such as the apprenticeship system or the network of collaborative technology transfer institutes. German public policy relies on the legal system to regulate a wide variety of inter-firm and labour contracts as well as to sustain neo-corporatist bargaining environments through the delegation of issue-area-specific bargaining rights to unions and other stakeholders within firms (Keller 1991).

In contrast, the United States has developed a liberal market economy. Business activity is organized primarily through 'markets or hierarchies' (Williamson 1975), with much weaker 'non-market' or associational coordination across firms (Schmitter and Streeck 1985). Financial and labour markets are largely deregulated, and corporate law is primarily enabling in nature. Because courts refuse to adjudicate incomplete contracts, market participants need to specify control rights in contracts to as full an extent as possible or, when this is not possible, use extremely high-powered performance incentives to align interests within and across organizations (Easterbrook and Fischel 1991; more generally Milgrom and Roberts 1992). Table 1 outlines the main institutional differences across the two countries.

Varieties of capitalism scholars argue that national institutional framework architectures advantage different organizational structures and subsequent innovation strategies within firms. I will now outline the German system of economic coordination and control in more detail, using somewhat stereotypical descriptions that, as we will see when discussing the biotechnology case in more detail, have begun to change in recent years.

First, how are *careers* for scientists and managers organized? In Germany most employees spend most of their careers within one firm, often after a formal apprenticeship or, in the case of many engineers and scientists, an internship arranged in conjunction with their university degree. While there are no formal laws stipulating long-term employment, German labour has used its power on supervisory boards as well as its formal consultative rights under codetermination law over training, work organization, and hiring, to demand unlimited employment contracts (Streeck 1984). Once the long-term employment norm for skilled workers was established, it spread to virtually all mid-level managers and technical employees. One result of long-term employment is that the active labour market for mid-career managers and scientists is limited (see Lehrer 1997; Monks and Minow 1995: 287–295).

The 'stakeholder' model of corporate governance has important repercussions for patterns of *company organization* in Germany (Charkham 1995; Lane 1989; Vitols et al. 1997). Long-term employment and codetermination rights for employees create incentives for management to create a broad consensus across the firm when making major decisions. Because unilateral decision making is limited, German firms cannot easily create strong performance incentives for individual managers. As a result, performance rewards tend to be targeted at groups rather than individuals. Finally, most career structures are well defined in German firms and based on broad education and experience within the firm, rather than short-term performance. *Ownership and financial relationships* in Germany are strongly influenced by corporate governance rules. Despite the recent expansion of equity markets, Germany remains a bank-centred financial system. Banks and other

Table 1
National
Institutional
Frameworks in
Germany and the
United States

	Germany	United States
Labour law	Regulative (coordinated system of wage bargaining; bias towards long-term employee careers in companies).	Liberal (decentralized wage bargaining; few barriers to employee turnover).
Company law	Stakeholder system (two tier board system plus codetermination rights for employees).	Shareholder system (minimal legal constraints on company organization).
Financial system	Primarily bank-based with close links to stakeholder system of corporate governance; no hostile market for corporate control.	Capital-market system closely linked to market for corporate control and financial ownership and control of firms.

large financial actors (e.g. insurance companies) maintain a strong over-sight role on firms through their seats on supervisory boards and through continuing ownership or proxy-voting ties with most large German indus-trial enterprises (Edwards and Fischer 1994; Vitols 1995). Most German firms rely on banks or retained earnings to finance investments. Banks can often adopt a longer term focus, partly because they know that German firms may credibly offer sustained commitments to employees and other stakeholders to the firm, and can often closely monitor the status of their investments through their seats on the supervisory board or by means of other direct contacts.

Proponents of the varieties of capitalism perspective argue that German patterns of market coordination facilitate the creation of organizational competencies necessary for firms competing in sectors characterized by incremental innovation processes within established industries, such as many segments within the metal-working, engineering, and chemicals sec-tors (Streeck 1992). Deep patterns of vocational training within firms, con-sensual decision making, long-term employment, and patient finance are all linked to the systematic exploitation of particular technologies in a wide variety of niche markets, a strategy Sorge and Streeck label 'diversified quality production' or 'DQP' (Sorge and Streeck 1988). On the other hand, the regulative nature of German economic institutions, combined with per-vasive non-market patterns of coordination within the economy, create con-straints against the organization of industries that best perform within shorter-term, market-based patterns of coordination (Soskice 1997). The US institutional environment, due to its more flexible, but short-term ori-ented, system of company organization and finance, is seen as facilitating more 'radical' or product-based innovation strategies.

The general implication of the varieties of capitalism view is that national patterns of specialization are created by *comparative institutional advan-tages* (Soskice 1994). Short of fundamental institutional change, policies designed to promote the creation of industries that are not favoured by the country's institutional frameworks will fail. This leads to the conclusion that country-specific policies should be crafted to 'fine-tune' their particu-lar institutionally derived location advantages, rather than attempt to craft policies to compete in industries requiring institutional supports at odds with the prevailing logic within the economy.

The Resource Orchestration Perspective

While industry specialization patterns from the 1980s and early 90s broadly support the varieties of capitalism view (Cantwell and Harding 1998; Casper et al. 1999), recent developments in Germany seem to contradict it. During the later half of the 1990s, the German economy has experienced the beginning of what many commentators, particularly within the business press, see as a renaissance in the performance of its high-technology industries (*Wirtschaftswoche* 1998). The most drastic reversal of fortune is occurring in biotechnology. Hampered by a hostile regulatory environment for genetic research throughout the 1980s and early 1990s, in addition to institutional constraints, there were very few commercial biotechnology labs created in Germany, either by large established pharmaceutical firms or start-ups (see Sylvia 1999). However, starting with a liberalization of genetic testing regulations in 1993, and beginning in 1995 with the introduction of substantial technology promotion programmes, over 400 new biotechnology start-up firms have been created in Germany in recent years, some 150 of which are life-science firms situated around German university and public research institutes (Ernst and Young 1998b). Similar expansions of commercial activity have taken place in other technology sectors, in particular software and telecommunications (Casper et. al. 1999).

Germany's recent successes in high-technology industries have led to the formulation of a different analysis of the sources of commercial innovation within the economy, focusing less on national institutional determinants of innovation processes and more on sector-specific technology policies. The implication of the resource orchestration view is that the government should search for obstacles blocking innovation processes within particular sectors and introduce new policies to transfer resources to, and orchestrate the coordination of the necessary linkages within the innovation chain. The new sentiment is found in a recent report by the IFO institute, a respected voice on German competitiveness issues: 'If there is an "innovation crisis" in Germany, then this "crisis" is due … to a high degree of inertia in shifting capital investments, human resources, and existing ingenuity talents from traditional to new high-tech areas promising higher growth rates in the future' (Büchtemann and Ludwig 1997: 36; see also Audretsch 1985).

Following this logic, the German government has introduced a range of new technology policies designed to create clusters of entrepreneurial start-up firms. University spin-offs have been one of the strongest sources of high-technology growth in the United States (Rosenberg and Nelson 1994), and have therefore become a focal point for German policies. The small-firm spin-off dynamic that has become commonplace within the United States has failed to develop within Germany.

In Germany, the relationship between universities and the private sector is strong, but the primary technology link has been with large firms (Abramson et al. 1997). Under German law, professors own most intellectual property and generally have long-term relationships with established firms. Universities have thus had little incentive to establish technology transfer labs. Research within the bio-medical sciences and other 'pure' research fields has until recently been conducted with minimal attention to possible commercial spin-offs.

Taking careful note of these and other 'obstacles' to the establishment of small entrepreneurial start-up firms, German public officials have crafted a dense network of support policies for university-centred spin-offs. Government intervention has focused particularly on biotechnology. As part of a federally funded 'BioRegio' competition that began in 1995, 17 different German regions have created government biotechnology promotion offices. Technology offices generally aim to help scientists and local entrepreneurs organize every phase of start-up formation within the biotechnology sector. This includes the hiring of consultants to persuade university professors or their students to commercialize their research findings and help them design viable business plans, subsidies to help defray the costs of patenting their intellectual property, and the provision of management consulting and partnering activities once new firms are founded. Most of the BioRegio programmes have used public funds to create new technology parks and 'incubator labs' to house fledging start-ups in and around universities or public research labs.

The technology transfer offices created through the BioRegio programmes are also responsible for the disbursement of an array of grants, loans, and subsidy programmes created in recent years for high-tech start-ups. In 1996, the federal government, wary of criticisms of the lack of venture capital in Germany, decided to provide 'public venture capital' in the form of 'sleeping' or silent equity partnerships from federal sources (see Adelberger forthcoming). The public agency created to oversee this programme, the *tbg*, has provided, on average, over 200 million DM to new start-up firms over each of the last three years, with biotech firms being the largest recipient of seed-capital (some 22 percent of start-ups as of March 1999, according to officials working within the *tbg*). In addition, the German Research Ministry has provided over DM 150 million in grants for 'pre-competitive' research and development by start-up firms within three regions selected as part of the federal 'BioRegio' contest.

The German government also worked with the financial community to introduce measures designed to stimulate the provision of higher risk investment capital and allow technology firms to undertake rapid growth trajectories commonly seen within American technology clusters. These reforms included the creation, in 1997, of a new stock exchange, the *Neuer Markt*, with substantially less burdensome listing requirements than those that exist for the main stock market, and the introduction, in March 1998, of a change in corporate law that allows firms to buy and sell their own shares more easily (a prerequisite for stock-option plans commonly used by US technology firms).

These new technology policies are taking effect in an environment that has seen no major changes to the broader economy-wide institutional frameworks emphasized by proponents of the varieties of capitalism perspective. There have been no reforms to German labour or company laws. Compared to the United States or the United Kingdom, Germany is still primarily a bank-centred financial system; at the end of 1996, German market capitalization was only 21 percent of GDP, compared to 151 percent in the United Kingdom and 121 percent in the United States (*Deutsche Bundesbank* 1997).

When the success of recent German technology policies is taken into account with the overall stability of German national institutional frameworks governing the economy, the resource orchestration perspective contains a markedly different view of the degree to which organizational structures within the economy are embedded within institutions. It suggests that sector-specific support structures can essentially circumvent the 'normal' institutional incentives and constraints within the economy. If correct, this has important repercussions for the debate on the sources of organizational competitiveness and on public policy more generally. A 'hybridization' of a country's institutional framework could occur (see Lane 1999; Glimstedt 1999). Firms with strategies that are advantaged by a country's 'normal' institutional infrastructure could continue to engage those institutions when creating their organizational structures. Firms seeking to generate organizational structures in institutionally impoverished areas could do so by engaging specialized institutions created through sector-specific technology policies. Public policy might expand a country's range of commercial activities by designing a plurality of institutional support systems, targeted at the unique needs of firms within particular sectors. Table 2 compares the primary differences across the varieties of capitalism and resource orchestration perspectives.

The recent expansion of German biotechnology and other high-tech industries demonstrates that a simplistic, static version of the varieties of capitalism approach is inadequate to explain instances of organizational change within the economy. Patterns of industrial organization are adapting within Germany to the innovative challenges posed by biotechnology and other new technologies, and technology policies have played a key role. However, empirical research on the biotechnology case will suggest that national institutional factors continue to shape sharply the incentives and constraints faced by firms. Instead of viewing resource orchestration policies and national institutional factors as independent causal factors, analysis must investigate how sector-specific policies work via long-standing economy-wide institutions to promote institutional adaptiveness. To develop this argument, the following analysis adopts a firm-centred view, first describing a series of organizational dilemmas shaped by technological characteristics of different market segments of biotechnology, and then examining how national and sector institutional variables shape opportunities for innovation in these segments in the United States and Germany.

Table 2 Comparison of the		Varieties of Capitalism	Resource Orchestration
Varieties of Capitalism and Resource Orchestration Perspectives	Which institutions are important?	National institutional frameworks (labour market regulations, company law, finance and corporate governance laws).	Sector-specific institutions (technology promotion frameworks and subsidies, technology transfer, other sector-specific regulations).
	Focus on public policy	Should be focused primarily on optimizing the effectiveness of economy-wide laws and regulations.	Should be focused primarily on sector-specific technology policies.
	Pattern of national specialization	Patterns of 'comparative institutional advantage' will create stark patterns of industry specialization across countries with differing national institutional frameworks.	National patterns of specialization should not be starkly differentiated across particular innovation types, but depend on the adequacy of sector-specific institutional support systems.

Technology Regimes and Organizational Dilemmas within Biotechnology

When considering biotechnology, public attention has focused primarily on one segment of this industry, therapeutics. This is the area where spectacular advances are occurring in the harnessing of molecular biology and genetic engineering techniques to design new treatments against disease. However, industry analysts have long noted that, even within bio-medical related fields, there are several market segments, including diagnostics, contract manufacturing and — of particular importance here — a wide assortment of 'platform technologies' (see Ernst and Young 1998a: 5–6). Firms in this last segment create enabling technologies that are then sold to other research labs. Products include consumable kits used to rationalize common molecular biology lab processes, such as the purification of DNA and other important molecules. Platform technology firms have also developed a number of information-technology-based applications that have been used to automate many aspects of the discovery process within therapeutics. These include extremely high throughput 'combinatorial chemistry' applications to aid the screening of potential therapeutic compounds and the development of genetic sequencing and modelling techniques to aid in the quest to fully decode and understand the human genome ('genomics').

Focusing on the segments of therapeutics and platform technologies, important differences in patterns of sub-sector specialization can be identified between Germany and the United States. Germany's new biotechnology firms, with few exceptions, have specialized in platform technology areas, while very few firms have become pure therapeutic research laboratories. For example, a recent European biotechnology survey asked over 300 firms to identify all the market sectors in which they conduct activities. While close to 40 percent of European biotech firms are developing therapeutic products, less than 20 percent of German firms are in this field. Conversely, about 30 percent of German firms are developing platform technologies, compared to less than 20 percent for the European industry as a whole (Ernst and Young 1998 a,b). When German biotech firms were asked to list their areas of research activities, therapeutics came in fifth, ranked well below contract research and manufacturing, platform technologies, diagnostics, and 'other services' (Ernst and Young 1998b: 17).

More impressionistic field research yields a much stronger trend towards specialization in platform technologies than indicated in this survey data. As part of a research project on German biotechnology, I have attended round-table presentations by leading German biotechnology firms at European and German industry conventions, conducted interviews at several of the leading German biotechnology firms, and also interviewed technology promotion officers in the four largest German biotechnology clusters. During this research, I failed to identify any German firms that conduct pure product-based therapeutics research similar to the typical applied biomedical research models often used by US drug discovery start-ups. Of the two German firms that have taken public stock listings and the four that are currently in the run-up stage, all are platform technology firms (*Wirtschaftswoche* 1998). Most German 'therapeutics' firms actually conduct genomics-based research for pharmaceutical firms or therapeutics research firms on a contractual basis. These firms may someday develop medical research competencies along the lines of leading US genomics firms. However, so far, only one prominent German genomics firm, the Genome Pharmaceutical Corporation near Munich, has developed internal medical research competencies, but only after this lab was financed by a large 'pre-competitive' research grant from the Bavarian government in late 1998.

As the location of the world's overwhelmingly dominant biotechnology sector, many American firms have also specialized in platform technologies, but are also present in very large numbers in therapeutic areas. Over 100 publicly traded biotechnology firms exist in the United States, most of which conduct active therapeutics research (see S.G. Cowen 1999). This does not include dozens of privately held firms, not to mention the many hundreds of firms that have failed or lost their autonomy through merger and acquisition activities (see Florida and Kenney 1988; Senker 1996).

An interesting empirical puzzle is thus why German firms are specializing in platform technologies while firms in the United States gravitate towards therapeutics research. One way to understand differences across the therapeutics and platform technology segments is to analyze their underlying technological and market characteristics. Differences in the underlying 'technological regime' underpinning these market segments can be used to identify a series of organizational dilemmas created for firms operating within each segment. We can then assess how institutional environments in the two countries have impacted the ability of firms to resolve these organizational problems and, if so, credibly pursue innovation strategies in a particular market segment. To examine technology regimes, I draw on a typology developed by Breschi, Malerba, and Orsenigo (Breschi and

Malerba 1997; Malerba and Orsenigo 1993). They examine four broad characteristics: opportunity conditions, levels of appropriability, technology trajectories within the industry (also known as 'cumulativeness'), and the nature of technological knowledge. I will now examine each of these areas, paying particular attention to the degree of cumulativeness and the nature of knowledge, characteristics where important differences exist across the two sub-sectors.

Opportunity conditions correspond to the likelihood that particular investments will yield commercially relevant innovations, and are generally high for both therapeutics and platform technology firms. Intellectual property in therapeutics is very fragmented across literally hundreds of separate research trajectories. For example, while scientists have uncovered tens of thousands of possible genetic targets within the human genome, the entire collection of drugs on the market today act through only 400 targets (S.G. Cowen 1998: 23). Though patents for therapeutic products are strong, intellectual property across these separate research clusters has not generally overlapped in such a way as to 'block' on-going research within competing research clusters. For example, in an extensive mapping of research clusters working to develop therapies for Alzeihmer's Disease, Pennan (1996) identified some 15 distinct research programmes racing against each other.

A similar situation exists within the platform technology field. Billion dollar plus annual research and development budgets of large pharmaceutical firms, combined with the smaller budgets of thousands of biotech start-ups and non-profit medical research labs create a vast market for products that simplify bio-medical research processes. Over time, the platform technology field might become more concentrated as a smaller number of truly effective technological approaches develop and are exploited by early innovators and consolidated into integrated 'solutions' that are sold to labs. However, because the segment has only developed into a major market niche in the last few years, it is still at the beginning of such a cycle, in which the opportunities for entry are extremely broad.

The *level of appropriability* relates to the ease with which the firm can capture rents created through innovation, and ranges from high to low (see Teece 1986). Appropriability conditions are often problematic for firms in both the therapeutics and platform technology segments, though they are somewhat offset by the huge size of potential markets for products created by each type of firm. While therapeutic firms can protect most intellectual property through patents, the expensive, long-term nature of drug development and the necessity for most firms to form alliances with pharmaceutical firms creates appropriability risk (McKlevey 1997). Within the pharmaceutical industry, only about 20 percent of total research and discovery expenditures are spent on the discovery of new therapeutic compounds. The remaining 80 percent of R&D is spent on the development of candidate compounds, including highly specialized activities such as several stages of preclinical and clinical trials and the submission of complex statistical studies necessary for regulatory approval. Lacking these competencies, virtually all drugs developed by biotechnology firms have been brought to market through alliances with established pharmaceutical companies. Therapeutic firms must manage risky, long-term alliances with pharmaceutical firms in a way that does not lead to a substantial transfer of rents generated by the firm's discoveries to integrated pharmaceutical firms.

Platform technology firms also face appropriability risks. Intellectual property is not as strong as that within therapeutics, meaning that several firms usually enter technology areas with particularly lucrative returns. Within the lab technology area, services seen as exotic a few years ago, such as the cloning of target strains of DNA for lab work (PCR), are now widely available. A similar phenomenon has occurred within the genomics field. Now, only a few years later, providing access to libraries of genetic sequences, a high-profile activity during the mid 1990s, has become a readily available service. The high profile (and value-added firms) today are moving into 'functional genomics', which attempts to embed particular genetic sequences with indicators of the biological activities associated with particular genes. Competition within particular product markets allows pharmaceutical firms and other major customers to negotiate lower prices for services than those expected by the biotechnology firm, especially for high-volume purchases.

A third technological characteristic, the *degree of cumulativeness*, relates to the volatility of technology within the firm's field of research. Technological trajectories vary on a scale from discrete to cumulative (see Breschi and Malerba 1997: 135–136). Discrete technological trajectories have two components. First, the competencies needed to organize sequential research projects are not stable. This implies that in a series of research projects necessary to bring a product to market, it is often difficult for a firm to foresee the particular competencies it will need to organize research project 'B' before the results of project 'A' are completed. Second, due to the radical nature of many emerging technologies, a high percentage of research projects will fail to meet their goals. Cumulative research trajectories, in contrast, are not competence destroying. The risk of particular research projects failing is lower, and competencies tend to remain stable and predictable across the sequence of projects leading to the development of saleable products.

Technological trajectories within therapeutics are extremely volatile. Firms are often constituted on the basis of theoretical expertise pertaining to particular therapeutic research areas, and then develop or acquire any number of particular application technologies needed to pursue projects as research progresses. Ethnographic accounts consistently document the widely changing course of therapeutic firm research activities over time, which often leads to repeated changes in the competence structure of the firm (see Werth 1993; Rabinow 1996). Failure rates and time horizons, as seen in Table 3, are high throughout the drug development process. No approval probability statistics exist for the discovery stage, as results here are wildly uncertain and varied across firms with particular research approaches. While technological uncertainty is a prime determinant of the high failure rate of particular projects, it is also increased by 'racing' activity across several firms (or networks of several firms) to obtain key research results (see Pennan 1996).

Platform technology firms develop more stable or cumulative technologies. Most firms begin with expertise in one or more process technologies that can be applied to a particular group of common molecular biology research activities. They then hope to expand into related areas on a sequential basis based on learning externalities generated through the completion of particular projects. For example, one of the first and the most successful German biotechnology firms, Qiagen, was founded in 1984 on the basis of the founder's doctoral thesis on the creation of nucleic acid filtration devices. Over the last 15 years, the firm has generated over 225 products that largely represent extensions of this initial technology. While competition is also fierce in the platform technology segment, the importance of service-oriented end-user relationships leads to more market fragmentation across firms, muting the winner-take-all atmosphere generated within many research races within therapeutics.

A final technological characteristic concerns the type of technological knowledge that is generated through research and development projects, the *knowledge property* (see Winter 1987). Once a particular research project is completed, a key question is whether the value of the results can be assessed by the firm's management and other outsiders to the particular project. If research results can be *codified*, then financiers and management can more easily monitor the activities of scientists and technicians within the firm. If research results remain *tacit*, then it becomes difficult for management and outsiders of the firm to assess the value of research results over the short to medium term, until projects are brought to market. Furthermore, work groups hold high amounts of 'know-how' that is difficult to transfer to other employees or leverage as intellectual property for financial investments.

Most knowledge within therapeutics research quickly becomes codified and assessable to participants across a research field. At the end of each 'race' or research stage the winners develop codified intellectual property in the form of patents or journal articles which, we will see, is often leveraged for additional research funding or sold on the market. In addition to scientific publications and patent documents, a number of industry analysts publish newsletters and quarterly 'score-cards' tracking the progress of particular firms. The codified nature of major research results, combined with the existence of large pre-existing markets for most major therapeutic projects, conduces towards the establishment of what Storper and Salais (1997) label 'generic' innovation strategies.

Platform technology firms often generate considerable long-term tacit knowledge within research groups. This is driven by the more cumulative nature of technological advance. Platform technology firms often generate revenues through serial projects that apply the firm's core technologies to help solve customers' particular problems. Incremental learning processes

900   Steven Casper

Table 3
Time Horizon and
Approval Rates
for Therapeutic
Drug
Development

Drug Development Stage	Time Horizon (in years)	Probability of Approval (in %)
Discovery	2–3	
Pre-clinical	1	5*
Clinical Stage 1	½–1	23
Clinical Stage 2	1–2	31
Clinical Stage 3	1–2	64
FDA approval	½–1	75

Source: SG Cowen 1998: 22, 33; *this figure from BIA 1999: 19.

conduce towards the accumulation of tacit knowledge within particular teams of scientists and technicians. Over time, the scientists and technicians involved in these projects make incremental improvements to technologies and add new competencies, most of which feed back into the firm's core technological know-how. Appropriability concerns also create a motive to avoid codification of important technical knowledge. End-user relationships are also more complex and service-oriented within platform technology companies; issues of technology integration between platform technology firms and major customers within the pharmaceutical sector are often critical and important to the establishment of profitable long-term end-user relationships (see again, Storper and Salais 1997).

Technological regime characteristics create three types of organizational risk. These include (a) problems created by the destruction of competencies within the firm as research progresses, (b) financial difficulties, and (c) dilemmas concerning employee motivation.

Competency Destruction Risks

This risk is primarily determined by the technological trajectory, and is much higher in therapeutics than most platform technologies. Most therapeutics research start-ups eventually fail and either enter into bankruptcy or are sold to other firms (see Senker 1996; Powell 1996). Internal competency destruction is also commonplace within successful therapeutics firms, which often change their research activities as projects evolve. When competency destruction is high, asset recycling becomes an important organizational problem (Bahrami and Evans 1995). Firms must have access to a pool of scientists, technicians, and other specialists with known reputations in highly specialized areas who can quickly be recruited to work on research projects. Because many projects will fail, coordination mechanisms to 'recycle' sophisticated assets across the matrix of public and private research clusters must be developed. If asset recycling is difficult, then specialists may choose not to commit to firms with high-risk research projects, fearing that if the project fails, the value of his or her research assets could significantly decline. Similarly, if extensive lateral career mobility across firms and non-profit research labs is not supported, then network externalities driving innovative research clusters would be difficult to sustain. Overall, the long-term career risk for managers and scientists of working within any given therapeutics firm must be low.

Financial Risks

While therapeutics and platform technology firms both require significant ongoing capital investments, they tend to generate different financial risks. Frequent failures and very high investment rates generated by the nature of technological volatility and short-term competition across research races create substantial financial risks for therapeutics firms. While reliable financing figures for each stage are not readily available, most industry guides estimate that the total cost of discovering and developing a new drug is between $100 and $200 million (PhRMA 1996). These costs increase dramatically as products are discovered and developed; while the research required for drug discovery can typically be financed by a few million dollars per year, the cost curve dramatically escalates once potential target compounds are discovered and clinical trials involving human participants begin. The 7–10 year time horizon between discovery and regulatory approval compounds these risks.

Firms may partially offset these risks by codifying key scientific results into intellectual property. Results generated by all aspects of therapeutics research may, if the firm chooses to codify and release the information, be widely reported and monitored throughout the research community. This allows investors the possibility of developing mechanisms to monitor each firm and to gradually extend financing, as warranted through positive results. Furthermore, while the odds of successfully bringing a product to market are low, the payoffs can be astronomical. Consumers have been repeatedly willing to support very high prices for effective new treatments, creating billion dollar plus returns for some drugs.

While platform technologies vary in the financial risks involved, they are generally lower than for therapeutics firms. Appropriability concerns may weaken the earnings of innovations and create pressure for firms to continually improve existing products or introduce new ones. Initial capital costs are often higher, especially for firms that require access to sophisticated lab equipment (e.g. gene sequencing devices or dedicated production equipment). However, many platform technology firms avoid this problem by beginning with relatively modest amounts of seed capital, which is used to rent time on sophisticated lab equipment owned by the basic research laboratories from which the new enterprise is spun out. Firms may obtain more substantial financing once they have reached a critical mass of customers and services to justify the construction of sophisticated capital assets in-house. Moreover, because most platform technology companies aim to sell services or products to other labs, time horizons are much shorter before the firm begins to generate income flows, and there are usually no significant regulatory approval costs and subsequent delays.

Employee Motivation Risks

Once a firm has obtained the necessary human and financial resources, it still has to create the organizational structures necessary to innovate. The key risk factor rather involves creating adequate incentives for employees to commit to what are often demanding, extremely competitive and time-intensive work environments that exist within both therapeutics and platform technology firms. Difficulties may also be created by 'hold-up' risks due to the extreme specialization of knowledge held by scientists working within biotech firms. Until key research results are codified by scientists, it is often difficult for mangers to access the quality of research carried out by teams of scientists. Scientists may refuse to codify results or work effectively within teams until adequate financial or reputational incentives are created by managers (see Werth 1994 for examples). Knowledge-related dilemmas may also emerge when employees are asked to invest in firm-specific skills that have a limited value outside the firm (see Miller 1992).

Employee motivation is particularly challenging for platform technology firms. While management needs to create a high-powered work environment to successfully compete, the existence of long-term tacit knowledge means that managers or other outsiders cannot easily monitor the activities of particular work groups or develop simple contractual structures rewarding employees for short-term achievements. Long-term relational contracts have to be developed between researchers and the management and owners of firms in order to create incentives for research groups to accurately report their results. When employees spend long amounts of time with the firm, there is also the risk that the cumulative nature of technological progress may generate substantial firm-specific know-how. Should the firm collapse, then the human capital of employees might be discounted on the open labour market. Knowing this, the firm's management, once the employee has made investments in firm-specific skills, could credibly demand that the employee accept remuneration at this discounted rate. Such opportunism is unlikely, however, given the overarching desire on the part of management to create high-powered incentives for employees to work in work-intensive environments. However, should the firm encounter financial difficulties, employees with substantial firm-specific skills are disadvantaged compared to those with more general skills.

Employee motivation problems within therapeutics firms are somewhat mitigated by the ability to codify most research results, while the turbulent nature of technological change and the subsequent high recycling of employee assets across the community of firms lowers the firm-specific knowledge risk. The chief employee motivation problem within therapeutic firms is to create high-powered work environments necessary to succeed in extremely competitive research races. Management also face a concern that scientists may attempt to 'hold up' the firm by refusing to codify research results until particular demands are met (see Werth 1994 for examples). Table 4 summaries this general discussion.

Table 4
Organizational
Dilemmas within
Biotechnology
Market Segments

	Therapeutics	Platform Technologies
Competency destruction risks	*High* — Due to discrete nature of technology; asset recycling a key problem.	*Low* — Due to cumulative nature of technology and lower failure rate.
Financial risks	*High* — Due to high failure rate, long time horizons, and high 'burn rate'; however codified knowledge facilitates short-term monitoring.	*Low to Medium* — Failure risk lower and time horizons shorter, but tacit knowledge makes monitoring difficult and many product segments have become extremely competitive.
Employee motivation risks	*Medium* — Firms face potential 'hold up' problem and must create high-powered incentives due to racing nature of research. But once scientists codify results performance may be easily monitored.	*High* — Long-term tacit knowledge makes monitoring difficult and cumulative research trajectories may create firm-specific knowledge risks for employees.

The Institutional Determinants of Organizational Governance within the US and German Biotechnology Industries

Innovative activity within the therapeutics and platform technology segments of the biotechnology industry requires that firms develop competencies to resolve quite different organizational dilemmas. The core institutional argument is that firms have to draw chiefly upon resources external to the firm if they are to successfully resolve these problems. In this respect, institutions function as 'tool kits' (Swidler 1986) that actors can draw upon to create governance mechanisms needed to structure their social interactions. We now examine how, particularly in the German case, technology policies have made it possible to develop credibly the organizational strategies needed to pursue entrepreneurial business strategies, but within institutional contexts sharply defined by long-standing national institutional frameworks. This will help to explain why German firms have tended to gravitate so strongly towards the platform technology segment while American firms, though strong in both areas, tend to be particularly dominant in therapeutics. To develop these points, I first discuss the orchestration of innovative competencies for therapeutics within the United States, and then turn to the German case.

Market-driven Innovation Networks in the United States

The orchestration of commercial innovation networks in the United States is consistent with the technological market characteristics embedded within the therapeutics sector. Starting with Genentech, the original biotech start-up formed in 1976, biotechnology firms quickly became enmeshed within a network of largely market-based relationships previously constructed to support the semiconductor and computer industries (see Kenney 1986).

Models of financing, firm organization, and corporate governance for start-ups were largely imposed onto the new industry, rather than being developed for it. Because institutional frameworks governing most substantive areas within the United States are broadly enabling in nature and tend to support market forms of business coordination, it is not surprising that such mechanisms were chosen. The US therapeutics sector has thrived, largely because flexible market-based governance mechanisms are able to resolve the major organizational dilemmas underpinning these activities. A brief review of how liberal market institutions impact the resolution of the key organizational dilemmas created by therapeutics research supports this claim.

Competency Destruction Risks

In the United States, the deregulated nature of most labour law creates an extremely active labour market. US courts have refused to enforce 'competition clauses' inserted into employment contracts to prevent poaching (Hyde 1998). While firms can ask employees to sign non-disclosure agreements covering specific technologies, scientists and managers are generally free to move from firm to firm as they see fit, while managers can shed assets through hiring and firing, as circumstances within the firm develop. This has facilitated the creation of extensive head-hunting operations within most US technology clusters and, within firms, the organization of career paths based on the probability of frequent employee turnover. Active labour markets facilitate rapid asset recycling to compensate for competency destruction within technology firms. (see Saxenian 1994 for a discussion of career paths within Silicon Valley).

Financial Risks

The initial funding of almost all US biotechnology firms stems from venture capitalists (see Florida and Kenney 1988), who are usually willing to accept high technological uncertainty and short- to medium-term financial losses in return for the prospect of very large gains in the future. However, it is also important for them to be able to segment the R&D activities of start-ups into several externally observable milestones (e.g. scientific publications, patents, alliances) so that they can make further investment decisions and eventually take the firm public. The codified nature of most scientific results in the therapeutics field fit easily into the venture capital models of corporate finance.

There are important institutional reasons why the venture capital market is so large in the United States. The property rights structure of firms is primarily financial in structure, and rooted in NASDAQ and other large capital markets of technology firms. Critical for venture capitalists is a liquid market for corporate control. Successful start-ups are provided with supplementary financing rounds and are eventually go public by means of an initial public offering (IPO) or are sold to a larger firm, usually creating a very high return for the venture capitalists. Without this exit option, it is difficult for venture capitalists to adopt a portfolio strategy by diversifying risks across several investments or creating a viable refinancing mechanism (Lerner and Gompers 1999). These profits may be used to offset the losses on other companies and thus make a portfolio strategy more viable.

Employee Motivation Risks

Short-term performance milestones complement the creation of high-powered performance incentives for employees. Managers of US high-technology firms face few labour or company law restrictions on hiring and firing or the organization of remuneration and performance incentives. Most companies motivate employees primarily with share options coupled with the announced intention of owners and venture capitalist to make the firm public within a few years. Where successful firms have gone public, share options can be worth from tens of thousands of dollars to junior staff to millions to senior scientists and owner/managers. The prospect of large financial rewards helps align the private incentives of scientists with those of companies and is a prime reason why US high-tech firms have become associated with extremely long work weeks and general dedication to projects. Most technology companies also have annual performance reviews that are largely based on individual performance. Within therapeutics firms, this is usually pegged to each scientist's contribution to codified intellectual property developed within the firm. To aid their longer-term reputation, should they re-enter the labour market, scientists are also regularly allowed to publish key results in scientific journals under their name, along with the firm's.

To fully appreciate the short-term, contingent nature of these relationships, a more systematic view should be taken. Each link of the competency chain must be credible before all actors will commit themselves to working on a particular entrepreneurial project. For example, as Zucker and Darby (1997) have shown, successful biotech firms are usually associated with 'star-scientists' from universities who contribute seed technology, provide informal consulting, and serve on the firm's scientific advisory board. Fledging firms with high-profile scientific backing are the most likely to gain the attention of venture capitalists with access to generous financing, managerial know-how, and the contacts needed to persuade high quality managers and scientists to work with the firm. This combination of assets enhances the probability of the firm succeeding in early research races, and through doing so, gaining access to further venture capital, and eventually to the investment banking community as well as joint ventures with large pharmaceutical firms.

While such virtuous circles are common with therapeutic start-ups, they can quickly become vicious. If the firm cannot recruit high quality researchers or attract start-scientists on its scientific advisory board, then it is unlikely that venture capitalists will support the firm. Similarly, when firms fail to meet important milestones, the short-term and market-driven nature of their organization facilitates their quick unravelling. Once a firm faces difficulties, venture capitalists may refuse to extend further financing, often forcing firms to sell valuable intellectual property to other firms at fire-sale prices, in order to stay alive. This could quickly lead to further difficulties as key researchers within the firm jump to other enterprises and star scientists affiliated with it turn their attention elsewhere. Such is the essence of a short-term, incentive based contracting scheme.

If, for institutional or other reasons, one or more links within the competency chain of an emerging therapeutics research enterprise is not credible, then it is unlikely that other participants will commit themselves to a particular project. This is the key factor explaining why German firms have not gravitated towards the therapeutics area. Up until as recently as the mid-1990s, institutional obstacles created major hurdles to the creation of viable governance mechanisms in each of the three areas discussed. While minor institutional reforms and sector-specific technology policies have lessened some restraints, key problems, particularly in the area of arranging human resource competencies within quickly changing technology areas, continue to undermine the viability of most therapeutics projects in Germany. Having explained the market-based construction of American biotechnology firms, we are now in a better position to interpret developments within Germany.

The Creation of New Technology Firms within German 'Non-market' Institutions

The one area where economy-wide institutional reforms have benefited entrepreneurial firms is finance. While large German firms continue to be governed through a stakeholder model of company law, in recent years, the management of many large companies have developed an interest in tapping international financial markets and broadening their shareholder base in order to generate shareholder value pressures, stock-option schemes and other mechanisms to increase short-term performance pressures within the firm. This has lead to an upsurge of investment banking activities and finance in Germany throughout the 1990s that facilitated the creation of a NASDAQ-modelled stock exchange for technology companies, the *Neuer Markt,* in 1997. While, as of Fall 1999, only one biotechnology firm — a genomics company — has had a successful IPO on the *Neuer Markt*, this market has successfully supported several dozen equity listings of German firms in other technology sectors.

Until very recently, venture capital was underdeveloped in Germany because of a lack of institutional mechanisms to support the rapid growth of firms through IPOs and other equity market activities, and a credible 'exit option' for venture capital syndicates. Spurred by government 'public venture capital' grants for new technology firms, the development of capital market institutions to support equity-based growth strategies has led to the inflow of venture capital firms. To increase their leverage, federal funds are provided only when firms can obtain matching funds from 'lead investors' within the private economy. While there were only two venture capital firms in Germany at the beginning of the 1990s, over 15 companies had set up shop there by early 1999 (Mietsch 1999). Due to the liberalization of German share-holding law in March 1998, most German biotech start-up firms offer stock options in order to foster intense work environments and are intent on leveraging the firm's equity for further financing along American-style high-technology growth trajectories. While high capital-gains taxes on stock options somewhat diminish their strength, German high-technology companies can now successfully mimic American-style employee motivation schemes.

Why, then, have most new German biotechnology firms not adopted higher-risk therapeutics strategies? The primary reason is that company and labour law continue to favour the construction of organizational structures that are dramatically at odds with those that have traditionally been best suited for therapeutic firms. In addition, the structure of German venture capital might be pushing firms into lower-risk market segments. However, it is also likely that Germany's current juxtaposition of long-term oriented labour market institutions and career development paths with more entrepreneurial patterns of start-up firm development and growth, could foster a comparative institutional advantage for firms specializing in platform technologies.

German start-up technology firms face difficulties in obtaining the necessary human resource competencies to innovate in volatile fields with frequent technological change. Labour market institutions pose obstacles to the creation of the coordination mechanisms needed to compensate for a high rate of competency destruction and firm failure. There are simply no large labour markets for experienced scientists and managers in Germany. Long-term employment strategies by large firms limit the development of labour markets for high quality staff. While large German firms can sell entire subsidiaries or business units or send some lower-productivity older employees into early retirement, co-determination law makes it difficult for firms to lay-off individual employees or groups of employees as part of the 'normal' course of business (see Becker et. al. 1999 for a discussion of Hoechst's difficulties in this area). Because labour markets for mid-career managerial and scientific expertise are relatively underdeveloped, the asset recycling mechanisms needed for therapeutics firms to successfully compete in technology races over the medium to long term do not exist. As a result, there is a high risk that senior managers and researchers will move from a large established company or prestigious university professorship to a start-up firm.

The continuing development of German biotechnology is unlikely to lessen the asset recycling problem. Unless employees throughout the German biomedical commercial and scientific research community begin to accept short-term incentive contracting arrangements, the extremely flexible labour markets to support therapeutics strategies seem unlikely to develop. Though it is too early to confirm empirically, most platform technology firms in Germany are likely to develop long-term employment patterns in order to build relational contracting structures with employees. If most German biotechnology firms become relatively stable, with low failure rates, then it is unlikely that they will eventually provide access to new pools of expert labour to work within therapeutics firms, since employment patterns will probably become predominately long term. This could limit job mobility across these firms, especially if many employees over the years invest in firm-specific skills.

While there is now financing for entrepreneurial firms in Germany, the governance of these investments is problematic. In addition to 'silent' venture capital, guaranteed by the federal government, much venture capital in Germany has been organized through 'innovation funds' administered by the banking sector, and, in particular, the public savings and investment banks (see the survey in Mietsch 1999: 241–255). As pointed out by Tylecote and Conesa (1999), banks in 'insider' dominated corporate governance systems tend to have excellent knowledge of particular firms, but usually they do not have the detailed *industry* knowledge that is necessary for investors to channel money into higher-risk technologies. Rather, financing for successful higher-risk activities is generally provided by specialized venture capitalist houses, often in conjunction with industry 'angels' who have detailed technical and market expertise within particular industries. While there are several credible venture capital houses in Germany, the extensive involvement of public funds in syndicates, backing most firms, creates limits on the reservoir of experience the firm can draw upon through its venture capital partners. Furthermore, public officials involved in the administration of federal subsidies as well as officials of public banks, when interviewed as part of field research conducted in early 1999, consistently stated that 'sustainability' was their core concern. Above all else, public officials want to avoid large numbers of corporate failures. In addition to risking moderate sums of public money, the political backlash created by a large number of high-tech failures could be embarrassing. Lacking the industry expertise to take an active role in the governance of these firms, it is not surprising that so many projects have been steered into lower-risk market segments.

It is this mix of entrepreneurial pressures and growth opportunities, combined with 'normal' patterns of primarily long-term and relationally based company organization that characterizes most of the new German high-tech enterprises. Seen in this light, it becomes clearer why so many of Germany's new biotechnology firms have headed into the platform technology field. The cumulative pattern of technology development helps to reduce the employment risk of joining a platform technology start-up. Government technology policies are ideally suited to these firms, since they provide incentives for universities to spin-off technologies and provide seed capital grants to incubate new fledgling enterprises. Once firms begin to establish themselves on the market, venture capitalists can and have provided access to resources needed to fuel growth.

However, it is also likely that Germany's new entrepreneurial firms enjoy a comparative institutional advantage in the platform technology area over US competitors. A contradiction exists within the incentive structures most American high-technology enterprises offer to employees, in that top management expect skilled employees to commit themselves to the very intense working conditions needed to successfully win innovation races with competitors, but they also reserve the right to hire and fire at will. This incentive conflict is reduced by offering very high-powered short-term performance incentives to employees. To monitor performance, employees need to work on projects that produce codified rather than tacit knowledge. Codified research results (patents, scholarly publications, prototypes, and the like) can easily be monitored by top management, venture capitalists and other stakeholders in the firm. This strategy is less viable, however, in areas where more cumulative technological trajectories create substantial amounts of tacit knowledge and firm-specific skills among employees.

To thrive, most platform technology firms must have access to financial and corporate governance institutions that can support entrepreneurial growth strategies. However, due to the complexity of the employee motivational problems, they require the formation of longer-term relational contracts with employees to encourage investments in firm-specific knowledge. Because German institutional frameworks strongly support the investment in firm-specific and long-term tacit knowledge within firms, it is not surprising that so many German firms have selected this area. If the long-term development of platform technology firms does create substantial amounts of long-term tacit knowledge, then there is a possibility that German institutional environments could allow more efficient governance structures to cope with these problems within the firm. Access to a superior institutional environment could lead to German firms eventually outperforming American firms in platform technologies.

Conclusion

Institutional change has clearly occurred within Germany. However, analysis of the activities of Germany's new firms supports a view of 'accommodation' or the incremental adaptation of German institutional frameworks to support an expansion of entrepreneurial technological firms within the economy, but not a fundamental shift towards a 'hybrid' model, as implied by the resource orchestration view. Germany's new technology policies have facilitated important extensions within the business system that, for the first time, allow the systematic promotion of entrepreneurial technology companies. However, the dominant strategies of market specialization and company organizational patterns found within these companies remains strongly influenced by incentives and constraints created by long-established national institutional structures. Most generally, German institutions tend to advantage innovation patterns in which knowledge cannot easily be codified and for which research trajectories are cumulative and have high degrees of firm-specific knowledge. Institutional frameworks within the United States advantage the construction of commercial innovative activities for which there is a large amount of competency destruction due to the discrete nature of technology trajectories, but knowledge can be codified.

Hybridization has occurred, not at the level of national institutional frameworks, but at that of business strategy. Technology firms in Germany may develop unique governance systems to support the development of technological trajectories that are broadly characteristic of the entrepreneurial high-tech sector, but they are difficult to sustain within liberal market economies. This returns to the concept of comparative institutional advantage. Recent public policy has precipitated the large-scale entry of German firms into new technologies, but it is clear that sector-specific policies and isolated institutional reforms cannot capture the institutional support structures needed to develop the predominately market-based US model within Germany. It seems unlikely that the German economy can develop a comparative institutional advantage by supporting firms actively in radically innovative technological areas.

While again recognizing that the creation of entrepreneurial technology models have become a powerful driver of innovation within the world economy, the analysis here stresses the need for firms and actors to experiment with institutions to develop unique applications. In other words, instead of viewing 'non-market' business institutions in Germany as obstacles, entrepreneurial firms in Germany might productively view these practices as 'tool kits' to selectively engage in developing novel business strategies. This perspective is potentially more powerful than those focusing on the need to mimic best practice elsewhere, as it realizes the possibility for German firms to craft comparative institutional advantages in new technology areas that differ in business strategy from common practice in the United States and other liberal market economies.

Unfortunately, the implications of this analysis for public policy are not clear-cut. While the biotechnology case certainly supports the varieties of capitalism perspective, this approach carries the strong implication that little or no change is possible, or even necessary. However, German technology policies have successfully stretched the fabric of the prevailing institutional frameworks in new directions. The forging of new technology transfer links through the BioRegio programmes, combined with financial subsidies and reforms to promote the creation of high-technology corporate governance, have combined to create extensions of the German model. However, we have also seen that this extension is strongly path dependent on prevailing forms of organization within the German economy, and in no sense can it be described as a 'break' with the long-established German patterns of company organization. While the widening of German capital markets and the creation of technology transfer channels have been clearly helpful, it is quite possible that many of Germany's new platform technology firms may have emerged without extensive public financial subsidies. Technology promotion is possible, but policies should be crafted in ways that are broadly consistent with the country's prevailing comparative institutional advantage.

An important theme for institutional research is to establish a theoretically useful analysis that can more easily incorporate changes, such as those presently occurring in Germany, into normal categories of analysis. A middle ground, so to say, must be established between extremely rigid institutional theorizing, implying that little change is likely, and the analysis suggestion that extreme discontinuity is possible. Static descriptions of existing institutional environments must be combined with micro-level accounts, tracing how firms, governments, and other actors within the economy experiment with, and at times re-configure, the institutional tool-kits at their disposal.

Note

* For helpful criticism, I would like to thank Karen Adelberger, Susanne Giesecke, Jerald Hage, Hannah Kettler, J. Rogers Hollingsworth, Ernst Homburg, Christel Lane, Marius Meeus, Bart Noteboom, David Soskice, Birgitte Unger, Frans van Waarden, Richard Whitley, and two anonymous reviewers. Financial support for field research was provided by the German Ministry for Education and Research (BMBF).

References

Adelberger, Karen
    'A developmental German state? Explaining growth in German biotechnology and venture capital'. *German Politics*, forthcoming.

Abramson, H. Norman, Proctor P. Reid, Ulrich Schmoch, and Jose Encarnacao, *editors*
1997 *Technology transfer systems in the United States and Germany.* Washington, D.C.: National Academy Press.

Audretsch, David
1985 'The innovation, unemployment, and competitiveness challenge in Germany'. WZB Discussion Paper FS IV 95–6.

Bahrami, Homa, and Stuart Evans
1995 'Flexible re-cycling and high-technology entrepreneurship'. *California Management Review* 37: 62–90.

Becker, Steffen, Wolfgang Menz, and Thomas Sablowski
1999 'In Netz gegangen: Industrielle Beziehungebn im Netzwerk-Konzern am Beispiel der Hoechst AG'. *Industrielle Beziehungen* 6: 9–35.

BioIndustry Association (BIA)
1999 *Industrial markets for UK biotechnology: Trends and issues*: London: BIA.

Breschi, Stefano, and Franco Malerba
1997 'Sectoral innovation systems: technological regimes, Schumpeterian dynamics, and spatial boundaries' in *Systems of innovation: technologies, institutions and organizations.* Charles Edquist (ed.), 130–155. London: Pinter.

Büchtemann, Christoph F., and Kurt Vogler-Ludwig
1997 *Das deutsche Ausbildungsmodell unter Anpassungszwang: Thesen zur Humankapitalbildung in Deutschland.* Munich: IFO Institute.

Cantwell, John, and Rebecca Harding
1998 'The internationalisation of German companies' R and D'. *National Institute Economic Review* 163: 99–115.

Casper, Steven, Mark Lehrer, and David Soskice
1999 'Can high-technology industries prosper in Germany: Institutional frameworks and the evolution of the German software and biotechnology industries'. *Industry and Innovation* 6: 6–23.

Casper, Steven, and Sigurt Vitols
1997 'The German model in the 1990s: Problems and prospects'. *Industry and Innovation* 4: 3–12.

912   Steven Casper

Charkham, Jonathan
1995   *Keeping good company: A study of corporate governance in five countries.* Oxford: Oxford University Press.

Crouch, Colin, and Wolfgang Streeck, *editors*
1997   *Modern capitalism or modern capitalisms?.* London: Pinter.

Deutsche Bundesbank
1997   'Quarterly Report'. November.

Easterbrook, Frank, and Daniel Fischel
1991   *The economic structure of corporate law.* Cambridge, MA: Harvard University Press.

Edwards, Jeremy, and Klaus Fischer
1994   *Banks, finance and investment in Germany:* Cambridge: Cambridge University Press.

Ernst and Young
1998a 'European life sciences 1998'. London: Ernst and Young.

Ernst and Young
1998b *'Aufbruchstimmung* 1998: First German biotechnology survey'. Munich: Ernst and Young.

Florida, Richard, and Martin Kenney
1988   'Venture capital, financial innovation and technological change in the USA'. *Research Policy* 17: 119–137.

Glimstedt, Henrik
1999   'Constructing and global, reconstructing the local: Reflexitive actors and economic action in the international context'. M.Sc., Stockhom School of Economics.

Hollingsworth, Rogers, and Robert Boyer, *editors*
1997   *Contemporary capitalism.* Cambridge: Cambridge University Press.

Hyde, Alan
1998   'Employment law after the death of employment'. *University of Pennsyvania Journal of Labor Law* 1: 105–120.

Katzenstein, Peter
1987   *Policy and politics in West Germany: Towards the growth of a semi-sovereign state.* Philadelphia: Temple University Press.

Katzenstein, Peter
1989   'Stability and change in the emerging third republic' in *Industry and politics in West Germany.* P. Katzenstein (ed.). Ithaca, NY: Cornell University Press.

Keller, Bernd
1991   *Einführung in die Arbeitspolitik.* München: Oldenbourg.

Kenney, Martin
1986   *Biotechnology: the university–industrial complex.* New Haven: Yale University Press.

Lane, Christel
1989   *Management and labour in Europe*: Aldershot: Edward Elgar.

Lane, Christel
1999   'The impact of German multinational companies' foreign direct investment activities on the German business system'. M.Sc., University of Cambridge.

Lehrer, Mark
1997   'German industrial strategy in turbulence: Corporate governance and managerial hierarchies in Lufthansa'. *Industry and Innovation* 4: 115–140.

Lerner, Josh, and Paul Gompers
1999   *The venture capital cycle.* Cambridge, MA: MIT Press.

Malerba, Franco, and Luigi Orsenigo
1993   'Technological regimes and firm behavior'. *Industrial and Corporate Change* 2: 45–71.

McKlevey, Maureen
1997   'Co-evolution in commercial genetic engineering'. *Industrial and Corporate Change* 6: 503–532.

Mietsch, Andreas
1999   *Bio-Technologie Das Jahr- und Adressbuch 1999.* Berlin: BIOCOM.

Milgrom, Paul, and John Roberts
1992   *Economics, organization, and management.* Englewood Cliffs: Prentice Hall.

Miller, Gary
1992   *Managerial dilemmas.* Cambridge: Cambridge University Press.

Monks, Robert, and Nell Minow
1995 *Corporate governance.* London: Blackwell.

Pennan, Hervé
1996 'R&D strategy in a techno-economic network: Alzheimer's disease therapeutic strategies'. *Research Policy* 25: 337–358.

PhRMA
1996 *Industry profile.* Washington DC: PhRMA.

Powell, Walter
1996 'Inter-organisational collaboration in the biotechnology industry'. *Journal of Institutional and Theoretical Economics* 152/1: 197–215.

Rabinow, Paul
1996 *Making PCR: A study of biotechnology.* Chicago: Chicago University Press.

Rosenberg R., and Richard Nelson
1994 'American universities and technical advance in industry'. *Research Policy* 23: 323–348.

Saxenian, Annalee
1994 *Regional advantage*: Cambridge, MA: Harvard University Press.

Schmitter, Philippe, and Wolfgang Streeck
1985 *Private interest government.* London: Sage.

Senker, Jacqueline
1996 'National systems of innovation, organizational learning, and industrial biotechnology'. *Technovation* 16: 219–229.

SG Cowen
1998 'Biotechnology in Europe'. *SG Cowen Perspectives*, 1 September.

SG Cowen
1999 'Biotechnology quarterly'. *SG Cowen Perspectives*, 1 January.

Sorge, Arndt, and Wolfgang Streeck
1988 'Industrial relations and technical change. The case for an extended perspective' in *New technology and industrial relations.* R. Hyman and W. Steeck (ed.), 19–47. Oxford: Blackwell.

Soskice, David
1994 'Innovation strategies of companies: a comparative institutional analysis of some cross-country differences' in *Institutionvergleich und Institutionsdynamik.* W. Zapf (ed.). Berlin: Sigma.

Soskice, David
1997 'German technology policy, innovation, and national institutional frameworks'. *Industry and Innovation* 4: 75–96.

Storper, Michael, and Robert Salais
1997 *Worlds of production: The action frameworks of the economy.* Cambridge, MA: Harvard University Press.

Streeck, Wolfgang
1984 'Co-determination: the fourth decade' in *International yearbook of organizational democracy*, Vol. 2. Bernhard Wilpert and Arndt Sorge (eds.), 391–422. New York: Wiley.

Streeck, Wolfgang
1992 'On the institutional preconditions of diversified quality production' in *Social institutions and economic performance.* Wolfgang Streeck (ed.). London and Newbury Park: Sage.

Streeck, Wolfgang
1996 'German capitalism: Does it exist? Can it survive?' in *Modern capitalism or modern capitalisms?.* Colin Crouch and Wolfgang Streeck (eds.). London: Pinter.

Swidler, Ann
1986 'Culture in action: symbols and strategies'. *American Sociological Review* 51: 273–286.

Silvia, Stephen, *editor*
1999 *Reversal of fortune: an assessment of the German biotechnology sector in comparative perspective.* (Economic Studies Program Series, Vol 5.) American Institute for Contemporary German Studies, The John Hopkins University.

Teece, David
1986 'Profiting from technological innovation: Implications for integration, collaboration, licensing, and public policy'. *Research Policy* 15: 285–305.

914   Steven Casper

Tylecote, Andrew, and E. Conesa
1999 'Corporate governance, innovation systems, and industrial policy'. *Industry and Innovation* 6: 25–50.

Vitols, Sigurt
1995 'Corporate governance versus economic governance: banks and industrial restructuring in the US and Germany'. WZB Discussion Paper, FS95-1, 312.

Vitols, Sigurt, Steven Casper, David Soskice, and Stephen Wolcock
1997 *Corporate governance in large British and German companies.* London: Anglo-German Foundation.

Werth, Barry
1994 *The billion-dollar molecule.* Touchstone, Simon & Schuster, New York.

Winter, Sidney
1987 'Knowledge and competence as strategic assets' in *The competitive challenge: Strategies for industrial innovation and renewal.* D. J. Teece (ed.). Cambridge, MA: Ballinger.

Whitley, Richard
1999 *Divergent capitalisms: The social structuring and change of business systems.* Oxford: Oxford University Press.

Williamson, Oliver
1975 *Markets and hierarchies.* New York: The Free Press.

Wirtschaftswoche
1998 'Schneller Aufstieg', 24 September 1998, pp.134–139.

Zucker, Lynn, and Michael Darby
1997 'Present at the revolution: transformation of technical identity for a large incumbent pharmaceutical firm after the biotechnological breakthrough'. *Research Policy* 26/4: 429–447.

[13]

Institutions, Sector Specialisation and Economic Performance Outcomes[*]

Sigrid Quack   Glenn Morgan

1.   Introduction

In this chapter, the sector is suggested as a useful starting point for an investigation of economic performance. Various authors have identified the sector as an important arena in which social and economic actors coordinate, co-operate and compete with each other within the national and international sphere (Porter 1990; Hollingsworth et al. 1994). The literature, however, has rarely addressed directly the issue of how institutions shape the evolution of and changes in the sector portfolios that constitute different national business systems. The sector will be understood here as a historical formation of complementary, interlinked and co-evolving economic activities of business organisations which produce a range of similar or related products and services, together with those who regularly transact with them in supplying, servicing, regulatory or customer roles (see e.g. Räsänen and Whipp 1992).

There are several reasons why sector specialisation provides a useful starting point for the analysis of the relationship between national institutions, global competition and economic performance. The emergence, evolution and decline of distinct forms of sector specialisation can, on the one hand, exemplify how national institutions shape over time collective capabilities and specific business recipes of companies in different national contexts, and thereby influence performance outcomes of sectoral and national economies. On the other hand, the sector provides a scene to study how economic actors are involved in the definition and re-definition of rules of business conduct and performance expectations which over time become engraved in the particular structures of competition and coordination. Finally, sectors have been drawn to a different extent and at

---

[*]   We would like to thank Dorothee Bohle, Jacqueline O'Reilly, Dieter Plehwe, Arndt Sorge and Richard Whitley for their helpful comments on an earlier version of this chapter.

different times into international markets. Thus the development of sector specialisation can exemplify how global competition feeds back into the economic organisation and performance of national business systems.

The chapter falls into three sections. We first review arguments about the relationship between the structural characteristics of national business systems and sector specialisation. In the following section, we move from the structural to the processual level and consider sector specialisation as an emergent process, e.g. how sectors emerge historically and how existing sectors adapt, transform or decline in response to changing business environments. In the last part, we ask what is the driving force behind processes of sector restructuring. We examine critically the notion of 'market performance' as selection criteria and suggest that performance depends on a more complex set of economic, social and political factors.

2.   National Institutions and Sector Specialisation

The literature on 'national business systems' (Whitley 1994; Whitley and Kristensen 1996, 1997) and 'varieties of capitalism' (Hollingsworth et al. 1994; Berger and Dore 1996; Hollingsworth and Boyer 1997) demonstrates how national institutions influence business organisation and economic coordination in different countries in distinct ways. The results of this literature are in line with earlier work by researchers related to the Aix-school (Maurice et al. 1980, 1986; Sorge 1991; for a recent review of the approach see Maurice and Sorge 1999) indicating that business organisations tend to concentrate on certain economic activities which have a close fit with their societal environment. This 'closeness of fit' argument can be applied to the relationship between institutions and sector specialisation in two directions: Firstly, it can be shown that the societal context provides an envelope of opportunities and constraints which tends to influence the development of capabilities and competencies of firms. Capabilities and competences of firms are here understood as sets of organisationally specific experiences, knowledge and expertise that enables them to carry out particular economic activities. Correspondence between firms' capabilities on the one hand and technological and organisational task requirements in certain industries and market segments on the other hand, then, can explain why firms in one country tend to cluster in certain sectors whereas in other countries they do so in other sectors. Secondly, it has also been shown that different societal contexts have distinct affinities to the social and political formation of collective actors which often play an important role in the institutionalisation of sectors. In the following, we examine how national systems of finance and innovation, labour market institutions, demand conditions and the role of intermediate/sectoral institutions correspond to distinct patterns of sector specialisation.

SECTOR SPECIALISATION AND ECONOMIC PERFORMANCE 29

2.1 *Financial Systems and Sector Specialisation*

Several studies have underlined the impact of national systems of finance and corporate governance on the time horizon of companies' investment and commitment of their resources to particular activities (Zysman 1983; Hutton 1995; Vitols 1997). Since the 1970s, the management of companies in Anglo-Saxon countries has, as a result of strong and liquid capital markets, become increasingly subject to strong pressures of outside stakeholders. These are mainly shareholders and institutional investors controlling dispersed share ownership which are predominantly interested in liquidity and short-term dividend growth (Lazonick and O'Sullivan 1996). In other European countries, the availability of long-term bank-based and/or state-controlled finance and considerable family and/or state ownership in companies, together with relative protection from hostile take-over through small or legally restricted markets for corporate governance, means that the management of companies can develop and pursue more long-term goals and strategies. Even though the interests and goals of the various stakeholder groups can vary widely in the latter systems, they tend to converge more easily towards medium- and long-term returns.

Since the 1970s, the increasing pressures for liquidity in Anglo-Saxon market-based financial systems have favoured mass production strategies which focus on short-term cost reduction and can be organised with large numbers of semi-skilled workers (Lane 1995; Porter 1990). Furthermore, it has been argued that the focus of Anglo-Saxon countries on short-term returns encourages the commitment of resources to activities which have low entry and exit costs (Whitley 1994) whereas it limits their readiness to invest in company specific R&D activities (Lazonick 1991; Whitley 1999). In contrast, the more long-term incentives of bank-based or state administered financial systems in continental European market economies have been related to their stronger commitment to capital-intensive industries (Whitley 1994). This context also favours flexible production strategies which focus on improvements in product and process quality. It facilitates the emergence of sectors which require long-term investment in company internal R&D and the development of company specific human resources (Sorge 1991; Streeck 1992). More recent studies, however, indicate that the links between financial systems and sector specialisation might be more complex. Service activities which are organised on a project basis, as is, for example, often the case in finance and construction, seem to flourish more easily under the 'time bound' investment rules of Anglo-Saxon countries than in continental European countries (Christopherson 1998; Campagnac et al. in this volume). Market-based financial systems seem also be more beneficial to the establishment of newly emerging firms in high-tech sectors with high uncertainty than bank-based systems (see Vitols 1995 for a comparison of Great Britain and Germany).

30   SIGRID QUACK AND GLENN MORGAN

2.2 Labour Market Institutions and Sector Specialisation

Various studies have shown links between labour market institutions, such as the system of training and education and the industrial relations system, and competitive strategies of companies from different countries (Maurice et al. 1980; Lane 1989; Whitley and Kristensen 1997). The success of German manufacturing sectors following flexible specialisation and diversified quality production strategies in the 1970s and 1980s, for example, has been regarded as closely related to the high level of qualification and polyvalent skill profile of their labour force (Sorge 1991; Streeck 1992). The limited success of these production strategies in the corresponding British and French sectors can — among other factors — be attributed to the fact that the societal pattern of organising human resources did not fit to the same extent to the task requirements inherent in these productions patterns as the German one (Sorge 1991). The concentration on competitive advantage in manufacturing, however, has as Christopherson (1998) argues, led to a neglect of aspects of training and employment policies which influence sector specialisation in the service sector. The strength of financial and legal services in the US reflects, among other factors, the specific organisation of the educational system which generates a large number of highly qualified professionals who carry their skills with them on an individual basis from project to project (see Porter 1990 for a similar statement with regard to the basis of success of the British finance industry).

National and labour market institutions also matter with regard to the ways in which companies make use of their employees' skills and seek their active participation in product and process development. Together with the industrial relations systems they influence how collective learning processes and innovation can be organised at the company and at the sectoral level. Employers associations and unions acting as 'discursive institutions' at the sectoral level can help to overcome what Sabel (1994) has called the 'dilemma of economic development'. A continued dialogue between corporate actors and interest organisations can help them to elaborate a new common understanding of changes in their environment. The presence of strong intermediate organisations, however, can make radical change also more difficult, exactly due to the need for extensive negotiations. This might be particularly the case when the transformation has a strong distributive element (see Lehrer and Darbishire in this volume).

2.3 Demand Conditions and Sector Specialisation

A further factor which influences sector specialisation, but has not received much attention in the institutional literature, is the role of demand conditions and

SECTOR SPECIALISATION AND ECONOMIC PERFORMANCE   31

vertical relationships among industries in stimulating sector specialisation. These factors have been assigned particular attention in Porter's (1990) work on the competitive advantage of nations. He shows that not only the size of the home market, but also the composition and pattern of growth of national demand influences sector specialisation. Demand patterns are related to specific geographic and climatic conditions (e.g. the Swiss tunnelling or the US heavy truck industry), social, political and legislative considerations (e.g. the environmental industries in Sweden and Denmark, and the low level of regulation in the City of London), and cultural conditions (e.g. the Italian textile and garment sector, and the Japanese focus on compact and multifunctional consumer electronics). Similarly, demand patterns interconnect developments in supplier and related industries. Demand patterns in Porter's view contribute not only to competitive advantage through economies of scale (e.g. size of the US American market), but also through pressures to upgrade products and improve productivity of production processes over time. National demand patterns which turn out to anticipate a broader shift of demand in international markets, can generate an important comparative advantage for the companies which are located in this country. The absence of such demand, on the other hand, can hinder the development of internationally successful sectors. According to Sorge (1991: 178) this was exactly what happened in the French machine tool industry which — despite having the necessary capabilities — could not fully exploit the comparative advantages of flexible specialisation because their customers continued to order products along the more standardised lines.

Financial systems, labour market institutions and demand factors together can explain quite well the differences in sector specialisation which have been observed between different industrialised countries (see Porter 1990; Kitschelt 1991). In both the US and UK, manufacturing tends to concentrate on large-scale production of consumer goods, and within the service sector, industries such as finance, legal advice, media and entertainment, etc. are strongly developed. The German institutional context, in contrast, has led to the flourishing of many specialised manufacturing equipment industries which focus on the high-quality end of the market, whilst the Japanese economy developed strength in consumer electronics. Within certain sectors, companies from Anglo-Saxon countries tend to focus more on the lower price end, whereas German firms tend to cover the more customised demand and Japanese firms combine low-cost with high-quality aspects.

2.4 *Institutions, Innovation and Sector Specialisation*

A number of authors have underlined the importance of innovation for sustained success of companies and sectors in international competition (Nelson and Winter

32   SIGRID QUACK AND GLENN MORGAN

1982; Porter 1990; Lazonick 1991). This applies not only to technological but also to organisational innovation. The impact of national institutional systems on technological innovation has been analysed in detail in the economic literature on 'national innovation systems' which cannot be referred to here in length (see e.g. Lundvall 1992; Nelson 1993; Storper 1996). The results indicate that institutions are of particular significance with regard to the rapid appropriation of knowledge, the organisation of collective learning and the management of uncertainties throughout the innovation process.

In general, institutional contexts which encourage collective investment in knowledge generation and use, both within and between firms, have been regarded as more likely to lead to stronger innovation than those that reproduce adversarial and spot market type relationships between economic actors. This argument, however, cannot explain the innovativeness of certain manufacturing sectors such as the computer and software industry in the US, and certain service sectors such as financial and legal services in both the US and UK context. It seems more appropriate to perceive of liberal market economies as not impeding innovation as such, but favouring certain types of innovation over others. This leads to the need to differentiate the impact of national business systems according to different types of technology (see e.g. Kitschelt 1991) and types of innovation (see e.g. Langlois and Robertson 1995). Sectors are likely to vary with regard to the level of complexity, the tightness of coupling, and the uncertainty involved in the innovation process (the latter, for example, leading to decentralised networks of innovation in sectors with high uncertainty such as gene technology). It also matters whether innovations depend on the development of company resources, or can be achieved through the integration of advances in basic research and science undertaken in universities or research centres outside of the firm. Whereas in some sectors large industrial and services firms might be the nexus of innovation, in others innovation will be brought about through a high rate of new entrepreneurial firm creation (Porter 1990; Whitley 1999).

Liberal market economies, for example, provide a range of incentives to entrepreneurs seeking to establish new companies (including substantial amounts of venture capital). These features, together with a high degree of employee mobility, are likely to favour the type of radical product and organisational innovation which is characteristic of industries and services which have developed a certain strength in the US and/or UK (Christopherson 1998; Hall 1997; Soskice 1997). In contrast, the long-termism inherent in the financial system and employment relationships in co-ordinated market economies favours strategies of incremental process and product innovation that build on the development of company internal resources (see e.g. Deakin et al. in this volume). The latter systems can mitigate against radical innovation. For example, it can be difficult to recruit experts from outside the firm or to change rapidly the skill profile of

SECTOR SPECIALISATION AND ECONOMIC PERFORMANCE   33

the employees. The limitation of CEOs by boards, works councils, etc. raises more problems for radical organisational innovation to be implemented than in Anglo-Saxon systems (Lehrer and Darbishire in this volume).

2.5 Variations in the Institutionalisation of Sectors

According to Hollingsworth et al. (1994: 9) there are two different sources for the historical development of sectors: Sectors can emerge from below through the independent interaction and cooperation between companies and their trading partners. Sectors can also be created from above through the imposition of boundaries and rules by public authorities. Between these two extremes, however, there is also the possibility of strong intermediate sectoral institutions (such as employers' associations, workers' unions, professional bodies, sector specific training institutions and research institutes) to evolve which provide a social fabric in which actors can develop a strong sectoral identity (Räsänen and Whipp 1992). Thus, a line can be drawn from the institutional context and historical processes of group formation to the degree and forms of sector specialisation in different societies. An institutional context that constitutes firms as isolated and self-sufficient actors, and in which the state refrains from direct intervention, as in the case of the UK, for example, is unlikely to generate a strong inter-sectoral specialisation with deep intra-sectoral clustering. In contrast, an institutional context which favours long-term, reciprocal obligations between firms and the evolution of intermediary organisations which take part in the co-ordination of flows and strategies will contribute to the emergence of strong and deeply clustered sectors such as in Germany. Finally, there are those countries, in which the state takes a strong interventionist role in the economic process (e.g. France and South Korea). In this case, the state tends to sponsor a small number of large companies with whom it has close relations.

This leads to the general point that sectoral identities and members vary in their institutionalisation across national contexts. The structure of sectors varies both within and across countries along a range of dimensions. Table 1 provides one conceptualisation of this variety based on studies reported in Whitley and Kristensen (1996, 1997). It distinguishes between economies in which there are a large number of sectors in operation and those characterised by a few dominant sectors. It also distinguishes between those societies in which most sectors tend to be dominated by large firms and those in which sectors show a higher degree of variation in firm size and patterns of interaction.

Differences in the structure and institutionalisation of sectors are likely to influence the nature of sector adaptation and innovation in response to new technology and globalising markets. Whereas in some techno-organisational task environments the dominance of a few large companies might facilitate the

Table 1: *Sector Specialisation and Organisation*

Characteristics of the Economy as a whole	Characteristics of Sectors	
	Small number of large firms	Highly integrated complex of firms
Large number of sectors	France	Germany
Small number of sectors	Finland	Denmark

accumulation and application of new knowledge, entrepreneurial activity of small companies can be more appropriate for innovation in other task environments. Faced with changing technological and organisational paradigms, large companies might become caught in their own routines and inertia while the innovations achieved by entrepreneurial firms can lead to a complete redefinition of sectoral identities and boundaries. This is exemplified by the changes occurring over the last decades in the computer industry. The structural evolution in this sector (as described by Malerba and Orsenigo 1996) also highlights that the role of actors other than firms (such as universities and research laboratories, the government, financial institutions, suppliers and consumers) undergoes significant changes over time, and that country differences in structural evolution lead to distinctive performance outcomes.

Sectors dominated by large companies are also more likely to be drawn to a greater extent into international markets and vice versa. The experiences and actions of large companies which are operating in national and international markets, and are often also combining a wide range of different business activities, are likely to feed back not only into the organisation and performance of national sectors (see Loveridge et al. and Whittington et al. in this volume) but also to reshape sectoral boundaries. Sectors, thus, do not have a once and for ever fixed shape but are rather fluid entities with changing identities over time.

3. Sector Specialisation as an Emergent Process

The previous discussion illustrated the relationship between the structural characteristics of national business systems and sector specialisation. The institutional environment provides an envelope of constraints and incentives but within them there is a variety of solutions possible. This raises the necessity of shifting from the structural level to the processual level in which one examines the ways in which certain opportunities for sectoral development are or are not taken. From this vantage point, the different economic actors with their strategies, goals and actions are the starting point of analysis to see how a) sectors emerge historically,

SECTOR SPECIALISATION AND ECONOMIC PERFORMANCE   35

b) adapt to changing business and market environment, and c) the role socially constructed performance standards play in this process.

In order to explain why specific sectors emerge in certain countries while other fail to develop we need to refer to historical macro-variables such as the timing of industrialisation and pre-existing social and political institutions. These national conditions supported and constrained learning processes of specific new sectoral capabilities and governance structures. It would be, however, a misconception to believe that the historical emergence of specific national sectors occurred independently from developments in other countries and the power relations between different nations (see e.g. Gerschenkron 1962). Whereas in some countries the evolution of specific sectors may have been largely insulated from events in other parts of the world, in other countries it clearly was not. The account of Van Iterson (in this volume), for example, demonstrates how the evolution of specific sectors in Netherlands was from the beginning linked to the integration of the country's largest companies in the world economy (see also Morgan 1998 for an account of the impact of the Colonial past on the emergence of specific sectors in Britain).

In many cases sectors have evolved around new basic technologies which had a certain fit to pre-existing national institutions and governance structures. Kitschelt (1991), for example, argues that countries seize their opportunities in new technologies primarily at junctures when national institutional endowments permit the development of efficient sectoral governance structures matched to the properties of the newly emerging technology. The British market-oriented society with its weak state, for example, could seize most energetically the opportunities offered by loosely coupled technologies emerging in the First Industrial Revolution whereas national economies in which the state was more strongly involved in industrial development provided more appropriate governance structures for the development of sectors with tightly coupled technologies requiring high investments (see e.g. the emergence of certain heavy industries and the chemical industry in Germany).

Business historians such as Gerschenkron (1962), Landes (1969), and more recently, Lazonick (1991) have also directed attention to how the emergence of and shifts in the relative importance of leading sectors have contributed to the rise and decline of national economies such as those of Britain, the US, Germany and Japan over the last two centuries. These authors, however, rather than focusing on technology as such, give more weight to the impact of national institutions on the development of specific organisational and managerial capabilities which became the basis for 'success' and 'failure' in specific economic sectors. In Germany, financial and educational institutions, as well as the involvement of the state, favoured the development of new science-based industries during the Second Industrial Revolution which required a more sophisticated managerial control of high-throughput processes. In contrast, the backwardness of the old industries in Britain retarded the development of appropriate institutions, and the persistence of family control and the rigidities of British class structure thwarted the development of organisational capabilities required for success in these new sectors.

Once sectors have come into being, the further development of their capabilities is often regarded as following path dependencies. With North (1990) path dependence can be defined as "a way to narrow conceptually the choice set and link decision making through time. It is not a story of inevitability in which the past neatly predicts the future." (North 1990: 98f). This means that the institutional factors outlined above plus internal routines which firms and organisations have established within the possibilities and constraints of their institutional framework will influence the type, speed and direction of change processes in which companies engage. For most of the time, learning and innovation will be of an incremental nature directed by institutional legacies and organisational routines. There is, however, some disagreement between different authors about how narrowly this corridor is defined by the institutional environment and how much autonomy individual firms and sectoral actors have to break out of existing organisational routines and to engage in 'revolutionary' (un-)learning. Very roughly, three approaches towards path dependency can be distinguished: a coherent, a dialectic and an experimental view.

In the *coherent version of path dependency* it is assumed that adaptation strategies of companies in a given sector take nationally distinct directions because, as a result of their institutional and societal context, they will develop different problem definitions, draw on distinct resources to manage the change process and are part of a nationally distinct logic to negotiate changes. This version of path dependency emphasises continuity and stability. The corridor which defines possible alternative developments is rather small. Change occurs merely through incremental learning and innovation. Only on rare occasions will industrial innovation sharply diverge from the path-dependent learning of institutional governance structures in new technology sectors. Economic depression, victory or loss in a major war, or a fundamental change in a country's position in the international system can serve as catalyst of a 'paradigm shift' yielding new technological trajectories and governance structures (see e.g. Kitschelt 1991).

The *dialectic approach towards path dependence* considers to a larger extent the variety, contradictions and tensions inherent to national business systems. It follows that the institutional and societal context gives shape to the basic patterns of companies' strategies, but does not determine them in detail. Companies have to some degree a choice which elements of their institutional environment they will enact in order to develop new strategies to cope with changes in their environment. The variety of institutionally supported forms of economic organisation within a national business system, thus, becomes an important resource for the ability of companies to adapt and innovate. Elements for such an analysis can be found in the work of Sorge (1991) who has suggested that business strategies and organisational/human resource patterns are enacted from a wider range of distinct and contrasting elements, and that the success of business strategies might lie in their

> "ability to combine, albeit selectively, distinct alternatives. Such alternatives to be combined may be, for instance, cost leadership and differentiation of the product range, production efficiency and product quality, (…) economies of scale and scope, (…)." (Sorge 1991: 184).

Herrigel's (1996) analysis of German industrial power as based on the evolving interactions between two competing industrial orders provides another example of such a dialectical approach towards path dependencies.

The *experimental view of path dependency* is quite common in evolutionary economics. In the tradition of Schumpter's concept of innovation as 'carrying out new combinations', various scholars have underlined the uncertainties which companies face when they have either to adapt existing or to develop new strategies. Some choices may be better than others, but no choice is clearly best ex ante. A diversity of responses of firms is regarded as good, since they explore the potential range of possible answers. Over the long run, competition would promote firms which chose well on the average and eliminate firms which consistently make mistakes. "In this view, the market system is (in part) a device for conducting and evaluating experiments in economic behaviour and organisation" (Nelson and Winter 1982: 277). This view highlights that diversity and pluralism of economic forms are a precondition for successful adaptation, innovation and selection. It points to the often unpredictable directions which sector specialisation takes as a result of complex interactions between national institutions, global markets and organisational choices.

Underlying these different versions of path dependency are not only distinct views of how much autonomy firms have to choose and experiment with alternative elements of organisational, human resource and product market strategies. These views also differ with respect to how much variety is allowed for within a national business system. Obviously, not all the firms within a given economy will correspond to the ideal profile identified as characteristic for this society; and not all companies will cluster in those sectors assumed to flourish particularly in a given society. Pockets of flexible specialisation production in the UK/US, for example, indicate that there is also an organisational beside the societal effect (Mueller 1994) and that even within arms-length systems it is possible to mobilise close and trustful relationships in certain localities. More recently, Hirst and

Zeitlin (1997) have tried to allow for this variety by developing the notion of 'mixed' or 'hybrid' systems of production. They underline that hybrid forms of production embedded in so-called dominant social systems of production have always existed. Social systems of production focusing on the customisation of products are dependent to some extent on the standardised production of components and parts; and social systems of production which centre on standardised production require customised machines. According to their view, firms in most countries and periods deliberately mix elements of mass production and craft or flexible specialisation. The resulting interpenetration of elements of flexible specialisation and mass production also means that firms often find it easier to shift strategies from one pole to another than abstract considerations of the models might suggest.

4. Performance Standards and Sector Specialisation

The previous sections examined the process of sectoral specialisation and why certain contexts favour particular types of sectors. What has not yet been clearly identified, however, is the underlying source of this process of sector specialisation. From a traditional economic perspective, one might assume that what is occurring is a process of market selection, i.e. certain firms/sectors located in particular institutional contexts out-perform those from elsewhere. In other words, it becomes possible to link institutionalist analysis at this level to traditional market economics. In this section, we critically examine the notion that 'market performance' can provide this explanatory framework.

4.1 *Competitive Advantage and Market Selection in Economics and Organisational Theory*

For neo-classical theory, the driving force behind the increasing division and specialisation of economic activity is the most efficient allocation of scarce resources to competing ends. This allocation is achieved through the 'invisible hand' of the market in which firms seek efficiency to survive. Positive profits are treated as the criterion of natural selection — the firms that make profits are selected or 'adopted' by the environment, and others are rejected or disappear. The concern of neo-classical approaches with matching demand and supply leads — even in applied competition theory — to a preoccupation with the question of how competitive prices can be achieved in equilibrium situations. Imperfect information and the use of market power are seen as important impediments to a socially efficient allocation of resources.

Within economics, however, there is a long history of complaints about the

SECTOR SPECIALISATION AND ECONOMIC PERFORMANCE   39

shortcomings of the neo-classical approach with regard to explanations of competitive advantage and performance. Authors from different theoretical backgrounds such as Hayek (1948) and Schumpeter (1942), or more recently Nelson and Winter (1982) and Langlois (1986) have pointed out that economic phenomena are in large measure the result of learning over time by economic agents. Competition, thus, cannot be accounted for by Walrasian general equilibrium models but should be analysed as a dynamic (and, as some argue, evolutionary) process. Institutionalists argue that the coordination of economic activity is not merely a matter of price-mediated transactions in the markets, but is supported by a wide range of economic and social institutions that are themselves an important topic of theoretical economic inquiry. Particular attention is given to how institutions shape the expectations, information systems and interpretative frameworks which are used by economic actors (see e.g. Loasby 1991). Taking into account more complex and uncertain environments and longer time horizons, the neo-classical perception of conscious maximisation of explicit objectives within the constraints of well-defined alternatives cannot be maintained any longer and needs to be replaced by other conceptions of rationality which allow for imperfections of knowledge under uncertainty (Shackle 1958), opportunism and bounded rationality (Williamson 1975, 1985), and learning from experience (Langlois 1986).

The accounts within new institutional economics of processes of competitive advantage and performance, however, are often still bound to the notion that in the end, it is the market which decides about the 'success' or 'failure' of individual business organisations or whole sectors. Transaction costs economics, for example, has relaxed a number of assumptions inherent in neo-classical orthodoxy. But it still maintains that the efficiency properties of alternative organisational forms determine their success or failure — even if it is only the fitter, and not necessarily the fittest in some absolute sense that is selected in 'weak form selection'.[1] Politically imposed impediments and disadvantaged parties may be able to delay transaction cost economising. These exceptions, however, are treated as 'noise' that will disappear in the long run (Williamson 1994). The hypothesis maintained is that firms producing products at the least cost drive out high-cost producers since markets favour low prices, and firms cannot withstand losses of profits or of customers, at least not for a long time.

As the business historian William Lazonick (1991:214) critically states, "Williamson's theory is a theory of an organisation that can only adapt to changes in the environment but does not offer a conception of how innovative organisations might attain and sustain competitive advantage by differentiating the quality and cost of their products from their competitors." Lazonick's work directs attention to the structures, behaviour and strategies of business organisations which generate the basis for what he calls value-creation. These issues, while often neglected in economic accounts of organisations as 'black boxes', have attracted increasing attention in organisational and management theory (for an overview of theoretical approaches towards organisational performance, see Clark 1996 and Meyer 1994). Performance implications, however, have often been dealt with only implicitly (see e.g. Whittington et al., in this volume, for an overview of the treatment of performance in the Chandlerian approach to structure and strategy approach) or, again, been referred to as a matter of market selection. The economist Edith Penrose (1959), for example, while being among the first to stress the importance of managerial organisation and organisational learning for performance still maintained that the selection between 'successful' and 'failing' organisations was merely a question of profitability and market selection.

A more recent example of these arguments can be found in Porter's (1990) theory of competitive advantage. In this version, the market is subdivided into segments in which competition works through different criteria: for example, price, quality at lowest price, customisation, delivery and/or technologically excellence at the cost of price, etc. It is up to companies' strategies to decide in which of these segments of the world market they want to position themselves. Within this market segment then again, competition will select the more efficient, qualitative, more customised or technologically excellent producers and drive out badly performing companies. These arguments assume that there are a variety of bases on which competition occurs; nevertheless, they remain wedded to the idea that it is through the market that performance is differentiated and selection occurs, leading to the development of strong firms and strong sectors, as a result of the theory of comparative advantage.

Furthermore, this approach assumes a relatively seamless transition between competition within the nation and competition in world markets, in the sense that, as trade barriers come down, firms utilise their home-based advantages in the larger international market. International competitive advantage of sectors or nations thus can be measured in terms of their exports and foreign investment to other nations. Success and failure in international markets feeds back into the national context, forcing some sectors and firms to close and enabling others to grow and expand. Processes of sector formation and reproduction in national contexts are therefore reconstituted under the impact of international competition. As particular markets for goods and services become opened up for international trade, selection mechanisms operate to restructure sector specialisation processes within national business systems.

4.2 *Institutionalist Approaches to Competitive Advantage and Market Selection*

It is characteristic of many institutionalist approaches towards comparative business organisation that their main concern, rather than challenging the notion

SECTOR SPECIALISATION AND ECONOMIC PERFORMANCE　41

of market selection per se, is to elucidate the variety of ways in which economic success can be achieved. In other words, they reject the notion that there is one best way to organise and propose instead the concept of 'functional equivalence'.[2] Their argument is that firms and sectors develop characteristics based on their national institutional context. In international markets, firms and sectors from different contexts may be equally successful even though their structures are different. Thus whilst some firms will be de-selected, there is no need to assume that those firms which survive and prosper need to have the same structure.

Sorge (1991), for example, argues that the primary requirement for a firm is to fit its task and societal environment, and that the degree of fit is essential for performance. But the success of a business strategy may also rest on its own impurity, i.e. on the selective combination of opposing contingent task requirements, and the institutional ability to reconcile conflicting contingencies. Despite this differentiated approach toward the links between institutions and performance, however, once more the market is identified as the selection mechanism which decides about the survival or disappearance of organisations, and thereby the emergence or disappearance of sectors: "...(T)he mentioned affinities are likely to come out in the process of a quasi-Darwinian selection in the intensifying international division of labour." (Sorge 1991: 168).

Sorge's argument reflects the ambivalence of the tradition of the 'societal effect' approach to sectoral specialisation and the role of performance. Maurice et al. (1986), in one of the first studies in the societal effect tradition, refused to give explicit performance judgements. According to their argument, firms with similar task environment may have very different organisational forms and organisational goals in different societies and still perform equally well. Nevertheless, the French-German comparison of Maurice et al. contains a subtext underlining the relative merits of the German system and the idea that competition on world markets between the two types of firm will lead to the de-selection of the French model. Equivocally they conclude that if "... different forms of the division of labour may lead to comparable levels of efficiency, it is none the less true that certain systems seem to be more efficient than others." (Maurice et al. 1986: 23). Thus the notion of functional equivalence seems to reach its limits when the two 'equivalents' are placed directly in competition (see Rose 1985). The implicit assumption is that at this point market selection will operate, causing the decline of certain firms and sectors from the less 'efficient' institutional context. Sorge attempts to reconcile these apparently contradictory elements:

> "The German model is definitely not the only or best model of operating within the respective product market segment, for instance, and the mass or the continuous process mode is not identical with French-style practices. The principle of functional equivalence, of different socio-organisational goals (Child 1972), still appears pertinent. However, the above discussion also points to the limits of the functional

equivalence perspective. Arrangements that are institutionalised and therefore transcend a functional purpose (...), have an affinity, nevertheless, with tasks, markets and overall strategies. The question of to what extent, and where, an institutionalized arrangement is not functionally neutral, is fairly open."
(Sorge 1991: 168).

4.3 *Performance and Institutional Contexts: Against Market Fundamentalism*

The ambiguities within the 'societal effects' approach to the question of market selection and performance point to the need to pursue further the question of what drives sector specialisation. The assessment of organisational performance makes sense only with regard to the attainment of objectives or goals — which raises the question of whose objectives and goals are the benchmarks against which performance is assessed. Goal setting and assessment of economic performance do not follow universal laws, but are influenced by socially constructed standards, rules and norms through which economic actors shape their environment. This means that performance standards may differ in time and space. Dominant standards are the result of selections between alternative and sometimes conflicting performance goals that are negotiated between different groups of social actors, which to a certain extent reflect influences of the national institutional context (see Morgan and Quack in this book). Thus the creation of sectoral specialisation and firm survival within national contexts cannot be simply read off as an outcome of neo-classical market selection.

If we compare the perception of desired performance outcomes in different societies we find variations which are related to differences in ownership patterns, governance principles and market relations. Whitley (1999) discusses the relative influence of owners, managers, different kinds of employees, business partners, and other groups in deciding upon dominant firms' objectives and performance standards. Four dominant goals and performance standards can be distinguished: personal and family wealth accumulation; high returns to portfolio managers and shareholders; growth in assets, turnover and markets; increasing technical excellence and reputation. In practice, these goals are always combined but usually one tends to dominate as a result of different interest groups' control over the strategic priorities of firms and the nature of the broader institutional environment. For example, the Anglo-Saxon business systems are likely to give priority to increases in share prices and dividends compared to the other goals; in contrast, business systems in which managers have a high degree of control over company development, and particularly when combined with strong employee and business partner influence, are likely to favour growth goals because salaries and rewards of managers are regarded as tied to the firm, and employees and business partners gain more from the expansion of the firm than from increased profits.

SECTOR SPECIALISATION AND ECONOMIC PERFORMANCE   43

National business systems are not only likely to influence the relative power and influence of different stakeholder groups. The formation of these social groups and their interests as such will also differ depending on the historical and social context (Kristensen 1997). For example, members of the highly mobile work force in the US, described above, should have much less interest in the development of the individual company they are working for than their counterparts in the German, and even more, in the Japanese system which focuses on long-term employment relationships. Differences in the educational and social background of British, French and German managers have been shown to lead to distinct management styles and a focus on generalist versus technical issues (Lane 1989). The social formation of supplier and business partner relations, and as a consequence, the type of interest they take in companies, has also been demonstrated to differ considerably depending on the national context (Lane 1997; Deakin et al. this volume).

These considerations mean that the driving force of sector specialisation in particular contexts cannot be simply ascribed to market selection mechanisms. Processes of selection and deselection are social constructions in the sense that actors have to decide on the goals which they want to achieve in particular contexts. These goals are not necessarily about short-term economic survival. Key stakeholders such as the state, lenders, shareholders and employees are involved in complex ongoing and conflictual decisions about the terms on which their own requirements are going to be met through the current strategy and structure of the firm and sector. Thus states can support the development of certain sectors, e.g. aerospace and defence, for straightforward political reasons. Such decisions do not negate market mechanisms but rather displace them to other parts of the social order, in the process restructuring and redefining the nature of survival and growth for firms. Similarly, lenders can evolve more complex goals than short-term profit maximisation, particularly when as with the case in Germany, a substantial part of the banking system is collectively, as opposed to privately, owned.

In this context it is important to underline that performance is always a multidimensional phenomenon — a construct in which certain aspects can become an issue for the actors involved in economic activity or not. Economic actors in sectoral or national business systems cannot maximise all dimensions of performance at the same time. In order to examine trade-offs between performance objectives, Traxler and Ungerer (1994) have suggested grouping them along four dimensions: Allocative efficiency represents the ability of an organisation to employ most efficiently the available resources at a given point in time. Dynamic efficiency (also referred to as 'adaptive efficiency' by North 1990: 80) describes the ability of organisations to adapt successfully to changing environments (see also Klein 1984; Lazonick 1991). Distributional performance deals with considerations of social peace and the egalitarian distribution of economic outcomes.

Stabilisation, finally, refers to the resources and capabilities on which an organisation can draw to overcome periods of economic difficulties.

These four dimensions of performance lead to conflicting goals. In evolutionary economics, tensions between allocative and dynamic efficiency have become known as 'Schumpeterian trade-off' (e.g. Nelson and Winter 1982; Langlois 1986). Authors from the institutionalist camp have referred to it as the conflict between achieving short and long-term profitability (Boyer and Hollingsworth 1997). Anglo-Saxon market capitalism has been in general ascribed a high propensity to maximise allocative efficiency whereas continental European capitalisms, and more recently Japan, with 'thick' institutional settings have been regarded as providing superior conditions for long-term success through higher developed capacities for adaptability to changing business environments (Aoki 1988; Katzenstein 1989; Streeck 1992).

Patterns of sectoral specialisation within national contexts, therefore, do not reflect a simple logic of market selection. Which sectors survive, how they develop and how they are structured can only be understood by examining the ways in which various groups of actors reach agreements and compromises on their economic, social and political interests within the particular institutional structure of their own society. These agreements are subject to periods of tension and instability which may result in restructuring and change or stasis and continuity. However, they certainly cannot be reduced to a process of neo-classical market selection.

4.4 *Markets as Social Structures: An Institutionalist Approach towards Market Selection*

By arguing against neo-classical market fundamentalism, as we have done in the previous section, we do not intend to deny the important role that markets play in shaping and selecting performance outcomes. We do, however, maintain that the market is not the only, and possibly not the most important site in which performance is assessed and performance outcomes are selected. Furthermore, we contend that the process of Darwinian selection with which the market is ascribed under the perfect competition model in orthodox economics constitutes a rare exception to what actually tends to happen in real markets (see Boyer 1997 for a more extensive discussion). Old and new institutionalist theory has pointed out that most markets for commodities call for sophisticated institutional arrangements as a prerequisite for their functioning (e.g. the state as guarantor of property rights, or non-price mechanisms to achieve market clearing, see e.g. Campbell and Lindberg 1990). We would argue that it is necessary to go one step further and to perceive of markets as consisting of social structures which emerge from recurrent exchange between different economic actors and are often shaped by

SECTOR SPECIALISATION AND ECONOMIC PERFORMANCE   45

power struggles over access to resources and choices of performance outcomes (see e.g. Swedberg 1994 for an overview on sociological approaches to markets). Boyer (1997) suggests that in studying the role of socially constructed markets as selection device, particular emphasis should be given to:

> "[T]he list of institutions, organizations, legislation, or associations that are organising the functioning of (...) markets, with detailed description of their responsibilities, objectives, tools and enforcement tools or incentives. (...) A characterisation of the forms of competition, according to the number of traders, the distribution of ownership, the distribution of market power, the possible explicit or implicit coordinating mechanisms, in order to solve overcapacity problems or to respond to uncertainty and/or structural changes." (Boyer 1997: 70).

Even though attempts to fill this research programme are still in their infancy, there is already considerable evidence for the existence of a variety of social market structures with distinct effects on the selection of 'successful' and 'unsuccessful' business organisations and corresponding effects for the development of different economic sectors. Interestingly enough, it is particularly in globalised financial sectors which are often regarded as prototype of anonymous and price-coordinated market selection that social and cultural aspects have been demonstrated to affect the workings of the market. Baker (1984), for example, demonstrated that price volatility in US securities markets was strongly influenced by the nature of networks operating in these markets. He showed that fragmented and larger networks of participants caused much more price volatility than smaller, more intense networks. Furthermore, it has been demonstrated by Podolny (1993, together with Philipps 1996) that market exchanges between US investment banks often involve not only the manifest transfer of goods and resources, but also a latent transfer of status. Status transfer has a significant impact on the resources which market participants can acquire, and thereby influences their performance. Thus, as far as the emergence, development and decline of sectors is influenced by market selections these selections should be regarded as the result of social and power relations between different market participants and their contest about different performance standards.

4.5 Towards 'Dis-embedded' Performance Standards in Global Markets?

It is tempting to suggest, as a number of institutionalist authors imply, that markets as social structures and socially constructed performance standards may work within tightly controlled national borders (as was characteristic of the golden age of Keynesianism) but once these borders are reduced in efficacy, then the global market 'red in tooth and claw' operates as a brutal form of selection between firms and nations, causing some sectors to disappear in particular countries and others to strengthen and grow. Three broad mechanisms are assumed to translate these market imperatives into action. The first is quite simply market competition itself which places firms from different institutional context into direct confrontation. Thus cheaper and/or more reliable products from one country cause the decline of that sector in another country. The second mechanism derives from global financial markets, which allows firms to shift resources out of their home base into other contexts offering better comparative advantage for the production of certain goods or services. The latter process allows firms to survive and prosper by outward investment but this destroys national sectors and the ties which link them together. From this perspective, whatever might have been the role for socially differentiated performance goals and outcomes under the accumulation regime of 'national Keynesianism', the situation in the era of globalisation is considerably different. Firms are measured by a single criterion of performance on the global market and failure to adjust to this leads to the decline of firms and sectors. The third mechanism which relates to this is the idea of the transfer of standards of performance across countries via multinational corporations (MNC), transnational corporate networks and international standard setting agencies.

This view, however, over-estimates the degree to which markets and firms can ever be completely 'dis-embedded' from national contexts or state or international regulation. Thus the terms on which firms compete in international markets have to come from somewhere: either national or regional or international bodies of some sort continue to regulate trade. What is at issue is not regulation per se but a series of practical questions such as what is the most appropriate level for regulation in particular sectors, what is the extent of regulation which is compatible with broader economic and political goals, who should have responsibility for implementing and monitoring regulation and who should pay for it. Whilst proponents of the free market might start from the presupposition that the market should rule, they recognise that in practice, this still requires some sort of framework. This framework therefore opens up the possibility of just the sort of bargaining over goals which has always existed at the national level. The fact that international institutions tend to be dominated by proponents of the free market only reinforces the point that power is used to make the market work by forcing countries to open up their boundaries; it is not inconceivable that it could therefore be used with more (or, perhaps, a different) political direction (see the arguments in Hirst and Thompson 1996; Boyer and Drache 1996; Berger and Dore 1996).

Similarly, the process of transfer of best practice always tends to be affected by different social contexts. Firstly, universal standards such as for example the ISO 9000 norms of product quality are likely to be implemented and enacted differently by social actors in distinct national and sectoral environments (see Hancké and Casper in this volume). Secondly, international regimes often delegate monitoring responsibilities back to the authority in the home country and are

SECTOR SPECIALISATION AND ECONOMIC PERFORMANCE 47

based on home-country control (Hirst and Thompson 1996; Lütz 1996). Thirdly, organisational procedures within multinational corporations still need to articulate different local, sectoral and national logics of action in order to be successful. The interesting question, thus, is not so much whether standards of performance are defined domestically or globally, but how the transfer processes work, how national, international and global rules of the game are articulated with each other and what changes in power are involved in these processes (see Loveridge and Mueller's chapter in this volume).

The fact that the last decade has seen the decline and in some cases loss of certain manufacturing sectors from advanced industrial societies or the systematic restructuring of others in the light of global competition should clearly not be under-estimated. However, nor should the significance of this be over-estimated. There remain considerable differences in the way in which sectors are opened up to international competition and the terms of this opening-up as well as the way in which firms and sectors adapt to this process. Governments and international regulators still play a role in the terms on which this occurs. Thus all Western governments continue to protect their agricultural sectors from cheaper foodstuffs from the developing world. Many of them continue to support certain key industries such as defence, energy, air transport and telecommunications (see the discussion in this volume by Lehrer and Darbishire, and Loveridge and Mueller) whilst at the same time encouraging them to become globally competitive. Even classically globally competitive sectors such as automobiles remain of central concern to governments, many of whom will seek to support home firms in this sector in order to sustain employment and the host of suppliers dependent on the sector. Service sectors are notoriously difficult to open up to international competition not just for purely technical reasons but because of entrenched professional groups. Thus certain patterns of sector specialisation which have been established historically are likely to continue long in to the future whatever the proponents of globalisation argue.

5. Conclusions

In this chapter, we have examined in detail the issue of sector specialisation. We have shown how institutional structures such as the nature of financial systems, innovation strategies, labour market institutions, demand conditions and patterns of intermediary associations influence sectoral specialisation in different national business systems. However, these structural factors exercise their influence through shaping the ways in which firms and individuals respond to opportunities and threats in their environment. This led us to consider whether ultimately the key issue was the process of market selection as assumed in neo-classical theory. Here, we argued that some institutionalists do in fact accept that this type of Darwinian market selection is at work between what they term 'functionally equivalent' aspects of business systems. Thus institutionalism can be linked to market economics ultimately through the recognition that there are various alternative forms of organising which have functional equivalence but it is likely that in particular circumstances one form will be more 'efficient' than another.

In this chapter, however, we have questioned this market fundamentalism. Instead, we have followed others in arguing that just as there are multiple functionally equivalent structures, there are multiple performance standards which are set for firms. Shareholder dominance is only one such standard and there are many examples of more complex balances of interest between different groups, creating performance standards that reflect social, political and economic interests. Therefore, the reasons why firms and sectors are sustained and developed in particular contexts needs to be related to the way in which certain performance standards are put in place by specific social actors in particular arenas. There are many arenas in which different choices for performance goals are negotiated and contested. The market — reconceptualised as a social structure — is only one of them. We also reject the idea that the opening up of national borders implies a declining significance for these sorts of processes and the final triumph of neo-classical markets. For the free market theorists, the decline of borders will lead inexorably to the creation of an international division of labour which reflects comparative economic advantages between countries and areas. Thus firms and sectors within countries which are unable to compete on the global market will decline whilst others will grow. In our view, this both over-generalises from a limited number of examples and under-estimates the continued role of political and social intervention at national, regional and global levels. There remain ways in which sectors can be protected or encouraged which will not disappear as a result of globalisation per se, though it may be that global institutions influenced by free market ideology may insist in the case of certain less powerful countries that they do not use these mechanisms. In general, however, it is important to examine the specific processes through which sectors within and across national boundaries are being restructured. It would be our expectation that this will reflect a complex inter-mixing of political, social and economic considerations, rather than some pure form of market selection (see e.g. the studies on financial services industries in Europe in Morgan and Knights 1997 as well as the discussions in this volume).

Notes

1. Other proponents of new economic institutionalism, like Langlois (1986: 13) ascribe a more far-reaching influence to social institutions. In this view, social institutions set the boundary conditions and provide filtering and selection mechanisms which shape the process of

SECTOR SPECIALISATION AND ECONOMIC PERFORMANCE   49

competition. In contrast to sociological conceptions described elsewhere in this article, however, social institutions are still regarded as distinct from the economic processes under consideration.

2. A distinction needs to be drawn between the notion of functional equivalence as used in contingency theory (referring to the use of different means to achieve identical goals), and a more broadly defined notion of 'functional equivalence' according to which not only the means, but also the goals pursued by economic actors can vary across countries (as referred to in this chapter).

References

Aoki, M. 1988. *Information, incentives and bargaining in the Japanese economy.* Cambridge: Cambridge University Press.

Baker, W. 1984. The Social Structure of a National Securities Market, *American Journal of Sociology* 89: 775–811.

Berger, S. and R. Dore (eds.). 1996. *National Diversity and Global Capitalism.* Cornell: Cornell University Press.

Boyer, R. 1997. The Variety and Unequal Performance of Really Existing Markets: Farewell to Doctor Pangloss?. In: Hollingsworth, J. R. and R. Boyer (eds.). 1997. *Contemporary Capitalism. The Embeddedness of Institutions*, 55–93. Cambridge: Cambridge University Press.

Boyer, R. and D. Drache. 1996. *States against Markets: the limits of globalization.* London: Routledge.

Boyer, R. and J. R. Hollingsworth. 1997. The Variety of Institutional Arrangements and Their Complementarity in Modern Economies. In: Hollingsworth, J. R. and R. Boyer (eds.). 1997. *Contemporary Capitalism. The Embeddedness of Institutions*, 49–54. Cambridge: Cambridge University Press.

Campbell, J. and L. Lindberg. 1990. Property Rights and the Organization of Economic Activity by the State, *American Sociological Review* 55: 634–647.

Clark, P. 1996. Organizational Performance. In: Warner, M. (ed.), *International Encyclopedia of Business and Management.* Volume 4, 3943–3955. London: Routledge.

Christopherson, S. 1998. Why do national labor market practices continue to diverge in a global economy? Paper presented to the EGOS Conference, July 1998, Maastricht.

Gerschenkron, A. 1962. *Economic Backwardness in Historical Perspective.* Cambridge, MA: Harvard University Press.

Hayek, F. A. 1948. *Individualism and Economic Order.* Chicago: University of Chicago Press.

Hall, P. 1997. The Political Economy of Adjustment in Germany. In: W. Zapf and M. Dierkes (eds.), *Institutionenvergleich und Institutionendynamik*, WZB-Year Book, 293–348, Berlin: Edition Sigma.

Herrigel, G. 1996. *Industrial constructions: The sources of German industrial power.* Cambridge: Cambridge University Press.

Hirst, P. Q. and G. F. Thompson. 1996. *Globalization in Question: The International Economy and the Possibilities of Governance.* Cambridge: Polity Press.

Hirst, P. and J. Zeitlin. 1997. Flexible Specialization: Theory and Evidence in the Analysis of Industrial Change. In: Hollingsworth, J. R. and R. Boyer (eds.), *Contemporary*

Capitalism. The Embeddedness of Institutions, 220–239. Cambridge: Cambridge University Press.

Hollingsworth, J. R., P. C. Schmitter and W. Streeck (eds.). 1994. *Governing Capitalist Economies. Performance and Control of Economic Sectors.* Oxford: Oxford University Press.

Hollingsworth, J. R. and R. Boyer (eds.). 1997. *Contemporary Capitalism. The Embeddedness of Institutions.* Cambridge: Cambridge University Press.

Hutton, W. 1995. *The State We're in.* London: Jonathan Cape.

Katzenstein, P. J. 1989. *Industry and Politics in West Germany: Toward the Third Republic.* Ithaca: Cornell University Press.

Kitschelt, H. 1991. Industrial Governance Structures, *International Organization* 45(4): 453–93.

Klein, B. 1984. *Prices, wages and business cycles. A dynamic theory.* New York: Pergamon Press.

Kristensen, P. H. 1997. National Systems of Governance and Managerial Prerogatives in the Evolution of Work Systems: England, Germany, and Denmark Compared. In: Whitley, R. and P. H. Kristensen (eds.), *Governance at Work: The Social Regulation of Economic Relations,* 3–46. Oxford: Oxford University Press.

Lane, C. 1989. *Management and Labour in Europe. The Industrial Enterprise in Germany, Britain and France.* Aldershot: Edward Elgar.

Lane, C. 1995. *Industry and Society in Europe.* Aldershot: Edward Elgar.

Lane, C. 1997. The social regulation of inter-firm relations in Britain and Germany: market rules, legal norms and technical standards, *Cambridge Journal of Economics* 21: 197–215.

Landes, D. 1969. *The Unbound Prometheus: Technological Change and Industrial Development in Western Europe from 1750 to the Present.* Cambridge: Cambridge University Press.

Langlois, R. N. (ed.). 1986. *Economics as a process. Essays in the New Institutional Economics.* Cambridge: Cambridge University Press.

Langlois R. N. and P. L. Robertson. 1995. *Firms, Markets and Economic Change.* London: Routledge.

Lazonick, W. 1991. *Business Organization and the Myth of the Market Economy.* Cambridge: Cambridge University Press.

Lazonick, W. and M. O'Sullivan. 1996. Organization, Finance and International Competition, *Industrial and Corporate Change* 5(1): 1–50.

Loasby, B. J. 1991. Equilibrium and evolution. *An exploration of connecting principles in economics.* Manchester: Manchester University Press.

Lundvall, B. A. (ed.). 1992. *National Systems of Innovation.* Pinter: London.

Lütz, S. 1998. The revival of the nation-state? Stock-exchange regulation in an era of globalized financial markets. *Journal of European Public Policy* 5: 153–168.

Malerba, F. and L. Orsenigo. 1996. The Dynamics and Evolution of Industries, *Industrial and Corporate Change* 5(1): 51–87.

Maurice, M., A. Sorge and M. Warner. 1980. Societal Differences in Organizing Manufacturing Units. A Comparison of France, West Germany and Great Britain, *Organization Studies* 1(1): 59–86.

SECTOR SPECIALISATION AND ECONOMIC PERFORMANCE 51

Maurice, M., F. Sellier and J.-J. Silvestre (eds.). 1986. *The social foundations of industrial power. A comparison of France and Germany.* Cambridge, MA: MIT Press.

Maurice, M. and A. Sorge (eds.). 1999. *Embedded organizations. Societal analysis of actors, organizations and socio-economic context.* Amsterdam: John Benjamins.

Meyer, M. W. 1994. Measuring Performance in Economic Organizations. In: N. J. Smelser and R. Swedberg (eds.), *The Handbook of Economic Sociology,* 556–580. New York: Princeton University Press.

Morgan, G. 1998. Varieties of Capitalism and the Institutional Embeddedness of International Economic Coordination. Paper presented to EGOS Conference, July 1998, Maastricht.

Morgan, G. and D. Knights (eds.). 1997. *Regulation and Deregulation in European Financial Services.* London: Macmillan.

Mueller, F. 1994. Societal Effect, Organizational Effect and Globalization, *Organization Studies* 15(3): 407–428.

Nelson, R. R. and S. G. Winter. 1982. *An Evolutionary theory of Economic Change.* Cambridge, MA: Harvard University Press.

Nelson, R. R. (eds.). 1993. *National Innovation Systems: A Comparative Analysis.* Oxford: Oxford University Press.

North, D. C. 1990. *Institutions, Institutional Change and Economic Performance.* Cambridge: Cambridge University Press.

Penrose, E. T. 1959. *The Theory of the Growth of the Firm.* Oxford: Oxford University Press.

Podolny, J. M. 1993. A Status-based Model of Market Competition, *American Journal of Sociology* 98: 829–872.

Podolny, J. M. and D. J. Phillips. 1996. The Dynamics of Organizational Status, *Industrial and Corporate Change* 5(2): 453–471.

Porter, M. E. 1990. *The Competitive Advantage of Nations.* New York: Free Press.

Räsänen, K. and R. Whipp. 1992. National Business Recipes: a Sector Perspective. In: R. Whitley (ed.), *European Business Systems. Firms and Markets in their National Contexts,* 46–60. London: Sage.

Rose, M. 1985. Universalism, culturalism and the Aix group: promise and problems of a societal approach to economic institutions, *European Sociological Review* 1(1): 65–83.

Sabel, C. 1994. Learning by Monitoring: The Institutions of Economic Development. In: N. J. Smelser and R. Swedberg (eds.), *The Handbook of Economic Sociology,* 137–165. Princeton, NJ: Princeton University Press.

Schumpeter, J. 1942. *Capitalism, Socialism, and Democracy.* New York: Harper and Brothers.

Shackle, G. L. S. 1958. *Time in Economics.* Amsterdam: North-Holland Publishing Company.

Sorge, A. 1991. Strategical Fit and Societal Effect: Interpreting Cross-National Comparisons of Technology, Organization and Human Resources, *Organization Studies* 12(2): 161–190.

Soskice, D. 1997. Innovation Strategies of Companies: A Comparative Institutional Approach of Some Cross-Company Differences. In: W. Zapf and M. Dierkes (eds.),

Institutionenvergleich und Institutionendynamik, WZB-Year Book, 271–289, Berlin: Edition Sigma.

Storper, M. 1996. Innovation as Collective Action: Conventions, Products and Technologies, *Industrial and Corporate Change* 5(3): 761–789.

Streeck, W. 1992. *Social Institutions and Economic Performance. Studies of Industrial Relations in Advanced Capitalist Economies.* London: Sage.

Swedberg, R. 1994. Markets as Social Structures. In: N. J. Smelser and R. Swedberg (eds.), *The Handbook of Economic* Sociology, 255–282. Princeton, NJ: Princeton University Press.

Traxler, F. and Ungerer, B. 1994. Industry or Infrastructure? A Cross-National Comparison of Governance: Its Determinants and Economic Consequences in the Dairy Sector. In: J. R. Hollingsworth, P. C. Schmitter and W. Streeck (eds.), *Governing Capitalist Economies. Performance and Control of Economic Sectors,* 183–214. Oxford: Oxford University Press.

Vitols, S. 1995. German Banks and the Modernization of the Small Firm Sector: Long-term Finance in Comparative Perspective. WZB-Discussion Paper FS I 95–309. Berlin: Wissenschaftszentrum Berlin für Sozialforschung.

Vitols, S. 1997. Financial Systems and Industrial Policy in Germany and Great Britain: The Limits of Convergence. In: D. Forsyth and . Notermands (eds.), *Regime Changes: Macroeconomic Policy and Financial Regulation in Europe from the 1930s to the 1990s,* 221–55. Providence, RI: Berghahn Books.

Whitley, R. 1994. Dominant Forms of Economic Organization in Market Economies, *Organization Studies* 15(2): 153–182.

Whitley, R. 1999. *Divergent Capitalisms: The Social Structuring and Change of Business Systems.* Oxford: Oxford University Press.

Whitley, R. and P. H. Kristensen (eds.). 1996. *The Changing European Firm. Limits to Convergence.* London: Routledge.

Whitley, R. and P. H. Kristensen (eds.). 1997. *Governance at Work: The Social Regulation of Economic Relations.* Oxford: Oxford University Press.

Williamson, O. E. 1975. *Markets and Hierarchies: Analysis and Anti-Trust Implications.* New York: Free Press.

Williamson, O. E. 1985. *The Economic Institutions of Capitalism.* New York: Free Press.

Williamson, O. E. 1994. Transaction Cost Economics and Organisation Theory. In: N. J. Smelser and R. Swedberg (eds.), *The Handbook of Economic Sociology,* 77–107. Princeton, NJ: Princeton University Press.

Zysman, J. 1983. *Governments, Markets and Growth.* Financial Systems and the Politics of Industrial Change. London: Cornell University Press.

Name Index